GOLD COINS
of the WORLD

"All passes. Art alone
Enduring, stays with us.
The bust outlasts the throne,
The coin, Tiberius."

GOLD COINS of the WORLD

(FIFTH EDITION)

COMPLETE FROM 600 A.D.
TO THE PRESENT

An Illustrated Standard Catalogue with Valuations

by ROBERT FRIEDBERG

Revised and Edited by

ARTHUR L. FRIEDBERG and IRA S. FRIEDBERG

THE COIN AND CURRENCY INSTITUTE, INC.

Book Publishers

116 WEST 32ND STREET ● NEW YORK, N.Y. 10001

OTHER BOOKS PUBLISHED BY
THE COIN AND CURRENCY INSTITUTE:

"PAPER MONEY OF THE UNITED STATES"
"COINS OF THE BRITISH WORLD"
"APPRAISING AND SELLING YOUR COINS" (U.S. and Canada)
"SO-CALLED DOLLARS" (U.S.)
"AMERICA'S FOREIGN COINS"

GOLD COINS OF THE WORLD
Complete from 600 A.D. to the present
An Illustrated Standard Catalogue with Valuations
Copyright, 1958, 1965, 1971, 1976, by
THE COIN AND CURRENCY INSTITUTE, INC.,
assigned to Arthur L. Friedberg and Ira S. Friedberg.
Copyright, 1980, by Arthur L. Friedberg and Ira S. Friedberg.
Library of Congress catalog card no. 80-66207
ISBN 0-87184-305-6

Manufactured in the United States of America
by Amos Press
Fifth Edition

Associate Editor
ARTHUR S. GOLDENBERG

CONTRIBUTORS

Our thanks and gratitude to the internationally known numismatists named below who have given graciously and generously of their precious time, their numismatic knowledge, and their accumulated experience in helping with this revision of "Gold Coins of the World," and who, in many instances, helped with the preceding editions: -

MANUEL E. AGUIAR, *New York, New York*
BJARNE AHLSTROM, *Stockholm, Sweden*
PIETRO BAJOCCHI, *Cairo, Egypt*
COLIN BRUCE, *Iola, Wisconsin*
REMO CAPELLI, *Rome, Italy*
JUAN R. CAYON, *Madrid, Spain*
SCOTT E. CORDRY, *San Diego, California*
ALBERT DELMONTE, *Brussels, Belgium*
JEAN-PAUL DIVO, *Luxembourg*
WILLIAM and THOMAS DONNER, *New York, New York*
AUGUSTO DRAGONI, *New York, New York*
JAMES F. ELMEN, *Beverly Hills, California*
THOMAS FAISTAUER, *Sao Paulo, Brazil*
GIUSEPPE DE FALCO, *Naples, Italy*
DAVID L. GANZ, *New York, New York*
NORMAN JACOBS, *Urbana, Illinois*
HANS KOCHMAN, *Sao Paulo, Brazil*
ERNST KRAUS, *New York, New York*
MASAMICHI OKA, *Tokyo, Japan*
CHARLES K. PANISH, *Norwalk, Connecticut*
JAMES C. RISK, *New York, New York*
HANS M. F. SCHULMAN, *Alicante, Spain*
PETER SEABY, *London, England*
BEN, HARVEY, LAWRENCE and NORMAN STACK, *New York, New York*
STANLEY P. STARSIAK, *New York, New York*
ROBERT L. STEINBERG, *Boca Raton, Florida*
LUIS VIGDOR, *New York, New York*
JEAN VINCHON, *Paris, France*
ROBERT E. WESTFALL, *New York, New York*
DAVID G. G. WORLAND, *Pymble, Australia*

We are ever indebted to the following distinguished numismatists whose valuable assistance helped make possible the previous editions of "Gold Coins of the World:" -

RAOUL BAJOCCHI, *Cairo, Egypt*
L. M. BJORKQUIST, *Stockholm, Sweden*
EMILE BOURGEY, *Paris, France*
ERICH and HERBERT A. CAHN, *Basel, Switzerland*
HENRY (dec'd) and WILLIAM B. CHRISTENSEN, *Madison, New Jersey*
MAURICE GRENIER-LA FOREX, *Paris, France*
LEONARD FORRER, (dec'd), *Amsterdam, The Netherlands*
JACK FRIEDBERG, *Scottsdale, Arizona*
MADELEINE GLUCK, *Stockholm, Sweden*
KARL-LUDWIG GRABOW, *Berlin, Germany*
HENRY GRUNTHAL, *New York, New York*
MORTIMER HAMMEL, *New York, New York*
HANS HOLZER, *New York, New York*
D. G. LIDDELL, *London, England*
ANTONIO MARINO, *New York, New York*
LEO MILDENBERG, *Zurich, Switzerland*
PETER MITCHELL, *London, England*
MARK M. SALTON-SCHLESSINGER, *New York, New York*
JACQUES SCHULMAN, *Amsterdam, The Netherlands*
PETER N. SCHULTEN, *Frankfurt, Germany*
HERBERT A. SEABY (dec'd), *London, England*
C. R. SINGHAL, *Chandigarh, India*
IVAN G. SPASSKY, *Leningrad, U.S.S.R.*
DAVID SPINK, *London, England*
SIGMUND WERKNER, *Innsbruck, Austria*
HOLLAND WALLACE, *Sausalito, California*

and to

THE AMERICAN NUMISMATIC SOCIETY OF NEW YORK
for use of their library

THE BRITISH MUSEUM *for furnishing certain illustrations*

COIN WORLD *for use of their library and for furnishing illustrations of recent issues. Special thanks to Margo Russell, Courtney L. Coffing, David T. Alexander and Jane Hutchins.*

5

CONTENTS

PREFACE

INTRODUCTION TO GOLD COINS

The collecting of gold coins seems to have become a part of mankind almost since the first gold coins were struck by the ancient Greeks about 700 B.C.

Since then, gold coins have been struck by almost every government that has come into existence. The term government as used here, is an extension of any coining authority—permanent or provisional, secular or ecclesiastical, national or local, republican or royal.

Formidable quantities of gold coins have thus been struck over the centuries, and fortunately many have survived to enrich the culture of our times and provide the numismatist with a lifetime of pleasure and study.

That so many gold coins have survived since ancient times —generally in a choice state of preservation—is no accident, and can be attributed to the nature of gold itself as a metal and then to the love of mankind for the metal.

The chemical and physical properties of gold are too well known to require elaboration here. For the numismatist, however, it is important to remember that gold was selected as the supreme coinage because its rarity made it precious, because its color is unique and because its lustre will last forever. Gold coins which have been buried or otherwise secreted for hundreds or even for 2000 years, when finally discovered, were found to be in the same brilliant and untarnished condition as when they were first hidden.

It is this age-old tendency for gold to go underground that continually results in the unexpected discovery of new, unpublished coins, some of which may cast important light on a personage or place otherwise unknown or beclouded in history.

Mankind has learned to love the metal for good reason. His bitter experience has shown that in the face of war, invasion, revolution, panic, inflation, or other economic disaster, the gold coin, small as it is in size, has alone survived as the symbol of security when all other familiar standards of value have fallen in the general ruin.

Knowing this, the peoples of the world have developed an especial reverence for the gold coin, always preserving it, and in the face of any danger, hiding it. Sometimes, the original owners did not or could not reclaim their treasure and the coins have been lost to the world until accidentally exposed many years later, by a plough share, or a surging tide or by dynamite.

Even today the wealth of nations is sometimes measured in terms of gold, and since this is so, and to demonstrate how little the long history of gold has really changed, it will be noted that the governments of the world, as in the past, have hidden their monetary gold underground, where it is carefully kept in the safe control of their Central Banks, under permanent armed guard and protected by the latest devices against theft, burglary or assault, and by heavy construction against all forms of disaster.

Although the literature of numismatics is extensive, there are no books in existence devoted to gold coins of the world as a class by themselves. Considering the passionate interest in gold coins, the author has found this condition remarkable. Having been a professional numismatist for most of his adult life, the author, as well as many thousands of other numismatists the world over, has sorely regretted the lack of such a book in the literature of numismatics.

In order to get a reference on any gold coin struck before the 20th century, it was necessary to hunt out the standard work (if it existed) on the country involved, which work, of course, was devoted also to silver and minor coins. Obviously, there are many hundreds of such books; most of them are printed in a foreign language and are out of print; many of them are rare and valuable and simply unobtainable.

It was thus a formidable undertaking looking up, or looking for, earlier issues of gold coins of the world, requiring special facilities or outside research assistance or many hours of tedious, and sometimes fruitless labors in the library.

The author had long dreamed of improving this condition by creating a single volume to encompass the entire gold coinage of the world, excluding ancient coins and coins of the Byzantine Empire. It seemed grandiose at first and impossible of ever bringing about, because of the colossal amount of coins to be found in 1300 years of coinage.

However, some preliminary calculations showed that with a certain economy of format, it would be possible to create a single, moderate size volume without sacrificing any vital information or the all-important illustrations.

Therefore, drawing on his own experience, and that of the valued contributors, the author spent over five years in gathering and collecting the information for this book which was first published in 1958.

THE SCOPE OF "GOLD COINS OF THE WORLD"

This book concerns itself with the gold coinage of the world that began when the coinage of antiquity ended and following the age of nomadic invasion, when new governments with recognizable names came into existence. The aim has been to start the coin issues of each place with the first distinctive coins that positively identify the place as we know its name today, thus making the coinage truly national in character; having determined the starting point for each place, the coinage has been treated chronologically until it comes to its natural end by the suspension of gold coinage of the particular place. Some of the issues continue up to the present time.

The earliest coins listed in this book are the Axumite issues of Ethiopia of about 300 A.D. Of the European issues the earliest coins are from around 600 A.D. and minted for the Italian city of Beneventum. Among the coins of the Western Hemisphere the earliest issues are the Spanish Colonial pieces of Colombia, about 1621.

THE GEOGRAPHY OF THIS BOOK

The proper national placement of certain place-names, which sometimes posed a dilemma, has been solved by arbitrarily focusing on a period of time best known to the present generation. The period between the two World Wars has thus been selected, (and 1937 as a normal year of that period), as a point of reference for the geo-political boundaries of the world. Therefore, the coins of a country in existence in 1937 have been listed under the name of that country, even though the coins may have been struck much earlier under foreign suzerainty.

Certain innovations have thus been made, as under this rule, the coinage of countries like Esthonia or Latvia are listed under their own names, rather than as a Swedish coinage, which is consistent, for example, with the traditional listing of Spanish-American coins under their American names, rather than under Spain.

The countries are arranged alphabetically. Under some of the countries — for example, Germany — a separate heading has been given to a state, principality, duchy or city that issued its own coinage. The index at the end of the book will be helpful in finding any locality which issued coins.

THE DESCRIPTIONS AND DATES

Every type of coin that falls within the scope of this book, and which the author could find, has been listed and described. The obverse of the coin is always described first. The description is followed by the various denominations and dates of that particular type. The use of a name only in the description indicates a standing figure. Otherwise, head, bust, etc. are used.

Coins without dates are followed by ND. In general, when a coin has from one to about four dates, all the dates have been listed; otherwise the first and last dates only have been used, but all years may not necessarily exist between these ultimate dates.

The author will be grateful for any omissions which are called to his attention, so that the coins can be included in future editions of this book.

THE ILLUSTRATIONS

About one half of the space in this book is devoted to the illustrations of the coins which are shown in actual size. At great additional expense, they have been incorporated within the text, where they belong, rather than at the end of the book as a separate section of plates. The description of the illustration is immediately below it.

An asterisk (*) alongside the denomination and date indicates that this is the coin illustrated above the description. In case there is only one denomination for the type of coin being illustrated, no asterisk has been used.

A variety of sizes of illustrations has purposely been used, as this will help to identify the denominations of those coins which are without the mark of value.

Most types from the very beginning have been illustrated — certainly since about 1700, the illustrations are virtually complete for all types. There are more than 3000 illustrations of gold coins in this book — more than have ever been illustrated in any one coin book of comparable size, and the author believes that almost all coins of general familiarity to numismatists have been shown.

THE VALUATIONS AND STATE OF PRESERVATION

The author publishes the valuations as a general guide to the value of the coins on the numismatic market. No one by himself can profess to know the numismatic value of every gold coin that has ever been struck. Hence, voluminous sales records have been consulted. These have been used in conjunction with the author's twenty years of experience in professional numismatics combined with the accumulated experience of the contributors, and it is believed that the present valuations reflect the true rarity, condition, demand and availability of the coins as of this printing.

These valuations represent an approximate figure at which the coins would change hands as between a well informed buyer and a well informed professional numismatist. They are based on recent sales records or are an extension into the present time of old sales records.

The valuation of rarities has been especially difficult because the coins have appeared so seldom. In some cases, they have not been valued at all and have been merely marked "rare." In other cases, the valuation has been determined by comparison of the coin with the known value of another coin of equal rarity or other similar attributes.

In any case, the valuation of a great rarity must be considered as purely nominal and at best can be an indication only that the coin is of extraordinary value. The author's experience in modern times has shown that when a great rarity has been put on the numismatic market, it has always tended to exceed its last known price because of an ever increasing demand for such coins.

In general, the numismatic value of a coin is determined partly by condition, partly by rarity and almost always by the inexorable law of supply and demand, which might sometimes cause a great divergence from the valuations in this book.

These valuations are for the average condition in which the coin is most frequently encountered, and for the commonest date or variety of the type. Coins in a superior condition or with rarer dates would command a higher price. In general, experience has shown that these average conditions are as follows:

For coins up to about 1800, the valuations are for fine to very fine specimens.

For coins from about 1800 to 1914, the valuations are for very fine specimens.

For coins from about 1914 to date, the valuations are for uncirculated (mint state) specimens or for choice specimens showing hardly any wear.

For coins marked "not placed in circulation," the valuations are for uncirculated or proof specimens.

THE BULLION VALUE OF GOLD COINS

Some gold coins, i.e. those commonly referred to as bullion coins, have little numismatic value and sell at a slight premium above the intrinsic value of the gold content of the coin. The value of these coins fluctuates in direct relation to the daily price of gold on the international market.

Bullion coins are designated in the text by the reference mark (B) following their price. It should be noted that the prices listed in the text are based on a gold price of $725 an ounce.

The reader can use Tables I and II in the Appendix to ascertain the current bullion value of these coins.

(For a more detailed discussion of these coins, see the introduction to ''Recent Issues Starting With 1960,'' page 419.)

PATTERNS, PROOFS, UNOFFICIAL ISSUES AND OFF-STRIKES

The author has attempted to include in the book all manner of gold coins which from time to time appear among numismatists. Among such coins are the fascinating series of patterns, proofs and essais. **These have been designated by the general term ''not placed in circulation.''** They are legitimate Government Mint issues and are among the rarest and most prized of gold coins, almost always appearing in proof condition.

Other coins have been plainly labelled as unofficially or privately made. These are not the official coins of any government and such coins have been manufactured exclusively for collectors, or for use in the gold markets of the world.

The question of including off-strikes in this book has posed a seemingly insoluble problem. (An off-strike is regarded as a coin struck in gold from the same die used to strike a non-gold coin). Off-strikes are generally the larger pieces of ducat coinage — from 3 Ducats up. Depending on what series was involved, they have sometimes been included, other times not, in keeping with traditional usage.

There is still no unanimity of opinion among numismatists whether to regard as legitimate, a gold coin weighing exactly what a 10 Ducat piece should weigh, but not bearing a mark of value and struck from the same die used to strike a silver Taler, similarly without the mark of value. Since most early gold coins are without the mark of value in any case (their true face value being their weight and purity), the question seems academic.

RESTRIKES

When the letter ''R'' appears after a number, it indicates that the coin is a restrike. Some countries, notably Austria, Hungary, Mexico and Spain, have issued newly struck versions of older coins, which bear the same design and date as the original although issued at a later time. Further information about restrikes can be found in the introduction to Part II, ''Recent Issues Starting With 1960.''

A BRIEF HISTORY OF THE LATIN MONETARY UNION

The Latin Monetary Union, which had a world-wide influence on the minting of gold coins, was formed in 1865 by France, Belgium, Italy and Switzerland. These countries were on a bimetallic monetary standard with a ratio between silver and gold of 15.5 to 1. This ratio was established by France in 1803 and had been adopted by Belgium, Italy and Switzerland for their coinage prior to forming the Union. Thus, the French monetary system was the predominating influence in the Union. The treaty provided that gold coins should continue to be struck with a fineness of .900 and that the denominations were to be of uniform weight and value.

Greece joined the Union in 1868. It, like the other countries, had been minting gold coins on the French standard prior to becoming a member of the Union.

France, through the Union, attempted to establish a universal monetary system based on the French unit. Although France was not entirely successful in this endeavor, a number of non-member countries did base their gold coinage on the standards of the Latin Monetary Union. However, these countries retained their own monetary unit and struck the gold coins according to specified weight and fineness. For instance, the 20 Peso of Guatemala had the same value as the French 100 Franc coin.

The following countries struck gold coins based on the standards set by the Latin Monetary Union:

Albania	Peru
Argentina	Philippines
Belgium	Poland
Bulgaria	Roumania
Colombia	Russia
Finland	Salvador
France	San Marino
Greece	Serbia
Guatemala	Spain
Honduras	Switzerland
Italy	Tunis
Monaco	Venezuela
Montenegro	Yugoslavia

World War I had a serious effect on the currencies of many nations which resulted in the discontinuance of gold coins in these countries for several years. An aftermath of these difficulties was the final dissolvement of the Latin Monetary Union in 1926. Nevertheless, some countries struck gold coins after that date based on the weight and fineness established by the Union. Among these issues are coins of Liechtenstein, Luxembourg, Roumania and Switzerland.

ABBREVIATIONS USED IN THIS BOOK

ND for no date
mm for mint mark
Obv. for obverse
Rev. for reverse

républicaine ou monarchique.

Pour le Lecteur Français.

PREFACE

QUELQUES NOTES SUR LES MONNAIES D'OR

Il semble que la collection de pièces d'or fait partie de l'humanité dès que les premières monnaies d'or ont été frappées par les anciens grecs, vers l'an 700 av. J. C. environ.

Dès lors, des pièces d'or ont été frappées par presque tous les gouvernements qui virent le jour. Le terme de gouvernement, tel que nous l'employons ici, s'étend à toute autorité frappant de la monnaie, fût-elle permanente ou provisoire, séculaire ou éclésiastique, nationale ou locale,

Des quantités énormes de pièces d'or ont ainsi été frappées au cours des siècles et heureusement un grand nombre a été conservé pour enrichir la culture de notre époque et fournir au numismate une vie remplie de plaisir et d'étude.

Le fait que tant de pièces d'or ont survécu depuis les temps anciens, généralement dans un état de conservation excellent, n'est pas un accident, mais une conséquence de la nature de l'or en tant que métal et de l'amour de l'humanité pour ce métal.

Les propriétés physiques et chimiques de l'or sont trop bien connues, elles ne seront plus traitées ici en profondeur.

Pour le numismate il est toutefois important de se souvenir que l'or a été choisi comme métal suprême pour les monnaies, parce que sa rareté le rend précieux, parce que sa couleur est unique et parce que son lustre dure éternellement. Les pièces d'or qui furent enfouies sous terre ou cachées dans n'importe quel endroit pendant des siècles, même jusqu'à 2000 ans, se révélèrent enfin, lorsqu'on les découvrit, inaltéréss dans leur condition, brillantes et non ternies, telles qu'on les avait cachées.

C'est cette vieille tendance de l'or à s'enfouir sous terre ce qui a pour résultat la découverte continuelle et inespérée de pièces nouvelles, inédites. Certaines d'entre elles peuvent jeter une lumière importante sur un personnage ou un endroit qui resterait sans celà inconnu ou embrumé dans le cours de l'histoire.

L'humanité a appris à aimer ce métal pour une bonne cause. L'expérience amère lui a montré qu'en face de la guerre, des invasions, des révolutions, de la panique, de l'inflation ou d'autres désastres économiques, la pièce d'or, toute petite qu'elle soit, n'est pas moins restéele seul symbole de la sécurité, alors que tous les autres standards de valeurs familiers se sont effondrés dans la ruine générale.

Sachant cela les peuples du monde entier ont développé une révérence spéciale pour la pièce d'or, la conservant toujours, prêts à la cacher devant tout danger. Parfois les propriétaires ne voulaient ou ne pouvaient plus réclamer leur trésor et les pièces furent ainsi perdues et oubliées jusqu'à ce que, maintes années plus tard, elles aient été mises à jour par hasard, grâce au soc d'une charrue, au flot de la marée ou à la dynamite.

Aujourd'hui encore, la richesse des nations quelque fois se mesure d'après la quantité d'or. Pour cette raison et afin de montrer combien la longue histoire de l'or a en réalité peu changée, on notera que les gouvernements du monde entier enfouissent aujourd'hui comme jadis leurs réserves d'or dans le sol. Il y reste conservé consciencieusement sous le contrôle sûr des Banques Centrales et des gardes permanentes armées. On le protège avec les dispositifs les plus efficaces contre le vol, le cambriolage et l'attaque et par des constructions massives contre toute sorte de désastre.

Bien que la littérature numismatique soit abondante, il n'existe encore aucun livre consacré exclusivement aux monnaies d'or du monde entier. Etant donné l'ntérêt passionné pour ces pièces, l'auteur a trouvé cette situation pour le moins remarquable. Numismate professionnel pendant la plupart de sa vie, l'auteur, de même que des milliers d'autres numismates, a regretté vivement l'absence d'un tel livre dans littérature numismatique.

Afin d'obtenir des informations sur les pièces d'or frappées avant le 20ème siècle, il a fallu consulter les travaux standards (s'ils existaient) du pays en question. Ces travaux spécialisés, bien entendu, traitaient aussi les pièces d'argent et d'autres métaux. Il existent, évidemment, de centaines de tels livres, la plupart écrits dans la langue du pays. L'édition en est très souvent épuisée et ils sont devenus rares et il est presque impossible de se les procurer.

C'était donc une entreprise formidable que de se mettre à étudier et à rechercher les émissions anciennes de monnaies d'or du monde entier. On avait besoin de privilèges spéciaux, d'assistants pour les recherches au dehors à part les longues heures de travail fastidieux et d'efforts parfois inutiles à la bibliothèque.

Depuis longtemps l'auteur rêvait d'améliorer cette situation en créant un seul volume qui comprendrait toutes les monnaies d'or du monde à l'exception des pièces antiques et de celles de tout l'empire byzantin. A première vue cette entreprise semblait prétentieuse et impossible à mener à

bout, en vue de la quantite inouie de pieces que l'on peut trouver au cours de 1300 ans.

Néanmoins quelques calculs préliminaires montrèrent qu'avec une certaine économie dans le format il serait possible de présenter un seul volume de dimensions modérées sans laisser de côté ni les renseignements essentiels, ni les illustrations très importantes.

Puisant dans sa propre expérience et dans celle de ses estimables collaborateurs, l'auteur a passé cinq années à réunir et sélectionner les renseignements pour ce volume, publié pour la première fois en 1958.

CADRE ET OBJET DE "PIÈCES D'OR DU MONDE"

Ce livre commence par les émissions de monnaies d'or à partir de la période des invasions nomades finissant l'antiquité, lorsque de nouveaux gouvernements avec de noms reconnaissables s'établirent. Le but livre était de commencer avec les toutes premières émissions distinctives de pièces de chaque endroit, qui identifient avec certitude chaque contrée telle que nous la connaissons aujourd'hui, ce qui donne à la monnaie un caractère vraiment national. Après avoir déterminé le point de départ pour chaque endroit, on a traité les monnaies dans l'ordre chronologique jusqu'à leur disparition naturelle par suspension de la frappe de monnaies en or en cet endroit particulier. Certaines émissions se poursuivent jusqu'à ce jour.

Les pièces les plus anciennes qui figurent dans ce livre sont les émissions Axumites d'Ethiopie de l'an 300 A.D. approximativement. Quant aux émissions européennes, les plus anciennes datent de l'an 600 A.D. environ; elles furent frappées pour la ville de Bénévent en Italie. Les premières monnaies de l'hémisphère occidentale sont les pièces coloniales espagnoles de la Colombie, vers 1621.

LES DATES GÉOGRAPHIQUES DANS CE LIVRE

L'emplacement national correct de certains noms d'endroits problématiques a été fixée arbitrairement en tenant compte de la période la mieux connue par la génération actuelle. C'est ainsi que la période entre les deux guerres mondiales a été choisie (1937 étant considérée une année normale de cette période) comme point de référence des frontières géo-politiques du monde. En conséquence, les pièces d'un pays existant en 1937 ont été classées sous le nom de ce pays, bien que ces pièces auraient pu être frappées bien avant sous une suzeraineté étrangère.

On a fait quelques innovations suivant ce principe. C'est ainsi que les monnaies de pays tels que l'Esthonie ou la Lettonie sont classées sous leurs propres noms, et non parmi les monnaies suédoises, ce qui est cohérent, par exemple, avec le classement traditionnel des pièces hispano-américaines sous leurs noms américains et non sous la rubrique de l'Espagne.

Les pays se suivent dans l'ordre alphabéthique. Sous quelques rubriques—par exemple l'Allemagne—des en-têtes spéciaux introduisent chaque Etat, principauté, duché ou ville qui émit ses propres monnaies. L'index à la fin de ce livre servira à retrouver toute localité qui a frappé de la monnaie.

LES DESCRIPTIONS ET LES DATES

Chaque type de pièce que l'auteur a pu trouver et qui entre dans le cadre de ce livre, a été classé et décrit. Le côté face (Avers.) est toujours décrit en premier. La description est suivie des diverses dénominations et dates de ce type en particulier. Un nom seul dans la description indique un personnage debout. Autrement, on se sert des mots tête, buste, etc.

Les pièces sans date sont suivies de ND. En général, lorsqu'un même type a été émis avec une à quatre dates environ, on énumère toutes ces dates. Dans les autres cas on s'est servi de la première et de la dernière, mais toutes les années n'existent pas forcément entre ces dates mentionnées.

L'auteur sera reconnaissant de toute omission qui sera portée à son attention, de sorte que les pièces en question puissent figurer dans les éditions à venir.

LES ILLUSTRATIONS

A peu près la moitié de la capacité de ce livre a été consacrée aux illustrations des pièces représentées en grandeur naturelle. Avec de grands frais supplémentaires elles ont été incorporées dans le texte, au lieu de les placer à la fin du livre sous forme d'une section de planches séparées. La description de la monnaie suit immédiatement au-dessous de l'illustration.

Un astérisque (*) à côté de la dénomination et de la date indique qu'il s'agit de la pièce illustrée au-dessus de la description. Dans le cas où il y a seulement une dénomination pour le type de pièce illustré, on ne s'est pas servi d'astérisque.

Des illustrations de tailles différentes ont été utilisées à dessein, pour aider à identifier les dénominations des pièces sans marques de valeur.

Depuis le début la plupart des types se trouve illustré, et après 1700 environ, les illustrations sont virtuellement complètes pour tous les types. Il y a plus de 3000 illustrations de pièces d'or dans ce livre—plus qu'on n'a jamais représentées dans un seul volume numismatique de dimensions comparables, et l'auteur pense bien avoir publié presque toutes les pièces avec lesquelles les numismates sont généralement familiers.

LES ÉVALUATIONS ET L'ÉTAT DE CONSERVATION

L'auteur a mis les évaluations comme guide général pour la valeur des pièces sur le marché numismatique. Personne ne peut prétendre de connaître par lui tout seul la valeur numismatique de toutes les monnaies d'or qui ont été frappées. Par conséquent, des catalogues de vente ont été consultés. L'auteur s'en est servi ainsi que de l'expérience de ses collaborateurs, pour compléter sa propre expérience de 20 ans dans le domaine de la numismatique professionnelle. De cette manière ces évaluations donnent sans doute un tableau fidèle de la véritable rareté, de la condition, de la demande et des disponibilités des pièces à la date de la publication.

Ces évaluations veulent être approximatives et l'on suppose que les pièces sont échangées entre un acheteur et un numismate professionnel tous deux bien informés. Elles sont basées sur des actes de ventes récentes et représentent une mise à jour de vieux compte-rendus de ventes.

L'évaluation de pièces rares est particulierement difficile car de telles pièces n'apparaissent pas souvent sur le marché. Dans certains cas ces monnaies n'ont pas été évaluées du tout, on les a simplement étiquetées de ''rare''. Dans d'autre cas les évaluations ont été déterminées par comparaison avec la valeur connue d'une autre pièce de rareté égale ou qui présente des attributs similaires.

De toute manière, l'évaluation d'une pièce de grande rareté doit être considérée comme purement nominale et ne saurait être qu'une indication que la pièce est d'une valeur extraordinaire. L'expérience de l'auteur à l'époque actuelle a montrée que quand une pièce de grande rareté

a été mise sur le marché, elle aura toujours la tendance à excéder son dernier prix connu car il y a une demande toujours croissante pour de telles pièces.

En général la valeur numismatique d'une pièce est déterminée d'une part par la condition, d'autre part par la rareté et presque toujours par la loi inexorable de l'offre et de la demande, ce qui peut causer parfois de larges divergences avec les évaluations de ce livre.

Ces évaluations s'entendent pour un état de conservation moyen et pour la date et la variété la plus commune de ce type. Des pièces de meilleure condition ou avec des dates plus rares demandent un prix plus élevé. La pratique a montré qu'en général ces conditions moyennes sont les suivantes:

Pour des pieces jusqu'a l'an 1800 environ les evaluations s'entendent pour des specimens en bel état à trés bel état.

Pour des pièces allant de 1800 a 1914 environ, les évaluations s'entendent pour des spécimens en très bel état.

Pour des pièces allant de 1914 environ jusqu'à nos jours, les évaluations s'entendent pour des spécimens qui n'ont pas circulé (fleur de coin) ou pour des spécimens de choix qui n'ont guère circulé.

Pour des pièces marquées ''non mises en circulation'', les évaluations s'entendent pour des spécimens n'ayant pas circulé ou des spécimens d'épreuve (flan bruni).

LA VALEUR DU CONTENU NET EN OR DES MONNAIES

Quelque monnaies d'or, par exemple, ceux communement voir le comme monnaies en lingots, ont une peu valeur numismatique et vendre à peu prime par-dessus la valeur intrinsèque du contenu d'or de la monnaie. La valeur des monnaies flotte en relation direct au prix journalier d'or en le marché international.

Monnaies en lingots sont designé dans le text par le renvoi (B) après leur prix. Il auraient été noter cela les prix sont cataloguent dans le texte fondent dans le prix d'or de $725 par once. Le lecteur sait utilise Tables I et II dans l'appendice afin d'obtenir la valeur lingots courant des monnaies.

(Pour une discussion plus de détail de les monnaies, voyez l'introduction à ''Recent Issues Starting With 1960,'' page 419.)

ESSAIS, ÉPREUVES, ÉMISSIONS NON-OFFICIELLES, FRAPPES HORS-SÉRIES

L'auteur a essayé de placer dans le livre toutes sortes de pièces d'or qui apparaissent de temps en temps chez les numismates. Parmi ces pièces figurent les séries fascinantes des épreuves et essais. **On les a designés avec le terme général ''non mises en circulation''.** Ce sont des émissions légitimes de la Monnaie du Gouvernement et elles comptent parmi les pièces d'or les plus rares et les plus recherchées, apparaissant presque toujours dans une condition exceptionnelle.

D'autres pièces ont été nettement reconnues non-officielles ou de facture privée. Aucun gouvernement n'a émis ces pièces officiellement. Elles ont été faites exclusivement pour les collectionneurs et pour les marchés mondiaux de l'or.

La question d'inclure les frappes hors-séries dans ce livre a posé un problème qui semblait tout d'abord insoluble. (Une pièce hors-serie est une pièce en or frappée de la matrice qui avait été employée pour des monnaies d'autres métaux). Ces frappes sont généralement des multiples du ducat—3 ducats et plus. D'après les séries intéressées elles ont été parfois inclues et parfois exclues de la classification, suivant l'usage et la tradition.

L'opinion n'est pas toujours unanime parmi les numismates

quand il s'agit de considérer comme légitime une pièce d'or qui pèse exactement 10 ducats sans toutefois porter aucune marque de valeur. Cette pièce a été frappée du même coin qui a servi pour frapper le taler d'argent, lui aussi sans marque de valeur. Etant donné que la plupart des pièces d'or ne portaient pas de marque de valeur (leur valeur réelle étant leur poids et leur pureté) la question semble purement académique.

REFRAPPES

Quand la lettre "R" se trouve après un numéro, cela indique que la pièce est une refrappe. Quelques pays, notamment l'Autriche, la Hongrie, le Mexique et l'Espagne ont émis des versions récemment frappées d'anciennes pièces qui portent le meme dessin et la meme date que les pieces originales bien qu'elles soient emises plus tard. Des renseignements additionels sur les refrappes peuvent être trouvés dans l'introduction à la Partie II, "Recent Issues Starting With 1960" (Emissions récentes commençant avec 1960).

BRÈVE HISTOIRE DE L'UNION MONÉTAIRE LATINE

L'Union Monétaire Latine qui a influencé la frappe de monnaies d'or à travers le monde a été formée en 1865 par la France, la Belgique, l'Italie et la Suisse. Ces pays basaient leur systeme monétaire bimetallique sur l'argent et l'or dans un rapport de 15.5 à 1. Ce rapport fut introduit en France en 1803 et l'Italie, la Suisse et la Belgique l'avaient adopté avant la fondation de l'Union. C'est pourquoi le système monétaire français a eu une influence prédominante dans l'Union. Le traité assurait la frappe de monnaies d'or dans une finesse de .900 demême que l'uniformité de la valeur et du poids de chaque dénomination.

La Grèce joignit l'Union en 1868. De même que les autres pays membres, la Grèce avait émis des monnaies d'or dans le standard français déjà avant de faire partie de l'Union.

En se servant de l'Union, la France tenta d'établir un système monétaire universel basé sur l'unité française. Elle n'a pas réussi entièrement à réaliser cette idée, pourtant de nombreux pays qui n'étaient pas membres adoptèrent le standard de l'Union Monétaire Latine comme base pour leurs monnaies d'or. Ces pays gardaient leur propre unité monétaire, mais ils frappèrent dorénavant les monnaies d'or d'après le poids et la finesse spécifiés. Par exemple, la pièce de 20 pesos de Guatemala avait la même valeur que celle de 100 francs français.

Les pays suivants ont frappé des monnaies d'or sur la base des standards fixés par l'Union Monétaire Latine:

Albanie	Monténégro
Argentine	Pérou
Belgique	Philippines
Bulgarie	Pologne
Colombie	Roumanie
Espagne	Russie
Finlande	Saint-Marin
France	Salvador
Grèce	Serbie
Guatemala	Suisse
Honduras	Tunisie
Italie	Vénézuela
Monaco	Yougoslavie

La première guerre mondiale a influencé profondément le système monétaire de bien de pays. Une discontinuité dans la frappe de monnaies d'or s'est manifestée dans ces pays pendant plusieurs années. Les difficultés se multiplièrent lorsque l'Union Monétaire Latine s'est effondrée en 1926. Pourtant après cette date quelques pays continuèrent à frapper des monnaies d'or en reconnaissant comme base le poids et la finesse fixés par l'Union. Parmi ces émissions se trouvent les pièces du Liechtenstein, du Luxembourg, de la Roumanie et de la Suisse.

ABRÉVIATIONS EMPLOYÉES DANS CE VOLUME

ND pour non daté
mm pour marque monétaire
Obv. pour côté face
Rev. pour revers

Für den deutschen Leser.

EINLEITUNG

EINFÜHRUNG ZU "GOLDMÜNZEN DER WELT"

Die ersten Goldmünzen wurden im 7. Jahrhundert vor Christus von den Griechen geprägt. Es hat wohl nicht lange gedauert, bis der Mensch begann, diese schönen und wertvollen Stücke zu sammeln.

Fast jede Regierung hat seither Goldmünzen geprägt. Der Begriff "Regierung" wird hier ausgedehnt auf jede Behörde, die Münzen prägen lässt, ob sie dauernd bestehe oder vorübergehend, ob sie weltlich sei oder geistlich, national oder regional, republikanisch oder königlich.

Riesige Mengen von Goldmünzen sind im Lauf der Jahrhunderte geschlagen worden, und glücklicherweise sind viele bis auf den heutigen Tag erhalten geblieben. Sie bereichern unsere Kultur und verschaffen dem Numismatiker ein Leben voll Freude und Arbeit.

Es ist kein Zufall, dass so viele Goldmünzen erhalten geblieben sind, im allgemeinen in ausgezeichnetem Zustand. Dies liegt an der unverwüstlichen Natur des Goldes und an der Liebe des Menschen zu diesem Metall. Es ist nicht nötig, sich hier mit den allgemein bekannten chemischen und physikalischen Eigenschaften des Goldes auseinander zu setzen. Der Numismatiker erinnere sich jedoch daran, dass das Gold als höchstgeschätzes Münzmaterial gewählt wurde, weil seine Seltenheit es wertvoll macht und seine Farbe und sein Glanz einzigartig sind. Goldmünzen können eingegraben, oder sonst auf irgendeine Weise versteckt während Jahrhunderten liegen oder sogar während 2000 und mehr Jahren: wenn sie entdeckt werden, glänzen sie makellos, wie wenn sie eben erst versteckt worden wären.

Diese uralte Tendenz des Goldes, unter die Erde zu verschwinden, zeitigt immer wieder unerwartete Entdeckungen neuer, unveröffentlichter Münzen. Manche von ihnen werfen Licht auf eine historische Persönlichkeit oder eine historische Stätte, die sonst im Dunkel bleiben würden.

Die Menschen haben gelernt, das Metall zu lieben. Bittere Erfahrungen haben ihnen gezeigt, dass die kleinen Goldmünzen angesichts von Krieg, Invasion, Revolutionen, Panik, Inflation oder anderer wirtschaftlicher Katastrophen allein das Symbol der Sicherheit geblieben sind, wenn alle anden bekannten Wertbegriffe dem Ruin anheimfielen.

Weil sie das erkannten, haben die Völker der Welt gelernt, die Goldmünzen besonders zu verehren. Sie haben sie aufbewahrt und vor einer drohenden Gefahr versteckt. Manchmal haben die ursprünglichen Besitzer ihren Schatz nicht wieder gehoben oder konnten ihn nicht wieder in Besitz nehmen. Die Münzen waren dann für die Welt verloren, bis sie zufällig, nach vielen Jahren, von einer Pflugschar, einer Flutwelle oder durch Dynamit zum Vorschein gebracht wurden.

Auch heute noch wird der Wohlstand einer Nation zuweilen an ihrem Goldbesitz gemessen. Dass dies so ist, beweist die Tatsache, dass die Regierungen, wie man das früher tat, ihr Münzgold unterirdisch verborgen halten, wo es sorgfältig unter der Kontrolle ihrer Zentralbanken aufbewahrt wird: es befindet sich unter der dauernden Obhut bewaffneter Wächter, geschützt durch alle Vorrichtungen gegen Diebstahl, Einbruch oder Ueberfall und durch solide Bauweise gegen alle Unglücksfälle. Dies alles zeigt, wie wenig sich eigentlich in der langen Geschichte des Goldes geändert hat.

Obwohl die numismatische Literatur gross ist, gibt es keine Bücher, welche die Goldmünzen der Welt als Gebiet für sich behandeln. Der Verfasser fand diesen Zustand angesichts des leidenschaftlichen Interesses an Goldmünzen merkwürdig. Er, der fast sein ganzes Leben lang ein berufsmässiger Numismatiker war, und viele tausend andere Numismatiker in der ganzen Welt haben das Fehlen eines solchen Buches in der numismatischen Literatur ausserordentlich bedauert. Um eine Auskunft über irgendeine Goldmünze zu erhalten, die vor dem zwanzigsten Jahrhundert geschlagen worden war, musste man das massgebende Werk des betreffenden Landes, falls ein solches existierte, ausfindig machen; dieses Buch war dann natürlich auch noch den Silbermünzen und dem Kleingeld gewidmet. Bekanntlich gibt es mehrere Hundert solcher Bücher; die meisten von ihnen sind in einer Fremdsprache geschrieben oder vergriffen. Viele von ihnen sind selten, wertvoll und nicht erhältlich. Es war also keine kleine Aufgabe, nach alten Büchern über Goldmünzen zu suchen und in ihnen die einschlägigen Stellen ausfindig zu machen. Oft erforderte diese Arbeit besondere Erlaubnisse oder Forschungsbeihilfen, sie zwang zu vielen Stunden von ermüdendem, oft erfolglosem Suchen in den Bibliotheken.

Der Verfasser träumte lange davon, diesem Umstand durch die Herausgabe eines einzigen Buches, welches die gesamten Goldmünzen der Welt — ausschliesslich der antiken und byzantinischen Münzen — umfassen sollte, Abhilfe zu schaffen. Dieses Unterfangen erschien zuerst vermessen, und, auch wegen der riesigen Menge von Münzen, die während 13 Jahrhunderten geschlagen worden waren, undurchführbar.

Die Vorbereitungen zeigten jedoch, dass es bei einer gewissen Sparsamkeit im Format möglich wäre, einen einzigen Band mässigen Ausmasses herauszubringen, ohne wesentliche Auskünfte oder wichtige Abbildungen zu opfern. Der Verfasser hat über fünf Jahre damit zugebracht, das Material für dieses Buch (1. Ausgabe 1958) zu sammeln und zu sichten.

DER INHALT DES WERKES "GOLDMÜNZEN DER WELT"

Dieses Buch befasst sich mit der Goldmünzenprägung der Welt vom Ende des Altertums an und folgt dann dem Zeitalter des Einbruchs der Nomaden, in dem neue Regierungen mit erkennbaren Namen entstanden. Dabei liess man die Münzprägung eines Ortes mit der ersten eindeutig von diesem Ort stammenden Münze beginnen, um so den nationalen und regionalen Charakter einer Münzserie deutlich zu machen. Innerhalb der Emission eines Ortes liess man die Münzen chronologisch aufeinander folgen, bis die betreffende Prägung eingestellt wurde. Einige Emissionen dauern bis heute an.

Die ältesten Münzen, die in diesem Buch aufgeführt werden, sind die axumitischen Prägungen vom Ende des 3.

Jahrhunderts. Die ältesten europäischen Münzen wurden um 600 in der italienischen Stadt Benevent geprägt. Unter den Münzen der westlichen Hemisphäre sind die frühesten Prägungen die spanischen Kolonialmünzen von Kolumbien aus den Jahren um 1620.

DER GEOGRAPHISCHE BEREICH DES BUCHES

Es ist oft schwierig zu entscheiden, in welchem Land man einen Ort, der im Lauf der Geschichte ein oder mehrere Male die Herrschaft gewechselt hat, unterbringen soll. Man hat deshalb einen der heutigen Generation bekannten Zeitpunkt herausgegriffen, nämlich das Jahr 1937. Die geographische Lage in diesem Jahr wurde für die Zuteilung einzelner Orte an bestimmte Nationen massgebend.

In einigen Fällen ist man jedoch nicht nach diesem System verfahren. So wurden Estland und Lettland unter ihrem eigenen Namen aufgeführt und nicht unter Schweden, wie es auch üblich ist, die hispano-amerikanischen Münzen unter Amerika, und nicht unter Spanien, aufzuführen.

Die Länder sind alphabetisch geordnet. Bei einigen Ländern, zum Beispiel bei Deutschland, setzte man eine separate Ueberschrift für ein Land, ein Fürstentum, ein Herzogtum, eine Stadt, die eigene Münzen herausgaben. Das Verzeichnis am Schluss des Buches wird zum Auffinden jedes Ortes, der Münzen geprägt hat, gute Dienste leisten.

DIE BESCHREIBUNGEN UND DATEN

Jeder Münztypus, der in den Rahmen dieses Buches passt und der dem Verfasser bekannt ist, ist hier aufgeführt und beschrieben. Der Avers der Münze wird immer zuerst beschrieben. Der Beschreibung folgen die verschiedenen Werte und Daten des betreffenden Typs. Wenn in der Beschreibung von Figuren die Rede ist, sind stehende Figuren gemeint; andernfalls wird die Figur näher bezeichnet (Kopf, Büste usw.) Hinter undatierten Stücken steht der Vermerk "ND". Wenn eine Münze weniger als fünf Prägedaten aufweist, werden alle angegeben. Sind es mehr Daten, werden nur das erste und das letzte angegeben, was nicht heisst, dass alle dazwischen liegenden Jahre Prägedaten der betreffenden Münze sind. Der Autor ist dankbar für jeden Hinweis auf eine von diesem Buch noch nicht erfasste Münze, die in einer neuen Auflage aufgeführt werden kann.

DIE ABBILDUNGEN

Etwa die Hälfte des verfügbaren Raumes in diesem Buch ist den Abbildungen der Münzen in ihrer Originalgrösse gewidmet. Unter grossen Kosten wurden sie im Text, dort, wo sie hingehören, eingefügt. Ein separater Bildteil am Schluss des Buches konnte so umgangen werden. Die Beschreibung einer Münze befindet sich unmittelbar unter ihrer Abbildung. Ein Sternchen (*) neben Nennwert und Datum zeigt an, dass es sich in der Beschreibung um das abgebildete Stück handelt. Falls es von einer Münze nur einen Nennwert gibt, wird das Sternchen weggelassen.

Da die Münzen in ihrer Originalgrösse abgebildet sind, ist es möglich, den Wert der Stücke, die keine Angabe des Nennwertes aufweisen, ungefähr abzuschätzen.

Die meisten Münztypen, beginnend mit den ersten Prägungen, sind abgebildet. Von 1700 an sind alle Münztypen ausnahmslos abgebildet. Abbildungen von mehr als 3000 Goldmünzen sind in diesem Buch vereinigt. Das sind mehr, als je in einem Buch der gleichen Grössenordnung abgebildet wurden. Der Verfasser glaubt, dass fast alle Münzen, die dem Numismatiker im allgemeinen geläufig sind, auch im Bild gezeigt wurden.

BEWERTUNGEN UND ERHALTUNGSGRAD

Der Verfasser veröffentlicht die Schätzwerte als allgemeine Anleitung für den Wert der Münzen auf dem numismatischen Markt. Niemand kann behaupten, den numismatischen Wert jeder einzelnen Münze, die je geschlagen wurde, zu kennen. Aus diesem Grunde wurden umfangreiche Auktionsergebnisse zu Rate gezogen. Die Auswertung dieser Unterlagen und die zwanzigjährige berufsnumismatische Erfahrung des Verfassers und seiner Mitarbeiter erlaubten es, Schätzwerte, Seltenheit, Zustand, sowie Angebot und Nachfrage der einzelnen Stücke zu bestimmen und zwar nach dem derzeitigen Stand.

Diese Zahlen sind approximative Werte. Ungefähr zu diesen Preisen werden Münzen von Numismatikern angekauft. Sie basieren auf neueren Verkaufsverzeichnissen oder sind die Angleichungen alter Verkaufsergebnisse an den heutigen Stand.

Die Bewertung von Raritäten war besonders schwierig, weil es für solche Münzen keine Bewertungsgrundlagen gibt. In einigen Fällen konnten sie überhaupt nicht bewertet werden; die Stücke wurden dann nur mit "selten" bezeichnet. In anden Fällen bestimmte man den Wert einer Münze durch den Vergleich mit einer ähnlich seltenen oder ähnlich kostbaren Münze. Auf alle Fälle können die Schätzungen der seltenen Stücke nur als grobe Richtlinien gelten. Der Verfasser weiss aus Erfahrung, dass solche Raritäten, wenn sie einmal auf den Markt kommen, oft enorm hohe Preise erzielen, weil eine ständig wachsende Nachfrage danach besteht.

Im allgemeinen wird der Wert einer Münze teils durch ihren Zustand, teils durch ihre Seltenheit und meistens durch das unerbittliche Gesetz von Angebot und Nachfrage bestimmt. Letzteres ist der Grund für grössere Abweichungen der erzielten Preise von den Schätzungen in diesem Buch. **Diese Schätzungen gelten für Münzen in einem durchschnittlichen Erhaltungsgrad, so wie man ihnen am häufigsten begegnet, und zwar für das häufigste Datum und den gebräuchlichsten Typ.** Münzen von besserem Erhaltungsgrad und von selteneren Datum würden einen höheren Preis erzielen. Erfahrungsgemäss gelten folgende Erhaltungsgrade als durchschnittlich:

Für Münzen bis 1800: der Grad "schön" - "sehr schön."

Für Münzen ungefähr von 1800 bis 1914: der Grad "sehr schön".

Von 1914 an: ungebrauchte Stücke oder solche, die kaum Abnützungsspuren aufweisen.

Die Bezeichnung "nicht im Umlauf befindlich" bezieht sich auch auf Stücke von polierter Platte.

DER "BULLION"-WERT DER GOLDMUENZEN

Einige Goldmuenzen, z.B. diejenigen, die im allgemeinen als "Bullion-Muenzen" bezeichnet werden, haben vergleichbar geringen numismatischen Wert und werden mit geringem Aufschlag auf den Wert des Goldgehaltes verkauft. Der Wert dieser Muenzen steigt und faellt in direktem Zusammenhang mit dem Tageswert von Gold am internationalen Markt.

"Bullion"-Muenzen sind im Text hinter dem Preis durch den Vermerk (B) gekennzeichnet. Es muss beachtet werden, dass die im Text aufgelisteten Preise auf dem Goldpreis von $725 per Unze basieren. Der Leser kann die Tabellen I und II im Anhang heranziehen, um den aktuellen "Bullion"-Wert dieser Muenzen zu ermitteln.

(Eine eingehendere Behandlung dieser Muenzen finden Sie in der Einfuehrung zu "Recent Issues Starting with 1960," page 419.)

PROBESTÜCKE, STÜCKE VON POLIERTER PLATTE, UNOFFIZIELLE PRÄGUNGEN UND ABSCHLÄGE

Der Verfasser hat versucht, in diesem Buch alle Goldmünzen zu besprechen, die von Zeit zu Zeit bei einem Numismatiker auftauchen. Dazu gehören auch die attraktiven Serien der Proben und Stücke von polierter Platte. **Diese sind mit dem allgemeinen Begriff "nicht in Umlauf gesetzt" gekennzeichnet.** Es sind gesetzliche, ungebrauchte Regierungsausgaben; sie gehören zu den am meisten geschätzten und seltensten Goldmünzen.

Andere Münzen sind einfach als nicht offizielle oder als privat hergestellte Stücke bezeichnet. Sie sind keine offiziellen Münzen irgendeiner Regierung und sind ausschliesslich für Sammler oder zum Gebrauch auf Weltgoldmärkten hergestellt worden.

Ein Problem bildete die Frage, ob man Abschläge in dieses Buch aufnehmen sollte oder nicht. (Als Abschlag bezeichnet man eine Goldmünze, die mit einem Nicht-Goldmünzenstempel geprägt wurde.) Abschläge sind im allgemeinen die grösseren Stücke der Dukaten-Münzprägung, von 3 Dukaten an aufwärts. Je nach Tradition wurden sie manchmal als gängige Münzen aufgefasst, manchmal nicht.

Die Numismatiker sind sich noch immer nicht einig, ob eine Goldmünze vom Gewicht eines 10 Dukaten-Stückes, ohne Nominalwert und mit dem Stempel eines Silbertalers geprägt, gesetzliches Zahlungsmittel ist oder nicht. Da die meisten frühen Goldmünzen sowieso ohne Wertbezeichnung sind (ihr Nominalwert resultiert aus ihrem Gewicht und ihrer Feinheit), ist dies eine rein akademische Frage.

NEUPRÄGUNGEN

Wenn der Buchstabe "R" nach der Nummer erscheint, bedeutet das, dass die Münze eine Neuprägung ist. Einige Länder, insbesondere Österreich, Ungarn, Mexiko und Spanien, haben Neuprägungen alter Münzen herausgebracht, die dieselbe Zeichnung und das gleiche Datum wie das Original haben, trotzdem sie zu einem späteren Zeitpunkt herausgegeben wurden. Weitere Auskunft über Neuprägungen sind in der Einleitung zum II. Teil zu finden, "Recent Issues Starting With 1960" (Neue Ausgaben seit 1960).

KURZE GESCHICHTE DER LATEINISCHEN MÜNZUNION

Die lateinische Münzunion, die einen weltweiten Einfluss auf die Goldmünzprägung hatte, wurde 1865 von Frankreich, Belgien, Italien und der Schweiz gegründet. Diese Länder hatten ihre Währung auf einem Zweimetallsystem aufgebaut, wobei Gold und Silber wertmässig in einem Verhältnis 1 : 15,5 standen. Dieses Verhältnis war 1803 von Frankreich festgesetzt worden und von Belgien, Italien und der Schweiz schon vor der Gründung der Union übernommen worden. Der Einfluss Frankreichs auf die Union war somit vorherrschend. Der Vertrag der Union sah vor, dass die Goldmünzen, in eine Feinheit von .900 geprägt werden sollten und dass die Wertbezeichnungen einheitlichen Werten und Gewichten entsprechen sollten.

Griechenland trat der Union 1868 bei. Wie andere Länder hatte es auch Gold nach der französischen Norm geprägt, schon bevor es Mitglied der Union wurde.

Frankreich versuchte mit Hilfe der Union, ein auf der französischen Einheit basierendes, universales Münzsystem durchzusetzen. Obwohl Frankreich dies nicht ganz gelang, richteten doch viele Länder ihre Goldmünzprägungen nach den Abmachungen der Lateinischen Münzunion. Dennoch behielten diese Länder ihre eigenen Münzeinheiten bei und prägten ihr Gold nach dem festgesetzten Gewicht und

Feinheit. Das 20 Peso-Stück von Guatemala, zum Beispiel, hatte den gleichen Wert wie das französische 100 Franken-Stück.

Die folgenden Länder prägten ihre Goldmünzen nach dem von der Lateinischen Münzunion eingeführten System:

Albanien	Montenegro
Argentinien	Peru
Belgien	Philippinen
Bulgarien	Polen
Finnland	Rumänien
Frankreich	Russland
Griechenland	Salvador
Guatemala	San Marino
Honduras	Schweiz
Italien	Serbien
Jugoslavien	Spanien
Kolumbien	Tunesien
Monaco	Venezuela

Die Auswirkungen des ersten Weltkrieges verursachten in manchen Ländern eine Unterbrechung der Goldmünzprägung von mehreren Jahren. Ein Nachspiel dieser Schweirigkeiten war schliesslich die Auflösung der Lateinischen Münzunion im Jahre 1926. Trotzdem gab es immer noch Länder, die nach diesem Zeitpunkt Goldmünzen mit Gewicht und Feinheit gemäss den Abmachungen der Union herausgaben. Darunter sind Münzen von Liechtenstein, Luxemburg, Rumänien und der Schweiz zu zählen.

ABKÜRZUNGEN

ND für ohne Jahr
mm für Münzkennzeichen
Obv. für Vorderseite
Rev. für Rückseite

Per il lettore Italiano.

PREFAZIONE

INTRODUZIONE ALLE MONETE AUREE

Raccogliere monete auree sembra sia stata una passione dell'uomo sin da quando le prime monete d'oro furono coniate dagli antichi greci, verso il 700 avanti Cristo.

Da allora, monete auree sono state coniate da quasi tutti i governi esistiti. Il termine governo, nel significato qui attribuitogli, si intende esteso ad ogni autorità che coniò monete, permanente o provvisoria, laica o ecclesiastica, nazionale o locale, repubblicana o monarchica.

Immense quantità di monete auree sono state così coniate attraverso i secoli. Fortunatamente molte sono a noi pervenute, contribuendo ad arricchire la cultura dei tempi odierni e fornendo al numismatico infinite possibilità di piacere e di studio.

Non è certo per caso che tante monete auree siano giunte fino a noi dai tempi antichi, generalmente in ottimo stato di conservazione. Ciò è dovuto alla natura dell'oro stesso ed all'amore dell'umanità per questo metallo.

Le proprietà fisiche e chimiche dell'oro sono troppo ben conosciute per essere qui ricordate. Per quanto riguarda la numismatica, è necessario ricordare che l'oro fu scelto come massimo simbolo monetario per il fatto che la sua rarità lo rese prezioso, per il suo colore singolare e per il suo splendore eterno.

Monete auree che furono sotterrate od altrimenti occultate per centinaia o migliaia di anni, quando furono ritrovate, erano ancora nelle identiche condizioni di quando furono nascoste.

E dobbiamo a questa vecchia tendenza dell'uomo a tesaurizzare, se continuamente abbiamo notizie di nuove, sconosciute monete, le quali in alcuni casi possono fornire importanti ragguagli su personaggi o luoghi altrimenti sconosciuti o avvolti nelle nebbie della storia.

L'uomo ha appreso ad amare l'oro per buone ragioni. La propria amara esperienza gli ha dimostrato che, di fronte alle guerre, invasioni, rivoluzioni, inflazioni o altri disastri economici, la moneta aurea, per quante piccole dimensioni possa avere, è sopravvissuta, unica, come simbolo di sicurezza, quanto tutti gli altri valori consueti erano trascinati nella rovina generale. Per questo motivo l'uomo ha sempre tenuto in speciale considerazione le monete auree, conservandole sempre, occultandole di fronte al pericolo. A volte, i possessori originari non vollero o non poterono reclamare i tesori che avevano nascosti e le monete furono sottratte alla circolazione, finché dopo molti anni vennero accidentalmente alla luce, per l'opera di un' aratro, di una marea, di un'alluvione o della dinamite.

Anche oggi la ricchezza di una nazione talvolta si misura in termini di oro, e per dimostrare quanto poco sia mutevole la storia di questo metallo sarà bene ricordare che i governi hanno, come nel passato sempre provveduto a cautelare le loro riserve auree nel sottosuolo, dove sono ben custodite sotto il controllo delle loro Banche Centrali, da guardie armate in permanenza e protette dagli ultimi ritrovati contro il furto, lo scasso a la rapina e da strutture resistenti ad ogni forma di disastro.

Sebbene le opere di letteratura numismatica siano innumerevoli, non esistono attualmente libri che si occupino delle monete d'oro, come di una categoria a se stante.

Considerato il grande interesse delle emissioni auree, l'autore ha trovato ciò alquanto sorprendente. Egli, numismatico professionista da molti anni, ha come migliaia di numismatici in tutto il mondo sentito la mancanza di tale opera nella letteratura numismatica. Per cercare un riferimento su una moneta d'oro coniata prima del 20mo secolo, era necessario trovare la letteratura esistente—se c'era—del paese in questione, la qual letteratura ovviamente era dedicata anche alle monete d'argento e di altri metalli. Come tutti sanno vi sono centinaia di tali libri; la maggior parte pubblicati in lingue straniere. Molti sono esauriti e perciò di grande valore e in alcuni casi introvabili. Pertanto lo studio delle emissioni auree si presentava compito alquanto arduo, e richiedeva mezzi speciali di ricerca o assistenza e molte ore di tedioso, spesso improduttivo lavoro di biblioteca.

L'autore riflettè a lungo sulla possibilità di migliorare tali condizioni creando un unico volume che comprendesse la totalità delle monete auree del mondo intero, eccezion fatta per quelle antiche greche e romane e per quelle bizantine.

Ciò sembrò a prima vista un progetto ambizioso, impossibile a realizzarsi, considerato l'enorme numero di monete coniate durante il periodo in esame.

Tuttavia calcoli preliminari dimostrarono che con una certa economia di formato, sarebbe stato possibile creare un solo volume, di dimensioni normali, senza sacrificare alcuna informazione vitale o le importantissime illustrazioni.

Attingendo alla propria esperienza, nonché a quella dei suoi stimati collaboratori, l'autore spese oltre cinque anni per raccogliere tutti i dati necessari per questo libro, la cui prima edizione fu pubblicata nel 1958.

LO SCOPO DI "LE MONETE AUREE DEL MONDO"

Questo libro tratta le emissioni monetarie auree di tutto il mondo dalla caduta dell'Impero Romano di Occidente, escludendo quelle dell'Impero di Bisanzio e quelle dei popoli nomadi. Cioè da quando stati, dai nomi ben definiti, apparvero alla ribalta della scena mondiale. Scopo del libro è di prendere in considerazione le monete dei vari luoghi di emissione, catalogandole sotto il nome usato oggi per identificare tali luoghi. Determinata l'epoca di inizio per ciascuna zecca, le emissioni sono elencate in ordine cronologico, fino alla fine della coniazione dell'oro nella zecca stessa.

Le monete più antiche elencate in questo libro sono quelle di Axum (Etiopia) risalenti a circa il 300 dopo Cristo. Le più antiche fra quelle europee risalgono a circa il 600 dopo Cristo, e sono quelle coniate nella città italiana di Benevento. Tra le monete del continente americano, le più antiche qui elencate sono i pezzi coloniali della Colombia risalenti a circa il 1621.

CONSIDERAZIONI GEOGRAFICHE DEL PRESENTE VOLUME

I mutamenti geopolitici verificatisi nel corso dei secoli, hanno sollevato un notevole problema per l'esatto inquadramento geografico di talune zecche nel quadro di qualche nazione. Questo problema è stato risolto col fissare arbitrariamente un periodo di tempo ben conosciuto alla generazione presente. Si è quindi scelto il periodo tra le due guerre mondiali e il 1937 come punto di riferimento per i confini geopolitici del mondo. Perciò le monete di una nazione esistente nel 1937 sono state elencate sotto il nome di detta nazione, anche se quando furono coniate la nazione aveva un nome geografico differente. Secondo questa regola le monete di nazioni come l'Estonia o la Lituania, sono assegnate all'Estonia o alla Lituania, anziché di essere catalogate come monete svedesi. Così come tradizionalmente si usava per le monete ispano-americane che conservavano la loro denominazione nazionale invece di quella spagnola.

I Paesi sono elencati in ordine alfabetico. Sotto i titoli di alcuni Paesi—ad esempio la Germania—un capoverso a parte è stato dedicato ad uno Stato, Principato, Ducato, o Città che battè zecca propria. L'indice al termine del libro potrà servire a identificare ogni località che coniò moneta.

DESCRIZIONI E DATE

Tutti i tipi di monete che rientrino nella finalità dell'opera e che l'autore ha potuto trovare, sono stati elencati e descritti. Il diritto viene sempre descritto per primo. La descrizione è seguita dall'elenco dei valori e date riguardanti quel tipo particolare di moneta. Quando sulla moneta è rappresentata una figura stante questa viene descritta col solo nome, negli altri casi vengono indicati il busto, la testa ecc. Le monete senza data sono seguite da ND, quelle datate, quando il tipo non varia e si conoscono solo poche date, queste sono tutte elencate. Quando le date sono molte si riportano solo la prima e l'ultima. L'autore sarà grato a tutti coloro che segnaleranno le varie omissioni e gli errori, affinche possano essere incluse o corretti nelle future edizioni di questo libro.

LE ILLUSTRAZIONI

Circa la metà dello spazio di questo libro è dedicato alle illustrazioni delle monete, riprodotte a grandezza naturale. Nonostante una notevole spesa suppletiva, esse sono state incorporate nel testo, nei punti cui si riferiscono, anziché alla fine del libro. La descrizione delle illustrazioni è messa sotto la figura. L'asterisco che segue la denominazione e la data indica che la moneta è illustrata. Di proposito sono state usate illustrazioni di monete di varia grandezza per facilitare la identificazione di quelle prive di indicazione di valore. La maggior parte dei tipi sin dall'inizio dell'emissione è stato illustrato; dopo il 1700 circa, tutti i tipi sono riprodotti. Il volume comprende oltre 3000 fotografie, più di quante se ne trovino in un libro di simile argomento e formato corrispondente, e l'autore ritiene che quasi tutte le monete auree conosciute ai numismatici siano state raffigurate.

VALUTAZIONE E STATO DI CONSERVAZIONE

Per ogni moneta l'autore indica il prezzo di stima in dollari, secondo il mercato numismatico attuale. Sarebbe assurdo pretendere di conoscere il valore numismatico delle monete auree di tutti i tempi; per fornire delle valutazioni obiettive, sono stati consultati un'enorme numero di cataloghi e risultati di vendite all'asta. Questi dati sono stati usati congiuntamente alla lunga esperienza dell'autore e dei suoi collaboratori, e si ritiene che le valutazioni riportate riflettano esattamente l'andamento del mercato al momento della stampa e rappresentano il valore approssimativo di scambio tra un collezionista ben informato e un numismatico professionista. Quando mancavano riferimenti di prezzi attuali si sono aggiornati quelli di vendite passate.

La stima delle monete rare si è presentata molto difficile, in alcuni casi esse non sono state valutate affatto, ma definite semplicemente rare. In altri casi la stima è stata determinata comparando la moneta in questione col valore accettato di un'altra di pari rarità. La stima di un pezzo di grande rarità deve considerarsi puramente indicativa di un notevole valore. L'autore si è reso conto attraverso la sua esperienza che, quando una moneta di grande rarità è stata immessa sul mercato, il prezzo realizzato ha sempre superato l'ultimo prezzo conosciuto. Ciò è dovuto al fatto che la domanda per tali monete aumenta sempre.

Di regola il valore numismatico di una moneta è determinato in parte dallo stato di conservazione, in parte dalla rarità e quasi sempre dalla legge inesorabile della domanda e dell'offerta, che a volta può causare differenze apprezzabili con le valutazioni del presente volume.

Le valutazioni devono intendersi per monete in uno stato di conservazione normale e per i tipi e le date più comuni. Per monete di conservazione eccezionale o con date rare è giustificato un prezzo più alto. Il criterio adottato è stato il seguente:

Per monete fino al 1800 circa, le valutazioni si riferiscono ad esemplari di bella-bellissima conservazione.

Per monete dal 1800 circa fino al 1914, le valutazioni si riferiscono ad esemplari di conservazione bellissima.

Per monete dal 1914 ad oggi, le valutazioni si riferiscono ad esemplari che non abbiano mai circolato o a pezzi scelti che non presentino usure.

Per monete indicate con la dizione "mai messe in circolazione" le valutazioni si riferiscono ad esemplari fior di conio o che siano fondo specchio.

IL VALORE AUREO DELLE MONETE D'ORO

Alcune monete d'oro, quelle che comunemente vanno sotto il nome di oro monetato, hanno scarso valore numismatico e si vendono al costo del loro intrinseco contenuto aureo con l'aggiunta di una modesta commissione di intermediazione.

Il valore di queste monete oscilla in ragione del prezzo del giorno dell'oro sui mercati internazionali.

L'oro monetato viene indicato nel testo con il riferimento (B) seguito dal prezzo. Occorre tener presente che i prezzi segnati sono basati su di un prezzo indicativo dell'oro di $725 l'oncia. Per ricavare il contenuto aureo di queste monete rimandiamo il lettore alle Tabelle I e II dell'apprendice.

(Per una trattazione piu' particolareggiata di queste monete leggasi l'introduzione a pag. 419 sotto ''Recent Issues Starting With 1960.'')

PROVE, FONDO SPECCHIO, EMISSIONI NON UFFICIALI E ANORMALI

L'autore ha cercato di includere nel testo ogni specie di monete auree che di tempo in tempo appaiano sul mercato. **Tra tali monete si trovano la serie affascinante delle "Prove" dei "Fondo specchio" e dei "Progetti", generalmente indicate col termine "Mai immesse in circolazione".** Devono essere considerate tra le più rare e pregiate e quasi sempre si trovano in perfetto stato di conservazione.

Altre monete sono state definite come emesse non ufficialmente, o privatamente, in quanto coniate esclusivamente per collezionisti o per uso nei mercati mondiali dell'oro.

L'includere i tipi a produzione anormale in questo volume ha creato un problema di ardua soluzione. (Esemplare di produzione anormale è considerata la moneta di oro battuta con un conio usato per monete di altro metallo). I numismatici non sono d'accordo se considerare ufficiale una moneta d'oro che pesi esattamente quanto un pezzo da 10 ducati, ma che non porti l'indicazione del proprio valore e che sia stata coniata con il conio usato per i talleri d'argento, ugualmente privo di indicazione di valore. Bisogna dire però che la maggior parte delle monete auree antiche non presenta l'indicazione del valore (essendo questo determinato dal peso e dalla purezza), la questione pertanto è puramente accademica.

RICONIAZIONI

Quando la lettera ''R'' appare dopo un numero, si tratta di riconio. Alcuni paesi quali l'Austria, Ungheria, Messico e Spagna, hanno riemesso nuove serie di vecchie monete che sebbene battute in epoche recenti o attuali, presentano stesse date e disegni dell'originale. Ulteriori informazioni in proposito si ritrovano nella parte II, "Recent Issues Starting With 1960" (Recenti emissioni a partire dal 1960).

BREVI CENNI SULL'UNIONE MONETARIA LATINA

L'Unione Monetaria Latina, che esercitò influenza mondiale nell' emissione delle monete auree, fu fondata nel 1865 dalla Francia, Belgio, Italia e Svizzera. Questi Paesi operavano in virtù di un sistema monetario bimetallico, con una proporzione tra argento ed oro di 15,5 a 1. Tale proporzione fu stabilita dalla Francia nel 1803, ed era stata adottata dal Belgio, Italia e Svizzera per le loro emissioni, anteriormente alla formazione dell'Unione. Quindi, il sistema monetario francese esercitava un influenza predominante in seno all'Unione. Il trattato stabiliva che le monete auree continuassero a venir coniate con una purezza di 900 millesimi e che i nominali mantenessero peso e valore uniforme.

La Grecia aderì all'Unione nel 1868. Questo Paese, come le altre nazioni, aveva coniato monete auree in conformità al sistema francese ancor prima di divenire membro dell'Unione.

La Francia tentò di stabilire, a mezzo dell'Unione, un sistema monetario universale basato sull'unità francese. Sebbene la Francia non ottenesse un successo completo in questo campo, svariati Paesi non membri basarono le loro emissioni auree sul sistema vigente nell'Unione Monetaria Latina.

Comunque, questi Paesi mantennero le loro unità monetarie e coniarono le monete auree secondo peso e purezza specifici. Ad esempio, i 20 Pesos del Guatemala avevano lo stesso valore del pezzo da 100 Franchi francese.

I seguenti Paesi coniarono monete auree basate sul sistema adottato dall'Unione Monetaria Latina:

Albania	Monaco
Argentina	Montenegro
Belgio	Perù
Bulgaria	Polonia
Colombia	Romania
Filippine	Russia
Finlandia	San Marino
Francia	San Salvador
Grecia	Serbia
Guatemala	Spagna
Honduras	Svizzera
Italia	Tunisi
Jugoslavia	Venezuela

La prima guerra mondiale ebbe serie ripercussioni sui valori monetarii di molte nazioni, provocando l'interruzione dell'emissione di monete auree in questi Paesi per una durata di vari anni.

Queste difficoltà comportarono poi lo scioglimento definitivo dell'Unione Monetaria Latina, avvenuto nel 1926.

Ciononostante, alcuni Paesi coniarono monete auree anche dopo questa data, basandosi sul peso e purezza stabiliti dall'Unione. Tra queste emissioni si trovano le monete del Lichtenstein, Lussemburgo, Romania e Svizzera.

ABREVIAZIONI USATE NEL TESTO

ND — senza data
mm — segno di zecca
Obv. — diritto
Rev. — rovescio

Para el Lector de Habla Hispana.

PROLOGO

INTRODUCCION A MONEDAS DE ORO

El coleccionar monedas de oro pareciera haber interesado a la humanidad prácticamente desde que las primeras monedas fueron acuñadas por los griegos cerca de 700 años antes de Jesucristo. Desde entonces, casi todos los gobiernos que han existido, han acuñado monedas de oro. El término gobierno según se emplea aquí, se refiere a toda autoridad permanente o provisional, secular o eclesiástica, nacional o local, real o republicana encargada del cuño.

Cantidades formidables de monedas de oro han sido acuñadas a través de los siglos y afortunadamente muchas de ellas han sobrevivido enriqueciendo la cultura de nuestra época y proporcionando al numismático una fuente de estudio y placer permanentes.

No es en forma accidental que tantas monedas de oro han sobrevivido y llegado a nuestros días desde el fondo de los tiempos antiguos — generalmente en excelente estado de conservación — y esto puede atribuirse a la naturaleza del oro propiamente y al amor de la humanidad por este metal.

Las propiedades fisicas y químicas del oro son bien conocidas y no vale la pena entrar en detalles sobre ellas en este artículo. Para el numismático sin embargo, es importante recordar que el oro fue seleccionado como el mejor material de cuño porque su escasez lo hacía precioso, porque su color es típico y porque su lustre y brillo son permanentes. Las monedas de oro que han sido enterradas u ocultadas por siglos y hasta por milenios, cuando son finalmente descubiertas se encuentran en la misma condición de brillo y lustre que tenían al ser escondidas.

Es esta vieja tendencia a enterrar el oro lo que resulta en inesperados descubrimientos de monedas nuevas y desconocidas, algunas de las cuales arrojan luz sobre algún sitio o personaje que de otra manera sería desconocido o permanecería envuelto en las nubes de la historia.

La humanidad ha aprendido a amar este metal por una buena razón: su amarga experiencia le ha demostrado que frente a guerras, invasiones, revoluciones, pánicos, inflación o cualquier otro desastre económico, la moneda de oro, pequeña como es en tamaño, ha sido única en sobrevivir como simbolo de seguridad cuando todos los otros estandards familiares de valores han sucumbido dentro de la ruina general.

Sabiendo ésto, los pueblos del mundo han desarrollado una especial reverencia por la moneda de oro, conservándola siempre, y escondiéndola ante el peligro. Algunas veces, los dueños originales no pudieron reclamar o no reclamaron su tesoro y las monedas estuvieron perdidas para el mundo hasta que fueron accidentalmente expuestas muchos años después por un golpe de arado, una marea embravecida o una explosión de dinamita.

Aún hoy, la riqueza de las naciones a veces se mide en términos de su oro, y ya que este es el caso y para demostrar lo poco que ha cambiado la larga historia del oro, llamamos la atención sobre el hecho de que los gobiernos del mundo en el pasado, han ocultado sus reservas de oro acuñado, bajo tierra, donde es cuidadosamente mantenido bajo el seguro control de sus Bancos Centrales, bajo permanente custodia armada y protegidos por las últimas novedades en aparatos preventores de robo o asalto así como por construcciones capaces de hacer frente a cualquier forma de desastre.

A pesar de que la literatura sobre numismática es extensa, no existen libros especiales sobre las monedas de oro en el mundo. Considerando el interés apasionado que existe sobre la materia, al autor le ha llamado mucho la atención este hecho. Habiendo sido un numismático profesional durante la mayor parte de su vida adulta, el autor, al igual que miles de otros numismáticos en el mundo entero, ha resentido, echando mucho de menos, la falta de un libro semejante en la literatura numismática.

Para poder obtener una referencia sobre cualquier moneda de oro acuñada antes del siglo veinte, era necesario ponerse a la búsqueda del material impreso estandard en el pais de que se trataba, material que como es de suponer se refería también a monedas de plata y a otras monedas menores. Es obvio que existen cientos de estos libros, la mayor parte impresos en lénguas extranjeras y en ediciones agotadas; muchos constituyen ejemplares raros y valiosos y son inobtenibles.

Era por lo tanto una empresa formidable ponerse a buscar o consultar material de referencia sobre las monedas de oro en el mundo ya que ello requería facilidades especiales, asistencia de otros en las investigaciones o muchas horas de trabajo tedioso y muchas veces estéril, en las bibliotecas.

El autor había acariciado por mucho tiempo la idea de mejorar este estado de cosas con la creación de un solo volumen que abarcara en forma total la acuñación de moneda en el mundo, con excepción de lo referente a monedas antiguas y monedas del Imperio Bizantino. Esto parecía enorme al principio y de imposible realización a causa de la cantidad colosal de monedas encontradas en 1300 años de acuñación.

Sin embargo, algunos cálculos preliminares demostraron que con una cierta economía de formato sería posible crear un solo volumen de tamaño moderado sin sacrificar ninguna información vital ni las ilustraciones que son tan importantes.

Por lo tanto, usando la fuente de su propia experiencia y la de sus valiosos colaboradores, el autor dedicado alrededor de cinco años a la recolección y reunión de la información para este libro, que se publicó por primera vez en 1958.

LO QUE ABARCA "LAS MONEDAS DE ORO DEL MUNDO"

Este libro se refiere a la acuñación de oro en el mundo que comienza al terminar la acuñación de la antigüedad e inmediatamente después de la era de las invasiones nómadas, cuando comenzaron a existir nuevos gobiernos con nombres determinados. El propósito ha sido comenzar a catalogar las emisiones de moneda de cada lugar, con las primeras monedas distintivas que identifican positivamente el lugar al que damos hoy día un determinado nombre, haciendo la acuñación verdaderamente nacional en carácter. Habiendo establecido el punto de partida en el caso de cada sitio, la acuñación ha sido tratada cronológicamente hasta llegar a su fin natural por la suspensión de acuñamiento de oro en cada lugar en particular. Algunas de las emisiones llegan hasta el presente.

Las monedas más antiguas consignadas en este libro son las acuñadas por los Axumitas de Etiopía alrededor del año 300 D.C. Las primeras acuñaciones europeas fueron hechas alrededor del año 600 D.C., en la ciudad italiana de Beneventum. Las primeras monedas acuñadas en el Hemisferio Occidental son las de las colonias españolas emitidas en Colombia alrededor del año 1621.

LA GEOGRAFIA DE ESTE LIBRO

La apropiada ubicación nacional de ciertos nombres de lugares que muchas veces significaba un dilema, ha sido resuelta por medio del enfoque arbitrario sobre la época mejor conocida de la generación actual. El período entre las dos guerras ha sido seleccionado (y el año de 1937 como un año normal de ese período), como punto de referencia en lo que se refiere a los límites geopolíticos del mundo. Por lo tanto las monedas de un país en existencia en 1937 han sido incluidas bajo el nombre de ese país a pesar de que hayan sido acuñadas en épocas anteriores y bajo soberanía extranjera.

Algunas innovaciones han sido así llevadas a cabo ya que bajo este sistema la acuñacion de moneda de países como Estonia o Latvia aparece bajo su propio nombre en vez de aparecer como acuñación de Suecia, lo que es consistente por ejemplo con la forma tradicional de incluir las monedas hispanoamericanas bajo sus nombres americanos, en vez de incluirlas como acuñación de España. El índice geográfico en el libro ayudará a localizar cualquier acuñación.

Los países figuran por orden alfabético. Bajos algunos de ellos — como, por ejemplo, Alemania — se da un título aparte a algún estado, principado, ducado o ciudad que acuñó su propia moneda. El índice que figura al final del libro servirá de gran auxilio para hallar cualquier localidad que haya acuñado monedas.

DESCRIPCIONES Y FECHAS

Cada tipo de moneda que cae dentro de las categorías contempladas por este libro, y que el autor pudo encontrar, ha sido anotado y descrito. El anverso de la moneda siempre está descrito en primer lugar. Su descripción es seguida por las varias denominaciones y fechas de ese tipo en particular. El uso de un nombre solamente en la descripción, indica una figura de pie. De otra manera, son usadas las palabras cabeza, busto, etc.

Las monedas sin fecha van seguidas de las letras ND. Por lo general, cuando una moneda tiene de una a cuatro fechas, todas las fechas han sido anotadas; de lo contrario se habrán anotado solamente la primera y última fechas y ésto no querrá decir que existan todos los años comprendidos entre ambas.

En un trabajo de esta magnitud y complejidad y considerando que se trata de una primera edición, es inevitable que algunos tipos o denominaciones de monedas hayan escapado a la atención del autor y que no hayan sido anotados a pesar de lo dicho acerca de la total integridad del trabajo.

El autor agradecerá cualquiera de las omisiones que sea llevada a su atención de manera que las monedas en cuestión puedan ser incluídas en ediciones futuras de este libro.

LAS ILUSTRACIONES

Cerca de la mitad del espacio de este libro está dedicado a ilustraciones de las monedas, que son presentadas en tamaño natural. Con gasto adicional considerable han sido incorporadas dentro del texto, donde pertenecen, en vez de al final del libro como un conjunto de láminas adicionales. La descripción de las ilustraciones se encuentra al pie de las mismas.

Un asterisco (*) al lado de la denominación y la fecha indica que esta es la moneda ilustrada en el espacio anterior a la descripción. En el caso de que haya una sola denominación para el tipo de moneda que se ilustra, no se ha usado el asterisco.

Una variedad de tamaños ha sido usado a propósito para las ilustraciones ya que ésto ayudará a identificar la denominación de las monedas que carecen de la marca del valor.

La mayor parte de los tipos, aún los más antiguos, han sido ilustrados y ciertamente, después de 1700, las ilustraciones son virtualmente completas en todos los tipos. Este libro incluye más de 3000 ilustraciones de monedas de oro, más de las que han sido nunca ilustradas en ningún otro libro de tamaño comparable y el autor cree haber ilustrado casi todas las monedas con que está generalmente familiarizado el numismático.

LAS EVALUACIONES Y EL ESTADO DE CONSERVACION

El autor publica las evaluaciones como una guía general acerca del valor de las monedas en el mercado numismático. Nadie por sí mismo puede pretender conocer el valor numismático de cada moneda de oro que ha sido acuñada. Para presentar este trabajo se han consultado voluminosos registros de ventas. Estos han sido usados en conjunción con la experiencia de veinte años del autor, en numismática profesional, combinada con la experiencia acumulada de los colaboradores. El autor cree las evaluaciones aquí presentadas reflejan la verdadera condición de curiosidad o rareza de la pieza, la condición, la demanda y la abundancia de las monedas hasta al imprimirse este libro.

Estas evaluaciones representan la cantidad aproximada en que las monedas cambiarían de mano entre un comprador bien informado y un numismático profesional. Están basadas en registros de ventas recientes o son una extensión dentro del tiempo presente de viejos registros de ventas.

La evaluación de piezas raras ha sido especialmente difícil porque las monedas han aparecido muy raras veces. En algunos casos no han sido evaluadas del todo y han sido marcadas simplemente "raras." En otros casos la evaluación ha sido determinada por comparación de la moneda con el valor conocido de otra moneda de igual rareza u otros atributos similares.

En todo caso, la evaluación de una verdadera rareza debe ser considerada como puramente nominal, y en el mejor de los casos puede ser solamente una indicación de que la moneda es de extraordinario valor. La experiencia del autor en los tiempos modernos le ha demostrado que cuando una verdadera rareza ha sido puesta en el mercado numismático, siempre ha tendido a exceder su último precio conocido a causa de la demanda siempre en aumento de esa clase de monedas.

En general el valor numismático de una moneda está determinado en parte por la condición, en parte por la rareza y casi siempre por la ley inexorable de la oferta y la demanda. Esta última puede a veces ser causa de gran divergencia entre los precios del momento y los anotados en este libro.

Estas evaluaciones se refieren a la condición corriente en que la moneda es más frecuentemente encontrada, y para la más corriente fecha y variedad del tipo. Las monedas en condición superior o con fechas más raras, exigirán un precio más elevado. En general la experiencia ha demostrado que estas condiciones corrientes son las siguientes:

Para monedas hasta cerca de 1800, las evaluaciones son para especímenes bien-muy bien conservados.

Para monedas de cerca de 1800 a 1914, las evaluaciones son para especímenes muy bien conservados.

Para monedas de cerca de 1914, a esta fecha, las evaluaciones son para especímenes flor de cuño o para especímenes escogidos que casi no muestren señales, de desgaste.

Para monedas marcadas "no puestas en circulación," las evaluaciones son para "no circulante" o cospel bruñido.

VALOR METALICO DE LAS MONEDAS DE ORO

Algunas monedas de oro, comunmente conocidas como monedas de bolsa, tienen poco valor numismático y se cotizan a precios ligeramente por encima del valor intrínseco del oro que contienen. El valor de estas monedas fluctua en directa relación al precio diario del oro en los mercados internacionales.

Monedas de bolsa están designadas en el texto por la marca de referencia (B) a continuación de sus precios. Nótese que los precios de lista en el texto han sido basados en oro a $725 la onza. El lector puede usar las Tablas I y II en el Apéndice para asertarse del valor metálico corriente de estas monedas.

(Para más detallada discusión de estas monedas, vea la introducción a "Recent Issues Starting with 1960," página 419.)

ENSAYOS, PRUEBAS, EMISIONES NO OFICIALES Y ACUÑACIONES ESPECIALES

El autor ha intentado incluir en el libro toda clase de monedas de oro de las que de tiempo en tiempo aparecen entre los numismáticos. Entre esas monedas puede incluirse la fascinante serie de ensayos y pruebas. **Estas han sido designadas con el término general de "no puestas en circulación."** Son emisiones legítimas de las oficinas gubernamentales del cuño, y pueden contarse entre las más raras y más apreciadas monedas de oro. Aparecen casi siempre en la condición de cospel bruñido.

Otras monedas han sido simplemente marcadas como extraoficialmente o privadamente hechas. Estas no son monedas oficiales de ningún gobierno y han sido manufacturadas exclusivamente para coleccionistas o para uso en los mercados de oro del mundo.

La inclusión de acuñaciones especiales en este libro ha presentado un problema aparentemente insoluble. (Una acuñación especial es considerada como una moneda acuñada en oro de la misma matriz o cuño que se ha usado para acuñar una moneda de otro metal.) Las acuñaciones especiales son generalmente múltiplos de ducados, de 3 ducados en adelante. De acuerdo con el uso tradicional, unas veces han sido incluidas y otras no, según la serie de que se trate.

No hay unanimidad de opinión entre los numismáticos acerca de si debe considerarse como legítimo una moneda de oro que pese exactamente lo que debería pesar una moneda de 10 ducados pero que no lleve la marca del valor y acuñada con la misma matriz usada para un tálero de plata, igualmente sin la marca del valor. Dado que la mayor parte de las monedas de oro tempranas no llevan en ningún caso la marca del valor (siendo su valor facial el peso y la pureza), la cuestión resulta académica.

REACUÑACIONES

Cuando la letra "R" aparece después de un número, ésto indica que la moneda es una reacuñación. Algunos países, notablemente Austria, Hungría, Méjico y España, han emitido nuevas acuñaciones de monedas de anteriores generaciones, conservando el mismo diseño y fecha de las originales aunque emitidas posteriormente. Adicional información sobre reacuñaciones puede ser obtenida en la introducción en la Parte II, "Recent Issues Starting With 1960" (Recientes Emisiones Comenzando Con 1960).

BREVE HISTORIA DE LA UNION MONETARIA LATINA

La Unión Monetaria Latina, que ha tenido influencia mundial en la acuñación de las monedas de oro, se formó en 1865 por Francia, Bélgica, Italia y Suiza. Estos países se hallaban bajo patrón monetario bimetálico, con una relación entre la plata y el oro de 15.5 a 1. Esta relación fue establecida por Francia en 1803, siendo después adoptada por Italia y Suiza para sus monedas antes de formarse la Unión. De esta manera, el sistema francés fue la influencia predominante en la Unión. El tratado dispuso que la acuñación de monedas de oro continuara con una ley de .900 y que las denominaciones debían tener el mismo peso y valor.

Grecia se adhirió a la Unión en 1868. Como los países ya en ella, había estado acuñando monedas bajo el sistema francés, antes de ser miembro de la Unión.

A través de la Unión, Francia intentó establecer un sistema monetario universal basado en la unidad francesa. Y aunque no triunfó por completo en su propósito, cierto número de países que no eran miembros de la Unión basaron sus monedas de oro en los tipos de la Unión Monetaria Latina. Sin embargo, estos países retuvieron su unidad monetaria propia y acuñaron sus monedas de acuerdo con peso y ley específicos. Por ejemplo, la moneda de 20 pesos de Guatemala tenía el mismo valor que la moneda francesa de 100 francos.

Los siguientes países acuñaron sus monedas de oro basados en los tipos establecidos por la Unión Monetaria Latina:

Albania	Italia
Argentina	Mónaco
Bélgica	Montenegro
Bulgaria	Perú
Colombia	Polonia
El Salvador	Rumanía
España	Rusia
Filipinas	San Marino
Finlandia	Serbia
Francia	Suiza
Grecia	Túnez
Guatemala	Venezuela
Honduras	Yugoeslavia

La Primera Guerra Mundial produjo un grave efecto sobre la circulación monetaria de varios países, los que discontinuaron las monedas de oro durante varios años. Resultado de estas dificultades fue, al fín, la disolución de la Unión Monetaria Latina en 1926. Sin embargo, algunos países acuñaron oro después de esa fecha basándose en el peso y la ley establecidos por la Unión. Entre estas acuñaciones se cuentan la de las monedas de Liechtenstein, Luxemburgo, Rumanía y Suiza.

ABREVIACIONES UTILIZADAS EN EL LIBRO

ND para sin fecha
mm para marca monetaria
Obv. para anverso
Rev. para reverso

GOLD COINS
of the WORLD

AFGHANISTAN

Prior to 1896 the type, style and workmanship of the coins were similar to those of Persia and the neighboring Indian states. The first modern style coins were the Dinars of 1896. This new denomination introduced for the first time the arms of Afghanistan, of which the dominant motif is the throne room. It should be noted that numbers 1-25, 27-28 and 36-38 are dated in A.H., or lunar years, while numbers 26, 29-35, and 39-44 are dated in S.H., or solar years.

Amirs of —

A. Durrani Dynasty

AHMAD SHAH, 1747-1772
Persian legend on each side.
1. 1 Mohur 1160-86 A.H. (1747-72 A.D.) 200.00
2. 1 Ashrafi 1171 A.H. (1758 A.D.) 90.00

TAIMUR SHAH (AS NIZAM), 1757-1772
Persian legend on each side.
3. 1 Mohur 1170-82 A.H. (1757-68 A.D.) 225.00

MIRZA SULAIMAN (CLAIMANT), 1772
Persian legend on each side.
4. 1 Mohur 1186. A.H. (1772 A.D.)..................... 650.00

TAIMUR SHAH (AS AMIR), 1772-1793

Persian legend on each side.
5. 1 Mohur 1186-1207 A.H. (1772-93 A.D.) 175.00

SHAH ZAMAN, 1793-1801
Persian legend on each side.
6. 1 Mohur 1208-16 A.H. (1794-1801 A.D.) 275.00

MAHMUD SHAH, 1801-1803, 1809-1818

Persian legend on each side.
7. 2 Mohur 1217-18 A.H. (1801-03 A.D.)........*...... 425.00
8. 1 Mohur 1217-25 A.H. (1801-10 A.D.) 175.00
9. 1 Ashrafi 1218-24 A.H. (1803-09 A.D.)............... 125.00

SHUJA SHAH, 1801, 1803-1809, 1839-1842

Persian legend on each side.
10. 2 Mohur 1218 A.H. (1803 A.D.) 500.00
11. 1 Mohur 1218-1258 A.H. (1803-42 A.D.) .....*...... 150.00
12. 1 Ashrafi 1222 A.H. (1807 A.D.) 100.00

QAISAR SHAH, 1803, 1807-1808
Persian legend on each side.
13. 1 Mohur 1218 A.H. (1803 A.D.) 325.00

ATA MOHAMMED (IN REBELLION), 1808-1813
Persian legend on each side.
14. 2 Mohur 1225 A.H. (1810 A.D.) 550.00
15. 1 Mohur 1225 A.H. (1810 A.D.) 300.00

AIYUB SHAH, 1818-1829
Persian legend on each side.
16. 1 Mohur 1238-39 A.H. (1823-24 A.D.) 225.00

B. Barakzai Dynasty

DOST MOHAMMED, 1823-1839, 1842-1863
Persian legend on each side.
17. 1 Tilla 1269 A.H. (1835 A.D.) 125.00

SHER ALI, 1863-1866, 1868-1878

Persian legend on each side.
18. 1 Mohur 1288 A.H. (1871 A.D.) ....*...... 225.00
19. 1 Tilla 1283-95 A.H. (1866-78 A.D.)................. 150.00

WALI SHER 'ALI, 1880
Persian legend on each side.
20. 1 Tilla 1297 A.H. (1880 A.D.) 250.00

ABDUR RAHMAN, 1880-1901

Persian legend on each side.
21. 1 Tilla 1298 A.H. (1811 A.D.) 175.00

Throne room. Rev. Toughra in wreath.
22. 2 Tilla 1309 A.H. (1892 A.D.) 275.00
23. 1 Tilla 1313-16 A.H. (1896-98 A.D.)..........*...... 175.00

HABIBULLAH, 1901-1919

Throne room. Rev. Toughra over crossed quivers.
24. 1 Tilla 1319-20 A.H. (1901-02 A.D.) 175.00

Star beneath throne room. Rev. Toughra over crossed quivers.
25. 1 Tilla 1336-37 A.H. (1918-19 A.D.)................. 225.00

AMANULLAH, 1919-1929
(The Afghanistani calendar was changed in 1920, when by Royal Decree, the corresponding A.H. year of 1338 was declared to be S.H. 1298.)

Throne room in star. Rev. Legend in wreath.

26.	2 Tilla 1298 S.H. (1920 A.D.)	175.00
27.	1 Tilla 1337 A.H. (1919 A.D.). Swords below throne .	90.00
28.	1 Tilla 1336,37 A.H. (1918,19 A.D.). Star below throne .... *	110.00

Throne room in star. Rev. Toughra in wreath.

29.	5 Amani 1299 S.H. (1921 A.D.) ....*	1250.00
30.	2 Amani 1299-03 S.H. (1921-25 A.D.)...............	175.00
31.	1 Amani 1299 S.H. (1921 A.D.)	125.00
32.	½ Amani 1299 S.H. (1921 A.D.) ....*	75.00

Large plain throne room. Rev. Toughra in wreath.

33.	2½ Amani 1306 S.H. (1928 A.D.)	750.00
34.	1 Amani 1304-06 S.H. (1926-28 A.D.)........*	125.00
35.	½ Amani 1304-06 S.H. (1926-28 A.D.)...............	100.00

HABIBULLAH GHAZI, 1929

(The name assumed by the brigand Bacha-i-Saquao, who held Kabul for nine months in 1929 but was captured and executed by Mohammed Nadir.)

In 1929 the calendar reverted back to the lunar year (A.H. dates).

Throne room in star. Rev. Legend in wreath.

36.	1 Habibi (30 Rupees) 1347 A.H. (1929 A.D.)........	350.00

MOHAMMED NADIR, 1929-1933

Large throne room. Rev. Toughra.

37.	20 Afghani 1349-50 A.H. (1931-32 A.D.)	350.00
38.	1 Tilla 1348-50 A.H. (1930-32 A.D.)..................	200.00

MOHAMMED ZAHIR, 1933-1973

In 1933, solar year dating (S.H. dates) resumed.

Throne room. Rev. Legend in wreath.

39.	1 Tilla 1313 S.H. (1935 A.D.)	350.00
40.	2 Tilla of 8 grams 1314-15 S.H. (1936-37 A.D.).......	425.00
41.	1 Tilla of 4 grams 1315 S.H. (1936 A.D.)	200.00

For later issues of Afghanistan, see the section, "Recent Issues Starting With 1960."

ALBANIA

Mints and mint marks:—R for Rome; V for Vienna. The 100 Franc pieces of 1928 and 1929 were unknown until about 1950. Albanian coinage is based on the Latin Monetary Union standard.

Presidents, and later, Kings of —
ZOG I, 1925-1939

Head with one, two or no stars below. Rev. Chariot.

1.	100 Francs 1926, 27	1200.00

Head. Rev. Eagle.

2.	20 Francs 1926, 27	250.00
3.	10 Francs 1927	225.00

Bust of Skanderbeg. Rev. Winged lion.

4.	20 Francs 1926. R mm.	350.00
5.	20 Francs 1926. Fasces mm.....................* ...	375.00
6.	20 Francs 1927. V mm. .... * ...	350.00

Bare head to left. Rev. Eagle. Not placed in circulation.

7.	100 Francs 1928	2250.00

Uniformed bust to right. Rev. Eagle. Not placed in circulation.

8.	100 Francs 1928	2250.00

Bare head to left in wreath. Rev. Eagle. Not placed in circulation.

9.	100 Francs 1928	2250.00

Bare head to left in wreath. Rev. Eagle with "Albania" added. Not placed in circulation.

10.	100 Francs 1929	2250.00

Bare head. Rev. Arms and dates 1912-1937. On the 25th year of Independence.

11.	100 Francs 1937	2100.00
12.	20 Francs 1937 ....*	450.00

Bare head. Rev. Arms and date, "27.IV.1938." On his wedding.

13.	100 Francs 1938	2100.00
14.	20 Francs 1938 .....*	400.00

Bare head. Rev. Arms and dates 1928-1938. On the 10th year of his rule.

15.	100 Francs 1938	2100.00
16.	50 Francs 1938	1500.00
17.	20 Francs 1938 .....*	600.00

ANNAM

The coins are dated in Annamese years. Most coins also exist in silver and are struck from the same dies. This series maintains a great popularity in France.

Emperors of —
MING MANG, 1820-1841

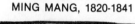

Chinese legend on each side. Rectangular bars.

1.	100 Ounces (1833)	Rare
2.	50 Ounces (1837, 38).	Rare
3.	40 Ounces (1840), ND.	Rare
4.	30 Ounces (1840)	Rare
5.	10 Ounces (1837)	3300.00
6.	5 Ounces (1837)	2200.00
7.	1 Ounce ND.	550.00
8.	5/10 Ounce ND .....*	400.00
9.	4/10 Ounce ND	275.00
10.	3/10 Ounce ND	200.00
11.	2/10 Ounce ND	200.00
12.	1/10 Ounce ND	150.00

Four Chinese characters on each side around square central hole.

13.	½ Piastre ND	450.00

Four Chinese characters around radiant sun. Rev. Dragon.

14.	1 Piastre (1834)	900.00
15.	½ Piastre (1834) .....*	575.00

Four Chinese characters around radiant sun. Rev. Heavenly bodies.

16.	⅛ Piastre ND	175.00

Two vertical Chinese characters. Rev. Eight precious symbols.

17.	⅛ Piastre ND	250.00

Two vertical Chinese characters. Rev. Five precious symbols.

18.	⅛ Piastre ND	165.00

Two vertical Chinese characters. Rev. The Three Abundances.

19.	¼ Piastre ND	450.00

THIEU TRI, 1841-1847

Chinese legend on each side. Rectangular bars.

20.	100 Ounces ND.	Rare
21.	50 Ounces ND.	Rare
22.	10 Ounces ND.	3300.00
23.	1 Ounce ND .....*	550.00
24.	5/10 Ounce ND.	400.00
25.	4/10 Ounce ND.	350.00
26.	3/10 Ounce ND.	350.00
27.	2/10 Ounce ND.	275.00
28.	1/10 Ounce ND.	275.00

Sun between two dragons. Rev. Four Chinese characters. With square central hole.

29. 7/10 Ounce ND .... * 725.00
30. 7/20 Ounce ND 350.00

Heavenly bodies flanked by four vertical characters. Rev. Long legend in form of a quatrain. With square central hole.

31. 5/10 Ounce ND 725.00
32. 5/20 Ounce ND 375.00

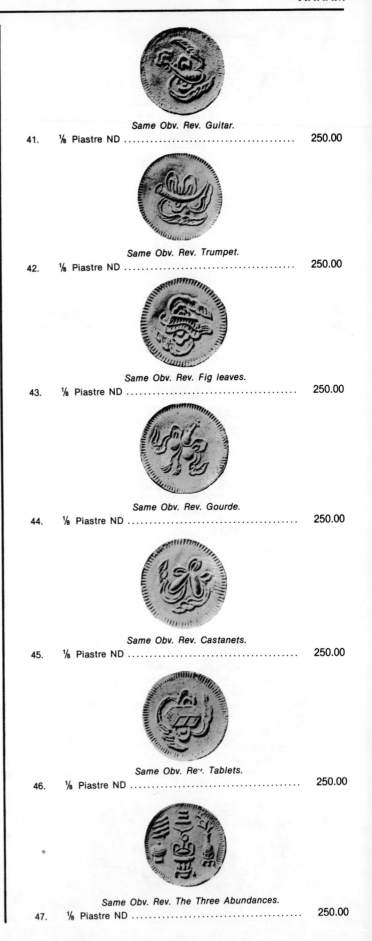

Eight Chinese characters. Rev. Facing dragon head. With square central hole.

33. 5/10 Ounce ND .... * 500.00
34. 5/20 Ounce ND 400.00

Four Chinese characters. Rev. Sun and moon between two vertical characters. With square central hole.

35. 1/4 Piastre ND 300.00

Four Chinese characters on each side around square central hole.

36. 1/2 Piastre ND 475.00

Four Chinese characters around radiant sun. Rev. Dragon.

37. 1 Piastre ND 700.00
38. 1/2 Piastre ND................................ * 400.00

Two vertical Chinese characters. Rev. Flaming sun.

39. 1/8 Piastre ND 250.00

Same Obv. Rev. Sceptre.

40. 1/8 Piastre ND............................ * 250.00
40a. 1/9 Ounce ND 350.00

Same Obv. Rev. Guitar.

41. 1/8 Piastre ND 250.00

Same Obv. Rev. Trumpet.

42. 1/8 Piastre ND 250.00

Same Obv. Rev. Fig leaves.

43. 1/8 Piastre ND 250.00

Same Obv. Rev. Gourde.

44. 1/8 Piastre ND 250.00

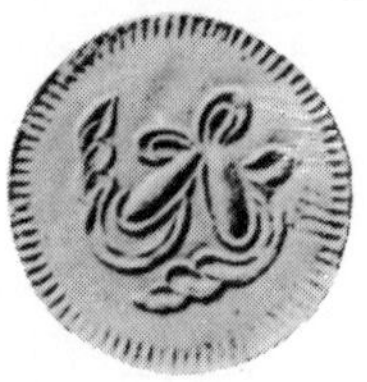

Same Obv. Rev. Castanets.

45. 1/8 Piastre ND 250.00

Same Obv. Rev. Tablets.

46. 1/8 Piastre ND 250.00

Same Obv. Rev. The Three Abundances.

47. 1/8 Piastre ND 250.00

TU DUC, 1847-1883

Four Chinese characters. Rev. Five Chinese characters. Rectangular bars.

48.	10 Ounces ND	3300.00
49.	5 Ounces ND	2200.00
50.	1 Ounce ND	550.00
51.	⁵/₁₀ Ounce ND	350.00
52.	⁴/₁₀ Ounce ND *	175.00
53.	³/₁₀ Ounce ND *	150.00
54.	²/₁₀ Ounce ND *	150.00
55.	¹/₁₀ Ounce ND *	125.00

Sun between two dragons. Rev. Four Characters. With square central hole.

56.	⁷/₁₀ Ounce ND	800.00

Heavenly bodies flanked by four vertical characters. Rev. Long legend in form of a quatrain. With square central hole.

57.	1 Ounce ND	900.00
58.	⁵/₁₀ Ounce ND *	1000.00

Eight Chinese characters. Rev. Facing dragon head. With square central hole.

59.	⁵/₁₀ Ounce ND	500.00

Legend on each side. With square central hole.

60.	½ Piastre ND	375.00
61.	¼ Piastre ND	275.00

Four Chinese characters. Rev. The Three Longevities. With square central hole.

62.	½ Piastre ND	475.00

Four Chinese characters. Rev. The Four Perfections. With square central hole.

63.	½ Piastre ND. (The Rev. is shown)	575.00

Four Chinese characters. Rev. The Five Happiness Symbols. With square central hole.

64.	¾ Piastre ND. (The Rev. is shown)	575.00

Four Chinese characters around radiant sun. Rev. Dragon.

65.	1 Piastre ND *	1100.00
66.	½ Piastre ND	600.00

Four characters around sun with blunt rays. Rev. Dragon coiled around similar sun.

67.	1½ Piastres (37½ Grams) ND *	4000.00
68.	1 Piastre (26 Grams) ND	1750.00
69.	¾ Piastre (19 Grams) ND	1500.00

DONG KHANH, 1885-1889

Five Chinese characters on each side.

70.   1 Ounce ND. Rectangular Bar 1000.00

Four Chinese characters. Rev. Blank. With square central hole.

71.   1/16 Piastre ND 175.00

Four Chinese characters. Rev. Sun, moon and two constellations. With square central hole.

72.   1/4 Piastre ND 675.00

THANH THAI, 1889-1905

Four Chinese characters. Rev. Five Chinese characters.

73.   1 Ounce ND. Rectangular bar...................... 650.00

Heavenly bodies flanked by four vertical characters. Rev. Long legend in form of a quatrain. With square central hole.

74.   1 Ounce ND.. 975.00

Four Chinese characters. Rev. Clouds and symbols for cosmic evolution. With square central hole.

75.   1/8 Piastre ND. (The Rev. is shown) 275.00

Four Chinese characters around radiant sun. Rev. Dragon.

76.   1/3 Piastre (10½ Grams). ND 275.00

Four Chinese characters. Rev. Sun, moon and characters. With square central hole.

77.   1/4 Piastre ND 275.00

Four Chinese characters. Rev. The Three Longevities. With square central hole.

78.   1/3 Piastre ND 275.00

Four Chinese characters around radiant sun. Rev. The Four Perfections around radiant sun.

79.   ½ Piastre ND 600.00

ARAB-ASIAN EMPIRES

The designation "Arab-Asian Empires" has been created especially for this book. Although they range over a vast expanse of earth, the coinages are basically similar in type, consisting mainly of native legends on each side of the coin. It was therefore felt that a single designation should encompass all such issues, except for those of Afghanistan, India, Persia and Turkey, which are catalogued separately.

Although it would have been possible to make a complete catalogue of the coins struck under each ruler (as has been done throughout this book), it was decided not to do so because all the coins look alike to the average Western eye (except for those trained in Oriental studies), and because the monotony of type and appearance remains unbroken over centuries of issue.

Caliphs, Sultans and Khans of —

A. ANONYMOUS CALIPHS
(Earliest Issues of North Africa and Spain)

Cross potent. Rev. Legend.

1.   1/3 Solidus ND (630-720 A.D.)........................ 175.00

Star. Rev. Legend.

2.   1/3 Solidus ND (630-720 A.D.)........................ 175.00

Legend on each side.

3.   1/3 Solidus ND (630-720 A.D.)........................ 175.00

Cross potent. Rev. Star.

4.   1/3 Solidus ND (630-720 A.D.)........................ 175.00

B. THE OMAYYAD CALIPHS OF DAMASCUS, 660-750 A.D.
(Successors to the first four Caliphs after Mohammed)

Arab legend on each side. With dates from about 38-132 A.H.

5.	1 Dinar ....*	60.00
6.	½ Dinar	55.00
7.	1/3 Dinar ....*	50.00
8.	1/4 Dinar	50.00

C. THE ABBASID CALIPHS OF BAGHDAD, 750-1517 A.D.

(This coinage was superseded by that of the Ottoman Sultans of Turkey.)

Arab legend on each side. With dates from about 133-923 A.H.

9.	3	Dinars..	600.00
10.	2	Dinars..	425.00
11.	1½	Dinars..	375.00
12.	1	Dinar.......................................*.....	50.00
13.	½	Dinar...	50.00
14.	¼	Dinar...	45.00

Bull. Rev. Horseman.

15.	1	Dinar..	Rare

D. THE ABBASID GOVERNORS OF EGYPT, 637-968 A.D.

(Including the lesser Dynasties of the Tulunuds, 868-905, and the Ikhshidis, 935-969).

Arab legend on each side. With dates from about 15-356 A.H.

16.	1	Dinar.....................................	60.00

E. THE FATIMID CALIPHS OF EGYPT, 969-1173 A.D.

Arab legend on each side. With dates from about 357-570 A.H.

17.	1	Dinar.......................................*.....	75.00
18.	¾	Dinar...	60.00
19.	½	Dinar...	50.00
20.	¼	Dinar...	45.00
21.	⅙	Dinar...	45.00

F. THE AYUBITE SULTANS OF EGYPT, 1173-1250 A.D.

Arab legend on each side. With dates from about 570-650 A.H.

22.	2	Dinars..	225.00
23.	1	Dinar.......................................*.....	100.00

G. THE MAMELUKE SULTANS OF EGYPT, 1250-1517 A.D.

Arab legend on each side. With dates from about 650-923 A.H.

24.	2	Dinars..	225.00
25.	1	Dinar.......................................*.....	85.00

H. THE OMAYYAD CALIPHS OF CORDOVA, 756-1024 A.D.

(Northwest Africa and Spain)

Arab legend on each side. With dates from about 138-415 A.H.

26.	1	Dinar.......................................*.....	200.00
27.	⅓	Dinar...	150.00

I. THE ALMORAVIDE AMIRS OF SPAIN, 1056-1147 A.D.

(Northwest Africa and Spain)

Arab legend on each side. With dates from about 448-541 A.H.

28.	1	Dinar.......................................*.....	165.00
29.	½	Dinar...	150.00
30.	¼	Dinar...	150.00

J. THE ALMOHADE CALIPHS OF SPAIN, 1130-1269 A.D.

(Northwest Africa and Spain)

Arab legend within square on each side. With or without dates from about 524-666 A.H.

31.	1	Dinar.......................................*.....	150.00
32.	½	Dinar...	135.00
33.	¼	Dinar...	100.00

K. THE SELJUK SULTANS OF WESTERN ASIA, 1040-1308 A.D.

(Dynasties in Persia, Syria and Asia Minor)

Arab legend on each side. With or without dates from about 431-708 A.H.

34.	1	Dinar...	80.00

L. THE MONGOL KHANS OF ASIA, 1251-1700 A.D.

Native legend on each side. With or without dates from about 750-1113 A.H.

35.	1	Dinar...	80.00

M. THE MONGOL KHANS OF KHOKAND AND BOKHARA, 1700-1875 A.D.

Native legend on each side. With dates from about 1113-1319 A.H.

36.	1	Tilla...	125.00

ARGENTINA

Mints and mint marks:—PTS monogram for Potosi; RA for Rioja. The 1 Escudo of 1813 remains unknown and its existence is in doubt. Many counterfeits exist of the large Rosas pieces. All gold coins of Argentina are considered rare except the 5 Peso piece, which is the equivalent of the 25 Franc piece struck on the Latin Monetary Union standard.

Radiant sun with human features. Rev. Arms.

1.	8 Escudos 1813. PTS mm.	14500.00
2.	8 Escudos 1826-35. RA mm.	4000.00
3.	4 Escudos 1813. PTS mm.	Unknown
4.	2 Escudos 1813. PTS mm.	Unique
5.	2 Escudos 1824, 25, 26. RA mm..........*	900.00
6.	1 Escudo 1813. PTS mm.	Rare

Uniformed bust of General Rosas. Rev. Mountain.

7.	8 Escudos 1836. Only six pieces known.	Rare

Mountain with crossed flags below and with legend "Repub. Argentina Confederada R." Rev. Arms.

8.	8 Escudos 1838, 40	3500.00

Similar Obv. but with legend "Republica Argentina R." Rev.

9.	8 Escudos 1840	4000.00

Uniformed bust of General Rosas. Rev. Arms.

10.	8 Escudos 1842	Rare
11.	2 Escudos 1842..........*	1000.00

Sun over mountain. Rev. Arms.

12.	2 Escudos 1843	1000.00

Shield. Rev. Arms.

13.	8 Escudos 1845	5500.00

Liberty head. Rev. Arms.

14.	5 Pesos (1 Argentino) 1881-89, 96..........*	250.00
15.	2½ Pesos (½ Argentino) 1881. Pattern. Only nine pieces were struck.	Rare
16.	2½ Pesos (½ Argentino) 1884	1000.00

AUSTRALIA

Mints and mint marks:—M for Melbourne; P for Perth; S for Sydney.

A. Early Issues of —

ADELAIDE ASSAY OFFICE

Crown and date. Rev. Value in beaded circle within two linear circles.

1.	1 Pound 1852	17500.00

Crown and date. Rev. Value in ornamental circle. The 5 Pound piece was not placed in circulation and no originals are known. The seven known pieces are re-strikes from the original dies.

2.	5 Pounds 1852	Rare
3.	1 Pound 1852..........*	3500.00

SOUTH AUSTRALIA GOLD INGOTS

Ingots of irregular shape stamped with a crown over SA and with other stamps denoting weight and fineness. Rev. Blank.

4.	Gold Ingot ND (1852)	Rare

PORT PHILIP COINAGE

Kangaroo and date in circle. Rev. Large value in circle.

5.	2 Ounces 1853, 54	*	Rare
6.	1 Ounce 1853		Rare
7.	½ Ounce 1853		Rare
8.	¼ Ounce 1853	*	Rare

B. British Sovereigns of —

VICTORIA, 1837-1901

Filletted young Head. Rev. "Sydney Mint One Sovereign" or "Half."

9.	1 Sovereign 1855-56		2500.00
9a.	½ Sovereign 1855-56		3500.00

Young head with oak leaf hair tie. Rev. "Sydney Mint One Sovereign" or "Half."

10.	1 Sovereign 1857-70	*	350.00
10a.	½ Sovereign 1857-66		300.00

(The remaining coins of Victoria and all those of the following rulers are of the same types as English gold coins, but with the distinguishing Australian mintmarks as indicated).

Young head. Rev. Arms, mintmark below.

11.	1 Pound 1871-87. S mm.		225.00
12.	1 Pound 1872-87. M mm.		225.00
13.	½ Pound 1871-87. S mm.		300.00
14.	½ Pound 1873-87. M mm.		300.00

Young head with mintmark below. Rev. St. George.

15.	1 Pound 1871-87. S mm.		150.00
16.	1 Pound 1872-87. M mm.		150.00

Jubilee head. Rev. St. George with mintmark on ground below horse.

17.	5 Pounds 1887. S mm. Proofs only		Rare
18.	2 Pounds 1887. S mm. Proofs only		Rare
19.	1 Pound 1887-93. S mm.		200.00(B)
20.	1 Pound 1887-93. M mm.		200.00(B)

Jubilee head. Rev. Arms, mintmark below.

21.	½ Pound 1887, 93. M mm.		200.00
22.	½ Pound 1887, 89, 91. S mm.		200.00

Veiled head. Rev. Similar to above.

22a.	5 Pounds 1893. S mm. Proofs only		Rare
22b.	2 Pounds 1893. S mm. Proofs only		Rare
23.	1 Pound 1893-1901. S mm.		200.00(B)
24.	1 Pound 1893-1901. M mm.		200.00(B)
25.	1 Pound 1899-1901. P mm.		200.00(B)
26.	½ Pound 1893-1901. M mm.		200.00
27.	½ Pound 1893, 97, 1900. S mm.		200.00
28.	½ Pound 1899, 1900. P mm.		200.00
29.	½ Pound 1893, 96, 99, 1900. M mm.		200.00

EDWARD VII, 1901-1911

Head. Rev. St. George with mintmark on ground below horse.

30.	5 Pounds 1902. S mm. Proofs only		Rare
31.	2 Pounds 1902. S mm. Proofs only		Rare
32.	1 Pound 1902-10. S mm.		200.00(B)
33.	1 Pound 1902-10. M mm.		200.00(B)
34.	1 Pound 1902-10. P mm.		200.00(B)
35.	½ Pound 1902-10. S mm.		200.00
36.	½ Pound 1906-09. M mm.		200.00
37.	½ Pound 1904, 08, 09. P mm.		200.00

GEORGE V, 1910-1936

Head. Rev. St. George with mintmark on ground below horse.

38.	1 Pound 1911-26. S mm.		200.00(B)
39.	1 Pound 1911-31. M mm.		200.00(B)
40.	1 Pound 1911-31. P mm.		200.00(B)
41.	½ Pound 1911-16. S mm.		200.00
42.	½ Pound 1915. M mm.		200.00
43.	½ Pound 1911, 15. P mm.		200.00

(Numbers 19, 20, 23-25, 32-34, 38-40 are bullion coins, i.e., coins whose price fluctuates according to the price of gold on the international market. The price listed is based on gold at $725 per ounce.)

AUSTRIA

(See remarks under Holy Roman Empire.)

Mints and mint marks for period from about 1750-1916.

A	mm for Vienna		M	mm for Milan
B, KB	mm for Kremnitz		V	mm for Venice
C	mm for Prague		W	mm for Vienna
D	mm for Salzburg			
E	mm for Karlsburg			
F	mm for Hall		Hand	mm for Antwerp
G	mm for Nagybanya		Small head	mm for Brussels
G.Y.F.	mm for Karlsburg (Hungarian)		Lion or lily	mm for Bruges
H	mm for Gunzburg		Tower	mm for Tournai

It will be seen that the series of coins struck under the Holy Roman Emperors is both long and extensive. It is regretted that lack of space did not permit a listing of the coinage of each mint, as has been done beginning with the reign of Joseph II. About 20 mints operated over a period of some 250 years, each with its own letter or symbol as a mint mark and a detailed listing of this formidable coinage would be beyond the scope of this book.

In many cases, some of the larger gold coins in the Austrian series are off-strikes. The denomination "Souverain" is traditionally applied to the coinage of the Austrian and Belgian Mints while its counterpart "Sovrano" is used for the coinage of the Milan and Venice Mints. The coins of Francis Joseph are especially noteworthy, since five different standards of gold coinage existed during his long reign, viz, Ducats, Sovranos, Krones, Florins and Corona.

A. Dukes of —

ALBERT II, 1330-1358

St. John. Rev. Lily.

1.	1 Goldgulden ND		600.00

RUDOLPH IV, 1358-1365
St. John. Rev. Lily.

2.	1 Goldgulden ND		2000.00

B. Holy Roman Emperors and Archdukes —

ALBERT V (ALBERT II OF HABSBURG) 1437-1439

Madonna. Rev. Orb in trilobe.

3.	1 Goldgulden ND		5000.00

FREDERICK III, 1439-1493
John the Baptist standing. Rev. Orb in trilobe.

4.	1 Goldgulden ND		3500.00

ARCHDUKE SIGISMUND, 1439-1496
Ruler standing. Rev. Four shields and floriated cross.

5.	1 Goldgulden ND		1500.00

MAXIMILIAN I, 1493-1519
Ruler standing. Rev. 4 shields and floriated cross.
5a. 1 Goldgulden ND..................................... 1500.00

St. Leopold. Rev. Arms.
6. 1 Ducat 1511, 14, 16, 18.......................... 4500.00

St. Leopold. Rev. Cross and shield.
7. 1 Goldgulden 1510, 11, 14-17 .... 3000.00

Double eagle. Rev. Carinthian shield.
8. 1 Goldgulden 1515, 16............................. 3500.00

Crowned bust. Rev. Carinthian shield.
9. 1 Ducat 1516-19 .... 3000.00

Bust with hat. Rev. Carinthian shield.
10. 4 Ducats 1518.................................... 15000.00

INTERREGNUM, 1519-1521
St. Leopold. Rev. 5 shields. Issued by the Wiener Hausgenossen.
10a. 1 Goldgulden 1519, 20........................... 7000.00

FERDINAND I, 1521-1564
Bust. Rev. Legend.
11. 4 Ducats 1529. Square........................... Rare
12. 3 Ducats 1529. Square........................... Rare
13. 2 Ducats 1529. Square........................... 5000.00

Bust. Rev. Cross and four shields.
14. 1½ Ducats 1529. Square.......................... 3500.00
15. 1   Ducat 1529. Square................*...... 2200.00
16. ½ Ducat 1529. Square............................ 1250.00

Austrian shield. Rev. Legend.
17. ½ Ducat 1529. Square............................ 1000.00
17a. ¼ Ducat 1529. Square........................... 850.00

(The above eight coins were struck during the Siege of Vienna.)

Bust. Rev. Double eagle.
18. 12 Ducats 1532.................................. Rare
19. 8 Ducats 1532.................................. Rare
20. 6 Ducats 1526.................................. Rare
21. 2 Ducats 1560.................................. 5000.00

Bust. Rev. Arms.
22. 1 Ducat 1525 .... 6000.00

Middle aged bust. Rev. St. Ladislas.
23. 1 Goldgulden 1531-58............................ 700.00

Ruler standing. Rev. Floriated cross and four shields.
24. 1 Goldgulden ND................................. 2500.00

Ruler standing. Rev. Arms.
25. 2 Ducats ND 2000.00
26. 1 Ducat ND..................................... 1000.00
27. 1 Ducat 1565. Posthumous 900.00

Bust. Rev. Legend. On his burial.
28. 1 Ducat 1565 .... 3000.00

ARCHDUKE CHARLES, 1564-1590

Ruler standing. Rev. Arms.
29. 12 Ducats 1579 .... Rare
30. 10 Ducats 1572, 76 .... Rare
31. 2 Ducats 1576-87 .... 3000.00
32. 1 Ducat 1565-90 ....*..... 600.00
33. 1 Ducat 1591, 92. Posthumous................ 600.00

Bust. Rev. Four shields.
34. 3 Ducats 1572................................ 5500.00

Fortuna standing. Rev. Five shields.
35. 3 Ducats 1573................................ 4500.00

ARCHDUKE FERDINAND, 1564-1595
Bust. Rev. Arms.
36. 3 Ducats ND 7000.00
37. 1 Ducat 1564-95 .... 900.00
38. ½ Ducat 1591 .... 1700.00

Bust. Rev. Eagle.
39. 20 Ducats 1590............................... Rare
40. 1 Ducat 1569-83 .... 850.00
41. ⅛ Ducat ND.................................. 600.00
42. 1 Gold Crown (Gulden) ND .... Rare

Bust of Maximilian I, Charles V and Ferdinand I. Rev. Double eagle.
43. 10 Ducats 1590............................... 15000.00
44. 8 Ducats ND .... Rare
45. 5 Ducats 1590................................ 12000.00

RUDOLPH II, 1576-1612
Bust. Rev. Double eagle.
46. 10 Ducats 1589-1611.......................... 14000.00
47. 5 Ducats 1587-1611........................... 8000.00
48. 4 Ducats 1589-1604........................... 7500.00
49. 3 Ducats 1580-1607........................... 5500.00
50. 2 Ducats 1598-1611........................... 1500.00
51. 1 Ducat 1577-1611............................ 650.00

Ruler standing. Rev. Double eagle.
52. 10 Ducats 1599-1610...............*.....13500.00
53. 5 Ducats 1587-1611........................... 7000.00
54. 4 Ducats 1589-1604........................... 7500.00
55. 3 Ducats 1598-1606........................... 5000.00
56. 2 Ducats 1598-1611........................... 1500.00
57. 1 Ducat 1577-1611............................ 650.00
58. The coin previously listed has been deleted.

Ruler standing. Rev. Arms.
59. 1 Ducat 1578-1608 .... 750.00

Busts of Maximilian I, Charles V and Ferdinand I. Rev. Double eagle.
60.	5 Ducats ND	....	13500.00

MATTHIAS II, 1612-1619
Bust. Rev. Arms. Struck as Archduke.

61.	10 Ducats ND	....	Rare
62.	6 Ducats 1608-11	....	10000.00
63.	5 Ducats 1608, 09	....	8500.00
64.	1 Ducat 1609-11	....	1250.00

Bust. Rev. Double eagle.

65.	25 Ducats 1615. Square	....	Rare
66.	20 Ducats 1612	....	Rare
67.	15 Ducats 1612, 17	....	Rare
68.	10 Ducats 1611-19	....	15000.00
69.	8 Ducats 1612	....	12000.00
70.	5 Ducats 1612-19	....	8500.00
71.	4 Ducats 1612	....	6500.00
72.	3 Ducats 1613, 17	....	4500.00
73.	2 Ducats 1613-19	....	2500.00
74.	1 Ducat 1612-19	....	1000.00

Armored bust. Rev. Busts of Maximilian I, Charles V and Ferdinand I.

75.	15 Ducats ND	....	Rare
76.	10 Ducats ND	....	Rare

ARCHDUKE MAXIMILIAN, 1612-1618
Ruler standing. Rev. Arms.

77.	1 Ducat ND	....	1250.00

Armored bust. Rev. Cross.

78.	½ Ducat ND	....	1100.00

ARCHDUKE FERDINAND, 1592-1618
Armored bust. Rev. Arms.

79.	8 Ducats 1618	....	Rare
80.	1 Ducat 1617	....	1250.00

Bust. Rev. Double eagle.

81.	5 Ducats 1602	....	8000.00
82.	1 Ducat 1598-1616	....	800.00

Ruler standing. Rev. Arms.

83.	1 Ducat 1598-1617	....	1250.00

FERDINAND II, 1618-1637
Ruler on throne. Rev. Double eagle.

84.	1 Ducat 1620-37	....	1250.00

Armored bust. Rev. Double eagle.

85.	20 Ducats 1622, 36	....	Rare
86.	15 Ducats 1636	....	Rare
87.	12 Ducats 1626	....	15000.00
88.	10 Ducats 1621-37	....	12500.00
89.	6 Ducats 1624, 27, 28	....	9500.00
90.	5 Ducats 1621-37	....	8500.00
91.	4 Ducats 1622-34	....	5500.00
92.	3 Ducats 1637	....	3000.00
93.	2 Ducats 1620-37	....	2000.00
94.	1 Ducat 1620-37	....	800.00
95.	½ Ducat 1633, 36	....	800.00

Laureate bust. Rev. Silesian eagle.

96.	1 Ducat 1623	....	850.00

Armored bust. Rev. Arms.

97.	20 Ducats 1636	....	Rare
98.	12 Ducats 1632	....	Rare
99.	10 Ducats 1621-37	....	8000.00
100.	9 Ducats 1632	....	7500.00
101.	8 Ducats 1632	....	7000.00
102.	6 Ducats 1628, 32	....	6500.00
103.	5 Ducats 1621-37	....................*	5500.00
104.	4 Ducats 1627. Square	....	7500.00
105.	3 Ducats 1634. Square	....	5500.00
106.	2 Ducats 1620-37	....	1500.00
107.	1 Ducat 1620-37	....	600.00

Ruler standing. Rev. Arms.

107a.	2 Ducats 1628	....	5000.00
108.	1 Ducat 1620-37	....	550.00

Bust facing. Rev. City view of Breslau, eagle above.

109.	10 Ducats 1626, 31	....	15000.00

Double eagle. Rev. Arms.

110.	4 Ducats 1621, 22	....	3500.00

INTERREGNUM IN THE TYROL, 1618-1619
Tyrolian eagle shield. Rev. Arms of Austria.

111.	1 Goldgulden 1618, 19	....	3500.00

ARCHDUKE LEOPOLD, 1619-1632
Busts of Leopold and Claudia. Rev. Eagle. Struck in 1626 on their marriage.

112.	20 Ducats ND	....	Rare
113.	8 Ducats ND	....	12000.00
114.	6 Ducats ND	....	10000.00
115.	6 Ducats ND. Square	....	10000.00
116.	5 Ducats ND	....	8500.00

Ruler standing. Rev. St. Leopold.

117.	1 Ducat 1631, ND	....	3000.00

Tyrolian shield. Rev. Arms.

118.	½ Ducat ND	....	1250.00

St. Leopold. Rev. Tyrolian shield.

119.	1 Ducat 1619	....	3000.00

FERDINAND III, 1627-1657

Youthful bust. Rev. Arms.

120.	12 Ducats 1629	....	Rare
121.	10 Ducats 1627-29	...................*	15000.00
122.	9 Ducats 1629	....	11000.00
123.	8 Ducats 1629	....	10000.00
124.	2 Ducats 1629-31	....	2500.00
125.	1 Ducat 1629-36	....	750.00

Armored bust. Rev. Arms.

126.	15 Ducats 1641	Rare
127.	12 Ducats 1641	15000.00
128.	10 Ducats 1638-57	12000.00
129.	8 Ducats 1638	10000.00
130.	7 Ducats 1638	8500.00
131.	6 Ducats 1638	8000.00
132.	5 Ducats 1638-57	7000.00
133.	4 Ducats 1638	6000.00
134.	2 Ducats 1637-57	2500.00
135.	1 Ducat 1637-57	800.00

Armored bust. Rev. Double eagle.

136.	20 Ducats 1645 .... *	Rare
137.	10 Ducats 1638-57 .... *	14000.00
138.	10 Ducats 1658. Posthumous	14000.00
139.	6 Ducats 1639-46	8000.00
140.	5 Ducats 1636-57	7000.00
141.	4 Ducats 1645	6000.00
142.	3 Ducats 1643, 56	4000.00
143.	2 Ducats 1637-57	2200.00
144.	1 Ducat 1637-57	1100.00
145.	½ Ducat 1637-49	800.00

Laureate bust. Rev. Three shields.

146.	1 Ducat 1637, 38	1500.00
147.	1 Ducat 1637, 38. Square	2500.00

Ruler standing. Rev. Dougle eagle.

148.	2 Ducats 1637-57 .... *	3500.00
149.	1 Ducat 1637-57	1500.00

PROTESTANT ASSEMBLY OF SILESIA, 1633-1635
Armored bust of Ferdinand III. Rev. Double eagle.

150.	3 Ducats 1634	6500.00
151.	1 Ducat 1634, 35	1500.00

ARCHDUKE FERDINAND CHARLES, 1632-1662

Bust. Rev. Eagle.

152.	6 Ducats 1632-37	8000.00
153.	5 Ducats 1632-37, ND	7500.00
154.	2 Ducats 1632-62, ND .... *	3500.00

Bust. Rev. Arms.

155.	1 Ducat 1632-62 .... *	2200.00
156.	½ Ducat 1632-62	2000.00

Bust with hat. Rev. Eagle.

157.	20 Ducats 1632-62	Rare

Ruler on horseback. Rev. St. Leopold.

158.	3 Ducats 1642	6000.00
159.	2 Ducats 1642 .... *	3300.00

Ruler standing. Rev. St. Leopold.

160.	1 Ducat 1632-62, ND	1500.00

FERDINAND IV, 1646-1654
Legend. Rev. Altar.

161.	1 Ducat 1646	700.00

ARCHDUKE SIGISMUND FRANCIS, 1662-1665
Bust with long hair. Rev. Eagle.

162.	20 Ducats ND	Rare

Bust with long hair. Rev. Crowned arms.

163.	1 Ducat ND	Rare

LEOPOLD I (THE HOGMOUTH), 1658-1705
Two angels with crown. Rev. Globe under two hands. On his Coronation.

164.	4 Ducats 1658	5500.00

Laureate bust. Rev. Tyrolian eagle.

165.	30 Ducats ND	Rare
166.	20 Ducats ND	Rare
167.	12 Ducats ND	Rare
168.	4 Ducats ND .... *	6500.00

Laureate bust. Rev. Double eagle.

169.	12 Ducats 1674 .... *	Rare
170.	10 Ducats 1658-1703 .... *	13000.00
171.	10 Ducats 1694. Square	Rare

172.	8 Ducats 1678	10000.00
173.	6 Ducats 1669-1703	8500.00
174.	5 Ducats 1659-1703	7500.00
175.	5 Ducats 1694. Square	10000.00
176.	4 Ducats 1692-1703	5000.00
177.	4 Ducats 1696-98. Square	5500.00
178.	3 Ducats 1694-1701	3000.00
179.	2 Ducats 1659-1705	2500.00
180.	2 Ducats 1660, 96. Square	4500.00
181.	1 Ducat 1658-1705	750.00
182.	1 Ducat 1691, 95, 99. Square	1000.00
183.	½ Ducat 1661-95	500.00
184.	⅓ Ducat 1675-98	450.00
185.	¼ Ducat 1669-1705	400.00
186.	⅙ Ducat 1669-99	400.00
187.	⅛ Ducat 1686-98	400.00
188.	¹⁄₁₂ Ducat 1675-99	350.00

Crowned bust. Rev. Double eagle.

189.	5 Ducats 1676-95	7500.00
190.	3 Ducats 1665 ....*	6500.00

Laureate bust. Rev. Arms.

191.	30 Ducats 1678	Rare
192.	20 Ducats 1670	Rare
193.	10 Ducats 1658-1703	15000.00
194.	6 Ducats 1662-1703	10000.00
195.	5 Ducats 1659-1703	8000.00
196.	4 Ducats 1658-95	6000.00
197.	4 Ducats 1661. Square	8500.00
198.	3 Ducats ND	4500.00
199.	2 Ducats 1659-1705	2500.00
200.	1 Ducat 1659-93 ....* ..	600.00
201.	¼ Ducat 1669, ND......................	350.00

Ruler on horseback. Rev. Double eagle.

202.	1 Ducat 1661	5000.00

JOSEPH I, 1705-1711
Bust. Rev. Tyrolian eagle.

203.	24 Ducats ND	Rare

Bust. Rev. Double eagle.

204.	10 Ducats 1705-09	Rare
205.	5 Ducats 1706-08	7000.00
206.	4 Ducats 1708	6000.00
207.	3 Ducats 1706-11	4000.00
208.	2 Ducats 1706-09. Round or square ....*	3000.00
209.	1 Ducat 1705-11	1000.00
210.	½ Ducat 1706-10	500.00
211.	⅓ Ducat 1706	300.00
212.	¼ Ducat 1706-11	300.00
213.	⅙ Ducat 1706-11	325.00
214.	⅛ Ducat 1706-09	300.00
215.	¹⁄₁₂ Ducat 1705-11	275.00

Bust. Rev. Arms.

216.	10 Ducats 1706..........................	Rare
217.	3 Ducats 1710	4400.00
218.	1 Ducat 1706, ND......................	1200.00

Ruler standing. Rev. Double eagle.

219.	1 Ducat 1710, 11	1250.00

Double Arms. Rev. Blank.

220.	⅛ Ducat 1710	400.00

CHARLES VI, 1711-1740

Armored bust. Rev. Double eagle.

221.	20 Ducats 1739........................	Rare
222.	12 Ducats 1740........................	15000.00
223.	10 Ducats 1712-40.....................	12500.00
224.	6 Ducats 1714, 28	8500.00
225.	5 Ducats 1713-39	7000.00
226.	4 Ducats 1713-30	5500.00
227.	3 Ducats 1717-38	4000.00
228.	2 Ducats 1715-35	2000.00
229.	2 Ducats 1734. Square.................	3000.00
230.	1 Ducat 1712-40 ....* ..	500.00
231.	½ Ducat 1728-40	350.00
232.	¼ Ducat 1720-38	300.00
233.	⅙ Ducat 1731	300.00
234.	⅛ Ducat 1729	250.00
235.	¹⁄₁₆ Ducat 1729	250.00

Globe. Rev. Sceptre.

236.	1 Ducat 1716	1500.00

Legend. Rev. Globe.

237.	1 Ducat 1723	850.00

Crowned bust with name and title as Charles III, King of Spain. Rev. Arms. With hand mint mark for Antwerp.

238.	2 Souverain d'or 1711...................	7500.00

Lion standing with same title. Rev. Arms. Hand mint mark.

239.	1 Souverain (Lion) d'or 1710	8000.00

Crowned bust with name and title as Charles VI, Holy Roman Emperor. Rev. Eagle and shield. Hand mint mark.

240.	2 Souverain d'or 1719, 20	8500.00

Laureate bust with titles as above. Rev. Arms. Hand mint mark.

241.	2 Souverain d'or 1724-26...............	8000.00

(For additional coins of Charles VI, as well as of the rulers following, see under Italy-Milan.)

CHARLES VII, 1740-1745
(Elector of Bavaria with title of Holy Roman Emperor).
Eagle. Rev. Crown.

242.	1 Ducat 1742	2200.00

MARIA THERESA, 1740-1780
Youthful bust. Rev. Elaborate arms.

243.	12 Ducats 1744	8000.00
244.	10 Ducats 1742-45	7000.00
245.	6 Ducats 1741-45	5500.00
246.	5 Ducats 1742-46	5000.00
247.	4 Ducats 1743	4000.00
248.	1 Ducat 1741-46	500.00

Mature bust. Rev. Double eagle.

249.	10 Ducats 1748-61 ....*	8000.00
250.	7 Ducats 1758	7000.00
251.	6 Ducats 1745-68	4500.00
252.	5 Ducats 1746-65	4000.00
253.	4 Ducats 1759-65	3300.00
254.	3 Ducats 1754-61	2750.00
255.	2 Ducats 1746-65	1100.00
256.	1 Ducat 1746-65	450.00
257.	½ Ducat 1748-65 ....* ...	300.00
258.	¼ Ducat 1749-65	250.00
259.	⅛ Ducat 1752	300.00
260.	⅛ Ducat 1749, 61	225.00

Head. Rev. Double eagle.

261.	¼ Ducat 1749, 51	300.00

Bust with widow's veil. Rev. Double eagle.

262.	5 Ducats 1777	5500.00
263.	4 Ducats 1778-80	3300.00
264.	2 Ducats 1767-80	1000.00
265.	1 Ducat 1765-80	600.00
266.	½ Ducat 1765-80	300.00
267.	¼ Ducat 1768-80	225.00

Arms. Rev. Value and date.

268.	⅛ Ducat 1778	250.00

Ruler standing. Rev. Crowned arms.

269.	1 Ducat 1744-65	450.00

Bust. Rev. Bust of Francis.

270.	1 Ducat ND.............................	600.00

Bust of the Imperial Couple. Rev. Crossed hammers.

271.	1 Mining Ducat 1751	1500.00

Bust with or without crown or veil. Rev. Arms.

272.	2 Souverain d'or 1756-80. W mm or with W........	1500.00
273.	2 Souverain d'or 1749-57. Hand mm.........*	1250.00
274.	2 Souverain d'or 1749-52. Lion mm..................	1500.00
275.	2 Souverain d'or 1758-80. Head mm................	1000.00
276.	1 Souverain d'or 1749-57. Hand mm..............	600.00
277.	1 Souverain d'or 1750-54. Lion mm.........*	550.00
278.	1 Souverain d'or 1757-77. Head mm........*	650.00

FRANCIS I, 1745-1765

Bust with long hair. Rev. Double eagle.

279.	6 Ducats 1747	8500.00
280.	5 Ducats 1745, 47	5000.00
281.	2 Ducats 1745, 46	1850.00
282.	1 Ducat 1745-65 ....* ...	400.00
283.	1 Ducat 1766-80. Posthumous...........	450.00
284.	¼ Ducat 1755-65	300.00

Draped laureate bust. Rev. Double eagle.

284a.	10 Souverains d'or 1751. Hand mm	12500.00

JOSEPH II, 1765-1790

Youthful bust. Rev. Double eagle. Struck as co-regent with Maria Theresa, 1765-80.

285.	3 Ducats 1773, 76, 78...................	4000.00
286.	2 Ducats 1768-80	850.00
287.	1 Ducat 1764-80 ....*	550.00
288.	¼ Ducat 1765, 77	250.00

Draped laureate bust. Rev. Double eagle.

289.	4 Ducats 1786. A mm...........................	4500.00
290.	1 Ducat 1781-84. C mm.	450.00
291.	1 Ducat 1781-86. F mm. ....*	350.00
292.	1 Ducat 1780, 82. A mm.	325.00
293.	1 Ducat 1781, 82. E mm.	325.00
294.	1 Ducat 1781, 82. G mm.	325.00

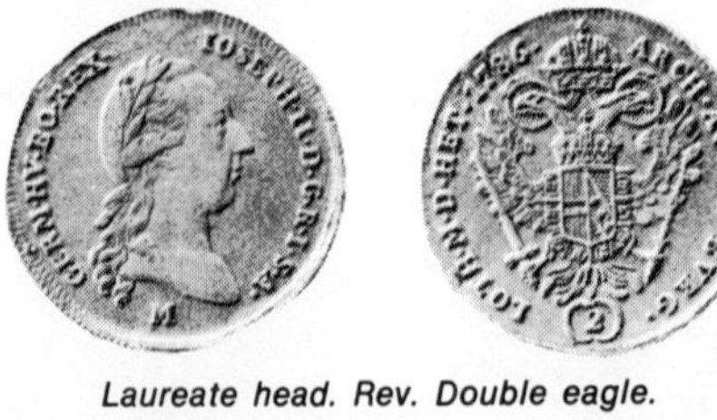

Laureate head. Rev. Double eagle.

295.	2 Ducats 1784, 86, 87. A mm...................	650.00
296.	2 Ducats 1786, 87. B mm.	650.00

297.	2 Ducats 1781-87. E mm..................	650.00
298.	2 Ducats 1786. M mm...............*	1250.00
299.	1 Ducat 1782-90. A mm..................	325.00
300.	1 Ducat 1786-90. B mm..................	325.00
301.	1 Ducat 1783-90. E mm..................	325.00
302.	1 Ducat 1787-90. F mm..................	325.00
303.	1 Ducat 1783-90. G mm..................	400.00
304.	1 Ducat 1786, 87, 88. M mm..........	1000.00
305.	½ Ducat 1787. A mm..................	Rare

Laureate head. Rev. Circular shield over cross. Prior to 1786, when gold was revalued, the 1 Souverain d'or struck at the Vienna mint (No. 306) was valued at 2 Souverains d'or. The 1 and ½ Souverains d'or which were struck at the Brussels mint (Nos. 308 and 311) were valued at 2 and 1 Souverains d'or, respectively, in Belgium.

306.	1 Souverain d'or 1784-87. A mm..............	850.00
307.	1 Souverain d'or 1786. F mm.............	1100.00
308.	1 Souverain d'or 1781-89. Head mm..........	750.00
309.	½ Souverain d'or 1786, 87, 89. A mm.......*	500.00
310.	½ Souverain d'or 1786-90. F mm..........	600.00
311.	½ Souverain d'or 1786, 88. Head mm.........	525.00
312.	1 Sovrano 1786-90. M mm...............*	800.00
312a.	1 Sovrano 1786. No mm. (Struck at Milan)	1200.00
313.	½ Sovrano 1787, 89, 90. M mm................	800.00

LEOPOLD II, 1790-1792
Laureate head. Rev. Arms.

314.	1 Ducat 1790................................	1250.00

Laureate head. Rev. Double eagle.

315.	4 Ducats 1790. A mm..................	Rare
316.	2 Ducats 1790. A mm..................	Rare
317.	1 Ducat 1790, 91. A mm............*	650.00
318.	1 Ducat 1791. B mm..................	550.00
319.	1 Ducat 1791, 92. E mm..............	600.00
320.	1 Ducat 1791, 92. F mm..............	700.00
321.	1 Ducat 1791, 92. G mm..............	600.00

Laureate head. Rev. Arms.

322.	1 Souverain d'or 1791. Head mm................	Rare
323.	1 Souverain d'or 1790, 91. A mm..............	3000.00
324.	1 Souverain d'or 1792. B mm..............	3000.00
325.	1 Souverain d'or 1972. E mm..............	3000.00
326.	1 Sovrano 1790, 91, 92. M mm............*	3500.00
327.	½ Souverain d'or 1791, 92. A mm..............	500.00
328.	½ Souverain d'or 1792. B mm..............	450.00
329.	½ Souverain d'or 1792. E mm., F mm..............	550.00
330.	½ Sovrano 1790, 91, 92. M mm............*	500.00
331.	¼ Sovrano 1791. M mm..................	Rare

FRANCIS (II, 1792-1806; I, 1806-1835)
Laureate head. Rev. Arms.

332.	1 Ducat 1792. A mm..................	1500.00

Laureate bust. Rev. Double eagle.

333.	4 Ducats 1793-1830. A mm..................	1500.00

Laureate head. Rev. Double eagle.

334.	2 Ducats 1799-1804. A mm..................	1800.00
335.	1 Ducat 1792-1831. A mm..................	300.00
336.	1 Ducat 1792-1830. B mm..................	300.00
337.	1 Ducat 1797-1807. C mm..................	500.00
338.	1 Ducat 1806, 08, 09. D mm..................	300.00
339.	1 Ducat 1792-1830. E mm..................	350.00
340.	1 Ducat 1793-1826. G mm............*	350.00
341.	1 Ducat 1819, 24. V mm..................	850.00
342.	½ Ducat 1796. E mm..................	2000.00

Older laureate head. Rev. Double eagle.

343.	1 Ducat 1831-35. A mm..................	225.00
344.	1 Ducat 1832-35. B mm..................	250.00
345.	1 Ducat 1833, 34, 35. E mm..................	250.00

Laureate head. Rev. Arms.

346.	1 Souverain d'or 1793. Head mm..................	1250.00
347.	1 Souverain d'or 1792-98. A mm..................	550.00
348.	1 Souverain d'or 1794, 95, 96. B mm..............	600.00
349.	1 Souverain d'or 1796. F mm..................	850.00
350.	1 Souverain d'or 1793. H mm..................	800.00
351.	1 Sovrano 1793-1800. M mm............*	750.00
352.	1 Sovrano 1793. V mm..................	800.00
353.	1 Sovrano 1796. MM monogram mm. (Mantua)	Rare
354.	½ Souverain d'or 1792-98. A mm..................	500.00
355.	½ Souverain d'or 1794, 95. B mm..............	650.00
356.	½ Souverain d'or 1795. E mm..................	1500.00
357.	½ Souverain d'or 1793-96. F mm..................	600.00
358.	½ Souverain d'or 1793, 98. H mm..................	850.00
359.	½ Sovrano 1800. M mm..................	700.00
360.	½ Sovrano 1793. V mm..................	750.00

Older laureate head. Rev. Double eagle.

361.	1 Sovrano 1822, 23, 31. A mm.................*	850.00
362.	1 Sovrano 1820-35. M mm................... *	750.00
363.	1 Sovrano 1822. V mm...................	1250.00
364.	½ Sovrano 1822, 23, 31. A mm................	550.00
365.	½ Sovrano 1820, 22, 31, 35. M mm.	500.00
366.	½ Sovrano 1822. V mm...................	650.00

Ruler kneeling before St. Mark. Rev. Christ. Struck at Venice in the style of the old Venetian Ducats.

367.	1 Zecchino ND	1000.00

FERDINAND I, 1835-1848

Laureate bust. Rev. Double eagle.

368.	4 Ducats 1835-48. A mm...............*	1500.00
369.	4 Ducats 1848. E mm...............	1800.00

Laureate head. Rev. Double eagle.

370.	1 Ducat 1835-48. A mm...............	150.00
371.	1 Ducat 1837-48. B mm...............	150.00
372.	1 Ducat 1835-48. E mm...............	150.00
373.	1 Ducat 1840-48. V mm...............	1000.00

Laureate head. Rev. Double eagle. The 1849-M ½ Sovrano is Posthumous.

374.	1 Sovrano 1837-47. A mm...............	1500.00
375.	1 Sovrano 1837-48. M mm...............	1800.00
376.	1 Sovrano 1837-47. V mm...............*	1500.00
377.	½ Sovrano 1837. A mm...............	Unknown
378.	½ Sovrano 1837-49. M mm...............*	1250.00
379.	½ Sovrano 1837-47. V mm...............	1500.00

FRANCIS JOSEPH, 1848-1916

Young laureate bust. Rev. Double eagle.

380.	4 Ducats 1854-59. A mm...............*	1400.00
381.	4 Ducats 1857. V mm...............	3500.00

Laureate bust with small side whiskers. Rev. Double eagle.

382.	4 Ducats 1860-65. A mm...............	1300.00
383.	4 Ducats 1864, 65. V mm.	3000.00

Older bust with heavier whiskers. Rev. Double eagle.

384.	4 Ducats 1866-72	1250.00

Oldest bust with thick whiskers. Rev. Double eagle.

385.	4 Ducats 1872-1914...............	650.00
386.	4 Ducats 1915. Proof restrike...............*	225.00

Young laureate head to left. Rev. Double eagle. With large date in legend and additional small date 1898. Struck in 1898 on the 50th year of his reign.

387.	1 Ducat 1848, 49, 50, 51...............	550.00

Young laureate head to right. Rev. Double eagle.

388.	1 Ducat 1852-59. A mm...............	200.00
389.	1 Ducat 1853-59. B mm...............	250.00
390.	1 Ducat 1853-59. E mm...............	250.00
391.	1 Ducat 1858. M mm...............	1250.00
392.	1 Ducat 1854-59. V mm...............*	1000.00

Laureate head with small side whiskers. Rev. Double eagle.

393.	1 Ducat 1860-65. A mm...............	200.00
394.	1 Ducat 1860-65. B mm...............	200.00
395.	1 Ducat 1860-65. E mm...............	200.00
396.	1 Ducat 1860-65. V mm...............*	850.00

Older head with heavier whiskers. Rev. Double eagle.

397.	1 Ducat 1866-72. A mm.	150.00
398.	1 Ducat 1866, 67. B mm.	200.00
399.	1 Ducat 1866, 67. E mm.	200.00
400.	1 Ducat 1866. V mm.	800.00

Oldest head with thick whiskers. Rev. Double eagle.

401.	1 Ducat 1872-1914	115.00
402.	1 Ducat 1915. Proof restrike ....*	85.00
403.	1 Ducat 1951. Unofficial Mint error for 1915	200.00

Laureate head. Rev. Double eagle.

404.	1 Sovrano 1853, 55, 56. M mm. ....*	3500.00
405.	1 Sovrano 1854, 55, 56. V mm.	4000.00
406.	½ Sovrano 1854, 55, 56. M mm.	1500.00
407.	½ Sovrano 1854, 55, 56. V mm. ......*	3000.00

Laureate head. Rev. Value and date in wreath.

408.	1 Krone 1858-66. A mm. ....*	1500.00
409.	1 Krone 1859. B mm.	Rare
410.	1 Krone 1858. E mm.	2000.00
411.	1 Krone 1859. M mm.	3000.00
412.	1 Krone 1858, 59. V mm.	4500.00
413.	½ Krone 1858-66. A mm.	1250.00
414.	½ Krone 1859, 60, 61. B mm.	1250.00
415.	½ Krone 1858, 59, 61. E mm.	1250.00
416.	½ Krone 1858. V mm.	4500.00

Head in circle of shields. Rev. Double eagle. On the Vienna Shooting Match.

417.	4 Ducats 1873	4500.00

Uniformed bust. Rev. Tourist Inn. On the building of the Charles Louis Inn on Mt. Raxalpe.

418.	6 Ducats 1877. (Same die as for the silver coin)....	Rare

Head. Rev. Double eagle and values.

419.	8 Florins-20 Francs 1870-92 ....*	185.00
419R.	8 Florins-20 Francs 1892. Restrike	175.00(B)
420.	4 Florins-10 Francs 1870-92	110.00
420R.	4 Florins-10 Francs 1892. Restrike	110.00(B)

Old laureate head. Rev. Double eagle.

421.	20 Corona 1892-1909 ....*	155.00
422.	10 Corona 1892, 93	1250.00
423.	10 Corona 1894-1909	100.00

Plain head. Rev. Double eagle.

424.	100 Corona 1909-15	1350.00
424R.	100 Corona 1915. Restrike	300.00(B)
425.	20 Corona 1909-15 ....*	350.00
425R.	20 Corona 1892, 1915. Restrike	155.00(B)
426.	20 Corona 1916	850.00
427.	20 Corona 1916. Change in arms	950.00
428.	10 Corona 1909-12	100.00
428R.	10 Corona 1912. Restrike	80.00(B)

Plain head. Rev. Female reclining on clouds. On the 60th year of reign.

429.	100 Corona 1908	1600.00

Plain head. Rev. Double eagle. On the 60th year of reign.

430.	20 Corona 1908	350.00
431.	10 Corona 1908 ....*	125.00

KARL I, 1916-1918
Head. Rev. Eagle.

432.	20 Corona 1918. Vienna Mint Cabinet	Unique

C. Republic of —

Large eagle. Rev. Value in circular wreath.

433.	100 Kronen 1923, 24 ....*	2850.00
434.	20 Kronen 1923, 24	1750.00

(Numbers 419R, 420R, 424R, 425R, 428R are bullion coins. The price listed is based on gold at $725 per ounce.)

Eagle. Rev. Value between branches.

435.	100 Schillings 1926-34		600.00
436.	25 Schillings 1926-34	*	150.00

Standing figure of the Maria Zell Madonna. Rev. Eagle.

437.	100 Schillings 1935-37	*	1600.00
438.	100 Schilling 1938		10000.00

St. Leopold holding model of Church. Rev. Eagle.

439.	25 Schillings 1935-37	*	850.00
440.	25 Schillings 1938		8000.00

D. Cities of —

BRIXEN

Bishops of —

CHARLES OF AUSTRIA, 1613-1624
Bust. Rev. Arms.

441.	7 Ducats 1614	Rare
442.	3 Ducats 1614	Rare

Bust. Rev. Three shields and two hooks.

443.	1 Ducat 1614, 18	1500.00
444.	½ Ducat 1618	1000.00

CASPAR IGNATZ OF KUENIGL, 1702-1747

Bust. Rev. Two shields.

445.	1 Ducat 1717, 45	2500.00

LEOPOLD MARIA JOSEPH OF SPAUR, 1747-1778
Bust. Rev. Arms.

446.	1 Ducat 1768	2250.00

DIETRICHSTEIN

Princes —

SIGISMUND LOUIS, DIED 1664
Bust. Rev. Double eagle.

446a.	10 Ducats 1653	Rare

446b.	6 Ducats 1638, 53	Rare
446c.	5 Ducats 1638	Rare
446d.	1 Ducat 1640, 51	2000.00

FERDINAND, 1655-1698
Bust with wig. Rev. Arms.

446e.	10 Ducats 1695	Rare
446f.	1 Ducat 1695, 96	2000.00

CHARLES LOUIS, DIED 1732
Bust. Rev. Arms.

446g.	1 Ducat 1726	1500.00

EGGENBERG

Princes —

JOHN CHRISTIAN AND JOHN SEYFRIED, 1649-1713
Two busts. Rev. Arms.

447.	15 Ducats 1652	Rare
448.	10 Ducats 1652, 54	8500.00
449.	5 Ducats 1652, 58	6500.00
450.	1 Ducat 1654	1500.00

KEVENHULLER

Counts —

JOHN JOSEPH, 1742-1776

Bust. Rev. Arms.

451.	1 Ducat 1761	2250.00

KLOSTERNEUBURG

Priors of —

THOMAS
St. Leopold. Rev. Castle.

452.	1 Ducat ND (1750)	Rare

MONTFORT

Counts —

ANTHONY III THE YOUNGER, 1693-1734

Crown over draped shield. Rev. Orb on eagle.

453.	1 Ducat 1715	Rare

Bust. Rev. Crown over draped shield.

454.	1 Ducat 1718	*	Rare
455.	½ Ducat 1722		2500.00
456.	¼ Ducat 1722, 28, 30	*	1000.00

ERNEST MAX JOSEPH, 1734-1758

Bust. Rev. Arms.

457.	1 Carolin 1735, 36		1850.00
458.	½ Carolin 1734, 35	*	1500.00
459.	1 Ducat 1745	*	3300.00

Bust. Rev. Cross of four crossed monograms around central "X".

460.	1 Carolin 1735	*	3750.00
461.	¼ Carolin 1736		1250.00

FRANCIS XAVIER, 1758-1780

Bust. Rev. Arms.

462.	1 Ducat 1758	3000.00

ORTENBURG

Counts —

CHRISTOPHER WIDMAN, 1640-1660
Bust. Rev. Arms.

463.	10 Ducats 1656	Rare
464.	2 Ducats 1657	Rare
465.	1 Ducat 1658	3000.00

PAAR

Princes —

JOHN WENZEL, 1741-1792
Bust. Rev. Arms.

465a.	1 Ducat 1771, 81	1500.00

SALZBURG

Archbishops of —

PILGRIM II, 1365-1396

Shield. Rev. St. John.

466.	1 Goldgulden ND	Rare

LEONARD, 1495-1519

Bust. Rev. Two shields, date below.

467.	4 Ducats 1513. Square		15000.00
468.	3 Ducats 1513, 19. Square	*	12000.00
469.	2 Ducats 1513. Square		8500.00

Bust. Rev. Arms between divided date.

470.	6 Ducats 1513.	a. Square..15000.00	b. Round ..15000.00
471.	5 Ducats 1513.	a. Square..12500.00	b. Round ..12500.00
472.	4 Ducats 1513.	a. Square..10000.00	b. Round ..12500.00
473.	3 Ducats 1513, 19.	a. Square.. 8500.00	b. Round... 8500.00

St. Rupert. Rev. Arms in enclosure.

474.	1 Ducat 1500-19	1500.00

St. Rupert. Rev. Shield.

475.	1 Goldgulden 1500-10	1800.00

MATTHEW LANG, 1519-1540

Bust. Rev. Two shields.

476.	3 Ducats 1521		9000.00
477.	2 Ducats 1521	*	4500.00

Bust. Rev. Saint standing.

478.	3 Ducats 1521		6750.00
479.	2 Ducats 1521	*	4500.00

Bust. Rev. Arms.

480.	10 Ducats 1522, 39	Rare
481.	8 Ducats 1522, 39	20000.00
482.	8 Ducats 1522. Square	Rare

483.	6 Ducats 1522, 39	15000.00
484.	5 Ducats 1522	12500.00
485.	5 Ducats 1522. Square	Rare
486.	4 Ducats 1521, 22	8500.00
487.	4 Ducats 1522. Square	Rare
488.	3 Ducats 1522	6500.00

Bust. Rev. Two saints seated.

489.	8 Ducats 1522	15000.00
490.	6 Ducats 1522	14000.00

Bust. Rev. Legend. On the end of rebellion.

491.	2 Ducats 1523. Square or round	10000.00
492.	1 Ducat 1523. Square or round ......*......	5500.00

Two saints seated. Rev. Arms

493.	10 Ducats 1539	15000.00
494.	6 Ducats 1539	9000.00

Saint standing. Rev. Arms.

495.	1 Ducat 1519-40	2000.00

ERNEST DUKE OF BAVARIA, 1540-1554
Saint seated. Rev. Arms.

496.	10 Ducats 1540, 46	15000.00

Saint standing. Rev. Arms.

497.	8 Ducats 1540	14000.00
498.	4 Ducats 1540, 50	8500.00
499.	1 Ducat 1541-54 ......*......	1850.00

Two saints seated. Rev. Arms.

500.	2 Ducats 1547, 48, 49	7500.00

Saint seated. Rev. Three shields.

501.	1 Goldgulden ND	3000.00

MICHAEL, 1554-1560
Saint seated. Rev. Two shields.

502.	8 Ducats 1554, 59	13000.00
503.	6 Ducats 1555	10000.00
504.	4 Ducats 1559	8000.00

Two saints seated. Rev. Arms.

505.	4 Ducats 1555	7500.00
506.	3 Ducats 1555 ......*......	4500.00

Saint standing. Rev. Arms.

507.	3 Ducats 1555	4000.00
508.	2 Ducats 1555, 59	3000.00
509.	1 Ducat 1555-59 ......*......	1850.00

JOHN JACOB KHUEN, 1560-1586

Saint standing. Rev. Arms.

510.	4 Ducats 1561, 63	7000.00
511.	3 Ducats 1561	4500.00
512.	2 Ducats 1561-67 ......*......	2200.00
513.	2 Ducats 1561. Thick flan	2500.00
514.	1 Ducat 1561-65	1500.00

Two saints seated. Rev. Arms.

515.	20 Ducats 1565	Rare
516.	12 Ducats 1565	Rare
517.	10 Ducats 1565	Rare
518.	6 Ducats 1565	12000.00
519.	4 Ducats 1565	10000.00

Saint seated with lions. Rev. Arms.

520.	20 Ducats 1572	Rare

Two saints seated. Rev. Two shields.

521.	8 Ducats ND	12500.00

Saint seated. Rev. Two shields.

522.	8 Ducats 1571	12000.00
523.	6 Ducats 1561, 63	8000.00

Two saints seated. Rev. Three shields.

524.	5 Ducats ND	8500.00
525.	4 Ducats ND	4500.00

Saint seated. Rev. Three shields.

526.	3 Ducats 1565, 67	*	8500.00
527.	1 Goldgulden 1566		3500.00

Saint seated with lions. Rev. St. Radiana with wolves.

528.	15 Ducats 1571		Rare

Double eagle. Rev. Arms.

529.	2 Ducats 1568, 69	*	2500.00
530.	1 Ducat 1568		1500.00

Saint with shield. Rev. Double eagle.

531.	2 Ducats 1569-85		1500.00
532.	1 Ducat 1569-82	*	1100.00

GEORGE, 1586-1587
Two saints seated. Rev. Arms.

533.	6 Ducats 1586		12500.00
534.	5 Ducats 1586		12500.00
535.	4 Ducats 1586		10000.00
536.	4 Ducats 1586. Square		Rare
537.	3 Ducats 1586, ND		8500.00
538.	2 Ducats ND		6000.00

Saint standing. Rev. Double eagle.

539.	2 Ducats 1586, 87	*	5500.00
540.	1 Ducat 1586		4500.00

Saint seated. Rev. Three shields.

541.	1 Goldgulden 1586		4500.00

WOLFGANG DIETRICH, 1587-1612

Two saints seated. Rev. Arms.

542.	20 Ducats ND		Rare
543.	12 Ducats ND		Rare
544.	10 Ducats 1587		Rare
545.	8 Ducats 1587, ND		10000.00
546.	7 Ducats ND		8500.00
547.	6 Ducats 1587, ND		8000.00
548.	5 Ducats ND		5500.00
549.	4 Ducats ND		5000.00
550.	4 Ducats ND. Square		Rare
551.	3 Ducats ND		3300.00
552.	3 Ducats ND. Square		4500.00
553.	2 Ducats ND		2000.00
554.	2 Ducats ND. Square	*	2750.00

Saint seated. Rev. Arms.

555.	2 Ducats 1598-1611	*	1250.00
556.	2 Ducats 1600. Square		1500.00
557.	1 Ducat 1600, 02		800.00
558.	1 Ducat 1600, 02. Square		1000.00

Arms. Rev. Shield.

559.	1 Ducat ND. Square		1250.00
560.	½ Ducat 1603, ND. Square	*	1000.00

Oval shield. Rev. Tower.

560a.	20 Ducats 1590		Rare
561.	14 Ducats 1590		Rare
562.	12 Ducats 1594		Rare
563.	12 Ducats 1594. Square		Rare
564.	10 Ducats 1590, 94		Rare
565.	9 Ducats 1594		12500.00
566.	8 Ducats 1594		10000.00

Saint with shield. Rev. Tower.

567.	16 Ducats 1593	Rare
568.	12 Ducats 1593	Rare
569.	10 Ducats 1593	14000.00
570.	10 Ducats 1593. Square	15000.00
571.	8 Ducats 1593	10000.00
572.	7 Ducats 1593	9000.00
573.	7 Ducats 1593. Square	10000.00
574.	6 Ducats 1593	8000.00
575.	5 Ducats 1593	6500.00
576.	5 Ducats 1593, ND. Square ....*	7000.00
577.	4 Ducats 1593, ND ....*	6500.00
578.	4 Ducats ND. Square	7000.00
579.	3 Ducats ND	4000.00
580.	3 Ducats ND. Square	5000.00

Saint with shield. Rev. Double eagle.

581.	2 Ducats 1587-97	1500.00
582.	1 Ducat 1587-97 ....*	1000.00

Saint seated. Rev. Tower.

583.	8 Ducats ND	10000.00
584.	5 Ducats ND	8000.00
585.	4 Ducats ND	5500.00
586.	4 Ducats 1587. Square	6000.00
587.	3 Ducats ND	5500.00

Four shields. Rev. Two shields.

588.	½ Ducat 1611. Square	1000.00
589.	½ Ducat 1599/1611. Square hybrid ....*	1200.00
590.	¼ Ducat 1599/1559. Square hybrid	1200.00

Four shields. Rev. Blank.

591.	¼ Ducat 1610. Square	700.00

MARCUS SITTICUS, 1612-1619

Bust. Rev. Two saints seated.

592.	14 Ducats 1612	Rare
593.	12 Ducats 1612	Rare
594.	8 Ducats 1613	12500.00

595.	6 Ducats 1615	8500.00
596.	5 Ducats 1615	5500.00
597.	4 Ducats 1615, 16, 18 ....*	5000.00

Saint seated. Rev. Tower.

598.	6 Ducats 1617	7000.00

Saint seated. Rev. Arms.

599.	10 Ducats 1613. Square	Rare
600.	10 Ducats 1617	12000.00
601.	8 Ducats 1613	10000.00
602.	7 Ducats 1618. Square	10000.00
603.	6 Ducats 1617, 18	7000.00
604.	6 Ducats 1616, 17. Square	8500.00
605.	5 Ducats 1612	6000.00
606.	5 Ducats 1612, 17. Square	7000.00
607.	4 Ducats 1612, 14, 15, 17	4500.00
608.	3 Ducats 1617	3500.00
609.	3 Ducats 1612. Square	4000.00
610.	2 Ducats 1612-16	1500.00
611.	2 Ducats 1612-16. Square	2000.00
612.	1 Ducat 1612-18	1000.00
613.	1 Ducat 1613-18. Square	1250.00

Two saints seated. Rev. Arms.

614.	2 Ducats ND. Square	2000.00

Saint standing. Rev. Arms.

615.	1 Goldgulden 1619	3500.00

Arms on each side.

616.	1 Ducat 1614, 15, 18. Square	1100.00
617.	½ Ducat 1612, 14, 18. Square	1000.00

PARIS, 1619-1653

Cathedral carried by two saints. Rev. Reliquary carried by eight Bishops.

618.	20 Ducats 1628	Rare
619.	16 Ducats 1628	Rare
620.	12 Ducats 1628	Rare
621.	10 Ducats 1628	8500.00
622.	10 Ducats 1628. Square	10000.00
623.	8 Ducats 1628	8500.00
624.	8 Ducats 1628. Square	Rare
625.	6 Ducats 1628	4500.00
626.	5 Ducats 1628	4500.00
627.	5 Ducats 1628. Square	7000.00
628.	4 Ducats 1628 ....*	2250.00
629.	4 Ducats 1628. Square	3000.00
630.	3 Ducats 1628	2750.00

Saint standing. Rev. Madonna.

631.	10 Ducats 1628, 31	15000.00
632.	8 Ducats 1625, 28	12500.00
633.	6 Ducats 1625, 28	8500.00
634.	4 Ducats 1624. Square	8500.00
635.	4 Ducats 1624, 25, 29, 38	5500.00
636.	3 Ducats 1631, 38, 42	4500.00
637.	3 Ducats 1624-42. Square	4000.00
638.	2 Ducats 1626	2250.00
639.	2 Ducats 1626. Square	2500.00

Saint seated. Rev. Arms.

640.	8 Ducats 1620	9000.00
641.	5 Ducats 1620	7500.00
642.	4 Ducats 1620	4500.00
643.	4 Ducats 1620. Square...........................	5500.00
644.	3 Ducats 1620	4500.00
645.	2 Ducats 1624-48	2250.00
646.	2 Ducats 1634-51. Square	3000.00
647.	1 Ducat 1620-53	1000.00
648.	1 Ducat 1627-51. Square .... *	1500.00
649.	½ Ducat 1643-52	800.00
650.	½ Ducat 1643-50. Square	850.00
651.	¼ Ducat 1652	425.00

Arms. Rev. Arms on cross.

652.	½ Ducat 1634-46	700.00
653.	¼ Ducat 1624	400.00

Arms. Rev. Five saints standing. On the 1100th year of Salzburg.

669.	12 Ducats 1682. Square....................... *		Rare
670.	10 Ducats 1682		10000.00
671.	10 Ducats 1682. Square........................		12000.00
672.	8 Ducats 1682. Square........................		10000.00
673.	7 Ducats 1682		8000.00
674.	6 Ducats 1682		7000.00
675.	5 Ducats 1682		5000.00
676.	4 Ducats 1682		4500.00
677.	3 Ducats 1682		2750.00

Arms under triangle. Rev. Legend. On the 1100th year of Salzburg.

678.	3 Ducats 1682	3000.00
679.	2 Ducats 1682 .... *	2000.00

Arms. Rev. Cathedral carried by two saints.

654.	50 Ducats 1654. Square...........................	Rare
655.	24 Ducats 1654	Rare
656.	20 Ducats 1654	Rare
657.	16 Ducats 1654	Rare
658.	12 Ducats 1654	Rare
659.	10 Ducats 1654	10000.00
660.	8 Ducats 1654	6500.00
661.	6 Ducats 1654, 55	4000.00
662.	5 Ducats 1654, 55 .... *	3500.00
663.	4 Ducats 1654, 55	3000.00

Two saints seated with Church. Rev. Arms.

680.	44 Ducats 1668		Rare
681.	25 Ducats 1668		Rare
682.	25 Ducats 1668. Square.........................		Rare
683.	20 Ducats 1668		Rare
684.	20 Ducats 1668. Square.........................		Rare
685.	15 Ducats 1668		Rare
686.	12 Ducats 1668		Rare
687.	12 Ducats 1668. Square.................... *		Rare
688.	10 Ducats 1668.		14000.00
689.	10 Ducats 1668. Square........................		Rare
690.	9 Ducats 1668.		10000.00
691.	8 Ducats 1668		8500.00
692.	6 Ducats 1668		4500.00
693.	5 Ducats 1668		4500.00
694.	4 Ducats 1668		4000.00
695.	3 Ducats 1668		3000.00

Saint seated. Rev. Arms.

664.	2 Ducats 1654, 59, 62...........................	1500.00
665.	1 Ducat 1654-68 .... *	850.00
666.	1 Ducat 1655, 57, 66. Square	1000.00
667.	½ Ducat 1654-66	650.00
668.	¼ Ducat 1654-68	300.00

Saint standing. Rev. Arms.

696.	10 Ducats 1686	15000.00

Saint seated. Rev. Arms.

697.	6 Ducats 1668	7500.00
698.	5 Ducats 1668	5500.00
699.	4 Ducats 1673. Square	6000.00
700.	3 Ducats 1670, 73	2500.00
701.	3 Ducats 1673. Square	4500.00
702.	2 Ducats 1668, 73 ....*	2000.00
703.	2 Ducats 1673. Square	2500.00
704.	1 Ducat 1668-87	1100.00
705.	1 Ducat 1668-74. Square	1100.00
706.	½ Ducat 1668-86	650.00
707.	½ Ducat 1668. Square	500.00
708.	¼ Ducat 1668-86	350.00

JOHN ERNEST, 1687-1709
Two saints seated with Church. Rev. Arms.

709.	50 Ducats 1687. Square	Rare
710.	20 Ducats 1687	Rare
711.	15 Ducats 1687	Rare
712.	12 Ducats 1687	Rare
713.	10 Ducats 1687	12500.00
714.	8 Ducats 1687	8500.00
715.	7 Ducats 1687	5500.00
716.	6 Ducats 1687	5000.00
717.	5 Ducats 1687	4500.00
718.	4 Ducats 1687	3000.00

Saint seated. Rev. Arms.

719.	10 Ducats 1687	12500.00
720.	3 Ducats 1690	3000.00
721.	2 Ducats 1688, 1707, 08	1850.00
722.	2 Ducats 1688. Square	2000.00
723.	1 Ducat 1687-1708	1250.00
724.	½ Ducat 1687-1707 ....*	700.00
725.	¼ Ducat 1687-1707 ....*	350.00

"WAS." Rev. "IRS." On the visit to Salzburg of Joseph I and Wilhelmina Amalia.

726.	1 Ducat 1699 ....*	1250.00
727.	¼ Ducat 1699	600.00

FRANCIS ANTHONY, 1709-1727
Bust. Rev. Arms.

728.	25 Ducats 1709	Rare
729.	20 Ducats 1709	Rare
730.	10 Ducats 1709, 11	Rare
731.	5 Ducats 1709	Rare
732.	1 Ducat 1710-26	1500.00

Bust. Rev. City view.

733.	25 Ducats 1711	Rare
734.	20 Ducats 1711	Rare

Bust. Rev. Horse in landscape.

735.	25 Ducats 1709	Rare
736.	20 Ducats 1709	Rare
737.	10 Ducats 1709	12000.00
738.	5 Ducats 1718, ND	5500.00

Saint seated. Rev. Arms.

739.	2 Ducats 1709. Square	3500.00
740.	1 Ducat 1709-26 ....*	1250.00
741.	½ Ducat 1709-27	700.00
742.	¼ Ducat 1709-25	250.00

LEOPOLD ANTHONY, 1727-1744

Bust. Rev. Arms.

743.	1 Ducat 1728-44	2000.00

Saint seated. Rev. Arms.

744.	2 Ducats 1734, 35	2500.00
745.	1 Ducat 1727-40	1500.00
746.	½ Ducat 1728	750.00
747.	¼ Ducat 1728-40	350.00

JACOB ERNEST, COUNT LIECHTENSTEIN, 1745-1747
Bust. Rev. Arms.

748.	1 Ducat 1745, 46, 47	3000.00

Saint seated. Rev. Arms.

749.	1 Ducat 1745, 46	2250.00
750.	¼ Ducat 1745	850.00

ANDREW JACOB, COUNT DIETRICHSTEIN, 1747-1753

Bust. Rev. Arms.

751.	2 Ducats 1750 ....*	4500.00
752.	1 Ducat 1748-51	2000.00
753.	½ Ducat 1751	1250.00
754.	¼ Ducat 1751	1000.00

Saint seated. Rev. Arms.

755.	2 Ducats 1752	3300.00
756.	1 Ducat 1747-52. Square	1800.00
757.	½ Ducat 1749	1500.00
758.	¼ Ducat 1749	850.00

SIGISMUND III, 1753-1771
Bust. Rev. Arms.

759.	2 Ducats 1755	2750.00
760.	1 Ducat 1754-63	1250.00
761.	½ Ducat 1755, 61	850.00
762.	¼ Ducat 1755, 70	750.00

Bust. Rev. Saint seated.

763.   5 Ducats 1759 .... 8000.00

Bust. Rev. Two shields.

764.   2 Ducats 1764 .... * 2500.00
765.   1 Ducat 1762-64 .... 1250.00

Bust. Rev. Draped arms.

766.   2 Ducats 1765-71 .... * 2250.00
767.   1 Ducat 1763-71, ND 1250.00

Bust. Rev. Saint seated with small Madonna.

768.   6 Ducats 1760 .... 1000.00

Bust. Rev. View of the Mint.

769.   3 Ducats 1766 .... 4500.00

Bust. Rev. City gate.

770.   10 Ducats 1767 .... Rare

Saint standing with small Madonna. Rev. Arms.

771.   1 Ducat 1763 .... 1000.00

Saint seated. Rev. Arms.

772.   1 Ducat 1753 .... 1000.00
773.   ¼ Ducat 1753 .... 750.00

SEDE VACANTE, 1772

Saint seated. Rev. Arms.

774.   1 Ducat 1772 .... 1250.00

JEROME OF COLLOREDO, 1772-1803

Bust. Rev. Arms.

775.   2 Ducats 1773 .... 2500.00
776.   1 Ducat 1772-1802 .... * 650.00
777.   1 Ducat 1803 .... Rare
778.   ½ Ducat 1776 .... 550.00
779.   ¼ Ducat 1776, 77, 82 .... 400.00

Bust. Rev. Temple.

780.   2 Ducats 1782 .... 2500.00
781.   1 Ducat 1782 .... 1250.00

FERDINAND, PRINCE AND ELECTOR, 1803-1806

Bust. Rev. Draped arms.

782.   1 Ducat 1803, 04 .... 1250.00

Bust. Rev. Crowned arms.

783.   1 Ducat 1805, 06 .... 1000.00

FRANCIS II (I), HOLY ROMAN AND AUSTRIAN EMPEROR, 1806-1810

Head. Rev. Eagle.

784.   1 Ducat 1806, 09 .... 950.00

TRAUTSON-FALKENSTEIN

Counts, and later, Princes —

PAUL SIXTUS I, 1589-1621
Arms. Rev. Double eagle.

785.   1 Ducat ND 2500.00

Bust. Rev. Arms.

786.   5 Ducats 1620 .... Rare

JOHN FRANCIS, 1620-1663
Bust. Rev. Arms.

787.   10 Ducats 1638 .... Rare
788.   1 Ducat 1634, 38 .... 2000.00
789.   ¼ Ducat 1635 .... 1250.00

FRANCIS EUSEBIUS, 1678-1728
Bust. Rev. Arms.

790.   1 Ducat 1708, 15 .... 2000.00

JOHN LEOPOLD, 1663-1724
Bust. Rev. Arms.

791.   1 Ducat 1719 .... 2000.00

VIENNA

Archbishops of —

CHRISTOPHER ANTHONY OF MIGAZZI, 1757-1803

Bust. Rev. Arms.

792.   1 Ducat 1781 .... 1750.00

WINDISCHGRAETZ

Counts —

LEOPOLD VICTOR JOHN, 1727-1746
Bust. Rev. Arms.

793.   10 Ducats 1732 .... Rare
794.   1 Ducat 1732, 33 .... 2250.00

JOSEPH NICHOLAS, 1746-1802
Bust. Rev. Arms.

795.   5 Ducats 1777 .... Rare
796.   1 Ducat 1777 .... 1850.00

BELGIUM

Mints and mint marks:—

Hand	mm for Antwerp
Small head	mm for Brussels
Lion or lily	mm for Bruges
Tower	mm for Tournai

Coins were struck at the above mints in the provinces of Brabant and Flanders when they were under Spanish and Austrian rule. Belgium became an independent country in 1830 and in 1832 it adopted the French monetary system for its coinage.

The coins listed as not being placed in circulation were all struck in proof condition and all are rare. Only 6 pieces were struck of the 100 Franc piece of 1912 with French legends and only 3 pieces of the same coin with Flemish legends.

A. United Provinces of —

Lion standing. Rev. Circle of eleven shields. Struck during the Insurrection against Austria.

1.   1 Lion d'or 1790 .... 4500.00

B. Kings of —

LEOPOLD I, 1831-1865

Laureate head. Rev. Value and date. This issue was not placed in circulation.

2.   40 Francs 1834-35, 38, 41 .... 10000.00
3.   20 Francs 1834-35, 38, 41 .... * 7500.00

Plain head. Rev. Arms.

4.   25 Francs 1848-50 (1849, 50 rare) 1500.00
5.   10 Francs 1849, 50 .... 1650.00

Plain head. Rev. Conjoined heads of the Duke and Duchess of Brabant. On their marriage. Without the mark of value.

6.   (100 Francs) 1853 .... 4000.00

Plain head. Rev. Value.

7.   20 Francs 1865 .... 200.00

LEOPOLD II, 1865-1909

Head. Rev. Arms. The 20 Francs of 1866 and the 10 Franc piece were not placed in circulation.

8.	20 Francs 1866-82 (1866 rare)	175.00(B)
9.	10 Francs 1867	1500.00

Conjoined heads. Rev. Female and lion standing. On the 50th year of independence. Without the mark of value.

9a. (100 Francs) 1880 .... 7500.00

ALBERT, 1909-1934

Uniformed bust. Rev. Arms. Only the 20 Franc piece was placed in circulation. The other denominations are patterns. 100 Franc pieces dated 1911 were not officially struck. They exist with milled and plain edges.

10.	100 Francs 1911, 12. French legends .... *	12000.00
11.	100 Francs 1912. Flemish legends	12000.00
12.	20 Francs 1914. French legends .... *	200.00
13.	20 Francs 1914. Flemish legends	200.00
14.	10 Francs 1911. French legends	2000.00
15.	10 Francs 1912. Flemish legends	2000.00

(Number 8 is a bullion coin. The price listed is based on gold at $725 per ounce.)

C. Cities of —

BORNE

Lords of —

WALRAM, 1356-1378
Bust of Emperor Charles IV. Rev. Lion.

16. 1 Florin ND .... Rare

BRABANT

Dukes of —

JOHN II, 1294-1312
St. John. Rev. Lily.

17.	1 Florin ND. With "DUX BRABA."	2500.00
17a.	1 Florin ND. With "DUX DALEN."	6000.00

JOHN III, 1312-1355

Ruler on throne. Rev. Cross.

18.	1 Chaise d'or ND	1500.00
19.	1 Chaise d'or ND. With name of Louis of Bavaria .... *	1100.00

St. John. Rev. Lily.

20. 1 Florin ND .... Unknown

JOAN AND WENCESLAS, 1355-1383
Bust of St. Peter. Rev. Cross.

21. 1 Peter d'or or ND 1500.00

Lamb. Rev. Cross.

22.	2 Mouton d'or ND	4000.00
23.	1 Mouton d'or ND. With "JOH-DUX" or "WEN-DUX" .... *	1800.00

Cavalier on horse. Rev. Cross.

24. 1 Cavalier d'or ND 1500.00

St. Servais seated under Gothic dais. Rev. Shield.

25. 1 Florin ND 5250.00

St. John. Rev. Lily.

26. 1 Florin ND .... Unknown

JOAN AND PHILIP, 1384-1389
Two shields. Rev. Cross.

27. 1 Grand Ecu d'or ND 15000.00

JOAN, 1383-1406

Knight on horse. Rev. Cross.

28. 1 Franc a cheval ND .... Unknown

Angel holding shield. Rev. Cross.

29. 1 Angel d'or ND 14000.00

Church of St. Peter at Louvain. Rev. Cross.

30. 1 Tourelle d'or ND 14000.00

ANTHONY OF BURGUNDY, 1406-1415
Shield supported by lions. Rev. Cross.

31.	1 Lion d'or ND	12000.00
32.	½ Lion d'or ND	12000.00

JOHN IV, 1414-1427
Arms. Rev. Cross.

33.	1 Ecu d'or ND......................................	Unknown

Ruler on throne. Rev. Cross.

34.	1 Chaise d'or ND..................................	1350.00

St. John standing. Rev. Four shields.

35.	1 Florin ND.......................................	4250.00

Lamb. Rev. Cross.

36.	½ Agnel d'or ND..................................	3750.00

PHILIP OF ST. POL, 1420-1430
Ruler on throne. Rev. Cross.

37.	1 Ecu d'or ND.....................................	1500.00

St. Peter standing. Rev. Five shields.

38.	1 Florin ND.......................................	4250.00

Bust of St. Peter over arms. Rev. Cross.

39.	1 Peter d'or ND	7500.00

PHILIP THE GOOD, 1430-1467
Ruler on throne. Rev. Cross.

40.	1 Chaise d'or ND..................................	900.00

Bust of St. Peter over arms. Rev. Cross.

41.	1 Peter d'or ND. Zevenbergen......................	900.00
41a.	1 Peter d'or ND. Louvain	3750.00

Ruler on horse. Rev. Cross.

42.	1 Cavalier d'or ND................................	1100.00
43.	½ Cavalier d'or ND................................	1800.00

Lion seated under dais. Rev. Arms.

44.	1 Lion d'or ND ....*	900.00
45.	½ Lion d'or ND	1200.00

St. Andrew standing with cross. Rev. Arms on cross.

46.	1 Florin ND.......................................	975.00

CHARLES THE BOLD, 1467-1477

St. Andrew standing with cross. Rev. Arms.

47.	1 Florin ND.................................*	750.00
48.	½ Florin ND.......................................	1500.00

MARIE OF BURGUNDY, 1477-1482
St. Andrew standing with cross. Rev. Arms on cross.

49.	1 Florin ND.......................................	750.00

St. Andrew standing with cross. Rev. Shield.

50.	½ Florin ND.......................................	3750.00

MAXIMILIAN AND PHILIP, 1482-1496
Christ on throne. Rev. Four shields.

51.	1 Florin 1492	4500.00

Ruler standing in ship. Rev. Cross.

52.	½ Noble 1488	1800.00

Maximilian standing. Rev. Arms on cross.

53.	2 Florins 1490 ....12000.00

St. Andrew standing with cross. Rev. Arms on cross.

54.	1 Florin 1482, 83	2250.00

St. Andrew standing with cross. Rev. Shield.

55.	½ Florin 1489, ND.................................	3000.00

St. Andrew standing with open book. Rev. Arms on cross.

56.	1 Florin 1489	2600.00

PHILIP III, 1494-1506
St. Philip with shield. Rev. Cross.

57.	1 Florin 1499-1502, ND	525.00
58.	½ Florin 1500, ND.................................	375.00
58a.	½ Florin 1500	1100.00

St. Philip standing. Rev. Four shields in angles of cross.

59.	1 Florin ND.......................................	975.00

Arms supported by lions. Rev. Cross.

60.	1 Toison d'or 1499, 1500, 04	9000.00

CHARLES V (CHARLES I OF SPAIN), 1506-1555
St. Philip with shield. Rev. Floriated cross.

61.	1 Florin (1506-55), ND............................	335.00
62.	½ Florin (1506-55), ND............................	400.00

Crowned bust. Rev. Arms on eagle.

63.	1 Real d'or ND ....*	2000.00
63a.	1 Carolus d'or ND	1000.00
64.	½ Real d'or ND	600.00

Crowned arms. Rev. Arms on floriated cross.

65.	1 Couronne d'or ND	525.00

Arms supported by lions. Rev. Cross.

66.	1 Toison d'or 1513, ND............................12000.00

PHILIP II OF SPAIN, 1555-1598

Bust. Rev. Arms.

67.	1 Real d'or (1555-98), ND	*	12000.00
68.	½ Real d'or (1555-98), ND		500.00

Arms. Rev. Floriated cross.

69.	2 Florins 1578		5000.00
70.	1 Couronne d'or 1580, 81, 86, ND	*	1300.00

St. Andrew standing with cross. Rev. Arms.

71.	1 Florin 1567-70	1200.00

FRANCIS ALENCON, 1581-1584
Arms. Rev. Cross.

72.	1 Couronne d'or 1582	7500.00

INDEPENDENT STATES OF BRABANT, 1584-1585
Lion seated under Gothic dais. Rev. Arms on cross.

73.	1 Lion d'or 1584, 85	4000.00
74.	½ Lion d'or 1585	7000.00

ALBERT AND ISABELLA OF SPAIN, 1598-1621
(Governors for the Crown).

Crowned busts facing each other. Rev. Arms.

75.	2 Ducats (1598-1621), ND	*	1500.00
76.	1 Ducat (1598-1621), ND		6000.00

Arms. Rev. Cross.

77.	2 Albertins (⅔ Ducat) 1600-11 (1610, 11 rare)	*	600.00
78.	1 Albertin (⅓ Ducat) 1600		600.00
79.	1 Couronne d'or 1614, 16		1200.00

Albert and Isabella on thrones. Rev. Arms.

79a.	4 Souverain d'or ND	Rare
80.	2 Souverain d'or 1612-20	3375.00

Conjoined busts. Rev. Arms.

81.	1 Souverain d'or ND	9750.00

Crowned shield and crowned initials. Rev. Cross.

82.	½ Souverain d'or ND	*	5250.00
83.	1 Couronne d'or 1614, 16, ND		1275.00

Albert and Isabella walking to right. Rev. Arms.

84.	⅔ Souverain d'or ND	8250.00

PHILIP IV OF SPAIN, 1621-1665

Crowned bust. Rev. Arms.

85.	2 Souverain d'or 1628-37. With lace collar		3750.00
85a.	2 Souverain d'or 1637-59. With flat collar	*	2250.00

Crowned lion standing. Rev. Arms.

86.	1 Lion d'or 1645-65	750.00

Cross. Rev. Arms.

87.	1 Couronne d'or 1622-57	1050.00

CHARLES II OF SPAIN, 1665-1700
Crowned child bust. Rev. Arms.

88.	2 Souverain d'or 1667-94	4000.00

Older bust with long curls. Rev. Arms.

89.	2 Souverain d'or 1697, 99	6000.00

Lion standing. Rev. Arms.

90.	1 Lion d'or 1666-84	2500.00

PHILIP V OF SPAIN, 1700-1712
Bust. Rev. Arms.

91.　　2 Souverain d'or 1704-06............................ 7500.00

AUSTRIAN RULERS
(For Austrian type coins struck at the Belgian Mints, see under Austria beginning with the year 1711).

BRUSSELS

Legend and "84". Rev. Blank. Square coins struck at Brussels while under siege by Alexander Farnese.

92.　　4 Florins 1584 .... *...... Rare
93.　　2 Florins 1584 .... Rare

FAGNOLLE

Counts —

CHARLES DE LIGNE, 1770-1803
Bust. Rev. Arms.

94.　　1 Ducat ND... 3800.00

FLANDERS

Counts of —

LOUIS DE CRECY, 1322-1346
St. John. Rev. Lily.

95.　　1 Florin ND.. 1500.00

LOUIS DE MALE, 1346-1384

Ruler seated on throne holding shield. Rev. Cross.

96.　　1 Chaise d'or ND. With eagle or lion on shield. *... 1300.00
97.　　½ Chaise d'or ND................................... 1500.00
98.　　¼ Chaise d'or ND................................... 600.00

Ruler on horse. Rev. Cross.

99.　　1 Franc a Cheval ND 2200.00

Ruler standing. Rev. Initials and cross.

100.　　1 Franc a Pied ND 2200.00

Lion seated. Rev. Initials and cross.

101.　　1 Lion Heaume ND ....*...... 3000.00
102.　　½ Lion Heaume ND 7500.00

Lamb. Rev. Cross.

103.　　1 Mouton d'or ND 2000.00

Helmeted shield. Rev. Initials and cross.

104.　　1 Vieil Heaume d'or ND ....*...... 7500.00
105.　　⅓ Vieil Heaume d'or ND 12000.00

PHILIP THE BOLD, 1384-1404
Ruler seated. Rev. Cross.

106.	1 Chaise d'or ND	1500.00

Ruler in ship. Rev. Cross.

107.	1 Noble ND	2700.00
108.	½ Noble ND	2250.00
108a.	¼ Noble ND	2700.00

Angel with two shields. Rev. Cross.

109.	1 Angel ND	* 7500.00
109a.	½ Angel ND	10000.00

Two shields. Rev. Cross.

110.	2 Heaume d'or ND	3750.00

JOHN, 1405-1419
Ruler in ship. Rev. Cross.

111.	1 Noble ND	4000.00

Lion with helmet seated. Rev. Cross.

111a.	1 Lion d'or ND	Rare

Helmeted shield. Rev. Cross.

111b.	1 Heaume d'or ND	Rare

PHILIP THE GOOD, 1419-1467

Ruler in ship. Rev. Cross.

112.	1 Noble ND	* 1800.00
113.	½ Noble ND	2500.00

Ruler on throne. Rev. Cross.

114.	1 Chaise d'or ND	750.00
115.	½ Chaise d'or ND	1000.00

Ruler on horse. Rev. Arms on cross.

116.	1 Cavalier d'or ND	1000.00
117.	½ Cavalier d'or ND	1500.00

Lion seated. Rev. Arms on cross.

118.	1 Lion d'or ND	* 1000.00
119.	½ Lion d'or ND	Unknown
120.	⅔ Lion d'or ND	2000.00
121.	⅓ Lion d'or ND	1200.00

St. Andrew. Rev. Arms on cross.

122.	1 Florin ND	825.00

Helmeted shield. Rev. Cross.

122a.	1 Heaume d'or ND	Rare

CHARLES THE BOLD, 1467-1477
St. Andrew. Rev. Arms.

123.	1 Florin ND	750.00
124.	½ Florin ND	975.00

MARIE OF BURGUNDY, 1477-1482

St. Andrew. Rev. Arms.

125.	1 Florin ND	825.00
125a.	½ Florin ND	1500.00

PHILIP THE HANDSOME, 1482-1506
St. John and lamb. Rev. Arms.

126.	1 Florin 1488, ND	975.00

St. Andrew and arms. Rev. Eagle on shield.

127.	½ Florin ND	1800.00

St. Philip and arms. Rev. Arms.

128.	1 Florin ND	450.00
129.	½ Florin ND	* 750.00

Arms supported by lions. Rev. Cross.

130.	1 Toison d'or ND	10000.00

CHARLES V (CHARLES I OF SPAIN), 1515-1555

Bust with sword and sceptre. Rev. Arms on eagle.

131.	1 Real d'or ND	* 2000.00
132.	1 Florin ND	700.00

Eagle on shield on cross. Rev. Arms.

133.	½ Real d'or ND	375.00

St. Philip and arms. Rev. Cross.

134.	1 Florin ND	450.00
135.	½ Florin ND	600.00

Arms between briquets. Rev. Cross.

136.	1 Couronne d'or 1541-52	750.00

Arms supported by lions. Rev. Cross.

136a.	1 Toison d'or ND	Rare

PHILIP II OF SPAIN, 1555-1598
Plain bust. Rev. Arms on floriated cross.

137.	2 Reales d'or 1586, ND	Unknown

Crowned bust. Rev. Arms in golden fleece.

138.	1 Real d'or ND	1300.00

Plain bust. Rev. Crowned arms.

139.	½ Real d'or ND	700.00

Arms. Rev. Floriated cross.

140.	1 Couronne d'or 1581, 85, 86, ND	1500.00

ALBERT AND ISABELLA OF SPAIN, 1598-1621
Rulers on thrones. Rev. Arms.

141.	2 Souverain d'or 1612-20, ND	5000.00

Initials and cross. Rev. Arms.

142.	1 Couronne d'or 1615, 20	2500.00

Crowned shield. Rev. Cross of St. Andrew.

142a.	2 Albertins 1601-07	1200.00
142b.	1 Albertin 1602	900.00

PHILIP IV OF SPAIN, 1621-1665
Crowned bust. Rev. Arms.

143.	2 Souverain dor 1634-36. With lace collar	5000.00
143a.	2 Souverain d'or 1638-47. With flat collar	2500.00

Lion standing. Rev. Arms.

144.	1 Lion d'or 1621-64	1000.00

Cross. Rev. Arms.

144a.	1 Couronne d'or 1625-42	1200.00

CHARLES II OF SPAIN, 1665-1700

Bust. Rev. Arms supported by lions.

145.	8 Souverain d'or 1694	*...... 12000.00
146.	4 Souverain d'or 1696, 1700	13000.00
146a.	2 Souverain d'or 1668, 1700	7000.00

Lion standing. Rev. Arms.

147.	1 Souverain d'or (Lion d'or) 1666-85, 1700	1000.00

GHENT

Royal figure in ship. Rev. Cross.

148.	1 Noble 1581, 82, 83	2000.00
149.	½ Noble 1581, 82, 83	1800.00
149a.	¼ Noble 1582, 83	2500.00

GRONSFELD

Barons —

THIERRY II OF BRONCKHORST, 1493-1508
St. John. Rev. Arms.

150.	1 Florin ND	1500.00

JOHN OF BRONCKHORST, 1508-1558
St. Martin. Rev. Lion.

151.	1 Florin ND	Rare

Horseman. Rev. Arms.

152.	1 Florin ND	Rare

JUSTUS MAXIMILIAN, 1617-1667

Arms. Rev. Legend.

153.	1 Ducat 1642, 57, 64	2000.00

HAINAUT

Counts —

WILLIAM II, 1337-1345
St. John standing. Rev. Lily.

154.	1 Florin ND	Rare

MARGUERITE D'AVESNES, 1345-1356
St. John standing. Rev. Lily.

155.	1 Florin ND	1050.00

WILLIAM III, 1356-1389
Ruler standing holding sceptre. Rev. Floriated cross.

156.	2 Royals d'or ND	Rare
157.	1 Royal d'or ND	Rare

Ruler on horse. Rev. Cross.

158.	1 Grand Cavalier ND	Rare
159.	1 Cavalier d'or ND	1800.00

Ruler standing holding club and sceptre. Rev. Cross.

160.	1 Franc a Pied d'or ND	Unique

St. John. Rev. Lily.

160a.	1 Florin ND	Rare

ALBERT OF BAVARIA, 1389-1404

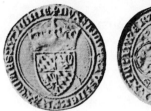

Arms. Rev. Cross.

| 161. | 1 Grand Couronne d'or ND | 4000.00 |
| 162. | 1 Couronne d'or ND ....* | 1500.00 |

WILLIAM IV, 1404-1417

Angel with shield. Rev. Cross.

| 163. | 1 Thuyne d'or ND | Rare |
| 163a. | 1 Angel d'or ND ....* | Unique |

Arms. Rev. Cross.

| 164. | 1 Couronne d'or ND | 1200.00 |

JACQUELINE, 1417-1433
Round shield. Rev. Cross.

| 165. | 2 Couronne d'or ND | Unknown |

JOHN IV, 1418-1427
Arms. Rev. Cross.

| 166. | 1 Couronne d'or ND | 8500.00 |

Angel holding two shields. Rev. Cross.

| 166a. | 1 Angel d'or ND | Unique |
| 166b. | ½ Angel d'or ND | Unique |

PHILIP THE GOOD, 1433-1467

Ruler on horse. Rev. Arms on cross.

| 167. | 1 Cavalier d'or ND | 1000.00 |
| 167a. | ½ Cavalier d'or ND | Rare |

Lion. Rev. Arms on cross.

168.	1 Lion d'or ND ....*	1200.00
169.	⅔ Lion d'or ND	Rare
170.	⅓ Lion d'or ND	2500.00

St. Andrew. Rev. Arms on cross.

| 171. | 1 Florin ND | 1000.00 |

St. Peter. Rev. Cross.

| 171a. | 1 Peter d'or ND | 1300.00 |

PHILIP II AND THE STATES GENERAL, 1577-1599
Bust. Rev. Arms.

| 172. | ½ Real d'or ND | Rare |

Arms. Rev. Cross.

| 173. | 1 Couronne d'or 1585 | Rare |

HOORN

Counts —

DIRK LOOF, 1358-1390
St. John. Rev. Lily.

| 174. | 1 Florin ND | Rare |

WILLIAM VII, 1358-1415
Half length bust. Rev. Double eagle.

| 175. | 1 Florin ND | Rare |

PHILIP MONTMORENCY, 1540-1568
St. Martin. Rev. Arms.

| 176. | 1 Florin ND | Rare |

LIEGE

Bishops of —

ENGELBERT OF MARK, 1345-1364
St. John. Rev. Lily.

| 177. | 1 Florin ND | 750.00 |

JOHN D'ARCKEL, 1364-1378

Lamb. Rev. Cross.

| 178. | 1 Grand Mouton d'or ND | Rare |

St. Peter and shield. Rev. Cross.

| 179. | 1 Peter d'or ND | Rare |

ARNOLD, 1378-1389
Bishop under dais. Rev. St. John.

| 180. | 1 Petit Florin ND | Rare |

St. Peter under dais. Rev. Two shields.

| 181. | 1 Florin ND | 6000.00 |

JOHN OF BAVARIA, 1389-1418
Ruler on throne. Rev. Cross.

| 182. | 1 Chaise d'or ND | Rare |

Ruler standing. Rev. Arms.

| 183. | 1 Florin ND | Rare |

St. John. Rev. Three shields.

| 184. | 1 Florin ND | 2250.00 |

St. John. Rev. Five shields.

185.   1 Florin ND...   Rare

Griffin and arms. Rev. Cross.

186.   1 Griffon d'or ND........................... * 3750.00
187.   ½ Griffon d'or ND...................................   Rare

JOHN HEINSBERG, 1419-1455
Ruler on throne. Rev. Cross.

188.   1 Chaise d'or ND..................................   6000.00

Griffin and arms. Rev. Cross.

189.   1 Griffon d'or ND..................................   Rare

St. Peter with shield. Rev. Cross.

190.   1 Peter d'or ND ....   Rare

Angel with shield. Rev. Arms. on cross.

191.   1 Angel d'or ND .... * ......   Rare
192.   ½ Angel d'or ND...................................   Rare

St. Lambert standing. Rev. Arms.

193.   1 Florin ND...   Rare

LOUIS BOURBON, 1456-1482
Lion with arms. Rev. Arms on cross.

194.   1 Lion d'or ND ....   Rare

Two lions with shield. Rev. Cross.

195.   1 Florin d'or ND...................................   Rare

St. Lambert standing. Rev. Arms.

196.   1 Florin ND...   1500.00

Madonna. Rev. Arms on cross.

197.   1 Florin ND...   Rare

JOHN OF HOORN, 1484-1505
St. Lambert standing. Rev. Arms.

198.   1 Florin ND...   450.00

St. John standing. Rev. Cross of four shields.

199.   1 Florin ND...   Rare

EBERHARD OF MARK, 1506-1538
Arms. Rev. Cross.

200.   2 Florins 1512, 13, 16............................   Rare
201.   1 Florin 1512, 13 .... Unknown

St. Lambert standing. Rev. Arms.

202.   1 Florin ND...   800.00

St. Lambert standing. Rev. Cross of four shields.

203.   2 Florins ND ....   Rare

CORNELIUS BERGHES, 1538-1544
St. Lambert standing. Rev. Arms.

204.   1 Florin ND.................................... Unknown

Christ on throne. Rev. Four shields.

205.   1 Florin ND...   3000.00

GEORGE OF AUSTRIA, 1544-1557
St. George and shield. Rev. Cross of four shields.

206.   1 Florin ND...   5000.00

GERHARD OF GROESBECK, 1564-1580
Arms. Rev. Double eagle.

207.   1 Florin 1568 ....   3000.00

Saint seated. Rev. Initials and cross.

208.   1 Florin ND...   Rare

ERNEST OF BAVARIA, 1581-1612
Arms and three shields. Rev. Double eagle.

209.   1 Florin 1581, 85 ....   3000.00

Bust. Rev. Arms.

210.   1 Florin 1612, ND.................................   3375.00

FERDINAND OF BAVARIA, 1612-1650
Bust. Rev. Arms.

211.   1 Florin 1612, 13 ....   1200.00

Arms. Rev. Legend on tablet.

212.   1 Ducat 1638 ....   1875.00

Arms. Rev. Cross.

213.   2 Ecus d'or 1613 ....   2000.00
214.   1 Ecu d'or 1613...................................   800.00

Arms. Rev. Initials and cross.

215.   1 Ecu d'or 1614, 31-44 ....   700.00

Ruler seated. Rev. Arms.

216.   1 Florin ND...   1500.00

MAXIMILIAN HENRY OF BAVARIA, 1650-1688
Arms. Rev. Legend on tablet.

217.   1 Ducat 1651-58 ....   1000.00

Bust Rev. Arms.

217a.   2 Ducats ND 4000.00
218.   1 Ducat 1663, 64, 68, ND 1200.00

JOHN LOUIS ELDERN, 1688-1694

Bust. Rev. Arms.

219.   2 Ducats 1690 .... * 5000.00
220.   1 Ducat 1690 .... Unknown

JOSEPH CLEMENT OF BAVARIA, 1694-1723
Bust. Rev. Arms.

221.   3 Ducats 1695, 1700 ....   5000.00

JOHN THEODORE OF BAVARIA, 1744-1763
Bust. Rev. Arms.

222.   1 Ducat 1749 ....   3000.00

SEDE VACANTE ISSUES
(Coins struck in the period between the death of one bishop and the coronation of another).

Bust of St. Lambert. Rev. Arms.

223.	2 Ducats 1688, 94, 1724	4000.00
224.	1 Ducat 1724, 44, 63, 71, 84, 92 ....*	1500.00
225.	½ Ducat 1724	Unknown

LOOS

Counts —

THEODORE III, 1336-1361
Lamb. Rev. Cross.

226.	1 Mouton d'or ND	4000.00

St. John. Rev. Lily.

227.	1 Florin ND.	2000.00

GODEFROID III, 1361-1363
St. John. Rev. Lily.

227a.	1 Florin ND.	Rare

MEGEN

Counts —

MARIA, 1572-1580
Ruler on throne. Rev. Arms in rose.

228.	2 Souverain d'or ND	5500.00

Ruler in ship. Rev. Rose.

229.	1 Noble ND	4000.00

Ruler in ship. Rev. Cross.

230.	1 Noble ND	4000.00

RECKHEIM

Counts —

WILLIAM OF VLODORP, 1556-1565

St. Peter. Rev. Madonna.

231.	1 Ducat ND.	1500.00

St. George. Rev. Madonna.

232.	1 Ducat ND.	2500.00

HERMAN OF ASPREMONT LYNDEN, 1590-1603
Helmeted arms. Rev. Double eagle.

232a.	1 Ducat ND.	2500.00

FERDINAND OF ASPREMONT LYNDEN, 1601-1665
Quartered arms. Rev. Soldier standing.

232b.	1 Ducat ND.	2500.00

RUMMEN

Counts —

ARNOLD OREY, 1355-1370
Ruler on horse. Rev. Cross.

233.	1 Franc a Cheval ND	3500.00

Lamb. Rev. Cross.

234.	1 Mouton d'or ND	4000.00

JOHN OF WEZEMAEL, 1415-1464

Lamb. Rev. Cross.

235.	1 Mouton d'or ND ....*	3000.00

St. John. Rev. Globe.

236.	1 Florin ND.	1500.00

Ruler seated. Rev. Cross.

236a.	1 Chaise d'or ND	3750.00
236b.	½ Chaise d'or ND	3000.00

STAVELOT

Abbots of —

CHRISTOPHER MANDERSCHEID, 1546-1576
Arms. Rev. Double eagle.

237.	1 Florin 1567, 68	2500.00

Ruler standing. Rev. Arms.

238.	1 Couronne d'or ND	Rare

THOREN

Abbesses of —

MARGUERITE IV BREDERODE, 1531-1579
Madonna seated. Rev. Arms.

239.	1 Ducat ND.	1500.00

Bust of Ferdinand II. Rev. Madonna.

240.	1 Ducat ND.	1200.00

Bust of Ferdinand II. Rev. Arms.

241.	1 Ducat ND.	1500.00

St. Michael. Rev. Ship.

242.	1 Angel ND. ....*	1700.00
243.	½ Angel ND.	3500.00

TOURNAI

Gold coins were struck at the Tournai mint by the Kings of France (Charles VI and Charles VII) and by the Spanish rulers of the provinces of Brabant and Flanders (Philip II, Albert and Isabella, and Philip IV).

VALKENBERG (FALKENBERG)

Barons —

REINHALD SCHONFORST, 1354-1355
St. John. Rev. Lily.

244.	1 Florin ND..	2250.00

FREDERICK IV OF MOERS, 1417-1448
St. John. Rev. Five shields.

245.	1 Florin ND..	2250.00

BOHEMIA

This is the ancient Kingdom occupying the territory now known as Czechoslovakia.

A. Kings of —

WENCESLAS II, 1278-1305
W in shield. Rev. Lion.

1.	1 Florin ND..	4300.00

JOHN OF LUXEMBOURG, 1310-1346
St. John. Rev. Lily.

2.	1 Florin ND..	2600.00

CHARLES IV, 1346-1378

Bust. facing. Rev. Lion.

3.	1 Goldgulden ND....................................	1400.00

WENCESLAS III, 1378-1419
Facing bust of St. Wenceslas. Rev. Lion.

4.	1 Ducat ND..	4750.00

Shield. Rev. Lion.

5.	1 Ducat ND..	4750.00

LADISLAS II, 1471-1516
St. Wenceslas. Rev. Lion in shield.

6.	1 Goldgulden ND....................................	2450.00

LOUIS II, 1516-1526
St. Wenceslas. Rev. Lion in shield.

7.	1 Ducat 1518, 21, ND..............................	1300.00

St. Wenceslas. Rev. Lion.

8.	1 Ducat ND..	1500.00

FERDINAND I, 1526-1564
St. Wenceslas. Rev. Lion.

9.	1 Goldgulden 1536-45, ND	900.00

MAXIMILIAN II, 1564-1576
Ruler standing. Rev. Arms.

10.	1 Ducat 1566, 73	900.00

RUDOLPH II, 1576-1612
Ruler standing. Rev. Arms.

11.	1 Ducat 1583, 88, 89, 94..........................	875.00

MATTHIAS II, 1612-1619
Bust. Rev. Legend.

12.	2 Ducats 1611.....................................	1200.00
13.	1 Ducat 1611......................................	600.00

Ruler standing. Rev. Double eagle.

14.	10 Ducats 1611-19	Rare
15.	5 Ducats 1611-19	Rare
16.	2 Ducats 1611-19	1750.00
17.	1 Ducat 1611-19	875.00

Ruler standing. Rev. St. Wenceslas.

18.	1 Ducat 1612-19	875.00

Stork. Rev. Legend.

19.	2 Ducats 1611.....................................	2100.00

FREDERICK V OF PALATINATE, 1619-1620

Ruler standing. Rev. Arms.

20.	10 Ducats 1620 ....*......		Rare
21.	5 Ducats 1620		Rare
22.	1 Ducat 1620		4800.00

Bust. Rev. Lion

23.	1 Ducat 1620	3000.00

Crowned bust. Rev. Arms on lion.

24.	2 Ducats 1620		4800.00
25.	1 Ducat 1620, ND..........................*......		4350.00

Lion. Rev. Three shields under hat.

26.	1 Goldgulden 1621.................................	1650.00

Legend. Rev. Crown. On the Coronation.

27.	2 Ducats 1619	1900.00

Crowned initial. Rev. Legend. On the Coronation.

| 28. | 1 Ducat 1619 ....*...... | 700.00 |
| 29. | ½ Ducat 1619 .... | 600.00 |

NATIONAL ASSEMBLY OF BOHEMIA AND MORAVIA, 1619-1620
Crowned Moravian Eagle. Rev. Obelisk.

30.	25 Ducats 1620	Rare
31.	10 Ducats 1620	Rare
32.	5 Ducats 1620	Rare

NATIONAL ASSEMBLY OF MORAVIA AND SILESIA, 1621
Silesian Eagle. Rev. Blank.

33.	25 Taler 1621	Rare
34.	12½ Taler 1621. Round	Rare
35.	12½ Taler 1621. Square..............................	Rare

FERDINAND II, 1619-1637

Ruler standing. Rev. Double eagle.

36.	12 Ducats 1632	Rare
37.	10 Ducats 1621-37 ....*......11000.00
38.	5 Ducats 1621-37	4800.00
39.	2 Ducats 1620-37	2150.00
40.	1 Ducat 1620-37	1000.00

Pax. Rev. Inscription.

| 41. | 1 Peace Ducat 1635 .... | 2450.00 |

FERDINAND III, 1637-1657

Bust in ruff collar. (See next column for Rev.)

Rev. Bohemian Lion in shield.

42.	100 Ducats 1629 ....*......	Rare
43.	50 Ducats 1629	Rare
44.	40 Ducats 1629	Rare

CHARLES VI, 1711-1740

Ruler standing. Rev. Globe and owl. From gold of the Eule Mines.

| 45. | 2 Ducats 1715-22 ....*..... | 4800.00 |
| 46. | 1 Ducat 1713-22 .... | 2200.00 |

Ruler standing. Rev. St. John on clouds. From gold of the Eule Mines.

47.	5 Ducats 1722. City view below St. John ...*......	Rare
48.	2 Ducats 1722-27	3500.00
49.	1 Ducat 1719-29	1575.00

MARIA THERESA, 1740-1780
Legend. Rev. Bohemian Lion. On the Coronation.

| 50 | 1 Ducat 1743 .... | 775.00 |

B. Cities of —

LOBKOWITZ

Princes —

FERDINAND AUGUST LEOPOLD, 1677-1715
Armored bust. Rev. Arms.

| 51. | 1 Ducat ND...................................... | 3500.00 |

OLMUTZ

Archbishops of —

FRANCIS OF DIETRICHSTEIN, 1599-1636

Madonna seated. Rev. Arms.

52.	1 Ducat 1626, 28, ND.............................	2200.00

Shield of Dietrichstein. Rev. Arms.

53.	½ Ducat 1636	1300.00

LEOPOLD WILLIAM OF AUSTRIA, 1637-1662
Bust. Rev. Arms.

54.	10 Ducats 1656, 58	Rare
55.	4 Ducats 1656..................................	7000.00

Bust. Rev. Two shields.

56.	1 Ducat 1658	1650.00

CHARLES II OF LIECHTENSTEIN-CASTELCORN, 1664-1695

Bust. Rev. Arms.

57.	10 Ducats 1678...............................	11000.00
58.	8 Ducats 1678	8000.00
59.	6 Ducats ND	6000.00
60.	5 Ducats 1672, 76, 78, ND	5250.00
61.	2 Ducats 1680, 84, 91........................*	3000.00
62.	1 Ducat 1684, ND..............................	1300.00
63.	⅛ Ducat 1671, ND.............................	475.00

CHARLES III, JOSEPH OF LORRAINE, 1695-1711
Bust. Rev. Arms.

64.	8 Ducats 1707.......................................	8750.00
65.	5 Ducats 1703, 04, 05, 07, ND	6125.00
66.	3 Ducats 1707	4000.00
67.	2 Ducats 1703, ND	2200.00
68.	1 Ducat ND.....................................	1300.00
69.	⅛ Ducat ND.....................................	650.00

WOLFGANG OF SCHRATTENBACH, 1711-1738

Bust. Rev. Arms.

70.	5 Ducats 1722 ....*	6000.00
71.	4 Ducats 1713	3000.00
72.	3 Ducats 1717, 25	2200.00
73.	1 Ducat 1725, 26, 28, 36, ND	1300.00

Bust with hat. Rev. Two shields.

74.	1 Ducat 1736, 37	1300.00

Bust and value. Rev. Three shields.

75.	¼ Ducat ND.....................................	425.00

JAMES ERNEST OF LIECHTENSTEIN-CASTELCORN, 1738-1745
Bust. Rev. Arms.

76.	1 Ducat 1739, 40	1000.00
77.	¼ Ducat ND.....................................	700.00

ANTHONY THEODORE COLLOREDO-WALLSEE, 1777-1811
Bust. Rev. Arms.

78.	1 Ducat 1779	1000.00

RUDOLPH JOHN OF AUSTRIA, 1819-1831
Bust. Rev. Arms.

79.	1 Ducat 1820	1300.00

ROSENBERG

Barons —

WILLIAM, 1581-1592
Bust right. Rev. Arms.

80.	4 Ducats 1585.....................................	7000.00
81.	2 Ducats 1585.....................................	5500.00

Arms. Rev. St. Christopher standing.

82.	2 Ducats 1584. Thick	6500.00
83.	1 Ducat 1582-88, 90........................*	1750.00

PETER WOK. 1592-1599

Arms. Rev. St. Christopher standing.

84.	1 Ducat 1592-95	1750.00

SCHLICK

Counts —

HENRY IV, 1612-1650

St. Anne and Virgin with shield. Rev. Eagle.

85.	10 Ducats 1627-46	*	Rare
86.	5 Ducats 1634, 46, 49		Rare
87.	1 Ducat 1628-38		2200.00

FRANCIS ERNEST, 1652-1675
St. Anne above arms and Madonna. Rev. Eagle.

88.	5 Ducats 1661, 62	7000.00

FRANCIS JOSEPH, 1675-1740
St. Anne. Rev. Eagle.

89.	1 Ducat 1716	1575.00

FRANCIS HENRY, 1740-1766
Madonna over arms. Rev. Eagle.

90.	1 Ducat 1759	2200.00

LEOPOLD HENRY, 1766-1770
Arms. Rev. Eagle.

91.	1 Ducat 1767	1575.00

SCHWARZENBERG

Princes —

JOHN ADAM, 1646-1683

Bust. Rev. Arms.

92.	1 Ducat 1682	2600.00

FERDINAND WILLIAM EUSEBIUS, 1683-1703

Bust. Rev. Arms.

93.	5 Ducats ND	*	7000.00
94.	1 Ducat 1693, 95		2100.00

ADAM FRANCIS, 1703-1732
Bust. Rev. Arms.

95.	1 Ducat 1710. Mint: Cologne	Rare
96.	1 Ducat 1721-32. Mint: Vienna	1600.00

JOSEPH ADAM, 1732-1782

Bust. Rev. Arms.

97.	1 Ducat 1768	2600.00

JOHN, 1782-1789

Bust. Rev. Arms.

98.	1 Ducat 1783	2200.00

TESCHEN

Dukes of —

See under GERMANY (SILESIA-TESCHEN)

VISHEHRAD

Abbots of —

CHARLES JOSEPH MARTINITZ
Two shields. Rev. Legend.

99.	1 Ducat 1734	1750.00

FERDINAND KINDERMANN SCHULSTEIN, 1782-1801
Arms. Rev. Legend.

100.	1 Ducat 1782	1750.00

PROCOP BENEDICT HENNIGER EBERG, 1802
Shields and insignia. Rev. Legend.

101.	1 Ducat 1802	2200.00

WALLENSTEIN

Duke of Friedland and Sagan

ALBERT WALLENSTEIN, 1625-1634
Facing bust. Rev. Arms with eagle.

102.	10 Ducats 1627, 29		Rare
103.	5 Ducats 1627		15000.00
104.	2 Ducats 1627		8750.00
105.	1 Ducat 1627, 28, 29		2600.00
106.	1 Goldgulden 1627, 28		8750.00

Bust right. Rev. Arms with eagle.

107.	10 Ducats 1628		Rare
108.	5 Ducats 1628		15000.00
109.	1 Ducat 1628		7000.00

Facing bust. Rev. Arms. With title as Duke of Mecklenburg.

110.	10 Ducats 1630 (very rare), 31	*	Rare
111.	5 Ducats 1629-31, 33, 34		14000.00
112.	2 Ducats 1631, 33, 34		8750.00
113.	1 Ducat 1629-31, 33, 34	*	3000.00

BOLIVIA

Mints and mint marks: — PTS monogram for Potosi. The bust on No. 18 is the same type as Chile No. 28.

A. Spanish Kings of —

CHARLES III, 1759-1788

Bust. Rev. Arms.

1.	8 Escudos 1778-88 (1778 Rare)		2500.00
2.	4 Escudos 1778-88 (1778 Rare)		2500.00
3.	2 Escudos 1778		5000.00
4.	2 Escudos 1779-88		1200.00
5.	1 Escudo 1778-88		500.00

CHARLES IV, 1788-1808
Bust of the previous King, Charles III. Rev. Arms.

6.	8 Escudos 1789, 90		1750.00
7.	4 Escudos 1790		2500.00
8.	2 Escudos 1789, 90		1000.00
9.	1 Escudo 1789, 90		275.00

Laureate bust. Rev. Arms.

10.	8 Escudos 1791	*	4000.00
11.	4 Escudos 1791		Rare
12.	2 Escudos 1791		3500.00
13.	1 Escudo 1791		750.00

Plain bust. Rev. Arms.

14.	8 Escudos 1791-1808		1250.00
15.	4 Escudos 1792-1808		1500.00
16.	2 Escudos 1793-1808		750.00
17.	1 Escudo 1793-1808		200.00

FERDINAND VII, 1808-1824
Uniformed bust. Rev. Arms.

18.	8 Escudos 1809	Unknown

Laureate head. Rev. Arms.

19.	8 Escudos 1817, 22, 23, 24	*	3000.00
20.	1 Escudo 1822, 23, 24		900.00

B. Republic of —

Uniformed bust of Bolivar. Rev. Arms.

21.	8 Escudos 1831-40	*	1500.00
22.	4 Escudos 1834		2700.00
23.	2 Escudos 1834, 35, 39		700.00
24.	1 Escudo 1831-39		350.00
25.	½ Escudo 1834, 39, 40		200.00

Small laureate head of Bolivar to right, his name below. Rev. Arms.

26.	8 Escudos 1841-47 ....*......	1250.00
27.	4 Escudos 1841	2750.00
28.	2 Escudos 1841	1100.00
29.	1 Escudo 1841, 42	350.00
30.	½ Escudo 1841-47	250.00

Plain head of Bolivar to left. Rev. Arms.

31.	8 Escudos 1851	1500.00
32.	1 Escudo 1851	Unknown

Laureate head of Bolivar to left, his name on neck. Rev. Arms.

33.	8 Escudos 1852	11000.00

Laureate head of Bolivar to right, his name on neck. Rev. Arms.

34.	8 Escudos 1852-57	2000.00
35.	1 Escudo 1852-56 ....*......	375.00
36.	½ Escudo 1852-56	200.00

Arms. Rev. Value, weight and fineness in wreath.

37.	1 Onza 1868 ....*......	12000.00
38.	1 Escudo 1868	1100.00
39.	½ Escudo 1868	700.00

Special Issue of 1952

These coins commemorate the revolution of October 31, 1952. The values are expressed by weight in grams. All coins are dated 1952. The reverses of all coins show the National arms. The obverses are as follows:

40.	35	Grams. Head of Villaroel	825.00
41.	14	Grams. Head of Busch	350.00
42.	7	Grams. Miner................................	250.00
43.	3½	Grams. Head of worker.........................	150.00

BRAZIL

Mints and mint marks:—

B or BBBB	mm for Bahia
R or RRRR	mm for Rio de Janeiro
PPPP	mm for Pernambuco (1702)
M or MMMM	mm for Minas Gerais (Vila Rica)

Brazilian gold coins were extensively counterstamped during the 18th and 19th centuries for use in other localities. Such coins may be found under Bahamas, Bermuda, British Guiana (Essequibo & Demerara), Grenada and Barlovento Islands, Guadeloupe, Jamaica, Martinique, Nevis, Saint Martin, Saint Vincent, Tobago, Trinidad, Virgin Islands and also under Portugal (Mary II, 1847).

Under the Portuguese Kings, the coins on the Colonial or Decimal standard (20000, 10000, 4000, 2000, 1000 and 400 Reis) show the denominations, whereas the coins on the National or Escudo standard (12800, 6400, 3200, 1600 and 800 Reis) are without the marks of value.

The first gold coin under the Empire, the "Coronation Piece" of 6400 Reis, 1822-R, was not approved for circulation by the Emperor, Peter I, and of the 64 originally struck, only 15 have survived.

The 10000 Reis pieces dated 1833-1840 have the same intrinsic value as the 6400 Reis pieces of similar head (Peter II as a child at the age of 7) dated 1832 and 1833, but are smaller and thicker.

It is interesting to note that of the two early gold types of the Republic, 20000 and 10000 Reis, 1889-1922, only the 10000 Reis piece shows the mark of value.

A. Dutch Government of Pernambuco, 1630-1654

G.W.C. monogram and value. Rev. Name and date. Square necessity coins struck by the Dutch West India Company (Geoctroyerde Westindische Compagnie).

1.	XII Guilders 1645, 46	3500.00
2.	VI Guilders 1645, 46 ....*......	2700.00
3.	III Guilders 1645, 46 ....*......	2700.00

B. Brazil — Colony, 1500-1818

ALFONSO VI, 1656-1667; PETER, PRINCE REGENT, 1667-1683, AND PETER II, 1683-1706

Primitive Brazilian counterstamps over Portuguese 4, 2 and 1 Cruzado pieces from the reigns of Philip I, II and III; John IIII (IV) and Peter, Prince Regent.

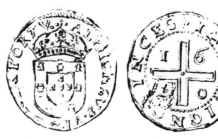

Crown bearing numeral of value (in Cruzados) counterstamped on reverse of Portuguese coins.

4.	Crowned 4 over 4 Cruzados ....*......	2700.00
5.	Crowned 2 over 2 Cruzados	2000.00
6.	Crowned 1 over 1 Cruzado	2250.00

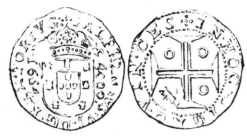

Portuguese counterstamps (value in Reis) for Portugal and Colonies.

7.	Crowned 4400 over 4 Cruzados.................*	3000.00
8.	Crowned 2200 over 2 Cruzados.....................	3000.00
9.	Crowned 1100 over 1 Cruzado....................	3000.00

Conjoined counterstamps (values in Cruzados and Reis) on the Cruzado coinage of Portugal.

10.	Crowned 4 and 4400 over 4 Cruzados..........*	2750.00
11.	Crowned 2 and 2200 over 2 Cruzados................	2750.00
12.	Crowned 1 and 1100 over 1 Cruzado................	3000.00

One, two or three counterstamps on the Cruzado coinage of Portugal; one counterstamp being a crowned globe, the others being the value in Cruzados and/or the value in Reis.

13.	Crowned Globe, 4 and/or 4400 over 4 Cruzados .*......	3500.00
14.	Crowned Globe, 2 and/or 2200 over 2 Cruzados........	2800.00
15.	Crowned Globe, 1 and/or 1100 over 1 Cruzado.........	2800.00

PETER II, 1683-1706

Arms and value. Rev. Plain cross in quadrilobe.

BAHIA.

16.	4000 Reis 1695. Large crown. No mm..................	700.00
17.	4000 Reis 1696-98. No mm.....................*......	600.00
18.	2000 Reis 1695. Large crown. No mm.................	3500.00
19.	2000 Reis 1696, 97. No mm.........................	500.00
20.	1000 Reis 1696. No mm............................	1500.00

RIO.

21.	4000 Reis 1699, 1700. No mm......................	600.00
22.	2000 Reis 1699, 1700. No mm......................	250.00
23.	1000 Reis 1699, 1700. No mm......................	200.00

PERNAMBUCO.

| 24. | 4000 Reis 1702 (over 1701). PPPP mm................. | 2000.00 |

Arms and value. Rev. Cross of Jerusalem.

RIO.

| 25. | 4000 Reis 1703-07. RRRR mm.................*..... | 1700.00 |
| 26. | 2000 Reis 1703. RRRR mm.......................... | 1700.00 |

Arms. and value. Rev. Cross of Jerusalem.

RIO.

27.	4000 Reis 1707-27 (1707 rare). RRRR mm.............	700.00
28.	2000 Reis 1723, 25, 26. RRRR mm....................	600.00
29.	1000 Reis 1708, 26. RRRR mm.	

BAHIA.

30.	4000 Reis 1714-27 (1714 rare). BBBB mm.............	700.00
31.	2000 Reis 1714-25. BBBB mm.................*.....	500.00
32.	1000 Reis 1714-26 (1714, 17 rare). BBBB mm.	800.00

MINAS GERAIS.

33.	20000 Reis 1724-27. MMMM mm	2750.00
34.	10000 Reis 1724-27. MMMM mm......................	2000.00
35.	4000 Reis 1724-27. MMMM mm......................	1750.00
36.	2000 Reis 1724-27. MMMM mm......................	1250.00
37.	1000 Reis 1724-27. MMMM mm......................	750.00

(Note: For 20000 Reis pieces dated 1724-27, MMMM mint mark, counterstamped with crowned Portuguese arms on reverse, see under Portugal, number 124.)

Crowned name and value. Rev. Cross of Jerusalem.

RIO.

| 38. | 400 Reis 1730. RRRR mm.......................... | 1250.00 |

MINAS GERAIS.

| 39. | 400 Reis 1724-26. MMMM mm.................*...... | 800.00 |

Laureate head. Rev. Oval arms.

RIO.

40.	12800 Reis 1727-31. R mm.....................*......	2500.00
41.	6400 Reis 1727-31. R mm..........................	2500.00
42.	3200 Reis 1727, 29. R mm.........................	2000.00
43.	1600 Reis 1727-30. R mm..........................	900.00
44.	800 Reis 1727, 30. R mm..........................	500.00

Laureate head. Rev. Italic arms.

RIO.

45.	12800 Reis 1731-33 (1733 rare). R mm.		2000.00
46.	6400 Reis 1732-50 (1732-34 rare). R mm.		650.00
47.	3200 Reis 1739, 41, 49. R mm.		1000.00
48.	1600 Reis 1736. R mm.		900.00
49.	800 Reis 1734, 36, 49. R mm.		350.00

BAHIA.

50.	12800 Reis 1727-32. B mm.		4000.00
51.	6400 Reis 1727-50 (1727-34 rare). B mm.	*	900.00
52.	3200 Reis 1727-50. B mm.		1500.00
53.	1600 Reis 1727-50. B mm.		1000.00
54.	800 Reis 1727-51. B mm.		700.00

MINAS GERAIS.

55.	12800 Reis 1727-33. M mm.		2750.00
56.	6400 Reis 1727, 31-34. M mm.		2500.00
57.	3200 Reis 1727-33. M mm.		1000.00
58.	1600 Reis 1727-33. M mm.		575.00
59.	800 Reis 1727-34. M mm.		300.00

Laureate head. Rev. Crown over date.

RIO.

60.	400 Reis 1734. R mm.	*	175.00

MINAS GERAIS.

61.	400 Reis 1730, 32-34. M mm.		175.00

Arms and value. Rev. Plain cross in quadrilobe. Without mint mark. Struck at Lisbon for the state of Maranhão.

LISBON.

62.	4000 Reis 1749. No mm.	*	600.00
63.	2000 Reis 1749. No mm.		300.00
64.	1000 Reis 1749. No mm.		200.00

JOSEPH I, 1750-1777

Laureate head. Rev. Italic arms.

RIO.

65.	6400 Reis 1751-77. R mm.		600.00
66.	3200 Reis 1755-73. R mm.	*	800.00
67.	1600 Reis 1752, 63, 72. R mm.		675.00
68.	800 Reis 1752, 63. R mm.		725.00

BAHIA.

69.	6400 Reis 1751-77. B mm.		700.00
70.	3200 Reis 1752-74. B mm.		1000.00
71.	1600 Reis 1752-77. B mm.		800.00
72.	800 Reis 1752-77. B mm.		675.00

Arms and value. Rev. Plain cross in quadrilobe. With IOSEPHUS or JOSEPHUS; DOMINVS or DOMINUS. Without mint mark. Struck at Lisbon, Rio and Bahia.

73.	4000 Reis 1751-77. No mm.	*	500.00
74.	2000 Reis 1752-73. No mm.		200.00
75.	1000 Reis 1749 (Rev. of John V), 52, 71, 74. No mm.		200.00

MARY I AND PETER III, 1777-1786

Conjoined busts. Rev. Italic arms.

RIO.

76.	6400 Reis 1777-86 (1777 rare). R mm.	*	600.00

BAHIA.

77.	6400 Reis 1777-86 (1777 rare). B mm.		725.00
78.	3200 Reis 1780-86. B mm.		1100.00
79.	1600 Reis 1780-82, 84. B mm.		675.00
80.	800 Reis 1782, 86. B mm.		675.00

Arms and value. Rev. Plain cross in quadrilobe. Without mint mark. Struck at Rio and Lisbon.

RIO.

81.	4000 Reis 1778. No mm.		500.00

LISBON, RIO.

82.	4000 Reis 1779, 81, 83, 86. No mm.		525.00
83.	2000 Reis 1778, 81-83 (1781-83 rare). No mm.		300.00
84.	1000 Reis 1778, 79, 81, 82 (1782 rare). No mm.		250.00

MARY I, 1786-1805

Bust with widow's veil. Rev. Italic arms.

RIO.

85.	6400 Reis 1786-89. R mm.		675.00

BAHIA.

86.	6400 Reis 1787-90 (1790 rare). B mm.	*	900.00

Bust in decorative headdress. Rev. Italic arms.

RIO.
87. 6400 Reis 1789-1805. R mm.....................*......   750.00
BAHIA.
88. 6400 Reis 1790-1804 (1790 rare). B mm. 825.00

*Arms and value. Rev. Plain cross in quadrilobe. Without
mint mark. Struck at Lisbon, Rio and Bahia.*

LISBON, RIO.
89. 4000 Reis 1787, 90, 92 (1790, 92 rare). No mm.........   675.00
90. 2000 Reis 1787, 92, 93. No mm.................*......   450.00
91. 1000 Reis 1787. No mm. 275.00
BAHIA.
92. 4000 Reis 1801-05. No mm. 600.00

JOHN, PRINCE REGENT, 1805-1818

Laureate bust. Rev. Oval arms.

RIO.
93. 6400 Reis 1805-17 (1815-17 rare). R mm........*......   650.00
94. 6400 Reis 1816, with PORT. BRAS. ET. ALG. R mm. ...   3500.00

*Arms and value. Rev. Plain cross in quadrilobe. Without
mint mark. Pieces from the Rio Mint have the date between two small flowers; those from the Bahia Mint have
the date between two points (1805-11) or between two
small flowers (1811-16), but cruder coinage.*

RIO.
95. 4000 Reis 1808-17. No mm......................*.....   500.00
96. 4000 Reis 1816, with BRAS. ET. ALG. No mm. 1000.00
BAHIA.
97. 4000 Reis 1805-11. Date between points. No mm. 600.00
97a. 4000 Reis 1811-16. Date between flowers. No mm. 700.00

C. Brazil — United Kingdom, 1818-1822

JOHN VI, 1818-1822 (Brazil)

Laureate bust. Rev. Arms of the United Kingdom.

RIO.
98. 6400 Reis 1818-22 (1821, 22 rare). R mm...............   2000.00

*Arms of the United Kingdom and value. Rev. Plain cross in
quadrilobe. Without mint mark. Pieces from the Rio Mint
have the date between two small flowers (1818-22), or
between two small crosses (1819); those from the Bahia
Mint have the date between two small crosses but cruder
coinage.*

RIO.
99. 4000 Reis 1818-22. No mm.....................*......   550.00
BAHIA.
100. 4000 Reis 1819, 20. No mm...........................   1500.00

*Crudely shaped rectangular gold bars, 1778-1833 (Colony,
United Kingdom and Empire), issued as current money at
Cuyabá, Goiás, Mato Grosso, Rio das Mortes, Sabará,
Serro Frio and Vila Rica, assay offices in Brazil, and
punched with various stamps, including arms and globe,
date, number, weight, fineness and the assayer's
monogram.*

101. CUYABA (1821-22).....................................   5000.00
102. GOIAS or GOVAS 4500.00
103. MATO GROSSO..   5000.00
104. RIO DAS MORTES or 960 or R. DAS MORT...........   5500.00
105. SABARA or 960 or V. DO SABARA....................   4000.00
106. SERRO FRIO or 960 or S.F...........................   4500.00
107. VILA RICA or 960 or V.R.......................*.....   4000.00
107a. I.C. OURO PRETO (1828) new name for Vila Rica ......   Unique

D. Brazil — Empire, 1822-1889

PETER I, 1822-1831

*Laureate bust with "Z. FERREZ" below. Rev. Imperial arms.
Without the mark of value. Coronation piece, not placed
in circulation.*

RIO.

108.   6400 Reis 1822. R mm................................. 28000.00

Bust in naval uniform. Rev. Imperial arms and value.

RIO.

109.   6400 Reis 1823-30 (1830 rare). R mm................... 2750.00
110.   4000 Reis 1823-27 (1827 rare). R mm...........*...... 1000.00

BAHIA.

111.   6400 Reis 1825, 26, 28. B mm. 3000.00
112.   4000 Reis 1825, 26, 28. B mm. 1500.00

PETER II, 1831-1889

*Child head. Rev. Imperial arms and value. With and without
the engraver's name.*

RIO.

113.   6400 Reis 1832. R mm. AZEVEDO F. below bust...... 1750.00
114.   4000 Reis 1832. R mm. AZEVEDO F. below bust...... 9000.00
115.   6400 Reis 1832, 33. R mm....................*...... 825.00
116.   4000 Reis 1832, 33. R mm........................... 4000.00

Child head. Rev. Imperial arms. Without the mark of value.

117.   10000 Reis 1833-40 (1839, 40 rare). 775.00

Bust in naval uniform. Rev. Imperial arms. Without the mark of value.

118.   10000 Reis 1841-48 (1844 rare)......................... 900.00

*Bust in Coronation Robe (Papo Tucano). Rev. Imperial arms.
Without the mark of value.*

119.   20000 Reis 1849-51..............................*...... 575.00
120.   10000 Reis 1849-51.................................. 500.00

Bearded young head. Rev. Imperial arms. Without the mark of value.

121.   20000 Reis 1851, 52.................................... 475.00

Bearded older head. Rev. Imperial arms. Without the mark of value.

121a. 20000 Reis 1853-89 (1862 rare) 475.00
122.   10000 Reis 1853-89. (1859, 63 rare)..................... 250.00
123.   5000 Reis 1854-59 (1857-59 rare). ....*...... 200.00

E. Brazil — Republic, 1889-

*Liberty head. Rev. The Stars of the Southern Cross. Without
the mark of value.*

124.   20000 Reis 1889-1922 (1892, 1906 rare)................. 1100.00

Liberty head. Rev. Arms of the Republic.

125. 10000 Reis 1889-1922 (1896, 98, 1914, 15, 22 rare)....... 900.00

For later issues of Brazil, see the section, "Recent Issues Starting With 1960."

BRITISH COLUMBIA

The two coins listed are of extreme rarity. They were struck in British Columbia as trials for a proposed coinage, but the actual issuance of the coins was forbidden by England.

Crown Rev. Value and date. These coins were not placed in circulation.

1. 20 Dollars 1862.................................... Rare
2. 10 Dollars 1862................................*...... Rare

BRITISH GUIANA

Brazilian gold coins of the period 1727-1804 counterstamped ED (Essequibo and Demerara) and with or without other counterstamps.

1. 6400 Reis 1727-1804.................................. 2000.00

BULGARIA

Bulgarian coinage is based on the Latin Monetary Union standard, excepting the Ducat coinage. The coins of 1894 are rare in perfect uncirculated condition; the coinage of that year is as follows: 100 Leva, 7500 pieces; 20 Leva, 175,000 pieces; 10 Leva, 75,000 pieces.

Kings of —

IVAN-ASSEN II, 1218-1241

Ruler and St. Dimitar. Rev. Christ standing. On the victory over the Byzantine Empire in the battle of Klokotnitza.

1. 1 Solidus ND....................................... Rare

FERDINAND, 1887-1918

Head. Rev. Arms.

2. 100 Leva 1894 .... 2000.00
3. 20 Leva 1894 ....*...... 175.00
4. 10 Leva 1894 ....*...... 125.00

Head. Rev. Crowned oval shield. On the 25th year of reign. The date 1912 is in very small numerals under the shield.

5. 100 Leva 1912 .... 2000.00
6. 20 Leva 1912 ....*...... 350.00

SPECIAL ISSUES

Uniformed bust. Rev. Arms with small crown counter-stamped at bottom.

7. 4 Ducats 1910, 12, 14, 18................... 1000.00

BORIS III, 1918-1943

Uniformed bust. Rev. Arms with small crown counter-stamped at bottom.

8.	4 Ducats 1926	1000.00

For later issues of Bulgaria, see the section, "Recent Issues With 1960."

BURMA

The coins are dated in the C.S. or Chula-Sakarat system, which started in the year 638 A.D. The beginning of the C.S. year corresponds with our March 13. To convert to A.D. dates, add 638 to the C.S. date for coins issued in the first nine months of the C.S. year and 639 for coins issued in the last three months. Due to major revisions, the numbering has been changed from previous editions.

Kings of —

MINDON MIN, 1852-1878

Peacock. Rev. Legend in wreath.

1.	1 Kyat (1 Mohur) 1214 C.S. (1853 A.D.). Restrike of Rupee in gold...............................		350.00
2.	1 Mu (2 Rupees) 1214 C.S. (1853 A.D.)		150.00
3.	1 Pe (1 Rupee) 1214 C.S. (1853 A.D.) .... *		100.00

Burmese lion, known as "Chinthe." Rev. Legend in wreath.

4.	1 Kyat (1 Mohur) 1228 C.S. (1866 A.D.)		525.00
5.	2 Mu, 1 Pe (¼ Mohur) 1228 C.S. (1866 A.D.) *		250.00
6.	1 Pe (1 Rupee) 1228 C.S. (1866 A.D.)		100.00

THEBAW, 1878-1885

Dragon lion, known as "To." Rev. Legend in wreath.

7.	5 Mu (½ Mohur) 1240 C.S. (1878 A.D.)	350.00

CAMBODIA

The bird Hamsa. Rev. Legend.

1.	1 Fuang ND (1846)...................................	300.00

Head of King Norodom I. Rev. Arms. Souvenir gold coins struck from dies used for silver coins.

2.	1 Piastre 1860		1750.00
3.	2 Francs 1860................................ *		500.00
4.	1 Franc 1860.......................................		350.00
5.	50 Centimes 1860		275.00
6.	25 Centimes 1860		200.00

CANADA

EDWARD VII, 1901-1910
Head. Rev. St. George. As the English Pound but with the distinguishing mintmark C on ground below horse.

1.	1 Pound 1908-10 (1908 rare)	375.00

GEORGE V, 1910-1936
Head Rev. St. George. As the English Pound but with the distinguishing mintmark C on ground below horse.

2.	1 Pound 1911-19 (1913, 16 rare)	225.00(B)

Crowned head. Rev. Arms.

3.	10 Dollars 1912-14....................................	750.00
4.	5 Dollars 1912-14 (1914 rare)	285.00

(Number 2 is a bullion coin. The price listed is based on gold at $725 per ounce.)

For later issues of Canada, see the section, "Recent Issues Starting With 1960."

CEYLON

Ruler standing. Rev. Ruler seated. Crude style. Struck during the period 840-1295 A.D.

1.	1 Stater ND .... *		225.00
2.	½ Stater ND		115.00
3.	¼ Stater ND		75.00
4.	⅛ Stater ND		60.00

Ruler kneeling. Rev. Legend. Crude style.

5.   1 Mas ND (840-1295 A.D.) 75.00

Ruler standing. Rev. Legend. Crude style.

6.   1 Mas ND (840-1295 A.D.) 75.00

"C" (For Colombo) and "VOC" monogram (Dutch East India Company) counterstamped on continental Dutch gold coins.

7.   2 Ducats 1691 . . . . Unique

Standing god. Rev. Granular surface.

8.   1 Pagoda ND (1760-94). 100.00

CHILE

Mints and mint marks:— S topped by small o for Santiago.

On the coins from 1846-1851, the Grecian helmet worn by Liberty on earlier years, is replaced by the Liberty Cap.

A. Spanish Kings of —

PHILIP V, 1700-1746
Bust. Rev. Arms. This issue was not placed in circulation. The last two coins were struck during the reign of Ferdinand VI.

1.   8 Escudos 1744 . . . . Rare
2.   4 Escudos 1744 . . . . Rare
3.   2 Escudos 1758 . . . . Unique
4.   1 Escudo 1754 . . . . Unique

FERDINAND VI, 1746-1760

Small bust. Rev. Arms.

5.   8 Escudos 1750-60 . . . . * 6000.00
6.   4 Escudos 1749-52 . . . . 4000.00
6a.   2 Escudos 1758 . . . . 3000.00
7.   1 Escudo 1754, 58, 59 . . . . 3000.00

Large bust. Rev. Arms.

8.   8 Escudos 1760 . . . . 4000.00

CHARLES III, 1759-1788

Bust of the previous King, Ferdinand VI. Rev. Arms.

9.   8 Escudos 1760-63 . . . . * 7000.00
9a.   4 Escudos 1762, 63 . . . . 6000.00
10.   1 Escudo 1761, 62 . . . . 1000.00

Bust. Rev. Arms without value.

11.   8 Escudos 1764-72 . . . . 7500.00
12.   4 Escudos 1763-65 . . . . 5000.00
13.   2 Escudos 1764 . . . . 2000.00
14.   1 Escudo 1763, 64, 66 . . . . 900.00

Bust. Rev. Arms with value.

15.   8 Escudos 1772-89 . . . . * 1100.00
16.   4 Escudos 1773-89 . . . . 2500.00
17.   2 Escudos 1773-88 . . . . 900.00
18.   1 Escudo 1772-88 . . . . 700.00

CHARLES IV, 1788-1808

Bust of the previous King, Charles III with title as "Carol IV." Rev. Arms.

19.   8 Escudos 1789-91 . . . . * 1100.00
20.   4 Escudos 1789-91 . . . . 3000.00
21.   2 Escudos 1789, 90 . . . . 1250.00
22.   1 Escudo 1790 . . . . 750.00

Bust of the previous King, Charles III with title as "Carol IIII." Rev. Arms.

23.   8 Escudos 1791-1808 . . . . * 1000.00
24.   2 Escudos 1791-1808 . . . . 1200.00
25.   1 Escudo 1791 . . . . 500.00

Bust of Charles IV. Rev. Arms.

26.   4 Escudos 1791-1808 .... 1250.00
27.   1 Escudo 1791-1808 .... 450.00

FERDINAND VII, 1808-1821
Bust of the previous king, Charles IV. Rev. Arms.

27a. 8 Escudos 1811 .... 10000.00

Large uniformed bust. Rev. Arms.

28.   8 Escudos 1808-11 .... 2500.00

Bust of the previous King, Charles IV. Rev. Arms.

29.   8 Escudos 1812-17 .... 1200.00
30.   4 Escudos 1810-17 .... * 2500.00
31.   2 Escudos 1810-17 .... 1100.00
32.   1 Escudo 1809-17 .... 700.00

B. Republic of —

Sun, mountains and volcanos. Rev. Crossed flags.

33.   8 Escudos 1818-34 .... * 750.00
34.   4 Escudos 1824-34 .... 1250.00
35.   2 Escudos 1818-34 .... 250.00
36.   1 Escudo 1824-34 .... 200.00

Hand on the book of the Constitution. Rev. Arms.

37.   8 Escudos 1835-38 .... * 750.00
38.   4 Escudos 1836, 37 .... 750.00
39.   2 Escudos 1837, 38 .... 300.00
40.   1 Escudo 1838 .... 150.00

Liberty as Pallas Athene standing at altar. Rev. Arms. The 8 Escudos from 1839-43 has a striated edge; from 1843-51 it has the month of issue inscribed on the edge.

41.   8 Escudos 1839-51 .... * 750.00
42.   4 Escudos 1839, 41 .... 3000.00
43.   2 Escudos 1839-51 .... 400.00
44.   1 Escudo 1839-51 .... 175.00

Liberty standing at altar. Rev. Arms.

45. 10 Pesos 1851-92 .... * 275.00
46.   5 Pesos 1851-73 .... 175.00
47.   2 Pesos 1857-75 .... 150.00

Liberty standing at altar. Rev. Value in wreath.

48.   1 Peso 1860-73 .... 75.00

Head of Liberty wearing cap. Rev. Arms.

49. 10 Pesos 1895 .... * 200.00
50.   5 Pesos 1895, 96 .... 125.00

Draped Liberty head with coiled hair. Rev. Arms.

51. 20 Pesos 1896-1917 .... * 200.00
52. 10 Pesos 1896, 98, 1901 .... * 125.00
53.   5 Pesos 1898, 1900 .... 125.00

SHANTUNG

Liberty head with coiled hair. Rev. Arms. Two values appear on these coins.

54.	100 Pesos — 10 Condores 1926, 32, 46-63 * ...	425.00(B)
55.	50 Pesos — 5 Condores 1926, 58, 61, 62, 65, 67, 68, 74	210.00(B)
56.	20 Pesos — 2 Condores 1926, 58, 59, 61 * ...	125.00(B)

(Numbers 54-56 are bullion coins. The price listed is based on gold at $725 per ounce.)

For later issues of Chile, see the section, "Recent Issues With 1960."

CHINA

The seventeen coins listed are the only ones which can be regarded as authentic Chinese gold coins, and of these seventeen, only numbers 4, 5, 10, 11 and 12 circulated to any extent. The many other Chinese "gold coins" which exist are either gold impressions from dies for silver coins or are outright fantasies.

A. Emperors of China

KUANG HSU, 1875-1908

Large dragon. Rev. Legend. The coins with reeded edge were reportedly not struck officially.

1.	1 Tael 1906, 07. Plain edge	5500.00
2.	1 Tael 1906, 07. Reeded edge	5000.00

B. Republic of China

Head of President Yuan Shi Kai. Rev. Dragon with Chinese legend reading "Empire of China."

3.	10 Yuans 1916	3000.00

Head of President Yuan Shi Kai. Rev. Legend and wreath.

4.	20 Yuans 1919 ....*	2750.00
5.	10 Yuans 1919	2500.00

Dragon and Phoenix. Rev. Legend.

6.	20 Yuans 1926	2750.00
7.	10 Yuans 1926 ....*	2250.00

YUNNAN

Five vertical characters flanked on each side by five dots. Rev. Blank.

8.	10 Yuans ND (1917)	1250.00
9.	5 Yuans ND(1917)	1250.00

Facing head of General Tang Chi Yao. Rev. Crossed flags.

10.	10 Yuans 1919. Numeral "1" below flags.......*	1350.00
11.	10 Yuans 1919. Without numeral	2000.00
12.	5 Yuans 1919. Numeral "2" below flags.......*	1250.00

Four characters around central dot. Rev. One character within grain wreath.

13.	10 Yuans ND (1925)	2000.00
14.	5 Yuans ND (1925)	2000.00

D. Nationalist China

For later issues of Nationalist China, see the section, "Recent Issues Starting With 1960."

COLOMBIA

Mints and mint marks: — Under the Spanish Kings, NR for Bogota; P or PN for Popayan; SF or FS for Santa Fe de Bogota. Under the Republic, the mints of Bogota, Popayan and Medellin used their names in full on the coins, with an occasional B or P for the first two.

All 5 Peso pieces of the 19th century are rare. During the latter part of the 19th century, the coinage was based on the Latin Monetary Union standard and in the 20th century, on that of the English Pound. Due to major revisions the numbering has been changed from previous editions.

A. Spanish Kings of —

PHILIP IV, 1621-1665
Arms. Rev. Cross. Crude Cob type.

1.	2 Escudos ND	300.00
2.	2 Escudos 1628, 33-35, 40-42, 50, 52-54	500.00

CHARLES II, 1665-1700
Arms. Rev. Cross. Cob type. Coins dated 1704 are posthumous issues.

3.	2 Escudos ND or partial date	450.00
4.	2 Escudos 1672, 77, 83, 87, 90, 94, 97, 98, 1701, 04	500.00
5.	1 Escudo ND	350.00

PHILIP V, 1700-1746
Arms. Rev. Cross. Cob type.

6.	8 Escudos 1744, 46, 48, ND. SF or FS mm	4200.00
7.	4 Escudos 1740, 45, 47, ND. FS mm	1500.00
8.	2 Escudos 1701-43, ND. SF or FS mm	600.00
9.	1 Escudo 1729-46, ND. FS mm	550.00

LOUIS I, 1723-1726
Arms. Rev. Cross. Cob type.

10.	2 Escudos 1725. SF or FS mm	1000.00

FERDINAND VI, 1746-1760
Arms. Rev. Cross. Cob type.

11.	8 Escudos 1749-56, ND. SF or FS mm	3500.00
12.	4 Escudos 1747, 51, 54-56. SF or FS mm	2500.00
13.	2 Escudos 1748, 50-54. SF or FS mm	600.00
14.	1 Escudo 1754, 55. SF or FS mm	500.00

Bust. Rev. Arms.

15.	8 Escudos 1756-59. NR mm	5000.00
16.	8 Escudos 1758, 59, 60. P or PN mm	5000.00
17.	4 Escudos 1757-59. NR mm	2000.00
18.	4 Escudos 1758-60. P or PN mm	2000.00
19.	2 Escudos 1756-59. NR mm............*	800.00
20.	2 Escudos 1758-61. P or PN mm	700.00
21.	1 Escudo 1756, 59 NR mm	700.00
22.	1 Escudo 1758, 59. P or PN mm	500.00

CHARLES III, 1759-1788

Bust of the previous King, Ferdinand VI. Rev. Arms.

23.	8 Escudos 1760-62. NR mm	3500.00
24.	8 Escudos 1760-71. P or PN mm	3500.00
25.	4 Escudos 1760. NR mm	Unknown
26.	4 Escudos 1760-62, 69. P or PN mm	2000.00
27.	2 Escudos 1760-62. NR mm	800.00
28.	2 Escudos 1760-71. P or PN mm............*	800.00
29.	1 Escudo NR mm	Unknown
30.	1 Escudo 1760, 62, 67, 69. P or PN mm	350.00

Bust with name as "Carolus." Rev. Arms without value. This type was not struck at the Popayan Mint.

31.	8 Escudos 1762-71. NR mm	4500.00
32.	4 Escudos 1769-71. NR mm	3500.00
33.	2 Escudos 1762-71. NR mm........*	800.00
34.	1 Escudo 1763, 67. NR mm	900.00

Bust with name as "Carol." Rev. Arms with value.

35.	8 Escudos 1772-89. NR mm	1000.00
36.	8 Escudos 1772-89. P or PN mm	1500.00
37.	4 Escudos 1775-87. NR mm	1500.00
38.	4 Escudos 1773-86. P or PN mm	1200.00
39.	2 Escudos 1772-89. NR mm	400.00
40.	2 Escudos 1771-89. P or PN mm........*	300.00
41.	1 Escudo 1772-89. NR mm	175.00
42.	1 Escudo 1772-89. P or PN mm	150.00

CHARLES IV, 1788-1808

Bust of the previous King, Charles III. Rev. Arms.

43.	8 Escudos 1789-91. NR mm	1100.00
44.	8 Escudos 1789-91. P or PN mm	1100.00
45.	4 Escudos 1789, 90. NR mm	2500.00
46.	4 Escudos 1790. P or PN mm	1200.00
47.	2 Escudos 1789, 90. NR mm	300.00
48.	2 Escudos 1789-91. P or PN mm........*	400.00
49.	1 Escudo 1789, 90. NR mm (1789 Rare)	200.00
50.	1 Escudo 1789, 90. P or PN mm	175.00

Bust. Rev. Arms.

51.	8 Escudos 1791-1808. NR mm....................	900.00
52.	8 Escudos 1791-1808. P or PN mm.................	900.00
53.	4 Escudos 1792-1807. NR mm....................	1500.00
54.	4 Escudos 1792-1802. P or PN mm.................	1500.00
55.	4 Escudos 1807, 08. P or PN mm..................	1750.00
56.	2 Escudos 1790-1805. NR mm....................	200.00
57.	2 Escudos 1791-1805. P or PN mm.........*.....	200.00
58.	1 Escudo 1792-1808. NR mm.....................	175.00
59.	1 Escudo 1792-1808. P or PN mm................	175.00

FERDINAND VII, 1808-1824

Bust of the previous King, Charles IV. Rev. Arms.

60.	8 Escudos 1808-20. NR mm.....................	1000.00
61.	8 Escudos 1808-20. P or PN mm............*.....	900.00
62.	4 Escudos 1818, 19. NR mm....................	2000.00
63.	2 Escudos 1808-11. NR mm	600.00
64.	2 Escudos 1817-19. P or PN mm...............	400.00
65.	1 Escudo 1808-20. NR mm.....................	200.00
66.	1 Escudo 1808-19. P or PN mm................	200.00

B. Republic of —

I. Coinage of the Republic of Colombia

Liberty head. Rev. Fasces within a double cornucopia and above, "Bogota" or "Popayan," the place of minting.

67.	8 Escudos 1822-37. Bogota	1250.00
68.	8 Escudos 1822-37. Popayan......................	750.00
69.	4 Escudos 1826. Bogota	1300.00
70.	2 Escudos 1824-36. Bogota	300.00
71.	1 Escudo 1823-33. Bogota	125.00
72.	1 Escudo 1823-36. Popayan ....*.....	150.00
73.	1 Peso 1825-36. Bogota.......................	100.00

II. Coinage of the Republic of New Granada

Draped Liberty head. Rev. Arms and "Bogota" or "Popayan"

74.	16 Pesos 1837-49. Bogota....................	750.00
75.	16 Pesos 1837-46. Popayan...................	750.00
76.	2 Pesos 1838-46. Popayan............*....	300.00
77.	1 Peso 1837-46. Bogota..............*....	200.00

Plain Liberty head. Rev. Arms with the value of the coins expressed by their weight in grams.

78.	16 Pesos 1848-53 Bogota. 25.8064 grams.....*......	2200.00
79.	10 Pesos 1854-57 Bogota. 16.400 grams.............	1600.00
80.	10 Pesos 1853 Popayan. 16.400 grams.	750.00
81.	2 Pesos 1849, 51 Bogota. 3.2258 grams.	700.00

Liberty head and "Nueva Granada." Rev. Value in wreath with B or P as mint marks.

82.	5 Pesos 1856, 57, 58. B mm.................*......	1000.00
83.	2 Pesos 1857, 58. P mm.	275.00
84.	1 Peso 1856, 58. B mm.	450.00

Liberty head and "Republica de la Nueva Granada." Rev. Arms with place of minting below.

85.	10 Pesos 1857, 58. Bogota...................*......	1000.00
86.	10 Pesos 1856, 57, 58. Popayan.....................	750.00

III. Coinage of the Granadine Confederation

Liberty head. Rev. Arms and place of minting.

87.	20 Pesos 1859. Bogota	5500.00
88.	10 Pesos 1859-61. Bogota...................*......	750.00
89.	10 Pesos 1858-62. Popayan	750.00
90.	5 Pesos 1859. Popayan	2500.00

Liberty head. Rev. Value in wreath.

91.	5 Pesos 1862. Medellin	Very Rare
92.	2 Pesos 1859, 60. Popayan ....*......	350.00
93.	1 Peso 1862. Medellin	600.00

IV. Coinage of the United States of Colombia

Liberty head with "Colombia" only in legend. Rev. Value and date in wreath. Medellin Mint.

94.	5 Pesos 1862, 63, 64.............................*......	5000.00
95.	1 Peso 1863, 64	1500.00

Liberty head with "Estados Unidos de Colombia" in legend. Rev. Value in wreath. Medellin Mint.

96.	5 Pesos 1863..................................*......	4000.00
97.	2 Pesos 1863.......................................	375.00
98.	1 Peso 1863..	200.00

Liberty head. Rev. Arms and place of minting.

99.	20 Pesos 1862-77. Bogota............................	1600.00
100.	20 Pesos 1862-75. Popayan	1500.00
101.	20 Pesos 1868-72. Medellin	1500.00
102.	10 Pesos 1862, 63. Bogota..........................	1000.00
103.	10 Pesos 1863-67. Popayan	700.00
104.	10 Pesos 1863-76. Medellin ....*......	700.00
105.	5 Pesos 1885. Medellin	2500.00
106.	2 Pesos 1871, 72, 76. Medellin.....................	175.00
107.	1 Peso 1872, 73. Medellin	150.00

Liberty head. Rev. Condor and place of minting.

108.	1 Peso 1872. Medellin	100.00
109.	1 Peso 1872-75. Bogota...................*......	100.00

V. Coinage of the Republic of Colombia (again)

Workman chipping at rock. Rev. Arms.

110.	5 Pesos 1913-19	100.00
111.	2½ Pesos 1913..	100.00

Large head of Bolivar. Rev. Arms.

112.	10	Pesos 1919-24	150.00
113.	5	Pesos 1919-24	100.00(B)
114.	2½	Pesos 1919, 20 ....*......	75.00

Small head of Bolivar. Rev. Arms.

115.	5	Pesos 1924-30 ....*......	100.00(B)
116.	2½	Pesos 1924-28	75.00

(Numbers 113 and 115 are bullion coins. The price listed is based on gold at $725 per ounce.)

For later issues of Colombia, see the section, "Recent Issues Starting With 1960."

COSTA RICA

Sun and five mountain peaks. Rev. Tree. The 4 Escudo piece of 1837 comes with or without a counterstamped 6-pointed star. The 1 Escudo piece comes with or without a counterstamped lion.

1.	8 Escudos 1828, 33, 37	3500.00
2.	4 Escudos 1828-49................................	1750.00
3.	2 Escudos 1828-50........................*......	500.00
4.	1 Escudo 1825-49.................................	300.00

Sun and three mountain peaks. Rev. Tree. With or without a counterstamped lion.

5.	½ Escudo 1825-49 (1825 rare).......................	175.00

Small star on larger radiant star. Rev. Tree.

6.	1 Escudo 1842.....................................	400.00

Indian leaning against column. Rev. Arms.

7.	½ Onza 1850 ....*......	750.00
8.	2 Escudos 1850-63................................	500.00
9.	1 Escudo 1850-55.................................	250.00
10.	½ Escudo 1850-64.................................	150.00

Arms. Rev. Value spelled out.

11.	10 Pesos 1870-72. Large size	600.00
11a.	10 Pesos 1876. Small size	2000.00
12.	5 Pesos 1867-70. Large size	350.00
13.	5 Pesos 1873, 75. Small size	1000.00
14.	2 Pesos 1866-68. Large size ....*	250.00
14a.	2 Pesos 1876. Small size	2000.00
15.	1 Peso 1864-68. Large size	150.00
16.	1 Peso 1871, 72. Small size	150.00

Arms. Rev. Value expressed in numerals.

17.	20 Pesos 1873	Rare
18.	5 Pesos 1873 ....*	4000.00

Head of Columbus. Rev. Arms.

19.	20 Colones 1897-1900	1100.00
20.	10 Colones 1897-1900 ....*	400.00
21.	5 Colones 1899, 1900	250.00
22.	2 Colones 1897-1928	110.00

For later issues of Costa Rica, see the section, "Recent Issues Starting With 1960."

COURLAND

Dukes of —

JAMES
Bust. Rev. Arms.

1.	1 Ducat 1646	4750.00

FREDERICK CASIMIR, 1682-1698

Bust. Rev. Eagle.

2.	1 Ducat 1689	3500.00

ERNEST JOHN
Bust. Rev. Arms.

3.	1 Ducat 1764	2000.00

PETER BIRON, 1769-1795

Head. Rev. Two shields.

4.	1 Ducat 1780	2000.00

CROATIA

*Head of the Duke of Aosta as king. Rev. Value over shield.
This coin was not placed in circulation. 170 pieces struck.*

1.	500 Kuna 1941	3500.00

CUBA

The coinage was struck at the Philadelphia Mint, and is without a mint mark. The 20 pesos of 1916 is extremely rare as proof specimens only were struck and only 10 are known. Cuban coinage is based on the U.S. gold standard.

Head of Marti. Rev. Arms.

1.	20 Pesos 1915	750.00
2.	20 Pesos 1916	40000.00
3.	10 Pesos 1915, 16	450.00
4.	5 Pesos 1915, 16 ....*	200.00
5.	4 Pesos 1915, 16 ....*	300.00
6.	2 Pesos 1915, 16 ....*	125.00
7.	1 Peso 1915, 16	450.00

For later issues, see the section, "Recent Issues Starting With 1960."

CURACAO

Gold coins of Brazil and Portugal with five round counter-stamps on Obv. — Gl, L, MH and B close to border, and GH in center. Rev. W stamped within a line circle.

1.	6400 Reis 1776. Rio mint	10000.00
2.	6400 Reis 1781	10000.00

CYPRUS

The gold coinage of Cyprus belongs to the series of the Crusader kings. Only two specimens are known of No. 1, and three of No. 5. It is believed that no more than 60 specimens are known of each of the others.

Kings of —

GUY DE LUSIGNAN, 1192-1194
King standing. Rev. Christ seated.

1.	1 Bezant ND	Very Rare

HUGH I, 1205-1218
King standing. Rev. Christ seated.

2.	1 Bezant ND	3250.00

HENRY I, 1218-1253
King standing. Rev. Christ seated.

3.	1 Bezant ND	3250.00

HUGH III, 1267-1284
King standing. Rev. Christ seated.

4.	1 Bezant ND	3250.00

JOHN I, 1284-1285
King standing. Rev. Christ seated.

5.	1 Bezant ND	Very Rare

CZECHOSLOVAKIA

(Formerly the ancient kingdom of Bohemia, which see).

*Half-length figure of St. Wenceslas. Rev. Shield. A special
1 Ducat piece, dated "1918-1923," was issued in 1923 to
commemorate the 5th anniversary of the Republic.*

1.	2 Ducats 1923-38, 51.........................*......	400.00
2.	1 Ducat 1923-38, 51.................................	135.00
3.	1 Ducat 1923. Serially numbered (from 1 to 1000) below the figure of St. Wenceslas	900.00

St. Wenceslas on horse. Rev. Shield.

4.	10 Ducats 1929-38, 51	2250.00
5.	5 Ducats 1929-38, 51.........................*......	1100.00

COMMEMORATIVES AND SPECIAL ISSUES

*Saint holding plow drawn by Devil. Rev. Arms. On the 10th
year of the Republic.*

6.	4 Ducats 1928 ....,.....	450.00
7.	2 Ducats 1928 ....*.......	300.00

*Standing figure with banner. Rev. Knight on horse. On the
1000th year of the introduction of Christianity into Bohemia.*

8.	5 Ducats 1929 ....*......	1250.00
9.	3 Ducats 1929	750.00
10.	1 Ducat 1929	375.00

Head of Dr. Miroslav Tyrs. Rev. Eagle. On the Sokol movement.

11.	1 Ducat 1932	350.00

Head of Dr. Antonin Svehla. Rev. Sower. Homage issue.

12.	1 Ducat 1933	350.00

*St. Catherine praying. Rev. Mining scenes. On the reopening
of the Kremnica Mines.*

13.	10 Ducats 1934 ....*......	6000.00
14.	5 Ducats 1934	3000.00
15.	2 Ducats 1934	1500.00
16.	1 Ducat 1934	500.00

*Bust of Wallenstein. Rev. Crowned shield. To commemorate
the ancient Wallenstein coinage.*

17.	10 Ducats 1934	Rare
18.	5 Ducats 1934	Rare

DANISH WEST INDIES

(Now the U.S. Virgin Islands.)

*Head of Christian IX of Denmark. Rev. Seated female. Two
values appear on these coins.*

1.	10 Daler—50 Francs 1904...........................	5500.00
2.	4 Daler—20 Francs 1904, 05.................*......	600.00

DANZIG

A. Polish Kings of —

SIGISMUND I, 1506-1548

Bust. Rev. City arms.

1.	1 Ducat 1546, 47, 48		1200.00

SIGISMUND II, 1548-1572

Bust right or left. Rev. City arms.

2.	1 Ducat 1549-58		1200.00

Bust. Rev. City arms.

3.	1 Ducat 1578-87		975.00

Christ standing. Rev. City arms.

4.	1 Siege Ducat 1577		1650.00

SIGISMUND III, 1587-1632

Bust. Rev. City arms.

4a.	15 Ducats 1614		15000.00
5.	10 Ducats 1613, 14		12000.00
6.	5 Ducats 1614, ND		7000.00
7.	4 Ducats 1617		1500.00
8.	3 Ducats 1617		1100.00
9.	2 Ducats 1619		750.00
10.	1 Ducat 1588-1632	*	400.00

LADISLAS IV, 1632-1648

Bust. Rev. City arms.

11.	4 Ducats 1640, 41	*	3500.00
12.	3 Ducats 1640, 41		1800.00
13.	2 Ducats 1634-47		1100.00
14.	1½ Ducats 1634, 47		1000.00
15.	1 Ducat 1633-48		750.00

Bust. Rev. City view.

16.	10 Ducats 1644, ND		4000.00
17.	8 Ducats 1644		3750.00
18.	6 Ducats ND		3750.00
19.	5 Ducats 1645		3750.00
20.	4 Ducats 1645		2500.00
21.	3 Ducats 1634-47	*	2250.00

JOHN CASIMIR, 1648-1668

Plain or crowned bust. Rev. City arms.

22.	2 Ducats 1652-58, ND	*	2500.00
23.	1½ Ducats 1661		1500.00
24.	1 Ducat 1649-68		925.00

Plain or crowned bust. Rev. City view.

25.	12 Ducats 1650		9000.00
26.	10 Ducats 1651		15000.00
27.	6 Ducats ND	*	4000.00
28.	5 Ducats 1654, 56, ND		2250.00
29.	4 Ducats 1650, ND		1650.00
30.	3 Ducats 1650, 58, ND		1650.00
31.	2 Ducats 1651		1100.00

MICHAEL KORYBUT, 1669-1673

Bust. Rev. City arms.

32. 1 Ducat 1670-73 .... 1100.00

Crowned bust. Rev. City view.

33. 3 Ducats ND 1850.00

JOHN SOBIESKI, 1674-1696

Plain or crowned bust. Rev. City arms.

34. 4 Ducats 1692 .... 3750.00
35. 2 Ducats 1692, ND 1850.00
36. 1 Ducat 1676-92 ....*...... 1100.00

Bust Rev. City view.

37. 5 Ducats ND 3750.00
38. 4 Ducats ND 2600.00
39. 3 Ducats ND 2000.00

AUGUST II OF SAXONY, 1697-1733

Bust. Rev. City arms.

40. 2 Ducats 1698 .... 2250.00
41. 1 Ducat 1698 ....*...... 975.00

AUGUST III OF SAXONY, 1733-1763
Bust. Rev. City arms.

42. 1 Ducat 1734 .... 1350.00

B. Free City of —

The 25 Gulden pieces of both 1923 and 1930 were struck in proof condition only. 1000 specimens were struck in 1923 and 4000 in 1930, but the later issue was not placed in circulation, and very few are known.

Neptune with trident. Rev. Arms between two columns.

43. 25 Gulden 1923 .... 4000.00

Neptune with trident. Rev. Arms supported by lions.

44. 25 Gulden 1930 .... 9000.00

DENMARK

It will be noted that some of the earlier coins are in imitation of English, German or Hungarian types.

Kings of —

(For additional coins of the Danish Kings, see under Norway).

HANS, 1481-1513

Ruler on throne. Rev. Arms.

1. 3 Nobles 1496 ....*...... Rare
2. 2 Nobles 1502 .... Rare
3. 1 Noble 1496, 1502 .... Rare

Ruler standing. Rev. Triple lion shield.

4. 1 Goldgulden ND .... Rare
5. ½ Goldgulden ND .... Rare

CHRISTIAN II, 1513-1523
Ruler on throne. Rev. Arms.

6. 1 Noble 1516, 18 .... Rare

Ruler standing. Rev. Triple lion shield.

7. 1 Goldgulden ND, Square .... Rare

Ruler on throne. Rev. Crowned shield. Posthumously struck in 1535 and 1536.

8. 2 Goldgulden ND ....*...... Rare
9. 1 Goldgulden ND .... Rare

FREDERICK I, 1523-1533

Ruler standing. Rev. Four shields around central shield.

10. 1 Goldgulden 1527 .... Rare

Small crowned bust. Rev. Triple lion shield.

11.	1 Goldgulden 1531.................................	Rare

Busts of the King and Queen. Rev. Arms.

12.	1 Noble 1532...	Rare

Ruler on throne. Rev. Arms.

13.	1 Noble ND	Rare

St. Andrew standing with cross. Rev. Cross of shields. Struck for Schleswig.

14.	1 Goldgulden 1531, ND............................	Rare

CHRISTIAN III, 1534-1559

Crowned head. Rev. Arms.

15.	1 Goldgulden 1557.................................	Rare

Cross of arms. Rev. Orb in circle. Struck for Schleswig.

16.	1 Goldgulden ND...................................	Rare

St. Andrew standing with cross. Rev. Cross of shields. Struck for Schleswig.

17.	2 Goldgulden 1546................................		Rare
18.	1 Goldgulden 1536, 46, ND	*	Rare

FREDERICK II, 1559-1588
Crowned F. Rev. Value.

19.	1 Goldgulden 1563. Square	6000.00
20.	1 Krone 1563. Square..............................	Rare

Crowned F. Rev. Fortuna standing on globe.

21.	1 Goldgulden 1563. Crudely shaped................	4000.00

Arms. Rev. Value.

22.	1 Ducat 1564. Square..............................	5000.00
23.	1 Krone 1564. Square..............................	6000.00
24.	1 Goldgulden 1564. Square	Rare

FS monogram crowned. Rev. Value.

25.	1 Portugaloser 1584		Rare
26.	1 Rosenoble 1584.............................	*	Rare
27.	2 Ducats 1584...................................		Rare
28.	1 Angelot 1584		Rare
29.	1 Krone 1584		Rare
30.	1 Goldgulden 1584.............................	*	Rare
31.	1 Hungarian Gulden 1584.........................		Rare

CHRISTIAN IV 1588-1648
Ruler standing. Rev. Arms.

32.	1 Goldgulden 1591, 92, 93, 1607, 08..........	5000.00

Ruler standing. Rev. Triple lion shield.

33.	1 Goldgulden 1603, 07, 08, 11...............	*	3000.00
34.	1 Ducat 1637		Rare

Ruler standing. Rev. Thirteen shields around central arms.

35.	3 Goldgulden 1608...............................		Rare
36.	2 Goldgulden 1608.........................	*	Rare

Ruler standing. Rev. Legend in square.

37.	1 Ducat 1640, 42, 46..............................	4000.00

Ruler standing. Rev. Hebrew legend.

38.	2 Ducats 1644, 45, 46, 48	......................*	3500.00
39.	1 Ducat 1644, 45, 46, 47, 48	....	1200.00
40.	½ Ducat 1644, 45, 46, 47	....	1500.00
41.	¼ Ducat 1646, 47, 48	....	1200.00

Ruler standing. Rev. C4 crowned.

42.	¼ Ducat ND	....	Rare

Ruler standing. Rev. Legend below pair of spectacles.

42a.	½ Ducat 1647	....	2500.00
42b.	¼ Ducat 1647	....	Rare

Large crowned bust. Rev. Triple lion shield.

43.	1 Goldgulden 1604-32	....	2500.00

Crowned bust. Rev. Value.

44.	8 Daler 1604. Square	....	8000.00
45.	6 Daler 1604. Square	.........................*	8000.00
46.	4 Daler 1604. Square	....	Rare
47.	3 Daler 1604. Square	....	Rare

Large crowned bust. Rev. Elephant.

48.	1 Rosenoble 1611-29	....	10000.00
49.	½ Rosenoble 1611	....	Rare

Plain bust. Rev. Two figures holding crown over arms and C4.

50.	Gold coin, 22.64 Grams ND	....	Rare
51.	Gold coin, 10.75 Grams ND	....	Rare
52.	Gold coin, 8.1 Grams ND	....	Rare

Crowned bust. Rev. Similar to above.

53.	Gold coin, 4.65 Grams ND	....	Rare

Triple lion shield. Rev. Crown.

54.	2 Kroner 1619-48	...........................*	4000.00
55.	1 Krone 1619	....	Rare
56.	½ Krone 1619	....	2000.00

C4 crowned. Rev. Arms.

57.	2 Ducats 1627	....	Rare
58.	1 Ducat 1627	....	Rare

C4 crowned. Rev. Legend below pair of spectacles.

58a.	1 Ducat 1647	....	Rare
59.	½ Ducat 1647	....	4000.00
60.	¼ Ducat 1647, ND	....	Rare

Large cross. Rev. Arms.

61.	2 Portugalosers 1592	....	Rare
62.	1 Portugaloser 1591, 92	....	Rare
63.	½ Portugaloser 1591, 92, 93	....	Rare
64.	¼ Portugaloser 1592, 93	....................*	Rare

Ruler on throne. Rev. Arms.

65.	1 Portugaloser 1603	....	Rare

Ruler standing. Rev. Fortuna on globe. Struck for Gluckstadt.

66.	1 Portugaloser 1623	....	Rare

Large cross. Rev. Crowned heart.

67.	¼ Portugaloser 1629	....	Rare

Ruler on horse. Rev. Arms.

68.	1 Portugaloser ND	....	Rare

Large bust. Rev. Ruler on horse in circle of shields.

69.	1 Portugaloser ND	....	Rare
70.	½ Portugaloser ND	....	Rare

FREDERICK III, 1648-1670

Laureate bust. Rev. Vase with flowers.

71.	5 Ducats 1648. Square	....	Rare
72.	4 Ducats 1648. Square	....	Rare
73.	3 Ducats 1648. Square	....	Rare
74.	2 Ducats 1648. Square	....	5000.00
75.	1 Ducat 1648. Square	.......................*	2500.00
76.	½ Ducat 1648. Square	....	1500.00

Laureate bust. Rev. Legend in circle.

77.	1 Ducat 1649, 50, 51, 53	....................*	2000.00
78.	½ Ducat 1652	....	3000.00

Laureate bust. Rev. Fortuna on globe.

79.	1 Ducat 1660-69	3000.00

Laureate bust. Rev. Arms.

80.	1 Portugaloser 1666	Rare
81.	5 Ducats 1665	Rare
82.	1 Ducat 1667, 68, 69 ....*	3000.00
83.	1 Krone 1667	Unknown

Laureate bust. Rev. Large crown.

84.	5 Ducats 1665, 66	Rare
85.	3 Ducats 1667	Rare
86.	2 Ducats 1657	Rare
87.	2 Kroner 1666 ....*	Rare
88.	1 Krone 1666	3000.00

Laureate bust. Rev. Small oval arms on cross.

89.	2 Portugalosers 1666	Rare
90.	½ Portugaloser 1665, 67	Rare
91.	12 Ducats 1665	Rare

Laureate bust. Rev. Crown and value.

92.	18 Marks 1668	3000.00

Laureate bust. Rev. Three shields on cross within circle of shields.

93.	2 Portugalosers ND...............................	Rare
94.	10 Ducats 1669. Thick	Rare

Laureate head. Rev. Double cross formed by F3 monogram.

95.	2 Ducats 1670	4000.00

Laureate bust. Rev. Crown and orb between sceptre and sword.

96.	2 Ducats ND	3500.00

Crowned bust. Rev. Square formed by four F's. The diameter of these coins is the same, the value being determined by the thickness and corresponding weight.

97.	10 Ducats 1653...................................	Rare
98.	5 Ducats 1653, 62	Rare
99.	3 Ducats 1662	Rare
100.	2 Ducats 1653, 62	Rare
101.	1 Ducat 1653-66, ND ....*	2000.00
102.	½ Ducat 1659, 64	1200.00
103.	¼ Ducat 1660, 64	1000.00

Laureate head. Rev. Similar to above.

104.	1 Ducat 1664, 67	2000.00

Crowned bust. Rev. Circle of shields around central arms.

105.	1 Portugaloser 1653, 55, 56	Rare
106.	½ Portugaloser 1653, 55, 57, 61	10000.00
107.	3 Ducats 1661	Rare

Crowned bust. Rev. Cross of crowned F's.

108.	1 Ducat 1653	Rare

Crowned bust. Rev. Three shields on crowned cross.

109.	1 Ducat 1669, 70	2000.00

Crowned bust. Rev. Ship.

110.	4 Ducats 1657, 58, 64 ....*	Rare
111.	3 Ducats 1666, 67	Rare
112.	2 Ducats 1657-67	3000.00

Crowned bust. Rev. Crowned shield on cross.

113.	1 Portugaloser 1662, 63, 64		Rare
114.	½ Portugaloser 1663, 64		Rare
115.	5 Ducats 1662	*	Rare
116.	4 Ducats 1663		Rare
117.	2 Ducats 1662, 63		3500.00

Crowned bust. Rev. View of Fort Aggershus.

| 118. | 1 Portugaloser ND | | Rare |

Triple lion shield. Rev. Crown.

| 119. | 2 Kroner 1657, 59 | | Rare |
| 120. | 1 Krone 1655, 57, 59, 60 | * | 3500.00 |

Triple lion shield. Rev. Crowned F3 over lion.

| 121. | ½ Portugaloser 1658 | | Rare |

Crowned F3. Rev. Sword cutting off hand reaching for crown.

122.	2 Portugalosers 1659		Rare
123.	1 Portugaloser 1659	*	8000.00
124.	½ Portugaloser 1659		6000.00
125.	6 Ducats 1659		Rare
126.	4 Ducats 1659		6000.00
127.	3 Ducats 1659		Rare

Crowned F3. Rev. Value.

| 128. | 6 Marks 1669 | | 1500.00 |
| 129. | 3 Marks 1665, 68, 70 | | 1000.00 |

Crown over double F3 monogram. Rev. Arms.

| 130. | ¼ Ducat 1670 | | 1000.00 |

Crossed sword and sceptre between crown and orb. Rev. Cross of St. Andrew.

| 131. | 1 Portugaloser 1663 | | Rare |
| 132. | 6 Ducats 1663 | | Rare |

CHRISTIAN V, 1670-1699

Crowned bust. Rev. Three crowns over triple C5 monogram.

| 133. | 2 Ducats 1673 | | Rare |
| 134. | 1 Ducat 1672, 73, 74, 76 | * | 3000.00 |

Laureate bust. Rev. Crowned C5 monogram.

135.	5 Ducats 1692		Rare
136.	2 Ducats 1670, 92, 94, ND	*	3500.00
137.	1 Ducat 1672-94, ND		Unknown
138.	½ Ducat 1675		2000.00
139.	¼ Ducat 1675		Unknown

Laureate bust. Rev. Three shields on cross.

| 140. | 1 Ducat 1671-74 | | 3000.00 |

Laureate bust. Rev. Three crowns over triple C5 monogram.

| 141. | 1 Ducat 1679, 80, 85 | | 2500.00 |

Laureate bust. Rev. C's and 5's around radiate triangle.

142.	5 Ducats 1692		Rare
143.	2 Ducats 1692, 94	*	3000.00
144.	1 Ducat 1694		1500.00

Laureate bust. Rev. Long cross over arms.

| 145. | 1 Ducat 1692 | | 2000.00 |

Laureate bust. Rev. Six crowns around C5 monograms.

| 146. | 2 Ducats ND | | Rare |

Armored bust. Rev. Crowned arms.

| 147. | 1 Ducat 1681, 83 | | 3000.00 |

Bust. Rev. Fortress.

148.	1 Ducat 1682	....	2500.00

Long haired bust. Rev. Arms in circle of shields.

149.	10 Ducats 1691	....	Rare
150.	5 Ducats 1687	....	Rare
151.	3 Ducats 1687	....	Rare
152.	2 Ducats 1687	....	4000.00
153.	1 Ducat 1687, ND	.........................*......	3000.00

Long haired bust. Rev. Crowned oval arms.

154.	2 Ducats 1691	....	Rare
155.	1 Ducat 1691, 92	.........................*......	2000.00

Long haired bust. Rev. Triple C5 monogram.

156.	1 Ducat 1691, 92, 93, 96, ND	....	2000.00

Bust. Rev. Large crown.

157.	10	Ducats 1693, 96	....	Rare
158.	3	Ducats 1694	....	Rare
159.	2½	Ducats 1696	....	Rare
160.	2	Ducats 1693, 94, 96	....	3000.00
161.	1	Ducat 1693, 94, 96	...............*......	1200.00
162.	½	Ducat 1694, 96	....	1000.00
163.	¼	Ducat 1694	....	Rare

Bust. Rev. Legend. From gold of the Kongsberg Mines.

164.	2 Ducats 1697	...........................*......	Rare
165.	1 Ducat 1697	....	Rare

Helmited bust. Rev. View of Fort Christiansborg in Guinea, Africa.

166.	4 Ducats 1688	....	Rare
167.	2 Ducats 1688	...........................*......	3000.00
168.	1 Ducat 1688	....	3000.00

Bust. Rev. Ship in Christiansborg harbor.

169.	2 Ducats 1699	...........................*......	4000.00
170.	1 Ducat 1699	....	2000.00

Laureate head. Rev. Elephant.

171.	3 Ducats 1678	....	Rare
172.	2 Ducats 1673	...........................*......	Rare

Laureate head. Rev. Value and date.

173.	3 Marks (¼ Ducat) 1676	....	1500.00

Laureate head. Rev. Six crowns around C5 monograms. The Rev. is shown.

174.	3 Ducats 1678	....	Rare
175.	2 Ducats 1678	...........................*......	Rare

Ruler standing. Rev. Fortuna on globe.

176.	1 Ducat 1682	....	4000.00

Ruler standing. Rev. C5 monogram crowned.

177.	10 Ducats ND	....	Rare

Ruler on horse. Rev. Elephant.

178.	3 Ducats 1673	....	Rare
179.	2 Ducats 1673	....	Rare

Ruler on horse. Rev. Crowned circular arms.

180.	1 Rider 1696 ....*	Unknown
181.	2 Ducats 1696, ND	Rare
182.	1 Ducat 1696	1500.00
183.	½ Ducat 1696	1200.00

Ruler on horse. Rev. Triple C5 monogram.

184.	4 Ducats ND	Rare
185.	2 Ducats ND	Rare
186.	1 Ducat 1692, ND..........................*	1500.00
187.	½ Ducat ND	Rare

Ruler on horse. Rev. Conjoined knight and lion. Without any legends.

188.	2½ Ducats ND	Rare
189.	1 Ducat ND.................................	Rare
190.	½ Ducat ND.............................	5000.00

Ruler on horse. Rev. Double C5 monogram. Without any legends.

191.	2 Ducats ND	2000.00
192.	1 Ducat ND.................................	1000.00
193.	½ Ducat ND.................................	Rare

Ruler on horse. Rev. Six crowns around C5 monograms. Without any legends.

194.	4 Ducats ND	Rare
195.	2 Ducats ND	Rare
196.	1½ Ducats ND	Rare

Crown over C5. Rev. Elephant.

197.	4 Ducats 1683	Rare
198.	2 Ducats 1673 ....*	4000.00
199.	1½ Ducats 1673	Rare
200.	1 Ducat 1673	Rare

Crown over double C5 monogram. Rev. Crowned arms.

201.	1 Ducat 1691	2000.00

Crown over initials. Rev. Value and date.

202.	3 Marks (¼ Ducat) 1675	800.00

Six crowns around C5 monograms. Rev. Elephant.

203.	3 Ducats 1673	Rare

Pyramid with or without base. Rev. View of Copenhagen harbor. On the king's death.

204.	2 Ducats ND ....*	3000.00
205.	1 Ducat ND.....................................	1500.00

FREDERICK IV, 1699-1730

Bust. Rev. Bust of Christian V. Coronation coins struck in 1699. The indicated 3 Ducat piece is 28 millimetres, all the others are 21 millimetres and of varying thickness, the value being determined by weight.

206.	4 Ducats ND	Rare
207.	3 Ducats ND (size 21)	Rare
208.	3 Ducats ND (size 28)	Rare
209.	2 Ducats ND	3500.00
210.	1 Ducat ND..............................*	1500.00

Bust. Rev. Three shields and three monograms around star.

211.	2 Ducats 1708, 09	Rare
212.	1 Ducat 1708, 09, ND......................*	2000.00

Bust. Rev. Three shields and three monograms around radiate triangle.

213.	10 Ducats 1699	Rare
214.	5 Ducats 1699, 1700............................	Rare
215.	4¾ Ducats, 1699	Rare
216.	2 Ducats 1708	Unknown
217.	1 Ducat 1708, 09, ND	Unknown

Bust. Rev. Crown over MDA, and below "Christiansborg."

218.	18 Marks 1701	Rare

Bust. Rev. Large crown and value (for the "Rixdalers").

219.	1 Ducat 1705, 06...........................*	2000.00
220.	4 Rixdaler (2 Courant Ducats) 1714	Rare
221.	2 Rixdaler (1 Courant Ducat) 1714, 15, 16	1000.00
222.	1 Rixdaler (½ Courant Ducat) 1715	800.00

Bust. Rev. Crowned arms in wreath.

223.	2 Ducats 1709	Rare
224.	1 Ducat 1709, 23, 26......................*	2000.00
225.	½ Ducat 1719	Rare

Bust. Rev. Crowned circular arms.

226.	1 Ducat 1718, 19	.....	4000.00
227.	½ Ducat 1710, 19	.....*	1000.00

Bust. Rev. Double F4 monogram.

228.	3 Ducats 1700	.....*	Rare
229.	2 Ducats 1701, 04	.....	3000.00
230.	1 Ducat 1700, ND	.....	1000.00
231.	½ Ducat ND	.....	Unknown
232.	¼ Ducat ND	.....	Rare

Ruler on horse. Rev. Cross of three shields and three monograms.

233.	2 Ducats ND	.....	Rare
234.	1 Ducat 1702, ND	.....*	1500.00
235.	½ Ducat ND	.....	Rare
236.	¼ Ducat ND	.....	Unknown

Ruler on horse. Rev. Arms.

237.	2 Ducats 1710, 11	.....*	Rare
238.	1 Ducat 1710, 11	.....	1000.00

Ruler on horse. Rev. Double F4 monogram.

239.	2 Ducats ND	.....	Rare
240.	1 Ducat ND	.....	Rare
241.	½ Ducat ND	.....	Rare
242.	¼ Ducat ND	.....	Rare

Bust. Rev. View of Fort Christiansborg.

243.	2 Ducats 1701, 04	.....	5000.00
244.	1 Ducat 1701, 02, 04, 08, 25, ND	.....	1500.00

Bust. Rev. Fortress and ship at Christiansborg.

245.	1 Ducat 1701	.....	2500.00

Bust. Rev. Ship and radiate sun, and below, "Christiansborg".

246.	5 Ducats 1704	.....	7000.00

Bust. Rev. Radiate sun over ship and below, "SOC. IND. OCC." (The Danish West Indies Company).

247.	2 Ducats 1708	.....	4000.00

CHRISTIAN VI, 1730-1746

Double C6 monogram. Rev. Fortress at Christiansborg.

248.	1 Ducat 1730, 38, 40	.....	1200.00

Bust. Rev. Arms on cross.

249.	1 Ducat 1732	.....	1500.00

Bust. Rev. Bust of Frederick IV.

250.	1 Ducat 1730	.....	Rare

FREDERICK V, 1746-1766

Bust. Rev. Bust of Christian VI. Coronation coins struck in 1746.

251.	2 Ducats ND	.....	3000.00
252.	1 Ducat ND	.....	2000.00

Bust. Rev. Crowned arms with ornaments and below, "EX AURO SINICO". Struck from Chinese gold.

253.	2 Ducats 1746	.....	3000.00
254.	1 Ducat 1746	.....*	2000.00

Laureate head. Rev. Type as above. Struck from Chinese gold.

255.	2 Ducats 1746	.....	Rare
256.	1 Ducat 1746	.....	2000.00

Bust. Rev. Ancient galley with banner. Struck from Chinese gold.

257.	2 Ducats 1746	.....	2500.00
258.	1 Ducat 1746	.....*	2000.00

Laureate head. Rev. Type as above. Struck from Chinese gold.

259.   1 Ducat 1746 ....   Rare

Bust. Rev. Crowned oval arms.

260.   2 Ducats 1747 ....   3000.00

Bust. Rev. Draped arms and below "EBEN EZER".

261.   1 Ducat 1758 ....   1200.00

Bust in helmet. Rev. Crown and value.

262.   12 Marks 1757, 58 ....   500.00

Laureate head. Rev. Fortress and ship at Christiansborg.

263.   2 Ducats 1746 ....   Rare
264.   1 Ducat 1746 ....*......   1200.00

Laureate head. Rev. Crowned oval arms.

265.   2 Ducats 1747 ....   2500.00
266.   1 Ducat 1747 ....   1500.00

Laureate head. Rev. Ship.

267.   2 Ducats 1753 ....   Rare
268.   1 Ducat 1753, 54, 56 ....*......   1500.00

Head. Rev. Crown and value.

269.   12 Marks 1757-65 ....   300.00

Ruler standing. Rev. Crowned oval arms.

270.   2 Ducats 1747 ....   2500.00
271.   1 Ducat 1747 ....*......   1500.00

Ruler standing. Rev. Fortress at Christiansborg.

272.   2 Ducats 1747 ....   2500.00
273.   1 Ducat 1747 ....*......   1500.00

Ruler on horse. Rev. Embellished arms with initials DWC for Danish West Indies Company.

274.   2 Ducats 1749 ....*......   Rare
275.   1 Ducat 1749 ....   1500.00

Ruler on horse. Rev. Double F5 monogram.

276.   2 Ducats 1748 ....   Rare
277.   1 Ducat 1748 ....*......   1000.00

F's and V's around triangle. Rev. Crown and value.

278.   12 Marks 1757, 63 ....   450.00

CHRISTIAN VII, 1766-1808

Bust. Rev. Crowned C7 monograms around triangle.

279.   1 Christian d'or 1775, ND 2000.00

Bust. Rev. "29 Januarii" in wreath.

280.   1 Ducat 1771 ....   1500.00

Bust. Rev. Crown and value.

281.   12 Marks 1781, 82, 83, 85 ....   1000.00

Wild man standing. Rev. Legend in square.

282.   1 Ducat 1771 .... 2000.00

Wild man standing. Rev. Value, weight and fineness in square tablet.

283.   1 Species Ducat 1791, 92, 94, 1802 .... 1000.00

FREDERICK VI, 1808-1839

Head. Rev. Value.

284.   2 Frederick d'or 1826, 27 .... 2500.00
285.   1 Frederick d'or 1827 .... *   2500.00

Head. Rev. Arms flanked by value.

286.   2 Frederick d'or 1828-36 .... 2000.00
287.   1 Frederick d'or 1828-38 .... 1500.00

Head. Rev. Arms supported by wild men.

288.   2 Frederick d'or 1836, 37, 38, 39 .... 2000.00

CHRISTIAN VIII, 1839-1848

Head. Rev. Arms supported by wild men.

289.   2 Christian d'or 1841-47 .... 2000.00
290.   1 Christian d'or 1843-47 .... *   2000.00

FREDERICK VII, 1848-1863

Head. Rev. Arms supported by wild men.

291.   2 Frederick d'or 1850-63 ....* 2000.00
292.   1 Frederick d'or 1853 .... 3000.00

CHRISTIAN IX, 1863-1906

Head. Rev. Arms supported by wild men.

293.   2 Christian d'or 1866, 67, 69, 70 ....* 2500.00
294.   1 Christian d'or 1869 .... 3000.00

Head. Rev. Seated female.

295.   20 Kroner 1873-1900 ....* 225.00
296.   10 Kroner 1873-1900 .... 225.00

FREDERICK VIII, 1906-1912

Head. Rev. Arms.

297.   20 Kroner 1908-12 ....* 200.00
298.   10 Kroner 1908, 09 .... 200.00

CHRISTIAN X, 1912-1947

Head. Rev. Arms.

299.   20 Kroner 1913-17 ....* 225.00
300.   10 Kroner 1913, 17 .... 235.00

DOMINICAN REPUBLIC

Head of Trujillo. Rev. Arms. On the 25th year of his rule.

1.   30 Pesos 1955 .... 700.00

For later issues of the Dominican Republic, see the section "Recent Issues Starting With 1960."

ECUADOR

Mints: —Quito and Birmingham. The unique 50 Franc piece of 1862 was discovered in 1956.

Liberty head. Rev. Sun over two mountain peaks. Issued while Ecuador was part of Colombia.

1.	2 Escudos 1833-35.................................	600.00
2.	1 Escudo 1833-35..................................	300.00

Liberty head. Rev. Sun and Zodiac over three mountain peaks.

3.	8 Escudos 1838-43................................	2000.00
4.	4 Escudos 1836-41.........................*......	1250.00

Head of Bolivar to right. Rev. Arms.

5.	8 Escudos 1844 .... Unknown

Larger head of Bolivar to left. Rev. Flag-draped arms, the poles showing below.

6.	8 Escudos 1845	3000.00

Type as above but the flagpoles do not show below the arms.

7.	8 Escudos 1845	3750.00

Head of Bolivar. Rev. Flag-draped oval arms.

8.	8 Escudos 1847-56.................................	3500.00

Head of Bolivar. Rev. Arms.

9.	50 Francs 1862 .... Unique

Head of General Sucre. Rev. Arms.

10.	10 Sucres 1899, 1900	350.00

Head of Bolivar. Rev. Arms.

11.	1 Condor 1928.....................................	300.00

EGYPT

NOTE: Some numbers have been changed from previous editions.

A. French Occupation of —

Toughra and accession date 1203 in Arabic (1789 A.D.). Rev. Arab legend and regnal year 13 or Arabic letter B (for Bonaparte). Struck during the rule of Selim III following Napoleon's invasion of Egypt.

1.	1 Sequin. Size 21 millimetres...............*......	90.00
2.	½ Sequin. Size 19 millimetres...............*......	400.00
3.	¼ Sequin. Size 17 millimetres.....................	80.00

B. Turkish Sultans —

(Earlier coins were of the same types as those of Turkey).

MAHMUD II, 1808-1839

Toughra. Rev. Dates and Mint. Coin bears the accession date 1223 and regnal year in Arabic numerals.

4.	100 Piastres. Years 30-31 (1837-38)	600.00
4a.	20 Piastres. Years 29-32 (1836-39)	250.00
4b.	10 Piastres. Years 29-30 (1836-37)	225.00
4c.	5 Piastres. Years 29-32 (1836-39)	200.00

ABDUL MEJID, 1839-1861

Toughra and value in plain field. Rev. Legend and date. All coins bear the accession date 1255 in Arabic numerals in addition to other Arabic numerals for the regnal year, which indicate the precise date of coinage.

5.	100 Piastres. Years 1-17 (1839-55)...... *		225.00
6.	50 Piastres. Years 1-16 (1839-54).............		200.00
7.	20 Piastres. Year 1 (1839)...................		300.00
8.	10 Piastres...............................		Unknown
9.	5 Piastres. Year 1-23 (1839-61).............		125.00

ABDUL AZIZ, 1861-1876

Same type as above. All coins bear the accession date 1277 in Arabic numerals in addition to other Arabic numerals for the regnal year, which indicate the precise date of coinage.

10.	500 Piastres. Years 8-15 (1868-75).............		15000.00
11.	100 Piastres. Years 2-16 (1862-76).............		275.00
12.	100 Piastres. Year 4 (1864). No Flower on Obverse .... *		750.00
13.	50 Piastres. Years 11-16 (1871-76)............		300.00
14.	25 Piastres. Years 8-15 (1868-75)............		150.00
15.	10 Piastres. Years 10-14 (1870-74)............		100.00
16.	5 Piastres. Years 3-15 (1863-75).............		75.00

Same type as preceding coins but bearing the toughra of Murad V and accession date 1293 (not to be confused with the next ruler's coins which bear the same accession date).

17.	100 Piastres. Year 1 (1876)...................		1500.00
18.	50 Piastres. Year 1 (1876)...................		1500.00

ABDUL HAMID, 1876-1909

Same type as above. All coins bear the accession date 1293 in Arabic numerals in addition to other Arabic numerals for the regnal year, which indicate the precise date of coinage. Only seven pieces were reported struck of number 18.

19.	500 Piastres. Year 1, 6 (1876, 81)		4000.00
19a.	100 Piastres. Year 8 (1883).................		350.00
20.	5 Piastres. Years 2-7 (1877-82).............		100.00

Toughra in lobed floral circle, value below. Rev. Legend and date. On larger flan than the preceding 100 Piastre pieces.

21.	100 Piastres. Year 12 (1888)..................		100.00
22.	10 Piastres. Years 17-34 (1891-1908)..........		90.00
23.	5 Piastres. Years 16-34 (1890-1908)..........		75.00

C. Independent Sultans —

HUSEIN KAMIL, 1915-1917

Arab legend. Rev. Value and date in English.

24.	100 Piastres 1916....................................	225.00

D. Kings of —

FUAD, 1917-1936

Civilian bust to right. Rev. Legend.

25.	500 Piastres 1922. Red gold		2000.00
26.	500 Piastres 1922. Yellow gold.....................		1700.00
27.	100 Piastres 1922. Red gold................... *		175.00
28.	100 Piastres 1922. Yellow gold.....................		165.00
29.	50 Piastres 1923-29		150.00
30.	20 Piastres 1923-29		80.00

Military bust to left. Rev. Legend.

31.	500 Piastres 1929-32 .... *		1750.00
32.	100 Piastres 1929, 30		200.00
33.	50 Piastres 1929, 30		125.00
34.	20 Piastres 1929, 30		100.00

FAROUK, 1937-1952

Military bust. Rev. Legend.

35.	500 Piastres 1938	2000.00
36.	100 Piastres 1938	185.00
37.	50 Piastres 1938 ......*	165.00
38.	20 Piastres 1938	125.00

E. Republic of (1953-1958) —

Ancient chariot and small Arabic date 1952. Rev. Legend and dates 1955 and 1374 in Arabic. On the Flight of Farouk and the formation of the Republic in 1952.

39.	5 Pounds 1955. Yellow gold	900.00
40.	1 Pound 1955. Yellow gold ....*	200.00
41.	5 Pounds 1957. Red gold	900.00
42.	1 Pound 1957. Red gold	200.00

F. United Arab Republic (1958-1971) —

Same design as coin numbers 39-42 above.

| 43. | ½ Pound 1958 | 115.00 |

For later issues of Egypt, see the section, "Recent Issues Starting With 1960."

ESTHONIA (REVAL)

Swedish Rulers of —

CHRISTINA, 1632-1654

Bust. Rev. City shield.

| 1. | 1 Ducat 1650 | 7000.00 |

CHARLES XI, 1660-1697

Bust. Rev. Arms.

2.	5 Ducats 1664-81	Rare
3.	4 Ducats 1664-81	Rare
4.	2 Ducats 1664-81	Rare
5.	1 Ducat 1664-81 ....*	7000.00

ETHIOPIA

The coins of the Axumite Kings of Ethiopia of about 300 A.D. are the earliest coins that appear in this book. This historical but little known coinage has been listed here since these coins are not included in the standard reference works on ancient coins. The ancient Kingdom of Axum was under Pagan rule until the period of Ousanas I, who converted to Christianity about 350 A.D.

A. Axumite Kings of —

ENDYBIS, ABOUT 300 A.D.

Helmeted bust on each side.

| 1. | ½ Aureus ND | 550.00 |

AFILAS, ABOUT 300 A.D.

Crowned bust. Rev. Helmeted bust.

| 2. | ½ Aureus ND | 400.00 |

Helmeted bust. Rev. Legend.

| 3. | 1/10 Aureus ND | 500.00 |

(Type: — The coins of the following kings of Axum are all of the same type and show a crowned bust on the obverse, and a helmeted bust on the reverse.)

OUSANAS I, ABOUT 350 A.D.

| 4. | ⅓ Solidus ND | 400.00 |

WAZEBA, ABOUT 375 A.D.

| 5. | ⅓ Solidus ND | Rare |

EZANAS AND/OR EZANA, ABOUT 400 A.D.

| 6. | ⅓ Solidus ND | 400.00 |

ANAFEON, ABOUT 500 A.D.

7. ⅓ Solidus ND 400.00

ESBEL OR ESBENA, ABOUT 550 A.D.

8. ⅓ Solidus ND 500.00

CALEB, ABOUT 575 A.D.

9. ⅓ Solidus ND 500.00

NEZANA, ABOUT 600 A.D.

10. ⅓ Solidus ND 600.00

OUSANAS II, ABOUT 600 A.D.

11. ⅓ Solidus ND .... Rare

OUSAS, ABOUT 600 A.D.

12. ⅓ Solidus ND 400.00

ALALMIRYIS, ABOUT 650 A.D.

13. ⅓ Solidus ND .... Rare

ELLA GABAZ, ABOUT 700 A.D.

14. ⅓ Solidus ND 600.00

JOEL, ABOUT 700 A.D.

15. ⅓ Solidus ND 600.00

ISRAEL, ABOUT 750 A.D.

16. ⅓ Solidus ND 400.00

JATHLIA, ABOUT 750 A.D.

17. ⅓ Solidus ND 600.00

GERSEM, ABOUT 850 A.D.

18. ⅓ Solidus ND 600.00

B. Modern Emperors of —

MENELIK II, 1889-1913

Crowned bust. Rev. Lion of Judah. Posthumously struck in 1916.

19.	2 Warks ND		1750.00
20.	1 Wark ND	*	750.00
21.	½ Wark ND		450.00
22.	¼ Wark ND		300.00
23.	⅛ Wark ND		200.00

EMPRESS ZAUDITU, 1916-1930

Crowned bust. Rev. Lion of Judah.

24.	4 Warks ND. Size 31 millimetres		3500.00
25.	2 Warks ND. Size 25 millimetres	*	2000.00
26.	1 Wark ND. Size 20 millimetres		1100.00

HAILE SELASSIE, 1930-1936 AND 1941-1974
Bust facing. Rev. Arms.

27. 4 Warks 1930 .... 1000.00

Head. Rev. St. George slaying dragon.

28.	1 Wark 1931	1800.00
29.	½ Wark 1931	900.00

For later issues of Ethiopia, see the section, "Recent Issues Starting With 1960."

FINLAND

A. Coinage under the Czars of Russia

Crowned eagle. Rev. Value. Struck under different Czars as indicated.

1.	20 Markkaa 1878-80. Alexander II	*	450.00
2.	20 Markkaa 1891. Alexander III		750.00
3.	20 Markkaa 1903, 04, 10-13. Nicholas II		375.00
4.	10 Markkaa 1878, 79. Alexander II	*	350.00
5.	10 Markkaa 1881, 82. Alexander III		325.00
6.	10 Markkaa 1904, 05, 13. Nicholas II		325.00

B. Coinage of the Republic

Lion. Rev. Value.

7.	200 Markkaa 1926	*	2250.00
8.	100 Markkaa 1926		1500.00

FRANCE

Additional coins of the French Kings will be found under some of the Italian States over which France had suzerainty.

Mints and mint marks:

A	mm for Paris	1610-1939
AA	mm for Metz	1693-1783
B	mm for Rouen	1610-1857
BB	mm for Strasbourg	1682-1870
C	mm for Saint Lô	1610-1656
C	mm for Caen	1694-1772
Ɔ	mm for Besançon	1694-1772
CC-CL	mm for Genoa (Italy)	1805-1811-1814
D	mm for Lyon	1610-1858
E	mm for Tours	1615-1774
F	mm for Angers	1610-1661
G	mm for Poitiers	1610-1772
H	mm for La Rochelle	1611-1837
I	mm for Limoges	1612-1837
K	mm for Bordeaux	1610-1878
L	mm for Bayonne	1610-1837
L crowned	mm for Lille	1686-1707
M	mm for Toulouse	1610-1837
MA	mm for Marseille	1787-1858
N	mm for Montpellier	1636-1791
O	mm for Riom	1625-1772
P	mm for Dijon	1637-1772
Q	mm for Narbonne	1650-1653
Q	mm for Peripignan	1711-1837
R	mm for Villeneuve Saint André	1620-1662
R	mm for Orléans	1718-1788
R crowned	mm for Rome (Italy)	1811-1814
R (1815)	mm for London (England)	1815
S	mm for Troyes	1615-1656
S	mm for Reims	1680-1772
T	mm for Nantes	1615-1837
U	mm for Turin (Italy)	1811-1814
V	mm for Troyes	1693-1772
W	mm for Lille	1693-1857
X	mm for Amiens	1615-1772
Y	mm for Bourges	1627-1772
Z	mm for Grenoble	1612-1772
9	mm for Rennes	1610-1772
&	mm for Aix	1613-1786
Cow	mm for Pau	1610-1789
Fish and mast	mm for Utrecht (Netherlands)	1811-1814

The French gold Franc, first issued in 1803, was the standard adopted by the Latin Monetary Union. France maintained this standard for its gold coins until 1914. It was not until 1929 that the first coins appeared based on the revaluation of the gold Franc.

A. Kings of —

(The coins from St. Louis IX through Henry IV are followed by an L and a number. These numbers identify the same coins in the French work by Lafaurie).

ST. LOUIS IX, 1226-1270
Shield in lobed circle. Rev. Floriated cross.

1. 1 Ecu d'or ND. L-197 .... Rare

PHILIP IV, 1285-1314

King on Gothic throne. Rev. Floriated cross in quadrilobe.

2. 1 Chaise d'or ND. L-213 .... 7500.00

King seated. Rev. Floriated cross in quadrilobe.

3. 1 Masse d'or ND. L-212 .... 4000.00

King seated. Rev. Floriated cross.

4. 1 Petit Royal d'or ND. L-211 .... 6500.00
5. 1 Denier d'or ND. L-214 .... * 6250.00

King standing. Rev. Floriated cross in quadrilobe.

6. 1 Petit Royal d'or ND. L-215 .... 11000.00

Lamb. Rev. Floriated cross in quadrilobe.

7. 1 Agnel d'or ND. L-216 .... 3000.00

LOUIS X, 1314-1316

Lamb. Rev. Floriated cross in quadrilobe.

8. 1 Agnel d'or ND. L-240 .... 4250.00

PHILIP V, 1316-1322
Lamb. Rev. Floriated cross in quadrilobe.

9. 1 Agnel d'or ND. L-241 .... 2500.00

CHARLES IV, 1322-1328

King standing under Gothic dais. Rev. Floriated cross in quadrilobe.

10. 1 Royal d'or ND. L-244 .... * 2750.00
11. ½ Royal d'or ND. L-245 .... Rare

Lamb. Rev. Floriated cross in quadrilobe.

12. 1 Agnel d'or ND. L-243 .... 2250.00

PHILIP VI, 1328-1350

King seated on Gothic throne. Rev. Floriated cross in quadrilobe.

13.   1 Parisis d'or ND. L-252 .... 7500.00

King seated on Gothic throne, a lion at feet. Rev. Floriated cross in quadrilobe.

14.   1 Lion d'or ND. L-253 .... 5000.00

King seated on throne under draped pavillion. Rev. Floriated cross in quadrilobe, diamond in center.

15.   1 Pavillion d'or ND. L-254 .... 4250.00

King with two sceptres on Gothic throne under dais. Rev. Floriated cross in enclosure.

16.   1 Double d'or ND. L-256 ....* 5000.00
17.   1 Single d'or ND. L-257 .... Unknown

King on Gothic throne. Rev. Floriated cross in quadrilobe, diamond in center.

18.   1 Chaise d'or ND. L-261 .... 2250.00

Armored King with shield on Gothic throne. Rev. Floriated cross in quadrilobe.

19.   1 Ecu d'or ND. L-262 .... 1600.00

King standing under Gothic dais. Rev. Floriated cross in quadrilobe.

20.   1 Royal d'or ND. L-251.............................. 2750.00

St. George on horse. Rev. Floriated cross in quadrilobe.

21.   1 George-Florin ND. L-260 .... 15000.00

Angel standing. Rev. Floriated cross in quadrilobe.

22.   1 Ange d'or ND. L-258 ....* 5000.00
23.   ½ Ange d'or ND. L-259 .... Unknown

Large crown. Rev. Floriated cross in quadrilobe.

24.   1 Couronne d'or ND. L-255 .... 12500.00

JOHN THE GOOD, 1350-1364

Armored King with shield on Gothic throne. Rev. Floriated cross in quadrilobe.

25.   1 Ecu d'or ND. L-292 .... 1500.00

King standing under dais flanked by lis. Rev. Floriated cross in quadrilobe.

26.   1 Denier d'or ND. L-293........................... Rare

King standing under dais. Rev. Floriated cross, diamond in center.
27.   1 Royal d'or ND. L-296 . . . .   1500.00

Armored King on horse. Rev. Floriated cross in quadrilobe.
28.   1 Franc a Cheval ND. L-297 . . . .   1500.00

Lamb. Rev. Floriated cross in ornate circle.
29.   1 Mouton d'or ND. L-294 . . . . * 2000.00
30.   ½ Mouton d'or ND. L-295 . . . .   15000.00

St. John standing. Rev. Fleur-de-lis.
31.   1 Florin ND. L-358 . . . .   1100.00

CHARLES V, 1364-1380
King standing under dais. Rev. Floriated cross, diamond in center.
32.   1 Royal d'or ND. L-369 . . . .   7000.00

King standing under dais. Rev. Floriated cross in ornate circle.
33.   1 Franc a Pied ND. L-371 . . . .   950.00

Armored King on horse. Rev. Floriated cross in quadrilobe.
34.   1 Franc a Cheval ND. L-370 . . . .   1600.00

CHARLES VI, 1380-1422

King on throne, two lions at feet. Rev. Floriated cross in ornate enclosure.

35.   1 Chaise d'or ND. L-428 . . . . * 16000.00
36.   ½ Chaise d'or ND. L-429 . . . .   18000.00

Arms between madonna and angel. Rev. Roman cross.
37.   1 Salut d'or ND. L-413 . . . . * 9000.00
38.   ½ Salut d'or ND. L-414 . . . .   Unknown

Lamb. Rev. Floriated cross in ornate enclosure.
39.   1 Mouton d'or ND. L-380 . . . .   1500.00

Crowned arms. Rev. Floriated cross in quadrilobe.
40.   1 Ecu d'or ND. L-378 . . . . * 850.00
41.   ½ Ecu d'or ND. L-379 . . . .   Rare

Crowned arms flanked by two coronets. Rev. Floriated cross in quadrilobe.
42.   1 Ecu d'or ND. L-426 . . . .   1000.00
42a.   ½ Ecu d'or ND. L-427 . . . .   Unknown

Crowned helmet over shield. Rev. Cross in ornate enclosure.
43.   1 Heaume d'or ND. L-398 . . . .   Rare
44.   ½ Heaume d'or ND. L-399 . . . . * 7000.00

HENRY V OF ENGLAND, 1415-1422
Lamb. Rev. Floriated cross in ornate enclosure.
45.   1 Mouton d'or ND. L-434 . . . .   6750.00

Arms between madonna and angel. Rev. Roman cross.
46.   1 Salut d'or ND. L-437 . . . .   10000.00
47.   ½ Salut d'or ND. L-438 . . . .   Unknown

HENRY VI OF ENGLAND, 1422-1453

Angel over two shields. Rev. Roman cross.

48.　1 Angelot ND. L-448 . . . . 5000.00

Madonna and angel over two shields. Rev. Roman cross.

49.　1 Salut d'or ND. L-447 . . . . 2000.00

CHARLES VII, 1422-1461
Armored king on horse. Rev. Floriated cross in quadrilobe.

50.　1 Franc a Cheval ND. L-455 . . . . Rare

King standing. Rev. Floriated cross in quadrilobe.

51.　1 Royal d'or ND. L-459 . . . . 1650.00

Lamb. Rev. Floriated cross in ornate enclosure.

52.　1 Mouton d'or ND. L-456 . . . . Unknown

Arms between madonna and angel. Rev. Roman cross.

53.　1 Salut d'or ND. L-461 (Type of Charles VI) 9000.00

Large crowned shield. Rev. Floriated cross in quadrilobe.

54.　1 Ecu d'or ND. L-457 . . . . 750.00

Crowned shield flanked by two lis or crowns. Rev. Floriated cross, a crown in each angle.

55.　1 Ecu Neuf ND. L-510 . . . . 750.00
56.　½ Ecu Neuf ND. L-511. (Crowns not in angles) 1000.00

Crowned shield flanked by two lis. Rev. Floriated cross, a crown or briquette in each angle.

57.　1 Ecu Briquette ND. L-512 . . . . 2000.00

LOUIS XI, 1461-1483
St. Michael slaying dragon. Rev. Floriated cross.

58.　3 Angelots ND. L-526 . . . . Rare
59.　½ Angelot ND. L-528 . . . . Rare

Crowned arms flanked by crowned lis. Rev. Floriated cross in quadrilobe.

60.　1 Ecu d'or ND. L-524 . . . . 750.00

Crowned arms. Rev. Large floriated cross.

61.　½ Ecu d'or ND. L-525 . . . . 900.00

Crowned arms, small radiate sun above. Rev. Floriated cross.

62.　1 Ecu au Soleil ND. L-529a (Perpignan) . . * 700.00
63.　½ Ecu au Soleil ND. L-530 . . . . 800.00

Quartered arms of Dauphine. Rev. Ornate cross.

64.　1 Ecu Delphinal ND. L-531 . . . . Rare

CHARLES VIII, 1483-1498

Crowned arms, small radiate sun above. Rev. Floriated cross.

65.　3 Ecus au Soleil ND. L-555 . . . . Rare
66.　1 Ecu au Soleil ND. L-554 . . . . * 575.00
67.　½ Ecu au Soleil ND. L-556 . . . . * 600.00

Crowned arms flanked by two ermines, sun above. Rev. Ornate cross.

68.　1 Ecu au Soleil de Bretagne ND. L-557 . . . . . * 650.00
69.　½ Ecu au Soleil de Bretagne ND. L-557bis . . . . Rare

Arms of Dauphine. Rev. Floriated cross.

70.   1 Ecu au Soleil du Dauphine ND. L-558............. 650.00

LOUIS XII, 1498-1515

Crowned arms, small radiate sun above. Rev. Floriated cross.

71.   1 Ecu d'or au Soleil ND. L-592..................... 600.00
72.   ½ Ecu d'or au Soleil ND. L-593..................... 825.00

Crowned arms flanked by two porcupines. Rev. Cross.

73.   1 Ecu d'or au Porcepic ND. L-598...........*...... 800.00
74.   ½ Ecu d'or au Porcepic ND. L-599 .... 8000.00

*Crowned arms flanked by two ermines, sun above. Rev.
Ornate cross.*

75.   1 Ecu au Soleil de Bretagne ND. L-594 .....*...... 950.00
76.   ½ Ecu au Soleil de Bretagne ND. L-595 .... 8000.00

*Crowned arms flanked by two ermines, a porcupine below.
Rev. Ornate cross.*

77.   1 Ecu au Porcepic de Bretagne ND. L-600a 850.00

*Arms of France and Dauphine quartered, sun above. Rev.
Floriated cross.*

78.   1 Ecu au Soleil du Dauphine ND. L-597............. 900.00

*Arms of France and Dauphine flanked by two porcupines.
Rev. Cross.*

79.   1 Ecu au Porcepic du Dauphine ND. L-601......... 3500.00

*Crowned arms, small radiate sun above. Rev. Cross of
Jerusalem.*

80.   1 Ecu au Soleil de Provence ND. L-596 .... Rare

FRANCIS I, 1515-1547

*Crowned arms flanked by two lis. Rev. Two crowns and two
F's in angles of cross.*

81.   1 Ecu d'or au Soleil ND. L-638..................... 600.00

*Crowned arms flanked by two crowned F's. Rev. Two F's
and two lis in angles of cross.*

82.   1 Ecu d'or au Soleil ND. L-642..................... 2000.00

*Crowned arms flanked by a G and a lis. Rev. Two F's and
two lis in angles of cross.*

83.   1 Ecu d'or au Soleil ND. L-644..................... 2250.00

*Crowned arms, sun above, mint mark below. Rev. Floriated
cross.*

84.   1 Ecu d'or au Soleil ND. L-739..............*..... 500.00
85.   ½ Ecu d'or au Soleil ND. L-740..................... 1500.00

*Crowned arms, sun above, mint mark below. Rev. Two F's
and two lis in angles of cross.*

86.   1 Ecu d'or au Soleil ND. L-741..................... 525.00
87.   ½ Ecu d'or au Soleil ND. L-742..................... 1100.00

Crowned arms, small radiate sun above. Rev. Floriated cross.

88.   1 Ecu d'or au Soleil ND. L-634..............*...... 500.00
89.   ½ Ecu d'or au Soleil ND. L-635..................... 800.00

Crowned arms, small radiate sun above. Rev. Two crowned F's in angles of cross.

90.	1 Ecu d'or au Soleil ND. L-636..............*......	500.00
91.	½ Ecu d'or au Soleil ND. L-637.....................	1000.00
92.	1 Ecu d'or au Soleil ND. The F's not crowned. L-644 bis.........................	1000.00

Crowned arms, small radiate sun above. Rev. Two F's and two lis in angles of cross.

93.	1 Ecu d'or ND. L-639 ....*......	450.00
94.	½ Ecu d'or ND. L-640	1000.00

Same type as above but with a small cross added to both the Obv. and Rev.

95.	1 Ecu d'or a la Petite Croix ND. L-746..............	550.00
96.	½ Ecu d'or a la Petite Croix ND. L-747.............	1500.00

Crowned arms, small radiate sun above. Rev. Four F's in angles of cross.

97.	1 Ecu d'or au Soleil ND. L-641......................	1250.00

Crowned arms flanked by two salamanders. Rev. Two F's and two salamanders in angles of cross.

98.	1 Ecu d'or au Salamanders ND. L-744, 745..........	2500.00

Crowned arms. Rev. Plain cross.

99.	1 Ecu d'or a la Croisette ND. L-749........*......	800.00
100.	½ Ecu d'or a la Croisette ND. L-750................	1650.00

Crowned arms flanked by two F's. Rev. Plain cross. This coin is doubtful.

101.	1 Ecu d'or a la Croisette ND. L-751................ Unknown

Arms of France and Dauphine. Rev. Floriated cross.

102.	1 Ecu d'or du Dauphine ND. L-645..................	600.00

Arms of France and Dauphine. Rev. Two crowned F's in angles of cross.

103.	1 Ecu d'or du Dauphine ND. L-646..................	600.00

Arms of France and Dauphine. Rev. One dolphin and one lis in angles of cross.

104.	1 Ecu d'or du Dauphine ND. L-647..................	750.00

Arms of France and Dauphine. Rev. Two crowns in angles of cross.

105.	1 Ecu d'or du Dauphine ND. L-648..................	400.00

Arms of France and Dauphine. Rev. Crowned F and dolphin in angles of cross.

106.	1 Ecu d'or du Dauphine ND. L-649..................	400.00

Arms of France and Dauphine. Rev. Two dolphins in angles of cross.

107.	1 Ecu d'or du Dauphine ND. L-650..................	400.00

Crowned arms of France and Dauphine. Rev. Two F's and two lis in angles of cross.

108.	1 Ecu d'or du Dauphine a la Petite Croix ND. L-753.	8500.00

Same arms as above. Rev. Floriated cross.

109.	1 Ecu d'or du Dauphine. L-752.....................	8500.00

Arms of France and Dauphine. Rev. Plain cross.

110.	1 Ecu d'or du Dauphine a la Croisette L-754........	4000.00

Crowned arms flanked by two ermines. Rev. Two F's and two ermines in angles of cross.

111.   1 Ecu d'or de Bretagne ND. L-651 .... 1500.00

Crowned arms flanked by an F and an ermine. Rev. Two F's and two ermines in angles of cross.

112.   1 Ecu d'or de Bretagne ND. L-652 .... 1000.00

HENRY II, 1547-1559

Crowned bust. Rev. Crowned arms.

113.   1 Ecu d'or à l'effigie 1549. L-807 .... * 5000.00
114.   ½ Ecu d'or à l'effigie 1549. L-808 .... 6000.00

Bust. Rev. Cross of four H's with two crescents and two lis in angles (see also under Frances II and Charles IX).

115.   2 Henri d'or 1553-62. L-809 .... 4750.00
116.   1 Henri d'or 1550-62. L-810 ....*...... 3500.00
117.   ½ Henri d'or 1550-60. L-811 .... 2500.00

Bust. Rev. Cross of four H's, with four lis in angles (see also under Francis II and Charles IX).

118.   2 Henri d'or 1550-61. L-812 .... 4500.00
119.   1 Henri d'or 1550-59. L-813 ....*...... 3500.00

Laureate bust. Rev. Gallia seated.

120.   2 Henri d'or ND. L-816 .... Rare
121.   1 Henri d'or ND. L-817 .... 9000.00
122.   ½ Henri d'or ND. L-818 ....*...... 8000.00

Crowned arms flanked by two crescents. Rev. Two H's and two crescents in angles of cross. The ½ Ecu is known only as an Essai in double thickness. The normal weight ½ Ecu is unknown.

123.   1 Ecu d'or aux Croissants 1552. L-814 ......*...... 7500.00
124.   ½ Ecu d'or aux Croissants 1552. L-815 .... Unknown

Crowned arms. Rev. Plain cross.

125.   1 Ecu d'or a la Croisette ND. L-806 .... 2500.00

FRANCIS II, 1559-1560

(There are no distinctive coins of Francis II. During his short reign of seventeen months, the coinage of Henry II was continued without change. Therefore, coins dated 1559 or 1560 actually bear the name or portrait of Henry II, although they may have been struck under Francis II).

CHARLES IX, 1560-1574

(The early coins of this reign are not distinctive, in that like those of Francis II, they continue to bear the name or portrait of Henry II. Therefore, certain coins dated 1560, 1561 or 1562, although they purport to be coins of Henry II, were actually struck under Charles IX. The distinctive coinage of Charles IX follows).

Crowned arms. Rev. Floriated cross. (The coins dated 1575 were struck under Henry III although they bear the name of Charles IX).

126.   1 Ecu d'or 1562-75. L-890 ....*...... 650.00
127.   ½ Ecu d'or 1561-75. L-891 .... 750.00

Arms of France and Dauphine. Rev. Floriated cross.

128.   1 Ecu d'or du Dauphine 1562-74. L-893......*...... 1100.00
129.   ½ Ecu d'or du Dauphine. L-894 .... Unknown

Crowned arms without the King's name. Rev. Floriated cross. Struck by the Protestants in Rouen.

130.   1 Ecu au Soleil 1562. L-890c...................... 775.00

HENRY III, 1574-1589

Crowned arms flanked by two H's. Rev. Ornate floriated cross. (For certain coins dated 1575, see under Charles IX).

131.	2 Ecu d'or 1589. L-959		Rare
132.	1 Ecu d'or 1578, ND. L-963	*	1100.00
133.	½ Ecu d'or 1578. L-964		2750.00

Crowned arms. Rev. Lobed floriated cross.

134.	1 Ecu d'or 1575-89. L-960	*	775.00
135.	½ Ecu d'or 1575-89. L-961		875.00

Crowned arms. Rev. Floriated cross, mint mark in center.

136.	1 Ecu d'or 1575, 88. L-960x, 962	700.00

CHARLES X, 1589-1590

Crowned arms. Rev. Floriated cross. (Coins with his name dated after 1590 were struck during the reign of Henry IV).

137.	1 Ecu d'or 1590-95. L-1015		775.00
138.	½ Ecu d'or 1590-94. L-1016	*	1650.00

HENRY IV, 1589-1610

Crowned arms flanked by two H's. Two H's and two lis in angles of floriated cross.

139.	2 Ecu d'or 1589. L-1047	Rare

Crowned arms. Rev. Lobed, floriated cross.

140.	1 Ecu d'or 1590-1610. L-1048	*	3000.00
141.	½ Ecu d'or 1590-1610. L-1049		4000.00

Crowned arms. Rev. Floriated cross with an H under each of the four lis.

142.	1 Ecu d'or 1589-1604. L-1051	*	4500.00
143.	½ Ecu d'or 1589-1603. L-1052		6000.00

Crowned arms in beaded circle. Rev. Floriated cross in beaded circle.

144.	1 Ecu d'or 1589-1610. L-1054	*	6000.00
145.	½ Ecu d'or 1589-1603. L-1055		Unknown

Crowned arms. Rev. Lobed floriated cross.

146.	1 Ecu d'or 1610-43	1100.00
147.	½ Ecu d'or 1610-43	1500.00

Crowned arms in circle. Rev. Floriated cross in circle.

148.	1 Ecu d'or 1615	*	1000.00
149.	½ Ecu d'or 1615		1400.00

Crowned arms. Rev. Floriated cross.

150.	1 Ecu d'or ND	575.00

Arms of France and Dauphine. Rev. Floriated cross.

151.	1 Ecu d'or 1641	4500.00
152.	½ Ecu d'or 1641	6000.00

Draped, laureate bust. Rev. Cross of eight L's.

153. 10 Louis d'or 1640 . . . . Rare

Laureate head. Rev. Cross of eight L's.

154. 10 Louis d'or 1640 . . . . 30000.00
155. 8 Louis d'or 1640 . . . . 25000.00
156. 4 Louis d'or 1640 . . . . 30000.00
157. 2 Louis d'or 1640-43 . . . . 6000.00
158. 1 Louis d'or 1640-43 . . . . * 2750.00
159. ½ Louis d'or 1640-43 . . . . 1500.00

LOUIS XIV, 1643-1715
Crowned arms. Rev. Lobed, floriated cross.

160. 1 Ecu d'or au Soleil 1643-51 . . . . 1250.00
161. ½ Ecu d'or au Soleil 1643-51 . . . . 4500.00

Child head with short curl. Rev. Cross of eight L's.

162. 2 Louis d'or 1644 . . . . 14000.00
163. 1 Louis d'or 1644 . . . . 2250.00
164. ½ Louis d'or 1644 . . . . * 2750.00

Child head with long curl. Rev. Cross of eight L's.

165. 2 Louis d'or 1644-52 . . . . 9000.00
166. 1 Louis d'or 1644-53 . . . . * 2000.00
167. ½ Louis d'or 1644-46 . . . . 3000.00

Youthful laureate head. Rev. Cross of eight L's.

168. 1 Louis d'or 1659-68 . . . . * 2000.00
169. ½ Louis d'or 1660-68 . . . . 6000.00

Youthful plain head. Rev. Cross of eight L's.

170. 1 Louis d'or 1668-80 . . . . * 2000.00
171. 1 Louis d'or 1688. Older head 2000.00
172. ½ Louis d'or 1669-80 . . . . 6000.00

Older laureate head. Rev. Cross of eight L's.

173. 1 Louis d'or 1683-89 . . . . 2000.00

Old laureate head. Rev. Crowned arms.

174. 2 Louis d'or 1690-93 . . . . 4500.00
175. 1 Louis d'or 1690-93 . . . . * 1750.00
176. ½ Louis d'or 1690-93 . . . . 2000.00

Old laureate head. Rev. Arms of France and Navarre-Bearn.

177. 1 Louis d'or 1690 . . . . 6000.00

Old laureate head. Rev. Four L's around mint mark.

178. 2 Louis d'or 1693-95 . . . . * 4500.00
179. 1 Louis d'or 1693-95 . . . . 1500.00
180. ½ Louis d'or 1693-95 . . . . 1750.00

Old laureate head. Rev. Eight L's over crossed insignia.

181. 2 Louis d'or 1701, 02 . . . . 4500.00
182. 1 Louis d'or 1701, 02 . . . . 1000.00
183. ½ Louis d'or 1701, 02 . . . . * 1500.00

Old laureate head. Rev. Four lis in angles of crossed insignia.

184.	2 Louis d'or 1704-09	....	5000.00
185.	1 Louis d'or 1704-09	.......................*	1500.00
186.	½ Louis d'or 1704-09	....	1650.00

Old laureate head. Cross of eight L's, sun in center.

187.	2 Louis d'or 1709-11	....	5750.00
188.	1 Louis d'or 1709-11	.......................*	1500.00
189.	½ Louis d'or 1709-11	....	2000.00

Cross of four lis. Rev. Two angels holding arms.

190.	1 Lis d'or 1656	....	7000.00

LOUIS XV, 1715-1774
Child head. Rev. Cross of eight L's.

191.	1 Louis d'or 1715	....	10000.00
192.	½ Louis d'or 1715	....	Unknown

Child head. Rev. Crowned arms over crossed insignia.

193.	2 Louis d'or 1716	....	10000.00
194.	1 Louis d'or 1716	...........................*	3500.00
195.	½ Louis d'or 1716	....	4500.00

Crowned child head. Rev. Cross of four shields.

196.	2 Louis d'or 1717, 18	...........................*	5250.00
197.	1 Louis d'or 1717, 18	....	6500.00
198.	½ Louis d'or 1717, 18	....	5500.00

Young laureate head. Rev. Maltese cross.

199.	1 Louis d'or 1718, 19	....	4000.00
200.	½ Louis d'or 1718, 19, 21	.....................*	5750.00

Laureate head. Rev. Crown over two L's.

201.	2 Louis d'or 1720, 22	....	Unknown
202.	1 Louis d'or 1720-22	........................*	2500.00
203.	½ Louis d'or 1720, 22	....	4500.00

Laureate head. Rev. Two script L's in palms, crown above.

204.	2 Louis d'or 1723-25	....	8500.00
205.	1 Louis d'or 1723-25	.......................*	2500.00
206.	½ Louis d'or 1723-25	....	5500.00

Draped bust. Rev. Crown over two shields.

207.	1 Louis d'or 1726-39	........................*	775.00
208.	½ Louis d'or 1726-39	....	650.00

Large head with band. Rev. Crown over two shields.

209.	2 Louis d'or 1740-65	....	2250.00
210.	1 Louis d'or 1740-65	....	1500.00
211.	½ Louis d'or 1740-65	........................*	1250.00

Old laureate head. Rev. Crown over two shields.

212.	2 Louis d'or 1765-74	*	4000.00
213.	1 Louis d'or 1765-74		3500.00
213a.	½ Louis d'or 1765-74		15000.00

LOUIS XVI, 1774-1793

Uniformed bust. Rev. Crowned arms within palms.

214.	1 Louis d'or 1774	6250.00

Uniformed bust. Rev. Crown over two oval shields.

215.	2 Louis d'or 1775-84		4000.00
216.	1 Louis d'or 1774-84	*	3000.00
217.	½ Louis d'or 1775-84		3500.00

Bare head. Rev. Crown over two oval shields. This coin was not placed in circulation.

218.	1 Louis d'or 1785	Unknown

Bare head. Rev. Crown over two square shields.

219.	2 Louis d'or 1786-92	*	950.00
220.	1 Louis d'or 1785-92		475.00
221.	1 Louis d'or 1786. Horn on head. BB mm.		3000.00

Bare head. Rev. Angel writing.

222.	24 Livres (Louis d'or) 1792, 93	6000.00

THE FIRST REPUBLIC

Angel writing. Rev. Value in wreath.

223.	24 Livres 1793	4250.00

NAPOLEON BONAPARTE, 1801-1815

Bare head with title of First Consul. Rev. Value and "Republique Francaise." Struck under the First Republic.

224.	40 Francs. Years 11, 12 (1803, 04)	*	400.00
225.	20 Francs. Years 11, 12 (1803, 04)		250.00

Bare head with title of Emperor. Rev. Value and "Republique Francaise."

226.	40 Francs. Years 12, 13, 14, 1806, 07. A mm	*	350.00
226a.	40 Francs. 1806. CL mm		800.00
227.	40 Francs. 1806, 07. I mm		800.00
228.	40 Francs. 1806, 07. M mm		800.00
229.	40 Francs. Year 14, 1806, 07. U mm. (Year 14 rare)		450.00
230.	40 Francs. Year 14, 1806, 07. W mm. (Year 14 rare)		500.00
231.	20 Francs. Years 12, 13, 14, 1806, 07. A mm		150.00
232.	20 Francs. Years 13, 14, 1806. I mm		400.00
233.	20 Francs. 1807. M mm		500.00
234.	20 Francs. Years 13, 14, 1806. Q mm		500.00
235.	20 Francs. Year 14, 1806, 07. U mm		850.00
236.	20 Francs. Year 14, 1806, 07. W mm		400.00

Laureate head with title of Emperor. Rev. Value and "Republique Francaise."

237.	40 Francs 1807, 08. A mm		500.00
238.	40 Francs 1808. H mm		500.00
239.	40 Francs 1808. M mm		600.00
240.	40 Francs 1808. U mm		1500.00
241.	40 Francs 1808. W mm		500.00
242.	20 Francs 1807, 08. A mm	*	150.00
243.	20 Francs 1808. K mm		1800.00
244.	20 Francs 1808. M mm		250.00
245.	20 Francs 1808. Q mm		1500.00
246.	20 Francs 1806, 08. U mm		800.00
247.	20 Francs 1808. W mm		300.00

Laureate head with title of Emperor. Rev. Value and "Empire Francais."

248.	40 Francs 1809-13. A mm.	325.00
249.	40 Francs 1809, 10, 12. W mm.	325.00
250.	40 Francs 1809. M mm.	1000.00
251.	40 Francs 1809. U mm.	2500.00
252.	40 Francs 1810, 11. K mm.	500.00
253.	40 Francs 1813. CL mm.	850.00
254.	20 Francs 1809-15. A mm.	195.00
255.	20 Francs 1809-15. L mm.	200.00
256.	20 Francs 1809-13. K mm.	250.00
257.	20 Francs 1809, 10, 11. H mm.	750.00
258.	20 Francs 1809-15. W mm.	195.00
259.	20 Francs 1809-12. M mm.	300.00
260.	20 Francs 1809-13. U mm. *	500.00
261.	20 Francs 1810-14. Q mm.	250.00
262.	20 Francs 1812, 13. R mm.	700.00
263.	20 Francs 1813, 14. CL mm.	400.00
264.	20 Francs 1813. Fish and mast mm.	300.00

LOUIS XVIII, 1814-1824

Uniformed bust. Rev. Arms.

265.	20 Francs 1814, 15. A mm.	190.00
266.	20 Francs 1814, 15. L mm.	210.00
267.	20 Francs 1814, 15. K mm.	210.00
268.	20 Francs 1814, 15. W mm.	235.00
269.	20 Francs 1814, 15. Q mm.	235.00
270.	20 Francs 1815. B mm.	275.00
271.	20 Francs 1815. R mm. (London) *	235.00

Bare head. Rev. Arms.

272.	40 Francs 1816-24. A mm (1823 Rare) *	400.00
273.	40 Francs 1816, 17. L mm.	600.00
274.	40 Francs 1822. H mm.	1200.00
275.	40 Francs 1816, 18, 19. W mm.	400.00
276.	40 Francs 1816. Q mm.	500.00
277.	40 Francs 1816. B mm.	1200.00
278.	20 Francs 1816-24. A mm.	190.00
279.	20 Francs 1816, 17, 18. L mm.	200.00
280.	20 Francs 1816, 17. K mm.	200.00
281.	20 Francs 1822. H mm.	250.00
282.	20 Francs 1816-24. W mm.	190.00
283.	20 Francs 1824. MA monogram mm.	500.00
284.	20 Francs 1818, 19, 20. T mm.	200.00
285.	20 Francs 1816-24. Q mm.	190.00
286.	20 Francs 1816. B mm.	190.00

CHARLES X, 1824-1830

Head. Rev. Arms.

287.	40 Francs 1824-30. A mm. (1826-27 Rare). *	400.00
288.	40 Francs 1830. MA monogram mm.	550.00
289.	20 Francs 1825-30. A mm.	190.00
290.	20 Francs 1825-30. W mm.	200.00
291.	20 Francs 1828. T mm.	300.00
292.	20 Francs 1826. Q mm.	300.00

LOUIS PHILIPPE I, 1830-1848

Bare head. Rev. Value and date.

293.	20 Francs 1830, 31. A mm.	185.00
294.	20 Francs 1831. B mm.	185.00
295.	20 Francs 1831. T mm.	450.00
296.	20 Francs 1831. W mm. *	185.00

Laureate head. Rev. Value and date.

297.	40 Francs 1831-39. A mm (1839 Rare) *	350.00
298.	40 Francs 1834, 35. L mm.	500.00
299.	40 Francs 1832, 33. B mm.	600.00
300.	20 Francs 1832-48. A mm.	190.00
301.	20 Francs 1834, 35. L mm.	200.00
302.	20 Francs 1832-46. W mm.	195.00
303.	20 Francs 1832. T mm.	450.00
304.	20 Francs 1832-35. B mm.	195.00

LOUIS NAPOLEON BONAPARTE, PRESIDENT, 1848-1852
(President of the Second Republic, and later Emperor Napoleon III)

Bare head. Rev. Value and date.

305.	20 Francs 1852	195.00

NAPOLEON III, 1852-1870

Bare head. Rev. Arms (100, 50 Francs); Value (20, 10, 5 Francs).

306.	100 Francs 1855-59. A mm. *	900.00
307.	100 Francs 1855-56, 58-60. BB mm.	950.00
308.	50 Francs 1855-59. A mm.	400.00
309.	50 Francs 1855-56, 58-60. BB mm.	450.00
310.	20 Francs 1853-60. A mm. *	175.00
311.	20 Francs 1855, 56. D mm.	175.00(B)
312.	20 Francs 1855-60. BB mm.	175.00(B)
313.	10 Francs 1854-60. A mm.	100.00
314.	10 Francs 1855-60. BB mm.	100.00
315.	5 Francs 1854-60. A mm.	110.00
316.	5 Francs 1859, 60. BB mm.	110.00

(Numbers 311 and 312 are bullion coins. The price listed is based on gold at $725 per ounce.)

Laureate head. Rev. Arms (100, 50, 20 Francs); Value (10, 5 Francs).

317.	100 Francs 1862, 64-70. A mm	1150.00
318.	100 Francs 1862-64, 66-69. BB mm	1250.00
319.	50 Francs 1862, 64-68. A mm	600.00
320.	50 Francs 1862-63, 66-69. BB mm	700.00
321.	20 Francs 1861-70. A mm .... *	175.00(B)
322.	20 Francs 1861-70. BB mm	175.00(B)
323.	10 Francs 1861-68. A mm	100.00
324.	10 Francs 1861-69. BB mm	100.00
325.	5 Francs 1862-68. A mm	110.00
326.	5 Francs 1862-69. BB mm	110.00

SECOND AND THIRD REPUBLICS—1848-1852 AND 1870-1940

Angel writing. Rev. Value and date.

327.	100 Francs 1878-1913	800.00
328.	50 Francs 1878-1904	1500.00
329.	20 Francs 1848, 49 (2nd Rep.)	195.00
330.	20 Francs 1871-98 (3rd Rep.) .... *	175.00(B)

Head of Ceres. Rev. Value in circle.

331.	20 Francs 1849, 50-51 (2nd Rep.) .... *	175.00
332.	10 Francs 1850, 51 (2nd Rep.)	125.00
333.	10 Francs 1878, 89 (3rd Rep.)	1500.00
334.	10 Francs 1895, 96, 99	125.00
335.	5 Francs 1878, 89. Patterns	1250.00

Head of the Republic. Rev. Rooster.

336.	20 Francs 1899-1915 .... *	175.00(B)
337.	10 Francs 1899-1915	60.00

Winged head of the Republic. Rev. Value.

338.	100 Francs 1929, 33, 35, 36	1200.00

(Numbers 321, 322, 330 and 336 are bullion coins. The price listed is based on gold at $725 per ounce.)

B. Cities and Provinces of —

AQUITAINE

A. English Rulers of —

EDWARD III, 1317-1355

Ruler walking. Rev. Cross.

339.	1 Guyennois ND	3250.00

Ruler seated. Rev. Cross.

340.	1 Ecu d'or ND	2500.00

St. John. Rev. Lily.

341.	1 Florin d'or ND	2500.00

Leopard. Rev. Cross.

342.	1 Leopard ND	3000.00

EDWARD, THE BLACK PRINCE, 1355-1375

Ruler standing under dais. Rev. Cross.

343.	1 Pavillion d'or ND .... *	5500.00
344.	½ Pavillion d'or ND	Unknown

Ruler walking. Rev. Cross.

345.	1 Guyennois ND	4250.00

Ruler seated. Rev. Cross.

346.	1 Chaise d'or ND	3500.00
346a.	½ Chaise d'or ND	Rare

Crowned bust facing. Rev. Cross.

347. 1 Hardi ND 4000.00

Leopard. Rev. Cross.

348. 1 Leopard ND 4000.00

RICHARD II, 1377-1399
Crowned bust facing. Rev. Cross.

349. 1 Hardi ND 4000.00
350. ½ Hardi ND 8500.00

HENRY IV, 1399-1413
Crowned bust facing. Rev. Cross.

351. 1 Hardi ND 7000.00

HENRY V, 1417-1422
Lamb. Rev. Cross.

352. 1 Mouton d'or ND 5000.00

Virgin and angel with shields. Rev. Cross.

353. 1 Salut d'or ND................................... 9000.00

HENRY VI, 1422-1436

Angel over two shields. Rev. Cross.

354. 1 Angelot ND...................................... 5000.00

Virgin and angel over two shields. Rev. Cross.

355. 1 Salut d'or ND................................... 1950.00

B. French Rulers of —

CHARLES, 1468-1474
Ruler on horse. Rev. Cross.

356. 1 Franc a Cheval ND .... Rare

Crowned bust facing. Rev. Cross.

357. 1 Hardi ND 3500.00
358. ½ Hardi ND 8000.00

Ruler standing with leopard. Arms on cross.

359. 1 Fort d'or ND.................................... Rare

ARLES

Archbishops of —

GAILLARD DE SAUMATE, 1317-1323
St. John. Rev. Lily. G. Arel Archp.

360. 1 Florin ND....................................... Unknown

STEPHAN DE LA GARDE, 1350-1359
St. John Rev. Lily. S. Arel Archp.

361. 1 Florin ND....................................... 850.00

WILLIAM II DE LA GARDE, 1360-1374
Ruler standing. Rev. Cross.

362. 1 Franc a Pied ND .... Rare

JOHN FERRER, 1499-1521
Arms. Rev. Cross.

363. 1 Ecu d'or ND..................................... Rare

AVIGNON

Popes of Rome at —

JOHN XXII, 1316-1334

St. John. Rev. Lily.

364. 1 Florin ND....................................... 1500.00

INNOCENT VI, 1352-1362
Pope seated. Rev. Crossed Keys.

365. 1 Zecchino ND 3500.00

URBAN V, 1362-1370

St. John. Rev. Lily.

366. 1 Florin ND....................................... 1500.00

CLEMENT VII, 1378-1394
Tiara and arms. Rev. St. Peter.

367. 1 Zecchino ND 2000.00

Tiara. Rev. Crossed Keys.

368. 1 Ecu ND 2500.00

JOHN XXIII, 1410-1415
Tiara. Rev. Cross.

369. 1 Ecu ND 1650.00

Pope seated. Rev. Tiara over arms.

370. 1 Ecu d'or ND .... Rare

Tiara and Arms Rev. Crossed keys.

371. 1 Ecu ND 1500.00

MARTIN V, 1417-1431

Tiara over shield. Rev. Crossed Keys.

372.   1 Ecu ND 2500.00

SIXTUS IV, 1471-1484
Tiara over arms. Rev. St. Peter.

373.   1 Ecu ND 3000.00

Tiara. Rev. Two keys.

374.   ½ Ecu d'or ND 3250.00

INNOCENT VIII, 1484-1492
Tiara. Rev. Crossed keys.

375.   1 Zecchino ND 2500.00

JULIUS II, 1503-1513

Legate's shield and arms. Rev. Cross.

376.   1 Ecu d'or ND 2750.00

JULIUS III, 1550-1555
Papal arms. Rev. Legate's arms.

377.   1 Ecu d'or ND 2750.00

PIUS IV, 1555-1559
Papal arms. Rev. Legate's arms.

378.   1 Ecu d'or 1562. With name of Alexander
       Farnese as legate 3250.00
379.   1 Ecu d'or ND. With name of Charles
       Bourbon as legate 3250.00

ST. PIUS V, 1565-1572
Pope seated. Rev. Cross.

380.   1 Ecu d'or ND 2750.00

Papal arms. Rev. Legate's arms.

381.   1 Ecu d'or ND 3000.00

Two shields. Rev. View of Avignon.

382.   1 Ecu d'or 1570 .... 5000.00

GREGORY XIII, 1572-1585
Two shields. Rev. View of Avignon.

383.   1 Ecu d'or ND 4500.00

Pope seated. Rev. Cross.

384.   1 Ecu d'or ND 1750.00

Papal arms. Rev. Two shields.

385.   1 Ecu d'or ND 1400.00

CLEMENT VIII, 1592-1605
Legate's arms. Rev. View of Avignon.

386.   8 Ecu d'or 1596 .... Rare
387.   4 Ecu d'or 1590 .... 9250.00

Bust. Rev. Legate's arms.

388.   10 Zecchini 1599 .... Rare
389.   4 Ecu d'or 1597, 98, 1602 ....* 9250.00
390.   2 Ecu d'or 1596, 98, 1600 .... 4750.00

PAUL V, 1605-1621

Bust. Rev. Legate's arms.

391.   4 Ecu d'or 1611 ....* 11000.00
392.   2 Ecu d'or 1608 .... 5250.00

GREGORY XV, 1621-1623
Bust. Rev. Arms.

393.   8 Ecu d'or 1622 .... 10000.00

URBAN VIII, 1623-1644

Bust. Rev. Arms.

394.   4 Ecu d'or 1632-43 ....* 5500.00
395.   2 Ecu d'or 1639, 40 .... 2500.00

INNOCENT X, 1644-1655
Bust. Rev. Legate's arms.

396.   4 Ecu d'or 1644-50 .... 5500.00
397.   2 Ecu d'or 1644 .... 3000.00

ALEXANDER VII, 1655-1667

Bust. Rev. Legate's arms.

398.   4 Ecu d'or 1657, 58, 62, 63 ....* 6500.00
399.   2 Ecu d'or 1664 .... 3500.00

BAR

Dukes of —

ROBERT, 1352-1411
St. John standing. Rev. Lily.

399a.   1 Florin ND...................................... 2000.00

EDWARD III, 1411-1415
Crowned bust facing. Rev. Lily.

400.   1 Florin ND....................................... 2500.00

BEARN

Counts —

GASTON, 1436-1471
Ruler on horse. Rev. Cross.

401.   1 Ecu d'or ND.................................... Rare

St. John. Rev. Lily.

402.   1 Florin ND....................................... 750.00

FRANCIS PHOEBUS, 1479-1483

Arms. Rev. Cross.

403.   1 Ecu d'or ND.................................... 2750.00
404.   ½ Ecu d'or ND.................................... Unknown

CATHERINE, 1483-1484
Arms. Rev. Cross.

405.   1 Ecu d'or ND.................................... 2750.00

BESANCON

CHARLES V (CHARLES I OF SPAIN), 1515-1556
Coins were struck in his name as late as 1673.

Ruler standing. Rev. Cross.

406.   1 Florin 1541 .... Unknown

Laureate head. Rev. Eagle.

407.   4 Pistolets 1579, 80 .... 6000.00
408.   2 Pistolets 1579-1673 ....*...... 5000.00

Crowned bust. Rev. Eagle.

409.   1 Pistolet 1578, 1653, 54........................ 2000.00

Ruler standing. Rev. Eagle.

410.   2 Pistolets 1662, 64 .... 5250.00

Ruler standing. Rev. Legend in cartouche.

411.   2 Ducats 1642, 54 .... Unknown
412.   1 Ducat 1655 .... Rare
413.   ½ Ducat 1655 .... 800.00

PHILIP IV OF SPAIN, 1621-1665
Armored bust. Rev. Name and date.

414.   4 Pistolets 1664 .... Rare

BOUILLON

Dukes of —

WILLIAM ROBERT DE LA MARCK, 1574-1588

Arms. Rev. Cross.

415.   1 Pistole 1587 .... Rare

CHARLOTTE, 1589-1591
Arms. Rev. Plain or elaborate cross.

416.   1 Ecu d'or 1589, 91............................. Unknown
417.   1 Pistole 1591 .... 3500.00

HENRY DE LA TOUR AND CHARLOTTE, 1591-1594
Arms. Rev. Cross of four towers.

418.   1 Pistole 1592 .... 4000.00

HENRY DE LA TOUR, 1591-1623
Bust. Rev. Arms.

419.   1 Ecu d'or 1614................................. 1750.00

Crowned arms. Rev. Cross of four towers.

420.   1 Pistole d'or 1597 .... 2250.00

Crowned arms. Rev. Cross.

421.   2 Ecu d'or 1610, 14, ND 3500.00
422.   1 Ecu d'or 1598, 1610, ND........................ 1000.00

GEOFFREY MAURICE, 1652-1671
Bust. Rev. Arms.

423.   1 Souverain d'or (1652-1691) .... Unknown
424.   ½ Souverain d'or (1652-1691) .... Unknown

BRITTANY

Dukes of —

PERIOD 800-1000
Bust. Rev. Cross.

425.   Electrum 1 Sou ND............................... Rare

CHARLES DE BLOIS, 1341-1364
Ruler standing. Rev. Cross.

426.   1 Royal d'or ND 3000.00

JOHN IV, 1345-1399
Ruler on horse. Rev. Cross.
427.　1 Ecu d'or ND...................................... 3500.00

JOHN V, 1399-1442
Ruler on horse. Rev. Cross.
428.　1 Ecu d'or ND...................................... 3000.00

FRANCIS I, 1442-1450

Ruler on horse. Rev. Cross.
429.　1 Ecu d'or ND...................................... 3000.00

FRANCIS II, 1458-1488
Ruler on horse. Rev. Cross.
430.　1 Ecu d'or ND...................................... 3000.00

ANNE, 1488-1491

Duchess on throne. Rev. Cross.
431.　1 Ecu d'or ND..................................11000.00

BURGUNDY

Dukes of —

EUDES IV, 1315-1350

St. John. Rev. Lily.
432.　1 Florin ND....................................... 1000.00

Ruler standing. Rev. Cross.
433.　1 Ecu d'or ND................................... Rare

PHILIP I, 1350-1361
St. John. Rev. Lily.
434.　1 Florin ND.. 900.00

PHILIP III, 1419-1467
Horseman. Rev. Arms on cross.
435.　1 Ecu d'or ND...................................... 2000.00

CAMBRAI

A. Archbishops of —

GUY IV, 1342-1348

St. John. Rev. Lily. "FLOR PSV CA or FLOR EPI CA."
436.　1 Florin ND.. 650.00

PETER IV, 1349-1368

Lamb. Rev. Floriated cross.
437.　1 Mouton d'or ND .... Rare

Ruler on horse. Rev. Cross.
438.　1 Franc a cheval ND 2250.00

Ruler standing. Rev. Cross.
439.　1 Royal d'or ND 4000.00

ROBERT OF GENEVA, 1368-1372

Ruler standing. Rev. Cross.
440.　1 Franc a pied ND................................. 4000.00

Ruler on horse. Rev. Cross.
441.　1 Franc a cheval ND 3000.00

GERARD III, 1372-1378
Ruler on horse. Rev. Cross.
442.　1 Franc a cheval ND 3750.00
442a.　1 Mouton d'or ND .... Rare

MAXIMILIAN OF BERGHES, 1556-1570

Arms. Rev. Cross.

443.	1 Ecu D'or ND............................	2500.00

Double eagle. Rev. Eagle shield.

444.	1 Florin ND...............................	1750.00

LOUIS OF BERLAYMONT, 1570-1596
Eagle shield. Rev. Double eagle.

445.	1 Florin 1578.............................	1750.00

B. Cathedral Chapter of —

St. John. Rev. Lily. "FLOR. CAPI. CA."

446.	1 Florin ND..	850.00

CHATEAU-RENAUD
Princes —

FRANCIS AND LOUISE MARGUERITE, 1605-1614
Bust of Francis. Rev. Arms.

447.	1 Florin ND..	950.00

LOUISE MARGUERITE, 1614-1631
Arms between two crosses of Jerusalem. Rev. Cross.

448.	1 Ecu d'or ND.....................................	2750.00

CHATELET-VAUVILLERS

NICHOLAS II, 1525-1562
Arms. Rev. Cross.

449.	1 Ecu Sol 1554, ND	Rare

DOLE (DOLA)

Spanish Kings of —

PHILIP II, 1556-1598
Crowned arms. Rev. Floriated cross.

450.	1 Ecu Pistolet 1563..............................	5500.00

PHILIP IV, 1621-1665
Floriated cross. Rev. Crowned arms between two small crowns.

451.	1 Corona or Ducat 1632	4500.00

DOMBES
Princes —

JOHN II, 1459-1482

Bust. Rev. Prince on horse.

452.	1 Franc a Cheval ND	Rare

PETER II, 1482-1503
Bust. Rev. Prince on horse.

453.	1 Franc a Cheval ND	Rare

LOUIS II, 1560-1582

Crowned arms. Rev. Cross.

454.	2 Ecu d'or or 1 Pistole 1574, 78	2750.00
455.	1 Ecu d'or or ½ Pistole 1574, 75...........*......	1850.00

FRANCIS II, 1582-1592
Prince kneeling before St. Mark. Rev. Christ.

456.	1 Zecchino ND	4000.00

Arms. Rev. Cross.

457.	1 Pistole 1587 ....Unknown

MARIE, 1608-1626
Arms. Rev. Cross.

458.	1 Ecu d'or 1616.................................	3500.00
459.	½ Ecu d'or 1611.................................	3500.00

GASTON AND MARIE, 1626-1627
Arms. Rev. Cross.

460.	1 Ecu d'or 1627.................................	Rare

GASTON, 1627-1650

Crowned shield. Rev. Lobed, floriated cross.

461.	2 Ecu d'or 1640.................................	Rare
462.	1 Ecu d'or 1640, 41.........................*......	2250.00

Laureate bust. Rev. Cross of eight L's. Posthumous issue.

463.	2 Louis d'or 1652............................*......10000.00
464.	1 Louis d'or 1652.................................	7500.00

ANNE MARIE LOUIS DE MONTPENSIER, 1650-1693
Ruler and Saint standing. Rev. Christ. Venetian style.

465.	1 Ducat ND.......................................	2250.00

EVREUX

Counts —

CHARLES OF NAVARRE, 1343-1387
Ruler standing before Gothic canopy. Rev. Cross.

466.	1 Ecu d'or ND....................................	3000.00

LIGNY

Counts —

JOHN, 1353-1364
Bust of St. Peter with lion shield. Rev. Cross.

467.   1 Ecu d'or ND................................... 2000.00

GUY, 1364-1371

Ruler standing under dais. Rev. Cross.

468.   1 Ecu d'or ND.. 2250.00

WALERAN III, 1371-1415
Lamb. Rev. Cross.

469.   1 Agnel d'or ND................................... 4250.00

Ruler standing under dais. Rev. Cross.

470.   1 Ecu d'or ND................................... 3500.00

LORRAINE

Dukes of —

JOHN I, 1346-1389

St. John standing. Rev. Lily.

471.   1 Florin ND.. 1500.00

RENE II, 1473-1508
St. Nicholas. Rev. Arms.

472.   1 Goldgulden ND.................................. 1500.00
473.   ½ Goldgulden ND.................................. 2000.00

ANTHONY, 1508-1544
Bust. Rev. Arms.

474.   6 Ducats ND .... Rare
475.   1 Florin 1526, 33 .... 3000.00

CHARLES III, 1545-1608
Arms. Rev. Cross.

476.   2 Pistoles 1587.................................. 3250.00
477.   1 Pistole 1587................................... 1750.00
478.   ½ Pistole 1587................................... 2000.00

Crowned bust. Rev. Arms.

479.   ½ Pistole ND 2250.00

Plain bust. Rev. Arms.

480.   4 Pistoles 1587.................................. 6000.00
481.   2 Pistoles 1587, 88 ....*...... 3500.00
482.   1 Ducat 1566-88................................. 2500.00
483.   ½ Ducat ND..................................... 2000.00

Bust. Rev. Circle of seven shields.

484.   1 Ducat 1588 .... 3250.00

HENRY II, 1608-1624
St. Nicholas. Rev. Arms.

485.   1 Goldgulden ND................................ 800.00
486.   ½ Goldgulden ND................................ 950.00

Bust. Rev. Arms.

487.   1 Goldgulden 1611, ND........................... 1750.00

CHARLES IV, 1625-1670

Arms. Rev. Cross.

488.   2 Pistoles 1631...........................*...... 3500.00
489.   1 Pistole 1639, ND 2500.00

Laureate head. Rev. Interlinked C's.

490.   1 Pistole 1661, 62, 68, 69......................... 4250.00

LEOPOLD I, 1697-1729
Laureate head. Rev. Two L's.

491.   1 Leopold d'or 1702...................... 4500.00

Laureate head. Rev. Arms.

492.	2 Leopold d'or 1720, 24 . . . . *	5000.00
493.	1 Leopold d'or 1719	3500.00
494.	½ Leopold d'or 1718	2250.00

FRANCIS III, 1729-1736

Bust. Rev. Arms supported by eagles.

495.	2 Ducats 1736 . . . . *	6000.00
496.	1 Ducat 1736	3500.00

METZ

St. Stephan standing. Rev. Arms.

497.	1 Goldgulden 1620-45, ND	700.00

Bust of St. Stephan. Rev. Arms.

498.	1 Goldgulden 1639, 45, ND	1750.00

MONTELIMART

Barons —

GAUCHER ADEMAR, 1346-1369
St. John. Rev. Lily.

499.	1 Florin ND.	3500.00

MONTPELLIER

Barons —

SANCHO OF MAJORCA. 1311-1324

Ruler seated. Rev. Double cross.

500.	1 Petit Royal d'or ND.	5000.00

NAVARRE

Kings of —

CHARLES II, 1349-1387
Crowned bust. Rev. Floriated cross.

501.	1 Gold Real ND	Rare

JOHN II, 1441-1479

Arms. Rev. Cross.

502.	1 Ecu d'or ND.	3500.00
503.	½ Ecu d'or ND . . . . *	2000.00

FRANCIS PHOEBUS, 1479-1483
Crowned bust. Rev. Arms.

504.	1 Ecu d'or ND	4500.00
505.	½ Ecu d'or ND.	3250.00

JOHN AND CATHERINE, 1484-1512

Arms. Rev. Small cross in quadrilobe.

506.	1 Ecu d'or ND . . . . *	2500.00
507.	¼ Ecu d'or ND.	2250.00

Two busts facing each other. Rev. Arms.

508.	1 Ducat ND.	4500.00

Crown over initials "I-K." Rev. Cross.

509.	½ Ecu d'or ND	2500.00

FERDINAND II OF ARAGON, 1512-1516
Crowned bust. Rev. Crowned arms.

510.	4 Ducats ND	Rare
511.	2 Ducats ND	3750.00
512.	1 Ducat ND.	1750.00
513.	½ Ducat ND.	1350.00

HENRY OF ALBRET, 1516-1555
Crowned arms. Rev. Floriated cross.

514.	1 Ecu au Soleil ND	2500.00

Crowned arms. Rev. Short cross.

515.	1 Ecu d'or ND	2750.00

JOAN, 1562-1572
Cross. Rev. Crowned arms.

516.	1 Ecu au Soleil 1561	3000.00

Crowned S between two I's. Rev. Crowned arms.

517.	1 Ecu d'or 1565.	Rare

HENRY II, 1572-1610

Busts of Henry and Margaret. Rev. Crowned arms.

518.	2 Ducats 1577	*	5000.00
519.	1 Ducat 1576, 77		2500.00

Crowned arms. Rev. Cross and four H's.

520.	1 Ecu d'or 1575-78	2750.00

N I C E

Arms. Rev. Legend. Siege coin.

521.	1 Scudo d'oro 1543	3500.00

O R A N G E

Princes —

RAYMOND III AND IV, 1335-1393
St. John. Rev. Lily.

522.	1 Florin ND	500.00

Ruler standing. Rev. Cross.

523.	1 Franc a Pied ND	825.00

JOHN II, 1475-1502
Helmet. Rev. Cross.

524.	1 Ecu d'or ND	2000.00

PHILIP WILLIAM, 1584-1618

Armored bust. Rev. Arms.

525.	1 Pistole 1616		4500.00
526.	½ Pistole 1617		3000.00
527.	4 Ecu d'or 1616	*	6500.00

MAURICE, 1618-1625
Bust. Rev. Arms.

528.	1 Grand Ecu d'or 1618	Rare

FREDERICK HENRY, 1625-1647

Bust. Rev. Arms.

529.	1 Grand Ecu d'or 1641, 45, ND	*	2500.00
530.	½ Grand Ecu d'or 1640, 43, ND		2750.00

Knight standing. Rev. Tablet. Dutch type.

531.	1 Ducat (1625-47)	2000.00

WILLIAM HENRY, 1650-1702
Prince kneeling before St. Mark. Rev. Christ.

532.	1 Zecchino ND	1250.00

P E R P I G N A N

French Kings of —

LOUIS XI, 1461-1483
Arms of France. Rev. Cross and P.

533.	1 Ecu au Soleil ND	625.00

CHARLES VIII, 1483-1498
Arms of France. Rev. Cross and P.

534.	1 Ecu au Soleil ND	600.00

P R O V E N C E

Counts —

CHARLES I OF ANJOU, 1246-1285

Bust. Rev. Arms.

535.	1 Augustale d'or ND	6500.00

K. Rev. Arms.

536.	1 Sou d'or ND	1350.00

K. Rev. Cross.

537.	1 Double Tarin ND	700.00

The Annunciation. Rev. Arms.

538.	1 Salut d'or ND		1500.00
539.	½ Salut d'or ND	*	2500.00

CHARLES II OF ANJOU, 1285-1309
The Annunciation. Rev. Arms.

540.   1 Salut d'or ND................................... 1100.00

JOANNA OF NAPLES, 1343-1352

Ruler standing. Rev. Cross.

541.   1 Franc a Pied ND 800.00

Crowned bust facing. Rev. Arms.

542.   1 Florin ND... Rare

St. John. Rev. Arms.

543.   1 Florin ND.. 750.00

St. John. Rev. Lily.

544.   1 Florin ND.. 600.00

Crown. Rev. Cross.

545.   1 Florin ND... Rare

LOUIS AND JOANNA, 1347-1382
St. John. Rev. Lily.

546.   1 Florin ND... 550.00

LOUIS I, 1382-1384

Crowned arms. Rev. Cross in enclosure.

547.   1 Ecu d'or ND...................................... 675.00

Ruler standing. Rev. Cross.

548.   1 Franc a Pied ND 1500.00

St. John. Rev. Arms.

549.   1 Florin ND.. 750.00

RENE, 1434-1480
Crowned arms. Rev. Cross of Jerusalem.

550.   1 Ecu d'or ND...................................... Rare
551.   ½ Ecu d'or ND...................................... Rare
552.   ¼ Ecu d'or ND...................................... Rare

Bust of St. Magdalene. Rev. Cross.

553.   1 Magdalin ND .... Rare

CHARLES III, 1480-1482
St. Magdalene standing. Rev. Cross with two bars.

554.   1 Magdalin (½ Ecu) ND ....Unknown

Bust of St. Magdalene. Rev. Cross with two bars.

555.   1 Magdalin ND 2750.00

RETHEL

Counts —

LOUIS III DE MALE, 1346-1384

Lamb. Rev. Cross.

556.   1 Mouton d'or ND 4250.00

CHARLES II GONZAGA, 1601-1637
Bust and date. Rev. Crowned arms.

557.   Gold 1 Ecu 1608................................... 7250.00

Ruler standing. Rev. Crowned arms.

558.   1 Florin ND... 2000.00

Ruler standing. Rev. Legend in cartouche.

559.   1 Florin ND... 1900.00

Arms. Rev. Double eagle.

560.   1 Florin ND... Rare

Crowned arms. Rev. Cross of Jerusalem.

561.   1 Florin 1608 .... Rare

ROUSILLON

Spanish Kings of —

FERDINAND II, 1479-1516
Crowned bust. Rev. Crowned arms between P-P.

562.   1 Principat ND 2500.00

CHARLES AND JOHANNA, 1516-1556
Crowned busts facing each other. Rev. Crowned arms between P-P.

563.   2 Ducats 1522.................................... 6000.00

SAINT POL

Counts —

GUY VI, 1360-1371
Count on horse. Rev. Cross and name of Count of Saint Pol.
564. 1 Franc a Cheval ND 3000.00

STRASBOURG

Madonna. Rev. Orb.
565. 2 Florins ND (1600)......................... 1500.00
566. 1 Florin ND (1600) .... * 1000.00

Inscription. Rev. Inscription. On the Centennial of the Reformation.
567.   1 Ducat 1617. Square............................ 2000.00

Arms. Rev. Legend in wreath.
568.   4 Ducats ND (1650)............................... Rare
569.   1 Ducat ND (1650) 1500.00

Madonna. Rev. Arms. Issued by the Cathedral Chapter.
570.   1 Ducat 1632 .... 1750.00

Seated female and child. Rev. Arms over three shields.
Issued under Bishop John v. Manderscheid, 1569-1592.
571.   6 Goldgulden 1575................................ Unique

Bust. Rev. Arms on mantle. Issued under Bishop Louis
Constantin de Rohan, 1756-1779.
572.   2 Ecu d'or 1759............................... Rare
573.   1 Ecu d'or 1759............................... 5500.00
574.   ½ Ecu d'or 1759............................... 6500.00

VERDUN

Bishops of —

ERIC OF LORRAINE, 1593-1611
Bust. Rev. Arms.
575.   1 Florin 1608 .... 2000.00

CHARLES OF LORRAINE-CHALIGNY, 1611-1622
Bust. Rev. Arms.
576.   1 Florin 1613 .... 2000.00

VIENNOIS

Dauphins of —

GUIGES VIII, 1319-1333
St. John. Rev. Lily.
577. 1 Florin ND... 850.00

HUMBERT II, 1333-1349
St. John. Rev. Lily.
578. 1 Florin ND... 750.00

CHARLES V, 1349-1364
St. John. Rev. Lily.
579. 1 Florin ND... 750.00

Ruler on horse. Rev. Cross.
580. 1 Franc a Cheval ND 1500.00

CHARLES VI, 1380-1409
Crowned arms. Rev. Elaborate cross.
581. 1 Ecu d'or ND..................................... 1500.00

CHARLES VII, 1422-1440
Crowned arms. Rev. Cross.
582. 1 Ecu d'or ND..................................... Unknown

LOUIS II, 1440-1456
Arms. Rev. Cross.
583. 1 Ecu d'or ND..................................... 800.00

GERMAN EAST AFRICA

Elephant. Rev. Eagle.
1.   15 Rupees 1916.................................... 1000.00

GERMAN NEW GUINEA

The two gold coins of this colony have always been popular and in demand. 1500 specimens were struck of the 20 Mark piece and 2000 of the 10 Mark piece.

Bird of Paradise. Rev. Value.
1.   20 Marks 1895..................................... 8500.00
2.   10 Marks 1895..................................... 8000.00

GERMANY

Mints and mint marks for the coinage of the German Empire from 1871-1918: —

    A mm for Berlin
    B mm for Hanover
    C mm for Frankfurt
    D mm for Munich
    E mm for Dresden
    F mm for Stuttgart
    G mm for Karlsruhe
    H mm for Darmstadt
    J mm for Hamburg

The colossal coinage of Germany is no way better evidenced than that it comprises about one third of this book. It must be remembered that Germany until 1871 was not a unified country and for hundreds of years consisted of a multitude of independent coin issuing localities, each one of which merits the same numismatic attention as a sovereign nation. This mingled secular coinage has been further enlarged by the extensive issues of many ecclesiastical rulers.

Even the issues of the German Empire from 1871-1918 were similar only in denominations for they still bore the heads and titles of the many different rulers whose states formed the Empire.

As a matter of fact, it can truly be said that there is no such thing as a "German" gold coin—only a Prussian coin or a Cologne coin, etc. Actually, it was not until the formation of the German Republic after World War I that a truly national German coinage came into existence, and under this coinage, there were unfortunately no gold coins.

A. Empire of —, 1871-1918

General Types for all the States

Obverse: Head of the ruler except for the free cities of Bremen, Hamburg and Lubeck, which have the city arms.

Reverse: "Deutsches Reich," value, date and eagle. Three varieties of this reverse design were used and the date on the coin automatically indicates the type of reverse:

FIRST REVERSE, 1871-1873 inclusive: Small eagle, and below, both the date and abbreviated value.

SECOND REVERSE, 1874-1889 inclusive: Small eagle, and below, the complete value with the date appearing at the right.

THIRD REVERSE, 1890-1915 inclusive: Large eagle.

(The illustrations above show a typical obverse as well as the three reverses in their correct numerical order.)

NOTE: The valuations in this section are for Very Fine to Extremely Fine specimens of the commonest dates.

ANHALT
Dukes of —
FREDERICK I, 1871-1904

1.	20 Marks 1875	1100.00
2.	20 Marks 1896, 1901	1000.00
3.	10 Marks 1896, 1901	1000.00

FREDERICK II, 1904-1918

4.	20 Marks 1904	900.00

BADEN
Grand Dukes of —
FREDERICK I, 1852-1907

5.	20 Marks 1872, 73	200.00
6.	20 Marks 1874	500.00
7.	20 Marks 1894, 95	200.00
8.	10 Marks 1872, 73	160.00
9.	10 Marks 1875-81, 88	200.00
10.	10 Marks 1890, 91, 93, 96, 97, 98, 1900, 01. Head left	180.00
11.	10 Marks 1902-07. Head right	200.00
12.	5 Marks 1877	300.00

FREDERICK II, 1907-1918

13.	20 Marks 1911-14	180.00
14.	10 Marks 1909-13	350.00

BAVARIA
Kings of —
LOUIS II, 1864-1886

15.	20 Marks 1872, 73	220.00
16.	20 Marks 1874-76, 78	220.00
17.	10 Marks 1872, 73	250.00
18.	10 Marks 1874-81	250.00
19.	5 Marks 1877, 78	400.00

OTTO, 1886-1913

20.	20 Marks 1895, 1900, 05, 13	185.00
21.	10 Marks 1888	260.00
22.	10 Marks 1890, 93, 96, 98, 1900. "Von" in title	160.00
23.	10 Marks 1901-07, 09-12. "V" in title	150.00

LOUIS III, 1913-1918

24.	20 Marks 1914	3000.00

BREMEN
Free City of —

25.	20 Marks 1906	1100.00
26.	10 Marks 1907	1100.00

BRUNSWICK
Dukes of —
WILLIAM, 1831-1884

27.	20 Marks 1875	725.00

HAMBURG
Free City of —

28.	20 Marks 1875-81, 83, 84, 87, 89	185.00
29.	20 Marks 1893-95, 97, 99, 1900, 13	185.00
30.	10 Marks 1873	1500.00
31.	10 Marks 1874. Arms of 1873	850.00
32.	10 Marks 1875-80, 1888. New type arms	150.00
33.	10 Marks 1890, 93, 96, 98, 1900-03, 05-13	150.00
34.	5 Marks 1877	275.00

HESSE
Grand Dukes of —
LOUIS III, 1848-1877

35.	20 Marks 1872, 73	300.00
36.	20 Marks 1874	400.00
37.	10 Marks 1872-73	300.00
38.	10 Marks 1875-77	225.00
39.	5 Marks 1877	800.00

LOUIS IV, 1877-1892

40.	20 Marks 1892	1000.00
41.	10 Marks 1878-80. H mm	425.00
42.	10 Marks 1888. A mm	600.00
43.	10 Marks 1890	550.00
44.	5 Marks 1877	850.00

ERNEST LOUIS, 1892-1918

45.	20 Marks 1893. Young head	650.00
46.	20 Marks 1896-1901, 03. Older head with one S in title	300.00
47.	20 Marks 1905, 06, 08, 11. With 2 S's in title	280.00
48.	10 Marks 1893. Young head	650.00
49.	10 Marks 1896, 98. Older head	550.00

LUBECK
Free City of —

50.	10 Marks 1901, 04. Small arms	850.00
51.	10 Marks 1905, 06, 09, 10. Large arms	800.00

MECKLENBURG-SCHWERIN
Grand Dukes of —
FREDERICK FRANCIS II, 1842-1883

52.	20 Marks 1872	1100.00
53.	10 Marks 1872	1250.00
54.	10 Marks 1878	1000.00

FREDERICK FRANCIS III, 1883-1897

55.	10 Marks 1890	500.00

FREDERICK FRANCIS IV, 1897-1918

56.	20 Marks 1901	1800.00
57.	10 Marks 1901	1500.00

MECKLENBURG-STRELITZ

Grand Dukes of —

FREDERICK WILLIAM, 1860-1904

58.	20 Marks 1873	3800.00
59.	20 Marks 1874	3700.00
60.	10 Marks 1873	5500.00
61.	10 Marks 1874, 80	4000.00

ADOLPH FREDERICK, 1904-1914

62.	20 Marks 1905	6000.00
63.	10 Marks 1905	5500.00

OLDENBURG

Grand Dukes of —

NICHOLAS FREDERICK PETER, 1853-1900

64.	10 Marks 1874	4000.00

PRUSSIA

Emperors of Germany and Kings of —

WILLIAM I, 1861-1888

65.	20 Marks 1871-73. A mm	180.00
66.	20 Marks 1872, 73. B mm	180.00
67.	20 Marks 1872, 73. C mm	180.00
68.	20 Marks 1874-79, 81-88. A mm	180.00
69.	20 Marks 1874, 75, 77. B mm	185.00
70.	20 Marks 1874, 76-78. C mm	185.00
71.	10 Marks 1872, 73. A mm	110.00
72.	10 Marks 1872, 73. B mm	110.00
73.	10 Marks 1872, 73. C mm	110.00
74.	10 Marks 1874, 75, 77-80, 82, 83, 86, 88. A mm	110.00
75.	10 Marks 1874-78. B mm	120.00
76.	10 Marks 1874-79. C mm	120.00
77.	5 Marks 1877, 78. A mm	325.00
78.	5 Marks 1877. B mm	325.00
79.	5 Marks 1877. C mm	350.00

FREDERICK III, 1888

80.	20 Marks 1888	185.00
81.	10 Marks 1888	140.00

WILLIAM II, 1888-1918

82.	20 Marks 1888, 89	185.00
83.	20 Marks 1890-1913. A mm ....*	180.00
84.	20 Marks 1905, 06, 08, 09, 10, 12. J mm	180.00
85.	20 Marks 1913-15. Uniformed bust (1915 Rare)	180.00
86.	10 Marks 1889	1800.00
87.	10 Marks 1890, 92-1907, 09-12 ....*	120.00

REUSS-OLDER LINE

Princes of —

HENRY XXII, 1859-1902

88.	20 Marks 1875	9500.00

REUSS-YOUNGER LINE

Princes of —

HENRY XIV, 1867-1913

89.	20 Marks 1881	2500.00
90.	10 Marks 1882	5500.00

SAXONY

Kings of —

JOHN, 1854-1873

91.	20 Marks 1872, 73	185.00
92.	10 Marks 1872, 73	140.00

ALBERT, 1873-1902

93.	20 Marks 1874, 76-78	185.00
94.	20 Marks 1894, 95	140.00

95.	10 Marks 1874, 75, 77, 78, 79, 81, 88	120.00
96.	10 Marks 1891, 93, 96, 98, 1900, 01, 02	120.00
97.	5 Marks 1877	325.00

GEORGE, 1902-1904

98.	20 Marks 1903	200.00
99.	10 Marks 1903, 04	170.00

FREDERICK AUGUST III, 1904-1918

100.	20 Marks 1905, 13, 14.	200.00
101.	10 Marks 1905-07, 1909-12	160.00

SAXONY ALTENBURG

Dukes of —

ERNEST, 1853-1908

102.	20 Marks 1887	1500.00

SAXONY-COBURG-GOTHA

Dukes of —

ERNEST II, 1844-1893

103.	20 Marks 1872	10000.00
104.	20 Marks 1886	1400.00

ALFRED, 1893-1900

105.	20 Marks 1895	1600.00

CARL EDWARD, 1900-1918

106.	20 Marks 1905	1500.00
107.	10 Marks 1905	1250.00

SAXONY-MEININGEN

Dukes of —

GEORGE II, 1866-1914

108.	20 Marks 1872	8000.00
109.	20 Marks 1882. Head right	5500.00
110.	20 Marks 1889. Head left	5000.00
111.	20 Marks 1900, 05	5500.00
112.	20 Marks 1910, 14. New older head	5500.00
113.	10 Marks 1890, 98	3300.00
114.	10 Marks 1902, 09, 14. New older head	3200.00

SAXONY-WEIMAR

Grand Dukes of —

CARL ALEXANDER, 1853-1901

115.	20 Marks 1892, 96	1750.00

WILLIAM ERNEST, 1901-1918

116.	20 Marks 1901	2500.00

SCHAUMBURG-LIPPE

Princes of —

ADOLPH GEORGE, 1860-1893

117.	20 Marks 1874	8250.00

GEORGE, 1893-1911

118.	20 Marks 1898, 1904	2250.00

SCHWARZBURG-RUDOLSTADT

Princes of —

GUNTHER, 1890-1918

119.	10 Marks 1898	1850.00

SCHWARZBURG-SONDERSHAUSEN

Princes of —

CHARLES GUNTHER, 1880-1909

120.	20 Marks 1896	2000.00

WALDECK

Princes of —

FREDERICK, 1893-1918

121.	20 Marks 1903	2700.00

WURTTEMBERG

Kings of —

CHARLES, 1864-1891

122.	20 Marks 1872, 73	180.00
123.	20 Marks 1874, 76	190.00
124.	10 Marks 1872, 73	140.00
125.	10 Marks 1874-81, 1888	140.00
126.	10 Marks 1890, 91	150.00
127.	5 Marks 1877, 78	300.00

WILLIAM II, 1891-1918

128.	20 Marks 1894, 97, 98, 1900, 05, 13, 14	180.00
129.	10 Marks 1893, 96, 98, 1900-07, 09-13	140.00

NOTE: Numbers 130-133 have been deleted

B. Coinage of the German Cities and States before the Empire.

AACHEN (AIX)

Seated Madonna with name of Reynald of Julich. Rev. Charlemagne standing.

134.	½ Goldgulden ND. (1402-23)	Rare

Madonna standing with name of Reynald of Julich. Rev. Charlemagne standing.

135.	½ Goldgulden ND. (1402-23)	Rare

Charlemagne seated. Rev. Church.

136.	5 Ducats ND (1500)	Rare

Charlemagne seated. Rev. Eagle with name of Maximilian II.

137.	1 Goldgulden 1572	2000.00
137a.	13 Ducats 1577	Rare

Charlemagne seated. Rev. Eagle with name of Rudolph II.

138.	1 Goldgulden 1582, 85, 91, 92	1250.00

Charlemagne seated. Rev. Eagle with name of Ferdinand II.

139.	1 Goldgulden 1634	1500.00
140.	1 Goldgulden 1634, square	2000.00

Bust of Charlemagne. Rev. Ferdinand III standing.

141.	1 Ducat 1641, 43, 45	1000.00

Ferdinand III standing. Rev. Value in tablet.

142.	1 Ducat 1646	1250.00

Bust of Charlemagne. Rev. Madonna standing.

143.	1 Ducat ND. (1637-57)	Rare

Madonna standing. Rev. Value in tablet.

144.	1 Ducat ND.	2000.00

Emperor Francis standing. Rev. Value in tablet.

145.	1 Ducat 1753	1500.00

ANHALT

Princes of —

WOLDEMAR VI AND BROTHERS, 1471-1508
St. Anne standing. Rev. Arms.

146.	1 Goldgulden ND	Rare

JOHN GEORGE AND BROTHERS, 1603-1618
Two busts. Rev. Three busts.

147.	4 Ducats 1614	Rare
148.	3 Ducats 1614, 16	Rare

Three helmets. Rev. Arms.

149.	1 Ducat 1615, 16, 18, ND	1500.00
150.	½ Ducat 1616, 18	1200.00

ANHALT-BERNBURG

Dukes of —

VICTOR FREDERICK, 1721-1765
Arms. Rev. Bear on wall.

151.	1 Ducat 1730-61	1500.00

Bust. Rev. Arms.

152.	5 Taler 1744	2200.00
153.	2½ Taler 1744	2000.00

ALEXIUS FREDERICK CHRISTIAN, 1796-1834

Bust. Rev. Arms.

154.	5 Taler or 1 Pistole 1796	1500.00

Bear on wall. Rev. Value and date.

155.	1 Harz-gold Ducat 1825	2250.00

ANHALT-COETHEN

Dukes of —

AUGUST LOUIS, 1728-1755
Arms supported by bears. Rev. Bear with shield.

156.	1 Ducat 1747, 51	1000.00

Head. Rev. Bear with shield.

157.	1 Ducat 1751	1250.00

ANHALT-PLOETZKAU

Dukes of —

AUGUST, 1603-1653
Altar with Phoenix. Rev. Fountain.

158.	3 Goldgulden 1620.....................	Rare
159.	2 Goldgulden 1620.....................	3000.00
160.	1 Goldgulden 1615, 17, 20	1500.00

ANHALT-ZERBST

Princes of —

CHARLES WILLIAM, 1667-1718
Bust. Rev. C.W.

161.	½ Ducat ND.........................	1250.00

JOHN LOUIS AND CHRISTIAN AUGUST, 1742-1747

Two busts. Rev. Arms.

162.	1 Ducat 1742 ....*	1250.00
163.	1 Ducat 1745. On the marriage of Catherine II of Russia, and with different legend	1500.00

FREDERICK AUGUST, 1747-1793
Bust. Rev. Arms.

164.	1 Ducat 1764	2500.00

ARENBERG

Dukes of —

LOUIS ENGELBERT, 1778-1820

Head. Rev. Arms.

165.	1 Ducat 1783	3000.00

ASPREMONT

Barons —

FERDINAND
Ruler standing. Rev. Arms.

166.	1 Ducat ND (1650)	3000.00

AUGSBURG

A. City Coinage

Legend. Rev. Ship. On the Reformation.

167.	1 Ducat 1717	1500.00

City view. Rev. Legend. On the Augsburg Confession.

168.	1 Ducat 1730	1800.00

B. Coinage with the heads or names of the Holy Roman Emperors.

St. Udalric seated. Rev. Orb. Name of Maximilian I.

169.	1 Goldgulden 1515..................	4000.00

Bust of Charles V. Rev. Arms.

170.	1 Goldgulden 1527, 31	3000.00

St. Udalric seated. Rev. Orb. Name of Charles V.

171.	1 Goldgulden 1520..................	3500.00

Eagle. Rev. Arms. Name of Charles V.

172.	1 Goldgulden ND (1517-58).........	850.00

Bust of Ferdinand I. Rev. Arms.

173.	1 Goldgulden 1558..................	3000.00

Eagle. Rev. Arms. Name of Ferdinand I.

174.	1 Goldgulden 1562, 63	2500.00

Bust of Maximilian II. Rev. Arms.

175.	1 Goldgulden 1562, 66	2000.00

Bust of Rudolph II. Rev. Arms.

176.	1 Goldgulden 1582..................	2000.00

Eagle. Rev. Pyre. Name of Rudolph II.

177.	1 Goldgulden 1609.................	3000.00

Seated female. Rev. Eagle. Name of Matthias II.

178.	1 Goldgulden 1613.................	1250.00

Bust of Ferdinand II. Rev. Arms.

179.	1 Goldgulden 1619.................	2000.00

Eagle. Rev. Arms. Name of Ferdinand II.

180.	1 Goldgulden 1623, 28.............	2000.00

St. Afra and St. Ulric standing. Rev. Eagle. Name of Ferdinand II.

181.	2 Ducats 1626	4500.00

St. Afra and pyre. Rev. Eagle. Name of Ferdinand II.

182.	4 Ducats 1630	8500.00
183.	1 Ducat 1629-38	1000.00

St. Afra and St. Ulric standing. Rev. Double eagle. Name of Ferdinand II.

184.	1 Goldgulden 1627, 28.............	3000.00

Bust of Ferdinand III. Rev. Arms.

185.	2 Ducats 1641, 43	4000.00
186.	1 Ducat 1637-57 ....*	1250.00

Busts of Ferdinand III and Eleanor. Rev. Arms.

187.	2 Ducats 1657	4500.00

St. Afra and pyre. Rev. Eagle. Name of Ferdinand III.
188.   1 Ducat 1638, 39, 42 .... 1850.00

Bust of Ferdinand IV. Rev. Legend in wreath. On his coronation.
189.   1 Ducat 1653 .... 3000.00

Legend. Rev. Eagle and trophies. Homage for Ferdinand IV.
190.   1 Ducat 1653 .... 1250.00

Sceptre and palms. Rev. Inscription.
191.   1 Ducat 1653 .... 1000.00

Bust of Leopold I. Rev. Arms.
192.   1 Ducat 1658-77 .... 1500.00

Bust of Leopold I. Rev. Pyre in wreath.
193.   1 Ducat 1677-92 .... 2000.00

Bust of Leopold I. Rev. Arms between river gods.
194.   2 Ducats 1700 .... 3500.00
195.   1 Ducat 1695, 97, 99, 1701 .... 1500.00

Bust of Leopold I. Rev. Female and pyre.
196.   1 Ducat 1701, 02 .... 2000.00

Bust of Leopold I and Margaret. Rev. Arms.
197.   3 Ducats 1672 .... 3500.00
198.   2 Ducats 1672 .... 2500.00

Bust of Leopold I. Rev. Bust of Eleanor.
199.   1 Ducat 1689, 90 .... 1750.00

Busts of Leopold and Eleanor. Rev. Arms.
200.   3 Ducats 1691 .... 3500.00
201.   2 Ducats 1691 .... 2500.00

Bust of Joseph I. Rev. Crown and insignia. On his coronation.
202.   1 Ducat 1690 .... 2000.00

Bust of Joseph I. Rev. Eagle.
203.   1 Ducat 1690 .... 1500.00

Two genii over legend. Rev. Sword. Joseph I as Emperor.
204.   1½ Ducats 1690 .... 2000.00

Two genii over legend. Rev. Crown. Joseph I as Crown Prince.
205.   1 Ducat 1690 .... 1500.00

Bust of Joseph I. Rev. Female and pyre.
206.   1 Ducat 1705, 07 .... 1850.00

Bust of Joseph I. Rev. Pyre between river gods and eagle.
207.   1 Ducat 1708, 11 .... 1500.00

Bust of Charles VI. Rev. Pyre between river gods and eagle.
208.   1 Ducat 1711 .... 1850.00

Bust of Charles VI. Rev. Pyre between river gods and eagle.
209.   1 Ducat 1714, 15 .... 1850.00

Bust of Charles VI. Rev. Flying eagle. On his coronation.
210.   1 Ducat 1711 .... 2000.00

Bust of Charles VI. Rev. Pyre between river gods.
211.   2 Ducats 1738 .... 3500.00
212.   1 Ducat 1737, 38 .... 2000.00

Bust of Charles VI. Rev. Female and pyre.
213.   1 Ducat 1726 ....*...... 1500.00
214.   ½ Ducat 1717 .... 1250.00

Bust of Charles VII. Rev. Female and pyre.
215.   1 Ducat 1742 .... 2250.00

Bust of Charles VII. Rev. Arms.
216.   1 Ducat 1743 .... 2250.00

Bust of Francis I. Rev. As indicated.
217.   3 Ducats 1745. City view 4500.00
218.   2 Ducats 1745. City view 3500.00
219.   3 Ducats 1745. Arms 4500.00
220.   2 Ducats 1745. Arms 3500.00

Bust of Francis I. Rev. Eagle and pyre between river gods.
221.   1 Ducat 1745 .... 2500.00

Bust of Francis I. Rev. Arms.
222.   1 Ducat 1762, 63 .... 2000.00

Bust of Joseph II. Rev. Arms.

223.   1 Ducat 1767 . . . .   1850.00

C. Bishops of —

ALEXANDER SIGISMUND OF THE PALATINATE, 1690-1737

Bust. Rev. Two shields.

224.   2 Ducats 1708 . . . . ★ 4000.00
225.   1 Ducat 1708 . . . .   2500.00

JOSEPH OF HESSE, 1740-1768
Bust with cap. Rev. Two shields.

226.   1 Ducat 1744 . . . .   2000.00

D. Swedish Kings of —

Conjoined heads of Gustav II Adolphe and Queen. Rev. Two shields.

226a.   3 Ducats 1632 . . . .   10000.00
227.   2 Ducats 1632 . . . . ★ 5000.00

Facing or profile bust of Gustav II Adolphe. Rev. Arms.

228.   1 Ducat 1632, 33, 34, 35 . . . .   750.00

BADEN

Margraves, and later, Grand Dukes of —

A. The Baden Line (Baden-Baden)

CHRISTOPHER, 1475-1527

St. Peter. Rev. Four shields and cross.

229.   1 Goldgulden ND . . . . ★ 1250.00
230.   1 Goldgulden 1505-09 . . . .   1500.00

St. Bernard standing. Rev. Arms.

231.   1 Goldgulden 1513, 18, 19 . . . . /. . .   2750.00

WILLIAM, 1622-1677
St. George on horse. Rev. Circle of arms.

232.   1 Goldgulden ND . . . .   Rare

Bust. Rev. Arms.

233.   1 Ducat 1674 . . . .   3000.00

LOUIS GEORGE AND FRANCISCA SIBYLLA AUGUSTA, 1707-1761

Conjoined busts. Rev. Two shields. On the Peace of Rastatt.

234.   1 Ducat 1714 . . . .   1750.00

B. The Durlach Line (Baden-Durlach)

GEORGE FREDERICK, 1604-1622

Bust. Rev. Quartered Arms.

235.   10 Ducats 1610 . . . . ★ . . . . . .   Rare
236.   2 Ducats 1610 . . . .   3500.00
237.   1 Goldgulden 1609 . . . .   2500.00

Ruler standing. Rev. Arms.

238.   1 Ducat 1622 . . . . Unknown

CHARLES WILLIAM, 1709-1738

Armored Bust. Rev. Arms supported by griffins.

239.   1 Ducat 1721 . . . .   2500.00
240.   ½ Ducat 1721 . . . . ★ 1500.00

Bust. Rev. Four shields and four initials around central shield.

241.   1 Carolin 1733, 34 . . . .   2500.00
242.   ½ Carolin 1734 . . . .   1500.00

Large bust. Rev. Draped arms.

243.   1 Ducat 1736 . . . .   2000.00
244.   1 Carolin 1734, 35 . . . .   2500.00

Arms. Rev. Legend in square tablet.

245.   2 Ducats 1737 . . . .   4000.00

Arms. Rev. Legend in circle.

246.   1 Ducat 1737 .... 2000.00

Arms. Rev. Legend in cartouche.

247.   ½ Ducat 1737 .... 1250.00

CHARLES AUGUST AND MAGDALENE WILHELMINA, 1738-1745

Crowned oval shield. Rev. Two shields surmounted by vase.

248.   1 Ducat 1738 .... 1500.00

Crowned oval shield. Rev. Two shields surmounted by flame.

249.   1 Ducat 1738 .... 1500.00

Crowned oval shield. Rev. Three line legend and date.

250.   1 Ducat 1738 .... 2500.00

Crowned oval shield. Rev. Standing female and column.

251.   1 Ducat 1738 .... 1850.00

CHARLES FREDERICK, 1746-1811
Large armored bust. Rev. Arms surrounded by legend and date.

252.   1 Ducat 1747 .... 1500.00

Large armored bust. Rev. Arms flanked by date.

253.   1 Ducat 1751 .... 1250.00

Large armored bust. Rev. Two shields crowned.

254.   ½ Ducat 1747 .... 1250.00

Crowned shield. Rev. Legend and date in circle.

255.   ¼ Ducat 1747 .... 750.00

Large head. Rev. Shield with supporters.

256.   1 Rhine-gold Ducat 1765, 67, 68 .... 3500.00

Bust of Amalie Frederika of Hesse. Rev. Two shields. On the birth of twin princesses.

257.   1 Ducat 1776 .... 2000.00

Two baby heads facing each other. Rev. Legend. On the birth of twin princesses.

258.   1 Ducat 1776 .... 1500.00

Bust. Rev. Draped arms. On the birth of Prince Charles.

259.   1 Ducat 1786 .... 2000.00

Head. Rev. River god.

260.   1 Rhine-gold Ducat 1807 .... 2500.00

LOUIS, 1818-1830

Head. Rev. Arms.

261.   10 Gulden 1819, 21, 23, 24, 25 ....* 1750.00
262.   5 Gulden 1819, 21, 22, 24-28 ....* 1500.00
263.   5 Taler or 500 Kreuzer 1830 .... 1500.00

LEOPOLD, 1830-1852

Obv. as indicated. Rev. Arms.

264.   1 Rhine-gold Ducat 1832-42. Small head 2000.00
265.   1 Rhine-gold Ducat 1843-46. Larger head 2000.00
266.   1 Rhine-gold Ducat 1847-52. Largest head 2000.00

FREDERICK, 1852-1907

Head. Rev. Arms.

267.   1 Rhine-gold Ducat 1854......................... 2200.00

BAMBERG

A. City of —

Two females standing. Rev. Legend. On the Union with Bavaria.

268.   1 Ducat 1802 .... 1500.00

B. Bishops of —

GEORGE III SCHENK, 1505-1522

St. Henry standing. Rev. Two shields.

269.   1 Goldgulden 1506, 11, 12, 13, 14.................. 4000.00

St. Henry and St. Kunigunde with church model. Rev. Two shields.

270.   1 Goldgulden 1507, ND 4500.00

JOHN PHILIP, 1599-1609

St. Henry and St. Kunigunde with church model. Rev. Two shields.

271.   2 Ducats 1601 .... Rare
272.   1 Ducat 1600, 01, 02 ....*...... 3500.00

JOHN GODFREY, 1609-1622
Arms. Rev. Legend. On his death.

273.   1 Goldgulden 1622............................... 2500.00

JOHN GEORGE II FUCHS, 1623-1633
Bust. Rev. St. Henry and St. Kunigunde with church model.

274.   1 Ducat 1628, 31 .... 3000.00
275.   1 Goldgulden 1624, 28........................... 2500.00

FRANCIS, 1633-1642

Madonna seated. Rev. Arms.

276.   1 Ducat 1635, 37, 38, 40 .... 1500.00

MELCHIOR OTTO VOIT, 1642-1653

Bust. Rev. Arms.

277.   1 Ducat 1647 .... 2000.00

PHILIP VALENTINE VOIT, 1653-1672
Bust. Rev. Two shields.

278.   1 Ducat 1657 .... 2000.00

LOTHAR FRANCIS, 1693-1729
(See under Mayence.)

FREDERICK CHARLES, 1729-1746
(See under Wurzburg.)

JOHN PHILIP ANTHONY, 1746-1753
Bust. Rev. Arms.

279.   1 Ducat 1750 .... 2200.00

Knight standing. Rev. Arms.

280.   1 Ducat 1746 .... 2000.00

FRANCIS CONRAD, 1753-1757

Bust. Rev. Arms. On the Homage of Bamberg.

281.   1 Ducat 1753 .... 2500.00

ADAM FREDERICK, 1757-1779

Bust. Rev. Knight standing. On the Homage of Bamberg.

282.   1 Ducat 1757 .... 1850.00

FRANCIS LOUIS, 1779-1795

Bust. Rev. Female and pyramid. On the Homage of Bamberg.

283.　　1 Ducat 1779 .... 1800.00

CHRISTOPHER FRANCIS, 1795-1802

Bust over legend. Rev. Female at altar. On the Homage of Bamberg.

284.　　1 Ducat 1795, ND.................................. 1500.00

BAVARIA

Dukes, and later, Kings of —

LOUIS IV, 1314-1347
Arms on cross. Rev. Three shields.

285.　　1 Goldgulden ND................................. 2000.00

Lamb. Rev. Floriated cross.

286.　　1 Mouton d'or ND .... Rare

Ruler on throne. Rev. Cross.

287.　　1 Chaise d'or ND................................. 2500.00

ALBERT IV, 1465-1508
Duke kneeling before Madonna standing. Rev. Arms.

288.　　1 Goldgulden 1506.............................. 1850.00

Duke kneeling before Madonna seated. Rev. Arms.

289.　　1 Goldgulden 1506................. .... 1750.00

WILLIAM IV, 1508-1550
Duke kneeling before Madonna seated. Rev. Arms. With titles of Albert.

290.　　1 Goldgulden 1508, 09, 10 .... 2000.00

WILLIAM IV AND LOUIS X, 1516-1545
Madonna seated. Rev. Arms.

291.　　1 Goldgulden ND................................. 4000.00

Madonna standing. Rev. Arms.

292.　　1 Goldgulden 1525, 32............................ 4000.00

ALBERT V, 1550-1579
Bust. Rev. Arms.

293.　　2 Ducats 1565, 68 .... 4500.00

Bust with hat. Rev. Arms.

294.　　1 Ducat ND...................................... 2000.00

Duke kneeling. Rev. Lion with arms.

295.　　2 Ducats ND 4500.00
296.　　1 Ducat ND...................................... 2000.00

WILLIAM V, 1579-1598
Arms. Rev. Date. On his wedding.

297.　　1 Ducat 1568 .... 2000.00

St. Henry standing. Rev. Arms.

298.　　1 Ducat 1596 .... 2500.00

MAXIMILIAN I, 1598-1651
St. Henry standing. Rev. Arms.

298a.　 8 Ducats 1598 .... 8500.00

Elector before Madonna. Rev. Arms.

299.　　2 Ducats 1642, 44, 45, 47 .... * 2000.00
300.　　1 Ducat 1638, 42-47............................ 1500.00

Madonna. Rev. Arms.

301.　　2 Ducats 1618 .... * 2000.00
302.　　1 Goldgulden 1625............................. 1500.00
303.　　1 Ducat 1632, 40 .... 1500.00

Elector standing. Rev. View of Munich.

304.　　5 Ducats 1640 .... * 4000.00
305.　　1 Ducat 1645 .... 2000.00

Elector standing. Rev. Madonna.

306.　　2 Ducats 1645 .... 3500.00
307.　　1 Ducat 1644, 46 .... 1500.00

Elector at table. Rev. Madonna over view of Munich.

308.　　4 Ducats 1610 .... 4000.00

FERDINAND MARIA, 1651-1679
Elector standing. Rev. Madonna and shield.

309.　　1 Ducat 1655-71 .... 1500.00

Elector standing. Rev. View of Munich.

310.　　1 Ducat 1677, 78 .... 2500.00

Bust. Rev. Madonna and shield.

311.　1 Goldgulden 1674-79............................. 1250.00

Bust. Rev. Arms.

312.　½ Ducat 1672, 78 .... 1250.00
313.　¼ Ducat 1672, 73, 76 .... 1000.00

Busts of Ferdinand and Adelaide. Rev. Arms. On their wedding.

314.　3 Ducats 1652 .... 4500.00

Madonna. Rev. Shield. On the birth of Prince Max Emanuel.

315.　½ Ducat 1662 .... 850.00

Bust of Adelaide. Rev. Arms. On the birth of Princess Louise.

316.　1 Ducat 1663 .... 1000.00

Family kneeling. Rev. Two shields. On the birth of Prince Louis Amadeus.

317.　4 Ducats 1665 .... 5000.00

Sun, moon and earth. Rev. Three shields. On the birth of Prince Cajetan Maria.

318.　2 Ducats 1670 .... 3500.00

St. Nicholas seated. Rev. Arms. On the birth of Prince Joseph Clemens.

319.　1 Ducat 1671 .... 2000.00

Two shields. Rev. Column. On the birth of Princess Violanta Beatrix.

320.　2 Ducats 1673 .... 2500.00

MAXIMILIAN EMANUEL, 1679-1726

Bust. Rev. Madonna standing.

321.　2 Ducats 1685, 87 ....*...... 4000.00
322.　1 Ducat 1687, 97 .... 2000.00

Bust. Rev. Madonna over arms.

323.　1 Goldgulden 1691, 98............................ 1850.00

Bust. Rev. Bust of Madonna over arms.

324.　1 Goldgulden 1699, 1700, 02, 03, 15........*...... 1250.00
325.　1 Goldgulden 1704. With pyre under bust.
　　　(Occupation of Augsburg) 2200.00

Head. Rev. Arms. Struck for the Lowlands.

326.　2 Souverain d'or 1712..................... 3000.00

Head. Rev. Madonna seated.

327.　2 Max d'or 1717 .... 1850.00
328.　1 Max d'or 1715-26 ....*..... 1000.00
329.　½ Max d'or 1715-25 .... 850.00

Palm tree. Rev. Shields of Bavaria and Poland. On the birth of Prince Charles Albert.

330.　2 Ducats 1697 .... 2500.00

Three sunflowers. Rev. Legend. On the birth of Prince Ferdinand Maria.

331.　2 Ducats 1699 .... 2200.00

Crowned lion. Rev. Arms. Struck for the Lowlands.

332.　1 Souverain d'or 1711-13......................... 2500.00

CHARLES ALBERT, 1726-1744

Head. Rev. Madonna seated.

333.　1 Carolin 1726-32............................. 1500.00
334.　½ Carolin 1726-31............................. 1000.00
335.　¼ Carolin 1726-31............................. 750.00

Bust. Rev. Madonna seated.

336.　1 Carolin 1732-35............................. 2000.00
337.　½ Carolin 1732-37............................. 1250.00
338.　¼ Carolin 1732-35............................. 1000.00

Bust. Rev. Arms supported by lions.

339.　1 Ducat 1737 ....Unknown

Head. Rev. Eagle. On the Vicariat.

340.　2 Goldgulden 1740............................. 2000.00
341.　1 Goldgulden 1740............................. 1500.00

Bust. Rev. Eagle. On the Vicariat.

342.　1 Ducat 1740 .... 1850.00

Madonna. Rev. Arms supported by lions.

343.　2 Ducats 1737 ....Unknown
344.　1 Ducat 1737, 39.........................*...... 2000.00

"AB". Rev. Legend. On his wedding.

345. 1 Ducat 1722 . . . . 2000.00

MAXIMILIAN III JOSEPH, 1745-1777

Bust. Rev. Eagle. On the Vicariat.

346. 1 Ducat 1745 . . . . 2200.00

Bust. Rev. Madonna.

347. 1 Max d'or 1747, 51 . . . . 2000.00

Busts of Maximilian and Marie Anne. Rev. Landscape. On their wedding.

348. 1 Ducat 1747 . . . . 2000.00

Bust. Rev. Carriage. Homage of the representatives of the people.

349. 1 Ducat 1747 . . . . 2000.00

Bust of Maximilian and Marie Anne. Rev. Bavaria before Pyramid.

350. 5 Ducats 1747 . . . . 5500.00

Bust. Rev. River god.

351. 1 Danube-gold Ducat 1756, 60, 62 . . . . 5000.00
352. 1 Inn-gold Ducat 1756, 60, 62 . . . . 6000.00
353. 1 Isar-gold Ducat 1756, 60, 62 . . . . 7500.00

Bust. Rev. Arms supported by lions.

354. 1 Ducat 1755-75 . . . . 2000.00

CHARLES THEODORE, 1777-1799

Head. Rev. Arms.

355. 3 Ducats 1787 . . . . 8000.00
356. 2 Ducats 1787 . . . . 4000.00
357. 1 Ducat 1778-98 . . . . * 1600.00

Head. Rev. River god, city in background.

358. 1 Danube-gold Ducat 1779, 80, 93 . . . . 3500.00
359. 1 Inn-gold Ducat 1779, 80, 93, 98 . . . . 4000.00
360. 1 Isar-gold Ducat 1779, 80, 93, 98 . . . . 5000.00

Head. Rev. Double Eagle. On the Vicariat.

361. 3 Ducats 1790, 92 . . . . * 5000.00
362. 2 Ducats 1790, 92 . . . . 4000.00
363. 1 Ducat 1790, 92 . . . . 1800.00

MAXIMILIAN JOSEPH (IV, 1799-1806), (I, 1806-1825)
Head. Rev. Arms.

364. 1 Ducat 1799-1805 . . . . 1800.00

Head. Rev. Wurzburg shield under palm tree.

365. 1 Goldgulden 1803 . . . . 2200.00

Bust or head. Rev. Arms supported by lions.

366. 1 Ducat 1806. Bust 2000.00
367. 1 Ducat 1811-25. Head 1500.00

Head. Rev. Wurzburg city view.

368. 1 Goldgulden 1815 . . . . 2000.00

Head. Rev. Wurzburg shield.

369. 1 Goldgulden 1817, ND 2500.00

Head. Rev. River god.

370. 1 Danube-gold Ducat 1821 . . . . 4000.00
371. 1 Inn-gold Ducat 1821 . . . . 4500.00
372. 1 Isar-gold Ducat 1821 . . . . 4500.00

Head. Rev. Speyer city view.

373. 1 Rhine-gold Ducat 1821 . . . . 3000.00

LOUIS I, 1825-1848

Head. Rev. Arms supported by lions.

374. 1 Ducat 1826-48 . . . . 1500.00

Head. Rev. River god.

375.	1 Danube-gold Ducat 1830	3000.00
376.	1 Inn-gold Ducat 1830	3000.00
377.	1 Isar-gold Ducat 1830	3500.00

Young or old head. Rev. Speyer city view.

378.	1 Rhine-gold Ducat 1830, 42, 46	2000.00

Head. Rev. Legend.

379.	1 Goldgulden 1826	2200.00

Head. Rev. Wurzburg city view.

380.	1 Goldgulden ND (1827, 43)	2000.00

Head. Rev. Wurzburg shield.

381.	1 Goldgulden ND (1843)	2000.00

MAXIMILIAN II, 1848-1864

Head. Rev. Arms.

382.	1 Ducat 1849-56	1250.00

Head. Rev. Wurzburg shield.

383.	1 Goldgulden ND (1850)	3500.00

Head. Rev. Wurzburg city view.

384.	1 Goldgulden ND (1850)	2800.00

Head. Rev. Speyer city view.

385.	1 Rhine-gold Ducat 1850-56, 63	1400.00

Head. Rev. Arms.

386.	1 Mining-Ducat 1855. Goldkronach	Rare

Head. Rev. Value.

387.	1 Krone 1857-64		4500.00
388.	½ Krone 1857-64	*	3800.00
389.	½ Krone 1864		6000.00

LOUIS II, 1864-1886

Head. Rev. Value.

390.	1 Krone 1864-69	*	6000.00
391.	½ Krone 1864-69		4500.00

Head. Rev. Wurzburg city view.

392.	1 Goldgulden ND (1864)	2500.00

Head. Rev. Wurzburg shield.

393.	1 Goldgulden ND (1864)	2200.00

Head. Rev. Crown in wreath.

394.	1 Ducat ND (1864)	1000.00

BENTHEIM

Counts —

MAURICE, 1625-1674
Bust. Rev. Arms.

395.	1 Ducat 1656	4000.00

ERNEST WILLIAM, 1643-1693
Arms. Rev. Value.

396.	2 Ducats 1669	5000.00
397.	1 Ducat 1669	2000.00

BRANDENBURG-ANSBACH
Margraves of —

JOACHIM ERNEST, 1603-1625

Margrave standing. Rev. Arms.

398.	4 Ducats 1622 .... *	Rare
399.	2 Ducats 1622	3500.00
400.	1 Ducat 1609, 19, 20, 23, 24	1200.00

Facing armored bust. Rev. Arms.

401. 1 Goldgulden 1610, 11, 19-21, 23, 24 .... 2000.00

Margrave on horse. Rev. Cross and five shields.

402. 1 Goldgulden 1623 .... 2000.00

FREDERICK, ALBERT AND CHRISTIAN, 1625-1634
Three busts. Rev. Arms.

403. 1 Ducat 1625-30, 32 .... 1500.00

ALBERT, 1634-1667
Bust. Rev. Arms.

404.	2 Ducats 1660	3500.00
405.	1 Ducat 1651, 52, 63	1200.00

JOHN FREDERICK, 1667-1686
Bust. Rev. Arms.

406.	3 Ducats 1672	4500.00
407.	2 Ducats 1672, 77, 83.	3000.00
408.	1 Ducat 1672	2000.00
409.	1 Ducat 1680, 83. PIETATE ET IVSTITIA ...	1250.00

Bust. Rev. Crossed initials.

410. 1 Ducat 1684 .... 1500.00

Arms. Rev. Piety and Justice.

411.	2 Ducats 1683	1250.00
412.	5/4 Ducat 1674	850.00
413.	1/4 Ducat 1680, 84	350.00

WILLIAM FREDERICK, 1703-1723
Bust. Rev. Arms.

414. 1 Ducat 1715 .... 2000.00

Bust. Rev. Two shields.

415. 1/4 Ducat 1717 .... 850.00

CHRISTIANE CHARLOTTE, 1723-1729

Bust. Rev. Crown over linked C's.

416. 1 Ducat 1726 .... 2200.00

CHARLES WILLIAM FREDERICK, 1729-1757
Bust. Rev. Eagle.

417.	2 Ducats 1729. Thick or broad	3000.00
418.	1 Ducat 1729	1500.00

Bust. Rev. Two shields.

419. 1 Ducat 1740, 47, 50 .... 1500.00

Bust. Rev. Eagle with shield.

420. 1 Ducat 1744 .... 1500.00

Bust. Rev. Eagle over arms.

421. 1 Ducat 1753 .... 1500.00

Falconier on horse. Rev. Falcon.

422. 1 Hunting Ducat ND 2500.00

Bust. Rev. Arms.

423.	1 Carolin 1734, 35	2200.00
424.	1/2 Carolin 1734, 35	1850.00

ALEXANDER, 1757-1791
Two shields. Rev. Legend. On his wedding.

425.	2 Ducats 1754	2200.00
426.	1 Ducat 1754	1500.00

Bust. Rev. Eagle shield.

427. 1 Ducat 1757 .... 1500.00

Bust. Rev. Arms.

428. 1 Ducat 1762 .... 1500.00

Bust. Rev. Crown above three arms.

429.	1 Ducat 1763	1500.00
430.	1 Ducat 1777 .... *	1850.00

Bust. Rev. Star of Order.

431. 1 Ducat 1779 .... 1800.00

Bust. Rev. Eagle shield with chain of Order.

432. 1 Carolin 1758, 66 .... 2200.00

Margrave on horse. Rev. Shields and trophies.

433. 1 Ducat 1765 .... 2000.00

Head. Rev. Eagle with two shields. On the union of Ansbach and Culmbach.

434. 1 Ducat 1769 .... 2000.00

Busts of Alexander and George Frederick. Rev. Altar. On the union of Ansbach and Culmbach.

435. 1 Ducat 1769 .... 1500.00

Knight at altar. Rev. Legend. On the homage.

436. 1 Ducat 1769 .... 1500.00

BRANDENBURG-BAYREUTH

Margraves of —

CHRISTIAN, 1603-1655
Margrave standing. Rev. Arms.

437.	4 Ducats 1609	4500.00
438.	2 Ducats 1609	2500.00
439.	1 Ducat 1609, 28-32	1500.00

Bust. Rev. Arms.

440.	1 Ducat 1631, 41, 42, 44, ND	1500.00

Bust. Rev. Arms. On the 50th year of his reign.

441.	1 Ducat 1653	2000.00

CHRISTIAN ERNEST, 1655-1712
Bust. Rev. Arms.

442.	1 Ducat 1659, 62, 77, 94, 1708, ND	1500.00
443.	½ Ducat 1685	1500.00

Busts of the Margrave and his wife. Rev. View of Cronach Mine.

444.	2 Ducats 1695	Rare

GEORGE WILLIAM, 1712-1726
Bust. Rev. Arms.

445.	2 Ducats 1720	5000.00
446.	1 Ducat 1720-22	2500.00

Bust. Rev. Legend. On his death.

447.	2 Ducats 1726	3000.00
448.	1 Ducat 1726	1800.00

GEORGE FREDERICK CHARLES, 1726-1735
Swan and tree. Rev. Legend. On the homage.

449.	1 Ducat 1727	1800.00

FREDERICK, 1735-1763
Bust. Rev. Arms.

450.	1 Ducat 1735, 46	1250.00

Margrave on horse. Rev. Order.

451.	1 Ducat 1746	1250.00

FREDERICK CHRISTIAN, 1763-1769
Bust. Rev. Arms.

452.	1 Ducat 1763	1500.00

Bust. Rev. Bible, cross and sword. On his birthday.

453.	1 Ducat 1764	1800.00

Margrave on horse. Rev. Crown over Order.

454.	1 Ducat 1767	1500.00

BRANDENBURG-FRANCONIA

Margraves of —

FREDERICK V, 1361-1397

Arms in enclosure. Rev. St. John.

455.	1 Goldgulden ND	1500.00

JOHN III, 1404-1420
Arms in enclosure. Rev. St. John.

456.	1 Goldgulden ND	Rare

FREDERICK VI, 1404-1440
Eagle. Rev. St. John.

457.	1 Goldgulden ND	2500.00

ALBERT ACHILLES, 1464-1486

St. John. Rev. Cross with five shields.

458.	1 Goldgulden ND. Mint: Schwabach	650.00

FREDERICK AND SIGISMUND, 1486-1495
St. John. Rev. Cross with four shields.

459.	1 Goldgulden ND. Mint: Schwabach	600.00

FREDERICK IV, 1495-1515
St. John. Rev. Cross with four shields.

460.	1 Goldgulden 1497-1515, ND. Mint: Schwabach	750.00

CASIMIR AND GEORGE, 1515-1527
St. John. Rev. Cross with four shields.

461.	1 Goldgulden 1515-26. Mint: Schwabach	1000.00

GEORGE, 1527-1536
Cross with five shields. Rev. St. John.

462.	1 Goldgulden 1528-35	850.00

GEORGE AND ALBERT, 1536-1543
Cross with five shields. Rev. St. John.

463.	1 Goldgulden 1538, 40, 41	1000.00

ALBERT ALCIBIADES, 1527-1554
Eagle. Rev. Blank. Square necessity coin.

464.	1 Ducat 1553	2200.00

Armored bust. Rev. Cross with five shields.

465.	1 Goldgulden 1549	3000.00

GEORGE FREDERICK, 1543-1603
Margrave standing. Rev. Arms.

466.	1 Ducat 1557. Mint: Schwabach	4000.00

Facing bust. Rev. Cross with five shields.

467.	1 Goldgulden 1571. Mint: Schwabach	3500.00

Margrave standing. Rev. Eagle.

468.   1 Ducat 1587-91, 94-97. Mint: Koenigsberg 1200.00

BRANDENBURG-PRUSSIA

(See under Prussia)

BRAUNAU

Arms. Rev. Blank. Octagonal siege coins of the Austrian War of Succession.

469.   2 Ducats 1743 .... 4000.00
470.   1 Ducat 1743 .... 2500.00
471.   ½ Ducat 1743 .... 1500.00

BREISACH

Legend. Rev. Imperial orb over three shields.

472.   1 Ducat 1633. Square siege coin................... 6500.00

BREMEN

A. City Coins with the heads or names of the Holy Roman Emperors

Eagle. Rev. Arms. Charles V.

473.   1 Goldgulden 1542, 46, 49 .... 4000.00

Eagle. Rev. Arms. Matthias II.

474.   1 Goldgulden 1613................................. 2500.00

Eagle. Rev. Arms supported by lions. Ferdinand II.

475.   1 Goldgulden 1635, 37............................. 2000.00

Eagle. Rev. Arms. Ferdinand II.

476.   1 Goldgulden 1627, 35............................. 2000.00

Ferdinand II standing. Rev. Arms.

477.   2 Ducats 1640, 52 .... 3500.00
478.   1 Ducat 1640-52 ....*...... 2200.00

Eagle. Rev. Arms supported by lions. Ferdinand III.

479.   2 Goldgulden 1649.........................*...... 7500.00
480.   1 Goldgulden 1640............................... 2500.00

Key. Rev. St. Peter. Leopold I.

481.   ¼ Ducat ND..................................... 1000.00

Eagle. Rev. Arms supported by lions. Leopold I.

482.   5 Ducats 1661 .... 6500.00
483.   3 Ducats 1667 .... 5500.00

Leopold I standing. Rev. Arms.

484.   5 Ducats ND .... Rare
485.   3 Ducats 1659 .... Rare
486.   2 Ducats 1659, 67 .... 4000.00
487.   1 Ducat 1659, 67.........................*...... 2000.00

Head of Leopold I. Rev. Arms.

488.   1 Ducat 1672 .... 2500.00

Bust of Leopold I. Rev. Arms supported by lions.

489.   4 Ducats ND .... Rare

Eagle. Rev. Arms supported by lions. Joseph I.

490.   1 Ducat 1710 .... 3000.00

Eagle. Rev. Arms supported by lions. Charles VI.

491.   1 Ducat 1723 .... 2500.00

Eagle. Rev. Arms supported by lions. Francis I.

492.   2 Ducats 1746................................... 3000.00
493.   1 Ducat 1745, 46..........................*...... 1500.00

B. Archbishops of —

HENRY II OF SCHWARZBURG, 1463-1497

St. Peter standing. Rev. Arms on cross.

494.   1 Goldgulden ND................................. 1500.00

JOHN III RODE, 1497-1511
St. Peter standing. Rev. Arms on cross.

495.	1 Goldgulden ND	2000.00
496.	½ Goldgulden ND	1800.00

St. Peter seated. Rev. Arms.

497.	1 Goldgulden ND	2000.00

CHRISTOPHER OF BRUNSWICK, 1511-1558
St. Peter standing. Rev. Arms on cross.

498.	1 Goldgulden ND	2200.00

St. Peter seated. Rev. Arms.

499.	1 Goldgulden 1521...............................	2500.00

GEORGE OF BRUNSWICK, 1558-1566
St. Peter standing. Rev. Arms.

500.	1 Goldgulden ND	2000.00

HENRY III OF LAUENBURG, 1567-1585
Bust. Rev. Arms.

501.	1 Ducat 1583	2500.00

St. Peter. Rev. Arms.

502.	1 Goldgulden 1584, ND	2000.00

JOHN FREDERICK OF HOLSTEIN-GOTTORP, 1596-1634
Bust. Rev. Cross.

503.	10 Ducats ND	Rare

St. Peter standing. Rev. Arms.

504.	1 Goldgulden 1612, 18............................	2200.00

BREMEN AND VERDEN

Swedish Rulers of —

Bust of Christina. Rev. Arms.

505.	10 Ducats 1650	Rare

BRESLAU

A. City of —

St. Wenceslas. Rev. Lion.

506.	1 Goldgulden 1517-31, ND	1200.00

St. John. Rev. Arms.

507.	1 Goldgulden 1531, 34............................	1200.00

St. Wenceslas. Rev. Arms.

508.	2 Ducats 1542....................................	3000.00
509.	1 Ducat 1531-60 ....*......	1000.00

Arms. Rev. Shield of Pfintzig. On the Shooting Fete.

510.	2 Ducats 1560....................................	3000.00

Maximilian II standing. Rev. Arms.

511.	1 Ducat 1572, 73	1250.00

Rudolph II standing. Rev. Arms.

512.	1 Ducat 1577	1800.00

Louis II standing. Rev. Arms.

513.	1 Ducat 1577	1800.00

Arms. Rev. Legend. On the Shooting Fetes.

514.	3 Ducats (1527-1614) Round........................	Rare
515.	3 Ducats (1527-1614) Square	Rare
516.	2 Ducats 1527, 77, 1614	3000.00
517.	1 Ducat 1614 ....*.....	1800.00

Bust of Matthias II. Rev. Arms.

518.	5 Ducats 1612.....................................	Rare
519.	5 Ducats 1612. Square............................	Rare
520.	4 Ducats 1612 ....*......	Rare
521.	3 Ducats 1612....................................	4500.00
522.	3 Ducats 1612. Square............................	3800.00
523.	2 Ducats 1611-13	2000.00
524.	2 Ducats 1612, 13. Square	2500.00
525.	1 Ducat 1611-13	1250.00

Bust of Matthias II. Rev. Crowned F over arms.

526.	2 Ducats 1617. Round and broad	2200.00
527.	2 Ducats 1617. Square and smaller ....*......	2500.00
528.	1 Ducat 1617	1250.00

Bust of Frederick V of Bohemia. Rev. Arms.

529.	2 Ducats 1620....................................	3500.00

Bust of Frederick V. Rev. Lion.

530.	1 Ducat 1620	2500.00

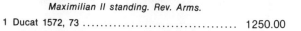

Bust of Ferdinand II. Rev. Arms.

531.	3 Ducats 1622	3500.00
532.	1 Ducat 1622	1400.00
533.	½ Ducat 1622	1000.00

Bust of Ferdinand II. Rev. Scales.

| 534. | 2 Ducats 1630 | 2500.00 |
| 535. | 1 Ducat 1630 ....*...... | 1250.00 |

Bust of Ferdinand III. Rev. Arms.

| 536. | 5 Ducats 1651 | 4500.00 |
| 536a. | 1 Ducat 1646 | 2000.00 |

B. Bishops of —

JACOB, 1520-1539

St. John. Rev. Arms.

| 537. | 1 Ducat 1524-39 | 2000.00 |

Bust. Rev. Arms.

| 538. | 3 Ducat 1531 | 4000.00 |

BALTHASAR, 1539-1562
Bust with hat. Rev. Arms.

| 539. | 5 Ducats 1551 | 6500.00 |

St. John. Rev. Three shields.

| 540. | 1 Ducat 1540-60 | 1250.00 |

CASPAR, 1562-1574

St. John. Rev. Arms.

| 541. | 1 Ducat 1562-73 | 1500.00 |

MARTIN GERSTMANN, 1574-1585
St. John. Rev. Arms.

| 542. | 2 Ducats 1574-77 | 3000.00 |
| 543. | 1 Ducat 1574-85 | 1000.00 |

ANDREW JERIN, 1585-1596

St. John. Rev. Arms.

| 544. | 1 Ducat 1585-92, ND | 1500.00 |

JOHN VI, 1600-1608

St. John. Rev. Arms.

545.	3 Ducats 1603. Square	Rare
546.	2 Ducats 1603. Square ....*.....	3500.00
547.	1 Ducat ND ....*.....	1250.00

CHARLES OF AUSTRIA, 1608-1624

Bust. Rev. Two shields.

| 548. | 1 Ducat 1611, 12 | 2000.00 |

Two shields. Rev. Legend. On the Shooting Fete.

549.	3 Ducats 1612	3500.00
550.	2 Ducats 1612	2500.00
551.	1 Ducat 1612 ....*......	1250.00

Bust. Rev. Three shields.

552.	10 Ducats 1615, 18	Rare
553.	7 Ducats 1614, 18	Rare
554.	6 Ducats 1614	Rare
555.	5 Ducats 1616	Rare
556.	4 Ducats 1618	Rare
557.	3 Ducats 1614, 18	4000.00
558.	1 Ducat 1614	1500.00

Bust. Rev. Arms.

| 559. | 1 Ducat 1618 | 1500.00 |
| 560. | ½ Ducat 1618 | 1000.00 |

Bust. Rev. Arms and two small shields.

561.	5 Ducats ND	Rare
562.	2 Ducats ND	3300.00
563.	1 Ducat ND	1250.00

CHARLES FERDINAND OF POLAND, 1625-1655

Bust right or left. Rev. Two shields or arms.

564.	15 Ducats 1631, 32	Rare
565.	10 Ducats 1631, 38, 39, 42	Rare
566.	6 Ducats 1632, 39	Rare
567.	6 Ducats 1632. Square	Rare
568.	5 Ducats 1632, 39	Rare
569.	5 Ducats 1632. Square	Rare
570.	4 Ducats 1632 ....*.....	Rare
571.	3 Ducats 1632, 53. Round... Rare Octagonal	Rare
572.	2 Ducats 1632, 53. Round... Rare Octagonal	Rare
573.	1 Ducat 1635	1500.00

SEBASTIAN OF ROSTOCK, 1664-1671
Bust. Rev. Arms.

574.	10 Ducats 1667	Rare
575.	2 Ducats 1655 ....*	2500.00
576.	1 Ducat 1655	1800.00

FREDERICK OF HESSE, 1671-1682

Bust. Rev. Arms.

577.	3 Ducats 1674	4000.00
578.	2 Ducats 1679-82 ....*	2500.00
579.	1 Ducat 1679-82	1800.00

FRANCIS LOUIS OF NEUBURG, 1683-1732

Bust. Rev. Arms.

580.	10 Ducats 1701	Rare
581.	6 Ducats 1730	Rare
582.	2 Ducats 1690, 93	3500.00
583.	1 Ducat 1686-1732 ....*	2000.00
584.	¼ Ducat ND.	700.00
585.	⅛ Ducat ND.	450.00

PHILIP OF SINZENDORF, 1732-1749

Bust. Rev. Arms.

586.	8 Ducats 1733	Rare
587.	1 Ducat 1738 ....*	2500.00

PHILIP GOTTHARD SCHAFFGOTSCH, 1747-1795
Bust. Rev. Arms.

588.	5 Ducats 1748	Rare
589.	1 Ducat 1748-77	1500.00

JOSEPH OF HOHENLOHE, 1795-1817

Bust. Rev. Arms.

590.	1 Ducat 1796	2000.00

BRETZENHEIM

Princes —

CHARLES AUGUST, 1769-1823

Bust. Rev. Arms on cross.

591.	1 Ducat 1790	3000.00

BRUNSWICK

City of —

Double Eagle. Rev. Lion.

592.	1 Goldgulden 1622, 29, 30	2000.00
593.	1 Ducat 1627, 48, 49, ND	1500.00

Double Eagle. Rev. Arms.

594.	1 Goldgulden 1628, 31	1800.00

Double Eagle. Rev. Value.

595.	1 Ducat 1626	2000.00

Double Eagle. Rev. Value on tablet.

596.	1 Ducat 1628-60	2000.00

BRUNSWICK-CALENBERG

Dukes of —

ERIC I, 1491-1540
Arms. Rev. Double Eagle.

597.	1 Goldgulden 1539...............................	2000.00

BRUNSWICK-GRUBENHAGEN

Dukes of —

WOLFGANG AND PHILIP II, 1567-1595
Arms. Rev. Bear and date.

598.	1 Goldgulden 1588.................................	1850.00

BRUNSWICK-LUNEBURG

Dukes of —

JULIUS ERNEST OF DANNENBERG, 1598-1636
Bust. Rev. Arms.

599.	1 Goldgulden 1619................................	2000.00
600.	1 Ducat 1625	2000.00

CHRISTIAN OF MINDEN, 1599-1633

Bust. Rev. Arms.

601. 1 Goldgulden 1621-1633 .... 1850.00

St. Andrew. Rev. Arms. Struck from Andreasberg gold.

602. 1 Goldgulden 1624, 29 .... 2000.00

AUGUST, 1610-1636
Bust. Rev. Arms.

603. 1 Ducat 1634 .... 1800.00

Ruler on horse. Rev. Arms.

604. 1 Goldgulden 1618 .... 2000.00

Standing ruler. Rev. Arms.

605. 1 Goldgulden ND 1800.00

FREDERICK, 1636-1648

Standing ruler. Rev. Arms.

606. 1 Ducat 1636-48, ND 2000.00

Armored bust. Rev. Arms.

607. 1 Ducat 1647 48, ND 1750.00

GEORGE OF CALENBERG, 1635-1641

Bust. Rev. Arms.

608. 1 Ducat 1635, 36, 37, 38, ND 1500.00

Arms. Rev. Orb.

609. 1 Goldgulden 1635 .... 2000.00

CHRISTIAN LOUIS OF CELLE, 1646-1665
Bust. Rev. Arms.

610. 1 Ducat 1646 .... 2000.00

Arms. Rev. Horse.

611. 1 Ducat 1650, 61 .... 1500.00

GEORGE WILLIAM OF CELLE, 1665-1705
Bust. Rev. Horse.

612.	4 Ducats 1688	Rare
613.	2 Ducats 1685, 88, 90, 99	3500.00
614.	1 Ducat 1685, 90	1500.00
615.	½ Ducat 1685, 90	850.00
616.	¼ Ducat 1690	550.00

Bust. Rev. Arms.

617.	10 Ducats 1665	Rare
618.	2 Ducats 1675, 99	2500.00
619.	1 Ducat 1664, 75	2000.00

Arms. Rev. Horse.

620.	4 Ducats 1681	Rare
621.	2 Ducats 1675, 99, 1700	2500.00
622.	1 Ducat 1684-97, ND .... *	1500.00
623.	½ Ducat 1685-90	650.00

JOHN FREDERICK OF CALENBERG, 1665-1679
Bust. Rev. Arms.

624. 1 Ducat 1659-1685 .... 2000.00

Bust. Rev. Palm tree on rock.

625.	4 Ducats 1673	Rare
626.	2 Ducats 1673	2500.00
627.	1 Ducat 1668-79 .... *	2000.00

ERNEST AUGUST, 1692-1698
Bust. Rev. Landscape.

628. 20 Ducats 1680 .... Rare

Bust. Rev. Arms.

| 629. | 10 Ducats 1681, 85 .... | Rare |
| 630. | 1 Ducat 1681, 85, 94 .... | 2500.00 |

Bust. Rev. Arms under hat.

| 631. | 2 Ducats 1694, 95 .... | 3000.00 |
| 632. | 1 Ducat 1694, 98 .... * ...... | 1500.00 |

Bust. Rev. Horse.

633.	2 Ducats 1695	3000.00
634.	1 Ducat 1695, 98	1500.00
635.	½ Ducat 1695	1000.00
636.	¼ Ducat 1695	650.00

Bust. Rev. Legend. On his death.

637. 1 Ducat 1698 .... 1800.00

GEORGE I OF ENGLAND, 1698-1727

Bust. Rev. Arms.

638.	2 Ducats 1698	2750.00
639.	1 Ducat 1712-23 .... *	1800.00
640.	1 Harz-gold Ducat 1712, 14	3000.00

Laureate bust. Rev. Four shields crossed.

641.	2 Ducats 1716, 18	....	2500.00
642.	1 Ducat 1715-27	...................*	1500.00
643.	1 Harz-gold Ducat 1715-27	....	2200.00

Laureate bust. Rev. Legend. On his death.

644.	4 Ducats 1727	....	Rare
645.	2 Ducats 1727	....	3000.00

Laureate head. Rev. Horse.

646.	1 Ducat 1713	....	1800.00
647.	½ Ducat 1724	....	1000.00
648.	¼ Ducat 1724	....	600.00

Arms. Rev. Horse.

649.	5	Taler 1699	Unknown
650.	2½	Taler 1699	Unknown
651.	2	Ducats 1698-1707	3000.00
652.	1	Ducat 1698-1714	2000.00
653.	1	Harz-gold Ducat 1710, 13, 14, 15 ....*	2200.00

Four shields crossed. Rev. Wild man.

654.	1 Ducat 1726	....	2500.00

GEORGE II OF ENGLAND, 1727-1760

Bust. Rev. Four shields crossed.

655.	1 Harz-gold Ducat 1729	....	2200.00

Bust. Rev. Arms.

656.	1 Ducat 1730, 32, 47	....	1500.00
657.	1 Harz-gold Ducat 1730, 47	...................*	2000.00
658.	½ Ducat 1730, 34, 37	..............*	1000.00
659.	¼ Ducat 1737	....	750.00

Head or Arms. Rev. Two values as indicated.

660.	4 Goldgulden or 8 Taler 1749-52	....	2200.00
661.	2 Goldgulden or 4 Taler 1749-55	...........*	1200.00
662.	1 Goldgulden or 2 Taler 1749-55	....	650.00

663.	½ Goldgulden or 1 Taler 1749-56	....	650.00
664.	¼ Goldgulden or ½ Taler 1754-57	....	400.00

Bust. Rev. Value.

665.	1 Ducat 1751	....	1800.00

Bust. Rev. Horse.

666.	¼ Ducat 1737	....	400.00

Arms. Rev. Horse.

667.	1 Ducat 1730-38	....	1500.00
668.	1 Harz-gold Ducat 1730-56	...........*	2000.00

Arms. Rev. Value.

669.	5 Taler 1758	....	1500.00

Horse. Rev. Value.

670.	1 Harz-gold Ducat 1751	....	2200.00

Four shields crossed. Rev. Horse.

671.	1 Ducat 1728, 30	....	1400.00
672.	1 Harz-gold Ducat 1727, 29	....	1800.00

Crowned initials. Rev. Horse.

673.	¼ Ducat 1730	....	450.00

GEORGE III OF ENGLAND, 1760-1820

Bust. Rev. Arms.

674.	The coin previously listed does not exist.		
675.	5 Taler 1768	....	1800.00

Arms. Rev. Horse.

676.	1 Harz-gold Ducat 1767-1818	....	1400.00

Arms. Rev. Value.

677.	5 Taler 1813, 14, 15	....	800.00

Horse. Rev. Value.

678.	1	Pistole 1803	*	1500.00
679.	10	Taler 1813, 14		2500.00
680.	5	Harz-gold Taler 1814	*	3000.00
681.	2½	Taler 1814, 15	*	1200.00
682.	1	Harz-gold Ducat 1815, 18	*	2000.00

(For coins of the succeeding English Kings, see under Hanover and under Charles II of Brunswick-Wolfenbuttel.)

BRUNSWICK-WOLFENBUTTEL

Dukes of —

(Old Line, 1514-1634 and New Line, 1635-1884.)
HENRY II, 1514-1568

Bust. Rev. Fortuna standing.

683.	1 Goldgulden 1558	2000.00

Bust. Rev. Arms.

684.	1 Ducat 1558	1800.00

Arms. Rev. Wild man.

685.	1 Ducat 1558	2200.00

JULIUS, 1568-1589
Busts of Julius and Hedwig. Rev. Arms.

686.	2 Ducats ND	4000.00

FREDERICK ULRIC, 1613-1634

Bust. Rev. Arms.

687.	1 Goldgulden 1625, 26	2500.00

Half length figure. Rev. Arms and wild man.

688.	10 Ducats 1615	Rare

Standing ruler. Rev. Arms.

689.	1 Goldgulden 1630	1800.00

Wild man and tree. Rev. Arms.

690.	1 Goldgulden 1615-31	2000.00
691.	1 Goldgulden 1621	2000.00

CHRISTIAN OF HALBERSTADT, 1616-1626
Armored arm with sword. Rev. Legend.

692.	10 Ducats 1622	Rare
693.	2 Ducats 1622	Rare
694.	1 Ducat 1622	3000.00

AUGUST, 1635-1666

Armored bust. Rev. Arms.

695.	1 Ducat 1638, 39	1400.00

Facing bust with cap. Rev. Arms.

696.	1 Ducat 1658	1500.00

RUDOLPH AUGUST, 1666-1704

Armored bust. Rev. Galley.

697.	1 Ducat 1680	2750.00

Bust. Rev. Legend. On his death.

698.	1 Ducat 1704	1500.00
699.	¾ Ducat 1704	800.00

Arms. Rev. Horse.

700.	2 Ducats 1669	2500.00
701.	1 Ducat 1669, 79	1500.00

RUDOLPH AUGUST AND ANTHONY ULRIC, 1685-1704

Two busts. Rev. Arms.

702.	1 Ducat 1691, 99	2000.00

Bust on each side.

703.	1 Ducat 1698, 99, 1701, ND	2200.00

ANTHONY ULRIC, 1704-1714
Bust. Rev. Arms.

704.	1 Ducat 1705	1500.00

Bust. Rev. Horse.

705.	2 Ducats 1707, 11		2500.00
706.	2 Harz-gold Ducats 1712		4000.00
707.	1 Ducat 1707, 11, 12	*	1500.00
708.	1 Harz-gold Ducat 1710		2000.00
709.	½ Ducat 1708, 09	*	1200.00

Initials. Rev. Horse.

710. 1 Ducat 1707, 09, 11.............................. 1500.00
711. ½ Ducat 1708, 09.........................*...... 600.00
712. 2 Harz-gold Ducats 1712........................ 3000.00
713. 1 Harz-gold Ducat 1710, 12.................... 1800.00

Prince Anthony Ulric in cradle. Rev. Legend.

714. 2 Ducats 1714................................... 2000.00

ELIZABETH JULIANA, 1656-1704
Bust. Rev. Legend. On her death.

715. 1 Ducat 1704................................... 1800.00

Bust. Rev. Salzdahlum Castle. On her death.

716. 2 Ducats 1704................................. 3000.00

FERDINAND ALBERT I, DIED 1687

Bust. Rev. Arms.

717. 2 Ducats 1678.........................*...... 3000.00
718. 1 Ducat 1680................................. 2000.00

LOUIS RUDOLPH, 1714-1735

Bust. Rev. Angel over city view of Blankenburg. On the Reformation.

719. 1 Ducat 1717................................. 1800.00

Bust. Rev. Horse and city view of Blankenburg.

720. 1 Ducat 1720................................. 2000.00

Bust. Rev. Arms.

721. 1 Ducat 1714................................. 1800.00

Bust. Rev. Horse.

722. 12 Ducats 1715............................... Rare
723. 1 Ducat 1725-34.............................. 1500.00
724. 1 Harz-gold Ducat 1732, 33, 34............... 2200.00

Bust of Albert Ernest of Oettingen. Rev. Legend.

725. 1 Friendship Ducat ND........................ 1800.00

Head. Rev. Helmet and Horse.

726. 1 Ducat 1726................................. 1800.00

Head. Rev. Helmet and horse.

727. 1 Ducat 1718-33.........................*..... 2000.00
728. 1 Harz-gold Ducat 1731, 32.................. 2200.00

Head. Rev. Star.

729. 1 Ducat 1726, 30, 33......................... 2000.00

Bust or head. Rev. Wild man with or without arms.

730. 2 Ducats 1731, 32, 33, ND.................... 3500.00
731. 1 Ducat 1733............................*...... 2000.00

Head. Rev. Legend. On his death.

732. 1 Ducat 1735................................. 1800.00

Arms. Rev. Horse.

733. 1 Ducat 1715................................. 1500.00

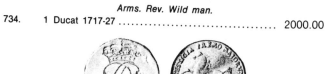

Arms. Rev. Wild man.

734. 1 Ducat 1717-27.............................. 2000.00

Initials. Rev. Horse.

735. 1 Ducat 1715, 18........................*...... 1500.00
736. 1 Ducat 1726................................. 1800.00
737. ½ Ducat 1715................................. 800.00
738. ¼ Ducat 1717-34, ND......................... 500.00

Initials. Rev. Wild man.

739. 1 Ducat 1720................................. 1500.00
740. ½ Ducat 1718-28.......................*...... 1000.00
741. ½ Ducat ND. Square.....................*...... 1250.00
742. ¼ Ducat 1728, ND............................ 500.00

Horse. Rev. Wild man.

743. 1 Ducat 1733................................. 1500.00

Initials. Rev. Helmet and horse.

744. ½ Ducat 1726, 27............................. 800.00

AUGUST WILLIAM, 1714-1731

Bust. Rev. Horse.

745.		2 Ducats 1716, 19, 22, 28 ....*	3000.00
746.		1 Harz-gold Ducat 1719, 21, 28, 29, 30	1500.00
747.		1 Ducat 1714-30	1250.00

Bust. Rev. Legend.

748.		2 Ducats 1730. Birthday issue	2500.00
749.		1 Ducat 1731. Death issue........................	1500.00

Bust. Rev. Legend. On the Reformation.

| 750. | | 1 Ducat 1717, 28 .... | 1500.00 |

Arms. Rev. Wild man.

| 751. | | 1 Ducat 1725, 28 .... | 1800.00 |

Arms. Rev. Horse.

| 752. | | 1 Harz-gold Ducat 1730.......................... | 2000.00 |

Wild man. Rev. Legend. On the jubilee of the dynasty.

| 753. | | 2 Ducats 1730 .... | 3000.00 |

Initials. Rev. Horse.

754.		2 Harz-gold Ducats 1727 ....*	Rare
755.		1 Ducat 1716	1500.00
756.		½ Ducat 1715-21 ....*	1000.00
757.		¼ Ducat 1717, 18	600.00

Bust. Rev. Legend. On the Augsburg Confession.

| 758. | | 1 Ducat 1730 .... | 2000.00 |

FERDINAND ALBERT II, 1735

Bust. Rev. Horse.

759.		1 Ducat 1735 ....*	2000.00
760.		1 Harz-gold Ducat 1735	2500.00

Bust. Rev. Legend. On his death.

| 761. | | 1 Ducat 1735 .... | 2200.00 |

Initials. Rev. Horse.

| 762. | | 1 Ducat 1735 .... | 2000.00 |

Arms. Rev. Horse.

| 763. | | 1 Ducat 1735 .... | 2500.00 |

ELIZABETH CHRISTINA, 1733-1797

Initials. Rev. Legend. On her wedding.

| 764. | | 1 Ducat 1733 .... | 1800.00 |

CHARLES I, 1735-1780

Armored bust. Rev. Arms.

765.	10	Taler 1742.................................	3000.00
766.	5	Taler 1742.............................*	2000.00

Armored bust. Rev. Horse.

767.	1	Harz-gold Ducat 1736.........................	2200.00
768.	1	Ducat 1736, 39...........................*	1500.00
769.	10	Taler 1742-64	1800.00
770.	5	Taler 1742-75	800.00
771.	2½	Taler 1742-77	500.00

Head. Rev. Horse.

772.	1	Ducat 1737-65 ....*	1800.00
773.	1	Harz-gold Ducat 1737, 39, 49.................	2200.00

774.	2 Pistoles 1767, 77. (10 Taler)......................	3000.00
775.	1 Pistole 1767, 76-78. (5 Taler).....................	1850.00
776.	½ Pistole 1767, 77. (2½ Taler)......................	1100.00

Initials. Rev. Legend. On his wedding.

777.	1 Ducat 1733	800.00

CHARLES WILLIAM FERDINAND, 1780-1806

Arms. Rev. Value.

778.	1 Ducat 1780	1250.00
779.	1 Harz-gold Ducat 1781-1801 .... *	2000.00
780.	10 Taler 1781-1806	2000.00
781.	5 Taler 1780-1806 .... *	1000.00
782.	2½ Taler 1781-1806 ....*	750.00

FREDERICK WILLIAM, 1806-1815

Arms. Rev. Value.

783.	10 Taler 1813, 14	1500.00
784.	5 Taler 1814, 15 ....*	1100.00
785.	2½ Taler 1815	1300.00
786.	1 Harz-gold Ducat 1814, 15	2000.00

CHARLES II, 1815-1830

Arms. Rev. Value. Struck during the regency of George IV of England. The coinage before 1822 shows his name as George only. The coinage of 1822 shows his name as George IV. Other coins of George IV will be found under Hanover.

787.	10 Taler 1817-22	1500.00
788.	5 Taler 1816-23 ....*	1000.00
789.	2½ Taler 1816-22	800.00

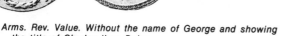

Arms. Rev. Value. Without the name of George and showing the title of Charles II as Duke.

790.	10 Taler 1824-30 ....*	2200.00
791.	5 Taler 1824-30	1200.00
792.	2½ Taler 1825-28	600.00
793.	1 Harz-gold Ducat 1825 ....*	2000.00

Uniformed bust. Rev. Arms.

794.	10 Taler 1827-29 ....*	2250.00
795.	2½ Taler 1829	1200.00

WILLIAM, 1831-1884

Horse. Rev. Value.

796.	10 Taler 1831	1800.00

Arms supported by wild men. Rev. Value.

797.	10 Taler 1831-34 ....*	1500.00
798.	5 Taler 1832, 34	1200.00
799.	2½ Taler 1832	700.00

Head. Rev. Arms.

800.	10 Taler 1850-57 ....*	1500.00
801.	2½ Taler 1851	850.00

Head. Rev. Value.

802.	1 Krone 1857, 58, 59.........................	1100.00

BUCHEIM

Counts —

JOHN CHRISTIAN, 1619-1657
Bust. Rev. Arms.

803.	1 Ducat 1650	Rare

COLOGNE

A. City coinage

Arms (Uniface).
804. Gold Bracteate ND (1300) .... Unknown

Christ on throne. Rev. Orb.
805. 1 Goldgulden ND (1400-1500) 900.00

Christ seated. Rev. Arms.
806. 1 Goldgulden 1515-34............................. 1100.00

The three Magi. Rev. St. Ursula in ship.
807. 6 Ducats ND (1600) .... Rare
808. 4 Ducats 1612 .... Rare

St. Ursula standing. Rev. Shield on cross.
809. 1 Goldgulden ND (1600) 2000.00

Value on tablet. Rev. Arms.
810. 1 Ducat 1634 .... 1250.00

B. Coinage with the heads or names of the Holy Roman Emperors.

Eagle. Rev. Arms. Maximilian II.
811. 1 Goldgulden 1567-73............................. 1000.00

Eagle. Rev. Arms. Ruldolph II.
812. 1 Goldgulden 1577-1611 .... 1000.00

Eagle. Rev. Arms. Ferdinand II.
813. 1 Goldgulden 1619-34............................. 1000.00

Ferdinand II standing. Rev. Arms.
814. 1 Ducat 1634-36 .... 900.00

Ferdinand III standing. Rev. Arms.
815. 1 Ducat 1636, 43-57............................... 1000.00

Bust of Leopold I. Rev. Arms.
816. 1 Ducat 1661-72 .... 1250.00

Leopold I standing. Rev. Arms.
817. 1 Ducat 1689, 93 .... 1250.00

Eagle. Rev. Wine glass. Leopold I.
818. 1 Ducat 1672 .... 1500.00

Bust of Joseph I. Rev. Arms.
819. 1 Ducat 1705, 08 .... 2000.00

Eagle. Rev. Arms. Joseph I.
820. 1 Ducat 1705 .... 2000.00

Bust of Charles VI. Rev. Eagle.
821. 1 Ducat 1724 .... 2000.00

Bust of Charles VI. Rev. Arms.
822. 1 Ducat 1717-39 .... 2000.00

Bust of Charles VI. Rev. Arms with supporters.
823. 12 Ducats 1727 .... Rare
824. 1 Ducat 1727, 31 .... 2000.00

Arms. Rev. Eagle. Charles VI.
825. 1 Ducat 1716 .... 2000.00

Arms. Rev. Wine bottle. Charles VI.
826. 1 Ducat 1716 .... 2500.00

Bust of Charles VII. Rev. Two shields.
827. 1 Ducat 1742 .... 3000.00

Bust of Francis I. Rev. Arms.
828. 1 Ducat 1750, 53, ND............................. 2000.00

Bust of Joseph II. Rev. Arms.
829. 1 Ducat 1767 .... 3000.00

C. Archbishops of —

WALRAM, 1346-1349
Ruler on throne. Rev. Cross.
830. 1 Ecu d'or ND..................................... 3000.00

St. John. Rev. Lily.
831. 1 Florin ND....................................... 1250.00

WILLIAM, 1349-1362
St. John. Rev. Lily.
832. 1 Florin ND....................................... 850.00
833. ½ Florin ND....................................... 1250.00
834. ¼ Florin ND....................................... 1000.00

ADOLPH II, 1363-1364
St. John. Rev. Lily.
835. 1 Florin ND....................................... 1500.00

ENGELBERT III, 1364-1368
St. John. Rev. Lily.
836. 1 Florin ND....................................... 1100.00

KUNO, 1368-1371
St. John on throne. Rev. Arms.
837. 1 Goldgulden ND................................... 700.00

St. Peter. Rev. Arms.
838. 1 Goldgulden ND................................... 600.00

St. Peter under canopy. Rev. Arms.
839. 1 Goldgulden ND................................... 600.00

FREDERICK III, 1371-1414
St. Peter under canopy. Rev. Arms.
840. 1 Goldgulden ND................................... 550.00

St. Peter on throne. Rev. Arms.
841. 1 Goldgulden ND................................... 600.00

St. John. Rev. Arms and two shields.
842. 1 Goldgulden ND................................... 600.00

St. John. Rev. Arms.
843. 1 Goldgulden ND................................... 600.00

THEODORE II, 1414-1463
Ruler standing. Rev. Arms.
844. 1 Goldgulden 1458, ND............................ 550.00

Christ. Rev. Four shields.
845. 1 Goldgulden ND................................... 600.00

St. Peter. Rev. Arms.

846.   1 Goldgulden ND 550.00

St. John. Rev. Arms.

847.   1 Goldgulden ND 550.00

Arms on cross. Rev. Three shields.

848.   1 Goldgulden ND 550.00
849.   1 Goldgulden 1436-56 .... 550.00

RUPERT, 1463-1480
Christ on throne. Rev. Cross and four shields.

850.   1 Goldgulden ND 550.00

Christ standing. Rev. Four shields.

851.   1 Goldgulden ND 550.00

Ruler standing. Rev. Arms.

852.   1 Goldgulden ND 550.00

HERMAN IV, 1480-1508
St. Peter. Rev. Arms.

853.   1 Goldgulden ND 600.00

Christ on throne. Rev. Arms.

854.   1 Goldgulden 1491-1508 .... 650.00

PHILIP II, 1508-1515
Christ on throne. Rev. Arms.

855.   1 Goldgulden 1508-15, ND 1250.00

HERMAN V, 1515-1546

Christ on throne. Rev. Arms.

856.   1 Goldgulden 1515-31 ....*...... 1500.00
857.   ½ Goldgulden 1516 .... 1650.00

ADOLPH III, 1547-1556
Christ on throne. Rev. Arms.

858.   1 Goldgulden 1547-49 .... 1100.00

ANTHONY, 1556-1558
Christ on throne. Rev. Arms.

859.   1 Goldgulden 1556, 57 .... 1500.00

JOHN GEBHARD, 1558-1562
Christ on throne. Rev. Arms.

860.   1 Goldgulden 1558 .... 2500.00

FREDERICK IV, 1562-1567
Christ on throne. Rev. Arms.

861.   1 Goldgulden 1563, 64, 65 .... 2000.00

SALENTIN, 1567-1577
Bust with long beard. Rev. Arms.

862.   2 Ducats 1577 .... 7500.00
863.   1 Ducat 1573, 75 .... 1800.00
864.   1 Goldgulden 1575 .... 2500.00

St. Peter standing. Rev. Arms.

865.   1 Goldgulden 1570 .... 2500.00

GEBHARD, 1577-1583
Bust. Rev. Arms.

866.   1 Goldgulden 1583 .... 3000.00

St. Peter. Rev. Arms.

867.   1 Goldgulden 1581, 82, 83 .... 3000.00

ERNEST, 1583-1612
St. Peter. Rev. Arms.

868.   1 Goldgulden ND 2500.00

FERDINAND, 1612-1650
Arms of Bavaria. Rev. Shield.

869.   1 Goldgulden 1634, 37 .... 2000.00

Madonna. Rev. Arms.

870.   1 Ducat ND 3000.00

Arms. Rev. Value in square.

871.   1 Ducat 1640 .... 2200.00

MAX HENRY, 1650-1688
Bust. Rev. Arms.

872.   1 Ducat 1644, 65, ND 2500.00

JOSEPH CLEMENT, 1688-1723

Joseph and Mary with the three Magi. Rev. Arms. Struck from Westphalian gold.

873.   3 Ducats 1696 .... 10000.00

Bust. Rev. Arms.

874.   1 Ducat 1694, 1722 .... 1500.00

Bust with hat. Rev. Arms.

875.   1 Ducat 1715 .... 1800.00

Bust. Rev. Madonna seated.

876.   1 Ducat 1694, 98 .... 1500.00

Bust. Rev. The three Magi.

877.   1 Ducat 1723 .... 2000.00

CLEMENT AUGUST, 1723-1761
Bust. Rev. Adoration of the three Magi.

878.   1 Ducat 1726, 42, 44 .... 1800.00

Bust. Rev. Seven shields on mantle.

879.   1 Carolin 1735 .... 2500.00
880.   ½ Carolin 1735, 36 .... 2000.00

Bust. Rev. Madonna seated.

881.   1 Ducat 1750 .... 2500.00

Facing or profile bust. Rev. Sun and legend.

882.   1 Ducat 1750 .... 1850.00

CONSTANCE

A. City of —

Eagle and CONST. Rev. Orb. Name of Maximilian.

883.   1 Goldgulden ND (1486-1508)...................... 5500.00

Eagle and CONSTANC. Rev. Similar to above.

884.   1 Goldgulden ND (1486-1508)...................... 5000.00

Arms. Rev. Double eagle. Name of Ferdinand II or III.

885.   2 Ducats ND. (1618-57). Square .... Rare
886.   1 Ducat 1629, 52, ND. Round or square............. 5000.00

B. Bishops of —

JOHN FRANCIS II SCHENK, 1704-1740

Two shields. Rev. Arms.

887.   2 Ducats 1737 .... 6000.00
888.   1 Ducat 1737 ....*...... 4500.00

FRANCIS CONRAD, 1750-1775
Bust. Rev. Arms.

889.   1 Ducat.. 2500.00

CORVEY

Abbots of —

CHARLES BLITTERSDORF, 1722-1737
St. Vitus. Rev. Arms.

890.   1 Ducat 1724, ND................................... 2000.00

CASPAR BOSELAGER, 1737-1758

St. Vitus. Rev. Arms.

891.   1 Ducat 1743, 53 .... 1800.00

PHILIP SPIEGEL, 1758-1776
St. Vitus. Rev. Arms.

892.   1 Ducat 1758, 59 .... 2000.00

COSEL

(Several so-called "Love Ducats" were struck under Saxon auspices, but they are more jetons than coins.)

DARMSTADT

Legend on each side. On the Reformation.

893.   1 Ducat 1817 .... 350.00

DIEPHOLT

St. Stephen. Rev. Eagle.

894.   1 Goldgulden ND (1600)........................... Rare

DIETRICHSTEIN

(The coinage of Dietrichstein will be found under Austria as numbers 446a.—446g.)

DORTMUND

(Coinage with the names, heads or standing figures of the Holy Roman Emperors.)

St. John standing. Rev. Orb. Name of Sigismund.

898.   1 Goldgulden ND (1410-39)........................ 2200.00

Frederick III standing. Rev. Orb.

899.   1 Goldgulden ND (1470-80)........................ 2000.00

Maximilian standing. Rev. Orb.

900.   1 Goldgulden ND (1500) 2000.00

Ferdinand II standing. Rev. Orb.

901.   1 Ducat 1632 .... 2500.00

Ferdinand III standing. Rev. Arms.

902.   1 Ducat 1636, 37, 39, 55.......................... 4000.00

Ferdinand III standing. Rev. Eagle over legend.
903.	1 Ducat 1635-55 .... 3000.00

Leopold I standing. Rev. Eagle.
904.	1 Ducat 1660, 63 .... 3000.00

Bust of Charles VI. Rev. Eagle.
905.	1 Ducat 1717 .... 4500.00

Bust of Charles VII. Rev. Eagle.
906.	2 Ducats 1742. Square......................* 7000.00
907.	1 Ducat 1742. Square.............................. 4000.00

EAST FRISIA

Counts, and later, Princes of —

UDO, 1421-1433

St. Luderus. Rev. Lion shield.
908.	1 Goldgulden ND (1433) 5000.00

ULRIC, 1441-1466
St. Peter. Rev. Orb.
909.	1 Goldgulden ND................................... 1000.00

St. John. Rev. Orb.
910.	1 Goldgulden ND................................... 1000.00

ENNO I, 1446-1491
St. John. Rev. Orb.
911.	1 Goldgulden ND................................... 850.00

EDZARD I, 1491-1528
St. John Rev. Orb.
912.	1 Goldgulden ND................................... 800.00

ENNO II, 1528-1540
Christ with globe. Rev. Harpyrie shield.
913.	1 Goldgulden ND................................... 850.00

St. John. Rev. Orb.
914.	1 Goldgulden ND................................... 850.00

Bust with hat. Rev. Arms.
915.	1 Goldgulden 1529................................. 4000.00

EDZARD II AND JOHN, 1566-1591
Bust of Emperor Maximilian II. Rev. Arms.
916.	1 Goldgulden 1568, 69............................. 2000.00

Bust of Emperor Rudolph II. Rev. Arms.
917.	1 Goldgulden 1571-90.............................. 1100.00

Charlemagne standing. Rev. Arms.
918.	1 Goldgulden 1574................................. 1500.00

Charlemagne on throne. Rev. Cross.
919.	1 Goldgulden ND................................... 1500.00

EDZARD II, 1591-1599
Bust of Emperor Rudolph II. Rev. Arms.
920.	1 Goldgulden 1594................................. 1250.00

St. Luderus. Rev. Arms.
921.	1 Goldgulden ND................................... 1250.00

ENNO III, 1599-1625
Bust. Rev. Cross.
922.	1 Goldgulden 1615................................. 1250.00

Christ standing. Rev. Arms.
923.	1 Goldgulden ND................................... 1100.00

Arms. Rev. Cross.
924.	½ Ducat ND.. 1000.00

CHRISTIAN EBERHARD, 1690-1708
Bust. Rev. Arms.
925.	1 Ducat 1702 .... 3250.00

GEORGE ALBERT, 1708-1734

Bust. Rev. Arms.
926.	1 Ducat 1715, 30, 31.............................. 3500.00

CHARLES EDZARD, 1734-1744
Armored bust. Rev. Arms.
927.	1 Ducat 1737 .... 3000.00

EICHSTAETT

Bishops of —

GABRIEL, 1496-1535
St. Walburga standing. Rev. Arms.
928.	1 Goldgulden 1511, 12............................. 7500.00

MARTIN, 1560-1590

St. Willibald standing. Rev. Arms.

929.	4 Goldgulden 1560................................	Rare
930.	1 Goldgulden 1560.........................*......	3500.00

St. Willibald standing. Rev. Eagle and name of Maximilian II.

931.	2 Ducats 1570....................................	4000.00

JOHN CONRAD, 1595-1612
Arms. Rev. Eagle and name of Rudolph II.

932.	14 Ducats 1596..................................	Rare
933.	8 Ducats 1596..................................	Rare
934.	6 Ducats 1596..................................	Rare

JOHN CHRISTOPHER, 1612-1636
St. Willibald standing. Rev. Two shields.

935.	1 Ducat 1633, 34	2500.00

St. Walburga standing. Rev. Two shields.

936.	1 Ducat 1633	2000.00

Saint standing. Rev. Eagle and name of Ferdinand II.

937.	1 Ducat 1635	2200.00

JOHN EUCHARIUS SCHENK, 1685-1697
Bust. Rev. Arms supported by lions.

938.	6 Ducats 1694	Rare

Bust. Rev. Eagle flying over arms.

939.	10 Ducats ND	Rare

FRANCIS LOUIS SCHENK, 1725-1736
Bust. Rev. Arms. Oval shaped.

940.	1 Ducat 1736	2500.00

JOHN ANTHONY II, 1736-1757
Bust. Rev. Arms.

941.	1 Ducat 1755	2200.00

St. Willibald standing. Rev. Arms.

942.	1 Ducat 1738	1500.00

St. Walburga standing. Rev. Arms.

943.	1 Ducat 1738	1400.00

EINBECK

City gate. Rev. Double eagle. Name of Ferdinand II.

944.	1 Goldgulden 1629................................	3800.00

ELBING

A. Swedish Kings of —

Bust of Gustav II Adolphe. Rev. Arms.

945.	1 Ducat 1630	4000.00

Bust of Charles X. Rev. Arms.

946.	1 Ducat 1657	5000.00

B. Polish Kings of —

Bust of John Casimir. Rev. Arms.

947.	1 Ducat 1661	2000.00

Bust of Michael Korybut. Rev. Arms.

948.	2 Ducats 1672.....................................	4000.00
949.	1 Ducat 1671	2000.00

EMDEN

St. Peter. Rev. Orb.

950.	1 Goldgulden ND. (1470)...........................	2200.00

Knight standing. Rev. Value in tablet or cartouche.

951.	2 Ducats 1694....................................	4000.00
952.	1 Ducat 1635-98, ND........................*......	2200.00

View of the city. Rev. Hand and sceptre.

953.	3¼ Ducats ND	3300.00
954.	2½ Ducats 1737, 43, 46.........................	2000.00
955.	2¼ Ducats 1750	1500.00
956.	2 Ducats ND	1500.00

Arms. Rev. Hands with bundle of arrows.

957.	4 Ducats ND. (1700)	3000.00

ERFURT

A. City of —

Wheel and date. Rev. Arms.

958.	1 Goldgulden 1620, 22, 70, ND....................	2000.00

B. Swedish Kings of —

Radiant Jehovah in Hebrew characters. Rev. Long legend.

959.	10 Victory Ducats 1631. Struck by Gustav II Adolphe.	Rare

King in bed. Rev. King in triumphal chariot. On the death of Gustav II Adolphe.

960.	4 Ducats 1634	Rare

Bust of Gustav II Adolphe. Rev. Crown over legend.

961. 1 Ducat 1632, 33, 34................................. 900.00

Bust of Gustav II Adolphe. Rev. Arms.

961a.	10 Ducats 1632	Rare
962.	8 Ducats 1632 .... *	Rare
962a.	5 Ducats 1632	Rare
963.	1 Ducat 1631-34 (1631 unique)	1000.00

(For the coinage of Christina of Sweden, which some sources now consider to have originated in Erfurt, see under Livonia.)

E S S E N

Abbesses of —

ANNA SALOME, 1646-1688
Arms. Rev. Madonna.

964. 1 Ducat 1672.................................... 6500.00

FRANCES CHRISTINE, 1717-1776

Arms. Rev. Madonna.

965. 1 Ducat 1754.................................... 5000.00

F R A N K F U R T

A. City coinage

Angel. Rev. Legend. On the Reformation.

966.	1 Goldgulden 1617.........................*	2000.00
967.	1 Goldgulden 1617. Square	2500.00

Two hands in prayer. Rev. Comet. On the appearance of a comet.

968. 1 Ducat 1618. Square............................... 3000.00

Eagle. Rev. Value on tablet, in cartouche or plain.

969.	2 Ducats 1633-37	1500.00
970.	1 Ducat 1633-1749, ND	550.00
971.	½ Ducat 1740	1250.00

Eagle. Rev. View of the city in a storm.

972. 2 Ducats 1705, 10 .... 3500.00

Eagle. Rev. Tower in a stormy sea.

973.	2 Ducats 1710, 11 ....*	3500.00
974.	1 Ducat 1710, 11	1800.00

Bible on rock at sea. Rev. Legend. On the Reformation.

975. 1 Ducat 1717.................................... 1600.00

Eagle. Rev. Floriated cross.

976. 1 Ducat 1762.................................... 3300.00

City view. Rev. Legend. Struck under French occupation.

977. 1 Ducat 1796.................................... 850.00

Legend on each side. On the Reformation.

978. 1 Ducat 1817 .... 300.00

Eagle. Rev. Value.

979. 1 Ducat 1853, 56 .... 1200.00

B. Coinage with the heads or names of the Holy Roman Emperors

St. John. Rev. Lily. Charles IV.

980. 1 Florin ND. (1347-78)............................. 1500.00

`St. John. Rev. Eagle on shield. Rupert of Palatinate.`

981. 1 Goldgulden ND. (1400-10) 2000.00

St. John. Rev. Orb. Sigismund.

982. 1 Goldgulden ND. (1410-33) 800.00

Charlemagne standing. Rev. Arms. Sigismund.

983. 1 Goldgulden ND. (1410-33) 1800.00

St. John. Rev. Orb. Albert II.

984. 1 Goldgulden ND. (1438-39) 1200.00

St. John. Rev. Orb. Frederick III.

985. 1 Goldgulden ND 600.00
986. 1 Goldgulden 1491, 92, 93 .... 500.00

St. John. Rev. Orb. Maximilian I.

987. 1 Goldgulden 1494-1515, ND 800.00

St. John. Rev. Lily. Charles V.

988. 1 Goldgulden 1521, 22 .... 1200.00

St. John. Rev. Orb. Charles V.

989. 1 Goldgulden 1527 .... 1500.00

St. John. Rev. Eagle. Rudolph II.

990. 1 Goldgulden 1611, 12 .... 1000.00

Bust of Matthias II. Rev. Crown.

991. 3 Ducats 1612 .... 3500.00
992. 2 Ducats or Goldgulden 1612 ....* 2000.00
993. 1 Goldgulden 1612 .... 1100.00

Matthias II on horse. Rev. Eagle.

994. 10 Ducat ND. (1612) .... Rare
995. 5 Ducat ND. (1612) .... Rare

Matthias II on horse. Rev. Circle of shields.

996. 5 Ducats ND. (1612) .... Rare
997. 3 Ducats ND. (1612) 3000.00

St. John. Rev. Eagle. Matthias II.

998. 1 Goldgulden 1617, 18, 19 .... 650.00

Ferdinand II on throne. Rev. Crown.

999.   3 Ducats 1619 .... 3500.00
1000. 1 Goldgulden 1619..........................* 1000.00

Bust of Ferdinand II. Rev. Wreath over crown.

1001. 2 Ducats ND. Square 2500.00

Legend. Rev. Arm with Crown. Ferdinand II.

1002. 2 Ducats 1619..................................... 2500.00
1003. 1 Ducat 1619 .... 1000.00

Crowned F. Rev. Legend. Ferdinand II.

1004. ½ Ducat 1619 .... 350.00

St. John. Rev. Eagle. Ferdinand II.

1005. 1 Goldgulden 1620, 21, 22 .... 850.00

St. John. Rev. Orb. Ferdinand II.

1006. 1 Goldgulden 1620, 21, 24, 25 .... 850.00

Hand with sceptre and arm with sword. Rev. Legend. On the coronation of Leopold I.

1007. 4 Ducats 1658 .... Rare
1008. 2 Ducats 1658 .... 3300.00
1009. 1 Ducat 1658 .... 1200.00
1010. ½ Ducat 1658 .... 800.00

Bust of Charles VI. Rev. Insignia.

1011. 2 Ducats 1711 .... 2700.00

Globe. Rev. Legend. Charles VI.

1012. 1½ Ducats 1711 .... 600.00
1013. ¾ Ducat 1711 .... 450.00

Legend. Rev. City view. On the election of Charles VI.

1014. 2 Ducats 1711 .... 2500.00

Bust of Charles VII. Rev. Female at altar.

1015.	4 Ducats 1742	Rare
1016.	2 Ducats 1742	3000.00
1017.	1 Ducat 1742	1500.00

Bust of Charles VII. Rev. Bust of Maria Amalia.

1018.	1 Ducat ND. (1742)	1500.00

Eagle. Rev. Legend. On the coronation of Charles VII.

1019.	1 Ducat 1742	1250.00

Bust of Francis I. Rev. Insignia on table.

1020.	1 Ducat 1745	1500.00

Eagle. Rev. Legend. On the election of Francis I.

1021.	1 Ducat 1745	800.00

Altar. Rev. Legend. On the coronation of Francis I.

1022.	1½ Ducats 1745	700.00
1023.	¾ Ducat 1745	450.00

Bust of Joseph II. Rev. Peace standing near fallen soldier.

1024.	2 Ducats 1764 ....*	2500.00
1025.	1 Ducat 1764	1250.00

Globe. Rev. Legend. On the coronation of Joseph II.

1026.	1½ Ducats 1764	800.00
1027.	¾ Ducat 1764	500.00

Head of Leopold II. Rev. Altar.

1028.	2 Ducats 1790	1800.00
1029.	1 Ducat 1790	1200.00

Crossed insignia. Rev. Legend. On the coronation of Leopold II.

1030.	1½ Ducats 1790	600.00
1031.	¾ Ducat 1790	400.00

Head of Francis II. Rev. Altar.

1032.	2 Ducats 1792	1500.00
1033.	1 Ducat 1792	1000.00

Bust. Rev. Two figures.

1034.	1 Ducat ND.....................................	1000.00

Crossed insignia. Rev. Legend. On the coronation of Francis II.

1035.	1½ Ducats 1792	800.00
1036.	¾ Ducat 1792	500.00

FREIBURG

Madonna. Rev. Arms.

1037.	1 Goldgulden 1622..............................	6500.00

Two shields and eagle. Rev. City view.

1038.	1 Ducat 1717	2500.00

FREISING

Bishops of —

JOHN FRANCIS, 1695-1727
St. Corbianus. Rev. Arms. On the Milennium.

1039.	2 Ducats 1724	3000.00

CLEMENT WENCESLAS, 1763-1768

Bust. Rev. Arms.

1040.	1 Ducat 1765, 66	2000.00

FUERSTENBERG

Princes —

JOSEPH, 1704-1762

Bust with wig. Rev. Arms with owl below.

1041.	1 Ducat 1750, 51	2200.00

CHARLES EGON I, DIED 1788

Bust. Rev. Arms.

1042.	1 Ducat 1772	2000.00

FUGGER

Counts —

ANTHONY, 1493-1560

Arms. Rev. Eagle.

1043.	1 Goldgulden ND................................	2000.00

MAXIMILIAN, 1619-1637
Arms. Rev. Eagle.

1044.	13 Ducats 1621		Rare
1045.	10 Ducats 1621		Rare
1046.	1 Goldgulden ND		2200.00

Three shields. Rev. Eagle.

1047.	1 Ducat 1622		2000.00

FULDA

Bishops of —

BALTHASAR, 1570-1606
Eagle. Rev. Arms and name of Rudolph II.

1048.	20 Ducats 1606		Rare

BERNARD GUSTAVE, 1671-1678

St. Boniface. Rev. Initials.

1049.	2 Ducats 1672		4000.00
1050.	1 Ducat 1672		2200.00
1051.	½ Ducat 1672	*	1500.00
1052.	¼ Ducat 1672		850.00

PLACIDUS, 1678-1700
Bust with hat. Rev. Arms.

1053.	10 Ducats 1680		Rare
1054.	8 Ducats 1688		Rare
1055.	7 Ducats 1688		Rare
1056.	2 Ducats 1692		3500.00
1057.	1 Ducat 1692		2000.00

CONSTANTINE, 1714-1726

Bust. Rev. Arms.

1058.	1 Ducat 1715-26		3300.00

Bust. Rev. Two shields.

1059.	1 Ducat 1716, 21		3000.00

ADOLPH, 1726-1737

Bust. Rev. Arms.

1060.	2 Ducats 1728, 30	*	3000.00
1061.	1 Ducat 1726, 28, 30		1800.00

Bust. Rev. Crossed initials.

1062.	1 Carolin or 10 Gulden 1734, 35		2000.00
1063.	½ Carolin or 5 Gulden 1734		1500.00

AMANDUS, 1737-1756

Bust. Rev. Arms.

1064.	8 Ducats 1738	*	Rare
1065.	1 Ducat 1738	*	2200.00

Bust. Rev. Sun and legend. On the Jubilee.

1066.	1 Ducat 1744		2000.00

ADALBERT, 1756-1759

Bust. Rev. Arms.

1067.	2 Ducats 1759		3000.00

HENRY VIII, 1759-1788

Arms. Rev. Legend.

1068.	1 Ducat 1779		2800.00

Bust. Rev. Legend.

1069.	1 Ducat 1779		3000.00

Bust. Rev. Arms.

1070.	1 Ducat 1779		3000.00

FURTH

Swedish Kings of —

Gustave II Adolphe standing. Rev. Arms.

1071.	1 Ducat 1632		Rare

GLATZ

Counts —

JOHN, 1537-1549

Two shields. Rev. Bohemian lion.

1072.	1 Ducat 1540, 41, 44, 46		2400.00

ERNEST, 1549-1554
Three shields. Rev. Bohemian lion.
1073.   1 Ducat 1549, 50, 54 ....   3000.00

GOSLAR

Arms under helmet. Rev. Double eagle. Name of Ferdinand II.
1074.   1 Goldgulden 1628, ND 2500.00

Bust of Ferdinand II. Rev. Arms.
1075.   1 Ducat ND. (1620) 2000.00

Ferdinand II standing. Rev. Arms.
1076.   1 Ducat ND. (1620) 4500.00

GOTTINGEN

Double Eagle. Rev. Arms.
1077.   4 Ducats 1660 ....   Rare

HAGENAU

Rose in shield. Rev. Double eagle. Name of Rudolph II.
1078.   1 Goldgulden 1604, 08, 10, 11 ....   6000.00

St. John. Rev. Eagle.
1079.   1 Goldgulden ND 6000.00

HALBERSTADT

CATHEDERAL CHAPTER OF THE BISHOPRIC
St. Stephan standing. Rev. Arms.
1080.   1 Goldgulden 1628, 29, ND 2000.00

St. Stephan standing. Rev. Shield.
1081.   2 Goldgulden 1631 ....   2750.00

HALL-IN-SUEBIA

Bust of Joseph I. Rev. Three shields.
1082.   1 Ducat 1705 ....   2500.00

Bust of Charles VI. Rev. Three shields.
1083.   1 Ducat 1712 ....   2500.00

Three shields. Rev. Legend. On the Peace of Baden.
1084.   1 Ducat 1714 ....   1800.00
1085.   ¼ Ducat 1714 ....   700.00

Bust of Charles VII. Rev. Three shields.
1086.   1 Ducat 1742 ....   2500.00

Bust of Francis I. Rev. Three shields.
1087.   1 Ducat 1746 ....   1800.00

Bust of Joseph II. Rev. Three shields.
1088.   1 Ducat 1777, ND 1800.00

HAMBURG

A. City coinage

City gate. Rev. Cross.
1089. 10   Ducats or 1 Portugaloser ND. (1553-1673) ....   Rare
1090.   5   Ducats or ½ Portugaloser ND. (1553-1673).* .....   Rare
1091. 2½ Ducats of ¼ Portugaloser ND. (1553-1673) ....   Rare

Christ blessing couple. Rev. The Wedding at Cana.
1092. 10 Ducats ND ....   Rare

Madonna on each side.
1093.   2 Ducats 1649, 60, 66 ....   3000.00
1094.   1 Ducat 1497-1667, ND 800.00

Madonna. Rev. Arms.
1095.   2 Ducats 1669-94 ....* 3500.00
1096.   1 Ducat 1668-75, 92 ....   800.00
1097.   ½ Ducat 1675 ....   1000.00

Madonna. Rev. Annunciation.
1098.   ¼ Ducat ND (1700) 600.00

Elbe River god. Rev. Father Time.
1099.   1 Ducat ND. (1700) 1500.00

Hammonia standing. Rev. Tablet.
1100.   1 Ducat 1807 ....   850.00

City gate. Rev. Tablet.

| 1101. | 2 Ducats 1808, 09, 10.........................* ...... | 1200.00 |
| 1102. | 1 Ducat 1808-11 .... | 900.00 |

Knight standing. Rev. Tablet.

| 1103. | 1 Ducat 1811-50. Old style.................... | 700.00 |
| 1104. | 1 Ducat 1851-72. New style.............* ... | 550.00 |

B. Coinage with the heads or names of the Holy Roman Emperors

St. Peter. Rev. Orb. Sigismund I.

| 1105. | 1 Goldgulden ND. (1435-37) .... | 1500.00 |

St. Peter. Rev. Orb. Frederick III.

| 1106. | 1 Goldgulden ND. (1440-93) .... | 1400.00 |

St. Peter. Rev. Orb. Maximilian I.

| 1107. | 1 Goldgulden ND. (1495-1519) .... | 1500.00 |

St. Peter. Rev. Orb. Charles V.

| 1108. | 1 Goldgulden 1553.................................. | 1800.00 |

St. Peter. Rev. Orb. Ferdinand I.

| 1109. | 1 Goldgulden 1553, 61............................. | 2800.00 |

St. Peter. Rev. Orb. Maximilian II.

| 1110. | 1 Goldgulden 1566.................................. | 1500.00 |

St. Peter. Rev. Orb. Rudolph II.

| 1111. | 1 Goldgulden 1581-89, 1600, 08, ND.............. | 1500.00 |

St. Peter. Rev. Orb. Matthias II.

| 1112. | 1 Goldgulden 1617, 19........................... | 1500.00 |

St. Peter. Rev. Orb. Ferdinand II.

| 1113. | 1 Goldgulden 1628................................. | 1700.00 |

Eagle. Rev. Arms. Leopold I.

1114.	5 Ducats 1696	Rare
1115.	2 Ducats 1689-1707	3000.00
1115a.	1 Ducat 1689-1707	1800.00
1116.	½ Ducat ND. (1692-1704)	500.00
1117.	¼ Ducat 1680, ND............................	500.00
1118.	1 Goldgulden 1675..........................	1800.00

Madonna. Rev. Eagle. Leopold I.

| 1119. | 2½ Ducats ND. (1692-1705) .... | 3000.00 |

Madonna and shield. Rev. Eagle. Leopold I.

| 1120. | 1 Ducat 1694, 1702............................. | 1700.00 |

Bust of Joseph I. Rev. Arms.

| 1121. | 2 Ducats 1705................................... | 3000.00 |
| 1122. | 1 Ducat 1705-10 .... | 1500.00 |

Eagle. Rev. Arms. Joseph I.

1123.	2 Ducats 1705..............................	1800.00
1124.	1 Ducat 1706-11	1000.00
1125.	¼ Ducat 1729..............................	500.00

Eagle. Rev. Arms. Charles VI.

| 1126. | 2 Ducats 1713-40 .... | 1700.00 |
| 1127. | 1 Ducat 1713-40 .... | 800.00 |

Eagle. Rev. Arms. Charles VII.

| 1128. | 2 Ducats 1742, 44, 45..................... | 1700.00 |
| 1129. | 1 Ducat 1742, 43, 44, 45.................. | 1000.00 |

Eagle. Rev. Arms. Francis I.

| 1130. | 2 Ducats 1746-64 .... | 1500.00 |
| 1131. | 1 Ducat 1746-65 .... | 800.00 |

Eagle. Rev. Arms. Joseph II.

| 1132. | 2 Ducats 1764-72 .... | 1500.00 |
| 1133. | 1 Ducat 1765-72 .... | 800.00 |

Eagle. Rev. Tablet. Joseph II.

| 1134. | 2 Ducats 1766-90 .... | 1500.00 |
| 1135. | 1 Ducat 1773-90 .... | 650.00 |

Eagle. Rev. Tablet. Leopold II.

| 1136. | 2 Ducats 1790-92 .... | 1500.00 |
| 1137. | 1 Ducat 1791, 92 .... | 850.00 |

Eagle. Rev. Arms. Francis II.

| 1138. | 4 Ducats 1797 .... | 3500.00 |

Eagle. Rev. Tablet. Francis II.

| 1139. | 2 Ducats 1793-1806.....................* ...... | 1800.00 |
| 1140. | 1 Ducat 1793-1806 .... | 1200.00 |

HAMLIN

City church. Rev. Double eagle. Name of Leopold I.

| 1141. | 1 Goldgulden 1638-68............................. | 3000.00 |

Ferdinand III standing. Rev. City church.

| 1142. | 1 Ducat 1656 .... | 3000.00 |

HANAU-LICHTENBERG

Counts —

JOHN REINHARD I, 1599-1625

Arms. Rev. Double Eagle.

| 1143. | 1 Goldgulden 1613, 14, 17, 18, ND............... | 2200.00 |

FREDERICK CASIMIR, 1641-1685
Jehova and wreath. Rev. Arms.

1144.   1 Ducat 1647 .... 1500.00

Arms. Rev. Legend in cartouche.

1145.   1 Ducat 1647 .... 1800.00

PHILIP REINHARD, 1666-1712
Bust. Rev. Arms.

1146.   1 Ducat ND... 2000.00

JOHN REINHARD II, 1712-1736
Bust. Rev. Arms.

1147.   1 Ducat 1733, ND.................................. 2000.00

WILLIAM IX, 1736-1785
Bust. Rev. Arms.

1148.   1 Ducat 1737 .... 2000.00

Bust of Wilhelmine of Denmark. Rev. Inscription.

1149.   1 Marriage Ducat 1764............................ 2200.00

HANOVER

A. City of —

Castle gate. Rev. Legend.
1150.   3½ Goldgulden 1590................................. Rare

Castle gate. Rev. Eagle.

1151.   3 Ducats 1666 .... Rare
1152.   3 Goldgulden 1654............................... Rare
1153.   1 Ducat 1640, 66, 67...................... * 2000.00
1154.   1 Goldgulden 1616-33............................ 2000.00

B. English Kings of —

(For earlier issues of the English Kings, see under Brunswick-Luneburg).

GEORGE IV, 1820-1830

Head. Rev. Value.

1155.   10   Taler 1821-30 .... * 1600.00
1156.   5   Taler 1821-30 .... 1200.00
1157.   2½   Taler 1821-30 .... 1000.00

Horse. Rev. Value.

1158.   5 Harz-gold Taler 1821..................... 4000.00
1159.   1 Harz-gold Ducat 1821, 24, 27.............. 1800.00

(For other coins with the name and title of George IV, see under Charles II of Brunswick-Wolfenbuttel.)

WILLIAM IV, 1830-1837

Head. Rev. Arms.

1160.   10   Taler 1832-37 .... 2000.00
1161.   5   Taler 1835 .... * 1500.00
1162.   2½   Taler 1832-37. Rev. Value .... * 900.00

Horse. Rev. Value.

1163.   1 Harz-gold Ducat 1831....................... 1500.00

C. Hanoverian Kings of —

ERNEST AUGUST, 1837-1851

Small head. Rev. Arms in circle.

1164.   10   Taler 1837, 38. B mm. 1400.00
1165.   10   Taler 1839, 44. S mm. 1300.00
1166.   5   Taler 1839. S mm........................ * ... 1000.00
1167.   2½   Taler 1839, 40, 43. S mm....................... 750.00

Large head. Rev. Plain arms. All with B mm.

1168.   10   Taler 1846-51 .... 1750.00
1169.   5   Taler 1845-51 .... * 850.00
1170.   5   Harz-gold Taler 1849, 50 .... * 1250.00
1171.   2½   Taler 1845-50 .... 750.00

GEORGE V, 1851-1866

Head. Rev. Arms.

1172.	10 Taler 1853-56		1300.00
1173.	5 Taler 1853, 55, 56	*	550.00
1174.	5 Harz-gold Taler 1853	*	1500.00
1175.	2½ Taler 1853, 55		650.00

Head. Rev. Value.

1176.	1 Krone 1857-66	1500.00
1177.	½ Krone 1857-65	1750.00

HATZFELD

Princes —

SEBASTIAN, 1569-1631
Bust. Rev. Two virtues standing.

1178.	1 Ducat 1597	3500.00

HERMAN, 1631-1677

Bust. Rev. Madonna.

1179.	1 Ducat ND	4000.00

MELCHIOR, 1631-1658
Bust of Ferdinand II. Rev. Madonna seated.

1180.	1 Ducat ND	3000.00

HESSE-CASSEL

A. Landgraves, and later, Electors of —

WILLIAM II, 1493-1509
St. Elizabeth. Rev. Five shields crossed.

1181.	1 Goldgulden 1506-08	6500.00

WILLIAM I AND PHILIP
St. Elizabeth. Rev. Five shields crossed.

1182.	1 Goldgulden 1510	7000.00

PHILIP, 1509-1567
St. Elizabeth. Rev. Lion shield within four small shields.

1183.	1 Goldgulden 1510, 11	6000.00

Arms. Rev. Legend.

1184.	½ Goldgulden 1564	2200.00

MAURICE, 1592-1632
Bust. Rev. Flags and symbols.

1185.	1 Goldgulden 1618	1800.00

Arms. Rev. Four shields.

1186.	1 Ducat 1624		2500.00
1187.	1 Goldgulden 1624, 26	*	2200.00

Lion. Rev. Two flags.

1188.	4 Ducats 1627	Rare

Legend. Rev. Crossed flags. On his death.

1189.	2 Ducats 1632	3000.00
1190.	1 Ducat 1632	1500.00

WILLIAM V, 1627-1637
Bust. Rev. Arms.

1191.	1 Goldgulden 1627	2000.00

Arms. Rev. Willow tree in storm.

1192.	2 Ducats 1632		2800.00
1193.	1 Goldgulden 1628-34	*	1400.00

Lion. Rev. Willow tree in storm.

1194.	2 Goldgulden 1637		3000.00
1195.	1 Goldgulden 1635-37	*	1500.00

Lion. Rev. Willow tree.

1196.	2 Ducats 1637	2500.00
1197.	1 Ducat 1637	1400.00

Legend. Rev. Willow tree. On his death.

1198.	2 Ducats 1637	2200.00
1199.	1 Ducat 1637	1400.00

AMALIA ELIZABETH, REGENT, DIED 1651
Arms. Rev. Rock in storm.

1200.	1 Mining Ducat ND	8000.00

Legend. Rev. Rock. On her death.

1201.	2 Ducats 1651	8000.00

WILLIAM VI, 1637-1663
Bust. Rev. Arms.

1202.	1 Ducat 1661, 63	3000.00

Bust. Rev. Legend. On his death.

1203.	1 Ducat 1663	1800.00

Lion. Rev. Willow tree in storm.

1204.	1 Goldgulden 1638	1800.00

Arms. Rev. Ship.

1205.	1¼ Ducats 1654	3000.00
1206.	1 Goldgulden 1652, 53	2200.00

HEDWIG SOPHIA, 1649-1683
Bust. Rev. Arms.

1206a.	1 Ducat 1669	4500.00

Arms. Rev. Legend. On her death.

1207.	2 Ducats 1683	3000.00

ELIZABETH HENRIETTA, DIED 1683
Bust. Rev. Crown on pedestal. On her death.

1208.	2 Ducats 1683	3000.00

WILLIAM VII, 1663-1670
Arms. Rev. Legend. On his death.

1209.	1 Ducat 1670	2200.00

CHARLES, 1670-1730
Bust. Rev. Spring.

1210.	½ Ducat ND	650.00

Bust. Rev. Lion and "Eddergold".
1211. ½ Edder-gold Ducat ND 2000.00

Head. Rev. Lion on pedestal with book.
1212. 2 Ducats ND 3000.00
1213. 1 Ducat 1720, ND.......................... * 1500.00
1214. 1 Ducat 1720. Without book on Rev................ 1500.00
1215. ¼ Ducat 1720 .... 500.00

Head. Rev. Arms.
1216. 2 Ducats ND 2800.00
1217. 1 Ducat 1724, 25, ND .... * 1400.00

Head. Rev. Swan.
1218. ¼ Ducat ND...................................... 550.00

Arms. Rev. Swan.
1219. 1 Ducat 1686 .... 2500.00

Legend. Rev. Edder River Landscape.
1220. 1 Edder-gold Ducat 1677...................... 6000.00

FREDERICK I
(See next page under B. Swedish Kings of —)
WILLIAM VIII, 1751-1760
Bust. Rev. Arms.
1221. 1 Ducat 1751, 54 .... 1800.00

Initials. Rev. Lion.
1222. ¼ Ducat 1752 .... 500.00

FREDERICK II, 1760-1785

Head. Rev. Star of Order.
1223. 2 Louis d'or 1773, 75-77, 80, 85 .... 2500.00
1224. 1 Louis d'or 1771, 77, 78, 83, 84, 85 ....* 1800.00

Armored bust. Rev. Landscape with river-god.
1225. 1 Edder-gold Ducat 1775......................... 5000.00

GEORGE WILLIAM, PRINCE
Bust. Rev. Arms.
1226. 1 Ducat 1768 .... 1500.00

Bust of Wilhelmine Caroline. Rev. Legend.
1227. 1 Ducat 1764 .... 1800.00

WILLIAM IX (I), 1785-1821
Head. Rev. Star of Order.
1228. 1 Louis d'or 1786, 87, 88, 90..................... 1500.00

Head. Rev. Lion and trophies.
1229. 5 Taler 1791-1801 .... 1250.00
1230. 5 Taler 1803, 05, 06. With title as elector William I *. 2000.00

Head. Rev. Arms.
1231. 5 Taler 1814-20 .... 2500.00

WILLIAM II, 1821-1831

Bust. Rev. Arms.
1232. 5 Taler 1821-29 .... 1500.00

WILLIAM II AND FREDERICK WILLIAM, 1831-1847

Arms. Rev. Value.
1233. 10 Taler 1838, 40, 41............................. 1800.00
1234. 5 Taler 1834-47 .... * 1250.00

Legend on each side.
1235. ½ Edder-gold Ducat 1835........................ 1350.00

FREDERICK WILLIAM I, 1847-1866

Head. Rev. Arms.
1236. 5 Taler 1851 .... 1850.00

B. Swedish Kings of —

FREDERICK I, 1730-1751

Bust. Rev. Swedish arms.

1237.   1 Ducat 1731, 46, 49, 50 .... 1500.00

Head. Rev. Swedish arms.

1238.   1 Ducat 1737, 46 .... 2000.00

Crown over linked FR. Rev. Lion-shield.

1239.   1 Ducat 1737 .... 1850.00

Crown over linked FR. Rev. Swedish arms.

1240.   1 Ducat 1737 .... 2200.00

Head. Rev. Lion standing.

1241.   ½ Edder-gold Ducat 1731 .... * 1500.00
1242.   ½ Ducat 1748 .... * 800.00
1243.   ¼ Ducat ND 600.00

Bust. Rev. Lion standing.

1244.   ½ Edder-gold Ducat 1731 .... 1500.00

Crown over linked FR. Rev. Lion standing.

1245.   ¼ Ducat 1744, 50 .... 600.00

HESSE-DARMSTADT

Landgraves, and later, Grand Dukes of —

LOUIS V, 1596-1626
Arms. Rev. Three helmets.

1246.   1 Goldgulden 1621 .... 3000.00
1247.   1 Ducat 1623 .... 3000.00

GEORGE II, 1626-1661
Bust. Rev. Arms.

1248.   1 Ducat 1651, 55, 56, 58 .... 3000.00
1249.   1 Goldgulden 1656 .... 3500.00

Oak tree. Rev. Legend. On his death.

1250.   1 Ducat 1661 .... 2800.00
1251.   ½ Ducat 1661 .... 1200.00

Legend. Rev. Laurel tree. On his death.

1252.   ½ Ducat 1661 .... 1500.00

LOUIS VI, 1661-1678
Bust. Rev. Arms.

1253.   1 Ducat 1675 .... 2300.00

ERNEST LOUIS, 1678-1739
Bust. Rev. Arms.

1254.   2 Ducats 1703, 06-10. Arms supported by lions 3000.00
1255.   2 Ducats 1704. Arms with 5 helmets 3000.00
1256.   1 Ducat 1702-06, 17, 18, ND. Arms supported by lions. 1850.00
1257.   ½ Ducat 1703. Arms supported by lions 800.00
1258.   ½ Ducat 1703. Arms between branches 800.00
1259.   ¼ Ducat 1705 .... 700.00

Bust. Rev. Female at altar. On the Reformation.

1260.   1 Ducat 1717 .... 2500.00

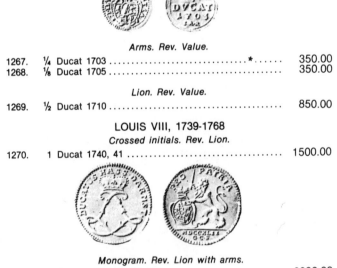

Bust. Rev. Crossed initials.

1261.   4 Ducats 1717 .... Rare
1262.   2 Ducats ND 3000.00
1263.   1 "Alchemy" Ducat ND 2500.00
1264.   1 Carolin 1733, ND .... * 1500.00
1265.   ½ Carolin 1733, ND 850.00
1266.   ¼ Carolin 1733, ND 1000.00

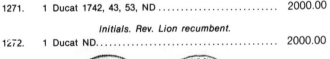

Arms. Rev. Value.

1267.   ¼ Ducat 1703 .... * 350.00
1268.   ⅛ Ducat 1705 .... 350.00

Lion. Rev. Value.

1269.   ½ Ducat 1710 .... 850.00

LOUIS VIII, 1739-1768
Crossed initials. Rev. Lion.

1270.   1 Ducat 1740, 41 .... 1500.00

Monogram. Rev. Lion with arms.

1271.   1 Ducat 1742, 43, 53, ND 2000.00

Initials. Rev. Lion recumbent.

1272.   1 Ducat ND 2000.00

Bust. Rev. Arms with and without palm-branches.

1273.   1 Ducat 1746, 48, 49, 51, 53, 55, ND ..Hesse-Darmstadt 2500.00

Bust. Rev. Lion with arms.
1274.   1 Ducat 1746 .... 2200.00

Crossed initials. Rev. Lion-shield within 7 shields.
1275.   2 Ducats 1760 .... 3500.00
1276.   1 Ducat 1760, 61 ....*...... 2000.00

Monogram. Rev. Horse and city view.
1277.   1 Ducat ND 1800.00

Monogram. Rev. Lion with monogram-shield.
1278.   1 Ducat ND 1800.00

Horse and city view. Rev. Lion with monogram-shield.
1279.   1 Ducat 1741 .... 1800.00

Stag and hunter. Rev. Stag and 3 dogs.
1280.   2 Ducats ND 3500.00

Crossed initials. Rev. Stag.
1281.   1 Ducat ND 2500.00

Crossed initials. Rev. Boar.
1282.   1 Ducat ND 2500.00

Monogram NB. Rev. Legend ALLES IN DER WELT etc.
1283.   1 Ducat ND 2600.00

LOUIS IX, 1768-1790
Bust. Rev. Arms, lions and value.
1284.   1 Ducat 1758, 72 .... 2500.00

LOUIS X (I), 1790-1830

Head. Rev. Arms.
1285.   10 Gulden 1826, 27 .... 4000.00

Inscription. Rev. Inscription.
1286.   1 Reformation Jubilee Ducat 1817 .... 600.00

LOUIS II, 1830-1848

Head. Rev. Arms.
1287.   10 Gulden 1840, 41, 42 .... 2500.00
1288.   5 Gulden 1835, 40, 41 ....*...... 1500.00
1289.   5 Rhine-gold Gulden 1835 ....*...... 6500.00

HESSE-HOMBURG
Landgraves of —
FREDERICK II, DIED 1708
Bust. Rev. Mountain.
1290.   1 Ducat 1690, ND (3 different bust-dies) 2800.00

HESSE-MARBURG
Landgraves of —
LOUIS III, 1567-1604
Bust. Rev. Arms.
1291.   1 Goldgulden 1591 .... 3000.00

HILDESHEIM
A. City of —

Bust of Charles V with hat. Rev. Arms. Struck during the 17th century.
1292.   5 Ducats 1528 .... 6000.00

Bust of Charles V. Rev. Arms.
1293.   4½ Goldgulden 1605, ND 6000.00

Orb. Rev. Arms.
1294.   1 Goldgulden 1573 .... 1800.00

Arms. Rev. Eagle. Name of Rudolph II.
1295.   1 Goldgulden 1602, 03, 06 .... 1500.00

Rudolph II on horse. Rev. Eagle.
1296.   10 Goldgulden ND. (1576-1610) .... Rare

Madonna. Rev. Arms.
1297.   1 Goldgulden 1624 .... 2000.00

Arms. Rev. Eagle. Name of Ferdinand II.
1298.   4 Goldgulden 1626 .... 4500.00
1299.   1 Goldgulden 1623, 27, 28 .... 1500.00
1300.   ½ Goldgulden 1623, 27 .... 1000.00

Arms. Rev. Eagle. Name of Leopold I.
1301.   1 Goldgulden 1672 .... 1800.00

B. Bishops of —
JODOCUS EDMUND, 1688-1702
Bust. Rev. Arms.
1302.   1 Ducat 1690, 94 .... 4000.00

SEDE VACANTE, 1761-1763
Arms. Rev. Value in cartouche.
1303.   ½ Pistole 1763 .... 1800.00

FREDERICK WILLIAM, 1763-1789

Bust right or left. Rev. Arms and value.

1304.	10 Taler or 2 Pistoles 1766	....	5000.00
1305.	5 Taler or 1 Pistole 1764, 65	...............*	2500.00
1306.	1 Ducat 1778	....	2000.00

Arms. Rev. Value in cartouche.

1307.	½ Pistole 1763	....	1250.00

Arms. Rev. Value.

1308.	1 Ducat 1784	....	1500.00

HOHENLOHE

Counts, and later, Princes —

ANONYMOUS
Bust of Rudolph II. Rev. Arms.

1309.	1 Ducat 1608	....	3800.00

Arms. Rev. Eagle.

1310.	1 Goldgulden 1615	....	2500.00

JOHN FREDERICK I OF OHRINGEN, 1676-1702

Knight on horse. Rev. Arms.

1311.	2 Ducats 1699	....	3500.00
1312.	1 Ducat 1699	......................*	1400.00

WOLFGANG JULIUS OF NEUENSTEIN, 1676-1698

Bust. Rev. Knight on horse.

1313.	1 Ducat 1697	....	2000.00

CHARLES LOUIS OF WEICKERSHEIM, 1708-1756
Bust. Rev. Arms.

1314.	1 Ducat 1737	....	1500.00

JOHN FREDERICK II OF OHRINGEN, 1708-1765
Bust. Rev. Three shields.

1315.	1 Ducat 1760	....	1500.00

CHARLES PHILIP OF NEUENSTEIN, 1733-1763
Bust. Rev. Arms.

1316.	1 Goldgulden 1735	....	1800.00

Bust. Rev. Phoenix over arms.

1317.	1 Ducat 1747	....	1500.00

PHILIP ERNEST OF SCHILLINGSFUERST, 1697-1753
Bust. Rev. Arms.

1318.	1 Ducat 1750	....	2200.00

JOSEPH ANTHONY OF PFEDELBACH, 1745-1764
Bust. Rev. Phoenix.

1319.	1 Ducat 1747	....	1500.00

LOUIS GOTTFRIED OF PFEDELBACH, 1685-1728
Arms. Rev. Legend. On the Reformation.

1320.	1 Ducat 1717	....	1500.00

LOUIS OF LANGENBURG, 1715-1765
Legend. Rev. Three female figures.

1321.	1 Ducat 1751	....	1500.00

LOUIS FREDERICK CHARLES OF OHRINGEN, 1765-1805
Bust. Rev. Arms.

1322.	1 Ducat 1770, 1804	....	2500.00

FREDERICK LOUIS OF INGELFINGEN, 1796-1806
Bust. Rev. Value.

1323.	1 Ducat 1796	....	2200.00

HOHENZOLLERN-HECHINGEN

Princes —

FREDERICK WILLIAM, 1671-1735

Bust. Rev. Arms.

1324.	1 Carolin 1734, 35	...........................*	3500.00
1325.	½ Carolin 1734, 35	....	2500.00

INGELHEIM

St. John. Rev. Orb. With name of Frederick III.

1326.	1 Goldgulden ND (1470-90)	....	1800.00

ISENBURG

Princes —

WOLFGANG ERNST I, 1596-1628
Arms. Rev. Double eagle.

1327.	2 Ducats 1618, 19	....	6500.00

CHARLES, 1803-1815
Head. Rev. Arms and value.

1328.	2 Ducats 1811	....	5500.00

JULICH-CLEVE-BERG

A. Dukes of Julich

WILLIAM I, 1356-1361
St. John. Rev. Lily.

1329.	1 Goldgulden ND	....	1600.00

WILLIAM II, 1361-1393
St. John. Rev. Lily.

1330. 1 Goldgulden ND 1700.00

Bust over arms. Rev. Two shields.

1331. 1 Goldgulden ND 2000.00

Bust over two shields. Rev. Eagle.

1332. 1 Goldgulden ND 2000.00

WILLIAM III, 1393-1402
Duke on throne. Rev. Cross.

1333. 1 Ecu d'or ND 4000.00

REYNALD IV, 1402-1423
Two angels with shield. Rev. Duke on horse.

1334. 1 Goldgulden ND 1200.00

St. John. Rev. Four or five shields.

1335. 1 Goldgulden ND 800.00

B. Dukes of Cleve

JOHN, 1347-1368
St. John. Rev. Lily.

1336. 1 Florin ND 1800.00

ADOLPH VII, 1394-1448
Helmeted arms on each side.

1337. 1 Goldgulden ND 1800.00

JOHN I, 1448-1481
Madonna. Rev. Helmet over two shields.

1338. ½ Goldgulden ND 2000.00

Standing ruler. Rev. Shield on cross.

1339. 1 Goldgulden ND 1500.00

JOHN II, 1481-1521
Standing ruler. Rev. Shield on cross.

1340. 1 Goldgulden ND 1250.00

Half length bust. Rev. Cross and four shields.

1341. 1 Goldgulden ND 1500.00

Bust of St. John. Rev. Five shields.

1342. 1 Goldgulden 1511, 17 .... 1500.00

St. John. Rev. Cross.

1343. 1 Philips-gulden 1501 .... 3300.00

St. John. Rev. Helmeted arms.

1344. 1 Goldgulden ND 1500.00

St. John. Rev. Arms on cross.

1345. 1 Goldgulden ND 1500.00

St. Martin standing. Rev. Arms.

1346. 1 Goldgulden 1503 .... 2800.00

C. Dukes of Berg

WILLIAM II, 1360-1408
Half length bust. Rev. Shield.

1347. 1 Goldgulden ND 2200.00

ADOLPH IX, 1408-1423
St. John. Rev. Four shields.

1348. 1 Goldgulden ND 1400.00

D. Dukes of Julich-Berg

ADOLPH IX, 1423-1437
St. John. Rev. Orb. Name of Sigismund I.

1349. 1 Goldgulden ND 1100.00

GERHART II, 1437-1475
St. John. Rev. Orb.

1350. 1 Goldgulden ND 1100.00

WILLIAM IV, 1475-1511
Arms on cross. Rev. Three shields.

1351. 1 Goldgulden ND 1200.00

Bust of St. Hubert. Rev. Arms on cross.

1352. 1 Goldgulden 1501, ND 1000.00

St. Hubert standing. Rev. Arms.

1353. 1 Goldgulden 1503 .... 1000.00

St. Hubert standing. Rev. Five shields. The last three dates are posthumous.

1354. 1 Goldgulden 1511, 12, 14 .... 1000.00

E. Dukes of Julich, Cleve and Berg

JOHN III, 1511-1539
St. Hubert. Rev. Arms.

1355. 1 Goldgulden 1511-16 .... 1500.00

WILLIAM V, 1539-1592
Five shields. Rev. Double eagle.

1356. 1 Goldgulden 1567, 68, 72, 81, 87, 89 .... 1500.00

JOHN WILLIAM I, 1592-1609
Five shields. Rev. Double eagle.

1357. 1 Goldgulden 1592, 93, 98, 1604, 05, 08, 09 .... 1400.00

INTERREGNUM, 1609-1624
Five shields. Rev. Double eagle.

1358. 1 Goldgulden 1613, ND 2200.00

SIEGE OF JULICH, 1610
Eight punch marks. Rev. Blank. Octagonal necessity coin.

1359. 40 Taler 1610 .... Rare

F. Palatine Dukes of Julich, Cleve and Berg

WOLFGANG WILLIAM, 1624-1653

Bust. Rev. Arms and value.

1360. 1 Ducat 1636, 43, 50 .... 2200.00

PHILIP WILLIAM, 1653-1679

Bust. Rev. Arms.

1361. 1 Ducat 1654-77 .... 3000.00

Bust. Rev. Sun over legend.

1362. 1 Ducat 1676 .... 2200.00

JOHN WILLIAM II, 1679-1716

Bust. Rev. Orb on shield.

1363. 1 Ducat 1682-1710 ....* 2200.00
1364. ¼ Ducat 1710, 11 .... 1250.00

Bust. Rev. Circle of nine shields.

1365. 2 Ducats 1707 ....* 3500.00
1366. 1 Ducat 1707, 08 .... 2000.00

Bust. Rev. Three shields.

1367. 2 Ducats 1708, 09, 11.......................... 3500.00
1368. 1 Ducat 1708, 09, 11............................ 2000.00

Head. Rev. Two shields on double eagle. Vicariat issue.

1369. 5 Ducats 1711.................................... 8000.00
1370. 3 Ducats 1711.................................... 6500.00
1371. 2 Ducats 1711............................* 4500.00
1372. 1 Ducat 1711 .... 3000.00

Bust. Rev. Bust of Marie Anne.

1373. 2 Ducats ND 3500.00

CHARLES PHILIP, 1716-1742
Bust. Rev. Initials.

1374. 10 Ducats 1717 .... Rare
1375. 5 Ducats 1717 .... Rare
1376. 1 Ducat 1720 .... 1500.00
1377. 1 Goldgulden 1718.............................. 1800.00

Head. Rev. Five shields.

1378. 1 Carolin 1732.................................... 2500.00

Head. Rev. Arms.

1379. 1 Carolin 1733...........................* 2000.00
1380. ½ Carolin 1733.................................. 1500.00
1381. ¼ Carolin 1735.................................. 1300.00

CHARLES THEODORE, 1742-1799

Bust. Rev. Arms.

1382. 1 Ducat 1749, 50 .... 3000.00

Bust. Rev. Three shields.

1383. 2 Ducats 1750...................................... 3500.00

Bust. Rev. Cross of St. Hubert.

1384. 1 Ducat 1750 .... 1850.00

KAUFBEUREN

Bust of Charles V. Rev. Orb.

1385. 1 Goldgulden ND (1517-58)................... 1800.00

Charles V standing. Rev. Pillars of Hercules.

1386. 1 Ducat 1542, 43 .... 2800.00

Orb. Rev. Arms.

1387. 1 Goldgulden 1541, 46............................ 3000.00

Arms. Rev. Cross.

1388. 1 Gold Crown ND (1545)......................... 1500.00

Seated female. Rev. Legend. On the Augsburg Confession

1389. 1 Ducat 1730 .... 1600.00

KEMPTEN

A. Abbots of —

RUPERT, 1678-1728

Four helmeted shields. Rev. St. Hildegarde in shield.

1390. 2 Ducats 1693 ....* 4000.00
1391. 1 Ducat 1692, 95 .... 2000.00

ANSELM, 1728-1747
Bust. Rev. Horse and arms.

1391a. 1 Ducat 1729 .... Rare

ENGELBERT, 1747-1760
Bust. Rev. Arms.

1392. 2 Ducats 1748 .... 3800.00
1393. 1 Ducat 1748 .... 2000.00

B. City of —

St. Magnus standing. Rev. Double eagle.

1394. 1 Goldgulden 1511-48............................ 2200.00

Angel. Rev. Legend. On the Reformation.

1395. 1 Ducat 1717 .... 1400.00

Obelisk. Rev. Sun over castle. On the Augsburg Confession.

1396. 1 Ducat 1730 .... 1400.00

KOENIGSEGG

Counts —

FRANCIS HUGO

Armored bust. Rev. Arms.

1397.   1 Ducat 1756 . . . .   5000.00

LANDAU

Arms, legend and punch marks. Rev. Blank. Square with clipped corners. Struck while besieged by the French.

1398.	4 Doppia 1713 . . . .*	Rare
1399.	2 Doppia 1713	Rare
1400.	1 Doppia 1713 . . . .*	5000.00

LEININGEN

Counts —

EMICHO V, 1375-1442

Half length figure under canopy. Rev. Arms in cartouche.

1401.   1 Goldgulden ND 6000.00

LEININGEN-WESTERBURG

Counts —

LOUIS, 1597-1622

Bust. Rev. Arms.

1402.   1 Goldgulden 1614, 17, 18, 19 . . . .   1500.00

LEIPZIG

Bust of Frederick the Bellicose. Rev. City view. On the 300th year of the Academy.

1403.   1 Ducat 1709 . . . .   1500.00

Bust of Martin Luther. Rev. Altar. On the Reformation.

1404.	2 Ducats 1717	1850.00
1405.	1 Ducat 1717	1250.00

LEUTKIRCH

City View. Rev. Church.

1406.   1 Peace Ducat 1748 . . . .   2200.00

LIMBURG-SONTHEIM

Barons —

FREDERICK, 1530-1596
Armored bust. Rev. Ship.

1407.   2 Ducats ND . . . .   Rare

LIPPE-DETMOLD

(The coinage of Lippe-Schaumburg will be found under Schaumburg-Lippe.)

Counts —

SIMON VII, 1613-1627

Eagle. Rev. Arms. Name of Matthias.

1408.   1 Goldgulden 1619 . . . .   3500.00

SIMON HENRY, 1666-1697
Bust. Rev. Arms.

1409.	3	Ducats 1685, 92	Rare
1410.	1½	Ducats 1685, 92	2500.00
1411.	1	Ducat 1673, 85	2000.00

FREDERICK ADOLPH, 1697-1718
Bust. Rev. Arms.

1412.	10 Ducats 1712, 15	15000.00
1413.	5 Ducats 1711, 15, 16	7500.00
1414.	2 Ducats 1714	4500.00
1415.	1 Ducat 1711-16, ND	2000.00

Bust. Rev. Legend.

1416.   1 Ducat 1710, ND 2000.00

Bust. Rev. Value.

1417.   ¼ Ducat 1714, 15 . . . .   750.00

SIMON HENRY ADOLPH, 1718-1734
Bust. Rev. Arms.

1418.	4 Ducats 1719	Rare
1419.	1 Ducat 1718, 19	2000.00

SIMON AUGUST, 1734-1782
Head. Rev. Arms.

1420.	1 Ducat 1765. Birthday issue	2000.00
1421.	1 Ducat 1767	1850.00

Busts of the Count and Countess. Rev. Two hands. On their wedding.
1422.   1 Ducat 1769 .... 1850.00

FREDERICK WILLIAM LEOPOLD, 1782-1802
Two shields. Rev. Legend. On the birth of the Crown Prince.
1423.   1½ Ducats 1796 .... 2000.00

LOEWENSTEIN-ROCHEFORT

Princes —

MAXIMILIAN CHARLES, 1672-1718
Flying eagle. Rev. Legend. On the birth of Leopold.
1424.   1 Ducat 1716 .... 2500.00

Bust. Rev. Arms.
1425.   1 Ducat 1692 .... 2500.00

CHARLES THOMAS, 1735-1789

Bust. Rev. Arms.
1426.   1 Ducat 1754 .... 2200.00

LOEWENSTEIN-WERTHEIM

Princes —

CHARLES LOUIS, 1737-1779

Bust. Rev. Arms.
1427.   1 Ducat 1767 .... 3000.00

JOHN LOUIS WOLRAD, 1730-1790
Bust. Rev. Lion.
1428.   1 Ducat ND... 3000.00
1429.   ¼ Ducat ND... 800.00

Bust. Rev. Arms.
1430.   1 Ducat 1768, 69, 71................................. 2500.00

Bust. Rev. Figure kneeling at altar. On the 50th year of reign.
1431.   1 Ducat 1780 .... 2200.00

DOMINICK CONSTANTINE, 1789-1806
Bust. Rev. Allegory. On his birthday.
1432.   1 Ducat 1791 .... 2500.00

FREDERICK CHARLES, 1799-1806

Bust. Rev. Arms.
1433.   2 Ducats 1799. Thick flan........................... 4000.00
1434.   1 Ducat 1799 ....* 3000.00

LUBECK

A. City of —

Double eagle. Rev. Blank.
1435.   ½ Ducat or Bracteate ND (1300)..................... Rare

"English" king in ship. Rev. Sun and eagle.
1436.   1 Rosenoble ND (1327-77)........................... Rare

St. John. Rev. Lily.
1437.   1 Ducat ND (1400-1500)............................. 750.00

St. John. Rev. Emperor seated.
1438.   1½ Ducats ND (1400-1500)........................... Rare

St. John. Rev. Madonna.
1438a. 1 Ducat 1497 .. .. 2500.00

St. John on each side.
1439.   1 Ducat ND (1500)................................. 1000.00

Orb. Rev. Double eagle.
1440.   1 Goldgulden 1583-1675 .... 1500.00
1441.   ¼ Ducat ND (1650)................................ 850.00

Double eagle. Rev. Arms.
1442.   1 Goldgulden 1589-1637 .... 1250.00

Birth of Christ. Rev. The Resurrection.
1443.   10 Ducats ND (1619-27)............................ Rare
1444.   5 Ducats ND (1619-27)............................. Rare

St. John. Rev. Cross.
1445.   ½ Portugaloser or 5 Ducats 1636.................. Rare

Royal figure seated. Rev. Double eagle.
1446.   ½ Portugaloser or 5 Ducats 1628.................. Rare

Royal figure standing. Rev. Double eagle.
1447.   4 Ducats 1638...................................... Rare

1448.	2 Ducats 1656-1716	*	2500.00
1449.	1 Ducat 1631-1759		1500.00
1450.	½ Ducat 1679-1714		800.00
1451.	¼ Ducat 1679-1728		500.00

Rock on sea. Rev. All-seeing eye.

1452.	1 Ducat 1707		1250.00

Double eagle. Rev. Legend. On the Reformation.

1453.	2 Ducats 1717		2500.00
1454.	1 Ducat 1717	*	1500.00

Bust of Charles VI. Rev. Double eagle.

1455.	1 Ducat 1729, 30		2000.00

Religion standing. Rev. Double eagle. On the Augsburg Confession.

1456.	1 Ducat 1730		1000.00

Tablet. Rev. Double eagle. With names of the Holy Roman Emperors.

1457.	1 Ducat 1790-1801		1250.00

B. Bishops of —

EBERHARD, 1567-1586
Bust. Rev. Arms.

1458.	10 Ducats ND		Rare

JOHN ADOLPH, 1585-1596
Arms. Rev. Cross.

1459.	1 Portugaloser or 10 Ducats ND		Rare
1460.	½ Portugaloser or 5 Ducats ND		Rare

JOHN FREDERICK, 1607-1634
St. Peter. Rev. Arms.

1461.	1 Goldgulden 1612		3000.00

Bust. Rev. Arms.

1462.	1 Portugaloser or 10 Ducats ND		Rare

CHRISTIAN ALBERT, 1655-1666
Armored bust. Rev. Arms. Posthumously struck.

1463.	1 Ducat 1689		2000.00

AUGUST FREDERICK, 1666-1705
Armored bust. Rev. Arms.

1464.	1 Ducat 1688, 89		1500.00

CHRISTIAN AUGUST, 1705-1726
Armored bust. Rev. Lion.

1465.	1 Ducat 1724, 26		2000.00

FREDERICK AUGUST, 1750-1785
Bust. Rev. Arms. For illustration, see Oldenburg No. 1808.

1466.	1 Pistole 1776		2500.00

LUNEBURG

St. John. Rev. Orb.

1467.	2 Goldgulden 1592		3500.00
1468.	1 Goldgulden ND (1419-1500)	*	750.00
1469.	1 Goldgulden 1581-99		850.00

St. John. Rev. Double eagle.

1470.	2 Goldgulden 1600		3000.00
1471.	1 Goldgulden 1600-35		800.00

St. John. Rev. Arms on cross.

1472.	3 Goldgulden ND (1600-50)		3000.00
1473.	2½ Goldgulden ND (1600-50)		2500.00

Bust of St. John. Rev. Orb.

1474.	1 Goldgulden 1626, 29		850.00

St. John. Rev. Face in crescent.

1475.	2 Goldgulden ND (1650)		3500.00
1476.	1 Goldgulden ND (1650)	*	1500.00
1477.	1 Ducat 1645, 47		2000.00

St. John. Rev. Crescent, hunters and fishermen.

1478.	6 Ducats ND (1650)		Rare

Castle gate. Rev. Double cross.

1479.	½ Portugaloser 1567, ND		Rare

Castle gate. Rev. Double eagle.

1480.	2 Goldgulden ND (1576-1610)		3000.00

Lion. Rev. Double eagle.

1481.	1 Goldgulden ND (1576-1610)		1500.00

MAGDEBURG

A. General City coinage

Arms. Rev. Inscription.

1482.	½ Siege Ducat 1551 square		3000.00

Arms. Rev. Cross.

1483.	10 Ducats ND (1573-1606)		Rare
1484.	5 Ducats ND (1573-1606)		Rare

Emperor Otto I on horse. Rev. Eagle.

| 1485. | 10 Ducats 1599 ....* .... | Rare |
| 1486. | 4 Ducats 1599 .... | Rare |

Arms. Rev. Value in square.

| 1487. | 1 Ducat 1673 .... | 2000.00 |

City view. Rev. Arms.

| 1488. | 2 Ducats 1675 .... | 3000.00 |

B. Coinage with the names of the Holy Roman Emperors

Female over city gate. Rev. Eagle. Maximilian II.

| 1489. | 1 Goldgulden 1571, 74, 76 .... | 1300.00 |

Female over city gate. Rev. Eagle. Rudolph II.

| 1490. | 2 Goldgulden 1594 .... | 3000.00 |
| 1491. | 1 Goldgulden 1571, 85, 1600, 05, 06 .... | 1500.00 |

Female over city gate. Rev. Eagle. Matthias.

| 1492. | 1 Goldgulden 1617 .... | 2000.00 |

Arms with helmet. Rev. Eagle. Matthias.

| 1493. | 1 Goldgulden ND .... | 2200.00 |

Arms with helmet. Rev. Eagle. Ferdinand II.

| 1494. | 1 Goldgulden 1624 .... | 1800.00 |

Female over city gate. Rev. Eagle. Ferdinand II.

| 1495. | 1 Goldgulden 1622, 24, 26-30 .... | 1200.00 |

Female over city gate. Rev. Eagle. Ferdinand III.

| 1496. | 2 Ducats 1639 .... | 1800.00 |

Eagle. Rev. Value on tablet. Ferdinand III.

| 1497. | 1 Ducat 1638, 41, 42 .... | 1250.00 |

C. Archbishops of —

JOACHIM FREDERICK, 1566-1598
Bust. Rev. Arms.

| 1498. | 2 Ducats 1590 .... | 2500.00 |

Eagle. Rev. Arms.

| 1499. | 1 Goldgulden 1586 .... | 2200.00 |

CHRISTIAN WILLIAM, 1598-1631
Bust. Rev. Arms.

| 1500. | 1 Goldgulden 1615, 23, ND .... | 2000.00 |
| 1501. | ½ Goldgulden ND .... | 1500.00 |

Bust. Rev. Three shields in circle of fourteen shields.

| 1502. | 2 Goldgulden ND .... | 2500.00 |

CATHEDRAL CHAPTER, 1638

St. Mauritius. Rev. Arms.

| 1503. | 1 Ducat 1638 .... | 1500.00 |

AUGUST, 1638-1680
Legend. Rev. St. Mauritius. On his enthronement.

| 1504. | 1 Ducat 1638 .... | 2000.00 |

Facing bust. Rev. Arms of Magdeburg.

| 1505. | 1 Ducat 1640, 41 .... | 2000.00 |

Bust. Rev. Arms of Saxony.

| 1506. | 1 Ducat 1671 .... | 1800.00 |

Initials. Rev. Legend. On the death of Anna Marie.

| 1507. | 1 Ducat 1669 .... | 1500.00 |

MANSFELD

Counts —

A. The Vorderort Line BORNSTEDT

BRUNO II, WILLIAM I AND JOHN GEORGE IV, 1604-1607
Three shields. Rev. St. George.

| 1508. | 1 Goldgulden 1606 .... | 1500.00 |

BRUNO II, WILLIAM I, JOHN GEORGE IV AND VOLRAT VI, 1605-1615
Three shields. Rev. St. George.

| 1509. | 1 Goldgulden 1611 .... | 1250.00 |

BRUNO II, WILLIAM I, JOHN GEORGE IV, VOLRAT VI AND JOBST, 1609-1615
Three shields. Rev. St. George.

| 1510. | 1 Goldgulden 1615, ND .... | 1250.00 |

WOLFGANG III AND JOHN GEORGE II, 1631-1638

St. George. Rev. Value on tablet.

| 1511. | 1 Ducat 1631, 32, 35, 38 .... | 1250.00 |

CHARLES ADAM, 1638-1662
St. George. Rev. Value on tablet.

| 1512. | 1 Ducat 1656 .... | 1250.00 |

FRANCIS MAXIMILIAN, 1644-1692
St. George. Rev. Arms and value.
1513. ¼ Ducat 1670, 71 .... 500.00

FRANCIS MAXIMILIAN AND HENRY FRANCIS, 1644-1692

St. George. Rev. Crowned arms.
1514. 1 Ducat 1687 .... 1250.00

HENRY, PRINCE OF FONDI, 1717-1780
Armored bust. Rev. Crowned arms.
1515. 1 Ducat 1747 .... 2000.00

Crowned arms on mantle. Rev. St. George.
1516. 1 Ducat 1774 .... 1250.00

FRANCIS GUNDACAR, 1780-1806
Crowned arms on mantle. Rev. St. George.
1517. 1 Ducat 1792 .... 1500.00

B. The Vorderort Line EISLEBEN

JOHN GEORGE I, PETER ERNEST I AND CHRISTOPHER II, 1558-1579
St. George. Rev. Three shields.
1518. 1 Goldgulden ND 1000.00

JOHN GEORGE II, 1619-1647
St. George. Rev. Three shields.
1519. 1 Goldgulden 1632, 35-37 .... 850.00

C. The Vorderort Line FRIEDEBURG

PETER ERNEST I, BRUNO II, HOYER CHRISTOPHER, GEBHARD VIII AND JOHN GEORGE IV, 1579-1587
Three shields. Rev. St. George.
1520. 1 Goldgulden 1587................................. 1000.00

PETER ERNEST I, BRUNO II, GEBHARD VIII AND JOHN GEORGE IV, 1587-1601
Three shields. Rev. St. George.
1521. 1 Goldgulden 1597................................. 1000.00

PETER ERNEST I, BRUNO II, WILLIAM I AND JOHN GEORGE IV, 1601-1604
Three shields. Rev. St. George.
1522. 1 Goldgulden 1603................................. 1100.00

D. The Vorderort Line ARTERN

VOLRAT VI, JOBST II AND WOLFGANG III, 1615-1617
Three shields. Rev. St. George.
1523. 1 Goldgulden 1616, 17............................. 850.00

VOLRAT VI, JOBST II, WOLFGANG III AND BRUNO III, 1616-1619
Three shields. Rev. St. George.
1524. 1 Goldgulden 1617, 18............................. 850.00

VOLRAT VI AND JOBST II
St. George. Rev. Three shields.
1525. 1 Goldgulden 1619................................. 850.00

VOLRAT VI, WOLFGANG III AND JOHN GEORGE II, 1620-1627

St. George. Rev. Three shields.
1526. 1 Goldgulden 1620, 21, 26 .... * 800.00
1527. ½ Goldgulden 1620................................. 1200.00

PHILIP ERNEST, WOLFGANG III AND JOHN GEORGE II
St. George. Rev. Three shields.
1528. 1 Goldgulden 1630................................. 1250.00

E. The Hinterort Line

VOLRAT V, JOHN I AND CHARLES I, 1560-1566
Arms. Rev. Helmet.
1529. 1 Goldgulden 1563................................. 1500.00

DAVID, 1603-1628
St. George. Rev. Crowned arms.
1530. 1 Ducat 1619 .... 1800.00

St. George. Rev. Legend above arms.
1531. 1 Goldgulden 1606, 18.............................. 1500.00

Arms with helmet. Rev. St. George.
1532. 1 Goldgulden 1622................................. 1500.00

ERNEST VI AND FREDERICK CHRISTOPHER, 1579 AND 1603-1611
Arms with helmet. Rev. St. George. Title of Rudolph II.
1533. 1 Goldgulden 1607................................. 1200.00

FREDERICK CHRISTOPHER AND DAVID, 1620-1628
St. George. Rev. Arms with helmet.
1534. 1 Ducat 1622 .... 1500.00

CHRISTIAN FREDERICK, 1632-1666
St. George. Rev. Value on tablet.
1535. 1 Ducat 1644, 47, 52.............................. 1000.00

MAYENCE (MAINZ)

A. Archbishops of —

GERLACH, 1346-1371
St. John. Rev. Lily.
1536. 1 Goldgulden ND................................... 600.00
1537. 1 Goldgulden ND. Mint: Eltville.................... 2500.00

Archbishop standing. Rev. Arms in enclosure.
1538. 1 Goldgulden ND. Mint: Bingen..................... 800.00

Archbishop standing. Rev. Rupert of Palatinate standing.
1539. 1 Goldgulden ND. Mint: Bingen..................... 2500.00

SEDE VACANTE, 1371
St. Martin standing. Rev. Wheel shield in enclosure.
1540. 1 Goldgulden ND. Mint: Bingen..................... 1000.00

JOHN I, 1371-1373
Archbishop standing. Rev. Arms in enclosure.

1541. 1 Goldgulden ND. Mint: Bingen.................... 600.00

Archbishop on throne. Rev. Wheel shield in enclosure.

1542. 1 Goldgulden ND. Mint: Hoechst 600.00

ELECTION DISPUTE AFTER THE DEATH OF JOHN I, 1373
St. Martin on throne. Rev. Wheel shield in enclosure.

1543. 1 Goldgulden ND (Anonymous). Mint: Bingen 750.00

ADOLPH I, 1373-1390

St. Martin on throne. Rev. Wheel shield in enclosure.

1544. 1 Goldgulden ND. Mints: Bingen, Hoechst.......... 600.00

St. John standing. Rev. 4 Arms in enclosure.

1545. 1 Goldgulden ND. Mints: Bingen, Hoechst.......... 600.00
1546. 1 Goldgulden ND. Mint: Udenheim................. 1000.00

Archbishop standing. Rev. Arms in enclosure.

1547. 1 Goldgulden ND. Mint: Oberlahnstein.............. 1250.00

CONRAD II, 1390-1396
Archbishop on throne. Rev. Wheel shield in enclosure.

1548. 1 Goldgulden ND. Mint: Bingen.................... 600.00

St. John standing. Rev. Wheel shield in enclosure.

1549. 1 Goldgulden ND. Mint: Bingen.................... 600.00

St. John standing. Rev. Arms of Mainz-Nassau in enclosure.

1550. 1 Goldgulden ND. Mint: Bingen.................... 600.00

St. John standing. Rev. 4 Arms in enclosure.

1551. 1 Goldgulden ND. Mints: Bingen, Hoechst.......... 600.00

ELECTION DISPUTE, 1396-1397
St. Martin on throne. Rev. Wheel shield in enclosure.

1552. 1 Goldgulden ND. Mints: Bingen, Hoechst.......... 600.00

JOHN II, 1397-1419
Archbishop on throne. Rev. Wheel shield in enclosure.

1553. 1 Goldgulden ND. Mint: Bingen.................... 500.00

St. John standing. Rev. Arms of Mainz-Nassau and small arms of Cologne and Trier.

1554. 1 Goldgulden ND. Mints: Bingen, Hoechst.......... 550.00

St. John standing. Rev. 5 Arms in enclosure.

1555. 1 Goldgulden ND. Mints: Bingen, Hoechst.......... 550.00

St. Peter standing. Rev. 5 Arms in enclosure.

1556. 1 Goldgulden ND. Mints: Bingen, Hoechst.......... 550.00

Bust of St. Peter under canopy. Rev. 5 Arms in enclosure.

1557. 1 Goldgulden ND................................... 600.00

St. Martin on throne. Rev. Wheel shield in enclosure.

1558. 1 Goldgulden ND. Mint: Hoechst 600.00

CONRAD III, 1419-1434
Archbishop standing. Rev. Wheel shield in enclosure.

1559. 1 Goldgulden ND. Mints: Bingen, Hoechst.......... 500.00

St. Peter standing. Rev. 5 Arms in enclosure.

1560. 1 Goldgulden ND. Mints: Bingen, Hoechst.......... 600.00

St. Peter standing. Rev. 4 Arms in enclosure.

1561. 1 Goldgulden ND. Mint: Bingen.................... 600.00

THEODORE I, 1434-1459
Archbishop standing. Rev. Wheel shield in enclosure.

1562. 1 Goldgulden ND. Mints: Bingen, Hoechst.......... 800.00

Arms on cross. Rev. 3 shields.

1563. 1 Goldgulden 1436-38, ND. Mints: Bingen, Hoechst . 600.00

THEODORE II, 1459-1461 AND 1475-1482
Christ on throne. Rev. Floriated cross with 4 shields.

1564. 1 Goldgulden ND. (1459-61). Mint: Mayence......... 600.00

Arms. on cross. Rev. 3 shields.

1565. 1 Goldgulden ND. (1475-82). Mints: Mayence,
     Hoechst, Rhenish 1250.00

ADOLPH II, 1461-1475
Christ on throne. Rev. Floriated cross with 4 shields.

1566. 1 Goldgulden ND. Mint: Mayence.................. 850.00

BERTHOLD, 1484-1504
Arms on cross. Rev. Christ on throne.

1567. 1 Goldgulden 1490. Mint: Rhenish 1250.00

4 Arms in enclosure. Rev. Christ on throne.

1568. 1 Goldgulden 1491-1504 .... 1000.00

JAMES, 1504-1508
4 Arms in enclosure. Rev. Christ on throne.

1569. 1 Goldgulden 1504-08............................. 1000.00

URIEL, 1508-1514
4 Arms in enclosure. Rev. Christ on throne over wheel shield.

1570. 1 Goldgulden 1506, 09, 12, 14, ND................. 850.00

Christ on throne over family shield. Rev. 4 Arms in enclosure.

1571. 1 Goldgulden ND................................. 1500.00

ALBERT, 1514-1545
Christ on throne. Rev. 4 Arms in enclosure.

1572. 1 Goldgulden 1515, 34-43, ND 2000.00

DANIEL BRENDEL, 1555-1582
Arms. Rev. Floriated cross and 4 shields.

1573. 1 Goldgulden 1571, 72............................ 2200.00

WOLFGANG, 1582-1601
Arms. Rev. 4 Arms in enclosure.

1574. 1 Goldgulden 1586, 87, 88, 93, 95................. 1250.00

Arms with infulae. Rev. 4 Arms in enclosure.

1575. 1 Goldgulden 1596................................ 2000.00

GEORGE FREDERICK, 1626-1629

Arms. Rev. Floriated cross, 3 shields and orb.

1576. 1 Goldgulden 1626, 27.......................... 2200.00

Arms. Rev. St. Martin on horse.

1577. 1 Goldgulden 1628................................ 1850.00

Arms. Rev. Value in tablet.
1578. 1 Ducat 1628, 29 .... 1000.00
1579. 1 Ducat 1628. Square........................... 1850.00

ANSELM CASIMIR, 1629-1647
Facing bust. Rev. Arms.
1580. 2 Ducats 1629 (from the ducat die) 2000.00
1581. 1 Ducat 1629 .... 1500.00

Facing bust. Rev. Crowned arms.
1582. 2 Ducats 1642 .... 2200.00

Bust right. Rev. Crowned arms.
1583. 2 Ducats 1642, 44, 46, 47 .... 2000.00
1584. 1 Ducat 1633, 38, 44, ND 1000.00

Bust right. Rev. Arms.
1585. 2 Ducats 1636 (from the ducat die) 2500.00
1586. 1 Ducat 1636, 38 .... 1250.00

Bust right. Rev. Arms with 3 helmets.
1587. 2 Ducats 1642...................................... 2500.00

Arms with 3 helmets. Rev. Legend in wreath.
1588. 2 Ducats 1638, 39, ND............................ 2200.00

Arms. Rev. Legend on tablet.
1589. 1 Ducat 1636, 41 .... 800.00

Crowned arms. Rev. Legend between branches.
1590. 1 Ducat 1642, 46 .... 900.00

Crowned arms in wreath. Rev. Legend between branches.
1591. 1 Ducat 1645, 46 .... 850.00

JOHN PHILIP, 1647-1673
Facing bust. Rev. Arms.
1592. 1 Ducat 1648-66 .... 1200.00

Bust right or left. Rev. Arms.
1593. 1 Ducat 1654, 55, 57, 67, 68, 70, 71 .... 700.00

LOTHAR FREDERICK, 1673-1675
Bust. Rev. Arms.
1594. 1 Ducat 1673...................................... 1250.00

DAMIAN HARTARD, 1675-1678
Bust. Rev. Arms.
1595. 1 Ducat 1676...................................... 1500.00

ANSELM FRANCIS, 1679-1695

Bust. Rev. Arms.
1596. 2 Ducats 1680 ....*...... 3500.00
1597. 1 Ducat 1684 .... 1500.00

LOTHAR FRANCIS, 1695-1729
Concordia seated. Rev. Arms under canopy. On the Peace
of Ryswick.
1598. 2 Ducats ND (1696).............................. 2500.00
1599. 1 Ducat ND (1696)............................... 1250.00

Arms. Rev. Altar and value.
1600. 2 Ducats 1696.................................... 2200.00
1601. 1 Peace Ducat 1696 ....*...... 1000.00

Minerva standing. Rev. Arms. On the Peace of Ryswick.
1602. 2 Ducats 1696 ....*...... 2500.00
1603. 1 Ducat 1696 .... 1250.00

Bust. Rev. Arms.
1604. 1 Ducat 1716, 28 .... 1500.00
1605. ¾ Ducat 1712 .... 1000.00

FRANCIS LOUIS, 1729-1732
Bust. Rev. Lion being led by hand from heaven.
1606. 1 Ducat 1730 .... 1500.00

PHILIP CHARLES, 1731-1743
Bust. Rev. Arms.
1607. 2 Ducats 1738.................................... 3250.00
1608. 1 Ducat 1738..................................... 2000.00

JOHN FREDERICK CHARLES, 1743-1763
Bust. Rev. Arms.
1609. 2 Ducats 1745, 48 .... 2500.00
1610. 1 Ducat 1745, 47, 53............................. 1500.00

Bust. Rev. Arms supported by dogs.
1611. 2 Ducats 1760 ....*...... 3500.00
1612. 1 Ducat 1759, 60 .... 1500.00

EMERIC JOSEPH, 1763-1774
Bust. Rev. Arms.

1613.   1 Ducat 1768, 69, 71................................. 1400.00

Bust. Rev. Legend.

1614.   1 Rhine-gold Ducat 1772......................... 3000.00

FREDERICK CHARLES JOSEPH, 1774-1802

Bust. Rev. Arms.

1615.   1 Ducat 1795 .... 1000.00

Bust. Rev. City view.

1616.   1 Ducat 1795 .... 1250.00

CHARLES, 1802-1813
(See under Rhine Confederation.)

B. Abbey of St. Alban —

St. Martin on horse and S-M-E. Rev. Shield with wheel in enclosure.

1617.   1 Goldgulden ND (1300-1400) .... Rare

St. Martin on horse and S-M-E. Rev. Arms.

1618.   1 Goldgulden ND 2000.00
1619.   ½ Goldgulden ND 2000.00

St. Martin on horse. Rev. Shield with wheel in enclosure.

1620.   2 Goldgulden ND (shield with ornaments).......... 2200.00
1621.   2 Goldgulden ND (Smaller shield).................. 2200.00
1622.   1 Goldgulden ND 1500.00

St. Martin on horse. Rev. Angel with arms.

1623.   1 Goldgulden 1584, ND............................ 1500.00

C. Swedish Rulers of —

Facing bust of Christina. Rev. Arms.

1624.   2 Ducats ND (1634)............................... Rare
(Note: For the coinage of St. Alban in Mayence, see under Saint Alban.)

MECKLENBURG

Dukes of —

JOHN ALBERT, 1547-1576
Bust with hat. Rev. Cross with five arms.

1625.   1 Ducat 1554 .... 2500.00

MECKLENBURG-GUSTROW

Dukes of —

JOHN ALBERT II, 1611-1636
Duke standing. Rev. Arms.

1626.   3 Ducats 1633 .... Rare
1627.   2 Ducats 1633 .... 4000.00
1628.   1 Ducat 1633 .... 1800.00

GUSTAVE ADOLPH, 1636-1695

Bust. Rev. Arms.

1629.   1 Ducat 1666, 68. Mint: Wismar.............* 2000.00
1630.   1 Ducat 1671, 72, 74, 75, 80, 85-89. Mint: Gustrow .. 2000.00

MECKLENBURG-SCHWERIN

Dukes, and later Grand Dukes of —

ADOLPH FREDERICK, 1592-1658
Bust. Rev. Arms.

1631.   1 Goldgulden 1615................................ 1800.00

Half length bust. Rev. Arms.

1632.   1 Goldgulden 1616................................ 2000.00

Bust. Rev. Arms.

1633.   1 Goldgulden 1625................................ 2000.00

Facing bust. Rev. Arms.

1634.   1 Ducat 1639 .... 1850.00

CHRISTIAN LOUIS I, 1658-1692
Bust. Rev. Arms.

1635.   2 Ducats 1681 .... 3500.00
1636.   1 Ducat 1670, 71, 81, 88......................... 2000.00

FREDERICK WILLIAM, 1692-1713
Initials. Rev. Arms.

1637.   1 Ducat 1696. NON EST MORTALE QVOD OPTO ... 2200.00
1638.   1 Ducat 1703. PROVIDE ET CONSTANTER.......... 1500.00

Bust. Rev. Arms.

1639.   2 Ducats 1703. PROVIDE ET CONSTANTER 2500.00
1640.   1 Ducat 1696. NON EST MORTALE QVOD OPTO ... 2000.00
1641.   1 Ducat 1701. QVO DEVS ET FORTVNA DVCVNT... 1500.00
1642.   1 Ducat 1703, 05. PROVIDE ET CONSTANTER *... 1500.00

Bust. Rev. Initials.

1643.   1 Ducat 1696 .... 2000.00

Arms. Rev. Ox head.

1644.	1	Ducat 1701	*	1850.00
1645.	¼	Ducat 1701		1000.00

Bust. Rev. The Duke and Duchess in boat.

1646.	2	Ducats 1704		2500.00
1647.	1	Ducat 1703, 04	*	1500.00

Bust. Rev. Value.

1648.	¼	Ducat ND	600.00

CHRISTIAN LOUIS II, 1747-1756
Bust. Rev. Arms.

1649.	2	Pistoles 1752	2000.00
1650.	1	Pistole 1754	1500.00

Bust. Rev. Value.

1651.	¼	Ducat 1756	650.00

FREDERICK, 1756-1785

Bust. Rev. Value.

1652.	2	Taler 1769, 78, 82, 83	1000.00

FREDERICK FRANCIS, 1785-1837

Arms. Rev. Value.

1653.	2	Taler 1792, 97	650.00

Head. Rev. Arms.

1654.	10	Taler 1828, 31, 32, 33		1800.00
1655.	5	Taler 1828, 31-33, 35	*	1500.00
1656.	5	Taler 1828. Mint visit		6000.00
1657.	2½	Taler 1831, 33, 35		1250.00
1658.	2	Taler 1830		2500.00
1659.	1	Ducat 1830	*	2500.00

PAUL FREDERICK, 1837-1842

Head. Rev. Arms.

1660.	10	Taler 1839	*	1700.00
1661.	5	Taler 1840		1500.00
1662.	2½	Taler 1840	*	1100.00

MECKLENBURG-STRELITZ

Dukes of —

ADOLPH FREDERICK III, 1708-1752

Bust. Rev. Faith before temple. On the Reformation.

1663.	1	Ducat 1717. A DEO	2000.00

Bust. Rev. Jerusalem on mountain. On the Reformation.

1664.	1	Ducat 1717. NEC INGENS etc.	1850.00

Bust. Rev. City on rock in ocean. On the Reformation.

1665.	1	Ducat 1717. CONSILIO STAT etc.	2000.00

Bust. Rev. Arms.

1666.	5	Taler 1747, 49	2500.00

Initials. Rev. Ox head.

1667.	5	Taler 1748	2500.00

Initials. Rev. Value.

1668.	2	Taler 1746, 47	1250.00
1669.	1	Taler 1746, 47, 49	1100.00

ADOLPH FREDERICK IV, 1752-1794

Head. Rev. Arms.

1670.	1 Pistole 1754		1500.00

Bust. Rev. Arms.

1671.	1 Pistole 1754		1500.00

MEMMINGEN

City view. Rev. Inscription. On the centennial of Peace of Westphalia.

1672.	1 Ducat 1748		2500.00

MINDEN

Bishops of —

HERMAN, 1566-1582
Arms. Rev. Double eagle.

1673.	1 Goldgulden ND		5000.00

ANTHONY, 1585-1599
Arms. Rev. Double eagle.

1674.	1 Goldgulden 1589, 95, ND		3000.00

MOERS

Counts —

FREDERICK II, 1375-1417
Three shields in enclosure. Rev. St. John.

1675.	1 Goldgulden ND		4000.00

FREDERICK III, 1417-1448
Five shields in enclosure. Rev. St. John.

1676.	1 Goldgulden ND		2500.00

Arms in enclosure. Rev. St. John.

1677.	1 Goldgulden ND. Mint: Falkenberg		3500.00

Arms in enclosure. Rev. St. Andrew over shield.

1678.	1 Goldgulden ND. Mint: Moers		3500.00

MUNSTER

Bishops of —

JOHN III, 1457-1466
Bust of St. Paul. Rev. Arms on cross.

1679.	1 Goldgulden ND		3500.00

HENRY III, 1466-1496

St. Paul seated. Rev. Three shields.

1680.	1 Goldgulden ND		2000.00

CONRAD II, 1497-1508
St. Paul standing. Rev. Eagle shield in enclosure.

1681.	1 Goldgulden ND		2500.00
1682.	½ Goldgulden ND		1500.00

St. Paul seated. Rev. Three shields.

1683.	1 Goldgulden ND		2000.00
1684.	½ Goldgulden ND		1800.00

ERIC I, 1508-1522
Knight on horse. Rev. Arms in enclosure.

1685.	1 Goldgulden ND		3500.00

FRANCIS, 1532-1553
St. Peter and St. Paul. Rev. Four shields in enclosure.

1686.	1 Goldgulden ND		2500.00

St. Paul seated. Rev. Four shields in enclosure.

1687.	1 Goldgulden ND		2500.00

JOHN IV, 1566-1574
St. Paul standing. Rev. Four shields in enclosure.

1688.	1 Goldgulden 1570		2200.00

FERDINAND, 1612-1650

Arms. Rev. Value.

1689.	2 Ducats 1640. Square		2750.00
1690.	1 Ducat 1638-47	*	1500.00

St. Paul standing. Rev. Arms.

1691.	1 Ducat 1633, 34		1500.00

CHRISTOPHER BERNARD, 1650-1678
Madonna. Rev. Arms.

1692.	2 Ducats ND		2500.00
1693.	1 Ducat ND		2000.00

Arms. Rev. Value.

1694.	1 Ducat 1652, 65		1500.00

Arms. Rev. City view.

1694a.	6 Ducats 1666		4500.00

Arms. Rev. Legend. On his death.

1695.	1 Goldgulden 1678		2200.00

FREDERICK CHRISTIAN, 1688-1706
Bust. Rev. Arms.

1696.	1 Ducat 1695		2500.00

FRANCIS ARNOLD, 1704-1718

Bust. Rev. Arms.

1697.	2 Ducats 1717	*	5000.00
1698.	1 Ducat 1717		2750.00

NASSAU

Counts, and later, Dukes of —

RUPERT, 1355-1390
St. John. Rev. Lily.

1699.	1 Goldgulden ND		3000.00

WALRAM, 1370-1393
St. Paul standing. Rev. Arms in enclosure.
1700. 1 Goldgulden ND 3000.00

PHILIP, 1371-1429
St. John. Rev. Arms in enclosure.
1701. 1 Goldgulden ND.................................. 3000.00

HENRY OF DILLENBURG, 1662-1702
Bust. Rev. Arms.
1702. 1 Ducat 1688..................................... 3000.00

CHARLES AUGUST, 1719-1753

Arms. Rev. Prince standing.
1703. 1 Ducat 1750...................................... 1500.00

Bust. Rev. Arms.
1704. 1 Ducat 1750...................................... 2000.00

FREDERICK AUGUST AND FREDERICK WILLIAM, 1803-1816

Arms. Rev. Value on tablet.
1705. 1 Ducat 1809...................................... 2000.00

WILLIAM, 1816-1839

Head. Rev. Arms.
1706. 1 Ducat 1818...................................... 2500.00

NOERDLINGEN

St. John. Rev. Orb. With name of Holy Roman Emperor as indicated.
1707. 1 Goldgulden ND. Sigismund 650.00
1708. 1 Goldgulden 1491-93, ND. Frederick III 850.00
1709. 1 Goldgulden 1494-1501, 06-08, 11, 13, 16. Maximilian I. 850.00

NORDHAUSEN

Theodosius seated. Rev. Arms.
1710. 1 Goldgulden 1619 .... Rare

NOSTIZ
Counts —

ANTHONY JOHN, 1683-1736
Bust. Rev. Arms supported by griffins.
1711. 1 Ducat 1719...................................... 2000.00

NUREMBERG

A. General City Coinage

St. Sebaldus. Rev. Arms in trefoil.
1712. 1 Goldgulden ND (1429) 2500.00

St. Lawrence. Rev. Eagle.
1713. 3 Goldgulden 1612 .... Rare
1714. 2 Goldgulden ND (1552), 1614, 86................... Rare
1715. 1 Goldgulden ND (1429-1506), 1506-1686 ......* 1250.00

St. Lawrence. Rev. Arms.
1716. 1 Goldgulden 1614-23 .... 1250.00

Two shields. Rev. Legend. On the Shooting Match.
1717. 1 Goldgulden 1579 .... 2500.00

St. Sebaldus with church model. Rev. Eagle.
1718. 1 Goldgulden 1623-86 .... 2200.00

St. Sebaldus with church model. Rev. Arms.
1719. 1 Goldgulden 1629-30 .... 1250.00

Eagle. Rev. Two shields.
1720. 1 Ducat 1635, 40 .... 1000.00

Eagle. Rev. Genius standing with two shields.

1721. 1 Peace Ducat 1635 .... 1500.00
1722. 1 Ducat 1637-86 .... * 850.00

Arms. Rev. Tablet.

1723. 1 Ducat 1635-45 .... 750.00

Legend and arms. Rev. Two hands over globe. On the Peace.

1724. 4 Ducats 1650. Square............................. 3500.00
1725. 3 Ducats 1650 .... 2500.00
1726. 3 Ducats 1650. Square............................. 2500.00
1727. 2 Ducats 1650 .... * 1500.00
1728. 1 Ducat 1650............................. 800.00

Eagle and hand. Rev. Legend.

1729. 1 Ducat 1650............................. 1000.00

Arms. Rev. Tablet.

1730. 1 Goldgulden 1660 .... 2200.00

Genius with two shields. Rev. City view.

1731. 5 Ducats 1677 .... 4000.00

Light and screen. Rev. Legend. On the Reformation.

1732. 2 Ducats 1717. Square........................* 2500.00
1733. 1 Ducat 1717............................. 1500.00
1734. 1 Goldgulden 1617 .... 1500.00

Three shields. Rev. City view.

1735. ½ Ducat 1773............................. 800.00

B. Coinage with the heads of the Holy Roman Emperors

Half figure of Sigismund. Rev. Eagle.

1735a. 1 Goldgulden ND 2000.00

Bust of Maximilian II. Rev. Two shields.

1736. 2 Goldgulden 1570 .... Rare
1737. 1 Goldgulden 1570 .... 3000.00

Bust of Rudolph II. Rev. Two shields.

1738. 1 Goldgulden 1580 .... 1850.00

Busts of Matthias and Anna. Rev. Three shields.

1739. 2 Goldgulden 1612 .... 2800.00
1740. 1 Goldgulden 1612 ....* 1500.00

Ferdinand II on horse. Rev. Genius with two shields.

1741. 10 Ducats 1630 .... Rare

Bust of Leopold I. Rev. Three shields.

1742. 1 Goldgulden 1658 .... 2500.00

Bust of Leopold I. Rev. Genius with two shields.

1743. 10 Ducats ND (1670)............................. 20000.00
1744. 6 Ducats ND (1670)............................. 10000.00
1745. 5 Ducats ND (1670)........................* 8000.00
1746. 4 Ducats ND (1670)............................. 5000.00

Arms. Rev. Eagle.

1746a. 10 Ducats 1694 .... 20000.00

City view. Rev. Pax with two genii.

1747. 6 Ducats 1698 .... 4500.00

1747a. 5 Ducats 1698 .... 4000.00

Bust of Charles VI. Rev. Three shields.

1748. 1 Ducat 1711............................ 1250.00

Bust of Charles VI. Rev. Altar.

1749. 1 Ducat 1712............................ 600.00

Bust of Charles VII. Rev. Noris standing.

1750. 1 Ducat 1742 .... 4500.00

Bust of Francis I. Rev. Noris standing.

1751. 1 Ducat 1745 .... 2500.00

Bust of Joseph II. Rev. Arms.

1752. 1 Ducat 1766 .... 1800.00

Bust of Leopold II. Rev. City view.

1753. 1 Ducat 1790 .... 2000.00

Bust of Francis II. Rev. City view.

1754. 1 Ducat ND (1792) 2000.00

C. The Lamb Coinage of Nuremberg

Arms. Rev. Lamb on globe.

1755. 2 Ducats 1632 ....*...... 1500.00
1756. 1 Ducat 1632 .... 1200.00
1757. ½ Ducat 1700. Square 500.00
1758. ¼ Ducat 1700, ND. Round **400.00**
1759. ¼ Ducat ND. Square 250.00
1760. ⅛ Ducat ND. Round 250.00
1761. ⅛ Ducat ND. Square 200.00
1762. ¹⁄₁₆ Ducat ND. Round 200.00
1763. ¹⁄₁₆ Ducat ND. Square 150.00
1764. ¹⁄₃₂ Ducat ND 150.00

Arms. Rev. Lamb under cross from heaven.

1765. 3 Ducats 1649. Square 3500.00
1766. 1 Ducat 1633. Round ....*...... 1800.00

Three shields. Rev. Lamb.

1767. 2 Ducats 1649 .... 2500.00
1768. 1 Ducat 1649 ....*...... 1800.00
1769. ½ Ducat 1692 .... 500.00

Three shields. Rev. Lamb on globe.

1770. 5 Ducats 1703 .... 4500.00
1771. 4 Ducats 1703 .... 3500.00
1772. 3 Ducats 1703. Round ....*...... 3000.00
1773. 3 Ducats 1700. Square 3200.00
1774. 2 Ducats 1700. Round 1300.00
1775. 2 Ducats 1700. Square 1300.00
1776. 1 Ducat 1700. Round 400.00
1777. 1 Ducat 1700. Square ....*...... 500.00
1778. ½ Ducat 1700. Round 250.00
1779. ½ Ducat 1700. Square 300.00
1780. ¼ Ducat 1700. Square 250.00
1780a. ¼ Ducat 1700. Round 250.00

City view. Rev. Lamb.

1781. 2 Ducats 1806. With laurel wreath 5000.00
1782. 1 Ducat 1806 ....*...... 2000.00

D. Nuremberg Coinage of the Swedish Kings

GUSTAVE II ADOLPHE, 1611-1632

Bust facing. Rev. Arms.

1784.	2 Ducats 1631. Thick	5000.00
1785.	1 Ducat 1631 ....*......	3000.00

Bust right. Rev. Arms.

1786.	6 Ducats 1632	Rare
1787.	2 Ducats 1632. Thick ....*......	4000.00
1788.	1 Ducat 1632	1200.00

Bust. Rev. Legend in wreath.

1789.	1 Ducat 1632	2000.00

King standing. Rev. Arms.

1790.	1 Ducat 1632	3000.00

Bust facing. Rev. Legend in square. On his death.

1791.	2 Ducats 1632	5000.00

OBERSTEINBACH

Two shields. Rev. Altar. On the Reformation.

1792.	1 Ducat 1717	1500.00

OETTINGEN

Counts, and later, Princes —

WOLFGANG I AND JOACHIM, 1477-1520
Arms. Rev. St. Wolfgang.

1793.	1 Goldgulden 1519, 20	4000.00

CHARLES WOLFGANG AND LOUIS XV, 1522-1549
Arms. Rev. Adoration of the three Magi.

1794.	1 Goldgulden 1522, 29, 34, 40, 41.................	4000.00

CHARLES WOLFGANG AND MARTIN, 1522-1549
Arms. Rev. Adoration of the three Magi.

1795.	1 Goldgulden 1529, 40............................	3000.00

MARTIN, 1520-1549

Half length bust of Charles V. Rev. Arms.

1796.	1 Goldgulden 1541.................................	4000.00

CHARLES WOLFGANG, LOUIS XV AND MARTIN, 1522-1549
Arms. Rev. Double eagle. Name of Charles V.

1797.	2 Goldgulden 1546.................................	4000.00
1798.	1 Goldgulden 1546.................................	3500.00

OETTINGEN-OETTINGEN

Princes —

ALBERT ERNEST I, 1659-1683
Bust. Rev. Arms.

1799.	2 Goldgulden 1677.................................	4500.00
1800.	1 Ducat 1675	2000.00

Bust. Rev. Legend and arms.

1801.	1 Goldgulden 1677.................................	3000.00

Monogram. Rev. Arms.

1802.	½ Ducat ND. Square	2000.00
1803.	¼ Ducat ND................................	1500.00

ALBERT ERNEST II, 1683-1731

Armored bust. Rev. Arms.

1804.	1 Ducat ND................................	3000.00

Bust. Rev. Legend. On his death.

1805.	1 Ducat ND (1731)................................	2000.00

OLDENBURG

Counts, and later, Dukes of —

ANTHONY GUNTHER, 1603-1667

Bust. Rev. Arms.

| 1806. | 3 Ducats 1660. Facing bust | 6000.00 |
| 1807. | 1 Ducat 1664. Profile bust | 1700.00 |

FREDERICK AUGUST, 1773-1785

Bust. Rev. Arms. This is the same coin as Lubeck No. 1466.

| 1808. | 1 Pistole 1776 | 2500.00 |

OSNABRUCK

A. Bishops of —

JOHN III, 1424-1437
St. Peter standing. Rev. Arms.

| 1809. | 1 Goldgulden ND | 6000.00 |

CONRAD IV, 1482-1508
St. Peter on throne. Rev. Arms in enclosure.

| 1810. | 1 Goldgulden ND | 1500.00 |

St. Peter standing. Rev. Arms in enclosure.

| 1811. | 1 Goldgulden ND .... * | 1500.00 |
| 1812. | ½ Goldgulden ND | 2000.00 |

ERIC II, 1508-1532
St. Peter on throne. Rev. Arms in enclosure.

| 1813. | 1 Goldgulden 1515, 23, 30 | 2200.00 |

St. Peter on throne. Rev. Cross with four arms.

| 1814. | 1 Goldgulden ND. Mint: Wiedenbruck | 2500.00 |

FRANCIS WILLIAM, 1625-1661
St. Peter standing. Rev. Arms.

| 1815. | 1 Ducat 1637 | 2000.00 |

Three shields on each side.

| 1816. | 1 Ducat ND. | 1600.00 |

ERNEST AUGUST I, 1662-1698

Bust. Rev. Arms.

| 1817. | 1 Ducat 1666-98 | 2500.00 |

Bust. Rev. Horse.

| 1818. | ¼ Ducat 1695 | 550.00 |

Bust. Rev. Horse and pillar.

| 1819. | 2 Ducats ND | 1800.00 |

B. Swedish Kings of —

Bust of Gustave II Adolphe. Rev. Crown over legend.

| 1820. | 1 Ducat 1633 | 1500.00 |

PADERBORN

Bishops of —

THEODORE ADOLPH, 1650-1660
Facing bust. Rev. Arms.

| 1821. | 1 Ducat 1651, 53 | 2200.00 |

FERDINAND II, 1661-1683
Bust. Rev. Arms.

| 1822. | 1 Ducat 1674 | 2000.00 |

HERMAN WERNER, 1683-1704
Bust. Rev. Arms.

| 1823. | 1 Ducat 1684, 93 | 2500.00 |

FRANCES ARNOLD, 1704-1718
Bust. Rev. Arms.

| 1824. | 1 Ducat 1713 | 2200.00 |

CLEMENT AUGUST, 1719-1761

Bust. Rev. Madonna and arms.

| 1825. | 1 Goldgulden 1720 | 2500.00 |

WILLIAM ANTHONY, 1763-1782

Bust. Rev. Arms.

| 1826. | 5 Taler or 1 Pistole 1767 .... * | 1800.00 |
| 1827. | 1 Ducat 1776, 77 | 2000.00 |

PALATINATE (PFALZ)

Electors of the —

RUPERT I, 1353-1390

St. John. Rev. Lily.

| 1828. | 1 Goldgulden ND. Mints: Bacharach, Heidelberg | 750.00 |

St. John. Rev. Arms in enclosure.

| 1829. | 1 Goldgulden ND. Mints: Bacharach, Heidelberg, Oppenheim | 850.00 |

RUPERT II, 1390-1398

St. John. Rev. Lion and wheel shield in enclosure.
1830.   1 Goldgulden ND. Mint: Neustadt.................   2750.00

St. John. Rev. Four arms in enclosure.
1831.   1 Goldgulden ND. Mints: Bacharach, Oppenheim ...   950.00

RUPERT III, 1398-1410

St. John. Rev. Five arms in enclosure.
1832.   1 Goldgulden ND. Mints: Bacharach, Neustadt......   2200.00

St. John. Rev. Eagle over 2 shields.
1833.   1 Goldgulden ND. Mint: Heidelberg.................   4000.00

LOUIS III, 1410-1436
St. Peter. Rev. 4 arms in enclosure.
1834.   1 Goldgulden ND. Mints: Bacharach, Heidelberg....   850.00

St. Peter. Rev. Five arms in enclosure.
1835.   1 Goldgulden ND. Mints: Bacharach, Heidelberg,
        Oppenheim..................................   900.00

Christ on throne. Rev. Cross with four arms.
1836.   1 Goldgulden ND. Mint: Bacharach 850.00

Elector standing. Rev. Arms in enclosure.
1837.   1 Goldgulden ND. Mints: Bacharach, Heidelberg,
        Neustadt (rare), Oppenheim,
        Ruesselsheim (rare) 700.00

LOUIS IV, 1436-1449

Arms on cross. Rev. Three shields.
1838.   1 Goldgulden 1436-38, ND. Mint: Bacharach 450.00

FREDERICK I, 1449-1476
Christ on throne. Rev. Cross with four arms.
1839.   1 Goldgulden ND. Mints: Bacharach, Heidelberg....   450.00

Arms on cross. Rev. Three shields.
1840.   1 Goldgulden ND. Mint: Bacharach 425.00

Elector standing. Rev. Arms in enclosure.
1841.   1 Goldgulden ND. Mint: Bacharach 1500.00

PHILIP, 1476-1508
Christ on throne. Rev. Arms on cross.
1842.   1 Goldgulden 1490, ND.......................   1400.00

Christ on throne. Rev. Four arms in enclosure.
1843.   1 Goldgulden 1492, 93, 97 ....   1850.00

Madonna on crescent. Rev. Three shields.
1844.   1 Goldgulden 1500, 02, 05 ....   3000.00

Shield on cross. Rev. Three shields.
1845.   1 Goldgulden ND. Mint: Bacharach 1300.00

Shield with 3 arms on cross. Rev. Three shields.
1846.   1 Goldgulden ND................................   1200.00

LOUIS V, 1508-1544
Madonna. Rev. Three shields.
1847.   1 Goldgulden 1508............................   3000.00

Christ on throne. Rev. Four shields in enclosure.
1848.   1 Goldgulden 1509, 13, 15 ....   1500.00

OTTO HENRY AND PHILIP, 1505-1556
Madonna on crescent. Rev. Arms in enclosure.
1849.   1 Goldgulden 1515. Mint: Neuburg.................   3000.00

Bust of Madonna. Rev. Arms.
1850.   1 Ducat 1516 ....   3500.00

FREDERICK II, 1508-1566

Half length bust. Rev. Four arms in enclosure

1851. 1 Goldgulden ND. Mint: Heidelberg 7000.00

FREDERICK III, 1557-1576

Half length bust. Rev. Arms and three shields.

1852. 1 Goldgulden 1567. Mint: Heidelberg 4500.00

Half length bust. Rev. Arms.

1853. 1 Goldgulden 1575 .... 5000.00

LOUIS VI, 1576-1592
Bust. Rev. Arms.

1854. 2 Goldgulden 1583 .... 8000.00

FREDERICK IV, 1592-1610

Half length bust. Rev. Three shields.

1855. 1 Goldgulden 1608 .... 4500.00

FREDERICK V, 1610-1632

Elector on horse. Rev. Three shields.

1856. 4 Ducats 1612. .... * ...... Rare
1857. 2 Ducats 1612 .... 8000.00
1858. 1 Ducat 1612. .... 3000.00

Lion. Rev. Three shields.

1859. 1 Goldgulden 1621. Mint: Heidelberg 2500.00

Lion. Rev. Arms.

1860. 1 Goldgulden 1621. Mint: Heidelberg 2500.00

CHARLES LOUIS, 1648-1680
Bust. Rev. Three shields. On the Vicariat.

1861. 1 Ducat 1657. .... 4000.00

Bust. Rev. Three shields.

1862. 1 Ducat 1659, 62, 73 .... * 2500.00
1863. ½ Rhine-gold Ducat 1674 .... 4000.00
1864. ½ Ducat 1673. .... 1500.00
1865. ¼ Rhine-gold Ducat 1674. .... 2000.00

CHARLES, 1680-1685
Bust. Rev. Three shields.

1866. 1 Ducat 1682. .... 3300.00

JOHN WILLIAM, 1690-1716
Bust. Rev. Ten shields.

1867. 2 Ducats 1707 .... 3300.00
1868. 2 Ducats 1707. "Hoc Bellonae Stipendium". 3000.00
1869. 1 Ducat 1707. .... 2000.00
1870. 1 Ducat 1707. "Hoc Bellonae Stipendium". 2000.00

Bust. Rev. Imperial globe in shield.

1871. 1 Ducat 1708. .... 2200.00
1872. ¼ Ducat 1711. .... 1200.00

Bust. Rev. Three shields.

1873. 1 Ducat 1708. .... 2500.00

Bust. Rev. Double eagle. On the Vicariat.

1874. 3 Ducats 1711 .... 6000.00
1875. 2 Ducats 1711. .... * 4500.00
1876. 1 Ducat 1711. .... 2200.00
1877. ¼ Ducat 1711. .... 1200.00

Bust. Rev. Arms.

1878. 1 Ducat 1683, 86, 1703 .... 2200.00
1879. ½ Ducat 1705, 08 .... 1500.00

Bust. Rev. Value.

1880. ¼ Ducat 1708. .... 1000.00

Head. Rev. Imperial globe in shield.

1881. ¼ Ducat 1710. .... 800.00

CHARLES PHILIP, 1716-1742

*Young bust of Prince Philip August. Rev. The Prince standing.
Struck by the city of Mannheim.*

1882.　1 Ducat 1725.............................. 1750.00

Head. Rev. Three shields.

1883.　1 Ducat 1737.............................. 2800.00

Bust. Rev. Double Eagle. On the Vicariat.

1884.　1 Ducat 1740.............................. 2500.00

Bust. Rev. City view of Mannheim.

1885.　1 Rhine-gold Ducat ND 3500.00

Bust. Rev. Three shields.

1886.　1 Ducat 1721.............................. 3000.00

Elector on horse. Rev. Five shields crossed.

1887.　1 Ducat 1721, 26 .... 2000.00

Head. Rev. Five shields crossed between four initials.

1888.　1 Carolin 1732 .... 2500.00
1889.　½ Carolin 1732 .... 2000.00

Head. Rev. Arms.

1890.　1 Carolin 1733, 35 ....*..... 1000.00
1891.　½ Carolin 1733, 36 .... 800.00
1892.　¼ Carolin 1735, 36 .... 600.00

Head. Rev. Crown over three arms supported by lions.

1893.　1 Carolin 1733 .... 3500.00

Bust. Rev. Crown over three arms supported by lions.

1894.　½ Carolin 1732 .... 3000.00

CHARLES THEODORE, 1743-1799

Bust. Rev. Four initials and arms.

1895.　1 Carolin 1748, 49 (very rare), 50 .... 2500.00

Bust. Rev. Three shields.

1896.　2 Ducats 1750. (Dusseldorf)........................ 4000.00

Bust. Rev. Arms.

1897.　1 Ducat 1749 (rare), 50, 51........................... 2500.00

Bust. Rev. St. Hubertus Order.

1898.　1 Ducat 1750...................................... 2200.00

Head. Rev. Arms.

1899.　1 Ducat 1764...................................... 2500.00

Head. Rev. Three shields.

1900.　1 Ducat 1769...................................... 2500.00

Head or bust. Rev. City view of Mannheim.

1901.　1 Rhine-gold Ducat 1763, 64, 67, 78 .... 2200.00

Conjoined heads of Charles and Elizabeth Augusta. Rev. Two shields.

1902.　1 Ducat 1742. Struck at Mannheim 1800.00

Small bust. Rev. Fortuna.

1903.   1 Lottery Ducat ND................................. 2200.00

Arms of Heidelberg. Rev. Long legend.

1904.   1 Homage Ducat 1746............................. 1800.00

City shield of Mannheim. Rev. Legend.

1905.   1 Homage Ducat 1744............................. 1500.00

City shield of Mannheim. Rev. Legend. On the 50th year of reign.

1906.   1 Ducat 1792.. 1500.00

(For other coins of Charles Theodore, see under BAVARIA)

(For other coins of Charles Theodore, see under BAVARIA)

PALATINATE-BIRKENFELD-ZWEIBRUCKEN

Counts —

CHRISTIAN IV, 1735-1775

Bust. Rev. Arms.

1907.   1 Ducat 1747, 51 .... 3000.00

CHARLES AUGUST, 1775-1795

Head. Rev. Arms.

1908.   2 Ducats 1788 .... 3500.00

Head. Rev. Arms supported by lions.

1909.   1 Ducat 1788, 90 .... 3000.00

PALATINATE-MOSBACH

Counts —

OTTO II, 1461-1499

Madonna. Rev. Arms.

1910.   1 Goldgulden 1496 .... 4000.00

PALATINATE-NEUBURG

Counts —

PHILIP WILLIAM, 1653-1690

Bust. Rev. Sun. On his daughter's marriage.

1911.   1 Ducat 1676.. 2800.00

Bust. Rev. Arms.

1912.   1 Ducat 1654.. 3000.00

PALATINATE-SIMMERN

Counts —

STEPHAN, 1410-1453

Count standing. Rev. Arms in enclosure.

1913.   1 Goldgulden ND. Mints: Simmern, Wachenheim (rare) 2200.00

FREDERICK I, 1453-1480

Count standing. Rev. Arms in enclosure.

1914.   1 Goldgulden ND 2500.00

RICHARD, 1569-1598

Count standing. Rev. Arms and value.

1915.	2 Ducats 1576	3750.00
1916.	1 Ducat 1576-79, 87..................*	1250.00

PALATINATE-SULZBACH

Counts —

CHRISTIAN AUGUST, 1632-1708
Bust. Rev. Arms.

1917.	1 Ducat 1682..........................	2200.00

Arms. Rev. Resurrection of Christ.

1918.	¼ Ducat ND	800.00

PALATINATE-VELDENZ

Counts —

GEORGE GUSTAVE, 1592-1634
Count standing. Rev. Arms.

1919.	1 Ducat 1596..........................	3000.00

LEOPOLD LOUIS, 1634-1694
Bust. Rev. Arms.

1920.	1 Ducat 1673..........................	3000.00

PALATINATE-ZWEIBRUCKEN

Counts —

LOUIS, 1459-1489
Count standing. Rev. Arms in enclosure.

1921.	1 Goldgulden ND. Mint: Wachenheim	2800.00

Arms on cross. Rev. Three shields.

1922.	1 Goldgulden ND. Mint: Wachenheim	3500.00

JOHN II, 1604-1635

Arms. Rev. Double Eagle.

1923.	1 Goldgulden 1611, 16-19, 24, ND....................	2500.00

PASSAU

Bishops of —

VIGILIUS FROESCHL, 1500-1517
St. Stephan. Rev. Cross.

1924.	1 Goldgulden 1508	3000.00

ERNEST, 1517-1540
St. Stephan. Rev. Arms.

1925.	1 Ducat 1522, 37	3000.00

URBAN, 1561-1598
St. Stephan. Rev. Double eagle.

1925a.	4 Ducats 1563	Rare
1926.	2 Ducats 1567	Rare
1927.	1 Ducat 1570...............................	2000.00

SEBASTIAN, 1673-1689

1928.	¼ Ducat 1674...............................	800.00
1929.	⅙ Ducat 1674...............................	700.00

JOHN PHILIP, 1689-1712

Bust. Rev. Arms.

1930.	2 Ducats 1698, 1701	3000.00
1931.	1 Ducat 1698, 1705, 06, 09.................*	2000.00

Monogram. Rev. Arms.

1932.	½ Ducat 1709..............................	1250.00

RAYMOND FERDINAND, 1713-1722
Bust. Rev. Arms.

1933.	1 Ducat 1716..........................	1800.00

Initials. Rev. Fox with arms.

1934.	½ Ducat 1716..........................	1000.00

JOSEPH DOMINIC, 1723-1761

Bust. Rev. Arms.

1935.	1 Ducat 1747..........................	2200.00

LEOPOLD ERNEST, 1763-1783

Bust. Rev. Arms.

1936.	1 Ducat 1779..........................	2200.00

POMERANIA

A. Dukes of —

BOGISLAUS X, 1474-1523
Madonna. Rev. Arms on cross.
1937. 1 Goldgulden 1499, ND 2500.00

JOHN FREDERICK, 1569-1600
Half length bust. Rev. Arms.
1938. 1 Ducat 1594, 96 .... 2000.00

PHILIP JULIUS, 1592-1625
Bust. Rev. Arms.
1939. 1 Goldgulden 1609, 11 .... 2000.00

PHILIP II, 1606-1618
Bust. Rev. Arms.
1940. 1 Goldgulden 1612, 13 .... 1800.00

Arms supported by wild men. Rev. David with his harp.
1941. 2 Goldgulden 1614 .... 2000.00

Bust. Rev. David with his harp.
1942. 2 Goldgulden 1614 .... 2000.00

Bust. Rev. Crossed sword and pen.
1943. 1 Goldgulden 1614, 15 .... 1500.00

Bust. Rev. Light.
1944. 2 Goldgulden 1615 .... 1800.00
1945. 1 Goldgulden 1615 .... 1500.00

Bust. Rev. Stag.
1946. 2 Goldgulden 1615 .... 2000.00
1947. 1 Goldgulden 1615, 16 .... 1500.00

Bust. Rev. Snail.
1948. 2 Goldgulden 1617 .... 2200.00
1949. 1 Goldgulden 1617, 18 .... 1500.00

Bust. Rev. Wreath with SOLI DEO GLORIA.
1950. 2 Goldgulden 1616 .... 2000.00
1951. 1 Goldgulden 1616-18 .... 1500.00

Bust. Rev. Legend. On the Reformation.
1952. 1 Goldgulden 1617 .... 2000.00

Man with lamb. Rev. Legend. On the Reformation.
1953. 1 Goldgulden 1617 .... 1600.00

FRANCIS, 1618-1620
Bust. Rev. Griffin.
1954. 1 Goldgulden 1618 .... 2000.00

BOGISLAUS XIV, 1620-1637
Bust. Rev. Griffin in shield.
1955. 1 Goldgulden 1632 .... Rare

Bust. Rev. Arms.
1956. 1 Goldgulden 1628 .... 1500.00

Bust and helmet. Rev. Griffin.
1957. 1 Goldgulden 1629 .... 1500.00

Duke standing. Rev. Arms.
1958. 1 Ducat 1629, 31, 33-36, ND 1500.00

Duke standing. Rev. Arms with three helmets.
1959. 1 Ducat 1633, ND 1800.00

Legend. Rev. Skull. On his burial.
1960. 1 Ducat 1654 .... 2000.00
1961. ½ Ducat 1654 .... 1000.00

B. Swedish Rulers of —

CHRISTINA, 1632-1654

Facing bust. Rev. Christ over arms.
1962. 1 Ducat 1641 .... 2200.00

Facing half length bust. Rev. Arms.
1963. 1 Ducat 1642 .... 2500.00

Facing bust. Rev. Arms.
1964. 1 Ducat 1642, 46, 53 .... 2500.00

Bust. Rev. Arms.
1965. 2½ Ducats 1653 .... 7500.00

CHARLES X, 1654-1660

Bust. Rev. Arms.
1966. 2 Ducats 1658 .... 6000.00

King standing. Rev. Arms.
1967. 1 Ducat 1654, 56, 58, 59 .... 3750.00

CHARLES XI, 1660-1697

Small bust in circle. Rev. Arms supported by wild men.
1968. 2 Ducats 1661 .... * 4500.00
1969. 1 Ducat 1662 .... 3500.00

Large bust not in circle. Rev. Arms supported by wild men.

1970.	3 Ducats 1674	6000.00
1971.	2 Ducats 1684, 90	5000.00
1972.	1 Ducat 1672-75, 82, 84, 86, 89, 90, 95, 97 .....*	2000.00
1973.	1 Ducat 1666. Without the wild men ....*	3000.00

Large bust. Rev. Crown, orb and crossed swords over sheaf.

1974.	2 Ducats 1692-94, 96, 97, ND	2800.00

CHARLES XII, 1697-1718

Half length bust. Rev. Lion between falling and broken columns.

1975.	2 Ducats 1706	4500.00

Half length bust. Rev. Five line legend in wreath.

1976.	2 Ducats 1706	4500.00

Bust with long hair. Rev. Arms.

1977.	1 Ducat 1706	2000.00

Bust with short hair. Rev. Arms.

1978.	1 Ducat 1706, 09	2500.00

ADOLPH FREDERICK, 1751-1771

Head. Rev. Griffin and value.

1979.	10 Taler 1759	4000.00
1980.	5 Taler 1758 (very rare), 59 ....*	2200.00

PRUSSIA

A. Brandenburg, Electors of —

JOACHIM AND ALBERT, 1499-1514
St. Paul standing. Rev. Cross and five shields.

1981.	1 Goldgulden ND. Mint: Brandenburg	6000.00
1982.	1 Goldgulden ND. Mint: Berlin	5000.00

JOACHIM I, 1499-1535
St. Paul standing. Rev. Cross and five shields.

1983.	1 Goldgulden 1516, 18, 19, 21. Mint: Frankfurt (Oder).	5500.00

St. John standing. Rev. Cross and five shields.

1984.	1 Goldgulden 1526. Mint: Frankfurt (Oder)	5000.00

JOACHIM II, 1535-1571
St. John. Rev. Cross and five shields.

1985.	2 Goldgulden 1540	8500.00
1986.	1 Goldgulden 1538-40	6500.00

Eagle. Rev. Double eagle.

1987.	1 Goldgulden 1552	6000.00

Five shields. Rev. Double eagle.

1988.	1 Goldgulden 1557	6000.00

Bust. Rev. Arms.

1989.	2 Ducats 1560	7500.00
1990.	1 Ducat 1560, 66	5500.00

Arms. Rev. Cross.

1991.	10 Ducats 1570	Rare

JOHN GEORGE, 1571-1598
Eagle. Rev. Five shields.

1992.	1 Goldgulden 1573, 87	5500.00

Armored bust. Rev. Arms and legend.

1993.	2 Ducats 1584	8000.00

Armored bust. Rev. Cross and shields.

1994.	10 Ducats 1584, 87	Rare
1995.	5 Ducats 1590	Rare

Armored bust. Rev. Arms.

1996.	1 Ducat 1590	5500.00

JOACHIM FREDERICK, 1598-1608
Elector standing. Rev. Eagle.

1997.	2 Ducats 1606	6500.00
1998.	1 Ducat 1605, 06	5500.00

Half length bust. Rev. Cross.

1999.	10 Ducats 1605	Rare

JOHN SIGISMUND, 1608-1619
Bust. Rev. Arms.

2000.	1 Goldgulden 1615	3500.00

Facing bust. Rev. Arms.

2001.	1 Goldgulden 1614, 17	2500.00

Half length bust. Rev. Arms.

2002.	1 Goldgulden 1617	4000.00

Bust. Rev. Arms.

2003.	1 Ducat ND	5000.00

Elector standing. Rev. Eagle.

2004.	1 Ducat 1611, 12, 14	2500.00

Elector standing. Rev. Arms.

2005.	2 Ducats 1615	5500.00

Bust. Rev. Cross.

2006.	10 Ducats 1612	Rare
2007.	5 Ducats 1611, 13, 14	Rare

GEORGE WILLIAM, 1619-1640
I. Berlin Mint with or without Mintmaster's Initials LM
Elector on horse. Rev. Sceptre within two circles of 24 shields.

2008.   10 Ducats 1620 (LM)................................. Rare

Bust. Rev. Sceptre shield.

2009.   1 Goldgulden 1620 (LM) 6000.00

Bust. Rev. Arms with 7 fields.

2010.   1 Goldgulden 1622 .... 3000.00

Bust. Rev. Arms with 12 fields.

2011.   2 Goldgulden 1621 .... 4000.00

Elector standing before desk with helmet. Rev. Five arms.

2012.   1 Ducat 1620 (LM).................................. 6500.00

Elector standing before desk with helmet. Rev. Sceptre within circle of 8 shields.

2013.   2 Ducats 1620 (LM)................................. 2800.00

Elector standing before desk with helmet. Rev. Arms.

2014.   2 Ducats ND (LM) 3700.00

II. Cologne Mint with Mintmaster's Initials LM or IP
Bust in elector's robes. Rev. Arms with 12 fields.

2015.	2 Ducats 1626 (IP) from the ducat die	4500.00
2016.	1 Ducat 1626 (IP)	3500.00
2017.	1 Goldgulden 1628 (LM)	3300.00

Elector standing. Rev. Sceptre within circle of shields.

2018.   1 Ducat 1639 (LM) 1850.00

Armored bust with sceptre. Rev. Arms.

2019.   1 Goldgulden 1628 (LM) 2000.00

Bust in elector's robes with sceptre. Rev. Arms.

2020.   2 Goldgulden ND (LM)............................. 4500.00

Bust in elector's robes with sceptre. Rev. Arms under elector's hat.

2021.   2 Goldgulden 1628 (LM) 4000.00

Elector standing at desk with helmet. Rev. Arms.

2022.   2 Ducats 1634 (LM), 36 (LM) 2000.00

Elector standing at desk with helmet. Rev. Oval arms.

2023.   2 Ducats 1635 (LM)................................. 2800.00

Elector standing at desk with helmet. Rev. Eagle with shields.

2024.   2 Ducats 1637 (LM), 38, 40 .... 2200.00

Elector on horse. Rev. Eagle with 14 shields.

2025.	10 Ducats 1634 (LM)	Rare
2026.	5 Ducats 1634 (LM)................................	Rare

III. Koenigsberg Mint with Initials DK or a heart
Elector standing. Rev. Arms under elector's hat.

2027.   1 Ducat 1625... 3000.00

Elector standing. Rev. Arms with 12 fields.

2028.   1 Ducat 1627 (heart) 3000.00

Elector standing. Rev. Arms with 5 fields under elector's hat.

2029.   1 Ducat 1631, 32 (heart)........................... 3000.00

Bust with elector's hat. Rev. Arms with 5 fields under elector's hat.

2030.	2 Ducats 1634 (heart).............................	4500.00
2031.	1 Ducat 1633, 34 (heart)..........................	2000.00
2032.	1 Ducat 1635-40 (DK)..............................	1800.00

Bust with elector's hat. Rev. Arms with 9 fields under elector's hat.

2033.	1 Ducat 1635 (DK and heart)................*****......	1800.00
2034.	1 Ducat 1638, 39 (DK).............................	1800.00

Bust. Rev. Arms with 9 fields under elector's hat.

2035.   1 Ducat 1639 (DK) 2600.00

FREDERICK WILLIAM, 1640-1688
I. Berlin Mint with initials LM, AB, LCS, CT, IL, or CS
Half length bust in elector's robes with sceptre. Rev. Arms with 25 fields.

2036.   5 Ducats 1650 (CT) 5500.00

Elector standing at desk with helmet. Rev. Arms with 25 fields.

2037.   5 Ducats 1652, 53, 55, 57 (CT) 5200.00

Elector standing at desk with helmet. Rev. Arms with 10 fields.

2038.   4 Ducats 1666 (IL)................................. 6000.00

Armored half length bust with sceptre. Rev. Arms with 25 fields.

2039.   5 Ducats 1653 (CT) 5000.00

Armored bust. Rev. Sceptre shield with the ribbon of the Order of the Garter between branches.

2040.   4 Ducats 1675 (CS) 12000.00

Elector standing. Rev. Eagle with 12 shields.

2041.   2 Ducats 1641 (LM)................................. 4500.00

Elector standing in wreath of flowers. Rev. Arms with 12 fields in wreath of flowers.

2042.   2 Ducats 1641 (sometimes with LM)................. 4500.00

Elector standing. Rev. Arms with 23 fields.

2043.	2 Ducats 1643, 44 (AB).............................	4000.00
2044.	2 Ducats 1646 (CT)	4000.00

Elector standing. Rev. Arms with 25 fields under elector's hat.

2045.   2 Ducats 1650, 54 (CT)............................. 4200.00

Armored half length bust. Rev. Arms with 25 fields under elector's hat.

2046.   2 Ducats 1654 (CT), 1665 (IL) 5500.00

Bust. Rev. Arms between palm-branches.

2047.   2 Ducats 1669 .... 5000.00

Bust with elector's hat. Rev. Arms between palm-branches.

2048.   2 Ducats 1670 .... 5000.00

Elector standing at desk. Rev. 6 shields and sceptre.

2049.   1 Ducat 1641 (LM)................................. 2500.00

Elector standing at desk. Rev. Arms with 9 fields.

2050.   1 Ducat 1641 (LM) 2200.00

Elector standing at desk. Rev. Arms with 12 fields.

2051.   1 Ducat 1643 (AB) 2200.00

Elector standing. Rev. Arms with 14 fields under elector's hat.

2052.   1 Ducat 1651 (CT) 2000.00

Elector standing knee-length. Rev. Arms with 14 fields under elector's hat.

2053.	5 Ducats 1654 (CT, from the ducat die)...............	6500.00
2054.	1 Ducat 1654, 56 (CT).............................	2000.00

Armored bust. Rev. Sceptre shield surrounded by 13 shields.

2055.	1 Ducat 1662 (AB)................................	2000.00
2056.	1 Ducat 1665, 66 (IL).............................	2000.00

Bust. Rev. Sceptre shield surrounded by 13 shields.

2057.	1 Ducat 1667 (IL).................................	2000.00

Draped bust. Rev. Sceptre shield between branches.

2058.	1 Ducat 1668, 73, 74 (IL), 75 (CS), 77 (CS)............	2200.00

Naked bust. Rev. Sceptre shield between branches.

2059.	1 Ducat 1669-72 (IL)	2200.00

Armored bust. Rev. Sceptre shield between branches.

2060.	1 Ducat 1679-82 (CS)	2200.00
2061.	1 Ducat 1683-85 (LCS)	1800.00

Armored and draped bust. Rev. Sceptre shield between branches.

2062.	1 Ducat 1685, 86 (LCS)............................	2500.00

Armored half length bust. Rev. Sceptre shield between branches.

2063.	1 Ducat 1686, 87	2800.00

Bust in elector's robes. Rev. Sceptre shield.

2064.	¾ Ducat 1656 (CT)	2700.00

Bust in elector's robes. Rev. Sceptre shield between branches.

2065.	½ Ducat ND......................................	2500.00

Bust in elector's robes. Rev. Arms with 14 fields.

2066.	⅓ Ducat 1655 (CT)	1250.00

Helmeted head. Rev. Crown over flying eagle.

2067.	½ Ducat 1668 (IL)	1500.00
2068.	¼ Ducat 1668 (IL)	1500.00

Bust. Rev. Crown over flying eagle.

2069.	¼ Ducat 1675 (IL)	1400.00

Bust. Rev. Ship. Trade coins for Guinea, Africa.

2070.	1 Ducat 1682 (CS)	3500.00
2071.	1 Ducat 1682, 83, 85, 86 (LCS) ....*	3500.00

Armored half length bust. Rev. Ship. For Guinea.

2072.	1 Ducat 1686-88 (LCS)	3000.00

Facing bust. Rev. Legend. On his 35th birthday and on the birth of Prince Charles Emil.

2073.	4 Ducats 1655 (AB)	Rare
2074.	3 Ducats 1655 (CT)	Rare
2075.	2 Ducats 1655 (with or without elector's hat).........	3000.00

Bust. Rev. City view of Stettin; above eagle and griffin. On the conquest of Stettin.

2076.	2 Ducats 1677 (CS). FORTIOR HIS SIGNIS............	2500.00
2077.	2 Ducats 1677 (CS). LUCE RESURGO NOVA	2500.00

Elector on horse. Rev. Legend. On the conquest of Stettin.

2078.	½ Ducat 1677.......................................	1200.00

Bust with elector's hat. Rev. Arms.

2079.	1 Ducat 1646 (CT). For Prussia	2200.00

Elector standing knee length. Rev. Crowned arms.

2080.	1 Ducat 1665 (IL). For Prussia......................	3000.00

Bust. Rev. Crowned arms.

2081.	1 Ducat 1665 (IL). For Prussia	4000.00

II. Halberstadt Mint with Initials LCS

Bust. Rev. Sceptre between branches.

2082.	1 Ducat 1679 (LCS)	5500.00

III. Koenigsberg Mint with Initials DK, HM, TT, CV, HS, BA, CM, CG, DS, NB

Bust. Rev. Arms.

2083.	5 Ducats ND (1657, DK)...........................	Rare
2084.	4 Ducats ND (1657, DK)...........................	Rare

Elector on horse. Rev. Rose in circle of shields.

2085.	5 Ducats ND......................................	Rare
2086.	3 Ducats ND......................................	Rare
2087.	2 Ducats ND.................................*	3500.00

Head. Rev. Head of Prince Charles Emil. On the 14th birthday of the Prince.

2088.	2 Ducats 1669 (CG)................................	3300.00

Bust. Rev. Crowned arms.

2089.	2 Ducats 1670-72 (TT)..............................	2800.00
2090.	2 Ducats 1673, 74 (CV).............................	2800.00
2091.	2 Ducats 1675, 79, 82-84 (HS)........................	3000.00
2092.	2 Ducats 1686 (BA)	4000.00

Bust with elector's hat. Rev. Arms.

2093.	1 Ducat 1641, 48, 49 (DK)..........................	1500.00

Facing bust. Rev. Arms.

2094.	1 Ducat 1643 (DK)	2200.00

Bust. Rev. Arms.

2095.	1 Ducat 1651 (CM)................................	1800.00
2096.	1 Ducat 1657 (DK), 1660 over 1657	1400.00

Bust in elector's robes. Rev. Arms.

2097.	1 Ducat 1657 (NB), 1658 (without NB)	2500.00

Armored bust. Rev. Arms.

2098.	1 Ducat 1661-63 (HM)..............................	3300.00

Crowned bust with sword. Rev. Arms with 5 fields.

2099.	1 Ducat 1664-66...............................*	2200.00
2100.	1 Ducat 1667 (CG)................................	2400.00

Bust. Rev. Eagle.

2101.	1 Ducat 1668 (CG and DS)............................	2200.00
2102.	1 Ducat 1673, 74 (CV)...............................	4000.00
2103.	½ Ducat 1670, 71 (TT), 1685 (HS) ....*	1500.00

Head. Rev. Crowned arms.

2104.	1 Ducat 1669 (CG and DS)..........................	2200.00

Bust. Rev. Crowned arms.

2105.	1 Ducat 1670-72 (TT)...............................	2500.00
2106.	1 Ducat 1679, 81, 82 (HS)..........................	2800.00

Bust. Rev. Crowned oval arms.

2107.	1 Ducat 1676, 83, 84 (HS)..........................	2500.00
2108.	1 Ducat 1685, 86 (BA)..............................	2500.00

Bust. Rev. Crowned round arms.

2109.	1 Ducat 1687 (HS)	2500.00

IV. Magdeburg Mint with Initials IE
Bust. Rev. Arms.

2110.	5 Ducats 1683 (IE).................................	Rare

V. Luenen Mint
Facing bust. Rev. Arms with 4 fields.

2111.	1 Ducat 1659 (M-M for Moneta Marcana)	6500.00

Bust. Rev. Arms with 4 fields.

2112.	1 Ducat 1660, 62	3300.00

Facing bust. Rev. Arms with 6 fields.

2113.	1 Ducat 1664......................................	3000.00

VI. Minden Mint with Initials HB
Bust in elector's robes. Rev. Arms with 26 fields.

2114.	1 Ducat 1652 (HB).................................	3000.00

Bust. Rev. Arms with 5 fields.

2115.	1 Ducat 1670 (HB).................................	2800.00

VII. Ravensberg Mint struck at Bielefeld
Arms. Rev. Value on tablet.

2116.	1 Ducat 1648.......................................	6500.00

Bust in elector's robes. Rev. Arms with 6 fields.

2117.	1 Ducat 1648.......................................	2500.00

FREDERICK III, 1688-1701 (I, 1701-1713)
I. Berlin Mint with Initials LCS, S or RF
Bust. Rev. Crossed initials.

2118.	1 Ducat 1688......................................	3000.00
2119.	1 Ducat 1697 (RF and LCS).........................	2000.00
2120.	1 Ducat 1697 (RF and LCS). Without Order of the Garter.................................	2500.00

Bust. Rev. Sceptre in shield.

2121.	1 Ducat 1689, 90 (LCS).............................	2000.00
2122.	1 Ducat 1696 (LCS). With Order of the Garter.........	2200.00

Head. Rev. Crossed initials.

2123.	2 Ducats 1698-1700 (RF and LCS)	3000.00
2124.	1 Ducat 1698, 99 (RF and LCS)	2200.00

Bust with mantle. Rev. Ship. Trade coin for Guinea, Africa.

2125.	1 Ducat 1688, 90 (LCS).............................	3300.00

Bust. Rev. Ship. Trade coin for Guinea.

2126.	1 Ducat 1692, 94-96 (S and LCS)	3500.00

II. Koenigsberg Mint with Initials HS, SD or CG
Laureate bust. Rev. Arms.

2127.	1 Ducat 1691, 93 (HS).............................	2500.00
2128.	1 Ducat 1695, 97 (SD)	2800.00
2129.	1 Ducat 1700 (CG).................................	2700.00

Laureate bust. Rev. Eagle.

2130.	½ Ducat 1700 (CG).................................	1500.00

III. Magdeburg Mint with Initials ICS
Bust. Rev. Sceptre in shield.

2131.	1 Ducat 1692 (ICS).................................	3000.00

IV. Minden Mint with Initials BH
Bust. Rev. Arms with 25 fields.

2132.	1 Ducat 1691 (BH)	3000.00

Bust. Rev. Sceptre in shield and eagle with crown.

2133.	1 Ducat 1695 (BH)	2800.00

Bust. Rev. Sceptre in shield.

2134.	½ Ducat 1695 (BH)	1400.00

(The coinage of Frederick III continues directly below under B, as Frederick I, King of Prussia.)

B. Kings of —

FREDERICK I, 1701-1713
Mints and the initials of the mint masters or engravers as they appear on the coins:

Berlin Mint: LCS, CS, L, CFL, M, R
Koenigsberg Mint: CG, GWM
Magdeburg Mint: HFH
Minden Mint: BH

Head. Rev. Cross of initials.

2135.	2 Ducats 1701. Thick. LCS	6500.00
2136.	1 Ducat 1701. LCS..........................*	2500.00

Bust over legend. Rev. Crown. On his Coronation.

2137.	1 Ducat 1701. Koenigsberg Mint	1800.00

Head. Rev. Crowned eagle.

2138.	1 Ducat 1701. CS.........................*	2600.00
2139.	1 Ducat 1703, 04. CFL and CS	2000.00

Bust. Rev. Initials in chain of Order.

2140.	1 Ducat 1705-12. L and CS	2000.00
2141.	1 Ducat 1707-09. HFH	4400.00
2142.	1 Ducat 1706. BH...............................	4400.00

Head. Rev. Flying eagle.

2143.	2 Ducats 1701. Thick. R and CS	6000.00
2144.	2 Ducats 1712. HFH	3000.00
2145.	1 Ducat 1710. R and CS...........................	3700.00
2146.	½ Ducat 1712. HFH	1500.00

Bust. Rev. Eagle shield.

2147.	2 Ducats 1713. CG	6000.00
2148.	2 Ducats 1703, 04. Thick. CG......................	5000.00
2149.	1 Ducat 1702-12. CG ....*	2400.00
2150.	1 Ducat 1713. GWM and CG........................	3800.00

Head. Rev. Crowned arms. Struck for Neuchatel.

2151.	1 Ducat 1713. JP	4000.00

Bust. Rev. Crown on altar. On his death.

2152.	1 Ducat 1713. L with or without CS	1800.00

FREDERICK WILLIAM AND SOPHIA DOROTHEA, 1706

Busts. Rev. Legend. On their wedding. Magdeburg Mint with initials HFH.

2153.	2 Ducats 1706 ....*	4000.00
2154.	1 Ducat 1706.............................*	1500.00
2155.	½ Ducat 1706, 12	1200.00
2156.	¼ Ducat 1706, 12	800.00
2157.	¼ Ducat 1706. With legend "Frid:Wilh:D.G.Rex. Boruss"	1400.00

FREDERICK WILLIAM I, 1713-1740

Mints and the initials of the mint masters or engravers as they appear on the coins:

Berlin Mint: IFS, IGN, EGN, L, M
Koenigsberg Mint: CG, M
Magdeburg Mint: HFH

Bust. Rev. Eagle flying to sun.

2158.	1 Ducat 1713. L and IFS.........	1400.00
2159.	¼ Ducat 1713. HFH	600.00

Bust. Rev. Eagle.

2160.	1 Ducat 1714. HFH.............................	2500.00
2161.	1 Ducat 1733. EGN	1400.00

Laureate head. Rev. Eagle flying to sun.

2162.	2 Ducats 1713. HFH.............................	4500.00
2163.	1 Ducat 1713. CG with or without M or L ......*	1400.00
2164.	1 Ducat 1713. HFH.............................	1800.00
2165.	½ Ducat 1713. HFH.............................	600.00
2166.	¼ Ducat 1713. HFH.............................	500.00

Bust. Rev. Initials and crown in chain of Order.

2167.	1 Ducat 1714. L and IFS.............................	1850.00

Bust. Rev. Arms with five fields.

2168.	1 Ducat 1714. L and IFS.............................	3000.00

Bust. Rev. Arms with six fields.

2169.	1 Ducat 1715, 16. L and IFS	2200.00
2170.	1 Ducat 1714-17. CG with M or L..................	1400.00
2171.	1 Ducat 1714. HFH.............................	1600.00

Bust. Rev. Arms with twelve fields.

2172.	1 Ducat 1714. HFH	2000.00

Bust. Rev. Arms with forty fields.

2173.	1 Ducat 1714. HFH.............................	1500.00
2174.	¼ Ducat 1715. HFH.............................	450.00

Laureate head. Rev. Arms with forty fields.

2175.	½ Ducat 1714. HFH.............................	550.00
2176.	¼ Ducat 1715. HFH.............................	350.00

Bust. Rev. Star of Order with legend.

2177.	1 Ducat 1717. L and IFS.........................	1600.00
2178.	1 Ducat 1733-40. EGN	1300.00
2179.	1 Ducat 1714. HFH.............................	1400.00

Bust. Rev. Star of Order without legend.

2180.	1 Ducat 1714-16. IFS	1500.00
2181.	1 Ducat 1714. CG and M	3000.00
2182.	1 Ducat 1715. No initials........................	3000.00
2183.	1 Ducat 1714, 16. Plain bust. HFH ....*	1600.00
2184.	1 Ducat 1717. Laureate bust. HFH................	1500.00
2185.	¼ Ducat 1716. HFH	450.00

Laureate head. Rev. Star of Order.

2186.	½ Ducat 1714. HFH.............................	800.00
2187.	¼ Ducat 1714, 16. HFH..........................	500.00

Bust with pigtail. Rev. Oval arms.

2188.	1 Ducat 1718-28. CG with or without M.............	1200.00
2189.	1 Ducat 1718. HFH with or without L	1200.00

Bust with pigtail. Rev. Star of Order with legend.

2190.	1 Ducat 1717, 18. HFH with or without M.............	1350.00

Bust with or without L. Rev. Oval arms with six fields.

2191.	2 Ducats 1724. IGN..............................	4000.00
2192.	2 Ducats 1732. EGN	5000.00
2193.	1 Ducat 1716. M and IFS.........................	1400.00
2194.	1 Ducat 1717, 18. IFS	1200.00
2195.	1 Ducat 1719-25. IGN	1000.00
2196.	1 Ducat 1725-32. EGN	1650.00
2197.	½ Ducat 1726. EGN	1000.00

Bust. Rev. Flying eagle.

2198.	2 Ducats 1733. EGN.............................	4000.00
2199.	1 Ducat 1733, 34. EGN...........................	1300.00

Bust. Rev. Cross of initials.

2200.	1 William D'or 1737-40. EGN on Obv. or Rev. ..*	3000.00
2201.	½ William D'or 1738-40. EGN......................	2000.00

FREDERICK II, THE GREAT, 1740-1786
Mints, mint marks and the initials of mint masters or mint officials as they appear on the coins:

Berlin Mint: A mm, EGN, CHI, ALS
Breslau Mint: B mm, AHE, AE
Cleve Mint: C mm
Aurich Mint: D mm

Head. Rev. Justice standing. On the Homage of Koenigsberg.

2202.	1 Ducat 1740. No initials............................	1100.00

Head. Rev. Legend. On the Homage of Berlin.

2203.	1 Ducat 1740. No initials............................	1100.00

Armored bust. Rev. Crowned eagle shield.

2204.	1 Ducat 1741-45. EGN	2200.00
2205.	1 Ducat 1743-48. AHE	2200.00

Armored bust. Rev. Crowned initials in chain of Order.

2206.	1 Ducat 1745. EGN	2500.00

Armored bust. Rev. Flying eagle over trophies.

2207.	1 Ducat 1745-49. EGN	2300.00
2208.	1 Ducat 1749. CHI.................................	2500.00

Armored bust. Rev. Eagle on globe over branches.

2209.	2 Ducats 1749. EGN	4000.00
2210.	1 Ducat 1749. EGN	3000.00

Armored bust. Rev. Eagle over trophies and value.

2211.	1 Ducat 1753, 54. A mm..........................	850.00

Bare bust. Rev. Eagle over trophies and value.

2212.	1 Ducat 1754, 57. B mm..........................	1500.00

Armored bust. Rev. Cross of initials.

2213.	1 Frederick D'or 1744-48. AE......................	2500.00

Armored bust. Rev. Crowned eagle between trophies. The last coin was struck in lower grade gold during the Seven Year War.

2214.	2 Frederick D'or 1749. ALS.........................	2800.00
2215.	2 Frederick D'or 1750-52. A mm	2800.00
2216.	2 Frederick D'or 1747-49. W on shield. AHE	3300.00
2217.	1 Frederick D'or 1741-46. EGN	1400.00

2218.	1 Frederick D'or 1750-52, 59. A mm........*......	1200.00
2219.	1 Frederick D'or 1749. Bust left. ALS..............	1500.00
2220.	1 Frederick D'or 1746-49. W on shield. AHE or AE..	1250.00
2221.	1 Frederick D'or 1750. AE	1250.00
2222.	1 Frederick D'or 1750, 64. B on shield. B mm or AE.	1250.00
2223.	½ Frederick D'or 1749. CHI........................	800.00
2224.	½ Frederick D'or 1750-52. A mm	550.00
2225.	1 Frederick D'or 1755, 56. A mm..................	1600.00

Head. Rev. Crowned eagle shield.

2226.	1 Frederick D'or 1750. A mm	1600.00

Armored bust. Rev. Eagle and lion's head between trophies.

2227.	1 Frederick D'or 1752, 53. D mm...................	3500.00

Head. Rev. Crowned eagle between trophies.

2228.	2 Frederick D'or 1753, 55. A mm..................	2000.00

Head. Rev. Eagle between trophies. The last three coins were struck in lower grade gold during the Seven Year War.

2229.	1 Frederick D'or 1752-58, 63. A mm	1500.00
2230.	½ Frederick D'or 1752-56. A mm	800.00
2231.	2 Frederick D'or 1756, 57. A mm..................	3000.00
2232.	1 Frederick D'or 1755, 56, 57. A mm	1000.00
2233.	½ Frederick D'or 1755. A mm	2500.00

Head. Rev. Crown over Two F's.

2234.	½ Frederick D'or 1750. A mm	800.00

Armored bust. Rev. Eagle over trophies.

2235.	2 Frederick D'or 1751, 52. B mm..................	2200.00
2236.	2 Frederick D'or 1752, 53. C mm..................	3300.00
2237.	1 Frederick D'or 1750-57. B mm	1500.00
2238.	1 Frederick D'or 1751-53. C mm ....*	1800.00
2239.	½ Frederick D'or 1750-53. B mm ....*	800.00
2240.	½ Frederick D'or 1753. C mm	1500.00

Head. Rev. Eagle over trophies.

2241.	1 Frederick D'or 1754, 55. C mm..................	3300.00

Young laureate head. Rev. Eagle over trophies.

2242.	2 Frederick D'or 1764-71, 75. A mm	2800.00
2243.	1 Frederick D'or 1764-76. A mm	1500.00
2244.	1 Frederick D'or 1764-75. B mm	1000.00
2245.	½ Frederick D'or 1765, 69, 70, 72-74. A mm	800.00
2246.	½ Frederick D'or 1765-75. B mm	850.00

Old laureate head. Rev. Eagle over trophies.

2247.	2 Frederick D'or 1776. A mm	2500.00
2248.	1 Frederick D'or 1775-86. A mm	1100.00
2249.	1 Frederick D'or 1776-78, 80-86. B mm	850.00
2250.	1 Frederick D'or 1781. With date "D.20.August" B mm.	Rare
2251.	½ Frederick D'or 1784, 86. A mm..................	700.00
2252.	½ Frederick D'or 1776, 77. B mm	1800.00

FREDERICK WILLIAM II, 1786-1797
Bust. Rev. Eagle above trophies.

2253.	1 Frederick D'or 1786, 88-97. A mm	1100.00
2254.	1 Frederick D'or 1787-97. B mm	1100.00

Crowned eagle shield. Rev. Value.

2255.	1 Ducat 1787, 90. A mm...........................	900.00

FREDERICK WILLIAM III, 1797-1840

Eagle shield. Rev. Legend, "Fuerstenzeche."

| 2256. | 1 Rhine-gold Ducat 1803. B mm . . . . | Rare |

Bust. Rev. Eagle above trophies.

2257.	2 Frederick D'or 1800-02, 06, 11, 13, 14. A mm . *	1650.00
2258.	1 Frederick D'or 1798-1813, 16. A mm.	1100.00
2259.	1 Frederick D'or 1800-05. B mm	1600.00
2260.	½ Frederick D'or 1802-04, 06, 14, 16. A mm	900.00

Bust Rev. Eagle.

| 2261. | 1 Frederick D'or 1797, 98. A mm. . . . . | 1250.00 |

Bust in uniform. Rev. Eagle above trophies.

| 2262. | 1 Frederick D'or 1817-19, 22. A mm . . . . | 1400.00 |
| 2263. | ½ Frederick D'or 1817. A mm . . . . | 800.00 |

Head. Rev. Eagle above trophies.

2264.	2 Frederick D'or 1825-32, 36-40. A mm	1500.00
2265.	1 Frederick D'or 1825, 27-34, 36-40. A mm.	1000.00
2266.	½ Frederick D'or 1825, 27-29, 32, 33, 37-40. A mm	850.00

FREDERICK WILLIAM IV, 1840-1861

Head. Rev. Eagle above trophies.

2267.	2 Frederick D'or 1841-46, 48, 49, 52. A mm. . . . . *	1350.00
2268.	1 Frederick D'or 1841-52. A mm	1000.00
2269.	½ Frederick D'or 1841-46, 49. A mm . . . . *	900.00

Older head. Rev. Eagle above trophies.

2270.	2 Frederick D'or 1853-55. A mm	1800.00
2271.	1 Frederick D'or 1853-55. A mm . . . . *	1000.00
2272.	½ Frederick D'or 1853. A mm	900.00

Older head. Rev. Value in wreath.

| 2273. | 1 Krone 1858, 59, 60, A mm . . . . | 2500.00 |
| 2274. | ½ Krone 1858. A mm . . . . | 2300.00 |

WILLIAM I, 1861-1888

Head. Rev. Value in wreath. The B mm is for Hanover.

2275.	1 Krone 1861-64, 66-68, 70. A mm . . . . *	2400.00
2276.	1 Krone 1867, 68. B mm.	2400.00
2277.	½ Krone 1862-64, 66-68. A mm	2000.00
2278.	½ Krone 1867. B mm	2400.00

QUEDLINBURG

Abbesses of —

DOROTHEA SOPHIA, 1618-1645
Arms of Quedlinburg. Rev. Arms of Saxony.

| 2279. | 1 Ducat ND . . . . | 2800.00 |

Crowned arms of Quedlinburg. Rev. Crowned arms of Saxony.

| 2280. | 1 Ducat ND . . . . | 2000.00 |

ANNE DOROTHEA, 1685-1704

Bust. Rev. Ship. On her death.

| 2281. | 2 Ducats 1704 . . . . | 2700.00 |

Bust. Rev. Setting sun. On her death.

| 2282. | 1 Ducat 1704. . . . . | 2200.00 |

RANTZAU

Counts —

CHRISTIAN I, 1650-1663

Bust. Rev. Arms.

2283.	2 Ducats 1656	7000.00
2284.	1 Ducat 1655, 56, 58 ....*	3500.00

DETLEF, 1663-1697
Bust. Rev. Arms.

2285.	1 Ducat 1689	3000.00

RATZEBURG

Bishops of —

AUGUST OF BRUNSWICK, 1610-1636

Duke on horse. Rev. Arms.

2286.	1 Goldgulden 1618	3000.00

Duke standing. Rev. Arms.

2287.	1 Ducat ND	2700.00

Bust. Rev. Arms.

2288.	1 Ducat 1634	3000.00

REGENSBURG (RATISBON)

A. General City Coinage

Arms. Rev. St. Wolfgang.

2289.	1 Goldgulden 1512, 54	6000.00

Trinity Church. Rev. Inscription.

2290.	1 Ducat 1627	1500.00

Arms. Rev. Legend. In honor of Bernard of Saxony.

2291.	1 Ducat 1633	2000.00

Arms. Rev. City view.

2292.	1 Ducat 1634	2000.00

Legend and arms. Rev. Light and hands. On the Reformation.

2293.	2 Ducats 1642	1800.00

Arms. Rev. Light. On the Reformation.

2294.	1 Ducat 1642	2000.00

Double eagle. Rev. Wreath.

2295.	1 Ducat 1653	2200.00

[diamond-shaped coins image]

Arms. Rev. Double eagle.

2296.	1 Ducat 1658		2200.00
2297.	½ Ducat ND. Square ....*		850.00
2298.	¼ Ducat ND		650.00
2299.	¼ Ducat ND. Square		600.00
2300.	⅛ Ducat ND. Square		500.00
2301.	⅛ Ducat ND. Square		500.00

[two coins image]

Lamb on column. Rev. Legend. On the Reformation.

2302.	1 Ducat 1717	1250.00

[two coins image]

Arms over legend. Rev. Vine. On the Reformation.

2303.	1 Ducat 1742	1500.00

Crossed keys. Rev. Crowned R.

2304.	1/16 Ducat ND (1750)	500.00
2305.	1/32 Ducat ND (1750)	400.00

Crossed keys. Rev. Double eagle.

2306.	1/32 Ducat ND (1750)	350.00

B. Coinage with the heads or names of the Holy Roman Emperors

Arms. Rev. Double eagle. Matthias.

2307.	1 Goldgulden 1617, 18	2000.00

Arms. Rev. Double eagle. Ferdinand II.

2308.	2 Ducats 1632	2800.00
2309.	1 Ducat 1632	2000.00

Inscription. Rev. Scales.

2310.	2 Ducats 1636	3000.00

Arms. Rev. Double eagle. Ferdinand III.

2311.	1 Ducat 1637-57	2000.00

Inscription. Rev. Inscription. Ferdinand IV.

2312.	1 Ducat 1653	1800.00
2312a.	½ Ducat 1653	1250.00

[two coins image]

Arms. Rev. Double eagle. Leopold I.

2312b.	10 Ducats 1667	15000.00
2313.	6 Ducats 1667	10000.00
2314.	4 Ducats 1664	6000.00
2315.	2 Ducats ND	3000.00
2316.	1 Ducat 1659-96 ....*......	2000.00
2317.	½ Ducat ND	1500.00

Arms. Rev. Double eagle. Joseph I.

2318.	5 Ducats ND	10000.00
2319.	1 Ducat 1706	2000.00

Bust of Charles VI. Rev. Arms.

2320.	2 Ducats ND	2800.00
2321.	1 Ducat 1712	1800.00
2322.	½ Ducat ND	1000.00

Bust of Charles VI. Rev. City View.

2323.	1 Ducat 1737, ND	1800.00

Arms. Rev. Double eagle. Charles VI.

2324.	3 Ducat ND (1740)	3500.00
2325.	½ Ducat ND (1740)	1000.00

Bust of Charles VII. Rev. City view.

2325a.	6 Ducats ND	Rare
2326.	2 Ducats ND (thick)...........................*......	10000.00
2327.	1 Ducat ND	2000.00

Bust of Charles VII. Rev. Arms.

2328.	2 Ducats ND (1742-45)	3000.00
2329.	½ Ducat ND (1742-45)	1200.00

Bust of Francis I. Rev. City view.

2330.	3 Ducats ND (1745-65) ....*...	4500.00
2331.	2 Ducats ND (1745-65)	3000.00
2332.	1 Ducat ND (1745-65)	2000.00
2333.	½ Ducat ND (1745-65)	1000.00
2334.	¼ Ducat ND (1745-65)	650.00

Bust of Francis I. Rev. Eagle flying over arms.

2335.	3 Ducats ND (1745-65)	4000.00
2336.	2 Ducats ND (1745-65)	3500.00

Bust of Joseph II. Rev. Arms.

2337.	3 Ducats ND (1765-90)	4500.00
2338.	1 Ducat ND (1765-90	1800.00

Bust of Joseph II. Rev. City view.

2339.	1 Ducat ND (1765-90) ....•.......	2000.00
2340.	½ Ducat ND	1000.00
2341.	¼ Ducat ND	600.00

City view. Rev. Double eagle. Joseph II.

2342.	8 Ducats ND..	7000.00
2343.	5 Ducats ND..	5000.00
2344.	2 Ducats ND (1765-90)	3500.00

Head of Leopold II. Rev. City view.

2345.	1 Ducat ND (1790-92)	Unknown

City view. Rev. Double eagle. Francis II.

2346.	1 Ducat ND (1792-1806)	1700.00

C. Bishops of —

JOHN III, 1507-1538
Arms. Rev. St. Peter standing.

2347.	1 Goldgulden 1523	4500.00

Arms. Rev. Madonna.

2348.	1 Ducat 1526...	4200.00

DAVID, 1567-1579
Arms. Rev. Double eagle.

2349.	1 Goldgulden ND	5000.00

ANTHONY IGNACE, 1769-1787
Bust. Rev. Arms.

2350.	1 Ducat 1770...	2200.00

CHARLES, 1804-1817
Bust. Rev. Arms.

2351.	1 Ducat 1809...	2000.00

R E U S S

Counts, and later, Princes —

A. Older Line

HENRY III, 1733-1768
Bust. Rev. Arms.

2352.	1 Ducat 1764...	2000.00

B. Younger Line

HENRY II, 1572-1635
Arms. Rev. Two helmets.

2353.	1 Goldgulden 1619, 22...............................	2200.00

HENRY XII, 1744-1784

Initials. Rev. Arms. On the Peace of Hubertusburg.

2354.	1 Ducat 1763...	1800.00

Bust. Rev. Arms.

2355.	1 Ducat 1764...	2200.00

REUSS-RODENTHAL

Counts —

HENRY V, 1668-1698
Bust. Rev. Arms.

2356.   1 Ducat 1679...................................... 3500.00

RHINE (CONFEDERATION)

CHARLES, ARCHBISHOP OF MAYENCE, 1802-1813

Bust. Rev. Arms.

2357.   1 Ducat 1809...................................... 1250.00

ROSTOCK

(The coinage is with the names of the Holy Roman Emperors.)

Griffin. Rev. Double eagle. Rudolph II.

2358.   1 Goldgulden 1606, 08-11, ND..................... 2000.00

Griffin. Rev. Double eagle. Matthias.

2359.   1 Goldgulden 1613-17 .... 2200.00

Griffin. Rev. Double eagle. Ferdinand II.

2360.   2 Goldgulden 1623................................ 4000.00
2361.   1 Goldgulden 1625-31............................. 1500.00

Arms. Rev. Double eagle. Ferdinand II.

2362.   1 Ducat 1632-34, 36.............................. 1250.00

Tablet and value. Rev. Double eagle. Ferdinand III.

2363.   2 Ducats 1639 .... 1850.00

Arms. Rev. Double eagle. Ferdinand III.

2364.   1 Ducat 1636, 39, 46, 55......................... 1250.00

Arms. Rev. Double eagle. Leopold I.

2365.   2 Ducats 1661, 95 .... 2200.00
2366.   1 Ducat 1661, 64, 65, 72, 77, 82, 94 .... 1500.00

Griffin. Rev. Double eagle. Leopold I.

2367.   ½ Ducat 1695..................................... 1200.00

Griffin. Rev. Double eagle. Leopold I.

2368.   1 Wedding Ducat 1704 .... 2000.00

Griffin. Rev. Value. Leopold II.

2369.   ¼ Ducat 1696..................................... 1000.00

Arms. Rev. Double eagle. Francis I.

2370.   1 Ducat 1762..................................... 2000.00

Arms. Rev. Double eagle. Joseph II.

2371.   1 Ducat 1783..................................... 1500.00

Arms. Rev. Double eagle. Francis II.

2372.   1 Ducat 1796..................................... 1500.00

ROTHENBURG

Legend. Rev. Fortress. On the Reformation.

2373.   1 Ducat 1717..................................... 1850.00

ROTTWEIL

Eagle. Rev. Orb in enclosure. Maximilian I.

2374.   1 Goldgulden ND (1486-1519) 8000.00

ST. ALBAN

(In Mayence)

St. Alban standing. Rev. Shield and donkey.

2375.   1 Goldgulden 1597 .... 2200.00
2376.   1 Goldgulden 1712, 16, 20, 25, 44, 78, 79, 80 ...*...... 1500.00

SALM-DHAUN

CURATORIAL COINAGE, 1606-1617
Arms. Rev. Double eagle. Matthias.

2377.   1 Goldgulden 1617................................ 3000.00

WOLFGANG FREDERICK, DIED 1638
Arms. Rev. Double eagle. Matthias.

2378.   1 Goldgulden 1619................................ 3000.00

SALM-KYRBURG

Counts, and later, Princes —

OTTO I, DIED 1607
Arms. Rev. Double eagle. Rudolph II.

2379.	2 Ducats ND	4500.00

JOHN PHILIP, OTTO LOUIS, JOHN CASIMIR AND OTTO
Arms with lion. Rev. Double eagle. Ferdinand II.

2380.	1 Goldgulden ND	4000.00

FREDERICK III, 1779-1794
Head. Rev. Arms.

2381.	1 Carolin 1782	2750.00
2382.	1 Ducat 1780, 82	2000.00

SAXONY

(The Albertine Line)

Electors, and later, Kings of —

ALBERT, 1464-1500
Orb in trefoil. Rev. St. John.

2383.	1 Goldgulden ND	800.00

Shield on cross. Rev. Shield with double eagle supported by lions. Struck for Frisia.

2384.	1 Goldgulden ND	3000.00

GEORGE, 1500-1539
St. John. Rev. Orb in trefoil.

2385.	1 Goldgulden ND	1850.00

Arms. Rev. St. Boniface. Struck for Frisia.

2386.	1 Goldgulden ND	2500.00

GEORGE AND HENRY, 1500-1505
St. John. Rev. Orb in trefoil.

2387.	1 Goldgulden ND	2000.00

MAURICE, 1547-1553
Arms. Rev. Legend. On the Siege of Leipzig.

2388.	10 Ducats 1547. Round	Rare
2389.	4 Ducats 1547. Square	Rare
2390.	2 Ducats 1547. Square	Rare
2391.	1 Ducat 1547. Square	2000.00

Shield. Rev. Arms.

2392.	2 Ducats 1552	3000.00
2393.	1 Ducat ND	2000.00

Elector standing. Rev. Five shields in quatrefoil.

2394.	1 Goldgulden 1548	2800.00

AUGUST, 1553-1586
Bust with sword. Rev. Arms.

2395.	2 Goldgulden 1554	3000.00

Bust with sword. Rev. Helmeted shield with lion.

2396.	1 Goldgulden 1558	2200.00

Bust with sword. Rev. Two shields and orb.

2397.	10 Goldgulden 1585	Rare

Bust. Rev. Arms.

2398.	1 Goldgulden ND	2000.00

Half length figure. Rev. Arms.

2399.	1¼ Ducats ND	2500.00
2400.	1 Goldgulden ND	2000.00

Half length figure. Rev. Five shields.

2401.	1 Goldgulden 1585, ND	1250.00

Arms within orb. Rev. Value.

2402.	1 Goldgulden 1584	1500.00
2403.	1 Goldgulden 1584. Square	1800.00

CHRISTIAN I, 1586-1591

Armored bust. Rev. Cross and four shields.

2404.	10 Ducats 1587, 90		Rare
2405.	5 Ducats 1587		Rare
2406.	2½ Ducats 1587		Rare
2407.	2 Ducats 1587, 90	*	5000.00
2408.	1 Ducat 1590		2500.00

Duke standing. Rev. Arms.

2409.	1 Ducat 1589, 90	1400.00

FREDERICK WILLIAM, REGENT, 1591-1601
Bust. Rev. Arms.

2410.	1 Ducat 1594	2000.00

SOPHIA, 1582-1622

Initials. Rev. "IHS".

2411.	1 Ducat 1616	325.00

CHRISTIAN II, 1601-1611
Half length figure. Rev. Cross and circle of shields.

2412.	20 Ducats 1610	Rare
2413.	10 Ducats 1606, 10	Rare
2414.	8 Ducats 1606	Rare

JOHN GEORGE I, 1611-1656
Half length figure with sword. Rev. Crossed swords.

2414a.	6 Ducats 1614. Square	Unique

Half length figure with sword, before helmet. Rev. Cross within circle of shields.

2415.	5 Ducats 1614	Rare

Half length figure with sword, a helmet in front. Rev. Arms.

2416.	2 Ducats 1616 (swan)		1800.00
2417.	2 Ducats 1625 (HI)		1800.00
2418.	2 Goldgulden 1620 (swan)		3300.00
2419.	1 Goldgulden 1615		2500.00
2420.	1 Goldgulden 1618-20 (swan)	*	1500.00
2421.	1 Goldgulden 1625, 32 (HI)		1800.00
2422.	1 Goldgulden 1641 (CR)		1800.00

Elector standing. Rev. Arms.

2423.	2 Ducats 1620 (swan)		3000.00
2424.	2 Ducats 1628, 29, 32 (HI)	*	3000.00
2425.	2 Ducats 1635 (CM)		3000.00
2426.	2 Ducats 1636-39 (SD)		3000.00
2427.	2 Ducats 1640-46, 52, 54 (CR)		3000.00
2428.	1 Ducat 1622 (swan)		1250.00
2429.	1 Ducat 1627-30, 32-34 (HI)		1100.00
2430.	1 Ducat 1635 (CM)		1500.00
2431.	1 Ducat 1635-40 (SD)		1500.00
2432.	1 Ducat 1640-46, 48, 49, 52, 53, 55 (CR)		1200.00
2433.	½ Ducat 1651-53, 55 (CR)		1500.00
2434.	¼ Ducat 1651 (CR)		1250.00

Bust of John George I. Rev. Bust of Frederick III. On the Reformation.

2435.	2 Ducats 1617		2200.00
2436.	1 Ducat 1617		1200.00

Elector on horse over arms. Rev. Legend. On the Vicariat.

2437.	5 Ducats 1619		5000.00
2438.	2 Ducats 1619		1800.00
2439.	1 Ducat 1619		1200.00

Arms. Rev. St. George. On the baptism of Prince Henry.

2440.	2 Ducats 1622		3000.00
2441.	1 Ducat 1622		1500.00

Bust of John George I. Rev. Bust of John. On the Augsburg Confession.

2442.	10 Ducats 1630		7500.00
2443.	5 Ducats 1630		4500.00
2444.	2 Ducats 1630	*	1800.00
2445.	1 Ducat 1630		1200.00

Legend. Rev. Patience standing. On the Peace of Prague.

2446.	1 Ducat 1635		1500.00

Facing bust with sword. Rev. Legend. On his death.

2447.	2 Ducats 1656		2000.00

JOHN GEORGE II, 1656-1680
Elector on horse. Rev. Legend. On the Vicariat.

2448.	2 Ducats 1657		2000.00
2449.	1 Ducat 1657		1500.00

Bust with sword; in front, elector's hat. Rev. Arms.

2450.	2 Ducats 1659, 60, 62		3300.00
2451.	1 Ducat 1659, 60, 62, 64, 65, 72	*	1250.00
2452.	½ Ducat 1659, 60, 62, 64, 65, 66		1000.00

Bust. Rev. Arms.

2453.	1 Goldgulden 1669		1600.00

Elector on horse. Rev. Shield on obelisk.

2454.	1 Ducat 1669		1250.00

Elector on horse. Rev. Arms.

2455.	1 Goldgulden 1670		2000.00

Bust. Rev. Arms on palm branches.

2456.	3 Ducats 1675, 79		4000.00
2457.	2 Ducats 1675, 76	*	2700.00

JOHN GEORGE III, 1680-1691

Bust. Rev. Arms on palm branches.

2458.	4 Ducats 1688		5500.00
2459.	2 Ducats 1681, 83, 85, 86, 88, 89, 91		3000.00
2460.	1½ Ducats 1681, 83, 84, 90, 91	*	2000.00

Bust with sword; in front, elector's hat. Rev. Arms on palm branches.

2461.	1 Ducat 1681, 83, 84, 86, 87, 90, 91	*	1500.00
2462.	½ Ducat 1683, 84, 88, 90, 91		850.00

Half length figure with sword, before elector's hat. Rev. Arms.

2463.	2 Ducats 1685		2500.00

Half length figure with sword. Rev. Arms.

2464.	2 Ducats 1685		2500.00

Bust. Rev. Crossed swords and four arms.

2465.	1 Ducat 1686		1400.00

Bust with sword, before helmet. Rev. Arms.

2466.	2 Ducats 1691	2500.00

Legend. Rev. Arms in clouds with flag. On his death.

2467.	1 Ducat 1691	1500.00

JOHN GEORGE IV, 1691-1694
Bust with sword, before elector's hat. Rev. Arms.

2468.	1 Ducat 1691-94	1600.00
2469.	½ Ducat 1691-94	850.00

Bust. Rev. Crossed swords and four arms.

2470.	3 Ducats 1692	3500.00
2471.	2 Ducats 1692-94	2500.00
2472.	1½ Ducats 1692, 93	2000.00

ANNA SOPHIA, DIED 1717
Ship. Rev. Legend under crown. On her death.

2473.	1 Ducat 1717	1800.00

FREDERICK AUGUST I (AUGUST II), 1694-1733
A. Coinage of the Dresden Mint.
Bust with sword. Rev. Arms.

2474.	2 Ducats 1695 (IK)	3300.00
2475.	1 Ducat 1694 (IK)	1500.00

Bust with sword. Rev. Lion with sword and arms.

2476.	1 Ducat 1695-97 (IK)	1500.00
2477.	¼ Ducat 1696 (IK)	600.00

Bust. Rev. Lion with sword and arms.

2478.	½ Ducat 1696 (IK)	750.00
2479.	¼ Ducat 1696 (IK)	600.00

Elector standing to right, before desk. Rev. Elector's hat over two arms.

2480.	2 Ducats 1696	2800.00

Elector standing to left, before desk. Rev. Altar.

2481.	2 Ducats 1696	2000.00

Bust. Rev. Crowned arms.

2482.	2 Ducats 1698, 1700-04, 07, 11, 14 (ILH)	2200.00
2483.	2 Ducats 1717, 23, 27, 33 (IGS)	2200.00
2484.	1 Ducat 1698-1704, 06, 07, 10, 11, 13, 14 (ILH)	1200.00
2485.	1 Ducat 1716-18, 20-33 (IGS)	1200.00
2486.	1 Ducat 1733 from the ½ ducat die (IGS)	1500.00
2487.	½ Ducat 1699, 1701, 07, 10 (ILH)	600.00
2488.	½ Ducat 1716, 17, 26, 29, 33 (IGS)	600.00
2489.	¼ Ducat 1700, 10 (ILH)	450.00
2490.	¼ Ducat 1717, 20-22, 27, 29, 33 (IGS)	450.00

Head. Rev. Crowned arms.

2491.	1 Ducat 1721	1800.00

Bust. Rev. Crowned initials.

2492.	2 Ducats 1708, 09 (ILH)	2500.00
2493.	1 Ducat 1708, 09 (ILH)	1250.00

Crowned initials. Rev. Crowned arms.

2494.	2 Ducats 1710	2500.00
2495.	1 Ducat 1710	1500.00
2496.	½ Ducat 1710	650.00
2497.	¼ Ducat 1710 from the ½ ducat die	750.00
2498.	¼ Ducat 1710	500.00

B. Coinage of the Leipzig Mint.
Elector on horse. Rev. Arms on drapery.

2499.	1½ Ducats 1697 (EPH)	1800.00
2500.	1 Ducat 1697 (EPH)	1250.00
2501.	1 Ducat 1697 (EPH) from the ½ ducat die	1250.00
2502.	1 Ducat 1697 (EPH) from the ¼ ducat die	1250.00
2503.	½ Ducat 1697 (EPH)	850.00
2504.	¼ Ducat 1697 (EPH)	650.00

King on horse. Rev. Arms on trophies.

2505.	2 Ducats 1702, 12 (EPH)	2500.00
2506.	1 Ducat 1702, 12 (EPH)	1250.00

Bust. Rev. Crown over two arms.

2507.	2 Ducats 1709 (EPH) from the ducat die	2500.00
2508.	1 Ducat 1702, 09 (EPH)	1250.00
2509.	½ Ducat 1702 (EPH)	800.00

Bust. Rev. Arms on star.

2510.	2 Ducats 1702	1850.00

Crowned bust on post. Rev. Crown over three arms.

2511.	1 Ducat 1702 (EPH)	2200.00

Crowned bust on post. Rev. Crowned initials and three arms.

2512.	1 Ducat 1703 (EPH)	1500.00
2513.	1 Ducat 1703 (EPH) from the ½ ducat die	1800.00
2514.	½ Ducat 1703 (EPH)	1700.00

C. Coinage on the Vicariat.
Elector on horse. Rev. Altar with insignia.

2515.	2 Ducats 1711	2200.00

Elector on horse. Rev. Two desks with insignia.

2515a.	4 Ducats 1711	Rare
2516.	2 Ducats 1711 (ILH)	2200.00
2517.	1 Ducat 1711 .... *	900.00

Elector on horse. Rev. Sword and sceptre crossed.

2518.	1 Ducat 1711	850.00

D. Commemorative Coinage.
Elector on horse. Rev. Arms on drapery. Expedition to Hungary.

2519.	2 Ducats 1695	1850.00
2520.	1 Ducat ND (1695), 1695	1000.00

King on horse. Rev. Crown over legend. On the Coronation.

2521.	2 Ducats 1697	1800.00
2522.	1 Ducat 1697 (O)	1000.00

Bust. Rev. Crown. On the Coronation.

2523.	2 Ducats 1697. FRID-AVG-etc.	2500.00
2524.	2 Ducats 1697. FRIDERICVS AVGVST etc.	2500.00
2525.	1 Ducat 1697	1000.00

Arm with Polish sabre. Rev. Crown over legend. On the Coronation.

2526.	1 Ducat 1697 (IK)	1100.00

Bust, AVGVSTVS-II:REX POLONIAE. Rev. Crown. On the Coronation.

2527.	1 Ducat ND. (1697) from the ½ ducat die	1500.00
2528.	½ Ducat ND (1697)	850.00

Bust of Frederick the Warlike with elector's hat and sword.
Rev. City view of Leipzig. Jubilee of the University.

2529.	2 Ducats 1709	2200.00
2530.	1 Ducat 1709	1000.00

Rock and seven planets. Rev. Legend. From gold of the Freiberg mines.

2531.	1 Ducat 1701	1500.00

Rock and triangle. Rev. Legend. From gold of the Freiberg mines.

2532.	1 Ducat 1709, 14	1500.00

Head. Rev. Crown on cushion. Treaty of Lublin.

2533.	1 Ducat 1715	1400.00

Legend. Rev. Two hearts. On the wedding of his son to Maria Josepha of Austria.

2534.	3 Ducats 1719 (IGS)	3000.00
2535.	2 Ducats 1719 (IGS)	2000.00
2536.	1 Ducat 1719 (IGS)	1250.00

FREDERICK AUGUST II, 1733-1763
A. Coinage of the Dresden Mint.

Bust. Rev. Crowned arms.

2537.	2 Ducats 1735-39 (FWoF)	2200.00
2538.	1 Ducat 1734 (IGS)...............................	1500.00
2539.	1 Ducat 1735-45, 48-51, 55, 56 (FWoF)	1000.00
2540.	1 Ducat 1757 (IDB)...............................	1000.00
2541.	1 Ducat 1760-63 (FWoF)	1000.00
2542.	1 Ducat 1757 (IDB) with FR (Fridericus Rex)	1200.00
2543.	½ Ducat 1735-37, 40, 43, 56 (FWoF)	500.00
2544.	½ Ducat 1750. (AVGVSTVS III REX POL)	1500.00
2545.	¼ Ducat 1734 (IGS)..............................	500.00
2546.	¼ Ducat 1735-37, 39, 40, 43 (FWoF)	500.00

B. Coinage of the Leipzig Mint.
Crowned bust. Rev. Crowned arms.

2547.	2	Ducats 1753, 54 (EDC)...........................	2500.00
2548.	1	Ducat 1752 (IGG)	1000.00
2549.	1	Ducat 1753, 54, 56 (EDC)	1000.00
2550.	10	Taler 1753 (G)................................	1500.00
2551.	10	Taler 1754, 55, 56 (EDC)	1500.00
2552.	5	Taler 1753 (G)	1000.00
2553.	5	Taler 1754-56, 58 (EC).........................	750.00
2554.	2½	Taler 1753 (G)	1000.00

C. Coinage on the Vicariat.
Bust. Rev. Double eagle with arms.

2555.	1 Ducat 1740	1250.00

Elector on horse. Rev. Throne.

2556.	1 Ducat 1741, 42	1000.00

Bust. Rev. Crown over two arms.

2557.	1 Ducat 1745	1250.00

Elector on horse. Rev. Flying eagle.

2558.	1 Ducat 1745	1000.00

FREDERICK CHRISTIAN, 1763
Hymen floating. Rev. Legend. On his wedding with Antonia of Bavaria.

2559.	1 Ducat 1747	1500.00

Bust. Rev. Crowned arms.

2560.	1 Ducat 1763 (FWoF)	1100.00

XAVIER, 1763-1768
Bust. Rev. Arms.

2561.	1 Ducat 1766-68 (EDC)...........................	875.00

FREDERICK AUGUST III (I, FROM 1806), 1763-1827
A. Coinage of the Dresden Mint.

Head. Rev. Arms.

2562.	1 Ducat 1764-78 (EDC)...........................	900.00
2563.	1 Ducat 1779-90 (IEC)...........................	1500.00

Bust. Rev. Arms.

2564.	1 Ducat 1791-1804 (IEC).........................	1000.00
2565.	1 Ducat 1805, 06 (SGH)..........................	1000.00

Armored bust. Rev. Two arms.

2566.	10 Taler 1777, 78 (EDC).........................	1500.00
2566a.	10 Taler 1779 (IEC).............................	1500.00

Head. Rev. Two arms.

2567.	10 Taler 1779-87, 90 (IEC)......................	1500.00
2568.	5 Taler 1777, 78 (EDC).........................	1000.00
2569.	5 Taler 1779, 82, 88 (IEC).....................	1000.00

Armored bust. Rev. Arms on branches.

2570.	10 Taler 1791-1803 (IEC)........................	1000.00
2571.	10 Taler 1804-1806 (SGH)........................	1000.00
2572.	5 Taler 1795, 1802, 03 (IEC)...................	1500.00
2573.	5 Taler 1805-06 (SGH)..........................	1000.00

B. Coinage of the Leipzig Mint.
Head. Rev. Arms.

2574.	1 Ducat 1764 (IFoF).............................	950.00

C. Coinage on the Vicariat.
Bust. Rev. Double eagle with arms.

2575.	1 Ducat 1792	1000.00

D. Coinage as Frederick August I.

Head. Rev. Arms.

2576.	10 Taler 1806-17 ....*	2500.00
2577.	5 Taler 1806-17	1800.00
2578.	1 Ducat 1806-22	1250.00
2579.	1 Ducat 1806. Without D in the D.G. of legend.*...	2000.00

Uniformed bust. Rev. Arms.

2580.	10 Taler 1818, 25-27............................	2200.00
2581.	5 Taler 1818, 25-27.........................*.....	2000.00
2582.	1 Ducat 1823-27	1500.00

ANTHONY, 1827-1836
Head. Rev. Arms.

2583.	10 Taler 1828-36	2500.00
2584.	5 Taler 1827-36	2000.00
2585.	1 Ducat 1827-36	1250.00

Bust of Frederick. Rev. Inscription. On Leipzig University Jubilee.

2586.	1 Ducat 1829	1200.00

FREDERICK AUGUST II, 1836-1854
Head. Rev. Arms in wreath.

2587.   1 Ducat 1836-38 .... 1250.00

Head. Rev. Inscription.

2588.   1 Hunting Ducat 1847 .... 1200.00

Head. Rev. Draped arms.

2589. 10   Taler 1836-53 .... 2000.00
2590. 5   Taler 1837-54 ....* 1500.00
2591. 2½   Taler 1842-54 .... 1250.00

JOHN, 1854-1873

Head. Rev. Value.

2592.   1 Krone 1857-63, 65, 67, 68, 70, 71 .... 2250.00
2593.   ½ Krone 1857, 58, 62, 66, 68, 70 ....* 2000.00

SAXONY-ALTENBURG

Dukes of —

JOHN PHILIP AND HIS BROTHERS, 1602-1639

Four busts. Rev. Arms.

2594.   1 Goldgulden 1614, 19, 22 .... 1250.00

JOHN PHILIP AND FREDERICK WILLIAM II
Bust of John Philip. Rev. Arms.

2595.   2 Ducats 1637, 38 .... 2000.00

Bust of John Philip. Rev. Bust of Frederick William.

2596.   1 Ducat 1638 .... 1800.00

JOHN PHILIP

Bust. Rev. Legend. On his death.

2597.   1 Ducat 1639 .... 2000.00

FREDERICK WILLIAM II, 1639-1669

Armored bust. Rev. Arms.

2598.   1 Ducat 1640, 41, 42, 44 .... 1500.00

Initials of Magdalene Sybil. Rev. Legend. On her death.

2599.   1 Ducat 1668 .... 1250.00

Armored bust. Rev. Legend. On his death.

2600.   1 Ducat 1669 .... 1800.00

SAXONY-COBURG-GOTHA

Dukes of —

ERNEST, 1826-1844

Head. Rev. Value and Arms.

2601.   1 Ducat 1831, 36, 42 .... 2000.00

SAXONY-EISENACH

Dukes of —

JOHN WILLIAM, 1690-1729
Armored bust. Rev. Arms and four initials.

2602.   1 Ducat 1700 .... 2000.00

Arms and four initials. Rev. Crane.

2603.   1 Ducat 1716 .... 1500.00

SAXONY-EISENBERG

Dukes of —

CHRISTIAN, 1675-1707
Armored bust. Rev. Two arms in clouds and heart on altar.

2604.   1 Ducat 1682 .... 2200.00

Bust. Rev. Arms.

2605.	2 Ducats 1682	2200.00
2606.	½ Ducat 1683. Thick	800.00
2607.	¼ Ducat 1683, ND. *	600.00

Armored bust. Rev. Table with sword and palm.

| 2608. | 1 Ducat 1686 | 1600.00 |

Bust. Rev. Oval arms.

2609.	2 Ducats 1697. Thick	2500.00
2610.	1 Ducat 1697 *	1250.00
2611.	½ Ducat ND.	850.00

Arms. Rev. Palm tree. "Alchemical" gold issue.

| 2612. | 1 Goldgulden 1684 | 1250.00 |

SAXONY-ERNESTINE

Electors of —

FREDERICK II, 1428-1464
St. John. Rev. Orb in trefoil.

| 2613. | 1 Goldgulden ND | 1500.00 |

FREDERICK III, ALBERT AND JOHN
St. John. Rev. Orb in quatrefoil.

| 2614. | 1 Goldgulden 1498-1500, ND | 1100.00 |

FREDERICK III, GEORGE AND JOHN, 1498-1507
St. John Rev. Orb.

| 2615. | 1 Goldgulden 1498, 99, ND | 1250.00 |

FREDERICK III, JOHN AND GEORGE
St. John. Rev. Orb.

| 2616. | 1 Goldgulden 1500, ND | 1500.00 |

FREDERICK III, 1486-1525
Bust with hat. Rev. Cross.

| 2617. | 2 Ducats 1522 | 12000.00 |

JOHN FREDERICK, 1532-1553
Bust. Rev. Double eagle. Name of Charles V.

| 2618. | 2 Goldgulden 1552 | 6500.00 |

SAXONY-GOTHA

Dukes of —

A. Old Gotha

JOHN FREDERICK, 1554-1595
Arms. Rev. Two angels with wreath.

| 2619. | 1 Ducat 1566, ND | 2500.00 |

Arms and date. Rev. Blank. On the Siege of Gotha.

| 2620. | 1 Ducat 1567. Square | 1850.00 |

JOHN CASIMIR, 1572-1633

Armored bust. Rev. Legend. On his death.

| 2621. | 2 Ducats 1633 | 2200.00 |

JOHN ERNEST, 1572-1638
Bust. Rev. Arms.

| 2622. | 1 Ducat 1635, 36, 37 | 850.00 |
| 2623. | 1 Ducat 1637, 38. With GOTT BESS etc. | 850.00 |

Bust. Rev. Legend. On his death.

| 2624. | 1 Ducat 1638 | 1100.00 |

B. New Gotha

ERNEST, 1640-1675

Name of Jehovah over legend. Rev. Arms over legend. On the Peace of Westphalia.

2625.	2 Ducats 1650	1500.00
2626.	1 Ducat 1650	1000.00
2627.	½ Ducat 1650 *	800.00

Arms. Rev. Legend.

| 2628. | ½ Ducat 1673 | 850.00 |
| 2629. | ¼ Ducat 1675 * | 450.00 |

Bust. Rev. Legend. On his death.

| 2630. | 1 Ducat 1675 | 1500.00 |

FREDERICK I, 1675-1691
Bust. Rev. Arms.

2631.   1 Ducat 1681 .... 1500.00

Laureate head of Magdalene Sybil. Rev. Legend. On her death.

2632.   1 Ducat 1681 .... 1800.00

Fortuna on globe. Rev. Arms.

2633.   1 Goldgulden 1684................................ 1250.00

Bust. Rev. Four arms and four initials.

2634.   1 Ducat 1689 .... 1200.00
2635.   ½ Ducat 1689, 90 .... 800.00

Head with wig. Rev. Ship.

2636.   1 Ducat 1690 .... 1400.00
2637.   ½ Ducat 1690 .... 1000.00

Head. Rev. Star of the Elephant Order, crossed initials and arms.

2638.   1 Ducat 1690 .... 1500.00

Bust. Rev. Arms.

2639.   ¼ Ducat 1682, 84 .... 400.00

Armored bust. Rev. Legend. On his death.

2640.   1 Ducat 1691 .... 850.00

FREDERICK II AND JOHN WILLIAM, 1691-1707

Busts of Bernard and Henry. Rev. Two hands in clouds.

2641.   1 Ducat 1692. Homage of Gotha................... 1500.00

FREDERICK II, 1691-1732
Bust. Rev. Arms.

2642.   2 Ducats 1699, 1707 .... 2500.00
2643.   1 Ducat 1694, 98, 99, 1707........................ 1200.00
2644.   ½ Ducat 1702 .... 500.00

Bust. Rev. Legend. On the Reformation.

2645.   2 Ducats 1717 .... 2500.00

Bust. Rev. Oak tree. On the Reformation.

2646.   1 Ducat 1717 .... 1500.00

Bust. Rev. Legend. On the Augsburg Confession.

2647.   2 Ducats 1730................................... 2200.00

FREDERICK III, 1732-1772

Bust. Rev. Arms.

2648.   1 Ducat 1732 .... 1850.00

Armored bust. Rev. Legend. On the religious peace.

2649.   2 Ducats 1755 .... 2200.00

Armored bust. Rev. Arms. On the religious peace.

2650.   1 Ducat 1755 .... 1500.00

SAXONY-GOTHA-ALTENBURG

FREDERICK IV, 1822-1825
Bust. Rev. Inscription. On Gotha Gymnasium.

2651.   1 Ducat 1824 .... 1500.00

SAXONY-HILDBURGHAUSEN

Dukes of —

ERNEST FREDERICK, 1715-1724
Bust. Rev. Legend. On the Reformation.

2652.   ½ Ducat 1717 .... 1000.00

ERNEST FREDERICK CHARLES, 1745-1780
Bust. Rev. Arms.

2653.   1 Ducat 1771 .... 1500.00

SAXONY-LAUENBURG

Dukes of —

FRANCIS II, 1581-1619
Bust. Rev. Arms.

2654.   1 Goldgulden 1609, 11, 12 .... 2500.00

JULIUS HENRY, 1656-1665

Bust. Rev. Arms.

2655.   2 Ducats 1662................................... 2500.00
2656.   1 Ducat 1657, 62..........................*...... 1500.00

Bust. Rev. Madonna.

2657.   1 Ducat 1659 .... 1600.00

JULIUS FRANCIS, 1666-1689

Bust. Rev. Arms.

2658.	2 Ducats 1673, 78-83, ND.....................	2500.00
2659.	1 Ducat 1670, 73, ND....................*	1500.00

FREDERICK AUGUST (1689-?)
Bust. Rev. Lion with shield.

2660.	¼ Ducat 1696	600.00

SAXONY-MEININGEN

Dukes of —

BERNARD, 1680-1706
Armored bust. Rev. Arms.

2661.	1 Ducat 1687, 88	1500.00

Armored bust. Rev. Meiningen Castle.

2662.	2 Ducats 1692.....................................	2500.00
2663.	1 Ducat 1692.....................................	1400.00

ERNEST LOUIS I, 1706-1724

Busts of the Duke and his wife. Rev. Two shields.

2664.	1 Ducat 1714. On the Marriage	1500.00
2665.	1 Ducat 1717. On the Reformation..........*	1500.00

CHARLES, 1763-1782
Two shields. Rev. Inscription.

2666.	2 Wedding Ducats 1780	2200.00

Initials. Rev. Inscription.

2667.	1 Wedding Ducat 1780............................	1300.00

SAXONY-ROEMHILD

Dukes of —

HENRY, 1680-1710
Bust. Rev. Arms.

2668.	1 Ducat 1698. Three varieties of the Rev...........	1800.00

SAXONY-SAALFELD

Dukes of —

JOHN ERNEST VIII, 1680-1729
Armored bust. Rev. Arms.

2669.	1 Ducat 1698, 1720, 21, 27.....................	1500.00
2670.	½ Ducat 1725, 27, 28..........................	1000.00
2671.	¼ Ducat 1725, 27, 28..........................	650.00

Armored bust. Rev. Bust of Luther. On the Reformation.

2672.	2 Ducats 1717....................................	2500.00
2673.	1 Ducat 1717....................................	1000.00

Armored half length bust. Rev. City view of Reichmansdorf.

2674.	1 Mining Ducat 1717, 19, 21, 22, 26-28..............	2000.00

CHRISTIAN ERNEST AND FRANCIS JOSIAS, 1729-1745

Initials in shields. Rev. Arms supported by lions.

2675.	1 Ducat 1740......................................	1800.00

Duke kneeling. Rev. Bust of his brother.

2676.	1 Ducat 1745.....................................	1500.00

Initials. Rev. Arms.

2677.	¼ Ducat 1738, 43	550.00

CHRISTIAN ERNEST, 1729-1745

Duke kneeling. Rev. Eagle and sun. On his death.

2678.	2 Ducats ND	850.00
2679.	1 Ducat ND.................................*	550.00

FRANCIS JOSIAS, 1745-1764

Lion with initials in shield. Rev. Arms.

2680.	1 Ducat 1746, 49	1800.00

Initials in shield. Rev. Arms.

2681.	¼ Ducat 1752	450.00

ERNEST FREDERICK, 1764-1800

Bust. Rev. City view of Reichmansdorf.

2682.	1 Mining Ducat 1766	2750.00

SAXONY-WEIMAR

Dukes of —

JOHN ERNEST AND HIS SEVEN BROTHERS, 1605-1640
Four busts on each side.
2683. 1 Goldgulden 1613-15, 17, 19 .... 850.00

JOHN ERNEST AND HIS FIVE BROTHERS

Arms. Rev. Shield.
2684. 1 Goldgulden 1623................................. 1400.00

BERNARD, DIED 1639
Arms. Rev. Christ standing.
2685. 1 Goldgulden 1634................................. 1800.00

WILLIAM, 1630-1662
Arms. Rev. Jehovah and legend.
2686. 1 Ducat 1651 .... 1100.00
2687. ½ Ducat 1651, 52 .... 600.00
2688. ¼ Ducat 1651 .... 450.00

Bust. Rev. Trophies and legend.
2689. 2 Ducats 1654 .... 2000.00
2690. ½ Ducat 1654 ....*...... 700.00

Arms. Rev. Legend.
2691. 1 Ducat 1651 .... 1100.00
2692. ½ Ducat 1651, 56..........................*...... 700.00
2693. ¼ Ducat 1658 .... 600.00

Arms of Henneberg. Rev. Legend.
2694. 1 Ducat 1661 .... 1500.00

Bust. Rev. Jena Castle.
2695. 1 Ducat 1661 .... 1500.00

Bust. Rev. Arms.
2696. ¼ Ducat 1662 .... 400.00

WILLIAM ERNEST, 1683-1728
Bust. Rev. Weimar Castle.
2697. 1 Ducat 1717 .... 1000.00

Table with book and lamp. Rev. Legend. On the Reformation.
2698. 2 Ducats 1717 .... 2500.00
2699. 1 Ducat 1717 ....*...... 1000.00

ERNEST AUGUST, 1728-1748
Hercules and lion. Rev. Mountain.
2700. 1 Ducat ND...................................... 1500.00

Initials in shield. Rev. Legend.
2701. 1 Ducat 1745 .... 1600.00

Bust amid trophies. Rev. Rose bush and sheep.
2702. 1 Ducat ND...................................... 1500.00

FREDERICK III, ADMINISTRATOR
Bust. Rev. Felicitas standing.
2703. 1 Ducat 1752 .... 1200.00

Bust. Rev. Arms.
2704. 1 Ducat 1754 .... 1500.00

ERNEST AUGUST CONSTANTINE, 1756-1758
Bust. Rev. City view of Eisenach.
2705. 1 Ducat 1756. Homage of Eisenach................ 2000.00

Bust. Rev. Hilarity.
2706. 1 Ducat 1756 .... 1400.00

Initials. Rev. Hilarity standing.
2707. 1 Ducat 1756 .... 1400.00

Armored bust. Rev. Arms and value.
2708. 1 Pistole ND 2200.00

ANNE AMALIA, 1758-1775
Bust. Rev. Arms.
2709. 1 Ducat 1764 .... 2500.00

Bust. Rev. Arms and value.
2710. 1 Pistole 1764 .... 2200.00

SAXONY-WEISSENFELS

Dukes of —

JOHN ADOLPH, 1680-1697
Initials of Joan Magdalene, his wife. Rev. Legend. On her death.
2711. 1 Ducat 1686 .... 2000.00

JOHN GEORGE, 1697-1712
Duke standing. Rev. Arms.
2712. 1 Ducat 1698 .... 2500.00

Bust. Rev. Two shields.
2713. 1 Ducat ND...................................... 2500.00

CHRISTIAN, 1712-1736
Bust. Rev. Stag.
2714. 1 Ducat 1726, ND................................ 1500.00

Bust. Rev. Luther kneeling. On the Reformation.
2715. 1 Ducat 1717 .... 1500.00

SAYN-SAYN

Counts —

HENRY, 1568-1606
Arms. Rev. Double eagle. Rudolph II.

2716.	2 Goldgulden 1592	6000.00
2717.	1 Goldgulden 1590	3000.00

SAYN-WITTGENSTEIN

Counts —

LOUIS, 1605-1634

Arms. Rev. Double eagle. Ferdinand II.

2718.	1 Goldgulden ND	2500.00

Arms. Rev. Orb.

2719.	1 Goldgulden ND. (Zwitter)	3000.00
2720.	1 Goldgulden ND. Title of Ferdinand II	2500.00

Three shields. Rev. Double eagle. Ferdinand II.

2721.	1 Goldgulden ND	2500.00

Three shields. Rev. Orb.

2722.	1 Goldgulden ND. SI DEUS PRO NOBIS etc	3000.00
2723.	1 Goldgulden ND. Title of Ferdinand II	2750.00

Two shields. Rev. Orb. Ferdinand II.

2724.	1 Goldgulden ND	2200.00

JOHN, 1634-1657

Bust. Rev. Arms.

2725.	1 Ducat 1654	4000.00

GUSTAVE, 1657-1701
Bust with wig. Rev. Castle, rock and goat.

2726.	2 Ducats 1687	6000.00

SCHAUENBURG

Counts —

ADOLPH XIII, 1576-1601
Count on horse. Rev. Arms.

2727.	20 Ducats 1592	Rare

Three shields. Rev. Orb. Rudolph II.

2728.	1 Goldgulden 1589, 92, 93, 95, 1600	2500.00

ERNEST III, 1601-1622
Arms. Rev. Double eagle.

2729.	1 Goldgulden 1603, 04, 08, 10, 12. Rudolph II	2500.00
2730.	1 Goldgulden 1616. Matthias	2500.00

Count on horse. Rev. Dragon over wall.

2731.	20 Ducats ND	Rare

Count on horse. Rev. Arms.

2732.	20 Ducats ND	Rare
2733.	10 Ducats ND. 45 or 51 millimetres	Rare
2734.	5 Ducats ND	Rare

SCHAUMBURG-LIPPE

Counts, and later, Princes —

WILLIAM, 1748-1777

Head. Rev. Arms.

2735.	10 Taler 1763	2500.00
2736.	1 Ducat 1762 ....*.....	1250.00

PHILIP ERNEST, 1777-1787
Arms. Rev. Legend.

2737.	1 Ducat 1777	1500.00

Bust. Rev. Tablet.

2738.	1 Ducat 1783	2000.00

GEORGE WILLIAM, 1807-1860

Head. Rev. Arms.

2739.	10 Taler 1829	4500.00

SCHLESWIG-HOLSTEIN

(See under Denmark, period 1523-1559)

SCHLESWIG-HOLSTEIN-GLUCKSBURG

Dukes of —

PHILIP ERNEST, 1698-1729
Arms. Rev. Initials.

2740.	1 Ducat 1716	2000.00

SCHLESWIG-HOLSTEIN-GOTTORP

Dukes of —

JOHN ADOLPH, 1590-1616
Duke standing. Rev. Arms.

2741.	1 Ducat 1601	2500.00

FREDERICK III, 1616-1659

Bust. Rev. Arms.

2742.	1 Goldgulden 1619	2500.00
2743.	1 Ducat 1642	2000.00

Duke standing. Rev. Arms.

2744.	1 Goldgulden 1627	2000.00

CHRISTIAN ALBERT, 1659-1694
Bust. Rev. Arms.

2745.	5 Ducats 1674	Rare
2746.	1 Ducat 1664, 74, 89	1800.00

Bust. Rev. Orb.

2747.	1 Goldgulden 1664	2000.00

Bust. Rev. Mountain.

2748.	1 Ducat 1689	2500.00

FREDERICK IV, 1694-1702

Arms and lions. Rev. Holm Fortress.

2749.	1 Ducat 1698	2000.00

Bust. Rev. Arms with two lions.

2750.	1 Ducat 1698, 1700	1500.00

Bust. Rev. Arms.

2751.	1 Ducat 1698	1800.00

Bust. Rev. Lions in shield and six arms.

2752.	1 Ducat 1698	2000.00

CHARLES FREDERICK, 1702-1739
Head. Rev. Lion shield.

2753.	¼ Ducat 1711	1250.00

Head. Rev. Arms supported by lions.

2754.	1 Ducat 1705	2000.00

Head. Rev. Arms.

2755.	1 Ducat 1706	3000.00

Bust. Rev. Arms.

2756.	1 Ducat 1712	2500.00

Bust. Rev. Lion shield.

2757.	1 Ducat 1710, 11, ND	2500.00

Arms. Rev. Initials.

2758.	1 Ducat 1710	2500.00

Lion shield. Rev. Initials.

2759.	¼ Ducat 1708	850.00

SCHLESWIG-HOLSTEIN-PLOEN

Dukes of —

JOHN ADOLPH, 1671-1704
Arms. Rev. Initials.

2760.	1 Ducat 1677	3000.00

Bust. Rev. Arms.

2761.	1 Ducat 1690	3000.00

FREDERICK CHARLES, 1722-1761

Bust. Rev. Arms.

2762.	1 Ducat 1760. Year under arms ....*	2500.00
2763.	1 Ducat 1760. Value under arms	2500.00

SCHLESWIG-HOLSTEIN-SONDERBURG

Dukes of —

JOHN THE YOUNGER, 1564-1622
Bust. Rev. Orb.

2764.	1 Goldgulden 1619	2000.00

ALEXANDER, 1622-1627
Arms. Rev. Orb.

2765.	1 Goldgulden 1624	2000.00

SCHWARZBURG

Counts —

THE SONS OF ALBERT VII, 1605-1613
Three helmets. Rev. Arms.

2766.	1 Goldgulden 1606	1600.00

Three helmets. Rev. Cross and five shields.

2767.	1 Goldgulden 1606, 08. Mint: Erfurt	1500.00
2768.	1 Goldgulden 1611, 13, 16, 18. Mint: Saalfeld	1500.00

SCHWARZBURG-RUDOLSTADT

Princes —

GUNTHER XLIII, 1718-1740
Arms. Rev. Legend. From gold of the Goldisthal Mines.

2769.	1 Ducat 1737	3500.00

LOUIS FREDERICK II, 1793-1807

Double eagle. Rev. Value.

2770.   1 Ducat 1803 .... 2500.00

SCHWARZBURG-SONDERSHAUSEN

Princes —

CHRISTIAN WILLIAM, 1666-1721
Bust. Rev. Shield.

2771.   ¼ Ducat 1684, 86 .... 550.00

Bust. Rev. Arms between wild man and wild woman.

2772.   1 Ducat 1679, 84, 89.............................. 1500.00

ANTHONY GUNTHER II, 1697-1716
Bust. Rev. Arms.

2773.   1 Ducat 1680 .... 1500.00

SILESIA

Protestant States of —

Silesian eagle. Rev. "Jehova" beneath radiate clouds.

2774.   1 Ducat 1634 .... 1850.00

SILESIA-JAEGERNDORF

Dukes of —

GEORGE FREDERICK, 1543-1603
Duke standing. Rev. Arms.

2775.   4 Ducats 1592. Thick .... Rare
2776.   2 Ducats 1592. Thick .... Rare
2777.   1 Ducat 1561, 92, 95, 96 .... 2200.00

Arms. Rev. Double eagle. Name of Ferdinand I.

2778.   1 Ducat 1563 .... 2500.00

Arms. Rev. Double eagle. Name of Rudolph II.

2779.   1 Ducat 1578 .... 2500.00

JOHN GEORGE, 1606-1621
Half-length bust. Rev. Oval arms with three helmets.

2780.   12 Ducats ND .... Rare
2781.   10 Ducats ND .... Rare
2782.   5 Ducats ND .... Rare
2783.   4 Ducats ND .... Rare

Half-length bust to right. Rev. Arms with three helmets.

2784.   10 Ducats 1611 .... Rare
2785.   8 Ducats 1611 .... Rare
2786.   7 Ducats 1611 .... Rare
2787.   5 Ducats 1611. Two sizes......................... Rare
2788.   4 Ducats ND .... Rare

Bust. Rev. Arms with three helmets.

2789.   4 Ducats 1610 .... Rare
2790.   3 Ducats 1610 .... Rare

Half-length bust facing. Rev. Arms with three helmets.

2791.   10 Ducats 1611 .... Rare

Duke standing. Rev. Crowned oval arms.

2792.   3 Ducats ND .... Rare
2793.   2 Ducats 1618, 20, 21, ND ....*...... 2750.00

Duke standing. Rev. Arms with three helmets.

2794.   1 Ducat 1610 .... 2200.00

Duke standing. Rev. Crowned arms.

2795.   1 Ducat 1611 .... 2000.00

Half-length bust. Rev. Crowned arms.

2796.   1 Ducat 1612, 20 .... 1500.00
2797.   1 Ducat 1614, 16, 17. With oval arms 1500.00

Crowned arms. Rev. Legend.

2798.   2 Ducats 1617. Thick 3300.00
2799.   1 Ducat 1620. Thick 2000.00
2800.   ½ Ducat 1615, 17, 20-22 ....*...... 1000.00

SILESIA-LIEGNITZ-BRIEG

Dukes of —

WENCESLAS, 1348-1364
Lily. Rev. St. John.

2801.   1 Goldgulden ND 1200.00

FREDERICK II, 1488-1547
Bust. Rev. Arms.

2802.   5 Ducats 1545 .... Rare
2803.   1 Ducat 1543, 44 .... 1500.00

JOACHIM FREDERICK, 1587-1602

Bust. Rev. Arms.

2804.   1 Ducat 1600 .... 1350.00

Bust. Rev. Legend. On his death.

2805.   5 Ducats 1602 .... Rare
2806.   2 Ducats 1602 .... 2500.00

JOHN CHRISTIAN AND GEORGE RUDOLPH, 1602-1621

Two busts facing. Rev. Crowned arms.

2807. 1 Ducat 1604-06 .... 1500.00

Two busts facing each other. Rev. Crowned arms.

2808.	2 Ducats 1608. Square	....	2500.00
2809.	2 Ducats 1609	.... *	2200.00
2810.	1 Ducat 1606-09	....	1200.00
2811.	½ Ducat ND	....	850.00

Two busts facing each other. Rev. Arms with three helmets.

2812.	10 Ducats 1609, 10, 17, 19	....	Rare
2813.	7 Ducats 1610	....	Rare
2814.	6 Ducats 1607, 17, 19, 21	....	Rare
2815.	5 Ducats 1608-10, 19, 21	....	3300.00
2816.	4 Ducats 1605, 07, 09, 10	.... *	2200.00
2817.	3 Ducats 1610, 13	....	1500.00
2818.	1 Ducat 1620	....	1000.00
2819.	½ Ducat 1620	....	700.00

Half-length bust to right over two arms. Rev. Half-length bust to left of George Rudolph over two arms.

2820. 10 Ducats 1609 .... Rare

Bust to right between two arms. Rev. Bust of George Rudolph to left between two arms.

2821.	10 Ducats 1611	....	Rare
2822.	6 Ducats 1611	....	Rare
2823.	5 Ducats 1611, 17	....	3500.00
2824.	4 Ducats 1611	.... *	2000.00
2825.	4 Ducats 1610, 11. Square	....	2200.00
2826.	3 Ducats 1611, 17, 19	....	1500.00
2827.	3 Ducats 1610. Square	....	1700.00
2828.	2 Ducats 1609-11	....	1500.00
2829.	2 Ducats 1610. Square	....	1800.00
2830.	1 Ducat 1610, 11, 19	....	1100.00

Crowned arms. Rev. Legend.

2831.	1 Ducat 1610. Thick	....	1500.00
2832.	½ Ducat 1610. Legend in 6 lines	.... *	800.00
2833.	½ Ducat 1610. Legend in 5 lines	....	800.00

Two busts facing each other. Rev. Crown over two arms.

2834. 1 Ducat 1612 .... 1250.00

Two busts facing each other over two arms. Rev. Legend.

2835.	1 Ducat 1619. Thick	....	1500.00
2836.	½ Ducat 1619	....	850.00
2837.	½ Ducat 1619. Square	....	1200.00

Crown over two arms. Rev. Legend.

2838.	¼ Ducat 1619	....	1200.00
2839.	¼ Ducat 1619. Square	....	1200.00

Bust to right between two arms. Rev. Bust of George Rudolph to left between two arms. Struck at Reichenstein.

2840.	4 Ducats 1614	....	Rare
2841.	2 Ducats 1614	....	3000.00
2842.	1 Ducat 1614	....	1850.00

Two busts facing. Rev. Arms with three helmets. Struck at Reichenstein.

2843.	10 Ducats 1617	....	Rare
2844.	8 Ducats 1617	....	Rare
2845.	6 Ducats 1615, 16	....	Rare
2846.	5 Ducats 1615, 16	....	Rare

JOHN CHRISTIAN, DIED 1639
Bust. Rev. Arms with three helmets.

2847.	7 Ducats 1621	....	Rare
2848.	5 Ducats 1622. Kreuzberg	....	Rare
2849.	4 Ducats 1622	....	Rare
2850.	3 Ducats 1622	....	Rare
2851.	3 Ducats 1622. Square	....	Rare

GEORGE RUDOLPH, DIED 1653
Bust. Rev. Crowned arms.

2852.	5 Ducats 1621	....	Rare
2853.	3 Ducats 1622	....	Rare
2854.	2 Ducats 1622	....	2000.00

Bust. Rev. Arms with three helmets.

2855.	8 Ducats 1621	....	Rare
2856.	7 Ducats 1621	....	Rare
2857.	6 Ducats 1621	....	Rare
2858.	1 Ducat 1621	....	1250.00

Facing bust. Rev. Legend. On his death.

2859. 2 Ducats 1653 .... 2500.00

GEORGE, LOUIS AND CHRISTIAN, 1639-1663

Three half-length busts. Rev. Arms with three helmets.

2860.	5 Ducats 1656, 58, 59............................	4500.00
2861.	4 Ducats 1652, 58, 59............................	4000.00
2862.	3 Ducats 1651, 58, 60............................	3000.00
2863.	2 Ducats 1651, 53, 57-59...............*	2000.00
2864.	1 Ducat 1651-62	1100.00
2865.	½ Ducat 1651, 52, 52/53, 52/54, 56	800.00

GEORGE III, 1639-1664

Crowned bust. Rev. Arms with three helmets.

2866.	1 Ducat 1660 ....*	1250.00
2867.	1 Ducat 1664. Reichenstein......................	1500.00

Facing bust. Rev. Legend. On his death.

2868.	2 Ducats 1664	2500.00

LOUIS, 1653-1663

Crowned bust. Rev. Arms with three helmets.

2869.	1 Ducat 1661 ....*	1500.00
2870.	1 Ducat 1662. With DUCES	1500.00

CHRISTIAN, 1639-1673

Crowned bust. Rev. Arms with three helmets.

2871.	1 Ducat 1660. With DUCES...............*	1500.00
2872.	1 Ducat 1661. Two different legends on Rev.	1500.00

Bust. Rev. Eagle.

2873.	10 Ducats 1666	Rare
2874.	5 Ducats 1672	Rare
2875.	3 Ducats 1666	Rare
2876.	2 Ducats 1666, 70, 72................*	2500.00
2877.	1 Ducat 1666, 70, 72...........................	1250.00

LOUISE, DIED 1680

Facing bust. Rev. Two arms.

2878.	¼ Ducat 1674	1000.00

GEORGE WILLIAM, 1672-1675

Bust. Rev. Eagle.

2879.	2 Ducats 1675..................................	3300.00
2880.	1 Ducat 1674, 75....................*	1200.00
2881.	¼ Ducat 1675	500.00

Facing bust. Rev. Eagle.

2882.	1 Ducat 1675. Thick	1500.00
2883.	½ Ducat 1675 ....*	850.00

Bust. Rev. Legend. On his death.

2884.	2 Ducats 1675..................................	3000.00

SILESIA-MUENSTERBERG
Duke of —
JOHN WEIKHARD, 1654-1677
Facing bust. Rev. Arms.

2885.	1 Ducat ND.....................................	2000.00

SILESIA-MUENSTERBERG-OELS
Dukes of —
ALBERT AND CHARLES, 1498-1511

St. James standing. Rev. Arms on cross.

2886.	1 Goldgulden ND.................................	2500.00

St. James standing. Rev. Cross and four arms.

2887.	1 Goldgulden 1510, 11.........................	1800.00

CHARLES I, 1498-1536
Bust. Rev. Arms.

2888.	2 Ducats 1528..................................	3500.00

St. James standing. Rev. Cross and four arms.

2889.	1 Goldgulden 1512-19....................*	1850.00
2890.	1 Goldgulden 1515, 22, ND. With name on Rev......	1750.00

Arms. Rev. St. Christopher.

2891.   1 Ducat 1520-22, 26-36 .... 1250.00

JOACHIM, HENRY II, JOHN AND GEORGE, 1536-1558

Arms. Rev. St. Christopher.

2892.   1 Ducat 1537-53 .... 1250.00

JOACHIM, HENRY III AND CHARLES II, 1552-1562

Arms. Rev. St. Christopher.

2893.   1 Ducat 1553-58, 60-62 .... 1300.00

JOHN, DIED 1565

Bust. Rev. Arms.

2894.   1 Ducat 1553-62 .... 2200.00

Bust. Rev. Five shields.

2895.   1 Ducat 1563, 64, 65 .... 1800.00

HENRY III AND CHARLES II, 1562-1587

Five shields. Rev. St. Christopher.

2896.   1 Ducat 1563-70 .... 1250.00

Arms. Rev. St. Christopher.

2897.   1 Ducat 1569 .... 1250.00

CHARLES II, 1548-1617

Bust. Rev. Arms.

2898.   2 Ducats 1593. Thick 3000.00
2899.   1 Ducat 1593 .... * 1500.00

Bust. Rev. Arms with three helmets.

2900.   10 Ducats 1612, 13, 16 .... Rare
2901.   9 Ducats 1612 .... Rare
2902.   6 Ducats 1611, 15, 16 .... Rare
2903.   5 Ducats 1611-13, 15, 16 .... * ...... Rare
2904.   4 Ducats 1613, 15 .... Rare
2905.   3 Ducats 1613, 14 .... 3000.00
2906.   2 Ducats 1614, 15 .... 2200.00

Bust. Rev. Five shields.

2907.   4 Ducats 1612 .... Rare
2908.   3 Ducats 1612 .... 3000.00

Bust. Rev. Crowned arms.

2909.   2 Ducats 1612 .... 3000.00
2910.   1 Ducat 1611-16 .... 1250.00

Eagle. Rev. Four shields.

2911.   ½ Ducat 1612 .... 850.00

Eagle. Rev. Crowned arms.

2912.   ½ Ducat 1616 .... 1000.00

Bust over arms. Rev. Legend. On his death.

2913.   12½ Ducats 1617 .... Rare
2914.   10   Ducats 1617 .... Rare
2915.   6   Ducats 1617 .... Rare

Bust. Rev. Legend. On his death.

2916.   2 Ducats 1617 .... 3000.00

HENRY WENCESLAS AND CHARLES FREDERICK, 1617-1639

Two busts facing each other. Rev. Arms with three helmets.

2916a. 6 Ducats 1620 .... Rare
2917.   5 Ducats 1620, 21 .... 5000.00
2918.   4 Ducats 1619, 21 .... 4000.00
2919.   3 Ducats 1619, 21, 22 .... * 2750.00

Half-length bust to right. Rev. Half-length bust of Charles Frederick to left. Five shields are on each side.

2920.	6 Ducats 1619	Rare
2921.	4 Ducats 1620	Rare
2922.	3 Ducats 1620, 21	Rare
2923.	2 Ducats 1621	2000.00

Bust to right. Rev. Bust of Charles Frederick to left.

2924.	1 Ducat 1619, 20, 21	1250.00

SILESIA-SCHWEIDNITZ

Dukes of —

BOICO II, 1326-1368
Lily. Rev. St. John.

2925.	1 Goldgulden ND	1500.00

SILESIA-TESCHEN

Dukes of —

ADAM WENCESLAS, 1579-1617
Half-length bust. Rev. Helmeted eagle-shield supported by angels.

2926.	5 Ducats 1611	Rare

Half-length bust. Rev. Eagle.

2927.	8 Ducats 1609	Rare
2928.	5 Ducats 1609	Rare

Bust. Rev. Eagle.

2929.	3 Ducats 1613. Square...........................	Rare

ELISABETH LUCRETIA, 1625-1653
Facing bust. Rev. Arms.

2930.	10 Ducats 1650	Rare
2931.	5 Ducats 1650	Rare

SILESIA-TROPPAU

Dukes of —

PRZEMISLAW, 1366-1433
Arms. Rev. Duke standing with flag and sword.

2932.	1 Goldgulden ND	3500.00

SILESIA-WURTTEMBERG-OELS

Counts —

SYLVIUS FREDERICK, 1673-1697

Bust. Rev. Arms.

2933.	2 Ducats 1677	3500.00
2934.	1 Ducat 1674, 75, 76 ....*......	1850.00

Bust. Rev. Bust of Eleonore Charlotte. On their wedding.

2935.	1 Ducat ND (1672)	1500.00

CHRISTIAN ULRIC, 1673-1704
Bust. Rev. Helmeted arms.

2936.	1 Ducat 1679, 98, 1701, 03	3000.00

Bust. Rev. Crowned arms.

2937.	1 Ducat 1681, 83	3000.00
2938.	½ Ducat 1683	1500.00
2939.	¼ Ducat 1685 ....*......	1000.00

Bust. Rev. Five shields and four initials crossed.

2940.	1 Ducat 1696	2000.00

Bust of Sybil Marie. Rev. Blank.

2941.	½ Ducat ND. Square	1000.00

Bust. Rev. Bust of Anne.

2942.	¼ Ducat ND. (1680)	1000.00

Bust. Rev. Bust of Sophia of Mecklenburg. On his wedding.

2943.	1 Ducat ND. (1700) Two different dies	2800.00

CHARLES OF JULIUSBURG, 1684-1745
Bust. Rev. Arms.

2944.	1 Ducat 1705	3300.00

CHARLES FREDERICK, 1704-1744
Bust. Rev. Arms.

2945.	1 Ducat 1708, 11, 13, 14	3500.00
2946.	¼ Ducat 1711	1000.00

Arms. Rev. Initials.

2947.	¼ Ducat 1708	750.00

SINZENDORF

Counts —

GEORGE LOUIS, 1632-1680
Bust with cap. Rev. Arms.

2948.	1 Ducat 1676	3000.00

PHILIP LOUIS, 1687-1742
Bust. Rev. Arms.

2949.	1 Ducat 1726	1800.00

JOHN WILLIAM, 1742-1766

Bust. Rev. Arms.

2950.	1 Ducat 1753	2200.00

SOLMS-LAUBACH

Counts —

CHRISTIAN AUGUST, 1738-1784
Bust. Rev. Arms and value.

2951.	1 Ducat 1761	2500.00

SOLMS-LICH

Counts —

ERNEST I, EBERHARD AND HERMAN ADOLPH, 1588-1590
Arms. Rev. Double eagle. Name of Rudolph II.

2952.	1 Goldgulden 1589...............................	3000.00

HERMAN ADOLPH, GEORGE EBERHARD, ERNEST II AND PHILIP, 1590-1610
Arms. Rev. Double eagle. Name of Rudolph II.
2953.   1 Goldgulden 1601................................   2500.00

ERNEST II, 1602-1619
Arms. Rev. Double eagle. Name of Matthias.
2954.   1 Goldgulden 1615................................   300.00

PHILIP, DIED 1631
Arms. Rev. Double eagle. Name of Matthias.
2955.   1 Goldgulden 1616................................   1500.00

Arms. Rev. Double eagle. Name of Ferdinand II.
2956.   1 Goldgulden 1623................................   1500.00

Arms. Rev. Emperor Matthias standing.
2957.   1 Ducat 1613 ....   3000.00

PHILIP REINHARD I, 1613-1635
Arms. Rev. Initials of Christian IV of Denmark.
2958.   2 Ducats 1627 ....   4000.00
2959.   1 Ducat 1627 ....   3000.00

CHARLES, DEPOSED 1918
Arms. Rev. Wreath. Privately issued.
2960.   1 Ducat 1908, 12 ....   500.00

SOLMS-ROEDELHEIM

Counts —

JOHN AUGUST AND HIS BROTHERS, 1632-1665
Arms. Rev. Value in wreath.
2961.   1 Ducat 1656 ....   3000.00

JOHN AUGUST, 1665-1680
Bust. Rev. Arms.
2962.   1 Ducat 1680 ....   3500.00

SPEYER

Bishops of —

PHILIP CHRISTOPHER, 1610-1652
Arms. Rev. Madonna.
2963.   2 Goldgulden 1612...............................   6000.00

LOTHAR FREDERICK, 1652-1675
Bust. Rev. Arms.
2964.   1 Ducat 1665 ....   3000.00

HENRY HARTARD, 1711-1719
Bust. Rev. Arms.
2965.   2 Ducats 1711 ....   3500.00

DAMIAN HUGO, 1719-1743

Arms. Rev. City view of Bruchsal.
2966.   2 Ducats 1726....................................   3000.00
2967.   1 Ducat 1726.............................* 2000.00

FRANCIS CHRISTOPHER, 1743-1770

Bust. Rev. Seated and kneeling figures.
2968.   1 Ducat 1745 ....   1800.00

AUGUST, 1770-1797

Three shields. Rev. Minerva with four genii.
2969.   1 Ducat 1770 ....   1600.00

STETTIN

Swedish Kings of —

Facing bust of Gustave Adolphe. Rev. Arms.
2970.   1 Ducat 1632 ....   1800.00

STOLBERG

Counts, and later, Princes—

A. The Stolberg Line (Stolberg-Stolberg)

LOUIS II AND HIS BROTHERS, 1555-1571
Arms. Rev. Double eagle. Name of Charles V.
2971.   1 Goldgulden ND.................................   5000.00

LOUIS II, 1535-1574
Arms. Rev. Double eagle. Name of Ferdinand I.
2972.   1 Goldgulden 1560. Mint: Augsburg...............   2200.00

Five shields in enclosure. Rev. Double eagle. Name of Maximilian II.
2973.   1 Goldgulden 1567. Mint: Frankfurt 2500.00

Five shields. Rev. Orb. Name of Maximilian II.
2974.   1 Goldgulden ND. Mint: Noerdlingen..............   2500.00

JOHN AND HENRY XXII, 1607-1612
Stag. Rev. Arms.
2975.   1 Goldgulden 1607, 09...........................   1500.00

Stag and column. Rev. Arms.
2976.   1 Goldgulden 1612...............................   1500.00

JOHN, 1606-1612
Stag. Rev. Legend. On his death.
2977.   1 Goldgulden 1612...............................   1500.00

HENRY XXII AND WOLFGANG GEORGE, 1612-1615
Stag. Rev. Arms.
2978.   1 Goldgulden 1613, 14, ND 1000.00

WOLFGANG GEORGE, 1615-1631
Arms. Rev. Stag.

2979.   1 Goldgulden 1619, 25, 26 .... 1000.00

CHRISTOPHER II AND HENRY VOLRAD, 1618-1632
Stag. Rev. Double eagle. Name of Matthias.

2980.   1 Goldgulden 1619................................ 2000.00

JOHN MARTIN, 1638-1669
Stag. Rev. Arms.

2981.   2 Ducats 1646.................................... 2200.00

Stag and column. Rev. Value on tablet.

2982.   1 Ducat 1647, 49, 53 .... 1500.00

CHRISTOPHER FREDERICK AND JOST CHRISTIAN, 1704-1738
Stag and column. Rev. Arms.

2983.   2 Ducats 1725.................................... 2000.00
2984.   1 Ducat 1706, 23, 25, 34 .... 1000.00
2985.   ¼ Ducat 1706 .... 750.00

Martin Luther at table. Rev. Legend. On the Reformation.

2986.   1 Ducat 1717 .... 1000.00

CHRISTOPHER FREDERICK, 1704-1738
Initials. Rev. Stag and column.

2987.   ½ Ducat 1715 .... 550.00
2988.   ¼ Ducat ND....................................... 350.00
2989.   ⅛ Ducat ND....................................... 300.00

JOST CHRISTIAN, 1704-1739
Initials. Rev. Stag and column.

2990.   ¼ Ducat ND....................................... 400.00
2991.   ⅛ Ducat ND....................................... 500.00

Stag and column. Rev. Arms.

2992.   ¼ Ducat ND....................................... 400.00

CHRISTIAN LOUIS II AND FREDERICK BOTHO, 1739-1761

Stag and column. Rev. Arms.

2993.	4 Ducats 1743....................................	Rare
2994.	2 Ducats 1743....................................	3000.00
2995.	1 Ducat 1740, 42, 43, 48, 50, 57............* ...	1500.00
2996.	½ Ducat 1745, 48, 50............................	500.00
2997.	¼ Ducat ND.......................................	500.00
2998.	⅛ Ducat ND.......................................	350.00

CHRISTOPHER LOUIS II, 1738-1761
Initials. Rev. Stag and column.

2999.   ¼ Ducat ND....................................... 500.00
3000.   ⅛ Ducat ND....................................... 300.00
3001.   1/16 Ducat ND..................................... 300.00
3002.   1/32 Ducat ND..................................... 300.00

FREDERICK BOTHO AND CHARLES LOUIS, 1761-1768

Stag and column. Rev. Arms.

3003.   2 Ducats 1764.................................... 3300.00
3004.   1 Ducat 1762, 64, 66..........................* ... 1500.00
3005.   ½ Ducat 1762, 66 .... 1000.00

FREDERICK BOTHO, 1739-1768
Initials. Rev. Stag and column.

3006.   ¼ Ducat ND....................................... 400.00
3007.   ⅛ Ducat ND....................................... 300.00

CHARLES LOUIS AND HENRY CHRISTIAN FREDERICK, 1768-1810

Stag and column. Rev. Arms.

3008.   1 Ducat 1768, 70, 88, 93, 96 ....* ... 1500.00
3009.   ½ Ducat 1768. From the ducat die 1600.00
3010.   ½ Ducat 1768 (very rare), 70.................... 1200.00

CHARLES LOUIS, 1796-1810
Bust. Rev. Arms.

3011.   1 Ducat 1796 .... 1500.00

B. The Wernigerode Line

LOUIS GEORGE, DIED 1618
Arms. Rev. Stag and column. On the Reformation.

3012.   1 Goldgulden 1617................................ 2000.00

HENRY ERNEST, 1638-1672
Stag. Rev. Arms.

3013.   1 Ducat 1661 .... 2000.00

ERNEST, DIED 1710
Bust. Rev. Legend. On his death.

3014.   1 Ducat 1710 .... 1850.00

FREDERICK CHARLES, 1710-1767
Head. Rev. Stag and column.

3015.   1 Ducat 1719 .... 2000.00

CHRISTIAN ERNEST, 1710-1771
Stag. Rev. Arms.

3016.   1 Ducat 1742, 59 .... 1500.00

Bust. Rev. Stag.

3017.   1 Ducat 1768..................................... 1500.00

Bust. Rev. Arms.

3018.   1 Ducat 1730..................................... 1500.00

HENRY ERNEST II, 1771-1778
Head. Rev. Stag.

3019.   1 Ducat 1778..................................... 2500.00

CHRISTIAN FREDERICK, 1778-1824
Stag. Rev. Value on tablet.

3020.   1 Ducat 1784, 95 .... 2500.00

Stag. Rev. Value and date in wreath. On the golden wedding.

3021.   1 Ducat 1818..................................... 1800.00

HENRY XII, 1824-1854
Bust. Rev. Stag and value.

3022.   1 Ducat 1824..................................... 1800.00

STRALSUND

City emblem. Rev. Orb. Ferdinand II.
3023. 1 Goldgulden 1628-31 . . . . 1200.00

City emblem. Rev. Double eagle. Ferdinand II.
3024. 1 Ducat 1632, 33, 35, ND 1200.00

City emblem. Rev. Double eagle. Ferdinand III.
3025. 1 Ducat ND, 1638, 40, 41, 44, 55 . . . . 1200.00

City emblem. Rev. Double eagle. Leopold I.
3026. 1 Ducat 1658, 62, 64, 66, 71, 77, 81 . . . . 2500.00

SUEBIAN LEAGUE

Arms. Rev. Two shields.
3027. 1 Ducat 1737 . . . . 3000.00

TEUTONIC ORDER

Grand Masters of —

A. Coinage in Prussia

HENRY VON PLAUEN, 1410-1413
Arms on cross. Rev. Madonna.
3028. 1 Ducat ND 6000.00

Grand Master standing. Rev. Madonna standing.
3029. 1 Ducat ND 6000.00

ALBERT OF BRANDENBURG, 1511-1525
Arms on cross. Rev. Madonna with shield.
3030. 2 Goldgulden 1521 . . . . 8000.00

Arms on cross. Rev. Madonna over shield.
3031. 1 Goldgulden ND 5500.00

B. Coinage in Mergentheim

WALTER VON CRONBERG, 1526-1543
Three shields. Rev. Madonna.
3032. 1 Goldgulden 1531 . . . . 6000.00

HENRY VON BOBENHAUSEN, 1572-1590
Three shields. Rev. Madonna.
3033. 1 Ducat 1575 . . . . 6000.00

MAXIMILIAN OF AUSTRIA, 1590-1618
Grand Master standing. Rev. Arms.
3034. 2 Ducats ND 3500.00
3035. 1 Ducat 1597, ND 1500.00

CHARLES OF AUSTRIA, 1619-1624
Head. Rev. Arms between arms of Brixen and Breslau.
3036. 1 Ducat ND 1800.00

Armored bust. Rev. Arms.
3037. 2 Ducats ND 2000.00

JOHN EUSTACE VON WESTERNACH, 1624-1627
Three shields. Rev. Double eagle.
3038. 1 Ducat 1626 . . . . 2000.00

JOHN CASPER I VON STADION, 1627-1641
Madonna. Rev. Arms.
3039. 1 Ducat ND . . . . Rare

JOHN CASPER II VON AMPRINGEN, 1664-1684
Armored bust. Rev. Madonna.
3040. 1 Ducat 1673 . . . . 2000.00

Arms. Rev. Madonna.
3041. 2 Ducats 1666 . . . . 3500.00
3042. 1 Ducat 1666 . . . . 1500.00

FRANCIS LOUIS OF THE PALATINATE-NEUBURG, 1694-1732
Bust. Rev. Arms.
3043. 1 Ducat 1696 . . . . 1800.00

Armored bust. Rev. Five shields.
3044. 1 Ducat 1699, 1701 . . . . 1800.00

CHARLES ALEXANDER OF LORRAINE, 1761-1780
Bust. Rev. Arms.
3045. 1 Ducat 1765 . . . . 2000.00

THURN AND TAXIS

Princes —

ANSELM FRANCIS, 1714-1739
Bust. Rev. Arms and lions.
3046. 1 Ducat 1734 . . . . 3000.00

TRIER (TREVES)

Archbishops of —

BOEMUND, 1354-1362

Lily. Rev. St. John.
3047. 1 Goldgulden ND 1250.00

CONRAD, 1362-1388
A. Coinage of the Coblenz Mint.
Lily. Rev. St. John standing.
3048. 1 Goldgulden ND 800.00

Arms in octofoil. Rev. St. John standing.
3049. 1 Goldgulden ND 800.00

Arms in trefoil. Rev. St. John standing.
3050. 1 Goldgulden ND 800.00

St. Peter on throne. Rev. Arms in octofoil.
3051. 1 Goldgulden ND 800.00

St. Peter on throne over shield of Minzenberg. Rev. Arms in trefoil.
3052. 1 Goldgulden ND 700.00

St. Peter on throne over shields of Minzenberg and Saarwerden. Rev. Arms in trefoil.
3053. 1 Goldgulden ND 850.00
3054. 1 Goldgulden ND. Arms in sexfoil 550.00

St. Peter on throne over shields of Minzenberg. Rev. Arms in sexfoil.
3055.   1 Goldgulden ND................................. 550.00

St. Peter on throne over shield of Minzenberg. Rev. Two shields in sexfoil.
3056.   1 Goldgulden ND................................. 500.00

St. Peter on throne over shields of Trier and Minzenberg. Rev. Arms in sexfoil.
3057.   1 Goldgulden ND................................. 550.00

St. John standing. Rev. Arms and three shields in trefoil.
3058.   1 Goldgulden ND................................. 600.00

B. Coinage of the Wesel Mint.
St. Peter standing under architecture. Rev. Arms in trefoil.
3059.   1 Goldgulden ND................................. 600.00

St. John standing. Rev. Arms and three shields in trefoil.
3060.   1 Goldgulden ND................................. 750.00

C. Coinage of the Trier Mint.
Arms with four shields in sexfoil. Rev. St. Peter on throne over crossed keys.
3061.   1 Goldgulden ND................................. 550.00

St. Peter on throne over crossed keys. Rev. Arms in sexfoil.
3062.   1 Goldgulden ND................................. 550.00

St. John standing. Rev. Arms and three shields in trefoil.
3063.   1 Goldgulden ND................................. 600.00

D. Coinage of the Deutz Mint.
Arms in sexfoil. Rev. Half-length bust of St. Peter under canopy over shield of Minzenberg.
3064.   1 Goldgulden ND. With title as Coadjutor of Cologne   550.00
3065.   1 Goldgulden ND. With title as Administrator.......   600.00
3066.   1 Goldgulden ND. With title as Vicarius 750.00

St. Peter standing under architecture over shield of Minzenberg. Rev. Arms in sexfoil.
3067.   1 Goldgulden ND. With title as Vicarius 600.00
3068.   1 Goldgulden ND. With title as Administrator.......   650.00

WERNER, 1388-1418
A. Coinage of the Coblenz Mint.
St. John standing. Rev. Arms and three shields in trefoil.
3069.   1 Goldgulden ND..................................   650.00
3070.   1 Goldgulden ND. Eagle under St. John 700.00

St. John standing over eagle. Rev. Arms in trefoil.
3071.   1 Goldgulden ND.................................   600.00

St. John standing over cross. Rev. Five shields in quatrefoil.
3072.   1 Goldgulden ND.................................   600.00

Half-length bust of St. Peter over shield of Minzenberg under architecture. Rev. Arms in sexfoil.
3073.   1 Goldgulden ND.................................   750.00

Half-length bust of St. Peter over shield of Minzenberg under architecture. Rev. Arms in trefoil.
3074.   1 Goldgulden ND.................................   600.00
3075.   1 Goldgulden ND. Without name of Werner.........   600.00

St. Peter standing under architecture. Rev. Arms in trefoil.
3076.   1 Goldgulden ND.................................   650.00

St. John standing. Rev. Angel over arms, two shields and ornament in trefoil.
3077.   1 Goldgulden ND.................................   550.00
3078.   1 Goldgulden ND. Without angel 550.00

B. Coinage of the Wesel Mint.
St. John standing. Rev. Arms and three shields in trefoil.
3079.   1 Goldgulden ND.................................   600.00

St. John standing. Rev. Arms in trefoil.
3080.   1 Goldgulden ND.................................   550.00

St. John standing. Rev. Five shields in quatrefoil.
3081.   1 Goldgulden ND.................................   600.00

St. Peter standing and shield of Minzenberg under architecture. Rev. Arms in trefoil.
3082.   1 Goldgulden ND.................................   600.00

Half-length bust of St. Peter over shield of Minzenberg under architecture. Rev. Arms in trefoil.
3083.   1 Goldgulden ND.................................   600.00

St. Peter standing. Rev. Arms in trefoil.
3084.   1 Goldgulden ND.................................   550.00

St. John standing. Rev. Angel over arms and two shields (and sometimes ornament) in trefoil.
3085.   1 Goldgulden ND.................................   750.00
3086.   1 Goldgulden ND. Without angel 600.00

C. Coinage of the Trier Mint.
Arms in sexfoil. Rev. St. Peter on throne over shield of Minzenberg.
3087.   1 Goldgulden ND.................................   600.00

Half-length bust of St. Peter over shield of Minzenberg under architecture. Rev. Arms in trefoil.
3088.   1 Goldgulden ND.................................   600.00

D. Coinage of the Offenbach Mint.
St. Peter standing under architecture. Rev. Arms in trefoil.
3089.   1 Goldgulden ND.................................   550.00

St. John standing. Rev. Arms, two shields and ornament in trefoil.
3090.   1 Goldgulden ND.................................   550.00

OTTO, 1418-1430
A. Coinage of the Coblenz Mint.
Half-length bust of St. Peter over shield of Ziegenhain under architecture. Rev. Arms in trefoil.
3091.   1 Goldgulden ND.................................   600.00

St. Peter standing behind shield of Ziegenhain. Rev. Arms and four shields in quatrefoil.
3092.   1 Goldgulden ND.................................   550.00

Archbishop standing. Rev. Arms in trefoil.
3093.   1 Goldgulden ND.................................   600.00

B. Coinage of the Wesel Mint.
Half-length bust of St. Peter over shield of Ziegenhain under architecture. Rev. Arms in trefoil.
3094.   1 Goldgulden ND.................................   500.00

St. Peter standing behind shield of Ziegenhain. Rev. Arms and four shields in quatrefoil.
3095.   1 Goldgulden ND.................................   500.00

C. Coinage of the Trier Mint.
St. Peter standing behind shield of Ziegenhain. Rev. Arms and four shields in quatrefoil.
3096.   1 Goldgulden ND.................................   650.00
3097.   1 Goldgulden ND. With three shields and rosette...   650.00

D. Coinage of the Offenbach Mint.
Archbishop standing. Rev. Arms in trefoil.
3098.   1 Goldgulden ND.................................   500.00

ULRIC, 1430-1436
Half-length bust of St. Peter over shield of Manderscheid. Rev. Arms in trefoil.
3099.   1 Goldgulden ND. Mint: Coblenz...................   650.00

RABAN, 1436-1439
Arms on cross. Rev. Three shields.
3100. 1 Goldgulden 1436, 37, 38, ND. Mint: Coblenz 750.00

JAMES, 1439-1456
Arms on cross. Rev. Three shields.
3101. 1 Goldgulden ND. Mint: Coblenz.................. 800.00

JOHN II, 1456-1503
Arms on cross. Rev. Three shields.
3102. 1 Goldgulden ND. Mint: Coblenz.................. 750.00
3103. 1 Goldgulden 1491, 1502. Mint: Wesel 750.00

Christ on throne over shield of Baden. Rev. Cross and four shields.
3104. 1 Goldgulden ND. Mint: Coblenz.................. 700.00

Arms and three shields in trefoil. Rev. Christ on throne over arms.
3105. 1 Goldgulden 1491, 1502. Mint: Coblenz 2000.00

JAMES II, 1503-1511
Arms and three shields in trefoil. Rev. Christ on throne over arms.
3106. 1 Goldgulden 1503, 04, 05 .... 3500.00

RICHARD GREIFFENKLAU, 1511-1531
Arms and three shields in trefoil. Rev. Christ on throne over arms.
3107. 1 Goldgulden 1511.............................. 3500.00

Christ standing. Rev. Arms and three shields in trefoil.
3108. 1 Goldgulden ND............................... 3500.00

Christ on throne. Rev. Arms and three shields in trefoil.
3109. 1 Goldgulden 1518............................. 3700.00

JOHN III, 1531-1540
Arms and three shields in trefoil. Rev. Christ on throne over arms.
3110. 1 Goldgulden 1538............................ 4000.00

JOHN VI, 1556-1567
Christ on throne over arms. Rev. Arms and three shields in trefoil.
3111. 1 Goldgulden 1563, 64...................... 3500.00

JAMES III, 1567-1581
Christ on throne over arms. Rev. Arms and three shields in trefoil.
3112. 1 Goldgulden 1571........................... 4000.00

JOHN VII, 1581-1599
Christ on throne. Rev. Arms and three shields in trefoil.
3113. 1 Goldgulden 1587, 90, 93-95 .... 2500.00

LOTHAR, 1599-1623
Christ on throne over arms. Rev. Arms and three shields in trefoil.
3114. 1 Goldgulden 1601, 05, 08, 09, 13, 17-19, ND.
　　　Mint: Coblenz............................. 1500.00

Bust of St. Peter over arms. Rev. Arms and three shields in trefoil.
3115. 1 Goldgulden 1619. Mint: Coblenz 1800.00
3116. 1 Goldgulden 1662. Kipper...................... 2200.00

St. Helen standing. Rev. Five shields in quatrefoil.
3117. 1 Goldgulden 1608, 10, 11. Mint: Trier 1500.00

PHILIP CHRISTOPHER, 1623-1652
Arms. Rev. Madonna.
3118. 1 Goldgulden 1632. Philipsburg................... 5000.00

CHARLES CASPAR, 1652-1676
Facing bust. Rev. Arms.
3119. 1 Ducat 1654, 56 .... 3500.00

JOHN HUGO, 1676-1711
Bust. Rev. Arms.
3120. 2 Ducats 1703............................... 4500.00
3121. 1 Ducat 1680, 84, 91, 92, 99 .... 2500.00
3122. ½ Ducat ND.............................. 1200.00

Bust. Rev. Three shields.
3123. 1 Ducat 1690 .... 3500.00

St. Peter and value. Rev. Three shields.
3124. 1 Goldgulden 1684, 94, 1700, 01 .... 2500.00

FRANCIS LOUIS, 1716-1729
Bust. Rev. Arms.
3125. 1 Ducat 1720, 22 .... 3500.00

Bust. Rev. Lion.
3126. 1 Ducat 1721....................................... 3000.00

FRANCIS GEORGE, 1729-1756
Bust. Rev. Arms supported by lions.
3127. 2 Ducats 1735, 45, 50, 52......................... 4500.00
3128. 1 Ducat 1735, 50, 52............................. 3500.00

JOHN PHILIP, 1756-1768
Bust. Rev. Arms supported by lions.
3129. 1 Ducat 1759. With VNIONE MIRIFICA
　　　SPLENDESCO.............................. 4500.00
3130. 1 Ducat 1760, 61, 62............................. 3500.00

CLEMENT WENCESLAS, 1768-1803
Bust. Rev. Arms.
3131. 1 Ducat 1770 .... 3300.00

U L M

Arms. Rev. Book. On the Reformation.
3132. 2 Ducats 1617................................... 6000.00

Tablet. Rev. Arms.
3133. 1 Ducat 1635, 36, 38, ND 3500.00

Wreath. Rev. Arms.
3134. 2 Ducats 1639................................. 6000.00
3135. 1 Ducat 1639................................. 2500.00

Bust of Joseph I. Rev. Arms.
3136. 1 Ducat 1705 .... 3300.00

Arms. Rev. Legend. Necessity coins.
3137. 6 Goldgulden 1704. Square .... Rare
3138. 1 Goldgulden 1704.....................*...... 2500.00

Arms. Rev. Legend. On the Reformation.
3139. 1 Ducat 1717 .... 1800.00
3140. ½ Ducat 1717 .... 1200.00

Arms. Rev. Altar or Book. On the Augsburg Confession.
3141. 2 Ducats 1730. Rev. Altar...................*...... 2000.00
3142. 1 Ducat 1730. Rev. Book...................... 1500.00
3143. ½ Ducat 1730. Rev. Book...................... 1000.00

Bust of Charles VII. Rev. Arms.
3144. 1 Ducat 1742 .... 3000.00

WALDECK

Counts, and later, Princes—

CHRISTIAN AND WOLRAD IV, 1588-1640

Arms. Rev. Double Eagle.

3145.   1 Goldgulden 1615-17, 22, ND 3500.00

GEORGE FREDERICK, JOHN AND HENRY WOLRAD, 1645-1664

Arms. Rev. Palm tree.

3146.   1 Ducat 1654 .... 2500.00

CHARLES AUGUST FREDERICK, 1728-1763
Head. Rev. Arms.

3147.   1 Ducat 1731, 32, 36, 42, 50 .... 2500.00
3148.   ½ Ducat 1736 .... 1500.00
3149.   ¼ Ducat 1741, 60, 61 .... 800.00
3150.   1 Carolin 1734. Head right 3000.00
3151.   1 Carolin 1750. Head left 3000.00
3152.   2 Ducats 1750. Head left 3500.00

Bust left. Rev. Arms.

3153.   10 Ducats 1752 .... Rare
3154.   1 Ducat 1762 .... 2000.00

Bust right. Rev. Arms.

3155.   1 Ducat 1762 .... 1850.00

Head. Rev. Cross of initials.

3156.   1 Carolin 1734 .... 3000.00

Head. Rev. Arms and initials.

3157.   ½ Carolin 1734 .... 1800.00

Bust. Rev. Cross of initials.

3158.   ½ Carolin 1735 .... 3000.00
3159.   ¼ Carolin 1735 .... 1800.00

FREDERICK, 1763-1812
Head. Rev. Arms.

3160.   1 Ducat 1781 .... 3500.00

WALLMODEN-GIMBORN

Counts —

LOUIS, DIED 1811

Initials. Rev. Value.

3161.   1 Ducat 1802 .... 4000.00

WERDEN AND HELMSTAEDT

Abbots of —

HENRY IV DUECKER, 1646-1667

Arms. Rev. Value.

3162.   1 Ducat 1647 .... 3500.00

WESTPHALIA

Kings of —

JEROME NAPOLEON, 1807-1813

Arms. Rev. Value.

3163.   10 Taler 1810 .... 3750.00
3164.   5 Taler 1810 ....* 2500.00

Laureate head. Rev. Value.

3165.   10 Taler 1811-13 ....* 2500.00
3166.   5 Taler 1811, 12 .... 3000.00

Laureate head. Rev. Value in wreath.

3167.   40 Francs 1813 .... 8000.00
3167R. 40 Francs 1813, Restrike 3000.00
3168.   20 Francs 1808-11 ....* 800.00
3169.   10 Francs 1813. Without wreath ....* 900.00
3170.   5 Francs 1813. Without wreath 900.00

WIED

Counts —

FREDERICK ALEXANDER, 1737-1791

Bust. Rev. Tree and all seeing eye.

3171.   1 Ducat 1744 .... 1500.00

Bust. Rev. Peacock.

3172. 1 Goldgulden 1751................................ 1400.00

Bust. Rev. City view of Neuwied.

3173. 2 Ducats 1752...................................... 3000.00
3174. 1 Pistole 1752. Rev. Arms ....* 2000.00

WISMAR

St. Lawrence. Rev. City arms.

3175. 1 Goldgulden 1558................................ 3750.00

St. Lawrence. Rev. Double eagle. Name of Rudolph II.

3176. 1 Goldgulden 1587, 91, 97, 1604, ND............... 3000.00

St. Lawrence. Rev. Double eagle. Name of Matthias.

3177. 1 Goldgulden 1616................................ 3000.00

St. Lawrence. Rev. Double eagle. Name of Ferdinand II.

3178. 1 Goldgulden 1626, 29, 32......................... 2500.00

Arms. Rev. Double eagle. Struck under Swedish rule.

3179. 1 Ducat 1672, 76 .... 4000.00
3180. 1 Ducat 1743 ....* 2000.00

WORMS

A. City of —

Bust of Madonna over shield. Rev. Double eagle.

3181. 1 Goldgulden 1510, ND............................ 4500.00

Dragon with shield. Rev. Double eagle.

3182. 1½ Goldgulden 1571. Square 5000.00
3183. 1 Goldgulden ND (1519-56)......................... 2500.00
3184. 1 Goldgulden 1614-22......................* 1250.00
3185. 1 Ducat 1651, 55................................. 4000.00

B. Bishops of —

GEORGE, 1580-1595
St. John. Rev. Lily.

3186. 1 Goldgulden 1588-93............................. 4000.00

WURTTEMBERG

Dukes, and later, Kings of —

ULRIC, 1498-1550

Duke standing. Rev. Arms.

3187. 2 Goldgulden ND..............................* ... 6500.00
3188. 1 Goldgulden ND..............................* ... 1200.00

Bust. Rev. Arms.

3189. 2 Ducats 1513.................................... 6500.00

Bust with hat. Rev. Arms.

3190. 2 Ducats 1537.................................... 6000.00
3191. 1 Ducat 1537..................................... 4000.00

AUSTRIAN OCCUPATION, 1519-1534
Bust of Charles V. Rev. Cross and four shields.

3192. 2 Goldgulden 1520................................ 7500.00
3193. 1 Goldgulden 1520................................ 5000.00

CHRISTOPHER, 1550-1568
Arms. Rev. Eagle. Charles V.

3194. 1 Goldgulden 1554, 55............................ 5500.00

LOUIS, 1568-1593
Arms. Rev. Eagle. Maximilian II.

3195. 2 Goldgulden 1575. Square 6500.00
3196. 1 Goldgulden 1575................................ 4000.00

Armored bust. Rev. Arms. Rudolph II.

3197. 2 Goldgulden 1592. Bust right 6000.00
3198. 1 Goldgulden 1592. Bust right 5000.00
3199. 1 Goldgulden 1593. Bust left 5000.00

FREDERICK, 1593-1608
Half-length armored bust. Rev. Arms.

3200. 2 Ducats 1597.................................... 7500.00
3201. 1 Ducat 1603, 05................................. 4000.00

Armored bust. Rev. Arms on cross.

3202. 2 Goldgulden 1606................................ 8500.00
3203. 1 Goldgulden 1597, 1606.......................... 6000.00

JOHN FREDERICK, 1608-1628
Half-length bust. Rev. Arms under eagle.

3204. 2 Ducats 1609, 15................................ 6000.00

Half-length bust. Rev. Arms on cross.

3205. 1 Goldgulden 1609................................ 4000.00

Bust. Rev. Four shields around orb.

3206. 1 Goldgulden 1614, 20, 21 .... 4000.00

Half-length figure. Rev. Arms under eagle.

3207. 2½ Ducats 1621 .... 7500.00

Half-length figure. Rev. Arms.

3208. 1 Ducat 1621 .... 3500.00

Duke on horse. Rev. Three wreaths.

3209. 2 Ducats 1623, 24, 27............................ 6000.00

EBERHARD III, 1628-1674

Armored facing bust. Rev. Arms.

3210.	2 Ducats 1640, 44, 48, 51	....	5000.00

Bust right. Rev. Arms.

3211.	1¼ Ducats 1631. Square	....	6000.00
3212.	1 Ducat 1639, 44, 51, 59, 68, 69	....	4000.00
3213.	½ Ducat 1659	....	2500.00

Armored facing bust. Rev. Palm tree. On the peace.

3214.	2 Ducats 1650	....	8000.00

Three shields. Rev. Flag.

3215.	½ Ducat ND	....	1500.00

FREDERICK CHARLES, 1677-1693
Armored bust. Rev. Arms.

3216.	2 Ducats 1681, 83	....	4500.00
3217.	1 Ducat 1681, 88	....	4000.00

Head. Rev. Arms.

3218.	½ Ducat 1688	....	1800.00

EBERHARD LOUIS, 1693-1733
Bust. Rev. Arms.

3219.	4 Ducats 1699, 1707	....	Rare
3220.	3 Ducats 1699		Rare

Bust. Rev. Crowned arms.

3221.	2 Ducats 1694, 1706	....	4500.00
3222.	1 Ducat 1694-97	....	2500.00
3223.	½ Ducat ND	....	1800.00

Bust. Rev. Helmeted arms.

3224.	2 Ducats 1699, 1707, ND	..........*	4500.00
3225.	1 Ducat 1732, 33, ND	....	2000.00

Duke on horse. Rev. Arms.

3226.	1 Goldgulden ND	....	2000.00

Bust. Rev. Shield in chain of Order.

3227.	1 Carolin 1731, 32, 33	....	1850.00
3228.	½ Carolin 1731, 32, 33	....	850.00
3229.	¼ Carolin 1731, 32, 33	....	750.00

CHARLES ALEXANDER, 1733-1737
Bust. Rev. Five shields.

3230.	1 Ducat 1736	....	3000.00

Bust. Rev. Arms. Homage issue.

3231.	2 Ducats 1733	....	4500.00

Bust. Rev. Arms.

3232.	1 Carolin 1734, 35, 36	..............*	1400.00
3233.	½ Carolin 1734, 35, 36	....	800.00
3234.	¼ Carolin 1734, 35, 36	....	700.00
3235.	1 Ducat 1733. Helmeted arms	....	2200.00
3236.	1 Ducat 1735, ND	....	2000.00
3237.	½ Ducat ND	....	1500.00

CHARLES RUDOLPH, 1737-1738
Bust. Rev. Arms.

3238.	1 Ducat 1737	....	2500.00
3239.	½ Ducat ND	....	2000.00
3240.	¼ Ducat ND	....	1500.00

CHARLES FREDERICK, 1738-1744

Bust. Rev. Arms.

3241.	1 Ducat 1739, 42	...................*	2500.00
3242.	½ Ducat ND	....	1500.00
3243.	¼ Ducat ND	....	1000.00

CHARLES EUGENE, 1744-1793
Bust. Rev. Crowned arms.

3244.	1 Ducat 1744, 47-50, 62, 90, 91, ND	....	2500.00

Bust. Rev. Helmeted arms.

3245.	1 Ducat 1746	....	2500.00

FC in shield. Rev. Altar. On his wedding.

3246.	1 Ducat 1749	....	2000.00

LOUIS EUGENE, 1793-1795
Bust. Rev. Arms.

3247.	1 Ducat 1794	....	3000.00

FREDERICK, 1795-1816
Bust. Rev. Legend. Struck in the presence of the king.

3248.	1 Ducat 1803, 04	....	5000.00

Draped bust. Rev. Arms.

3249.	1 Ducat 1804. Bust right	....	2500.00
3250.	1 Ducat 1808. Bust left	....	2200.00

Head. Rev. Arms.

3251.	1 Frederick d'or 1810	....	3000.00
3252.	1 Ducat 1813	...............*	2500.00

WILLIAM, 1816-1864

Head. Rev. Large supported arms without legend.

3253.   1 Ducat 1818 .... 2000.00

Head. Rev. Small supported arms with legend.

3254.   1 Ducat 1840-48 .... 800.00

Head. Rev. Arms.

3255.   10 Gulden 1824, 25 .... 2850.00
3256.   5 Gulden 1824, 25, 35, 36, 39 .... 1500.00

Head. Rev. Date and four line legend. On the King's visit to the mint.

3257.   10 Gulden 1825 .... 8000.00

Head. Rev. Seated female and children. On the 25th year of reign.

3258.   4 Ducats 1841 .... 1850.00

Head. Rev. The Mint in Stuttgart. On the King's visit.

3259.   4 Ducats 1844. The value is on the edge 6500.00

WURZBURG

A. Bishops of —

GERHARD, 1372-1400
Arms. Rev. St. John standing.

3260.   1 Goldgulden ND 3500.00

LAWRENCE, 1495-1519

St. Kilian. Rev. Arms.

3261.   2 Goldgulden 1506 .... 5500.00
3262.   1 Goldgulden 1506, 07, 08, 13, ND .... * 2000.00

MELCHIOR ZOBEL, 1544-1558
Three shields. Rev. Eagle.

3263.   2 Goldgulden 1553 .... 5000.00
3264.   1 Goldgulden 1553 .... 3000.00

FREDERICK, 1558-1573
Three shields. Rev. Eagle.

3265.   1 Goldgulden 1572 .... 6500.00

JULIUS ECHTER, 1573-1617

St. Kilian over arms. Rev. Madonna over eagle.

3266.   4 Goldgulden ND .... Rare
3267.   2 Ducats ND 3300.00
3268.   1 Ducat ND .... * 2000.00

Three shields. Rev. Legend. Homage issue.

3269.   1 Goldgulden 1583 .... 1850.00

St. Kilian standing. Rev. Date over arms. Name of Rudolph II.

3270.   2 Goldgulden 1575, 78, 79 .... 3000.00
3271.   1 Goldgulden 1575 .... 1600.00

St. Kilian standing. Rev. Arms with 3 helmets. Name of Rudolph II.

3272.   2 Goldgulden 1581, 83, 85, 89, 90, 1608, 11, 13, ND. 3000.00
3273.   1 Goldgulden 1581, 83, 86, 89, 90, 92, 94,
          1601, 08, 11 .... * 1800.00
3274.   1 Goldgulden 1613, 15. Name of Matthias II 1800.00

Arms with 3 helmets. Rev. Legend. On his death.

3275.   2 Goldgulden 1617 .... 3300.00
3276.   1 Goldgulden 1617 .... 1600.00

JOHN GODFREY, 1617-1622

Arms. Rev. Legend around shield.

3277.	2 Goldgulden ND. Square. AUGUSTUM PATRIAE etc. ....*	3500.00
3278.	1 Goldgulden ND. AUGUSTUM PATRIAE etc.	2000.00
3279.	1 Goldgulden ND. ORE ET CORDE, etc.	2000.00
3280.	1 Goldgulden 1617, 18, 19	1800.00

Arms with 4 helmets. Rev. Legend. On his death.

3281.	1 Goldgulden 1622................................	2000.00

PHILIP ADOLPH, 1623-1631

St. Kilian. Rev. Arms.

3282.	2 Goldgulden ND...........................	3500.00
3283.	1 Goldgulden 1626, ND ....*	1850.00

Arms. Rev. Legend. On his death.

3284.	1 Goldgulden 1631................................	2200.00

FRANCIS, 1631-1642
Arms. Rev. Wreath.

3285.	1 Goldgulden 1631, ND	2500.00

Arms. Rev. Legend. On his death.

3286.	1 Ducat 1642	2200.00

JOHN PHILIP I, 1642-1673
Bust right over arms. Rev. Three mountain peaks.

3287.	2 Ducats ND	3500.00
3288.	1 Ducat ND....................................	1550.00

Facing bust over arms. Rev. Three mountain peaks.

3289.	2 Ducats ND	6500.00
3290.	1½ Ducats ND ....*	2800.00
3291.	1 Ducat ND....................................	1600.00

Bust right over arms. Rev. Legend over shield.

3292.	1 Goldgulden ND................................	2000.00

Facing bust over arms. Rev. Legend over shield.

3293.	1 Goldgulden ND................................	1500.00

Arms. Rev. Legend over shield.

3294.	1 Goldgulden ND................................	2000.00

JOHN HARTMANN, 1673-1675
Bust over arms. Rev. Legend over shield.

3295.	1 Goldgulden ND................................	2200.00

PETER PHILIP, 1675-1683
Bust. Rev. Legend over shield.

3296.	1 Goldgulden ND................................	1850.00

CONRAD WILLIAM, 1683-1684
Bust. Rev. Arms.

3297.	1 Ducat ND....................................	2000.00

JOHN GODFREY II, 1684-1689
Facing bust. Rev. Legend over shield.

3298.	1 Goldgulden ND................................	2000.00

Arms. Rev. Flag in cartouche.

3299.	1 Goldgulden ND................................	2000.00

JOHN PHILIP II, 1699-1719
Bust. Rev. Three Saints.

3300.	1 Ducat 1702	1800.00

Bust. Rev. Arms with three helmets.

3301.	2 Ducats 1705...................................	3300.00
3302.	1 Ducat 1700	1800.00

Bust. Rev. Coat of arms.

3303.	2 Ducats 1705...................................	3300.00

Bust. Rev. Tree.

3304.	1 Ducat 1703	2000.00

Bust. Rev. Madonna over arms.

3305.	3 Ducats 1707	6000.00
3306.	2 Ducats 1707 ....*......	3800.00

Arms. Rev. Flag in shield.

3307.	1 Goldgulden ND..............................	1400.00

Arms supported by lions. Rev. Madonna over shield.

3308.	1 Goldgulden ND..............................	1400.00

JOHN PHILIP FRANCIS, 1719-1724
Bust. Rev. Lion with sword and scales before city view.

3309.	2 Ducats ND	6000.00
3310.	2 Ducats ND. Without the city view	7500.00

Bust. Rev. Arms.

3311.	2 Ducats ND	5500.00
3312.	2 Ducats 1719. On his election	5500.00

Bust. Rev. Arms in cartouche.

3313.	1 Ducat ND...................................	1500.00

Bust. Rev. Altar with Wurzburg shield.

3314.	1 Goldgulden ND..............................	1500.00
3315.	1 Goldgulden ND. With "QUIA TU ES" etc..........	1400.00

CHRISTOPHER FRANCIS, 1724-1729
Arms. Rev. St. Christopher. With D.G.EL.EP.

3316.	2 Ducats ND	1850.00
3317.	1 Ducat ND...................................	1250.00

Arms. Rev. Ship entering harbor. With D.G.EL.EP.

3318.	1 Ducat ND...................................	1600.00

Bust. Rev. St. Christopher. With D.G.EP.

3319.	2 Ducats ND	2000.00

Arms. Rev. St. Christopher. With D.G.EP.

3320.	1 Ducat ND...................................	800.00

Arms. Rev. Initials on mantle.

3321.	1 Ducat 1725, 27, 28.........................	1500.00

Arms. Rev. Sword and stola.

3322.	½ Ducat ND...................................	600.00

Arms. Rev. Mountain. "NON FULMEN" etc.

3323.	1 Goldgulden ND..............................	1500.00

Arms. Rev. Mountain and city view. "FELIX A DEO" etc.

3324.	1 Goldgulden 1724. With flag-shield	1500.00
3325.	1 Goldgulden 1724. With flag and sceptre crossed..	1500.00

FREDERICK CHARLES, 1729-1746

Bust. Rev. Arms.

3326.	10	Gulden or 1 Carolin 1735, 36 ....*......	3500.00
3327.	5	Gulden or ½ Carolin 1735...................	2500.00
3328.	2½	Gulden or ¼ Carolin 1735, 36	1500.00

Bust. Rev. Initials on mantle.

3329.	10	Gulden or 1 Carolin 1735, 36	3500.00

3330.	5	Gulden or ½ Carolin 1735....................	2500.00
3331.	2½	Gulden or ¼ Carolin 1736....................	1500.00

Bust. Rev. Arms supported by lions.

3332.	2 Ducats 1729, 30, 31..........................	3000.00

Bust. Rev. Arms.

3333.	1 Ducat 1731, 32, 33..........................	1800.00

Arms supported by lions. Rev. Initials on mantle.

3334.	1 Ducat 1729, 30	1250.00

Arms. Rev. Franconia standing and lion.

3335.	2 Goldgulden 1729............................	3000.00
3336.	1 Goldgulden 1729............................	1500.00

Bust. Rev. Flag shield.

3337.	1 Goldgulden ND..............................	1850.00
3338.	1 Goldgulden ND. Shield with flowers ......*......	1850.00

Arms. Rev. Initials on mantle.

3339.	½ Ducat 1729	1100.00

ANSELM FRANCIS, 1746-1749
Arms. Rev. Hands over city shield.

3340.	1 Goldgulden ND..............................	1500.00

Angel and three lambs. Rev. Legend.

3341.	1 Ducat 1747. On his consecration	1850.00

CHARLES PHILIP, 1749-1754
Bust over arms. Rev. Arms with three helmets.

3342.	1 Goldgulden ND................................	2000.00

Arms with three helmets. Rev. Griffin.

3343.	1 Goldgulden ND................................	2000.00

ADAM FREDERICK, 1755-1779
Bust. Rev. Arms and legend.

3344.	1 Goldgulden 1755..............................	1500.00

Bust. Rev. Arms without legend.

3345.	1 Ducat 1755-70	1400.00

Bust in square. Rev. Arms in square.

3346.	1 Ducat 1772	1400.00

Bust in square. Rev. Madonna in square.
3347.   1 Ducat 1773-79 .... 1250.00

Bust and arms. Rev. Palm tree and shield.
3348.   1 Goldgulden 1773, 74, 77, 78 .... 1500.00

Fame over arms. Rev. Three females.
3349.   1 Goldgulden ND (1755). Homage issue............ 2000.00

Bust over arms. Rev. Franconia standing and dove. On the Peace of Hubertusburg.
3350.   1 Goldgulden 1764............................. 1500.00

FRANCIS LOUIS, 1779-1795

Bust over arms. Rev. Palm tree and shield.
3351.   1 Goldgulden 1779................................. 1400.00

Bust over arms. Rev. Arms.
3352.   1 Goldgulden 1782, 86, 91, 94 .... 1600.00

Bust. Rev. Three Saints over arms.
3353.   1 Ducat 1785 .... 1500.00

Bust. Rev. St. Kilian standing and value.
3354.   2 Goldgulden 1786.........................*...... 1850.00
3355.   1 Goldgulden 1786............................... 1300.00

Bust. Rev. St. Burkhard standing and value.
3356.   1 Goldgulden 1790............................ 1500.00

GEORGE CHARLES, 1795-1803
Bust. Rev. Arms and value.
3357.   1 Carolin 1795................................... 2500.00

Arms. Rev. Palm tree and shield.
3358.   1 Goldgulden 1795................................. 1500.00

Bust. Rev. City view and value.
3359.   1 Goldgulden 1798............................. 1850.00

FERDINAND, GRAND DUKE, 1806-1814

Bust. Rev. Palm tree and shield.
3360.   1 Goldgulden 1807, 09............................ 2000.00

Head. Rev. Shield and value.
3361.   1 Goldgulden 1812, 13............................. 1850.00

Head. Rev. Altar and shield.
3362.   1 Goldgulden 1814................................. 2000.00

B. Swedish Rulers of —

Bust of Gustav II Adolphe. Rev. Arms.
3363.   1 Ducat 1631, 32 .... 1200.00

GREAT BRITAIN

The English gold Pound enjoyed enormous popularity and prestige during its years of issue and was known and accepted throughout the world. In order to identify themselves more closely with this unit of currency, many other countries struck their own local coins in the same weight and fineness as the Pound. Such coins can be noted in the appendix under "The Principal Gold Coins of the World."

Additional English type gold coins will be found among the various parts of the British Empire, namely, Canada, Australia, India, and South Africa. These coins bear the distinguishing mint mark of the issuing country. The coinage of the London Mint is without a mint mark.

Kings of —
OFFA, KING OF MERCIA, 757-796

Arabic legend. Rev. Arabic legend and "OFFA REX." Struck in the style of the contemporary Arabian Dinars.
1.   1 Dinar ND.. Unique

Bust. Rev. Standing figure.
2.   Gold Penny ND.................................... Unique

WIGMUND, ARCHBISHOP OF YORK, 837-854

Facing bust. Rev. Cross in wreath.
3.   1 Solidus ND..................................... Unique

AETHELRED II, 979-1016

Bust in helmet. Rev. Long cross.

4. 1 Gold Penny ND.................................... Unique

EDWARD THE CONFESSOR, 1042-1066
Diademed bust. Rev. Cross.

5. 1 Gold Penny ND.................................. Unique

HENRY III, 1216-1272

Ruler on throne. Rev. Long cross.

6. 1 Gold Penny ND.................................... Rare

EDWARD III, 1327-1377

Ruler on throne. Rev. Ornamental cross.

7. 1 Florin ND.. Rare

Crowned leopard with banner. Rev. Ornamental cross.

8. ½ Florin or Leopard ND............................. Rare

Leopard on helm. Rev. Ornamental cross.

9. ¼ Florin or Helm ND............................... Rare

Ruler in ship. Rev. Ornamental cross.

10. 1 Noble ND...................................*..... 3000.00
11. ½ Noble ND 1500.00

Arms. Rev. Ornamental cross.

12. ¼ Noble ND 1000.00

RICHARD II, 1377-1399

Ruler in ship. Rev. Ornamental cross.

13. 1 Noble ND 2250.00
14. ½ Noble ND..................................*...... 1250.00

Arms. Rev. Ornamental cross.

15. ¼ Noble ND 1000.00

HENRY IV, 1399-1413

Ruler in ship. Rev. Ornamental cross. The heavy Nobles weigh 120 grains, the light Nobles 108 grains. The smaller coins are in proportion.

16. 1 Noble ND. Heavy type......................... Rare
17. 1 Noble ND. Light type....................*...... 4500.00
18. ½ Noble ND. Heavy type......................... Rare
19. ½ Noble ND. Light type......................... Rare

Arms. Rev. Ornamental cross.

20. ¼ Noble ND. Heavy type....................*..... Rare
21. ¼ Noble ND. Light type......................... 2000.00

HENRY V, 1413-1422

Ruler in ship. Rev. Ornamental cross.

22.	1 Noble ND	2000.00
23.	½ Noble ND.................................*	1250.00

Arms. Rev. Ornamental cross.

24.	¼ Noble ND	450.00

HENRY VI, 1422-1461

Ruler in ship. Rev. Ornamental cross.

25.	1 Noble ND	2250.00
26.	½ Noble ND.................................*	1500.00

Arms. Rev. Ornamental cross.

27.	¼ Noble ND	600.00

HENRY VI RESTORED, 1470-1471

St. Michael slaying dragon. Rev. Cross and arms on ship.
Restoration coinage.

28.	1 Angel ND.................................*	1500.00
29.	½ Angel (Angelet) ND	3000.00

EDWARD IV, 1461-1470 AND 1471-1483
Ruler in ship. Rev. Ornamental cross.

30.	1 Noble ND. Heavy type	Rare
31.	1 Noble ND. Light type	Unique

Ruler in ship, rose at side. Rev. Radiate rose within royal emblems.

32.	1 Rose Noble or Ryal ND...............*	2000.00
33.	½ Rose Noble or ½ Ryal ND	2500.00

Arms. Rev. Radiate rose.

34.	¼ Ryal ND	900.00

St. Michael slaying dragon. Rev. Cross and arms on ship.

35.	1 Angel ND.................................*	1500.00
36.	½ Angel (Angelet) ND	2500.00

EDWARD V, 1483

St. Michael slaying dragon. Rev. Cross and arms on ship.

37.	1 Angel ND. Mint mark boar's head........*	Rare
38.	½ Angel ND	Unique

RICHARD III, 1483-1485

St. Michael slaying dragon. Rev. Cross and arms on ship.

39.	1 Angel ND	2000.00
40.	½ Angel ND.................................*	Rare

HENRY VII, 1485-1509

Ruler on throne. Rev. Arms on large rose.

41.	2 Sovereigns ND ....*......	Rare
42.	1 Sovereign ND..............................*......	Rare

Ruler in ship. Rev. Shield on large rose.

43.	1 Ryal ND	Rare

St. Michael slaying dragon. Rev. Cross and arms on ship.

44.	1 Angel ND.................................*......	1250.00
45.	½ Angel ND..	1250.00

HENRY VIII, 1509-1547

Ruler on throne. Rev. Arms on large rose.

46.	1 Sovereign ND....................................	8500.00

Ruler on throne. Rev. Arms with supporters.

47.	1 Sovereign ND..............................*......	5000.00
48.	½ Sovereign ND.................................	1250.00

St. Michael slaying dragon. Rev. Cross and arms on ship.

49.	1 Angel ND...	1000.00
50.	½ Angel ND.................................*......	1000.00
51.	¼ Angel ND...	1000.00

St. George on horse. Rev. Cross and rose on ship.

52.	1 George Noble ND......................*......	Rare
53.	½ George Noble ND...............................	Rare

Crowned arms. Rev. Rose, initials and floriated cross.

54.	1 Crown of the Rose ND	Rare

Crown over double rose. Rev. Crowned arms.

55.	1 Crown ND ....*......	850.00
56.	½ Crown ND	850.00

EDWARD VI, 1547-1553

Ruler on throne. Rev. Arms with supporters. With name and title of Henry VIII, although the figure is that of Edward VI.

57.	½ Sovereign ND....................................	1750.00

Ruler on throne. Rev. Arms on large rose. With his own name and title.

58.　　2 Sovereigns ND ....　　Rare
59.　　1 Sovereign ND............................*......　　Rare

Ruler on throne. Rev. Arms with supporters. With his own name and title.

60.　　1 Sovereign ND................................　　5000.00

Half-length figure. Rev. Arms.

61.　　1 Sovereign ND.............................*......　　3750.00
62.　　½ Sovereign ND.................................　　3000.00
63.　　1 Crown ND....................................　　2750.00
64.　　½ Crown ND....................................　　2750.00

Crowned child bust. Rev. Arms.

65.　　½ Sovereign ND..............................*......　　2500.00
66.　　1 Crown ND....................................　　2250.00
67.　　½ Crown ND....................................　　2000.00

Child bust without crown. Rev. Arms.

68.　　½ Sovereign ND.................................　　2500.00
69.　　1 Crown ND....................................　　2250.00
70.　　½ Crown ND....................................　　2000.00

Crowned bust with King's name on each side.

71.　　½ Sovereign ND.................................　　Rare

Crown over double rose, with name of Henry VIII. Rev. Crowned arms.

72.　　1 Crown ND....................................　　1000.00
73.　　½ Crown ND....................................　　1000.00

St. Michael slaying dragon. Rev. Cross and arms on ship.

74.　　1 Angel ND.....................................　　Rare
75.　　½ Angel ND.....................................　　Unique

MARY, 1553-1554

Queen on throne. Rev. Arms on large rose.

76.　　1 Sovereign 1553, 54, ND.........................　　5500.00

Queen in ship. Rev. Radiate rose.

77.　　1 Ryal 1553, ND.................................　　Rare

St. Michael slaying dragon. Rev. Cross and arms on ship.

78.　　1 Angel ND................................*......　　1750.00
79.　　½ Angel ND.................................　　Rare

PHILIP AND MARY, 1554-1558

St. Michael slaying dragon. Rev. Cross and arms on ship.

80.　　1 Angel ND................................*......　　4750.00
81.　　½ Angel ND.....................................　　Rare

ELIZABETH I, 1558-1603

Queen on throne. Rev. Arms on large rose.

82.	1 "Fine" Sovereign ND	4750.00

Queen in ship. Rev. Radiate rose.

83.	1 Ryal ND	6500.00

St. Michael slaying dragon. Rev. Cross and arms on ship.

84.	1 Angel ND ....*	900.00
85.	½ Angel ND	800.00
86.	¼ Angel ND	700.00

Crowned bust. Rev. Crowned arms.

87.	1 Sovereign ND. Hammered coinage	2500.00
88.	½ Sovereign ND. Hammered coinage	2400.00
89.	½ Sovereign ND. Milled coinage ....*	4000.00
90.	1 Crown ND. Hammered coinage	1500.00
91.	1 Crown ND. Milled coinage	3250.00
92.	½ Crown ND. Hammered coinage ....*	1400.00
93.	½ Crown ND. Milled coinage	2750.00

JAMES I, 1603-1625

Ruler on throne. Rev. Arms on large rose.

94.	1 Rose Ryal ND	4000.00

Ruler on throne. Rev. XXX over arms.

95.	30 Shillings (Rose Ryal) ND	6000.00

Ruler in ship. Rev. Radiate rose.

96.	1 Spur Ryal ND	5750.00

Crowned bust. Rev. Crowned arms. With "Exurgat" legend.

97.	1 Sovereign ND	2750.00
98.	½ Sovereign ND ....*	Rare

Crowned bust. Rev. Crowned arms. With "Tueatur Venita Deus" legend.

99.	1 Crown ND	Rare
100.	½ Crown ND ....*	2000.00

Crowned bust. Rev. Crowned arms. With "Faciam Eos" legend.

101.	1 Unite (20 Shillings) ND	1250.00
102.	½ Unite (10 Shillings) ND	600.00
103.	1 Crown ND	450.00
104.	½ Crown ND	450.00

Laureate bust. Rev. Crowned arms.

105.	1 Laurel (Unite) ND	1000.00
106.	½ Laurel ND ....*	750.00
107.	¼ Laurel ND	600.00

St. Michael slaying dragon. Rev. Arms.

108.	¼ Angel ND	Rare

St. Michael slaying dragon. Rev. Large arms on ship.

109.	1 Angel ND ....*	1750.00
110.	½ Angel ND	Rare

St. Michael slaying dragon. Rev. Large ship with three masts.

111.	1 Angel ND	2500.00

Crowned facing lion over arms with XV. Rev. Radiate rose.

112.	15 Shillings (Spur Ryal) ND	7500.00

Crowned rose. Rev. Crowned thistle.

113.	1 Thistle Crown or 4 Shillings ND	375.00

CHARLES I, 1625-1649

St. Michael with or without X for value in field. Rev. Three masted ship.

114.	10 Shillings (1 Angel) ND	*	2500.00
115.	10 Shilling ND. Smaller size and finer style. By Nicholas Briot		Unique

Crowned bust. Rev. Scroll type legend. (The Declaration). The 20 and 10 Shilling values are indicated by Roman numerals on the Obv.

116.	3 Pounds (Triple Unite) 1642-44. Oxford Mint*	9000.00
117.	3 Pounds 1642. Shrewsbury Mint	Rare
118.	20 Shillings (1 Unite) 1642-46. Oxford Mint	3000.00
119.	20 Shillings 1645. Bristol Mint	Rare
120.	10 Shillings (½ Unite) 1642-44. Oxford Mint	3000.00
121.	10 Shillings 1645. Bristol Mint	Rare

Crowned bust and Roman numerals for value. Rev. Arms.

122.	20 Shillings ND. Tower Mint	1500.00
123.	20 Shillings ND. Briot's coinage	Rare
124.	20 Shillings ND. Chester Mint	Unique
125.	20 Shillings ND. Truro Mint	Rare
126.	20 Shillings ND. Weymouth Mint	Rare
127.	20 Shillings ND. Salisbury Mint	Unique
128.	10 Shillings ND. Tower Mint ....*	1000.00
129.	10 Shillings ND. Tower Mint. Briot's Coinage	3000.00
130.	5 Shillings ND. Tower Mint	500.00
131.	5 Shillings ND. Tower Mint. Briot's coinage*	Rare

CIVIL WAR
Siege of Colchester

Castle, date and value. Rev. Blank.

132.	10 Shillings 1648	Unique

SIEGE OF PONTEFRACT

Crown over CR. Rev. Castle.

133.   1 Unite 1648 .... Rare

Crown over legend. Rev. Castle in circle, with name of Charles II.

134.   1 Unite 1648 .... Rare

THE COMMONWEALTH OF ENGLAND, 1649-1660

Shield of St. George. Rev. Shields of St. George and Ireland. With Roman numerals for value.

135.	20 Shillings 1649-60	2000.00
136.	10 Shillings 1649-60 .... *	2000.00
137.	5 Shillings 1649-60	1250.00

OLIVER CROMWELL, 1656-1660

Laureate head. Rev. Arms. The half broad is not now believed to be contemporary.

138.	50 Shillings 1656	Rare
139.	1 Broad 1656	4000.00
140.	½ Broad 1656 .... *	5000.00

CHARLES II, 1660-1685

Laureate head with or without value as indicated. Rev. Arms.

141.	20 Shillings ND. Without value .... *	2500.00
142.	20 Shillings ND. With value	2250.00
143.	10 Shillings ND. Without value	2000.00
144.	10 Shillings ND. With value .... *	1500.00
145.	5 Shillings ND. Without value	2000.00
146.	5 Shillings ND. With value	1750.00

Laureate head. Rev. Cross of four shields. With or without the various symbols below the head as indicated.

5 Guineas

147.	1668-84. No symbol	4500.00
148.	1668, 69, 75. Elephant	4000.00
149.	1675-84. Elephant and castle	4000.00

2 Guineas

150.	1664-84. No symbol	1750.00
151.	1664, 78. Elephant	1750.00
152.	1676-84. Elephant and castle	2000.00

1 Guinea

153.	1663-84. No symbol	1000.00
154.	1663-78. Elephant .... * ...	1500.00
155.	1674-84. Elephant and castle	1000.00

½ Guinea

156.	1669-84. No symbol	650.00
157.	1676-84. Elephant and castle	1250.00

JAMES II, 1685-1688

Laureate head. Rev. Cross of four shields. With or without the various symbols below the head as indicated.

5 Guineas

158.	1686, 87, 88. No symbol .... *	4000.00
159.	1687, 88. Elephant and castle	4500.00

2 Guineas

160.	1687, 88. No symbol	2250.00

1 Guinea

161.	1685-88. No symbol	650.00
162.	1685-88. Elephant and castle	850.00

½ Guinea

163.	1686, 87, 88. No symbol	700.00
164.	1686. Elephant and castle	1750.00

WILLIAM AND MARY, 1688-1694

Conjoined head. Rev. Crowned arms. With or without the various symbols below the heads as indicated.

5 Guineas

165.	1691-94. No symbol	4500.00
166.	1691-94. Elephant and castle	5500.00

2 Guineas

167. 1693, 94. No symbol 2250.00
168. 1691, 93, 94. Elephant and castle 2750.00

1 Guinea

169. 1689-94. No symbol 800.00
170. 1692. Elephant 1250.00
171. 1689-94. Elephant and castle 950.00

½ Guinea

172. 1689-94. No symbol 650.00
173. 1692. Elephant .... Rare
174. 1691, 92. Elephant and castle .... * 750.00

WILLIAM III, 1694-1702

Laureate head. Rev. Cross of four shields. With or without the various symbols below the head as indicated.

5 Guineas

175. 1699, 1700, 01. No symbol 4500.00
176. 1699. Elephant and castle............................ 5500.00

2 Guineas

177. 1701. No symbol .... * 2500.00

1 Guinea

178. 1695-1701. No symbol................................. 750.00
179. 1695-1701. Elephant and castle........................ 1500.00

½ Guinea

180. 1695-1701. No symbol................................. 750.00
181. 1695, 96, 98. Elephant and castle 1250.00

ANNE, 1702-1714

Draped bust. Rev. Cross of four shields. With or without the various symbols below the bust as indicated.

5 Guineas

182. 1705-14. No symbol 4500.00
183. 1703. Vigo .... Rare

2 Guineas

184. 1709-14. No symbol 2250.00

1 Guinea

185. 1702-14. No symbol 750.00
186. 1703. Vigo......................................* 7500.00
187. 1707, 08, 09. Elephant and castle 1500.00

½ Guinea

188. 1702-14. No symbol 575.00
189. 1703. Vigo 5000.00

GEORGE I, 1714-1727

Laureate head. Rev. Cross of four shields. With or without the symbol below the head as indicated.

5 Guineas

190. 1716, 17, 20, 26. No symbol.......................... 7500.00

2 Guineas

191. 1717, 20, 26. No symbol.............................. 2750.00

1 Guinea

192. 1714-27. No symbol 650.00
193. 1721, 22, 26. Elephant and castle..............* 2250.00

½ Guinea

194. 1715-27. No symbol 400.00
195. 1721. Elephant and castle............................ Rare

¼ Guinea

196. 1718. No symbol 225.00

GEORGE II, 1727-1760

Laureate head. Rev. Crowned arms. With or without "E.I.C." or "Lima" below the head as indicated.

5 Guineas

197. 1729-41. Young head, plain.......................... 3500.00
198. 1729. Young head, E.I.C. 3500.00
199. 1748, 53. Old head, plain............................ 3500.00
200. 1746. Old head, Lima................................ 4000.00

2 Guineas

201. 1734-39. Yound head, plain.......................... 1250.00
202. 1739, 40. Middle aged head, plain..................... 1250.00
203. 1748, 53. Old head, plain............................ 1500.00

1 Guinea

204. 1727-38. Young head, plain...................* 625.00
205. 1729, 31, 32. Young head, E.I.C....................... 1000.00
206. 1739-46. Middle aged head, plain.................... 750.00
207. 1739. Middle aged head, E.I.C. ....* 1250.00
208. 1745. Middle aged head, Lima....................... 1750.00
209. 1747-60. Old head, plain.....................* 625.00

½ Guinea

210. 1728-39. Young head, plain.......................... 450.00
211. 1729-39. Young head, E.I.C.......................... 1000.00
212. 1740-46. Middle aged head, plain................... 425.00
213. 1745. Middle aged head, Lima....................... 1500.00
214. 1747-60. Old head, plain............................ 400.00

GEORGE III, 1760-1820

Laureate head. Rev. Arms.

5 Guineas

215. 1770, 73, 77. Patterns only .... Rare

2 Guineas

216. 1768, 73, 77. Patterns only .... Rare

1 Guinea

217. 1761. 1st young head ....* 2000.00
218. 1763, 64. 2nd young head. Longer, curlier hair 1500.00
219. 1765-73. 3rd young head. Laurel divides legend 500.00
220. 1774-79, 81-86. 4th head. Larger head; laurel * ......
   divides legend 300.00

Laureate head. Rev. Spade shaped shield.
221. 1787-99. 5th head, smaller. "Spade Guinea" 400.00

Laureate head. Rev. Arms within the Order of the Garter.
222. 1813. 6th head, smaller. "Military Guinea".............. 1250.00

Laureate head. Rev. Arms.

½ Guinea

223. 1762, 63. 1st young head............................. 750.00
224. 1764-66, 68, 69, 72-75. 2nd young head. Laurel
   divides legend ....* 400.00
225. 1774, 75. 3rd head. Laurel in legend.................... 550.00
226. 1775-79, 81, 84-86. 4th head. Hair on both shoulders ... 250.00
227. 1787-98, 1800. 5th head. "Spade" shield rev. 225.00
228. 1801-03. 6th type, long hair. "Garter" rev. 225.00
229. 1804, 06, 08-11, 13. 7th type, short hair. "Garter" rev. .. 225.00

Laureate head. Rev. Crown.

⅓ Guinea

230. 1797-1800. 1st head. Date in legend ....* 150.00
231. 1801-03. 1st head. Date below crown................... 150.00
232. 1804, 06, 08-11, 13. 2nd head, short hair. Date
   below crown.............................* 150.00

¼ Guinea

233. 1762. Type similar to No. 224 .... 150.00

Laureate head. Rev. St. George slaying dragon.
234. 5 Pounds 1820. Plain or lettered edge. Patterns only... 50000.00
235. 2 Pounds 1820. Plain or lettered edge. Patterns only... 15000.00
236. 1 Sovereign 1817-20. (1819 rare)................* 600.00

Laureate head. Rev. Arms.
237. ½ Sovereign 1817, 18, 20..................... 400.00

GEORGE IV, 1820-1830

Bare head. Rev. Arms.
238. 5 Pounds 1826. Proofs only...................... 15000.00
239. 2 Pounds 1825, 26. Proofs only ....* 6500.00

Bare head. Rev. St. George slaying dragon.
240. 2 Pounds 1823..................................... 2000.00

Laureate head. Rev. St. George slaying dragon.
241. 1 Sovereign 1821-25 .... 600.00

Bare head. Rev. Arms.
242. 1 Sovereign 1825-30 .... 600.00

Laureate head. Rev. Arms.

243.	½ Sovereign 1821. Ornately garnished shield .*.....	850.00
244.	½ Sovereign 1823-25. Plain shield ....*......	450.00
245.	½ Sovereign 1826-28. Bare head. Type similar to No. 242	450.00

WILLIAM IV, 1830-1837

Head. Rev. Arms.

246.	5 Pounds 1831. Proofs only.......................	Rare
247.	2 Pounds 1831. Proofs only.................*......	9250.00
248.	1 Sovereign 1831-33, 35-37.........................	700.00
249.	½ Sovereign 1831, 34. Small size (1831-Proof only) .	675.00
250.	½ Sovereign 1835-37. Large size....................	625.00

VICTORIA, 1837-1901

Young head. Rev. Una and the lion.

| 251. | 5 Pounds 1839. Plain and lettered edge. Proofs only | 25000.00 |

Young head. Rev. Arms.

| 252. | 1 Sovereign 1838, 39, 41-66, 68-74 .... | 275.00 |

Young head. Rev. St. George slaying dragon.

| 253. | 1 Sovereign 1871-74, 76, 78-80, 84, 85.............. | 225.00 |

Young head. Rev. Arms.

| 254. | ½ Sovereign 1838, 39, 41-67, 69-80, 83-85 .... | 225.00 |

Jubilee bust. Rev. St. George slaying dragon.

255.	5 Pounds 1887.....................................	1750.00
256.	2 Pounds 1887.....................................	850.00
257.	1 Sovereign 1887-92 ....*......	200.00(B)
258.	½ Sovereign 1887-93. Rev. Arms....................	200.00

Old veiled bust. Rev. St. George slaying dragon.

259.	5 Pounds 1893.............................*......	1850.00
260.	2 Pounds 1893.....................................	950.00
261.	1 Sovereign 1893-96, 98-1901.....................	200.00(B)
262.	½ Sovereign 1893-1901	200.00

EDWARD VII, 1901-1910

Head. Rev. St. George slaying dragon.

263.	5 Pounds 1902....................................	2250.00
264.	2 Pounds 1902....................................	1000.00
265.	1 Sovereign 1902-10 ....*.....	200.00(B)
266.	½ Sovereign 1902-10	200.00

GEORGE V, 1910-1936

Head. Rev. St. George slaying dragon.

267.	5 Pounds 1911. Proofs only........................	4000.00
268.	2 Pounds 1911. Proofs only........................	2000.00
269.	1 Sovereign 1911-17, 25.....................*.....	200.00(B)
270.	½ Sovereign 1911-15	200.00

(Numbers 257, 261, 265 and 269 are bullion coins. The price listed is based on gold at $725 per ounce.)

GEORGE VI, 1936-1952

Head. Rev. St. George slaying dragon.

271.	5 Pounds 1937. Proof........................*	2250.00
272.	2 Pounds 1937. Proof................................	1100.00
273.	1 Sovereign 1937. Proof	1000.00
274.	½ Sovereign 1937. Proof	500.00

ELIZABETH II, 1952-

Head. Rev. St. George slaying dragon. A few specimen sets of 5 Pound, 2 Pound, Sovereign and ½ Sovereign pieces were struck in 1953 for presentation and to maintain the series. None were made available and all are now in official custody.

| 275. | 1 Sovereign 1957-59, 62-68........................ | 200.00(B) |

(Number 275 is a bullion coin. The price listed is based on gold at $725 per ounce.)

For later issues of Great Britain, see the section, "Recent Issues Starting With 1960."

GREECE

Greek coinage is based on the Latin Monetary Union standard. The coins of 1852 are of extraordinary rarity. Although 8 specimens were struck of the 40 Drachmai piece and 16 specimens of the 20 Drachmai piece, the author knows of the existence of only a few of the 40 Drachmai coins and one of the 20 Drachmai.

Only 76 pieces were struck of the 100 Drachmai piece of 1876 and 182 pieces of the 50 Drachmai.

A. Kings of —

OTTO, 1831-1863

Young head. Rev. Arms.

| 1. | 20 Drachmai 1833................................... | 1250.00 |

Head with moustache. Rev. Arms. These coins are Essais.

| 2. | 40 Drachmai 1852...........................* ..... | Rare |
| 3. | 20 Drachmai 1852................................... | Unique |

GEORGE I, 1863-1913

Young head. Rev. Arms. Coins dated 1869 and 1875 are Essais and are very rare.

4.	100 Drachmai 1876.....................................	12500.00
5.	50 Drachmai 1876...........................*	6000.00
6.	20 Drachmai 1876...................................	375.00

Young head. Rev. Value and date.

| 7. | 10 Drachmai 1876................................... | 900.00 |
| 8. | 5 Drachmai 1876................................... | 1100.00 |

Old head. Rev. Arms.

| 9. | 20 Drachmai 1884................................... | 175.00 |

GEORGE II, 1935-1947

Head. Rev. Value. On the re-establishment of the Kingdom. Not placed in circulation.

| 10. | 100 Drachmai 1935...........................* ..... | 8500.00 |
| 11. | 20 Drachmai 1935................................... | 7000.00 |

For later issues of Greece, see the section, "Recent Issues Starting With 1960."

B. Cities and Islands of —

CHIOS

A. Genoese Doges of —

MARTIN AND BENEDICT II ZACCHARIA, 1319-1324

Shield. Rev. Cross.

14.   ¼ Zecchino ND 1500.00

Cross. Rev. Christ on throne.

15.   ¼ Zecchino ND 1500.00

THE CAMPOFREGOSI, 1415-1421 AND 1436-1458

Ruler kneeling before St. Lawrence. Rev. Christ.

16.   1 Zecchino ND 850.00

B. Milanese Dukes of —

PHILIP MARIA, 1421-1436

Ruler kneeling before St. Peter. Rev. Christ.

17.   1 Zecchino ND. S mm for Chios.................. 850.00
18.   1 Zecchino ND. P mm for Pera ....*...... 1500.00

C. French Kings of —

CHARLES VII, 1458-1461

Ruler kneeling before St. Lawrence. Rev. Christ.

19.   1 Zecchino ND 1500.00

D. Venetian Coinage for —

LEONARDO LOREDANO, 1501-1521
Ruler kneeling before St. Mark, legend completely around. Rev. Christ.

20.   1 Zecchino ND 800.00

FOKIA (PHOCAEA)

Mytilene Lords of —

DORINO GATTILUSIO, 1400-1449

Ruler kneeling before Saint. Rev. Christ.

21.   1 Zecchino ND 1200.00

MYTILENE

Lords of —

THE GATTILUSI, 1376-1462

Ruler kneeling before Saint. Rev. Christ.

22.   1 Zecchino ND 1500.00

GRENADA

Gold coins of Brazil counterstamped three times along the outer edge of the obverse with a G and with or without a plugged hole in the center.

1.   6400 Reis 1727-1804 .... 2000.00

GUADELOUPE

Gold coins of Brazil or Portugal counterstamped with a "G" (plain or crowned) and with or without a fleur-de-lis or "82.10."

1.   82 Livres, 10 Sous 1727-1804 .... 2000.00

GUATEMALA

Mints and mint marks:—G or NG (New Guatemala) for Guatemala. Almost every coin issued under the Spanish Kings is a rarity.

During the latter part of the 19th century, the coinage was based on the Latin Monetary Union standard, and is unique in that so many denominations were struck—the equivalent of 100, 80, 50, 40, 25, 20, 10, 5 and 2½ Franc pieces (20 Pesos to 4 Reales). Of all the countries in the Union, only Guatemala struck so tiny a coin as the 2½ Franc equivalent.

The only coins of the 20th century were struck in 1926 and are based on the U.S. gold dollar. In the 1926 issues, 49,000 pieces were reported struck of the 20 Quetzals, 18,000 of the 10 Quetzals, and 48,000 of the 5 Quetzals.

A. Spanish Kings of —

PHILIP V, 1700-1746
Bust. Rev. Arms.

1.	8 Escudos 1733-45	Rare

FERDINAND VI, 1746-1760

Crude bust of the previous King, Philip V. Rev. Arms.

2.	8 Escudos 1750	Rare
3.	1 Escudo 1751.......................................	3000.00

Bust. Rev. Arms with star hanging at bottom.

4.	8 Escudos 1754, 55.........................*	Rare
5.	1 Escudo 1755.......................................	2000.00

Bust. Rev. Arms with the Golden Fleece hanging at bottom.

6.	8 Escudos 1756, 57.........................*	Rare
7.	1 Escudo 1757.......................................	1700.00

CHARLES III, 1759-1788
Crude small bust. Rev. Arms.

8.	8 Escudos 1761	Rare

Crude large bust. Rev. Arms without value.

9.	8 Escudos 1765, 68, 70	Rare
9a.	4 Escudos 1765	Rare
9b.	1 Escudo 1765, 70..................................	3000.00

Normal style bust. Rev. Arms with value.

10.	8 Escudos 1778-85 ....*	10000.00
11.	4 Escudos 1778, 81, 83	7000.00
12.	2 Escudos 1783, 85	3000.00
13.	1 Escudo 1778, 83..................................	2000.00

CHARLES IV, 1788-1808

Bust of the previous King, Charles III. Rev. Arms.

14.	8 Escudos 1789, 90..........................*	9000.00
15.	4 Escudos 1789	5500.00
16.	2 Escudos 1789	3500.00
17.	1 Escudo 1789, 90, 91	1300.00

Bust. Rev. Arms.

18.	8 Escudos 1794, 97, 1801......................*	9000.00
19.	4 Escudos 1794, 97, 1801...........................	4000.00
20.	2 Escudos 1794, 1801	3000.00
21.	1 Escudo 1794, 97, 1801...........................	1000.00

FERDINAND VII, 1808-1822

Laureate head. Rev. Arms.

22.	8 Escudos 1808, 11, 17	10000.00
23.	4 Escudos 1813, 17..........................*	7000.00
24.	2 Escudos 1808, 11, 17	2000.00
25.	1 Escudo 1817.....................................	2000.00

B. Republic of —

Sun over five mountain peaks. Rev. Tree.

26.	8 Escudos 1824, 25	....	Rare
27.	4 Escudos 1824, 25, 26	.....................*	Rare
28.	2 Escudos 1825-47	....	1250.00
29.	1 Escudo 1824, 25	....	850.00
30.	½ Escudo 1824-26, 43	....	300.00

Head of Carrera with title as "PTE" (President). Rev. Arms.

31.	16 Pesos 1863. Size 35½ millimetres	....	Rare
32.	16 Pesos 1864, 65. Size 33 millimetres	.......*	5000.00
33.	8 Pesos 1864	....	2000.00
34.	4 Pesos 1861, 62	....	1200.00
35.	2 Pesos 1859	....	250.00

Obv. similar to above. Rev. Value in wreath.

36.	1 Peso 1859, 60	....	90.00
37.	4 Reales 1860-64	....	45.00

Head of Carrera with title as "Fundator" (Founder). Rev. Arms.

38.	20 Pesos 1869	....	1250.00
39.	16 Pesos 1867, 69	....	2500.00
40.	10 Pesos 1869	....	800.00
41.	8 Pesos 1869	....	1700.00
42.	5 Pesos 1869	.........................*	400.00
43.	4 Pesos 1866, 68, 69	....	400.00

Liberty head with flowing hair. Rev. Arms.

44.	20 Pesos 1877-78	....	7000.00
45.	5 Pesos 1872-78	...................*	675.00

Liberty head with coiled hair. Rev. Arms. The mark of fineness (0.900) may appear on the obverse or reverse. These coins were not placed in circulation.

46.	10 Pesos 1894	....	12000.00
47.	5 Pesos 1894	.............................*	4000.00

Quetzal on column. Rev. Arms.

48.	20 Quetzals 1926	....	850.00
49.	10 Quetzals 1926	....	500.00
50.	5 Quetzals 1926	...........................*	350.00

HAWAII

Head of King Kalakua. Rev. Arms. Souvenir gold and platinum coins struck from dies used for silver coins.

1.	½ Dollar 1884. Gold	....	Rare
2.	½ Dollar 1884. Platinum	....	Rare
3.	¼ Dollar 1884. Gold	....	Rare
4.	¼ Dollar 1884. Platinum	....	Rare
5.	⅛ Dollar 1883. Gold	....	Rare
6.	⅛ Dollar 1883. Platinum	....	Rare

(The two coins following were privately struck in England by Reginald Huth).

Head of Queen Liliuocalania to right. Rev. Map of the islands.

7.	20 Dollars 1893	....	Rare

Head of Queen Liliuocalania to left. Rev. Crown over value and date.

8.	20 Dollars 1893	....	Rare

HEJAZ

Kings of —

HUSEIN IBN ALI, 1916-1924

Arab legend in panels on each side.

1.	1 Dinar 1923	....	250.00

HOLY ROMAN EMPIRE

(See under Austria, Bohemia and Hungary).

For the sake of as much simplicity as could be gained, this most complicated and involute of all coinage systems has been divided among Austria, Bohemia and Hungary. Necessity has forced this arrangement, since the Holy Roman Empire was a political concept and not a geographical entity with clearly defined borders.

Under Austria will be found those coins of the Hapsburg Emperors which are of similar type, whether the coins were struck in Austria proper or in the various mints of Bohemia or Hungary (including Transylvania). These similar type coins differ from each other only in the minor aspect of mint marks, mint symbols or in variations of the armorial devices or legends.

Under Bohemia and Hungary will be found the coins of these same Hapsburg Emperors, but of types which are peculiar only to their own areas, and these coins differ markedly in design from those listed under Austria.

Other coins, with either the portraits or names of the Holy Roman Emperors will be found throughout the cities and states of Germany, as well as in several other European countries.

The coinage of the Holy Roman Empire as such ended in 1806, at which time the incumbent Emperor Francis II became Francis I of the newly created Austro-Hungarian Empire, which in turn lasted until the First World War.

HONDURAS

The coinage of Honduras was based on the Latin Monetary Union standard and 20 Pesos were equivalent to 100 Francs.

Arms. Rev. Tree. With plain or reeded edges. These coins are patterns and were not placed in circulation.

1.	10 Pesos 1871	*	Rare
2.	5 Pesos 1871		Rare
3.	1 Peso 1871		2500.00

Liberty head. Rev. Arms. Most coins have overstruck dates.

4.	20 Pesos 1888, 95, 1908	10000.00
5.	10 Pesos 1889	Rare
6.	5 Pesos 1883, 88, 90, 95-97, 1900, 02, 08, 13 *	1500.00
7.	1 Peso 1888, 89, 95, 96, 99, 1901, 02, 07, 13, 19, 20, 22 *	650.00

HUNGARY

The Hungarian Goldgulden and Ducat of the standing Emperor type were among the most popular coins of Europe and were circulated and accepted throughout the Continent. Many cities and states imitated this type for their own local coinage.

The St. George coins of Kremnitz have always been carried on the person to bring good luck to the bearer and keep him from harm. The coins of Transylvania are notable for the striking portraits and costuming that appear on them.

A. Kings of —

CHARLES ROBERT, 1308-1342
St. John. Rev. Lily.

1.	1 Goldgulden ND	750.00

LOUIS I, 1342-1382

St. John. Rev. Lily.

2.	1 Goldgulden ND	600.00

St. John. Rev. Arms.

3.	1 Goldgulden ND	600.00

St. Ladislas. Rev. Arms.

4.	1 Ducat ND	550.00

MARIA, 1382-1387
St. Ladislas. Rev. Arms.

5.	1 Ducat ND	850.00

SIGISMUND, 1387-1437

St. Ladislas. Rev. Quartered arms.

6.	1 Ducat ND	450.00

ALBERT OF AUSTRIA, 1438-1439
St. Ladislas. Rev. Quartered arms.

7.	1 Ducat ND	500.00

LADISLAS OF POLAND, 1440-1449
St. Ladislas. Rev. Quartered arms.

8.	1 Ducat ND	425.00

JOHN HUNYAD, 1446-1453
St. Ladislas. Rev. Quartered arms.

9.	1 Ducat ND	500.00

LADISLAS V, 1453-1457
St. Ladislas. Rev. Quartered arms.

10.	1 Ducat ND	400.00

MATTHIAS CORVINUS, 1458-1490

St. Ladislas. Rev. Quartered arms.

11.	1 Ducat ND	400.00

St. Ladislas. Rev. Madonna seated.

12.	1 Ducat ND	350.00

LADISLAS II, 1490-1516

St. Ladislas. Rev. Madonna seated.

13.   1 Ducat 1506, 07, ND 550.00

St. Ladislas. Rev. Madonna standing.

14.   1 Ducat 1510-16 .... 600.00

St. Ladislas on horseback. Rev. Arms.

15.   10 Ducats 1506 .... 5500.00
16.   8 Ducats 1506 .... 6000.00

LOUIS II, 1516-1526
Ruler on horse. Rev. Madonna seated.

17.   2 Ducats 1525 .... 2500.00

St. Ladislas. Rev. Madonna standing.

18.   1 Ducat 1518-25 .... 500.00

Youthful King seated. Rev. Legend.

19.   5 Ducats 1544 ....* 2500.00
20.   3 Ducats 1544 .... 1500.00
21.   2 Ducats 1544 .... 1000.00

JOHN ZAPOLYA, 1526-1540
Madonna seated. Rev. Arms.

22.   1 Ducat 1539 .... 500.00

St. Ladislas. Rev. Arms.

23.   1 Ducat 1540 .... 450.00

St. Ladislas. Rev. Madonna standing.

24.   1 Ducat 1526-40 .... 400.00

FERDINAND I, 1521-1564
St. Ladislas. Rev. Madonna standing.

25.   2 Ducats 1535-60 .... 1500.00
26.   1 Ducat 1521-64 .... 500.00
27.   1 Ducat 1565. Posthumous 600.00

St. Ladislas. Rev. Arms.

28.   1 Ducat 1545-58 .... 450.00

MAXIMILIAN II, 1564-1576
St. Ladislas. Rev. Madonna standing.

29.   2 Ducats 1567, 72 .... 1000.00
30.   1 Ducat 1564-76 .... 650.00
31.   1 Ducat 1577, 78. Posthumous 850.00

Ruler standing. Rev. St. Ladislas.

32.   1 Ducat 1564-76 .... 600.00

RUDOLPH II, 1576-1612
St. Ladislas. Rev. Madonna standing.

33.   3 Ducats 1580 .... 2000.00
34.   1 Ducat 1578-1608 .... 500.00

MATTHIAS II, 1612-1619

Ruler standing. Rev. Madonna.

35.   5 Ducats 1614 ....* 6000.00
36.   2 Ducats 1612-19 .... 1850.00
37.   1 Ducat 1612-19 .... 750.00
38.   ¼ Ducat 1615 .... 250.00

Bust. Rev. Double eagle between K-B or N-B.

39.   15 Ducats 1617 .... Rare
40.   5 Ducats 1617 .... Rare

FERDINAND II, 1618-1637

Ruler standing. Rev. Madonna.

41.   5 Ducats 1632 .... 5500.00
42.   2 Ducats 1622-37 .... 1500.00
43.   1 Ducat 1620-37 ....* 500.00
44.   ¼ Ducat 1630-35 .... 250.00

Bust. Rev. Double eagle between K-B or N-B.

45.   10 Ducats 1626-35 ....* 12500.00
46.   5 Ducats 1632-37 .... 7500.00

FERDINAND III, 1627-1657
Ruler standing. Rev. Madonna.

47.   2 Ducats 1637-57 .... 2000.00
48.   1 Ducat 1637-57 .... 700.00
49.   1 Ducat 1658, 59. Posthumous 750.00

Bust. Rev. Double eagle between K-B or N-B.

50.   10 Ducats 1629-57 .... 12500.00

LEOPOLD I (THE HOGMOUTH), 1658-1705

Ruler standing. Rev. Madonna.

51.   1 Ducat 1658-1704 .... 550.00

Laureate bust. Rev. Madonna on crescent.

52.	10 Ducats 1687	15000.00
53.	8 Ducats 1695	12500.00
54.	5 Ducats 1675, 87	8000.00
55.	4 Ducats 1687, 95	6000.00
56.	3 Ducats 1695	4000.00
57.	2 Ducats 1695	1850.00

Laureate bust. Rev. Madonna seated, two shields below.

| 58. | 1 Ducat 1675 | 750.00 |

Bust and value. Rev. Madonna.

59.	¼ Ducat 1684-99 ....*	300.00
60.	⅛ Ducat 1673-98	300.00
61.	1/12 Ducat ND. With blank Rev.	185.00

REBELLION OF THE MALCONTENTS, 1703-1707
Arms and date. Rev. Value in cartouche.

| 62. | 5 Ducats 1704 | 8000.00 |

Arms. Rev. Madonna.

| 63. | 1 Ducat 1704-07 ....* | 1250.00 |
| 64. | 1 Ducat 1705. Square | 2000.00 |

JOSEPH I, 1705-1711

Ruler standing. Rev. Madonna.

| 65. | 1 Ducat 1705-11 | 450.00 |

CHARLES VI, 1711-1740

Ruler standing. Rev. Madonna.

66.	1 Ducat 1712-40 ....*	500.00
67.	½ Ducat 1740	450.00
68.	¼ Ducat 1712-40	400.00

Bust. Rev. Madonna.

69.	1 Ducat 1736-40	600.00
70.	⅙ Ducat 1712-40	200.00
71.	⅛ Ducat 1739	200.00
72.	1/12 Ducat 1739	200.00

MARIA THERESA, 1740-1780

Ruler standing. Rev. Madonna.

| 73. | 2 Ducats 1763-65 ....* | 1000.00 |
| 74. | 1 Ducat 1741-65 | 450.00 |

Bust. Rev. Madonna.

| 75. | 1 Ducat 1753-65 | 600.00 |

Old veiled bust. Rev. Madonna.

| 76. | 1 Ducat 1765-80 | 500.00 |

JOSEPH II, 1765-1790
Ruler standing. Rev. Madonna.

| 77. | 2 Ducats 1781-85 | 400.00 |
| 78. | 1 Ducat 1781-85 | 400.00 |

LEOPOLD II, 1790-1792
Ruler standing. Rev. Madonna.

| 79. | 1 Ducat 1790-92 | 550.00 |

JOSEPH II AND LEOPOLD II
Two busts. Rev. Inscription. On visit to the mines.

| 80. | 1 Ducat 1764 | 1100.00 |

FRANCIS II, 1792-1835
Ruler standing. Rev. Madonna.

| 81. | 1 Ducat 1792-1835 | 350.00 |

FERDINAND I, 1835-1848
Ruler standing. Rev. Madonna.

| 82. | 1 Ducat 1837-48. Latin legends | 325.00 |
| 83. | 1 Ducat 1848. Magyar legends | 350.00 |

FRANCIS JOSEPH, 1848-1916
Ruler standing. Rev. Arms supported by angels.

| 84. | 1 Ducat 1868-70. KB mm | 350.00 |
| 85. | 1 Ducat 1868, 69. GYF mm | 250.00 |

Laureate head. Rev. Crowned arms.

| 86. | 1 Ducat 1877-81 | 650.00 |
| 86R. | 1 Ducat 1870. Restrike | 85.00(B) |

Laureate head. Rev. Arms and two values.

87.	8 Florins-20 Francs 1870-92. KB mm ....*	190.00
87R.	8 Florins-20 Francs 1887. KB mm. Restrike	175.00(B)
88.	8 Florins-20 Francs 1870, 71. GYF mm	225.00
89.	4 Florins-10 Francs 1870-92. KB mm.......*	150.00
89R.	4 Florins-10 Francs 1870. KB mm. Restrike	110.00(B)
90.	4 Florins-10 Francs 1870. GYF mm	300.00

(Numbers 86R, 87R and 89R are bullion coins. The price listed is based on gold at $/25 per ounce.)

Ruler standing. Rev. Arms.

91.	100 Korona 1907, 08	2500.00
91R.	100 Korona 1907, 08. Restrike. "UP" on reverse.......	600.00(B)
92.	20 Korona 1892-1916.........................*......	170.00
92R.	20 Korona 1892, 95. Restrike.............	155.00(B)
93.	20 Korona 1914, 16. Slight change in arms	450.00
94.	10 Korona 1892-1915 ....*......	85.00
94R.	10 Korona 1892, 98. Restrike..................	80.00(B)

Head. Rev. Coronation scene. On the 40th year of his reign.

95.	100 Korona 1907..........................	1500.00
95R.	100 Korona 1907. Restrike. "UP" next to date........	650.00(B)

(Numbers 91R, 92R, 94R and 95R are bullion coins. The price listed is based on gold at $725 per ounce.)

*Crowned bust. Rev. Madonna and child. On the 1000th year
of the Hungarian Kingdom.*

96.	9 Ducats 1896...................................	5500.00

St. John. Rev. Lily. On the 1000th year of the Hungarian Kingdom.

97.	1 Goldgulden 1896.............................	1750.00

CHARLES, 1916-1918
Head. Rev. Arms. Not placed in circulation.

98.	20 Korona 1918...................................	Rare

REGENCY, 1919-1944

Arms. Rev. Value. Not placed in circulation.

99.	20 Pengo 1928, 29 ....*......	Rare
100.	10 Pengo 1928...................................	Rare

For later coins of Hungary, see the section, "Recent Issues Starting With 1960."

B. Cities of —

BATTHYANI

Princes —

CHARLES, 1764-1772

Bust. Rev. Arms.

107.	10 Ducats 1764	Rare
108.	5 Ducats 1764	4500.00
109.	1 Ducat 1764, 65, 70.....................*......	800.00

LOUIS, 1787-1806
Bust. Rev. Arms.

110.	10 Ducats 1788	Rare
111.	5 Ducats 1789	4500.00
112.	1 Ducat 1791	1250.00

ESTERHAZY

Princes —

NICHOLAS, 1762-1790
Bust. Rev. Arms.

113.	1 Ducat 1770	1500.00

KREMNITZ

*St. George slaying dragon. Rev. Christ in boat. Struck during
the period 1600-1800.*

114.	10 Ducats ND ....*......	5500.00
115.	6 Ducats ND	4000.00
116.	5 Ducats ND	3500.00
117.	3 Ducats ND	2250.00
118.	2 Ducats ND	1500.00
119.	1 Ducat ND....................................	1250.00

TRANSYLVANIA (SIEBENBURGEN)

Voivodes (Princes) of —

JOHN I ZAPOLYA, 1538-1540
Ruler standing. Rev. Madonna.

120.	1 Ducat 1540	1250.00

St. Ladislas standing. Rev. Madonna.

121.	1 Ducat 1539, 40	850.00

Madonna. Rev. Arms.

122.	1 Ducat 1539	850.00

ISABELLA AND JOHN SIGISMUND, 1556-1559
Madonna. Rev. Arms.

123.	5 Ducats 1557	7500.00
124.	1 Ducat 1556-60	1250.00
125.	½ Ducat 1558, 59	1000.00
126.	¼ Ducat 1559	650.00

St. Ladislas. Rev. Arms.

127.	1 Ducat 1556	1500.00

Arms. Rev. Legend.

128.	10 Ducats 1557	10000.00
129.	10 Ducats 1557. Square....................	12000.00
130.	5 Ducats 1557	6000.00

JOHN SIGISMUND, 1559-1571

Madonna. Rev. Arms.

131.	4 Ducats 1577. Thick flan................	5000.00
132.	2 Ducats 1562	2000.00
133.	1 Ducat 1560-72 ....*	1250.00

St. Ladislas standing. Rev. Arms.

134.	1 Ducat 1556-59	1000.00

Arms and ISRV. Rev. Blank.

135.	10 Ducats 1562, 65	5000.00

STEPHAN BATHORI, 1571-1575
Madonna. Rev. St. Ladislas.

136.	1 Ducat 1572-79	1250.00

CHRISTOPHER BATHORI, 1576-1581

Arms. Rev. Legend.

137.	10	Ducats 1577, 83 ....*	8000.00
138.	5	Ducats 1577, 83	4000.00
139.	4	Ducats 1577	3300.00
140.	2	Ducats 1577	1850.00
141.	1½	Ducats 1577	1750.00

Madonna. Rev. Arms.

142.	1 Ducat 1579	1500.00

Madonna. Rev. St. Ladislas.

143.	1 Ducat 1577-80	1500.00

ELIZABETH BOCSKAI, 1577

Lion seated. Rev. Legend.

144.	10 Ducats 1577 ....*	12500.00
145.	5 Ducats 1577	5000.00
146.	3 Ducats 1577	3000.00
147.	2 Ducats 1577	2250.00

SIGISMUND BATHORI, 1581-1602
Bust. Rev. Eagle.

148.	10 Ducats 1598	10000.00
149.	9 Ducats 1598	10000.00

Bust. Rev. Arms supported by angels.

150.	10 Ducats 1590	10000.00

Madonna. Rev. St. Ladislas.

151.	5 Ducats 1590. Thick flan.................	4000.00
152.	1 Ducat 1581-97 ....*	1250.00

St. Ladislas. Rev. Eagle.

153.	1 Ducat 1598	1250.00

Arms. Rev. Legend.

154.	10 Ducats 1583	8500.00

MOSES SZEKELY, 1602-1603

Two lions with sword. Rev. Legend.

155.	10 Ducats 1603	12500.00

STEPHAN BOCSKAI, 1604-1606

Bust. Rev. Arm with sword.

156. 10 Ducats 1605 .... 9000.00

Crossed swords. Rev. Double eagle. Struck by Rudolph II during siege of Hermannstadt.

157. 10 Ducats 1605 .... Rare

Bust. Rev. Arms.

158. 10 Ducats 1606 .... 9000.00
159. 5 Ducats 1606 .... 4500.00

Bust. Rev. Crossed swords.

160. 1 Ducat 1606 .... 1850.00

Head with fur cap. Rev. Arms.

161. 2 Ducats 1606 .... 3000.00
162. 1 Ducat 1606 ....*...... 1850.00

Madonna. Rev. St. Ladislas.

163. 1 Ducat 1605, 06, 07, ND 1250.00

Madonna. Rev. Arms.

164. ½ Ducat 1606 .... 650.00
165. ¼ Ducat 1606 .... 450.00

SIGISMUND RAKOCZI, 1607-1608

Bust. Rev. Legend.

166. 10 Ducats 1607 .... 12500.00

Bust. Rev. Eagle on castles.

167. 1 Ducat 1607, 08 .... 2000.00

Madonna. Rev. Arms.

168. ¼ Ducat 1608 .... 400.00

GABRIEL BATHORI, 1608-1613
Bust. Rev. Three shields.

169. 10 Ducats 1609 .... 9500.00

Bust. Rev. Eagle.

170. 6 Ducats 1613. Thick flan 7500.00
171. 1 Ducat 1611, 12, 13 ....*...... 1500.00

Bust. Rev. Arms.

172. 2 Ducats 1610, 12 .... 2500.00
173. 1 Ducat 1609-12, ND 1250.00

Head with cap. Rev. Arms.

174. 1 Ducat 1613 .... 1500.00

Bust. Rev. Crossed swords.

175. 1 Ducat 1613 .... 1500.00

Madonna. Rev. St. Ladislas.

176. 1 Ducat 1609 .... 1250.00

Three shields. Rev. Legend.

177. 10 Ducats 1611, 12, 13 .... 7500.00
178. 8 Ducats 1612 .... 5000.00

Madonna. Rev. Arms.

179. ½ Ducat 1612, 13 .... 450.00
180. ¼ Ducat 1610, 12, 13 .... 300.00

MICHAEL WEISS (1613)

Legend on each side.

181. 10 Ducats 1612 ....*...... 12500.00
182. 1 Ducat 1612, 13 .... 3000.00

GABRIEL BETHLEN, 1613-1629
Bust with cap. Rev. Arms.

183. 2 Ducats 1613 .... 2500.00
184. 1 Ducat 1613-18 .... 1250.00

Bust with cap. Rev. Arm with sword.

185. 10 Ducats 1616 .... 9500.00

Bust. Rev. Elaborate arms.

186. 1 Ducat 1618 .... 1250.00

Bust. Rev. Three shields.

187. 10 Ducats 1619 .... 9500.00
188. 1 Ducat 1619 .... 1250.00

Bust. Rev. Arms.

189. 10 Ducats 1620, 21, 22, 28, ND 8000.00
190. 5 Ducats 1622 .... 5500.00
191. 3 Ducats 1627 .... 4000.00
192. 1 Ducat 1620, 22, ND ....*...... 1250.00

Bust. Rev. Madonna.

193.   1 Ducat 1620-27 .... 1250.00

Bust. Rev. Madonna in flames.

194.   2 Ducats 1628 .... 2500.00
195.   1 Ducat 1627, 28, 29 .... 1500.00

Madonna. Rev. Arms.

196.   1 Ducat 1627 .... 1250.00
197.   ¼ Ducat 1619-27 .... 300.00

CATHERINE BETHLEN, 1629-1630
Bust. Rev. Madonna.

198.   1 Ducat 1630 .... 6000.00

Bust. Rev. Arms.

199.   1 Ducat 1630 .... 5500.00

STEPHAN BETHLEN, 1630

Bust. Rev. Arms.

200.   1 Ducat 1630 .... 3250.00

GEORGE RAKOCZI I, 1630-1648

Bust. Rev. Legend.

201.   20 Ducats 1637, 39 .... Rare
202.   10 Ducats 1631, 36, 37, 39 .... * 7500.00
203.   5 Ducats 1631, 36, 37, 39 .... 4500.00

Bust. Rev. Arms.

204.   10 Ducats 1645, 47 .... 8500.00
205.   6 Ducats 1647 .... 6000.00

Bust. Rev. Eagle and castles.

206.   2 Ducats 1632 .... 3000.00
207.   1 Ducat 1631-39 .... 1250.00

Bust with fur cap. Rev. Arms.

208.   10 Ducats 1646, 48 .... 8000.00

Bust with fur cap. Rev. Eagle on castles.

209.   1 Ducat 1646 .... 1250.00

Bust with cap. Rev. Madonna.

210.   1 Ducat 1646, 48 .... 1000.00

Bust. Rev. Madonna.

211.   1 Ducat 1645, 48 .... 1000.00

Madonna. Rev. Arms.

212.   ¼ Ducat 1642, 47 .... 400.00

GEORGE RAKOCZI II, 1648-1660

Bust with fur cap. Rev. Arms.

213.   13 Ducats 1657. Square .... Rare
214.   12 Ducats 1657. Square .... Rare
215.   10 Ducats 1652, 57, 60. Square or hexagonal. * 12500.00
216.   10 Ducats 1648-60. Round 8500.00
217.   7 Ducats 1654 .... 8000.00

Bust with fur cap. Rev. Madonna.

218.   1 Ducat 1648-57 .... 1000.00

Bust with fur cap. Rev. Eagle and castles.

219.   1 Ducat 1657 .... 1250.00
220.   1 Ducat 1657. Square 2000.00

Madonna. Rev. Arms.

221.   ¼ Ducat 1650, 53 .... 400.00

ACHATIUS BARCSAI, 1658-1660

Bust. Rev. Arms.

222.   10 Ducats 1659, 60 .... 8500.00
223.   10 Ducats 1659. Square or hexagonal 12500.00
224.   2 Ducats 1659 .... 3000.00
225.   1 Ducat 1659 .... * 2000.00

Arms. Rev. Legend.

226.   10 Ducats 1660 .... 8500.00
227.   10 Ducats 1660. Square 12500.00

228.	9 Ducats 1660. Square.............................	12500.00
229.	7 Ducats 1660. Square.............................	8000.00
230.	5 Ducats 1660. Square.............................	5500.00
231.	5 Ducats 1660	5000.00
232.	1 Ducat 1660	1850.00

Arms on each side.

233.	10 Ducats 1660	9500.00

JOHN KEMENY, 1661-1662

Bust with fur cap. Rev. Arms.

234.	10 Ducats 1661 ....*	12500.00
235.	5 Ducats 1661	8000.00
236.	3 Ducats 1661	5000.00
237.	2 Ducats 1661	4500.00
238.	2 Ducats 1661. Square............................	5000.00
239.	1 Ducat 1661	1850.00

MICHAEL APAFI, 1661-1690

Bust with fur cap. Rev. Arms.

ROUND COINS

240.	100 Ducats 1677	Rare
241.	30 Ducats 1677, 83	Rare
242.	10 Ducats 1662-74	8000.00
243.	5 Ducats 1662-73	4250.00
244.	4 Ducats 1665	4000.00
245.	1 Ducat 1662, 82	2000.00

SQUARE OR HEXAGONAL COINS

246.	10	Ducats 1662, 63, 75, 81.................*	12000.00
247.	6	Ducats 1668	7500.00
248.	4½	Ducats 1668	7000.00
249.	3	Ducats 1663	5000.00
250.	2	Ducats 1662, 68	3500.00
251.	1	Ducat 1663, 68	1500.00

Bust. Rev. Arms.

ROUND COINS

252.	10 Ducats 1672-89	8000.00
253.	5 Ducats 1677, 87	4000.00
254.	4 Ducats 1677, 89	3500.00
255.	1 Ducat 1673-90	1850.00

SQUARE OR HEXAGONAL COINS

256.	25 Ducats 1687...................................	Rare
257.	10 Ducats 1684, 89	12500.00

258.	6 Ducats 1686	8000.00
259.	5 Ducats 1689	7500.00
260.	4 Ducats 1678	5500.00
261.	3 Ducats 1684	5000.00
262.	2 Ducats 1689	3500.00
263.	1 Ducat 1678-89	1500.00

Bust in center within circle of ten other busts. Rev. Arms in center within circle of ten other arms.

264.	100 Ducats 1674, 75	Rare

EMERIC TOKELY, 1682-1690

Bust with fur cap. Rev. Arm with sword.

265.	10 Ducats 1683...................................	10000.00
266.	8 Ducats 1683...................................	8500.00
267.	4 Ducats 1683...................................	6500.00

Bust with fur cap. Rev. Arms.

268.	1 Ducat 1690	3000.00

FRANCIS RAKOCZI II, 1704-1711

Arms. Rev. Palm tree.

269.	1 Ducat 1705	2000.00

CHARLES VI, 1711-1740
Head. Rev. Arms.

270.	¼ Ducat ND......................................	300.00

Arms. Rev. Globe.

271.	¼ Ducat ND......................................	300.00

MARIA THERESA, 1740-1780
Arms. Rev. Value.

272.	¼ Ducat 1749	300.00
273.	⅛ Ducat 1778	250.00
274.	1/16 Ducat 1778	250.00

Bust. Rev. Arms.

275.	1 Ducat 1740-80	800.00

INDIA

A. British Sovereigns of —

(Note: Restrikes have been issued by the Bombay and Calcutta mints of all of the coins of British India with the exception of numbers 3, 6, 8 and 15.)

WILLIAM IV, 1830-1837

Head. Rev. Lion and palm tree. Issued by the East India Company.

1.	2 Mohurs 1835	*......	1500.00
2.	1 Mohur 1835		500.00

VICTORIA, 1837-1901

Head. Rev. Lion and palm tree. Issued by the East India Company.

3.	1 Mohur 1841	450.00

Thin face with title of Queen. Rev. Value.

4.	1 Mohur 1862-70	*......	250.00
5.	10 Rupees 1862-70		160.00
6.	5 Rupees 1862-70	*......	150.00

Plump face with title of Queen. Rev. Value.

7.	1 Mohur 1870	*......	300.00
8.	10 Rupees 1870		250.00
9.	5 Rupees 1870		190.00

Thin face with title of Empress. Rev. Value.

10.	1 Mohur 1877-89	*......	280.00
11.	5 Rupees 1879		190.00

Plump face with title of Empress. Rev. Value.

12.	10 Rupees 1878, 79	230.00
13.	5 Rupees 1879	190.00

GEORGE V, 1910-1936

Head. Rev. Value.

14.	15 Rupees 1918	375.00

Head. Rev. St. George. This is the same type as the English Pound but with the distinguishing Indian mint mark "I" on ground below horse.

15.	1 Pound 1918	200.00(B)

(Number 15 is a bullion coin. The price listed is based on gold at $725 per ounce.)

B. Private Tola Coinage of —

Gold coins issued by various Indian banking houses during the present generation. There are many varieties and the pieces may be round, square, diamond shaped, or scalloped. The Tola weighs a little more than 11.50 Grams and is thus similar to the Mohur. Tola coinage is undated.

16.	10 Tola piece	2450.00
17.	5 Tola piece	1225.00
18.	1 Tola piece	245.00
19.	½ Tola piece	125.00
20.	¼ Tola piece	65.00

C. Native States of —

AGRA

Indian legend on each side. Oblong shape.

21.	1 Mohur. About 1550-1600	400.00

AJMIR AND DELHI

Goddess seated. Rev. Legend.

22.	1 Stater. About 1010-1160	190.00

ARCOT

Persian legend on each side. Coinage of the British East India Company in the name of Alamgir II of Hindustan. With dates from about 1172-1214 A.H. (1758-99).

23. 1 Mohur 250.00
24. ½ Mohur .... * 125.00
25. ¼ Mohur 65.00

ASSAM

Bengali legend on each side. Octagonal shaped coins struck during the period 1540-1820.

26. 1 Mohur .... * 250.00
27. ½ Mohur 125.00
28. ¼ Mohur 62.50
29. ⅛ Mohur 37.50
30. 1/16 Mohur 32.50
31. 1/32 Mohur 32.50

AWADH

Kings of —

GHAZI-UD-DIN-HAIDAR, 1819-1827

Persian legend on each side. In the name of Shah Alam II.

31a. 1 Mohur 1234 A.H. (1819) 300.00

Persian legend. Rev. Two fish crowned, supported by tigers.

32. 1 Mohur 1234-42 A.H. (1819-27) .... * 280.00
33. ¼ Mohur 1234 A.H. (1819) 155.00

NAZIR-UD-DIN-HAIDAR, 1827-1837

Inscription. Rev. Arms.

34. 1 Mohur 1243-44 A.H. (1827-29) 280.00

MOHAMMED ALI SHAH, 1837-1842

Persian legend. Rev. Two females standing and supporting crown.

35. 1 Mohur 1253-57 A.H. (1837-41) 250.00
35a. ½ Mohur 1256 A.H. (1840) 130.00

AMJAD ALI SHAH, 1842-1847

Persian legend. Rev. Umbrella over crown over fish.

36. 1 Mohur 1259-62 A.H. (1843-45) 250.00
37. ½ Mohur 1262 A.H. (1845) .... * 125.00

WAJID ALI SHAH, 1847-1856

Persian legend. Rev. Arms supported by mermaids holding clubs and banners.

38. 1 Mohur 1264-72 A.H. (1847-56) .... * 250.00
39. ½ Mohur 1267-72 A.H. (1850-56) .... * 125.00
40. ¼ Mohur 1265-71 A.H. (1848-54) 90.00
41. ⅛ Mohur 1266 A.H. (1849) 70.00
41a. 1/16 Mohur 1270 A.H. (1853) 60.00

BAHAWALPUR

Bust of Rajah Sadik Mohammed V. Rev. Arms.

42. 1 Ashrafi 1343 A.H. (1925) 625.00

BAJRANGGARH

Indian legend on each side. Struck under Jai Singh.

43. 1 Mohur (1798-1818). Octagonal 300.00

BARODA

Bust of Gaikwar Sayaji Rao III (1875-1933). Rev. Nagari legend.

44. 1 Mohur 1945-59 Samvat (1888-1902) .... * 375.00
45. ⅓ Mohur 1942 Samvat (1885) 250.00
46. ⅙ Mohur 1943-59 Samvat (1886-1902) .... * 125.00

BENARES

Persian legend on each side. Coinage of the British East India Company in the name of Shah Alam II of Hindustan. With dates from about 1212-1235 A.H. (1797-1819).

47. 1 Mohur 250.00

BENGAL

Indian legend on each side. Royal coinage struck during the period 1302-1518.

48.	1 Mohur..	150.00

Indian legend on each side. Coinage of the East India Company struck during the period 1750-1820.

49.	2 Mohurs......................................	500.00
50.	1 Mohur..	250.00
51.	¼ Mohur..	65.00

BHARTPUR

Persian legend on each side.

52.	1 Mohur (1805-55).................................	300.00

Crude head of Queen Victoria. Rev. Persian legend.

53.	1 Mohur 1910-16 Samvat (issued 1858, 59)..........	600.00

BHOPAL

Persian legend on each side. Coinage of the Begums.

54.	1 Mohur (1834-67)................................	250.00

BIKANIR

GANGA SINGH, 1887-1942

Bust of the Maharajah. Rev. Nagari legend.

55.	1 Mohur 1994 Samvat (1937)........*......	400.00
56.	½ Mohur 1994 Samvat (1937)........................	300.00

BOMBAY

Arms of the British East India Company. Rev. "Bombay" and date.

57.	1 Mohur 1765.....................................	900.00
58.	½ Mohur 1765.....................................	450.00
59.	¼ Mohur 1765.....................................	375.00

Persian legend on each side. Coinage of the East India Company in the name of Shah Alam of Hindustan.

60.	1 Mohur 1182 A.H. (1768).........................	250.00

Persian legend. Rev. English name, date and value.

61.	15 Rupees (1 Mohur) 1770	1125.00

BUNDI

Persian legend. Rev. Regnal year. Struck in the name of Mohammed Akbar II.

62.	1 Mohur (1822-26).................................	250.00

CALCUTTA

Persian legend on each side with a large C on Rev. Coinage of the British East India Company in the name of Shah Alam II of Hindustan.

63.	1 Mohur 1216 A.H. (1801).........................	250.00

CANNANORE

Ali Rajahs of —

Persian legend on each side.
63a.　2 Fanams 1194 A.H. (1780)........................ 150.00

CARNATIC

Nawabs of —

Three figures. Rev. Symbol amid grains.
63b.　1 Pagoda ND (1752-95)........................... 100.00

CHEDI (WESTERN)

Goddess seated. Rev. Legend. Coinage of Governors struck during the period 1000-1100.
64.　　1 Stater 155.00

CHOLAS

Ruler standing on each side. Crude tribal coinage struck during the period 1000-1300.
65.　　1 Stater 200.00

Two fish and tiger seated. Rev. Inscription. Struck under Rajendra I, 1012-44.
65a.　1 Fanam ND....................................... 35.00

COCHIN

A. Portuguese Kings of —

JOHN III, 1521-1557

St. Thomas standing. Rev. Arms.
66.　1 Pardau San Tome ND. C mm..................... 2500.00

B. Netherlands, Colony of —

Crude symbols on each side. Struck during the period 1740-80.
66a.　1 Fanam.. 27.50

COROMANDEL COAST

Symbols on each side. Struck during the period 1700-1800.
67.　　1 Fanam.. 27.50

CUTCH-BHUJ

MAHARAJAH DESALJI II, 1819-1860
Persian legend on each side.
67a.　25 Kori 1912-14 Samvat (1855-57)................... 190.00

MAHARAJAH PRAGMALJI II, 1860-1875

Persian legend with name of Queen Victoria, Christian date in Arabic numerals and value. Rev. Indian legend with Maharajah's name, Samvat date, and value.
68.　100 Kori 1866.............................. * 525.00
69.　50 Kori 1866-74.................................. 350.00
70.　25 Kori 1862-70.................................. 250.00

COOCH-BIHAR

Legend in square. Rev. Legend. Struck under Rajah Narendra Narayana, 1839-54.
71.　　1 Mohur... 400.00

Arms supported by lion and elephant. Rev. Legend. Struck under Rajah Jitandra Narayana, 1912-1922.
72.　　1 Mohur. Years 402, 404 (1912, 14)................. 400.00

DATIA

GOVIND SINGH, 1907-1948
Bust. Rev. Arms.
73.　　½ Mohur ND....................................... 400.00

DELHI

Sultans of —

MOHAMMED I, 1193-1206
Indian legend within square on each side. With dates from about 589-602 A.H.
74.　　1 Tanka. Large flan. Ghazni mint 475.00

Ruler on horse within circle. Rev. Legend.

75. 1 Tanka .... Unique

Crude figure of Lakshmi seated. Rev. Nagari legend.

76. ½ Tanka 200.00

SHAMS-UD-DIN ILTUTMISH, 1210-1235
Ruler on horse. Rev. Persian legend.

77. ½ Tanka ND .... Rare

ALA-UD-DIN MASUD, 1242-1246
Indian legend within square on each side. With dates from about 639-644 A.H.

78. 1 Mohur 470.00

NASIR-UD-DIN MAHMUD I, 1246-1266

Persian legend within circle on each side. With dates from about 644-664 A.H.

79. 1 Mohur 250.00

Indian legend within square on each side.

80. 1 Mohur 250.00

GHIYAS-UD-DIN BALBAN, 1266-1287
Persian legend within circle on each side. With dates from about 664-686 A.H.

81. 1 Mohur 250.00

KAIQUBAD, 1287-1290
Persian legend on each side.

82. 1 Mohur 250.00

JALAL-UD-DIN FIRUZ II, 1290-1296

Indian legend on each side. With dates from about 689-695 A.H.

83. 1 Mohur 250.00

ALA-UD-DIN MOHAMMED, 1296-1316
Persian legend on each side. With dates from about 695-715 A.H.

84. 1 Mohur. Round 425.00
85. 1 Mohur. Square.......................... 250.00

SHIHAB-UD-DIN UMAR, 1316
Persian legend on each side.

86. 1 Mohur 715 A.H. 250.00

QUTB-UD-DIN MUBARAK, 1316-1320

Persian legend on each side. With dates from about 716-720 A.H.

87. 1 Mohur. Round 250.00
88. 1 Mohur. Square..................... * 275.00
89. ⅓ Mohur. Square.......................... 110.00

NASIR-UD-DIN KHUSRU, 1320
Persian legend on each side.

90. 1 Mohur 720 A.H. 250.00

GHIYAS-UD-DIN TUGHLUK, 1320-1325
Persian legend on each side. With dates from about 720-725 A.H.

91. 1 Mohur 250.00

MOHAMMED III, 1325-1351

Arabic legend on each side. With dates from about 725-752 A.H.

92. 1½ Mohurs 375.00
93. 1 Mohur .... * 250.00
94. ½ Mohur .... * 125.00

FIRUZ III, 1351-1388

Persian legend on each side. With dates from about 752-790 A.H.

95. 1 Mohur 250.00

FATH KHAN, 1351-1388
(Son of Firuz III)
Persian legend on each side.

96. 1 Mohur 250.00

TUGHLUK II, 1388-1389
Persian legend on each side. With dates from about 790-791 A.H.

97. 1 Mohur 250.00

FIRUZ WITH ZAFAR, 1389
Persian legend on each side.

98. 1 Mohur 791 A.H. 250.00

ABU BAKR, 1389-1390
Persian legend on each side. With dates from about 791-793 A.H.

99. 1 Mohur 250.00

MOHAMMED IV, 1390-1393
Persian legend on each side. With dates from about 792-795 A.H.

100. 1 Mohur 250.00

MAHMUD II, 1393-1413
Persian legend on each side. With dates from about 795-815 A.H.

101. 1 Mohur 250.00

NUSRAT SHAH, 1395-1399
Persian legend on each side. With dates from about 779-802 A.H.
102. 1 Mohur 250.00

MUBARAK II, 1421-1434
Persian legend on each side. With dates from about 824-837 A.H.
103. 1 Mohur 250.00

MOHAMMED V, 1434-1445
Persian legend on each side. With dates from about 837-849 A.H.
104. 1 Mohur 250.00

SHER, 1538-1545
Persian legend on each side. With dates from about 945-952 A.H.
105. 1 Mohur 400.00

ISLAM, 1545-1552
Persian legend on each side. With dates from about 952-960 A.H.
106. 1 Mohur 400.00

MOHAMMED ADIL, 1552-1556

Persian legend on each side. With dates from about 960-964 A.H.
107. 1 Mohur 525.00

DIU

Mint mark:—D-O

Portuguese Kings of —

PETER, PRINCE REGENT, 1667-1683
St. Thomas standing. Rev. Crowned arms. Crude style.
107a. San Tome of 5 Xerafins 1684 .... 1500.00
107b. San Tome of 2½ Xerafins 1684 .... 1100.00

JOHN V, 1706-1750

St. Thomas standing. Rev. Crowned arms. Crude style.
108. San Tome of 5 Xerafins 1717-28 ....* 1100.00
108a. San Tome of 2½ Xerafins 1717-26 .... 925.00

JOSEPH I, 1750-1777

Crowned arms. Rev. Cross of St. Thomas. Crude style.
109. San Tome of 10 Xerafins 1752-57 ....* 1250.00
109a. San Tome of 5 Xerafins 1755, 57 .... 800.00

EAST INDIA COMPANY

(For other issues of the Company, see under British sovereigns of India, numbers 1-3. In addition, the Company struck native type coins at the mints of Arcot, Benares, Bengal, Bombay, Calcutta, Madras, Murshidabad and Surat, which see).

Arms supported by lions; English legend. Rev. Urdu legend.
110. 1 Mohur ND (1820)................................. 250.00

Lion with crown on plain ground; English legend. Rev. Urdu legend.
111. ½ Mohur ND (1820)...............................* 150.00
112. ¼ Mohur ND (1820)..........................* 125.00

Lion standing on shield; English legend. Rev. Urdu legend.
113. ⅓ Mohur ND (1820)................................. 150.00

GOA

Mint mark:—G-A

A. Chiefs of —
Lion, sun and moon. Rev. Legend. Struck during the period 1185-1215.
114. 1 Pagoda ND 220.00

B. Portuguese Kings of —

MANUEL I, 1495-1521

MEA under crown. Rev. Globe.
115. ½ Esphera ND 1250.00

JOHN III, 1522-1557

St. Thomas standing. Rev. Crowned arms.
115a. 1 Indian San Tome ND 4375.00

St. Thomas seated. Rev. Crowned arms.

116.   1 Pardau San Tome ND.......................... 2500.00

SEBASTIAN, 1558-1578
St. Thomas standing. Rev. Crowned arms.

116a.   1 San Tome ND 2500.00

PHILIP I, 1581-1599
St. Thomas standing. Rev. Crowned arms.

116b.   1 San Tome ND 2750.00

PHILIP III, 1621-1640

St. Thomas standing. Rev. Crowned arms.   2500.00

116c.   San Tome of 5 Xerafins 1632, 33 ....

ALFONSO VI, 1657-1667

St. Thomas standing. Rev. Crowned arms.

117.   1 San Tome 1660.................................. 2500.00

PETER, PRINCE REGENT, 1667-1683

St. Thomas standing. Rev. Crowned arms.

118.   San Tome of 5 Xerafins 1670-80 .... 1500.00

Crowned arms. Rev. Cross.

118a.   San Tome of 1 Xerafin 1679 .... 650.00

PETER II, 1684-1706
Crowned arms. Rev. Cross of Jerusalem.

119.   San Tome of 1 Xerafin 1705 .... 800.00

JOHN V, 1707-1750
St. Thomas standing. Rev. Crowned arms.

120.   San Tome of 10 Xerafins 1713-17 .... 1250.00
120a.   San Tome of 5 Xerafins 1713-17 .... 925.00
120b.   San Tome of 2½ Xerafins 1713-17 .... 550.00

Crowned arms. Rev. Cross of St. Thomas. With or without legend.
121.   San Tome of 10 Xerafins 1728-37 ....* 1100.00
122.   San Tome of 5 Xerafins ND......................... 925.00

Crowned arms. Rev. Cross of Jerusalem.
123.   San Tome of 1 Xerafin 1711-28....................... 425.00

JOSEPH I, 1751-1777

Crowned arms. Rev. Cross of St. Thomas.
124.   San Tome of 12 Xerafins 1762-80 ....*...... 850.00
125.   San Tome of 8 Xerafins 1763-80, ND................. 1000.00
126.   San Tome of 4 Xerafins 1763-80 .... 750.00
127.   San Tome of 2 Xerafins 1762-80 .... 500.00

Royal crown. Rev. Cross of St. Thomas.
127a.   San Tome of 2 Xerafins 1766-80 .... 500.00
127b.   San Tome of 1 Xerafin 1766, 68, ND 250.00

Shield. Rev. Cross of St. Thomas.
127c.   San Tome of 1 Xerafin 1769 .... 250.00

MARY I AND PETER III, 1778-1787
Crowned arms. Rev. Cross of St. Thomas
127d.   San Tome of 12 Xerafins 1778-86 .... 850.00
127e.   San Tome of 8 Xerafins 1778, 82 .... 1000.00
127f.   San Tome of 4 Xerafins 1778 .... 750.00
127g.   San Tome of 2 Xerafins 1778, 86 .... 500.00

MARY I, 1787-1807

Crowned arms. Rev. Cross of St. Thomas.
128.   San Tome of 12 Xerafins 1787-1809 .... 850.00
129.   San Tome of 8 Xerafins 1786-1804 ....*...... 1000.00
130.   San Tome of 4 Xerafins 1795-1804 ....*...... 750.00
130a.   San Tome of 2 Xerafins 1799 .... 500.00

JOHN, PRINCE REGENT, 1807-1819
Crowned arms. Rev. Cross of St. Thomas.
131.   San Tome of 12 Xerafins 1807-16 .... 850.00
131a.   San Tome of 8 Xerafins 1819 .... 1000.00
131b.   San Tome of 2 Xerafins 1815 .... 500.00

JOHN VI, 1819-1826
Crowned arms. Rev. Cross of St. Thomas.
132.   San Tome of 12 Xerafins 1819-25 .... 1000.00
132a.   San Tome of 8 Xerafins 1819 .... 1250.00
132b.   San Tome of 4 Xerafins 1819 .... 1000.00
132c.   San Tome of 2 Xerafins 1819 .... 650.00
132d.   San Tome of 1 Xerafin 1819 .... 500.00

MARY II, 1834-1853

Crowned arms. Rev. Cross of St. Thomas.
133.   San Tome of 12 Xerafins 1840, 41 .... 1250.00

GUJARAT

Persian legend on each side.

134.	1 Mohur 914-77 A.H. (1459-1573) .... *	250.00
135.	½ Mohur 914 A.H. (1508)	125.00

GWALIOR

Persian legend on each side.

135a.	1 Mohur 1130 A.H. (issued 1843-86)	375.00

Turbaned bust of the Rajah Madho Rao III, 1886-1925. Rev. Arms.

136.	⅓ Mohur 1959 Samvat (1902)	345.00

HINDUSTAN

The coinage of the Mogul Emperors of Hindustan is the most extensive and varied of Indian coinages. The largest gold coins of the entire world were struck by these Emperors. The whereabouts of most of these large coins is now unknown, but they are all reported as having been seen in contemporary literature. The largest coin of all is the 200 Mohur piece of Shah Jahan. The actual coin was last reported seen in India in the early part of the 19th century, and a cast of the coin is now in the British Museum (see the back cover of the book).

The Mogul Emperors also issued the famous set of Zodiac Mohurs. There are many variations of the Zodiac figures and the illustrations in this book are of typical examples.

Mogul Emperors of —

HUMAYUN, 1530-1554

Persian legend on each side. With dates from about 937-960 A.H.

137.	1/10 Mohur	60.00
138.	1/20 Mohur	40.00

AKBAR, 1556-1605
(Coinage with dates from about 963-1014 A.H.)

Persian legend on each side.

139.	100 Mohurs	Unknown
140.	50 Mohurs	Unknown
141.	20 Mohurs. Round	Unknown
142.	20 Mohurs. Square	Unknown

143.	5 Mohurs	5000.00
144.	2 Mohurs. Round	Unknown
145.	2 Mohurs. Square.............................	Unknown
146.	1 Mohur. Round ....* ..	155.00
147.	1 Mohur. Square ....* ..	155.00
148.	1 Mohur. Oblong with scalloped corners....*	470.00
149.	½ Mohur. Lozenge shaped	340.00
150.	½ Mohur. Square	155.00
151.	¼ Mohur. Round	135.00
152.	¼ Mohur. Square	135.00
153.	1/10 Mohur	40.00
154.	1/20 Mohur	40.00

Persian legend within square on each side.

155.	1 Mohur....................................	155.00

Persian legend within octagon on each side.

156.	1 Mohur....................................	220.00

Hawk standing. Rev. Persian legend.

157.	1 Mohur....................................	750.00

Duck standing. Rev. Persian legend.

158.	1 Mohur....................................	750.00

Male and female figures standing, the male holding bow and arrows. Rev. Persian legend.

159.	½ Mohur...................................	700.00

JAHANGIR, 1605-1627
(Coinage with dates from about 1014-1037 A.H.)

Turbaned bust with or without fruit or goblet in front of face. Rev. Lion to right or left under radiate sun.

160.	1 Mohur....................................	750.00

King seated cross-legged. Rev. Persian legend.

161.   ¼ Mohur.. 375.00

Small figure seated cross-legged. Rev. Lion under radiate sun.

162.   1 Mohur....................................... 1200.00

Large figure seated cross-legged. Rev. Radiate sun in square within panelled Persian legend.

163.   1 Mohur....................................... 1200.00

Sign of the Zodiac as noted. Rev. Persian legend. The famous Zodiac Mohurs.

164.   1 Mohur. Twins (Gemini)..................... 1500.00
165.   1 Mohur. Goat (Capricorn) 1500.00
166.   1 Mohur. Scales (Libra) 1500.00
167.   1 Mohur. Bull (Taurus)..................... 1500.00
168.   1 Mohur. Crab (Cancer)..................... 1700.00
169.   1 Mohur. Female (Virgo) 1500.00
170.   1 Mohur. Ram (Aries)....................... 1750.00
171.   1 Mohur. Lion (Leo)........................ 1875.00
172.   1 Mohur. Scorpion (Scorpio) 1750.00
173.   1 Mohur. Archer (Sagittarius) 1750.00
174.   1 Mohur. Water carrier (Aquarius).......... 1875.00
175.   1 Mohur. Fish (Pisces)..................... 1750.00

Persian legend on each side.

176.   5 Mohurs.............................*...... 3750.00
177.   1 Mohur. Round ....*...... 125.00
178.   1 Mohur. Square.....................*...... 190.00

SHAH JAHAN, 1628-1658
(Coinage with dates from about 1037-1068 A.H.)
Persian legend on each side.

179.   1 Mohur. Round 125.00
180.   1 Mohur. Square............................. 190.00
181.   ½ Mohur.................................... 220.00

Persian legend within square on each side.

182.   200 Mohurs............................*..... Unknown
183.   1 Mohur............................*...... 125.00

Persian legend within lozenge or diamond on each side.

184.   1 Mohur................................... 125.00

Persian legend within circle on each side.

185.   1 Mohur................................... 155.00

MURAD BAKHSH, 1658

Persian legend within square on each side.

186.   1 Mohur 1068 A.H............................ 280.00

AURANGZIB, 1659-1707
(Coinage with dates from about 1069-1118 A.H.)

Persian legend on each side.

187.   100 Mohurs................................. Unknown
188.   1 Mohur.................................... 250.00
189.   ¼ Mohur............................*...... 65.00

Persian legend within square on each side.

190.   1 Mohur................................... 250.00

AZAM SHAH, 1707
Persian legend on each side.

191.   1 Mohur 1118, 19 A.H........................ 280.00

KAM BAKHSH, 1708
Persian legend on each side.

192.   1 Mohur 1120 A.H........................... 350.00

SHAH ALAM BAHADUR I, 1707-1712

Persian legend on each side. With dates from about 1119-1124 A.H.

193.	1 Mohur. Usual size		125.00
194.	1 Mohur. Broad type	*	190.00

JAHANDAR, 1712
Persian legend on each side.

195.	1 Mohur 1124 A.H.		125.00

FARRUKH-SIYAR, 1713-1719

Persian legend on each side. With dates from about 1124-1131 A.H.

196.	1 Mohur		125.00
197.	¼ Mohur	*	50.00
198.	⅛ Mohur	*	40.00

RAFI-UD-DARJAT, 1719
Persian legend on each side.

199.	1 Mohur 1131 A.H.		500.00

SHAH JAHAN II, 1719
Persian legend on each side.

200.	1 Mohur 1131 A.H.		280.00

201.	The coin previously listed does not exist		—

IBRAHIM, 1720
Persian legend on each side.

202.	1 Mohur 1132 A.H.		250.00

MOHAMMED SHAH, 1719-1748
Persian legend on each side. With dates from about 1131-1161 A.H.

203.	1 Mohur		250.00
204.	¼ Mohur		65.00
205.	1/64 Mohur		30.00

AHMED SHAH, 1748-1754
Persian legend on each side. With dates from about 1161-1167 A.H.

206.	1 Mohur		250.00
207.	1/64 Mohur. Rev. Blank		35.00

ALAMGIR II, 1754-1759
Persian legend on each side. Wtih dates from about 1167-1173 A.H.

208.	1 Mohur		250.00
209.	¼ Mohur		65.00
210.	1/64 Mohur		30.00

Persian legend within square on each side.

211.	1 Mohur		250.00

SHAH JAHAN III, 1759-1760
Persian legend on each side.

212.	1 Mohur 1173, 74 A.H.		250.00

SHAH ALAM II, 1759-1806

Persian legend on each side. With dates from about 1173-1221 A.H.

213.	1 Mohur. Usual size	*	250.00
214.	1 Mohur. Broad type		325.00
215.	1/16 Mohur		50.00
216.	1/64 Mohur		30.00

Persian legend within circle on each side, the whole within a floral wreath formed by roses, thistles and shamrocks.

217.	1 Mohur		375.00

BIDAR BAKHT, PRETENDER, 1788
Persian legend on each side.

218.	1 Mohur 1202, 03 A.H.		250.00

HYDERABAD

Persian legend on each side. Coinage of the Nizams, struck during the period 1700-1903, and with dates from about 1114-1321 A.H.

219.	1 Mohur	*	250.00
220.	½ Mohur		150.00
221.	¼ Mohur		100.00
222.	⅛ Mohur		70.00
223.	1/16 Mohur		45.00

The Char Minar building. Rev. Legend. Struck under the Nizam Mir Mahbub Ali Khan, 1869-1911.

224.	1 Mohur 1321-29 A.H. (1903-11)	*	250.00
225.	½ Mohur 1321-29 A.H. (1903-11)		150.00
226.	¼ Mohur 1321-29 A.H. (1903-11)		100.00
227.	⅛ Mohur 1321-29 A.H. (1903-11)		70.00

Type similar to above but struck under the Nizam Mir Usman Ali Khan, 1911-1948.

228.	1 Mohur 1343-65 A.H. (1924-46)	250.00
229.	½ Mohur 1337-53 A.H. (1919-34)	130.00
230.	¼ Mohur 1337 A.H. (1919)	110.00
231.	⅛ Mohur 1337-43 A.H. (1919-24)	70.00

IKARI

Goddess seated. Rev. Legend. Coinage of Governors struck during the period 1500-1700

232.	1 Pagoda ND	125.00

JAIPUR

Urdu legend on each side. Maharajah coinage struck during the period 1806-1855.

233.	1 Mohur	250.00

Urdu legend on each side. Struck in the names of the ruling English sovereigns (Queen Victoria and King George V) during the period 1858-1943.

233a.	1 Mohur	250.00

JAISALMIR

Persian legend on each side. Rajah coinage struck during the period 1860-1899

234.	1 Mohur. Regnal year 22	250.00

JAUNPUR

Persian legend on each side. Royal coinage struck during the period 1400-1500.

235.	1 Mohur	250.00

JEJAKABHUKTI (BUNDELKHAND)

Goddess seated. Rev. Legend. Coinage of Governors struck during the period 1055-1240.

236.	1 Stater	160.00

JIND

Indian legend on each side. Rajah coinage struck during the period 1840-1865.

237.	1 Mohur	250.00

JODHPUR

Persian legend. Rev. Arab legend. Rajah coinage struck during the period 1802-1858.

238.	1 Mohur	280.00

Urdu legend on each side. Struck in the names of the ruling English sovereigns (Queen Victoria and Kings George V and George VI) during the period 1858-1947.

238a.	1 Mohur (1858-1947)	280.00
238b.	½ Mohur (1876-1895)	160.00
238c.	¼ Mohur (1876-1895)	125.00

JUNAGADH

Urdu legend on each side. Struck under Mahabat Khan.

238d.	1 Kori 1292 A.H. (1875)	435.00

Urdu legend on each side. Struck under Nawab Bahadur Khan III.

239.	1 Kori 1309 A.H. (1891)	*	375.00
240.	½ Kori 1309 A.H. (1891)		280.00

KACHAR

Bengali legend on each side. Struck between 1583 and 1720.

240a.	1 Mohur ND	3125.00

KALINGA

Recumbent bull. Rev. Date. Coinage of Governors struck during the period 1050-1150.

241.	1 Fanam	50.00

The Monkey god Hanuman. Rev. Blank.

242.	1 Fanam (1050-1150)	50.00

KALPI

Native legend on each side. Shah coinage struck during the period 1500-1600.

243.	1 Mohur. Square	250.00

KALYANI

Temple. Rev. Blank. Coinage of Governors struck during the period 1100-1200.

244.	1 Pagoda	140.00

The Monkey god Hanuman. Rev. Blank.

245.	1 Pagoda (1100-1200)	140.00

KANAUJ

King standing. Rev. Goddess. Royal coinage struck during the period 600-900.
246.   1 Stater 100.00

KASHMIR

King standing. Rev. Goddess seated. Royal coinage struck during the period 700-800.
247.   1 Stater 155.00

Indian legend on each side.
248.   1 Mohur (1450-1550) 125.00

KISHANGARH

Urdu legend on each side. In the name of Shah Alam II.
249.   1 Mohur 1197 A.H. (struck 1782-1858) 400.00

KOTAH

Urdu legend on each side. Struck in the name of Mohammed Bahadur during the period 1837-1857.
250.   1 Mohur ....* 280.00
251.   ½ Mohur ....* 220.00
251a.   ¼ Mohur 155.00

Urdu legend on each side. Struck in the name of Queen Victoria during the period 1858-1902.
251b.   1 Mohur 280.00

KULBARGA

Persian legend on each side. Bahmani coinage struck during the period 1400-1500.
252.   1 Mohur 155.00

MADRAS

Urdu legend on each side. Coinage of the British East India Company struck during the period 1750-1820.
253.   1 Mohur 250.00
254.   ½ Mohur 125.00
255.   ⅓ Mohur 85.00

Vishnu seated. Rev. Star.
256.   1 Pagoda (1750)................................. 95.00

Vishnu standing. Rev. Star.
257.   1 Pagoda (1750)................................. 75.00

Vishnu standing. Rev. Grains.
258.   1 Pagoda (1750)................................. 60.00

Three gods standing. Rev. Grains.
259.   1 Pagoda (1750)................................. 75.00

Four-armed god. Rev. Grains.
260.   1 Pagoda (1750)................................. 75.00

Siva and Parvati seated. Rev. Grains.
261.   1 Pagoda (1750)................................. 75.00

Pagoda amid stars. Rev. Vishnu.
262.   2 Pagodas (1810) ....* 220.00
263.   1 Pagoda (1810)............................* 170.00

MAHAKOSALA

Rampant lion. Rev. Legend. Coinage of Governors struck during the period 1140-1190.
264.   1 Stater 155.00

MALACCA

Portuguese Kings of —

PHILIP III, 1623-1640
St. Thomas standing. Rev. Crowned arms.
264a. San Tome of 1 Xerafin 1634. A-M mm.................. 750.00

MALDIVE ISLANDS

Urdu legend on each side. Struck by Hasan Nur Al-Din, 1778-1798.
264b.   1 Mohur 1207 A.H. (1793)........................... 925.00

MALWA

Persian legend on each side. Royal coinage struck during the period 1400-1600.
265.   1 Mohur. Round 275.00
266.   1 Mohur. Square...........................* 250.00
267.   1 Mohur. Octagonal........................... 250.00

MANIPUR

Indian legend on each side. Rajah coinage struck during the period 1760-1780.
268.   1 Mohur. Square.............................. 250.00
269.   ½ Mohur. Square.............................. 125.00
270.   ¼ Mohur. Square.............................. 65.00

MASULIPATAN

Three gods standing. Rev. Grains.
272.   1 Pagoda (1750)................................. 30.00

MEWAR-UDAIPUR

Persian legend and design on each side. Maharajah coinage struck during the period 1842-1910.

273.   1 Mohur 250.00

Nagari legend on each side.

274.   1 Mohur (1851-1930) 250.00

MOGUL EMPIRE

(See under Hindustan)

MURSHIDABAD

Urdu legend on each side, with oblique or straight milling or with plain edge. Coinage of the British East India Company in the name of Shah Alam II of Hindustan. With dates from about 1182-1204 A.H. (1768-1832).

275.   1 Mohur ....* 250.00
276.   ½ Mohur 125.00
277.   ¼ Mohur 65.00
278.   ⅛ Mohur ....* 35.00
279.   ¹⁄₁₆ Mohur 25.00

MYSORE

RAJAH RANADHIRA WODEYAR, 1638-1659
Vishnu seated. Rev. Legend.

280.   1 Fanam ND.. 20.00

HAIDAR ALI, 1761-1782
Persian legend on each side.

281.   1 Mohur 1195 A.H. (1781) 675.00
281a. 1 Pagoda ND... 75.00
281b. 1 Fanam 1189-96 A.H. (1775-82) 40.00

Siva and Parvati seated. Rev. Initial on grains.

282.   1 Pagoda ND ....* 60.00
282a. ½ Pagoda ND 45.00
283.   1 Fanam ND.. 30.00

Half-length figure of Vishnu. Rev. Initial on grains.

284.   ½ Pagoda ND 70.00

TIPU SULTAN, 1782-1799

Persian legend on each side. Beginning in 1787 A.D. dates are given in solar years (A.M.) rather than in lunar years (A.H.)

285.   4 Pagodas (1 Mohur) 1198-99 A.H.,
         1215-19 A.M. (1784-91) ....* 500.00
286.   2 Pagodas (½ Mohur) 1216-19 A.M. (1788-91)........ 300.00
287.   1 Pagoda 1215-23 A.M. (1787-95) ....* 90.00

Initial. Rev. Persian legend.

288.   1 Pagoda 1197-1200 A.H., 1215-23 A.M. (1783-95)* ... 100.00
289.   1 Fanam 1197-1200 A.H., 1215-23 A.M. (1783-95)..... 25.00

KRISHNA RAJAH WODEYAR, 1799-1868

Siva and Parvati seated. Rev. Nagari legend.

290.   1 Pagoda ND (1811-30).....................* 70.00
291.   ½ Pagoda ND (1811-30)............................. 50.00
292.   1 Fanam ND (1799-1830) 20.00

NAWANAGAR

Crude Persian legend on each side. Struck under Vibhaji II, 1852-1895.

293.   1 Kori ....* 220.00
293a. ½ Kori 200.00

NEGAPATNAM

(Dutch East India Company)

Crude four-armed god. Rev. Grains.

294.   1 Pagoda (1660-1780) 90.00

Vishnu standing. Rev. Grains.

295.   1 Pagoda (1660-1780) 60.00

Crude human figure. Rev. Legend and "OC" (East India Company).

296.   3 Fanams (1690-95) 125.00
297.   1 Fanam (1690-95) 50.00

ORISSA

Elephant. Rev. Scroll. Coinage of Governors struck during the period 1200-1400.

298.	1 Pagoda	155.00

Crude figure. Rev. Legend.

299.	1 Pagoda	80.00
300.	½ Pagoda	50.00

PATIALA

Native legend on each side. Rajah coinage struck in the name of Ahmad Shah Durrani during the period 1831-1894.

301.	1 Mohur	300.00
301a.	½ Mohur	225.00
301b.	¼ Mohur	150.00
301c.	⅛ Mohur	125.00

PONDICHERRY

(French East India Company)
Crown and stars. Rev. Fleur-de-lis.

302.	1 Pagoda (1715-74)	550.00

Goddess. Rev. Crescent amid grains.

303.	1 Pagoda (1715-74)	375.00

Two goddesses. Rev. Crescent amid grains.

304.	1 Pagoda (1715-74)	375.00

Vishnu between two figures. Rev. Crescent amid grains.

305.	1 Pagoda (1715-74)	375.00

PULICAT

(Dutch settlement on the Coromandel Coast)

Crude four-armed god. Rev. Legend.

306.	1 Pagoda (1646-1781)	Unique

Crude symbol. Rev. Grains.

307.	1 Fanam (1646-1781)	65.00

PUNJAB

Persian legend on each side. Sikh coinage struck during the period 1750-1875.

308.	1 Mohur	*	250.00
309.	1 Rupee 1205 A.H.		30.00

RADHANPUR

ZORAWAR KHAN, 1825-1874
Persian legend on each side.

310.	1 Mohur 1277 A.H. (1860)	525.00

RAJKOT

Radiant sun. Rev. Arms and tridents.

311.	1 Mohur 1945	750.00

REWA

GULAB SINGH, 1918-1944
Arms supported by lions. Rev. Nagari legend. On his coronation.

311a.	1 Mohur 1975 Samvat (1918)	400.00

SOUTH INDIA

Lotus flower. Rev. Blank. Crude concave coins struck during the period 600-1000.

312.	1 Tanka	90.00

SURAT

Persian legend on each side. Coinage of the British East India Company in the name of Shah Alam II of Hindustan. This issue was struck in 1825.

313.	1 Mohur	*	100.00
314.	½ Mohur		125.00
315.	¼ Mohur		62.50
316.	¹⁄₁₆ Mohur		50.00

Very small crowned head amid legend. Rev. Legend with
date 1802 on small oval panel.

317.	1 Mohur ....*	375.00
318.	¼ Mohur .... *	200.00

TELLICHERRY

Native legend on each side.

319.	1 Pagoda (1806).....................	80.00

Native legend on each side with date on reverse.

320.	⅕ Rupee 1809........................	155.00

TIPERAH

Bengali legend on each side. Rajah coinage struck during
the period 1460-1467 A.D.

321.	1 Mohur.......................	675.00

Lion. Rev. Bengali legend in square.

321a.	1 Mohur 1412-1791 Samvat (1490-1869).............	550.00
321b.	¼ Mohur 1682 Samvat (1760)......................	675.00

Arms. Rev. Bengali legend.

322.	1 Mohur 1279-1306 Tiperah Era (1869-96)...........	465.00

TONK

Persian legend on each side. Rajah coinage struck during
the period 1834-1885.

323.	2 Mohurs..................... *	340.00
324.	1 Mohur.............................	100.00

TRAVANCORE

Pellets and lines on each side.

325.	1 Viraraya Fanam (1700-1890)	15.00

Pellets. Rev. Symbol.

326.	1 Anantaraya Fanam (1790-1860). Without leaf spray	15.00
326a.	1 Anantaraya Fanam (1860-90). With leaf spray* ...	15.00
327.	½ Anantaraya Fanam (1790-1820)	15.00

Crescent. Rev. Symbol.

328.	1 Kali Fanam (1740-1881)	15.00

MAHARAJAH RAMA VARMA IV, 1860-1880

Shell in wreath. Rev. "R.V." and "1877" in wreath, "Travancore" above.

329.	2 Pagodas 1877	450.00
330.	1 Pagoda 1877....................................	340.00

PRESENTATION ISSUES

Tamil legend. Rev. Blank. Struck on smaller and thicker
flans than later issues.

331.	2 Pagodas (1829-50)..........................*	375.00
332.	1 Pagoda (1829-50)................................	280.00
333.	½ Pagoda (1829-50)...............................	155.00
334.	¼ Pagoda (1829-50)...............................	125.00

Shell in wreath. Rev. Tamil legend in wreath.

335.	2 Pagodas (1870-1931)	375.00
336.	1 Pagoda (1870-1931).........................*	250.00
337.	½ Pagoda (1870-1931)	125.00
338.	¼ Pagoda (1870-1931)	100.00

Bust of the Maharajah Sri Rama Varma V, 1880-1885. Rev.
Arms supported by elephants.

339.	1 Sovereign 1881	625.00
340.	½ Sovereign 1881	850.00

TUTICORIN

Crude symbols on each side.

341.	1 Fanam (1675-1760)	50.00

UJAIN

Native legend on each side. Rajah coinage struck during
the period 1750-1800.

342.	1 Mohur...	300.00

VENGI

Boar and umbrella. Rev. Blank. Coinage of Governors struck
during the period 1000-1100.

343.	1 Pagoda..	125.00

VIJAYANAGAR

God and Goddess seated. Rev. Legend. Royal coinage struck during the period 1400-1600.

344.	1 Pagoda .... *	60.00
345.	½ Pagoda	40.00

Deity seated. Rev. Legend.

346.	1 Pagoda	50.00

Eagle and elephants. Rev. Legend.

347.	1 Pagoda	95.00
348.	½ Pagoda .... *	75.00

Vishnu standing. Rev. Legend.

349.	1 Pagoda .... *	60.00
350.	½ Pagoda	40.00

IRELAND

English Kings of —

CHARLES I, 1626-1649

The following coins, issued by the Lords Justices of Ireland, are sometimes called "Inchiquin Money" or "Ormonde Money." Only two specimens are known of the 2 Pistoles piece and ten of the 1 Pistole piece.

Stamped with weight "8 dwtt. 14 gr." on both sides.

1.	2 Pistoles ND ....Very Rare

Stamped with weight "4 dwtt. 7 gr." on both sides.

2.	1 Pistole ND ....Very Rare

Stamped with weight "4 dwtt. 7 gr." Rev. "4 dwtt. 6 gr."

3.	1 Pistole ND ....Very Rare

ITALY

Mints and mint marks or symbols for the Italian and Sardinian Kingdoms during the period 1821-1878.

(Later coinage was struck only at the Rome Mint):—

R	mm for Rome
Eagle's head	mm for Turin
Anchor	mm for Genoa
T and BN	mm for Turin
M and BN	mm for Milan

National Italian coinage from 1806 to 1927 was based first on the French monetary system and later on the standard of the Latin Monetary Union. The Italian gold Lira was subsequently re-valued and the first coins on the new standard were struck by the Vatican in 1929 and by Italy in 1931.

The Italian series is second only to the German in its extent and variety, since there was no truly national coinage until 1861. Prior to that time, Italy had a multitude of autonomous local coinages dating back to about 600 A.D.

The Florentine Florin, the Genoese Genovino (and later Ducat) and the Venetian Ducat (and later Zecchino) were the principal gold coins of the late Middle Ages, 1200 and later. They were universally known and respected for the purity of their gold which was from about .990 to 1000 fine, and the size, weight and purity of these coins became the prototypes for the principal part of later Continental coinage.

The enduring nature of the Ducat can be seen from the fact that it was struck as an official government coin as recently as 1972. The country of issue was the Netherlands and it is interesting to note that the specifications of the Ducat of 1972 were about the same as the original Ducat which Venice introduced to the world about 1200.

A. Republic of —, 1797-1805

Head of Napoleon as founder and president. Rev. Value in wreath or circle.

1.	1 Doppia 1803 (year 2)........................ *	Rare
2.	½ Doppia 1803 (year 2)............................	Rare

Head of Napoleon. Rev. Scales.

3.	20 Lire 1804	Rare

B. Kings of —, 1805-1814 and 1861-1945

NAPOLEON, 1805-1814

Head. Rev. Arms. Milan Mint with M mm.

4.	40 Lire 1807	3000.00
5.	40 Lire 1808-14 .... *	400.00
6.	40 Lire 1808. Without M mm........................	1500.00
7.	20 Lire 1808-14	300.00

(For French type coins struck at the Italian Mints, see under France).

VICTOR EMANUEL II, 1861-1878
(For the earlier coins of this ruler, see under Sardinia and Emilia).

Head. Rev. Arms.

8.	100 Lire 1864. T mm.	8000.00
9.	100 Lire 1872, 78. R mm.	8000.00
10.	50 Lire 1864. T mm.	Rare
11.	20 Lire 1861-70. T mm.	150.00
12.	20 Lire 1870-78. R mm.	150.00
13.	20 Lire 1872-75. M mm. *	150.00
14.	10 Lire 1861. T mm.	8000.00
15.	10 Lire 1863-65. T mm. *	200.00
16.	5 Lire 1863, 65. T mm.	300.00

HUMBERT I, 1878-1900

Head. Rev. Arms.

17.	100 Lire 1880	15000.00
18.	100 Lire 1882, 83, 88, 91 (1888, 91 Rare)	4000.00
19.	50 Lire 1884, 88	3000.00
20.	50 Lire 1891	5000.00
21.	20 Lire 1879-97 *	150.00

VICTOR EMANUEL III, 1900-1944

Head. Rev. Eagle. All coins of 1902, 1908, 1910 are rare.

22.	100 Lire 1903, 05	7000.00
23.	20 Lire 1902. With and without small anchor at bottom of Obv. indicating gold from Eritrea..	Rare
24.	20 Lire 1903, 05, 08, 10 *	1000.00

Head. Rev. Allegorical scene. On the 50th year of the Kingdom.

25.	50 Lire 1911	1000.00

Uniformed bust. Rev. Agricultural scene. The 1910, 1926, 1927 issues are rare.

26.	100 Lire 1910, 12, 26, 27	3250.00
27.	50 Lire 1910, 12, 26, 27	1250.00
28.	20 Lire 1910, 12, 26, 27 *	650.00
29.	10 Lire 1910, 12, 26, 27	2500.00

Head. Rev. Fasces. On the first year of the Fascist march on Rome.

30.	100 Lire 1923	1750.00
31.	20 Lire 1923	500.00

Head. Rev. Naked male holding winged Victory. On the 25th year of reign and on the 10th year of entry into World War I.

32.	100 Lire 1925	4000.00

Head. Rev. Italia on prow of ship.

33.	100 Lire 1931, 32, 33	500.00

Head. Rev. Figure holding Fasces.

34.	50 Lire 1931, 32, 33	350.00

Head right. Rev. Figure holding Fasces. After the conquest of Ethiopia, with the title of Emperor added to that of King.

35.	100 Lire 1936 *	5500.00
36.	100 Lire 1937. Size reduced	15000.00

Head left. Rev. Eagle over two medallions.

37.   50 Lire 1936 .... 3250.00

C. States and Cities of —

ACHAIA

Princes of —

ROBERT OF ANJOU, 1346-1364

Lily. Rev. St. John standing.

38.   1 Florin ND.. 2500.00

AMADEUS VI OF SAVOY, 1367-1383
Helmeted arms. Rev. St. John.
39.   1 Florin ND.. 3000.00

Arms. Rev. Cross.
40.   1 Scudo d'oro ND 10000.00

LOUIS OF SAVOY, 1402-1418
Ruler on horse. Rev. Helmet.
41.   1 Florin ND.. 7500.00

AMALFI

Rulers of —

PRINCE GUAIMARIO V AND MANSONE IV, 1042
Cufic legend on each side.
42.   1 Tari ND.. 1000.00

AUTONOMOUS, 1050-1100
Cufic legend on each side.
43.   1 Tari ND.. 400.00

DUKE ROGER BORSA, 1085-1111
Cufic legend on each side.
44.   1 Tari ND.. 600.00

GISULFO II, 1098
Head of St. Andrea. Rev. Cufic legend.
44a.   1 Tari ND.. 5000.00

DUKE WILLIAM I, 1111-1127
W. Rev. Cross.
45.   1 Tari ND.. 600.00

COUNT ROGER II, 1105-1154

R. Rev. Cross

46.   1 Tari ND.. 550.00

KING WILLIAM II, 1162-1189

W. Rev. Rex.

47.   1 Tari ND... 700.00

KING TANCRED, 1189-1194
ACD Monogram. Rev. Rex.
48.   1 Tari ND... 700.00

KING TANCRED AND WILLIAM, 1193
Rex and TCD Monogram. Rev. W.
49.   1 Tari ND... 2000.00

KING HENRY VI, 1194-1197
Bust. Rev. Cross.
50.   1 Tari ND... 3000.00

QUEEN CONSTANCE AND FREDERICK II, 1197-1198
Palm Tree. Rev. Cross.
51.   1 Tari ND... Rare

KING FREDERICK II, 1198-1250
FRE. Rev. Star.
52.   1 Tari ND... 1750.00

F. Rev. Rex.
53.   1 Tari ND... 1750.00

IMP. Rev. Cross Potent.
54.   1 Tari ND... 5000.00

ANCONA

Anonymous Rulers of —

Knight standing. Rev. St. Quiriacus standing.
55.   2 Ducats ND (1500-1600)........................... Rare
56.   1 Ducat ND (1500-1600)........................... 10000.00

(For additional coins of Ancona, see under Vatican-Ancona).

ANTIGNATE

Lords of —

JOHN BENTIVOGLIO II, 1494-1509
Bust with cap. Rev. Legend.
57.   4 Ducats 1494 .... Rare
58.   ½ Ducat 1494 .... 10000.00

Bust with cap. Rev. Arms.
59.   2 Ducats ND 7500.00
60.   1 Ducat ND.................................*......10000.00

ARQUATA

Marcheses of —

JULIUS SPINOLA, 1681-1691
Bust. Rev. Arms.

61.   ½ Doppia 1681 ....   Rare

GERARD SPINOLA, 1682-1694
Bust. Rev. Arms.

62.   1 Doppia 1682 ....   Rare

ASTI

A. Kings of —

LOUIS XII OF FRANCE, 1498-1513
Crowned bust. Rev. Crowned arms.

63.   2 Ducats ND ....   Rare
64.   1 Ducat ND ....   Rare

Porcupine. Rev. Crowned arms.

65.   1 Ducat ND ....   Rare

B. Lords of —

CHARLES OF ORLEANS, 1407-1422 AND 1447-1465
Arms. Rev. Cross.

66.   1 Scudo d'oro ND 9000.00

LOUIS OF ORLEANS, 1465-1498
Ruler on horse. Rev. Arms.

67.   1 Ducat ND 7000.00

Arms. Rev. Cross.

68.   1 Scudo d'oro ND 13000.00

EMANUEL FILIBERT, 1542-1553
Arms. Rev. Cross.

69.   1 Scudo d'oro ND 7500.00

BARDI

Marcheses of —

FREDERICK LANDI, 1590-1627
Bust. Rev. St. Francis kneeling.

70.   5 Doppie 1622 ....   Rare

Bust. Rev. St. John standing.

71.   2 Doppie 1623 ....   Rare

Bust. Rev. Double eagle in shield.

72.   2 Doppie ND ....   Rare
73.   1 Doppia ND ....*......   Rare

Bust. Rev. St. Theresa.

74.   1 Doppia ND ....   Unknown

BARLETTA

Dukes of —

CHARLES I, 1266-1278

Bust. Rev. Arms.

75.   1 Real ND ....*......   Rare
76.   ½ Real ND ....   Rare

K. Rev. Arms.

77.   1 Tari ND 650.00

BELGIOJOSO

Princes of —

ANTHONY BARBIANO

Bust. Rev. Arms.

78.   1 Zecchino 1769 ....   5000.00

BELMONTE

Princes of —

ANTHONY PIGNATELLI

Bust. Rev. Arms.

79.   1 Zecchino 1733 ....   8000.00

BENEVELLO

Counts of —

JOHN ANTHONY FALLETTI, 1520-1544
Arms on cross. Rev. Eagle.

80.   1 Scudo d'oro ND ....   Rare

BENEVENTUM

Dukes, and later, Princes of —

ANONYMOUS, 569-706
Bust. Rev. Cross.

81.	1 Solidus ND	1200.00
82.	⅓ Solidus ND	1000.00

ROMUALD II, 706-731

Bust. Rev. Cross.

83.	1 Solidus ND.............*	1750.00
84.	⅓ Solidus ND	800.00

AUDELAO, 731
Bust. Rev. Cross.

85.	1 Solidus ND	Rare
86.	⅓ Solidus ND	Rare

GREGORY, 732-739
Bust. Rev. Cross.

87.	1 Solidus ND	1400.00
88.	⅓ Solidus ND	700.00

GODESCALCO, 739-742

Bust. Rev. Cross.

89.	1 Solidus ND.............*	1750.00
90.	⅓ Solidus ND	800.00

GISULF II, 742-751
Bust. Rev. Cross.

91.	1 Solidus ND	1750.00
92.	⅓ Solidus ND	800.00

LUITPRAND AND SCAUNIPERGA, 751-755

Bust. Rev. Cross.

93.	1 Solidus ND.............*	Rare
94.	⅓ Solidus ND	Rare

LUITPRAND, 755-758
Bust. Rev. Cross.

95.	1 Solidus ND	1750.00
96.	⅓ Solidus ND	800.00

INTERREGNUM, 758

Bust. Rev. Cross.

97.	1 Solidus ND.............*	3000.00
98.	⅓ Solidus ND	2500.00

ARICHIS II, DUKE, 758-774
Bust. Rev. Cross.

99.	1 Solidus ND	1750.00
100.	⅓ Solidus ND	800.00

ARICHIS II, PRINCE, 774-787

Bust. Rev. Cross.

101.	1 Solidus ND.............*	1200.00
102.	⅓ Solidus ND	600.00

GRIMOALD III, 788-806
Bust. Rev. Cross.

103.	1 Solidus ND. With monogram of Charlemagne	1500.00
104.	1 Solidus ND. Without monogram	1000.00
105.	⅓ Solidus ND. With monogram of Charlemagne	600.00
106.	⅓ Solidus ND. Without monogram	500.00

SICO, 817-832
Bust. Rev. St. Michael.

107.	1 Solidus ND	1500.00

Bust. Rev. Cross.

108.	⅓ Solidus ND	500.00

SICARDO, 832-839
Bust. Rev. Cross.

109.	1 Solidus ND	1200.00
110.	⅓ Solidus ND	500.00

RADELCHIS, 839-851
Bust. Rev. Cross.

111.	1 Solidus ND	1800.00

BERGAMO

CHARLEMAGNE, 773-800
Cross Potent. Rev. Cross and four globes.

112.	⅓ Solidus ND	Rare

BOLOGNA

(For additional coins struck at Bologna, see under Cispadane Republic, Emilia and Vatican).

A. Republic of —, 1376-1500

St. Peter standing. Rev. Lion.

113.	1 Bolognino d'oro ND	2000.00

St. Peter seated. Rev. Lion.

114.	2 Bolognino d'oro ND	....	Rare
115.	1 Bolognino d'oro ND	....	5000.00

B. Governors of —

JOHN I BENTIVOGLIO, 1401-1402
St. Peter. Rev. Lion.

116.	1 Bolognino d'oro ND	....	3000.00

PHILIP MARIA VISCONTI, 1438-1443
St. Peter. Rev. Lion.

117.	1 Florin ND	....	Rare

JOHN II BENTIVOGLIO, 1463-1506
St. Peter. Rev. Lion.

118.	2 Bolognino d'oro ND	....	2500.00
119.	1 Bolognino d'oro ND	....	3750.00

CHARLES V OF SPAIN
Head. Rev. Pillars of Hercules.

120.	1 Ducat 1530	....	Rare
120a.	½ Ducat 1530	....	Rare

BOZZOLO

Princes of —

JULIUS CAESAR GONZAGA, 1593-1609
Bust. Rev. Chameleon.

121.	5 Doppie (Gold Piastre) ND	....	Rare
122.	1 Doppia ND	....	16000.00

Bust. Rev. Arms.

123.	1 Doppia ND	....	16000.00

Soldier. Rev. Arms.

124.	1 Ducat ND	....	8000.00

SCIPIO GONZAGA, 1609-1670
Arms. Rev. Crowned female.

125.	1 Doppia 1618	....	12000.00

Bust. Rev. St. Peter kneeling before Christ.

126.	6 Doppie 1639	....	Rare
127.	4 Doppie 1639	....	Rare

Bust. Rev. Arms.

128.	5 Doppie ND	....	Rare
129.	1 Doppia ND	....	10000.00

Bust. Rev. Two shields.

130.	1 Doppia ND	....	10000.00

Soldier. Rev. Tablet.

131.	1 Ducat ND	....	4000.00

Duke standing. Rev. Eagle.

132.	1 Ducat ND	....	Rare

BRESCELLO

Lords of —

ALFONSO II D'ESTE, 1570-1595
Arms. Rev. Cross.

133.	1 Scudo d'oro ND	....	Rare

BRINDISI

Kings of —

FREDERICK II, 1197-1250

Bust. Rev. Eagle.

134.	1 Augustalis ND	....	8000.00
135.	½ Augustalis ND	....	5000.00

Eagle in circle. Rev. Legend divided by cross.

136.	10 Tari ND	....	2500.00
137.	6 Tari ND	..................*	1500.00

CHARLES I OF ANJOU, 1266-1278
Bust. Rev. Arms.

138.	1 Real ND	....	15000.00

Ruler on horse. Rev. Cross.

139.	5 Tari ND	....	10000.00
140.	1 Tari ND	....	2000.00

K, Rev. Cross.

141.	Multiple Tari ND	....	800.00
142.	The coin previously listed does not exist	....	—

Name. Rev. Cross.

143.	Multiple Tari ND	....	1000.00

CAGLIARI

Spanish Kings of —

CHARLES V
Arms. Rev. Cross.

144.	1 Scudo d'oro ND (1517-56)	....	5000.00

PHILIP V

Arms. Rev. Cross.

145.	1 Scudo d'oro 1701, 02, 03	....	1000.00

CHARLES III
Arms. Rev. Cross.

146.	1 Scudo d'oro 1710, 11, 12	....	1200.00

CAMERINO

Dukes of —

JOHN MARIA VARANO, 1511-1527

Bust. Rev. Arms.

147.	1 Ducat ND..........................	Rare

JULIA VARANO, 1527-1534
Head. Rev. Arms.

148.	1 Scudo d'oro ND	Rare

Arms. Rev. Cross.

149.	1 Scudo d'oro ND	1250.00

JULIA VARANO AND GUIDOBALD II DELLA ROVERE, 1534-1539

Arms. Rev. Cross.

150.	1 Scudo d'oro ND	1800.00

CAMPI

Marcheses of —

CHARLES CENTURIONI, 1654-1663
Bust. Rev. Eagle.

151.	1 Doppia 1661	16000.00

JOHN BAPTIST CENTURIONI, 1663-1715
Bust. Rev. Arms.

152.	½ Doppia 1668	10000.00

Busts of John and his wife, Julia. Rev. Arms.

153.	1 Doppia 1668	Rare

CARMAGNOLA

Marcheses of —

LOUIS II DI SALUZZO, 1475-1504

Bust with cap. Rev. Arms.

154.	1 Doppia ND .... *	Rare
155.	1 Ducat ND..........................	12000.00

Bust with cap. Rev. Helmet.

156.	1 Ducat ND	12000.00

Busts of Louis and Margaret. Rev. Eagle.

157.	10 Scudi d'oro 1503	Rare

MICHAEL ANTHONY DI SALUZZO, 1504-1528

St. Constantine on horse. Rev. Cross.

158.	1 Scudo d'oro ND	3000.00

St. Constantine. Rev. Helmet.

159.	1 Scudo d'oro ND	6000.00

Eagle. Rev. Cross.

160.	1 Scudo d'oro ND	3500.00

FRANCIS DI SALUZZO, 1529-1537
Arms. Rev. Cross.

161.	1 Scudo del sole ND	3500.00

GABRIEL DI SALUZZO, 1537-1548
Saint Constantine on horse. Rev. Helmeted shield.

162.	10 Scudi d'oro ND....................	Rare

CASALE

Marcheses of —

WILLIAM I PALEOLOGO, 1464-1483
St. Theodore. Rev. Helmeted shield.

163.	1 Ducat ND..........................	12000.00

WILLIAM II PALEOLOGO, 1494-1518
Bust with cap. Rev. Stag.

164.	4 Ducats ND	Rare

Bust with cap. Rev. Arms.

165.	2 Ducats ND	Rare

Bust. Rev. Plant.

166.	2 Ducats ND	Rare

Arms. Rev. Cross.

167.	1 Scudo d'oro ND	10000.00

Double eagle. Rev. Cross.

168.   1 Scudo d'oro ND 2200.00

BONIFACE II PALEOLOGO, 1518-1530
Bust with cap. Rev. Saint on horse.

169.   1 Ducat ND..   Rare

Double eagle. Rev. Cross.

170.   1 Scudo d'oro ND 2200.00

JOHN GEORGE PALEOLOGO,1530-1533
Double eagle. Rev. Cross.

171.   1 Scudo d'oro ND 6000.00

Arms. Rev. Cross.

172.   1 Scudo d'oro ND 6000.00

ANONYMOUS, 1500-1600
Double eagle. Rev. Cross.

173.   1 Scudo d'oro ND 6000.00

CHARLES V OF SPAIN, 1533-1536
Arms. Rev. Cross.

174.   1 Scudo d'oro ND 10000.00

FREDERICK II GONZAGA AND MARGARET PALEOLOGO, 1536-1540
Arms. Rev. Cross and initials.

175.   1 Scudo d'oro ND ....   Rare

FRANCIS III GONZAGA AND MARGARET PALEOLOGO, 1540-1550

Arms. Rev. Cross and initials.

176.   1 Scudo d'oro ND 6000.00

WILLIAM GONZAGA AND MARGARET PALEOLOGO, 1550-1566

Arms. Rev. Cross and initials.

177.   1 Scudo d'oro 1563-67, ND 2200.00

WILLIAM III GONZAGA, 1566-1587

Arms. Rev. Cross and initials.

178.   1 Scudo d'oro 1578, ND 2000.00

Bust right or left. Rev. Arms.

179.   2 Doppie 1578-86, ND...........................*..... 6000.00
180.   1 Doppia 1578, ND .... *...... 8000.00

Bust. Rev. Cross.

181.   1 Scudo d'oro 1578-82 .... 8000.00

VINCENT I GONZAGA, 1587-1612

Bust. Rev. Arms.

182.   2 Doppie 1588-1601................................ 10000.00

Arms. Rev. Cross.

183.   1 Scudo d'oro ND 6000.00

Eagle. Rev. Ruler standing.

184.   1 Ducat ND.. 6000.00

FRANCIS IV GONZAGA, 1612-1613

Busts of Francis and Margaret. Rev. Flower.

185.   1 Doppia 1612.....................................   Rare

Cross. Rev. Arms on Mt. Olympus.

186.   1 Doppia 1612.....................................   Rare

FERDINAND GONZAGA, 1613-1626

Bust. Rev. Arms.

187.   2 Doppie 1617, 21, ND............................. 7000.00
188.   1 Doppia 1617, ND ....*...... 8500.00

Bust. Rev. Stag.

189.	5 Doppie ND	Rare

VINCENT II GONZAGA, 1626-1627
Bust. Rev. Arms.

190.	2 Doppie 1627	Rare
191.	1 Doppia ND	10000.00

CHARLES I GONZAGA, 1627-1637
Bust. Rev. Arms.

192.	2 Doppie 1629, 31, 36........................	10000.00
193.	1 Doppia 1632	12500.00

CHARLES II GONZAGA, 1637-1655
Busts of Charles and Maria. Rev. Arms.

194.	2 Doppie ND	Rare
195.	1 Doppia ND	Rare

FERDINAND CHARLES GONZAGA, 1665-1708
Bust. Rev. Arms.

196.	2 Doppie ND	Rare

CASTEL SEPRIO

DESIDERIUS, 757-773
Cross potent. Rev. Star.

197.	⅓ Solidus ND	Rare

CHARLEMAGNE, 773-800
Cross potent. Rev. Cross and four globes.

198.	⅓ Solidus ND.................................	Rare

CASTIGLIONE DELLE STIVIERE

Princes of —

FRANCIS GONZAGA, 1593-1616
Bust. Rev. Arms.

199.	5 Doppie 1614	Rare
200.	½ Doppia ND	8000.00
201.	⅛ Doppia ND	2000.00

FERDINAND GONZAGA, 1616-1678
Eagle. Rev. Soldier.

202.	1 Florin 1639	Rare

St. Nazarius. Rev. Value.

203.	1 Florin ND..................................	Rare

St. Ferdinandus. Rev. Value.

204.	1 Florin ND..................................	Rare

Madonna. Rev. Value.

205.	1 Florin ND..................................	Rare

Lion. Rev. Value.

206.	1 Florin ND..................................	Rare

CASTIGLIONE DEI GATTI

Counts of —

HERCULES AND CORNELIUS PEPOLI, 1700

Tablet. Rev. Double eagle.

207.	1 Ducat ND...................................	12000.00

ALEXANDER AND SICINIUS PEPOLI, 1703-1713
Tablet. Rev. Double eagle.

208.	1 Ducat ND...................................	12000.00

CASTRO

Dukes of —

PETER LUIGI FARNESE, 1545-1547

Arms. Rev. Cross.

209.	1 Scudo d'oro ND	2000.00

CHIVASSO

Marcheses of —

THEODORE I PALEOLOGO, 1307-1338
Lily. Rev. St. John.

210.	1 Florin ND..................................	10000.00

CISPADANE REPUBLIC

Madonna. Rev. Trophies. Struck at Bologna.

211.	20 Lire or 1 Doppia 1797	Rare

CISTERNA

Princes of —

JAMES DAL POZZO, 1667-1677
Bust. Rev. Arms.

212.	10 Scudi d'oro 1677	Rare
213.	2 Doppie 1677................................	Rare

CORREGGIO

Princes of —

GILBERT, CAMILLO, AND FABRIZIO, 1569-1597
Eagle and arms. Rev. Madonna.

214.	1 Doppia ND	15000.00
215.	1 Scudo d'oro ND	10000.00

Eagle and arms. Rev. St. Quirinus.

216.	1 Scudo d'oro ND	1500.00

Double eagle. Rev. St. Quirinus.

217.	1 Scudo d'oro ND	Rare

Arms. Rev. Young St. Quirinus in oval.

218.	1 Scudo d'oro ND	Rare

Soldier standing. Rev. Madonna.

219.	1 Ducat ND...................................	Rare

Tablet. Rev. Madonna.
219a.   1 Ducat ND.................................... Rare

CAMILLO AND FABRIZIO, 1580-1597
Arms. Rev. Bust of St. Quirinus.
220.   144 Soldi (Scudo d'oro) ND 6000.00

CAMILLO, 1597-1605

Ruler standing. Rev. Arms.
221.   1 Ducat 1599, ND.................................. 1250.00

Ruler standing. Rev. Double eagle.
222.   1 Ducat ND....................................... 1250.00

Ruler standing. Rev. Madonna.
223.   1 Ducat ND....................................... 1250.00

SIRUS, 1605-1630
Soldier. Rev. Tablet.
224.   1 Ducat 1609 .... 1250.00

CORTONA

LOMBARDIC PERIOD, 600-800
Cross. Rev. Legend.
225.   ⅓ Solidus ND.. 4000.00

CREMONA

Lords of —

FRANCIS II SFORZA, 1521-1535
Saint standing. Rev. Serpent.
226.   1 Scudo d'oro ND .... Rare

CUNEO

SIEGE OF 1641
Arms. Rev. Column and flag.
227.   5 Doppie 1641 .... Rare
228.   1 Doppia 1641 .... Rare

DESANA

Counts of —

LOUIS TIZZONE II, 1510-1525
Bust. Rev. Arms.
229.   2 Ducats ND .... Rare

Arms. Rev. St. Peter seated.
230.   2 Scudi d'oro ND................................. Rare
231.   1 Scudo d'oro ND 15000.00

Eagle. Rev. Cross.
232.   1 Scudo d'oro ND................................. 15000.00

PETER BERARD, 1516-1529
Bust. Rev. Arms.
233.   1 Scudo d'oro ND .... Rare

Arms on cross. Rev. Cross.
234.   1 Scudo d'oro ND .... Rare

AUGUSTIN TIZZONE, 1559-1582
Bust. Rev. Arms.
235.   1 Doppia 1581 .... Rare

DELFINO TIZZONE, 1583-1598
Arms. Rev. St. Lawrence.
236.   1 Scudo d'oro ND 5000.00

ANTHONY MARIA TIZZONE, 1598-1641
Bust. Rev. Arms.
237.   2 Doppie ND 20000.00
238.   1 Doppia ND 15000.00
239.   1 Florin ND..................................... Unknown

Bearded bust. Rev. Arms.
240.   2 Doppie ND .... Rare
241.   1 Doppia ND .... Rare

Head. Rev. Female at column.
242.   2 Doppie ND .... Rare

Head. Rev. St. Dorothea standing.
243.   1 Doppia ND 15000.00
Bust. Rev. Double eagle.
244.   1 Florin ND...................................... Rare
Bust. Rev. Arms.
244a.   1 Florin ND..................................... Rare
Arms. Rev. St. Peter.
245.   1 Florin ND..................................... Rare
Arms. Rev. Double eagle.
246.   1 Florin ND..................................... 7000.00
247.   1 Ducat ND...................................... 6000.00
Arms. Rev. Cross.
248.   1 Scudo d'oro ND .... Unknown
Soldier standing. Rev. Tablet.
249.   1 Ducat 1603 .... 4000.00
Ruler standing. Rev. Tablet.
250.   1 Ducat ND...................................... 3500.00
Arms. Rev. St. Catherine seated.
251.   1 Ducat ND...................................... Rare
Eagle. Rev. St. Lawrence.
252.   1 Ducat ND...................................... Rare
Double eagle. Rev. St. Louis standing.
253.   1 Ducat ND...................................... Rare

CHARLES JOSEPH FRANCIS TIZZONE, 1641-1676
Ruler standing. Rev. Tablet.
254.   1 Ducat ND...................................... 6000.00

Soldier standing. Rev. Tablet.
255.   1 Ducat ND...................................... 6000.00

EMILIA

VICTOR EMANUEL II, KING ELECT, 1859-1861

Head. Rev. Value in wreath. Bologna Mint with B mm.

256.	20 Lire 1860		Rare
257.	10 Lire 1860 ....*......		4500.00

FERRARA

Dukes of —

LIONEL D'ESTE, 1441-1450
Sail on mast. Rev. Christ.

258.	1 Ducat ND...............................	Rare

Pillow and helmet. Rev. Arms.

259.	½ Ducat ND....................................	Rare

BORSO D'ESTE, 1450-1471
Christ. Rev. Arms.

260.	1 Ducat ND...............................	Rare

Bust. Rev. Christ.

261.	1 Ducat ND......................................	Rare

HERCULES I D'ESTE, 1471-1475
Duke kneeling before saint. Rev. Christ.

262.	1 Doppia ND	Rare

Head. Rev. Hercules and bull.

263.	1 Doppia ND	Rare

Head. Rev. Hercules and lion.

264.	1 Doppia ND	Rare

Bust. Rev. Christ.

265.	1 Ducat ND......................................	5000.00

Duke standing. Rev. St. Maurelius seated.

266.	½ Ducat ND....................................	Rare

Eagle. Rev. Animal.

267.	½ Ducat ND....................................	Rare

ALFONSO I D'ESTE, 1505-1534

Plain or bearded bust. Rev. Christ and the Pharisee.

268.	2 Zecchini ND......................................	Rare

Arms. Rev. Calvary cross.

269.	1 Scudo d'oro ND	1000.00

HERCULES II D'ESTE, 1534-1559

Arms. Rev. Mary Magdalene at cross.

270.	1 Scudo d'oro 1534, ND	1500.00

Bust. Rev. Hercules with lion skin.

271.	10 Scudi d'oro 1546	Rare

ALFONSO II D'ESTE, 1559-1597

Arms. Rev. Cross.

272.	1 Scudo d'oro 1576, ND	1000.00

Duke standing. Rev. Arms.

273.	1 Ducat 1596, 97, ND.............................	800.00

Bust. Rev. Eagle.

274.	½ Ducat ND......................................	Rare

FLORENCE

A. Republic of —, 1189-1531

Lily. Rev. St. John.

275.	1 Florin ND (1252-1422) .... *	700.00
276.	1 Florin ND. Broad type. (1422-1531)	1400.00
277.	¼ Florin ND (1252-1422)	5000.00

Lily. Rev. St. John baptizing Christ.

278.	2 Florins ND (1504-31)	Rare

Arms. Rev. Cross. Struck during the Siege of Florence, 1530.

279.	1 Scudo d'oro ND	Rare

B. Tuscan Grand Dukes of —

ALEXANDER, 1531-1536

Arms. Rev. Cross.

280.	1 Scudo d'oro ND	1000.00

COSIMO I, 1536-1574
Bust. Rev. Cross.

281.	1 Gold Piastre ND	Rare

Bust. Rev. St. John standing.

282.	1 Gold Piastre 1571, 72	Rare
283.	1 Ducat ND .... *	Rare

Bust. Rev. St. John preaching to disciples.

284.	½ Gold Piastre 1571, 72	Rare

Arms. Rev. Cross.

285.	1 Gold Piastre ND	Rare
286.	1 Scudo d'oro ND .... *	1000.00
287.	½ Scudo d'oro ND	2500.00

Bust of St. John. Rev. Arms.

288.	¼ Scudo d'oro ND	4000.00

FRANCIS I, 1574-1587
Bust. Rev. St. John standing.

289.	1 Gold Piastre (5 Doppia) 1574-84..................	Rare

Head. Rev. The Annunciation.

290.	1 Doppia 1580, 82	Rare

Arms. Rev. Cross.

291.	1 Scudo d'oro ND	3000.00

FERDINAND I, 1587-1608
Bust. Rev. Bees in flight.

292.	14 Scudi d'oro 1587	Rare

Bust. Rev. The Annunciation.

293.	2 Doppie 1591....................................	Rare
294.	1 Doppia 1587-91................................	12000.00
295.	½ Doppia 1587, 93	8000.00

Bust. Rev. Cross of St. Stephan.

296.	½ Doppia 1587.....................................	16000.00

Bust. Rev. Cross.

297.	¼ Doppia ND .... *	6000.00
298.	⅛ Doppia ND	6000.00

Bust. Rev. St. John baptizing Christ.

299.	1 Gold Piastre 1589, 92, 96	Rare

Lily. Rev. St. John standing.

| 300. | 2 Ducats 1595 | 15000.00 |
| 301. | 1 Ducat 1595, 96, 97, 1608 ....* | 1000.00 |

Arms. Rev. Ornate cross.

| 302. | 1 Doppia 1607 | 5000.00 |

Arms. Rev. Floriated cross.

| 303. | 1 Scudo d'oro ND | 1000.00 |
| 304. | ¼ Doppia ND | 5000.00 |

Arms. Rev. Bust of St. John.

| 305. | ⅛ Doppia ND | 3000.00 |

Arms. Rev. Cross of St. Stephan.

| 306. | ⅛ Doppia ND | 3000.00 |

Arms. Rev. The Annunciation.

| 307. | 1 Doppia 1588 | 10000.00 |

Arms. Rev. St. John seated.

| 308. | 1 Florin 1588 | 8000.00 |

St. John standing. Rev. Cross of St. Stephan.

| 309. | 1 Florin 1588 | 8000.00 |

COSIMO II, 1609-1621
Bust. Rev. St. John baptizing Christ.

| 310. | 1 Gold Piastre 1610 | Rare |

Bust. Rev. Cross.

| 311. | ¼ Doppia 1609 | Rare |

Arms. Rev. Cross.

| 312. | 1 Doppia 1608, ND (1608 Rare) ....* | 2000.00 |
| 313. | 1 Scudo d'oro ND ....* | 6000.00 |

Lily. Rev. St. John standing.

| 314. | 1 Florin 1608, 10, 11, 14 | 800.00 |

FERDINAND II, 1621-1670
Bust. Rev. St. John standing.

| 315. | 1 Gold Piastre 1628 | Rare |

Arms. Rev. Cross.

316.	1 Doppia ND	1200.00
317.	½ Doppia ND	3000.00
318.	⅛ Doppia ND	2500.00

Lily. Rev. St. John standing.

| 319. | 1 Zecchino 1655, ND | 2500.00 |

Arms. Rev. Bust of St. John.

| 320. | ¼ Doppia 1663, 68 ....* | 2500.00 |
| 321. | ⅛ Doppia ND | 1000.00 |

COSIMO III, 1670-1723

Arms. Rev. Cross.

322.	2 Doppie 1676	8000.00
323.	1 Doppia 1711, 16	6000.00
324.	½ Doppia ND	4000.00

Lily. Rev. St. John seated.

| 325. | 1 Ruspone 1719 | Rare |
| 326. | 1 Florin 1712-23 ....* | 700.00 |

JOHN GASTON, 1723-1737

Lily. Rev. St. John seated.

327.	1 Ruspone 1724 ....*	4500.00
328.	1 Zecchino 1723-36	500.00
329.	½ Zecchino 1726	6000.00

Lily. Rev. Bust of St. John.

330. ½ Zecchino 1726 .... 1100.00

FRANCIS III, 1737-1765
Lily. Rev. St. John seated.

331. 1 Ruspone 1743-64 .... 1500.00
332. 1 Zecchino 1737-43 .... 750.00

Head. Rev. Arms.

333. 1 Ducat 1738, 41 .... 12000.00

PETER LEOPOLD, 1765-1790

Lily. Rev. St. John seated.

334. 1 Ruspone 1765-90 .... 1800.00
335. 1 Zecchino 1779-89 ....*...... 700.00

FERDINAND III, 1791-1801
Lily. Rev. St. John seated.

336. 1 Ruspone 1791-1801 .... 1800.00
337. 1 Zecchino 1791-97 .... 700.00

LOUIS I, 1801-1803
Lily. Rev. St. John seated.

338. 1 Ruspone 1801, 03................................. 2000.00

CHARLES LOUIS AND MARIE LOUISE, 1803-1807

Lily. Rev. St. John seated.

339. 1 Ruspone 1803-07 .... 2500.00

St. Zanobius kneeling before Christ. Rev. St. John standing. Struck for the Levant.

340. 1 Zecchino ND 10000.00

FERDINAND III, 1814-1824
Lily. Rev. St. John seated.

341. 1 Ruspone 1815-23 .... 2000.00
342. 1 Zecchino 1816, 21 .... 700.00

LEOPOLD II, 1824-1859

Lily. Rev. Arms.

343. 80 Florins or 200 Paoli 1827, 28 .... 3750.00

Lily. Rev. St. John seated.

344. 1 Ruspone 1824-36 .... 1500.00
345. 1 Zecchino 1824-53 .... 750.00

(For the last coin of this type, see under Tuscany).

FORLI
Lords of —

HIERONYMUS RIARIO, 1480-1488
Double eagle. Rev. St. Mercurialus standing.

346. 1 Ducat 1480 .... Rare

FRINCO

Arms. Rev. Cross. Anonymous Princely coinage.

347. 1 Scudo d'oro ND (1581-1601)...................... Rare

GAETA
Dukes of —

ALFONSO I, 1436-1458

Ruler on horse; letter B to left of ruler. Rev. Arms.

348. 1 Ducatone d'oro ND (5.23 grams) ....*...... 8000.00
349. 1 Ducat ND.. 8000.00

GAZZOLDO
Counts of —

HANNIBAL DEGLI IPPOLITI, 1632-1666

Bust. Rev. St. Hippolitus.

350. 2 Doppie 1662..................................... Rare

GENOA

A. Doges of —

The following coins are all of the same type and show a castle on the Obv. and a cross on the Rev., with the common legend Conradus. The Doges can be identified on the coins by a number representing their order of succession or by their initials or name. All are without dates.

ANONYMOUS DOGES, 1200-1350

351.	1 Genovino	*	2000.00
352.	1 Quartarola		1200.00
353.	1 Soldo	*	3000.00

GUELPH GOVERNMENT, 1318-1333

353a.	1 Genovino	3500.00

GHIBELLINE GOVERNMENT, 1334-1336

353b.	1 Genovino	3000.00

SIMON BOCCANEGRA, 1339-1344 AND 1356-1363

354.	1 Genovino. With "Dux Primus." and "Dux Ianue"	*	1500.00
354a.	1 Genovino. With "Dux Quartus."		1500.00
355.	⅓ Genovino		1200.00
356.	¼ Genovino		1200.00

GABRIEL ADORNO, 1363-1370

357.	1 Genovino. With "Dux V."	1700.00

DOMINIC DI CAMPOFREGOSO, 1370-1378

358.	1 Genovino	10000.00

ANTONIOTTO ADORNO, 1378

359.	1 Genovino. With "Dux Septim."	12000.00

NICHOLAS GUARCO, 1378-1383

360.	1 Genovino. With "Dux Otavus."	4800.00

LEONARD DI MONTALDO, 1383-1384

361.	1 Genovino. With "Dux Decem."	4000.00

THEODORE II DI MONFERRATO, 1409-1413 (?)

361a.	1 Genovino	8000.00

GEORGE ADORNO, 1413-1415

362.	1 Genovino. With "Dux XVII."	4200.00

BARNABAS DI GOANO, 1415

363.	1 Genovino. With "Dux XVIII."	9000.00

THOMAS DI CAMPOFREGOSO, 1415-1421 (FIRST RULE)

364.	1 Ducat. With "Dux XVIIII."	2500.00

PHILIP MARIA OF MILAN, 1421-1425

365.	1 Ducat	1500.00

THOMAS DI CAMPOFREGOSO, 1436-1442 (SECOND RULE)

366.	1 Ducat. With "Dux XX."	10000.00
367.	1 Ducat. With "Dux XXI."	1750.00

THE EIGHT CAPTAINS OF LIBERTY, 1442-1443

368.	1 Ducat	Rare

RAFFAEL ADORNO, 1443-1447

369.	1 Ducat. With "Dux XXII."	5000.00
370.	1 Ducat. With "Dux XXIII."	10000.00
371.	½ Ducat	Rare
372.	¼ Ducat	Rare

JOHN CAMPOFREGOSO, 1447

373.	1 Ducat	12000.00

374.	½ Ducat	Rare

LOUIS CAMPOFREGOSO, 1447-1450 AND 1461-1462

375.	1 Ducat. With "Dux XXV."	8000.00
376.	1 Ducat. With "Dux XXVII."	Rare

PETER CAMPOFREGOSO, 1450-1458

377.	1 Ducat. With "Dux XXVI."	1700.00

PROSPERO ADORNO, 1461

378.	1 Ducat	Rare

PAUL CAMPOFREGOSO, 1463-1464

379.	1 Ducat	8000.00
380.	½ Ducat	Rare

FRANCIS I OF MILAN, 1464-1466

381.	1 Ducat. With "F.S."	*	3000.00
382.	½ Ducat. With "F.S."		10000.00

GALEAZZO MARIA OF MILAN, 1466-1476

383.	1 Ducat. With G.S."	1500.00
384.	½ Ducat. With "G.S."	8000.00
385.	¼ Ducat. With "G.S."	Rare

PROSPERO ADORNO AND TWELVE CAPTAINS, 1478

386.	1 Ducat	Rare

BAPTIST CAMPOFREGOSO, 1478-1483

387.	1 Ducat. With "Dux XXX."	1500.00

PAUL CAMPOFREGOSO, 1483-1488

388.	1 Ducat. As Governor	Rare
389.	1 Ducat. As Doge. With "Dux XXXI."	10000.00
390.	½ Ducat	Rare

AUGUSTIN ADORNO, 1488-1489

391.	1 Ducat. With "Aug Adurnus."	Rare

JOHN GALEAZZO OF MILAN, 1489-1494

392.	3 Ducats	Rare
393.	2 Ducats	Rare
394.	1 Ducat	5000.00

LOUIS MARIA OF MILAN, 1494-1499

395.	1 Ducat. With "LV."	15000.00

ANTONIOTTO ADORNO, 1522-1527

396.	1 Ducat. With "Antoniotus."	4000.00
397.	½ Ducat. With "Antonitu."	10000.00
398.	2 Scudi d'oro	Rare
399.	1 Scudo d'oro. With "Antoniotus." *	1500.00
400.	½ Scudo d'oro	8000.00

B. French Kings of —, 1396-1528

(Same type as above).

CHARLES VI, 1396-1409

401.	1 Genovino	15000.00
402.	⅓ Genovino	Rare

CHARLES VII, 1458-1461

403.	1 Ducat	7000.00

LOUIS XII, 1499-1513

404.   1 Ducat.. Rare

Crowned arms of France with name of Genoa in title. Rev.
Floriated cross.

405.   1 Ecu d'or ND.................................. 3000.00

FRANCIS I, 1515-1528

Castle flanked by F and lis. Rev. Floriated cross.

406.   1 Ecu d'or ND.................................. 10000.00
407.   ½ Ecu d'or ND.................................. Rare
408.   ¼ Ecu d'or ND.................................. Rare

*Castle flanked by F and lis. Rev. Two F's and two lis in
angles of floriated cross.*

409.   1 Ecu d'or ND.................................. Rare
410.   The coin previously listed does not exist.............. —

C. The Biennial Doges of —, 1528-1797

Castle. Rev. Cross.

411.   10   Scudi d'oro 1633 .... Rare
412.   1   Scudo d'oro 1541-55, ND 800.00
413.   ½   Scudo d'oro 1541-55, ND 8000.00
414.   25   Doppie 1636 .... Rare
415.   12½   Doppie 1632, 34, 36, 37 .... Rare
416.   5   Doppie 1600-20 .... 15000.00
417.   2½   Doppie 1596 .... Rare
418.   2   Doppie 1592-1638 .... * 5000.00
419.   1   Doppia 1557-1638 .... 2000.00
420.   ½   Doppia 1557-1638 .... 2000.00
421.   ¼   Doppia 1623-38 .... 2500.00
422.   ⅛   Doppia 1623-38 .... 2200.00

Madonna. Rev. Cross.

423.   25   Doppie 1638-1714 .... Rare
424.   20   Doppie 1645 .... Rare
425.   12½   Doppie 1638-1711 .... Rare
426.   10   Doppie 1641-94 .... Rare
427.   5   Doppie 1639-97 .... 10000.00
428.   4   Doppie 1720 .... 9000.00
429.   2½   Doppie 1697 .... 8500.00
430.   2   Doppie 1638-1722 .... * 6000.00
431.   1   Doppia 1640-1748 .... 3000.00
432.   ½   Doppia 1639-1749 .... 1000.00
433.   ¼   Doppia 1641 .... 1800.00
434.   ⅛   Doppia 1641 .... 1800.00

Doge kneeling before St. John. Rev. Christ.

435.   1 Zecchino ND .... Rare

Arms. Rev. St. George on horse.

436.   1 Zecchino 1718-23 ....12000.00
437.   ½ Zecchino 1723 .... Rare

Arms. Rev. St. John standing.

438.   1 Zecchino 1724-39 .... * 1000.00
439.   ½ Zecchino 1724-36 .... 2000.00

*Arms supported by griffins. Rev. Madonna. The denomina-
tions do not appear on the first four pieces.*

440.   100   Lire 1758-67 .... Rare
441.   50   Lire 1758-67 .... * 14500.00
442.   25   Lire 1758-67 .... 9500.00
443.   12½   Lire 1758-67 ....14500.00
444.   96   Lire 1792-97 .... 2000.00
445.   48   Lire 1792-97 .... * 3000.00
446.   24   Lire 1792-95 .... 4000.00
447.   12   Lire 1793-95 .... 5000.00

D. The Republic (Ligurian) of —, 1798-1805

Liguria seated. Rev. Fasces.

448.   96 Lire 1798-1805 .... * 2750.00
449.   48 Lire 1798, 1801, 04 .... 2500.00
450.   24 Lire 1798 .... 8000.00
451.   12 Lire 1798 .... 8000.00

GORIZIA

Counts of —

HENRY II, 1304-1323
St. John. Rev. Lily.

452.   1 Florin ND.................................... 6000.00

ALBERT IV, 1338-1374
St. John. Rev. Lily.

453.   1 Florin ND.................................... 6000.00

HENRY III, 1338-1364
St. John. Rev. Lily.

454.   1 Florin ND.................................... 6000.00

MAINHARD, 1364-1385
St. John. Rev. Lily.

455.   1 Florin ND.................................... 6000.00

St. John. Rev. Arms.

456.   1 Florin ND.................................... 6000.00

GUASTALLA

Dukes of —

CAESAR I GONZAGA, 1557-1575
Arms. Rev. Cross.

457. 1 Scudo d'oro ND 5000.00

FERDINAND II GONZAGA, 1575-1630
Bust. Rev. The Annunciation.

458. 10 Doppie 1610 .... Rare

Ruler standing. Rev. Arms.

459. 1 Ducat ND.. 2500.00

Arms. Rev. Cross.

460. 1 Scudo d'oro ND 2500.00

GUBBIO

Lords of —

FRANCIS MARIA I DELLA ROVERE, 1508-1538
St. Ubaldus seated. Rev. Arms.

461. 1 Scudo d'oro ND .... Rare

FRANCIS MARIA II DELLA ROVERE, 1574-1634

Bust. Rev. Arms.

462. 1 Scudo d'oro ND 10000.00

IVREA

DESIDERIUS, 756-774
Monogram. Rev. St. Michael.

462a. ⅓ Solidus ND....................................... Rare

LEGHORN (LIVORNO)

Tuscan Grand Dukes of —

FERDINAND II, 1621-1670

Head. Rev. View of the Port of Leghorn.

463. 1 Ducat 1655, ND................................... Rare

COSIMO III, 1670-1723

Ruler standing. Rev. Legend in tablet.

464. 1 Ducat 1674, 75, 76, 91 .... 2500.00

Arms. Rev. Rose bush. These coins are also referred to as "Pezza d'oro della rosa."

465. The coin previously listed does not exist............... —
466. 1 Doppia or Rosina 1717, 18, 21 ....*...... 5000.00
467. ½ Doppia or Rosina 1718, 20...................... 4000.00

Bust. Rev. View of the Port of Leghorn.

468. 1 Ducat ND....................................... Rare

Ruler standing. Rev. Fame over globe.

469. 1 Ducat ND....................................... 10000.00

LOANO

Princes of —

JOHN ANDREW II, 1622-1640
Bust. Rev. Eagle.

470. 2 Doppie 1639.................................... Rare
471. 1 Doppia 1639................................... Rare

Tablet. Rev. Madonna.

472. 1 Ducat ND...................................... 12000.00

JOHN ANDREW III, 1654-1737
Bust. Rev. Arms and cross.

473. 1 Doppia 1665................................... Rare

LOMBARDY

Provisional Government of —

Italia standing. Rev. Value. Struck at Milan.

474. 40 Lire 1848 ....*...... 2000.00
475. 20 Lire 1848 .... 2000.00

LUCCA

A. Dukes of —

ANONYMOUS, 650-749
Monogram. Rev. Cross.

476. ⅓ Solidus ND........................ 2750.00

Star. Rev. Cross.

477. ⅓ Solidus ND........................ 1500.00

ASTOLF, 749-756
Rose. Rev. Cross.

478. ⅓ Solidus ND........................ 2500.00

Star. Rev. Cross.

479. ⅓ Solidus ND........................ Rare

DESIDERIUS, 757-773
Star. Rev. Cross.

480. ⅓ Solidus ND........................ Rare

CHARLEMAGNE, 773-814
Bust. Rev. Star.

481. ⅓ Solidus ND........................ Rare

Star. Rev. Cross.

482. ⅓ Solidus ND........................ Rare

FREDERICK II, 1190-1250

Bust of Christ facing or left. Rev. Monogram and name of Otto IV.

483. 1 Grosso d'oro ND .... Rare

ANONYMOUS, 1300-1350

Bust of Christ. Rev. St. Martin on horse.

484. 1 Florin ND........................ 12000.00

B. Republic of —, 1369-1799

Bust of Christ. Rev. St. Peter.

485. 1 Florin ND (1387-1400)................ Rare

Bust of Christ. Rev. St. Martin on horse.

486. 1 Ducat ND (1400-1500)..........*..... 4000.00
487. 1 Zecchino 1572, ND 1500.00

Arms. Rev. Bust of Christ.

488. 4 Scudi d'oro 1748..............*..... 8000.00
489. 2 Scudi d'oro 1749, 50............... 1250.00
490. 1 Scudo d'oro 1552-1749, ND......... 500.00
491. ½ Scudo d'oro 1551, 52, ND.......... 1750.00

Head of Christ. Rev. Four letters crossed.

492. ½ Scudo d'oro ND 2000.00

Arms. Rev. St. Paulinus seated.

493. 1 Doppia 1758..................... 13500.00

MACCAGNO

Counts of —

GIACOMO III MANDELLI, 1618-1645
Soldier. Rev. Arms.

494. 1 Ducat 1622, 23 .... 3000.00

Saint with shield. Rev. Eagle.

495. 1 Ducat 1622...................... 2250.00

Saint with shield. Rev. Orb.

496. 1 Ducat ND........................ 3000.00

St. Stephan kneeling. Rev. Arms.

497. 1 Ducat 1622...................... 3000.00

Arms. Rev. Eagle.

498. 1 Ducat 1622, ND.................. 3000.00

Arms. Rev. Orb.

499. 1 Ducat 1622...................... 3250.00

Ruler standing. Rev. Arms.

500. 1 Doppia ND...................... 30000.00
501. 1 Ducat 1622, ND...........*..... 3500.00

Ruler standing. Rev. Eagle.

502. 1 Ducat ND........................ 3000.00

Soldier. Rev. Tablet.

503. 1 Ducat 1623, ND.................. 3000.00

Madonna. Rev. Tablet.

504. 1 Ducat ND........................ 3000.00

Bust of Saint. Rev. Eagle.

505. 1 Ducat ND........................ 3000.00

Bust. Rev. Arms.
506.   1 Doppia 1625, ND 30000.00

Bust. Rev. Eagle.
507.   1 Ducat ND.................................. 3000.00

Bust. Rev. Orb.
508.   1 Ducat ND.................................. 3000.00

MANFREDONIA

MANFRED, 1258-1266

Eagle. Rev. Legend.
509.   10 Tari ND................................. 3000.00
510.   8 Tari ND.................................. 2000.00
511.   6 Tari ND.................................. 1200.00
512.   4 Tari ND.......................*..... 500.00
513.   3 Tari ND.................................. 400.00

MANTUA

Marcheses, and later, Dukes of —

LOUIS II GONZAGA, 1445-1478

Bust. Rev. Sacred vessel.
514.   1 Ducat ND....................... Rare

Ruler standing. Rev. St. George on horse.
515.   1 Ducat ND....................... Rare

Sun. Rev. Sacred vessel.
516.   ⅓ Ducat ND................................. 6000.00

FREDERICK I GONZAGA, 1478-1484

Bust. Rev. Sacred vessel.
517.   1 Ducat ND....................... Rare

FRANCIS II GONZAGA, 1484-1519

Bust. Rev. Arms.
518.   2 Ducats ND....................... Rare

Bust. Rev. Crucible in flames.
519.   2 Ducats ND....................... Rare
520.   1 Ducat ND.............................*......10000.00

Bust with hat. Rev. Sacred vessel.
521.   1 Ducat ND....................... Rare

Madonna. Rev. Altar.
522.   ½ Ducat ND................................. 10000.00

FREDERICK II GONZAGA, 1519-1540
Head. Rev. Ruler on horse.
523.   3 Ducats ND....................... Rare
524.   2 Ducats ND....................... Rare

Head. Rev. St. Catherine.
525.   1 Ducat ND.................................10000.00

Head. Rev. Mt. Olympus.
526.   2 Ducats ND.............................*......12000.00
527.   1 Ducat ND....................... Rare

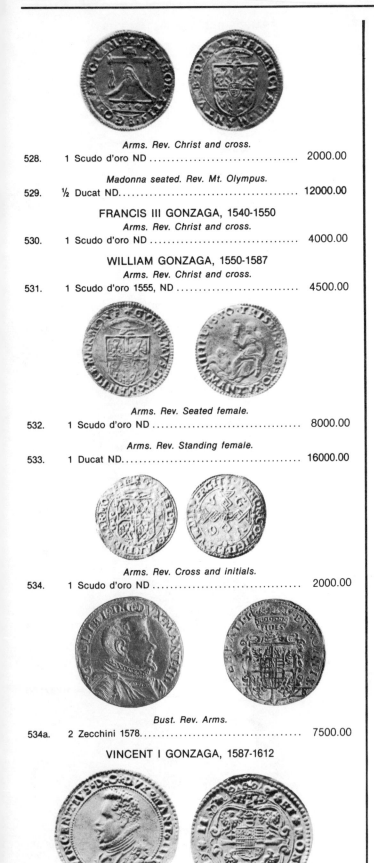

Arms. Rev. Christ and cross.
528.   1 Scudo d'oro ND 2000.00

Madonna seated. Rev. Mt. Olympus.
529.   ½ Ducat ND... 12000.00

FRANCIS III GONZAGA, 1540-1550
Arms. Rev. Christ and cross.
530.   1 Scudo d'oro ND 4000.00

WILLIAM GONZAGA, 1550-1587
Arms. Rev. Christ and cross.
531.   1 Scudo d'oro 1555, ND 4500.00

Arms. Rev. Seated female.
532.   1 Scudo d'oro ND 8000.00

Arms. Rev. Standing female.
533.   1 Ducat ND... 16000.00

Arms. Rev. Cross and initials.
534.   1 Scudo d'oro ND 2000.00

Bust. Rev. Arms.
534a.   2 Zecchini 1578.................................... 7500.00

VINCENT I GONZAGA, 1587-1612

Bust. Rev. Arms.

535.   7 Doppie 1589.................................... Rare
536.   4 Doppie 1590.................................... Rare
537.   2 Doppie 1590, ND ....*...... Rare

Bust. Rev. Tree.
538.   2 Doppie 1590.................................... Rare

Bust. Rev. St. George on horse.
539.   10 Doppie ND .... Rare

Bust. Rev. Arms on cross.
540.   2 Zecchini ND.................................... Rare

Ruler standing. Rev. Arms.
541.   1 Ducat 1595.................................... 4000.00

Soldier standing. Rev. Arms.
542.   1 Ducat ND....................................... 2000.00

Bust of Virgil. Rev. Half moon.
543.   ⅛ Scudo d'oro ND 15000.00

Eagle. Rev. Compass and clock.
544.   ¼ Ducat 1596 .... 1800.00

Eagle. Rev. Crescent and legend.
545.   ¼ Ducat 1596 ....*...... 4000.00
546.   ⅛ Ducat 1596 ....*...... 3000.00

FRANCIS IV GONZAGA, 1612
St. Andrew and St. Longinus. Rev. Arms.
547.   5 Doppie 1612.................................... Rare

Bust. Rev. Arms.
548.   2 Doppie 1612.................................... Rare
549.   1 Doppia 1612.................................... Rare

FERDINAND GONZAGA, 1612-1626

Bust. Rev. Sun.
550.   12 Zecchini 1617................................. Rare
551.   6 Doppie 1613, 14, 15........................... Rare
552.   4 Doppie ND ....*...... 35000.00

Bust. Rev. Two angels.

553.	2 Doppie 1613, 14, 15........................*	5000.00
554.	1 Doppia 1614, 16	10000.00

Bust. Rev. St. Andrew and St. Longinus.

555.	1 Doppia 1613.................................	16000.00

Bust. Rev. St. Longinus.

556.	1 Doppia 1616, ND	12000.00

Bust. Rev. Madonna.

557.	12 Doppie 1614...............................	Rare
558.	6 Doppie 1614...............................	Rare

Bust right or left. Rev. Arms.

559.	6 Doppie 1616................................	Rare
560.	2 Doppie 1621, ND ....*	6500.00
561.	1 Doppia 1617, ND	7500.00
562.	½ Zecchino ND	4000.00

St. Andrew and St. Longinus. Rev. Arms.

563.	2 Doppie 1613................................	Rare

Arms on each side.

564.	6 Doppie 1620................................	Rare

Cardinal standing. Rev. Madonna.

565.	1 Scudo d'oro 1613, ND	12500.00

Madonna. Rev. Rose.

566.	1 Zecchino ND	3500.00

VINCENT II GONZAGA, 1626-1627

Bust. Rev. Arms.

567.	2 Doppie 1627.................................	20000.00

Legend. Rev. Ship.

568.	1 Scudo d'oro ND	Rare

CHARLES I GONZAGA, 1627-1637
Bust. Rev. Sun in zodiac.

569.	8 Doppie 1628................................	Rare
570.	6 Doppie 1628, 32............................	Rare
571.	5 Doppie 1636................................	Rare

Bust. Rev. Arms.

572.	2 Doppie 1629, 31, 36.....................*	Rare
573.	1 Doppia ND	Rare

CHARLES II GONZAGA, 1637-1665
Busts of Charles and Maria. Rev. Madonna.

574.	12 Scudi d'oro ND..................................	Rare
575.	8 Doppie ND	Rare
576.	5 Doppie ND	Rare
577.	4 Doppie ND	Rare

Busts of Charles and Maria. Rev. Arms.

578.	2 Doppie ND	12000.00

Bust. Rev. Sun in shield.

579.	12 Scudi d'oro 1649	Rare
580.	10 Zecchini 1649.......................*	Rare
581.	6 Doppie 1649................................	Rare

Bust. Rev. Arms.

582.	2 Doppie ND	Rare
583.	1 Doppia ND	Rare

FERDINAND CHARLES GONZAGA, 1665-1707

Busts of Ferdinand and Isabella Clara. Rev. Sun.

584.	12 Doppie 1666	Rare
585.	6 Doppie 1666	Rare
586.	5 Doppie 1666	Rare
587.	4 Doppie 1666	Rare
588.	2 Doppie 1666 ....*	Rare

Busts of Ferdinand and Isabella Clara. Rev. Madonna.

589.	6 Doppie 1666	Rare

Bust. Rev. Sun and rock.

590.	8 Doppie 1679	Rare

Bust. Rev. Arms.

591.	2 Doppie ND	Rare

MASSA DI LUNIGIANA

Dukes of —

ALBERIC CYBO MALUSPINA, 1559-1623

Bust. Rev. Arms.

592.	2 Doppie 1582, 88, 89, ND ....*	10000.00
593.	1 Doppia 1588, ND	8000.00

Bust. Rev. Temple.

594.	2 Doppie 1588, ND	14000.00

Bust. Rev. Fire.

595.	1 Doppia ND	8000.00

Bust. Rev. Arms and eagle.

596.	2 Doppie 1593, 98, ND	12000.00
597.	1 Doppia 1593	8000.00

Arms. Rev. Eagle.

598.	1 Doppia ND	8000.00

Arms. Rev. Anvil.

599.	1 Scudo d'oro ND	6000.00

St. Peter. Rev. Arms.

600.	1 Scudo d'oro ND	6000.00

Arms. Rev. Cross.

601.	1 Scudo d'oro 1569, ND	6000.00

Arms. Rev. Pyramid.

602.	½ Scudo d'oro ND	5000.00

Arms. Rev. Rose bush.

603.	½ Scudo d'oro ND	8000.00

CHARLES I CYBO MALUSPINA, 1623-1662
Bust. Rev. Arms.

604.	5 Doppie ND	Rare

MASSA-LOMBARDY

Marcheses of —

FRANCIS D'ESTE, 1562-1578

Bust. Rev. Two temples.

604a.	1 Doppia ND	Rare

Bust. Rev. Eagle.

605.	1 Scudo d'oro ND	Rare

Eagle. Rev. Cross.

606.	1 Scudo d'oro ND	15000.00

MESSERANO

Princes of —

ANONYMOUS, 1492-1521
Madonna. Rev. St. Theonestus.

607.	1 Ducat ND...	2000.00

Eagle. Rev. Cross.

608.	1 Scudo d'oro ND	4000.00

LOUIS II AND PETER LUCAS II, 1521-1528
Arms. Rev. Cross.

609.	1 Scudo d'oro ND	3000.00

LOUIS II, 1528-1532
Bust. Rev. Horse.

610.	1 Doppia ND	20000.00

Head. Rev. Arms.

611.	1 Ducat ND...	10000.00

Head. Rev. St. Theonestus seated.

612.	1 Ducat ND...	7000.00

Eagle. Rev. Cross.

613.	1 Scudo d'oro ND	2000.00

PETER LUCAS II, 1528-1548
Eagle. Rev. Cross.

614.	1 Scudo d'oro ND	3500.00

FILIBERT FERRERO, 1532-1559
Arms. Rev. Cross.

615.	1 Scudo d'oro ND	5000.00

BESSO FERRERO, 1559-1584
Bust. Rev. Arms.

616.	1 Doppia 1582......................................	Rare

Arms. Rev. Cross.

| 617. | 1 Scudo d'oro ND | 2500.00 |

FRANCIS FILIBERT FERRERO, 1584-1629
Bust. Rev. Arms.

| 618. | 1 Doppia 1594, ND | 10000.00 |

Bust. Rev. The Annunciation.

| 619. | 2 Doppie ND | Rare |
| 620. | 1 Doppia ND | Rare |

Ruler standing. Rev. Arms on eagle.

| 621. | 1 Ducat 1596, ND | 2500.00 |

Ruler standing. Rev. Tablet.

| 622. | 1 Ducat 1598 | 2500.00 |

PAUL BESSO FERRERO, 1629-1667
Bust. Rev. Arms.

| 623. | 5 Doppie 1638 | Rare |
| 624. | 1 Scudo d'oro 1640 | 5000.00 |

Soldier. Rev. Tablet.

| 625. | 1 Ducat ND | 2500.00 |

Tablet. Rev. Eagle.

| 626. | 1 Ducat ND | 2500.00 |

FRANCIS LOUIS FERRERO, 1667-1685
Bust. Rev. Arms.

| 627. | 1 Doppia 1667 | Rare |

Bust. Rev. Four shields crossed.

| 628. | 5 Doppie 1672 | Rare |

CHARLES BESSO FERRERO, 1685-1690
Bust. Rev. Arms.

| 629. | 1 Doppia 1689 | Rare |

MESSINA

A. Norman Kings of —

ROGER II, 1102-1154
Cufic legend on each side.

630.	3 Tari ND	500.00
631.	2 Tari ND	200.00
632.	1 Tari ND	150.00

WILLIAM I, 1154-1166
Cufic legend on each side.

| 633. | 2 Tari ND | 200.00 |
| 634. | 1 Tari ND | 150.00 |

WILLIAM II, 1166-1189
Six globes. Rev. Cross.

| 635. | 1 Tari ND | 200.00 |

W. Rev. Star.

| 636. | 1 Tari ND | 150.00 |

Star. Rev. Cufic legend.

637.	3 Tari ND	*	250.00
638.	2 Tari ND		150.00
639.	½ Tari ND		100.00

TANCRED, 1190-1194
Globe. Rev. Cross.

| 640. | 2 Tari ND | 200.00 |
| 641. | 1 Tari ND | 150.00 |

B. German and Anjou Kings of —

HENRY VI OF HOHENSTAUFEN, 1194-1197
Bust. Rev. Cross and four globes.

| 642. | 1 Tari ND | Rare |

E. Rev. Cross.

| 643. | 1 Tari ND | 250.00 |

HENRY VI AND FREDERICK II OF HOHENSTAUFEN, 1195
FE. Rev. Cross.

644.	3 Tari ND	500.00
645.	2 Tari ND	300.00
646.	1 Tari ND	300.00

Five globes. Rev. Cross.

| 647. | 3 Tari ND | 300.00 |

FREDERICK II OF HOHENSTAUFEN, 1198-1250
FRE. Rev. Cross.

| 648. | 1 Tari ND | 200.00 |

Cross on hill. Rev. Cross.

| 649. | 1 Tari ND | 500.00 |

Eagle. Rev. Cross.

650.	10 Tari ND		2000.00
650a.	2 Tari ND	*	250.00
651.	1 Tari ND		150.00

Five globes. Rev. Cross.

| 652. | 1 Tari ND | 150.00 |

CHARLES I OF ANJOU, 1266-1282
Bust. Rev. Arms.

| 653. | 1 Real ND | 15000.00 |

C. Spanish Kings of —

CONSTANCE AND PETER III OF ARAGON, 1282-1285

Arms. Rev. Eagle.

| 654. | 1 Ducat or Oncia ND | 7500.00 |

JAMES OF ARAGON, 1285-1296
Arms. Rev. Eagle.

| 655. | 1 Ducat ND | Rare |

FREDERICK III, 1296-1337
Arms. Rev. Eagle.

656. 1 Ducat ND... Rare

JOHN, 1458-1479
Ruler seated. Rev. Eagle.

657. 1 Real ND.. 5000.00

FERDINAND II, 1479-1516
Bust. Rev. Eagle.

658. 2 Ducats ND .... Rare

Ruler on throne. Rev. Eagle.

659. 1 Ducat ND...................................* 3000.00
660. ½ Ducat ND... 3000.00

CHARLES V, 1516-1556
Bust. Rev. Eagle.

661. 2 Ducats ND .... Rare
662. 1 Ducat ND.. Rare
663. ½ Ducat ND... Rare

Cross of St. Andrew. Rev. Shield.

664. 1 Scudo d'oro 1541-44 .... 3000.00
665. ½ Scudo d'oro 1541-43 .... 3000.00

Cross of St. Andrew. Rev. Eagle.

666. 1 Scudo d'oro 1544-54 ....* 3000.00
667. ½ Scudo d'oro 1544-51 .... 3000.00

PHILIP II, 1556-1598
Bust. Rev. Eagle.

668. 1 Scudo d'oro 1557................................ Rare

MILAN

A. Dukes of —

DESIDERIUS, 757-773
Cross. Rev. Star.

669. ⅓ Solidus ND...................................... Rare

CHARLEMAGNE, 774-814
Cross potent. Rev. Cross.

670. ⅓ Solidus ND...................................... Rare

Cross. Rev. Star.

671. ⅓ Solidus ND...................................... Rare

FIRST REPUBLIC, 1250-1310
Saints Protaxius and Gervasius standing. Rev. St. Ambrose standing.

672. 1 Florin ND... Rare

Bust of St. Ambrose. Rev. M.

673. ½ Florin ND.. 1500.00

LUCHINUS AND JOHN VISCONTI, 1339-1349
St. Ambrose seated. Rev. Dragon with shield.

674. 1 Florin ND.......................................10000.00

GALEAZZO II AND BARNABAS VISCONTI, 1354-1378

Helmeted arms on each side.

675. 1 Florin ND... 5000.00

GALEAZZO II VISCONTI, 1354-1378

Ruler on horse. Rev. Helmeted arms.

676. 1 Florin ND... 2000.00

BARNABAS VISCONTI, 1354-1385

Helmeted arms. Rev. Serpent and initials.

677. 1 Florin ND... 5000.00

JOHN GALEAZZO VISCONTI, 1385-1402
Ruler on horse. Rev. Helmeted arms.

678. 1 Florin ND... 2500.00

Bust. Rev. Serpent.

679. 10 Florins ND .... Rare

JOHN MARIA VISCONTI, 1402-1412
Ruler on horse. Rev. Helmeted arms.

680. 1 Florin ND...12000.00

PHILIP MARIA VISCONTI, 1412-1447

Ruler on horse. Rev. Helmeted arms.

681. 1 Florin ND... 1500.00

SECOND REPUBLIC, 1447-1450
St. Ambrose standing. Rev. M.

682. 1 Florin ND...12000.00

FRANCIS I SFORZA, 1450-1466

Bust. Rev. Ruler on horse.

683.   1 Ducat ND... 5000.00

Ruler on horse. Rev. Helmeted arms.

684.   1 Ducat ND... 16000.00

Ruler on horse. Rev. Serpent.

685.   1 Ducat ND... 16000.00

GALEAZZO MARIA SFORZA, 1466-1476
Bust. Rev. Arms.

686.   10 Ducats ND .... Rare

Bust. Rev. Helmeted arms.

687.   2 Ducats ND .... Rare
688.   1 Ducat ND.....................................*...... 5000.00

Bust. Rev. Lion.

689.   2 Ducats ND .... Rare

BONA DI SAVOIA
AND JOHN GALEAZZO MARIA SFORZA, 1476-1481
Bust on each side.

690.   2 Zecchini ND..................................... Rare

Bust. Rev. Lion.

691.   2 Zecchini ND..................................... Rare

JOHN GALEAZZO MARIA SFORZA, 1481

Bust. Rev. Arms.

692.   10 Ducats ND ....*........ Rare
693.   2 Ducats ND ....*......20000.00

JOHN GALEAZZO MARIA AND LOUIS MARIA SFORZA,
1481-1494
Bust on each side.

694.   10 Ducats ND .... Rare
695.   2 Ducats ND .... Rare

Bust of John. Rev. Arms.

696.   1 Ducat ND... Rare

LOUIS MARIA SFORZA, 1494-1500

Bust. Rev. Ruler on horse.

697.   10 Ducats ND .... Rare
698.   2 Gold Testones ND.........................*...... 16000.00

FRANCIS II SFORZA, 1522-1535
Bust. Rev. Bust of St. Ambrosius.

699.   10 Scudi d'oro ND................................... Rare
700.   6 Scudi d'oro ND.................................... Rare

Ruler on horse. Rev. Arms.

701.   2 Scudi d'oro ND................................... Rare

Arms. Rev. Cross.

702.   1 Scudo d'oro ND 5000.00

B. French Rulers of —

LOUIS XII, 1500-1513
Bust. Rev. Arms.

703.   10 Ducats ND .... Rare

Crowned bust. Rev. St. Ambrosius on horse.

704.   2 Ducats ND .... Rare

St. Ambrosius seated. Rev. French coat-of-arms.

705.   2 Ducats ND .... Rare

FRANCIS I, 1515-1522
Armored bust. Rev. Crowned arms.

706.   2 Ducats ND .... Rare

Crowned arms with small head of St. Ambrosius above. Rev. Floriated cross.

707.   1 Scudo d'oro ND 3000.00

C. Spanish Rulers of —

CHARLES V, 1534-1556
Bust. Rev. The Pillars of Hercules.

708.	2 Scudo d'oro ND	Rare

PHILIP II, 1556-1598
Bust. Rev. Arms.

709.	3 Doppie 1555, 79, 82............................	Rare
710.	2 Doppie ND	Rare
711.	1 Doppia ND	14000.00

Bust. Rev. St. Ambrosius on horse.

712.	2 Doppie 1562..................................	Rare

Bust. Rev. Bust of St. Ambrosius.

713.	3 Doppie 1591..................................	Rare

Bust. Rev. The Crucifixion.

714.	4 Doppie ND	Rare

Radiate head right or left. Rev. Arms.

715.	2	Doppie 1562, 88, 95.............................	Rare
716.	1	Doppia 1578-98, ND........................*	3000.00
717.	1½	Scudi d'oro ND	Rare
718.	1	Scudo d'oro ND	2500.00

Arms. Rev. Cross.

719.	1 Scudo d'oro ND	4500.00

PHILIP III, 1598-1621

Bust. Rev. Arms.

720.	2 Doppie 1610, 17, ND....................*	7000.00
721.	1 Doppia 1617, ND	8000.00

PHILIP IV, 1621-1665
Bust. Rev. City view.

722.	4½ Doppie 1630...................................	Rare

Bust. Rev. Arms.

723.	20 Zecchini 1643.................................	Rare
724.	2 Doppie 1630, ND ....*	3000.00
725.	1 Doppia 1630, ND	7000.00

CHARLES II, 1665-1700

Busts of Charles and Maria Anna. Rev. Arms.

726.	2 Doppie 1666.....................................	8000.00

Young bust. Rev. Arms.

727.	1 Doppia 1676.....................................	8000.00

Old bust. Rev. Arms.

728.	1 Doppia 1698.....................................	8000.00

D. Austrian Rulers of —

(For Austrian type coins struck at Milan with "M" mm, see under Austria. Italian type coins are listed here).

CHARLES VI, 1711-1740
Head. Rev. Arms.

729.	2 Scudi d'oro 1720, 24............................	Rare

Head. Rev. Double eagle.

730.	1 Scudo d'oro 1723, 24	Rare

Bust. Rev. Arms.

731.	12 Scudi d'oro ND.................................	Rare

MARIA THERESA, 1740-1780
Bust. Rev. St. Ambrosius standing.

732.	1 Zecchino ND	Rare

Bust. Rev. Arms.

733.	2 Doppie 1778, 79		4000.00
734.	1 Doppia 1778, 79, 80...........................		3000.00
735.	1 Zecchino 1778, 79, 80....................*		3000.00

JOSEPH II, 1780-1790

Bust. Rev. Legend. On his Inauguration.

736.	1 Doppia 1781...................................		6000.00
737.	1 Zecchino 1781...........................*		2000.00

Bust. Rev. Arms.

738.	1 Doppia 1781-85 ....*		3500.00
739.	1 Zecchino 1781-88		1500.00

FRANCIS II, 1792-1797

Bust. Rev. Legend. On his Inauguration.

| 740. | 1 Doppia 1792 .... * ...... | 6000.00 |
| 741. | 1 Zecchino 1792 .... | 3000.00 |

MIRANDOLA
Dukes of —

JOHN FRANCIS PICO, 1499-1533
Book. Rev. The Resurrection.

| 742. | 3 Zecchini ND .... | Rare |

Bust. Rev. The Resurrection.

| 743. | 1 Doppia ND .... | Rare |

Plain bust right. Rev. St. Francis kneeling.

| 744. | 1 Doppia ND .... | 7000.00 |

Bust with hat to left. Rev. St. Francis kneeling.

| 745. | 1 Doppia ND .... | 10000.00 |

Bust with hat. Rev. Arms.

| 746. | 1 Zecchino ND .... | 10000.00 |

Head. Rev. Arms.

| 747. | 1 Zecchino ND .... | 10000.00 |

Head. Rev. Shield.

| 748. | 1 Zecchino ND .... | Rare |

Head. Rev. Two Apostles standing.

| 749. | 1 Zecchino ND .... | 10000.00 |

Arms. Rev. Legend.

| 750. | 1 Zecchino ND .... | 6000.00 |

GALEOTTO PICO II, 1533-1550
Arms. Rev. Cross.

| 751. | 1 Scudo d'oro ND .... | 6500.00 |

LOUIS PICO II, 1550-1568

Arms. Rev. Cross.

| 752. | 1 Scudo d'oro ND .... * ...... | 1250.00 |
| 753. | ½ Scudo d'oro ND .... | 2500.00 |

GALEOTTO PICO III, 1568-1590
Arms. Rev. Cross.

| 754. | 1 Scudo d'oro ND .... | 8000.00 |

ALEXANDER PICO, 1602-1637
Bust. Rev. Arms.

| 755. | 24 Scudi d'oro 1618 .... | Rare |

MODENA
Dukes of —

HERCULES I D'ESTE, 1471-1505
Head. Rev. St. Geminianus seated.

| 756. | 1 Ducat ND.. | Rare |

Head with cap. Rev. St. Geminianus seated.

| 757. | 1 Ducat ND.. | Rare |

MAXIMILIAN I OF AUSTRIA, 1513-1514
Bust. Rev. St. Geminianus seated.

| 758. | 1 Ducat ND.. | Rare |

ALFONSO I D'ESTE, 1505-1534
Bust. Rev. St. Geminianus seated.

| 759. | 1 Ducat ND.. | Rare |

Cross. Rev. St. Geminianus seated.

| 760. | 1 Scudo d'oro ND .... | 6500.00 |

HERCULES II D'ESTE, 1534-1559

Cross. Rev. St. Geminianus seated.

| 761. | 1 Scudo d'oro ND .... | 1250.00 |

ALFONSO II D'ESTE, 1559-1597
Cross. Rev. St. Geminianus seated.

| 762. | 1 Scudo d'oro ND .... | 4500.00 |

CAESAR D'ESTE, 1598-1628

Ruler standing. Rev. Arms.

| 763. | 1 Ducat 1598, 1600, ND...................... * ...... | 1000.00 |
| 764. | ¼ Ducat ND.. | Rare |

Head. Rev. Patience standing.
765.   1 Doppia 1605, 09 .... 8000.00

Bust. Rev. Female standing.
766.   2 Doppie 1608.................................... 16000.00

Bust. Rev. Soldier seated.
767.   4 Doppie 1612............................. Rare

Bust. Rev. Eagle.
768.   2 Doppie ND 7000.00

Arms. Rev. Cross.
769.   1 Scudo d'oro ND 4000.00

FRANCIS I D'ESTE, 1629-1658

Bust. Rev. Ship.
770.   24 Scudi d'oro 1631, ND............................ Rare
771.   20 Scudi d'oro ND .... Rare
772.   16 Scudi d'oro 1631, ND............................ Rare
773.   12 Scudi d'oro 1633, 46, ND .... Rare
774.   10 Scudi d'oro ND .... Rare
775.   8 Scudi d'oro 1631, 33, ND ....*...... Rare
776.   6 Scudi d'oro ND................................ 10000.00

Bust. Rev. Madonna.
777.   8 Scudi d'oro 1631 .... Rare
778.   4 Scudi d'oro 1632, 34, ND ....*..... 4000.00
779.   2 Scudi d'oro 1631, ND 5500.00

Bust. Rev. Arms.
780.   1 Doppia 1651.................................. 13000.00
781.   ½ Doppia 1651................................. 6000.00

Bust. Rev. Eagle.
782.   4 Scudi d'oro ND.............................. Rare
783.   2 Scudi d'oro ND.............................. 10000.00
784.   1 Scudo d'oro ND 5000.00
785.   ½ Scudo d'oro ND 3500.00

Ruler standing. Rev. Tablet.
786.   1 Ducat 1649.................................. 2100.00

Ruler standing. Rev. Eagle.
787.   1 Doppia 1639..................................... 6000.00
788.   1 Ducat 1649 ....*...... 4000.00

Ruler standing. Rev. Eagle with shield.
789.   1 Ducat 1649 .... 4000.00

Legend. Rev. Eagle.
790.   5 Lire or ⅓ Scudo d'oro ND .... Rare
791.   103 Soldi or ⅓ Scudo d'oro ND ....*...... 500.00

ALFONSO IV D'ESTE, 1658-1662
Bust. Rev. Sword.
792.   12 Scudi d'oro 1659 .... Rare

Bust. Rev. Eagle.
793.   2 Doppie 1660.................................. Rare
794.   1 Doppia 1660, ND .... Rare

FRANCIS II D'ESTE, 1662-1694

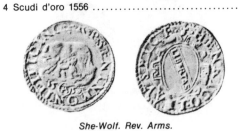

Ruler standing. Rev. Eagle.
795.   1 Ducat ND.. 5000.00

MONTALCINO

SIENESE RULE, 1555-1559
Madonna. Rev. She-Wolf.
796.   4 Scudi d'oro 1556 .... Rare

She-Wolf. Rev. Arms.
797.   1 Scudo d'oro 1556, 57, 58, 59..................... 8000.00

S. Rev. Arms.
798.   ½ Scudo d'oro ND 8000.00

MONTANARO

Abbots of —

BONIFACE FERRERO, 1529-1543
Arms. Rev. Cross.
799.   1 Scudo d'oro ND .... Rare

Eagle. Rev. Cross.

800.	1 Scudo d'oro ND	Rare

SEBASTIAN FERRERO, 1546-1547
Bust. Rev. Arms.

801.	3 Scudi d'oro ND	Rare

Arms. Rev. Cross.

802.	1 Scudo d'oro ND	Rare

JOHN BAPTIST, 1581-1582
Soldier standing. Rev. Arms.

803.	2 Doppie ND	Rare
804.	1 Doppia ND	Rare

Arms. Rev. Cross.

805.	1 Scudo d'oro ND	Rare

MUSSO

Marcheses of —

JOHN JAMES OF MEDICI, 1528-1530
Arms. Rev. Cross.

806.	1 Scudo d'oro ND	Rare

Bust. Rev. Reclining figure.

807.	1 Zecchino ND	Rare

NAPLES

(KINGDOM OF THE TWO SICILIES; SEE ALSO SICILY)

A. Anjou Rulers of —

CHARLES I, 1266-1278

The Annunciation. Rev. Arms.

808.	1 Salut d'or ND . . . . *	2000.00
809.	½ Salut d'or ND	15000.00

CHARLES II, 1285-1309
The Annunciation. Rev. Arms.

810.	1 Salut d'or ND	2000.00

JOANNA I, 1343-1347
Ruler seated. Rev. Cross.

811.	1 Ducat ND	Rare

St. John. Rev. Arms.

812.	1 Florin ND	2500.00

JOANNA AND LOUIS, 1352-1362
St. John. Rev. Lily.

813.	1 Florin ND	3000.00

LOUIS, 1382-1384
St. John. Rev. Arms.

814.	1 Florin ND	2000.00

B. Aragon Rulers of —

ALFONSO I, 1442-1458

Ruler on horse. Rev. Arms.

815.	1 Ducatone ND (31 Millimetres)	4500.00
816.	1 Ducat ND (27 Millimetres) . . . . *	4500.00

FERDINAND I, 1458-1494
Crowned bust. Rev. Victory in chariot.

817.	5 Ducats ND	Rare

Crowned bust. Rev. Arms.

818.	2 Ducats ND	Rare
819.	1 Ducat ND . . . . *	2000.00

ALFONSO II, 1494-1495
Crowned bust of Ferdinand I. Rev. Arms.

820.	1 Ducat ND	6000.00

Crowned bust. Rev. Arms.

820a.	1 Ducat ND	8000.00

FERDINAND II, 1495-1496

Crowned bust. Rev. Arms.

821.	1 Ducat ND	7000.00

FREDERICK III, 1496-1501

Crowned bust. Rev. Animal over shield.

822.	1 Ducat ND	7000.00

C. French Rulers of —

CHARLES VIII, 1495
Arms. Rev. Cross of Jerusalem.

823. 1 Scudo d'oro ND .... Rare

Arms between initials. Rev. Cross of Jerusalem in quadrilobe.

824. 2 Scudi d'oro ND .... Rare
825. 1 Scudo d'oro ND .... * ...... Rare

LOUIS XII, 1501-1503

Crowned bust. Rev. Arms.

826. 1 Ducat ND... 2000.00

D. Spanish Rulers of —

FERDINAND AND ISABELLA, 1504

Crowned busts facing each other. Rev. Arms.

827. 1 Ducat ND 20000.00

FERDINAND THE CATHOLIC, 1504-1516

Crowned bust. Rev. Arms.

828. 1 Ducat ND....................................... 6000.00

CHARLES AND JOANNA, 1516-1519

Arms. Rev. Cross.

829. 1 Ducat ND....................................... 500.00

CHARLES V, 1519-1556

Bust. Rev. Peace standing.

830. 4 Scudi d'oro ND............................... Rare
831. 2 Scudi d'oro ND.........................* 6000.00

Bust. Rev. Pallas seated.

832. 2 Scudi d'oro ND................................. 15000.00

Crowned young bust right. Rev. Arms.

833. 1 Ducat ND .... Rare

Crowned young bust left. Rev. Arms.

833a. 1 Ducat ND 8500.00

Crowned older bust. Rev. Arms.

833b. 1 Ducat ND 15000.00

Laureate head. Rev. Arms.

834. 1 Ducat ND.................................... 1750.00

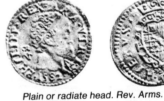

Arms. Rev. Cross.

835. 1 Scudo d'oro ND 800.00

PHILIP II, 1556-1598

Plain or radiate head. Rev. Arms.

836. 1 Scudo d'oro 1582, 83, 85, 97, ND........... 1500.00
Plain head with "Princeps Hispaniae". Rev. Arms.
836a. 1 Scudo d'oro ND................................. 8000.00

PHILIP III, 1598-1621
Bare head. Rev. Arms.

837. 1 Scudo d'oro ND .... Unknown

Radiate bust. Rev. Arms.

838. 1 Scudo d'oro ND .... Rare

PHILIP IV, 1621-1665

Plain head right. Rev. Arms.

839. 2 Scudi d'oro 1626 .... Unknown
840. 1 Scudo d'oro 1622-36 ....* 2000.00

Armored bust left. Rev. Arms.

841. 1 Scudo d'oro 1642, 47-49 .... 6000.00

CHARLES II, 1667-1700

Bust. Rev. Arms.

842.   1 Ducat 1665 .... Unknown

E. Bourbon Rulers of —

CHARLES, 1734-1759

Bust. Rev. Arms and value.

843.   6 Ducati 1749-55 .... * 800.00
844.   4 Ducati 1749-55 .... 800.00
845.   2 Ducati 1749-54 .... 800.00

FERDINAND IV (I), 1759-1825

(Ferdinand IV from 1759-1816 and Ferdinand I from 1817-1825).

Youthful bust. Rev. Arms.

846.   6 Ducati 1759-67 ....
847.   4 Ducati 1760-67 .... * 500.00
848.   2 Ducati 1762 .... 650.00
                                                           600.00

Older bust. Rev. Arms.

849.   6 Ducati 1768-81 .... * 500.00
850.   4 Ducati 1769-76 .... 600.00
851.   2 Ducati 1771 .... 600.00

Oldest bust. Rev. Arms.

852.   6 Ducati 1783, 84, 85 .... 2000.00

Bust of Queen Maria Caroline. Rev. Two figures at altar.

853.   2 Ducati 1768 .... 2000.00

Bust. Rev. Legend.

854.   2 Ducati 1772 .... 2000.00

Crowned bust. Rev. Male standing at column.

855.   30 Ducati 1818 .... * 4000.00
856.   15 Ducati 1818 .... 2000.00
857.   3 Ducati 1818 .... * 700.00

JOACHIM MURAT, 1808-1815
(Napoleonic Dynasty)

Head. Rev. Value.

858.   40 Franchi 1810 .... Rare
859.   40 Lire 1813 .... 1250.00
860.   20 Lire 1813 .... * 800.00
861.   20 Lire 1813. N mm. .... Rare

FRANCIS I, 1825-1830

Head. Rev. Male standing at column.

862.   30 Ducati 1825, 26 .... 7000.00
863.   15 Ducati 1825 .... Rare
864.   6 Ducati 1826 .... * 6000.00
865.   3 Ducati 1826 .... * 3500.00

FERDINAND II, 1830-1859

Head with or without beard. Rev. Male standing at column
with or without wings.

866.   30 Ducati 1831-56 .... * 4500.00
867.   15 Ducati 1831-56 .... * 2500.00
868.   6 Ducati 1831-56 .... * 1500.00
869.   3 Ducati 1831-56 .... 1200.00

NOVARA

Marcheses of —

PETER LUIGI FARNESE, 1538-1547

Arms. Rev. Cross.

870.	1 Scudo d'oro ND	....	Rare

PADUA

FRANCIS I, 1355-1388
St. Prosdocimus. Rev. Arms.

871.	1 Ducat ND	....	Rare

PALERMO

A. Fatimid Caliphs of —
AL-MANSUR, 946-953
Cufic legend on each side.

872.	1 Tari	....	150.00

AL-MU'IZZ, 953-975
Cufic legend on each side.

872a.	1 Tari	....	150.00

AL-AZIZ, 975-996
Cufic legend on each side.

872b.	1 Tari	....	150.00

AL-HAKIM, 996-1021

Cufic legend on each side.

873.	1 Tari	....	150.00

AL-ZAHIR, 1021-1036
Cufic legend on each side.

874.	1 Tari	....	150.00

ANONYMOUS
ERTINA. Rev. Si Mirio.

875.	1 Tari (1021)	....	600.00

ABU TAMIM MUSTANSIR, 1036-1094

Cufic legend on each side.

875a.	1 Tari	....	500.00

B. Kings of —

ROGER II, 1105-1154
Cufic legend on each side.

876.	2 Tari ND	....	250.00
877.	1 Tari ND	....	150.00

T. Rev. Cufic legend.

878.	1 Tari ND	....	150.00

WILLIAM II, 1166-1189
Cufic legend. Rev. Cross.

879.	1 Tari ND	....	150.00

FREDERICK II, 1198-1250
Eagle. Rev. Cross.

880.	2 Tari ND	....	250.00

CHARLES II, 1665-1700

Shield on breast of eagle. Rev. Small head in border under palms.

881.	1 Scudo Riccio 1697	....	3500.00

CHARLES III, 1720-1734
Head. Rev. View of Sicily.

882.	2 Ducati 1723	....	Rare

Bust. Rev. Sceptre and sword above globe.

883.	4 Ducati 1727	....	Rare
884.	2 Ducati 1727	....	15000.00

Head. Rev. Phoenix.

885.	1 Oncia 1720-34	....	500.00

CHARLES BOURBON, 1734-1759

Bust. Rev. Bourbon shield on eagle.

886.	2 Oncia 1734-54	....	1000.00

Bare head. Rev. Phoenix.

887.	1 Oncia 1734-59	....	300.00

FERDINAND IV (III OF SICILY), 1759-1815

Radiate head. Rev. Triskelis.

888.	2 Oncia 1814	....	10000.00

PARMA AND PIACENZA

(For the Papal coinage of Parma, see under Vatican-Parma).

A. Republic of —, 1448-1449

Christ and Madonna. Rev. St. John and St. Hillary standing.

889.   1 Ducat ND...................................... Rare

B. Dukes of —

(Unless otherwise stated, all coins are for Parma. Those coins struck for Piacenza are so indicated at the end of the description).

OCTAVIUS FARNESE, 1547-1586

Arms. Rev. Security seated.

890.   1 Scudo d'oro 1552-57, ND................. * 1750.00
891.   1 Scudo d'oro 1552. For Piacenza 3250.00

Pallas seated. Rev. Arms.

892.   ½ Scudo d'oro 1552, ND 4000.00

Head. Rev. She-wolf. For Piacenza.

893.   2 Doppie 1582, 86, 87, ND................. * 7250.00
894.   1 Doppia 1582, 85, 86, 89, ND 3500.00

ALEXANDER FARNESE, 1586-1591
Bust. Rev. The three Graces standing.

895.   7 Scudi d'oro 1588 .... Rare
896.   4 Doppie 1588.. Rare

Bust. Rev. Arms.

897.   2 Doppie ND .... Rare

Bust. Rev. Security standing.

898.   1 Doppia ND .... Rare

Bust. Rev. She-wolf. For Piacenza.

899.   2 Doppie 1590-99, ND........................... 4500.00

Bust. Rev. Christ and Madonna.

899a.   2 Doppie ND .... Rare

RANUCCIO FARNESE I, 1592-1622
Bust of Alexander Farnese. Rev. The three Graces standing.

900.   8 Scudi d'oro 1594 .... Rare

Ruler standing. Rev. Arms.

901.   1 Ducat 1602, 03 .... 1000.00

Ruler standing. Rev. Madonna.

902.   1 Ducat ND...................................... 3500.00

Bust. Rev. Ship. For Piacenza.

903.   2 Doppie 1592...................................... 10000.00

Bust. Rev. Wind blowing. For Piacenza.

904.   4 Doppie 1601.................................... Rare
905.   2 Doppie 1595, 1612, 13, 14 .... 8000.00
906.   1 Doppia 1595-1612........................ * 8000.00

Bust. Rev. She-wolf. For Piacenza.

907.   2 Doppie 1599-1622.............................. 3500.00

Ruler standing. Rev. Tablet.

908.   1 Ducat 1601 .... Rare

ODOARDO FARNESE, 1622-1646

Bust. Rev. Madonna.

909.   8 Doppie 1639..................................... Rare
910.   6 Doppie ND .... Rare
911.   2 Doppie 1625, 39, ND.................... * 5000.00
912.   1 Doppia ND 8500.00

Bust. Rev. Mars and Pallas standing.

913.   8 Doppie 1629..................................... Rare

Bust. Rev. The three Graces standing.

914.   3 Doppie 1633..................................... Rare

Bust. Rev. Lily. For Piacenza.

915.　2 Doppie 1623, 24 . . . .　Rare

Bust. Rev. St. Anthony on horse. For Piacenza.

915a　8 Doppie 1629 . . . .　Rare
916.　6 Doppie 1626, 29 . . . .　Rare

Bust. Rev. She-wolf. For Piacenza.

917.　2 Doppie 1626, 31 . . . . * . . . . . .　4500.00
918.　1 Doppia 1626 . . . .　4000.00

RANUCCIO FARNESE II, 1646-1694
Bust. Rev. Madonna.

919.　2 Doppie 1658, ND . . . .　9000.00

Bust. Rev. Saint standing.

920.　1 Doppia 1687 . . . .　9000.00

Head. Rev. Wind blowing.

921.　1 Doppia 1692 . . . .　9000.00

Bust. Rev. Mars and Pallas standing.

922.　10 Doppie 1673 . . . .　Rare
923.　8 Doppie 1660, 79 . . . .　Rare

Bust. Rev. St. Anthony on horse. For Piacenza.

924.　10 Doppie 1676 . . . .　Rare

FRANCIS FARNESE I, 1694-1727

Head. Rev. Arms.

925.　1 Doppia 1695 . . . .　15000.00

FERDINAND BOURBON, 1765-1802

Head. Rev. Arms.

926.　8 Doppie 1786-96 . . . .　10000.00
927.　6 Doppie 1786 . . . .　10000.00

928.　4 Doppie 1784-96 . . . .　5000.00
929.　3 Doppie 1784, 86 . . . .　Rare
930.　1 Doppia 1784-96 . . . . * . . . . .　750.00
931.　½ Doppia 1785-97 . . . .　600.00
932.　1 Zecchino 1784 . . . .　2000.00

MARIE LOUISE, 1815-1847

Head. Rev. Arms.

933.　40 Lire 1815, 21 . . . . * . . . . .　950.00
934.　20 Lire 1815, 32 . . . .　1250.00

PASSERANO

ANONYMOUS, 1581-1598
Eagle. Rev. Cross.

935.　10 Scudi d'oro 1582 . . . .　Rare

Arms. Rev. Cross.

936.　2 Scudi d'oro 1597 . . . .　Rare

PAVIA

Kings of —

ROTARI, 636-652
Bust. Rev. Victory standing.

937.　⅓ Solidus ND . . . .　2500.00

CUNIBERT, 686-700
Bust. Rev. St. Michael standing.

938.　⅓ Solidus ND . . . .　2500.00

Bust. Rev. Victory standing.

939.　⅓ Solidus ND . . . .　2500.00

LUITBERT, 700-701

Bust. Rev. St. Michael standing.

940.　⅓ Solidus ND . . . .　2250.00

ARIBERT, 701-712
Bust. Rev. St. Michael standing.

941.　⅓ Solidus ND . . . .　2500.00

LUITBRAND, 712-744
Bust. Rev. St. Michael standing.

942.　⅓ Solidus ND . . . .　2000.00

RACHIS, 744-749
Bust. Rev. St. Michael standing.

943.　⅓ Solidus ND . . . .　Rare

ASTOLF, 749-756
St. Michael standing. Rev. Christogram.

944. ⅓ Solidus ND...................................... Rare

DESIDERIUS, 756-774
Cross. Rev. Star.

945. ⅓ Solidus ND...................................... Rare

CHARLEMAGNE, 744-800
Cross. Rev. Star.

946. ⅓ Solidus ND...................................... Rare

PHILIP MARIA, 1402-1412
Horseman. Rev. Arms.

947. 1 Florin ND... Rare

FRANCIS I, 1447-1450
Ruler on horse. Rev. Crowned serpent.

948. 1 Ducat ND... Rare

SIEGE OF PAVIA, 1524-1525
Legend. Rev. Legend incused. Square shape.

949. 1 Ducat 1524...................................... Rare

PERUGIA

(Roman Republic, 1799).
Eagle facing, and below "Perugia." Rev. Value in wreath.

950. 1 Gold Scudo. Year VII (1799)..................... Rare

(For additional coins of Perugia, see under Vatican).

PESARO

Dukes of —
JOHN SFORZA, 1489-1510
Bust. Rev. St. Paul standing.

951. 1 Zecchino ND .... Rare

CONSTANCE II SFORZA, 1510-1512
Arms. Rev. St. Paul standing.

952. 1 Scudo d'oro ND .... Rare

FRANCIS MARIA DELLA ROVERE, 1513-1538
Arms. Rev. St. Francis standing.

953. 1 Scudo d'oro ND 6000.00

Plan of fortress. Rev. St. Francis standing.

954. 1 Scudo d'oro ND 7000.00

GUIDOBALD II DELLA ROVERE, 1538-1574

Three pyramids. Rev. Legend.

955. 1 Ducat ND.. 8000.00
956. ½ Ducat ND...............................*...... 4000.00

FRANCIS MARIA II DELLA ROVERE, 1574-1624
Crowned arms. Rev. St. Francis kneeling.

956a. 2 Scudi d'oro ND........................... 15000.00

PIACENZA

DESIDERIUS, 756-774
Cross. Rev. Star.

956b. ⅓ Solidus ND..................................... Rare

PIOMBINO

Princes of —

NICHOLAS LUDOVISI, 1634-1665
Madonna. Rev. Arms.

957.   2 Doppie 1651................................... Rare
957a. 1 Doppia 1644.................................. Rare

JOHN BAPTIST LUDOVISI, 1665-1699

Bust. Rev. Arms.

958. 1 Doppia 1695.................................. Rare
959. 1 Zecchino 1695, 96 ....*...... Rare

PISA

A. Kings of —

ANONYMOUS, 650-749
Cross. Rev. Star.

960. ⅓ Solidus ND..................................... Rare

Star. Rev. Cross.

961. ⅓ Solidus ND..................................... Rare

ASTOLF, 749-756
Cross. Rev. Star.

962. ⅓ Solidus ND.................................... Rare

DESIDERIUS, 757-778
Cross. Rev. Star.

963. ⅓ Solidus ND..................................... Rare

CHARLEMAGNE, 774-800
Cross. Rev. Star.

964. ⅓ Solidus ND..................................... Rare

B. Republic of —

Madonna. Rev. Eagle.

965. 1 Zecchino ND (1313-1494)........................ 4000.00

Madonna. Rev. Cross.

966. 1 Zecchino ND (1495-1509)........................ 4500.00

C. French Rulers of —

CHARLES VIII, 1494-1495
Madonna and child. Rev. Crowned arms.

967. 1 Zecchino ND .... Rare

D. Tuscan Grand Dukes of —

FERDINAND I, 1587-1609
Madonna in clouds. Rev. Cross of Pisa.

968. 2 Doppie 1595................................... 8000.00
969. 1 Doppia 1595.................................. 3500.00

FERDINAND II, 1621-1670

Madonna in clouds. Rev. Cross of Pisa.

970.	2 Doppie ND	8000.00
971.	1 Doppia 1641-55, ND ....*	2000.00
972.	½ Doppia 1643, ND	1500.00

COSIMO III, 1670-1723

Madonna in clouds. Rev. Cross of Pisa.

973.	1 Doppia ND	8000.00

PISTOIA

Rose. Rev. Cross.

974.	⅓ Solidus ND (700-800)............................	Rare

POMBIA

DESIDERIUS, 756-774
Cross. Rev. Star.

974a.	⅓ Solidus ND......................................	Rare

POMPONESCO

Marcheses of —

JULIUS CAESAR GONZAGA, 1583-1593
Arms. Rev. Cross.

975.	1 Scudo d'oro ND	Rare

PORCIA

Princes of —

HANNIBAL ALFONSO EMANUEL, 1704
Bust. Rev. Arms.

976.	1 Ducat 1704	Rare

RAVENNA

Kings of —

ASTOLF, 749-756
Bust. Rev. Cross.

977.	1 Solidus ND.......................................	Rare
978.	⅓ Solidus ND......................................	Rare

REGGIO-EMILIA

Dukes of —

HERCULES I D'ESTE, 1471-1505
Hercules lifting Antaeus. Rev. St. Prospero standing.

979.	1 Ducat ND................................... 10000.00

ALFONSO I D'ESTE, 1505-1534

Bust. Rev. St. Prospero seated.

980.	1 Ducat ND...................................	Rare

HERCULES II D'ESTE, 1534-1559

Arms. Rev. Christ with cross.

981.	1 Scudo d'oro 1550-58, ND	1250.00

ALFONSO II D'ESTE, 1559-1597
Arms. Rev. Christ with cross.

982.	1 Scudo d'oro 1560-72............................	1250.00

Bust. Rev. Nude male with shield.

983.	2 Doppie 1567.....................................	Rare

Bust. Rev. Eagle.

984.	10 Scudi d'oro 1572	Rare

RETEGNO

Barons of —

ANTHONY THEODORE TRIVULZIO, 1676-1678
Ruler on horse. Rev. Bundle of corn ears.

985.	1 Zecchino 1676...................................	5000.00

Bust. Rev. Arms.

986.	10 Zecchini 1677.....................................	Rare

Soldier standing. Rev. Tablet.

987.	2 Ducats 1677	6000.00
988.	1 Ducat 1677	5000.00

ANTHONY CAIETAN TRIVULZIO, 1679-1705

Bust. Rev. Arms.

989.	10 Zecchini 1686....................................	Rare

Soldier standing. Rev. Legend.

990.	2 Doppie ND	Rare

Soldier standing. Rev. Tablet.

991.	2 Ducats 1686, ND..........................	*......	5000.00
992.	1 Ducat 1686, ND............................		4000.00

ANTHONY PTOLEMY TRIVULZIO, 1708-1767

Bust. Rev. Arms.

993.	1 Ducat 1724, 26	5500.00

RIFREDI

PISAN RULE, 1363
Madonna. Rev. Eagle.

994.	1 Zecchino ND	Rare

ROME

(See Vatican).

RONCO

Marcheses of —

NAPOLEON SPINOLA, 1647-1672

Bust. Rev. Eagle.

995.	4 Ducats 1647.....................................	Rare
996.	1 Ducat 1668 ....*......	12000.00

CHARLES SPINOLA
Bust. Rev. Eagle on arms.

997.	1 Doppia ND (1699)...............................	Rare

SABBIONETA

Dukes of —

VESPASIAN GONZAGA, 1562-1565
Arms. Rev. Cross.

998.	1 Scudo d'oro ND	10000.00

Head. Rev. Madonna.

999.	½ Scudo d'oro ND	10000.00

Three shields. Rev. Cross.

1000.	1 Scudo d'oro ND	12000.00

LUIGI CARAFA AND ISABELLA GONZAGA, 1591-1637
Madonna. Rev. Arms on eagle.

1001.	1 Ducat ND.....................................	12000.00

SALERNO

Princes of —

SICONOLFO, 839-849
Bust. Rev. Cross.

1002.	1 Solidus ND.....................................	1600.00

GISULF I, 935-974

Cufic legend on each side.

1003.	1 Tari ND..	400.00

GUAIMARIO IV, 999-1015
Cufic legend on each side.

1004.	1 Tari ND..	400.00

1005.	The coin previously listed will now be found as No. 875a.

GISULF II, 1052-1075
Latin and Cufic legends on each side.

1006.	1 Tari ND..	500.00

ROBERT, 1059-1085

Cufic legend on each side.

1007.	1 Tari ND..	550.00

ROGER II, 1127-1130
Cufic legend on each side.

1008.	1 Tari ND..	350.00

WILLIAM II, 1166-1189

W. Rev. Star and Cufic legend.

1009.	1 Tari ND..	850.00

TANCRED, 1189-1194
ACD REX. Rev. Cufic legend.

1010.	1 Tari ND..	850.00

SAN GIORGIO

Marcheses of —

JOHN DOMINIC MILANO, 1732
Bust. Rev. Arms.

1011.	2 Zecchini 1732.....................................	Rare
1012.	1 Zecchino 1732.....................................	10000.00

SAN JACOPO AL SERCHIO

FLORENTINE RULE, 1256
St. John standing, trefoil mm. Rev. Lily.

1013.	1 Florin ND...	1150.00

SARDINIA

(HOUSE OF SAVOY)

Counts, and later, Kings of —

AMADEUS VI, 1343-1383
Lily. Rev. St. John.

1014.	1 Florin ND...	Rare

AMADEUS VII, 1383-1391

Helmeted shield. Rev. St. John.

1015.	1 Florin ND...	Rare

Ruler on throne. Rev. Arms.

1016.	1 Florin ND...	Rare

Helmeted shield. Rev. Cross.

1017.	1 Scudo d'oro ND	Rare

AMADEUS VIII (DUKE), 1391-1439

Ruler kneeling before St. Maurice. Rev. Helmeted shield.

1018.	1 Ducat ND...	Rare

LOUIS I, 1434-1465

Ruler on horse. Rev. Helmeted shield and "Fert."

1019.	1 Ducat ND...	5000.00

Arms and "Fert." Rev. Cross.

1020.	1 Scudo d'oro ND	*	10000.00
1021.	½ Scudo d'oro ND		Rare

Arms in enclosure. Rev. Cross.

1022.	1 Scudo d'oro ND	12000.00

AMADEUS IX, 1465-1472
Ruler on horse. Rev. Arms.

1023.	1 Ducat ND...	16000.00

Arms in enclosure. Rev. Cross.

1024.	1 Scudo d'oro ND	Rare

FILIBERT I, 1472-1482
Ruler on horse. Rev. Arms.

1025.	1 Ducat ND...	10000.00

CHARLES I, 1482-1490

Ruler on horse. Rev. Helmeted shield and "Fert."

1026.	1 Ducat ND...	10000.00

Bust with cap. Rev. Helmeted shield.

1027.	1 Ducat ND...	13500.00

Bust with cap. Rev. Arms and "Fert."

1028.	1 Ducat ND...	12000.00

PHILIP II, 1496-1497
Ruler on horse. Rev. Arms.

1029.	1 Ducat ND...	Rare

FILIBERT II, 1497-1504

Bust with cap. Rev. Arms and "Fert."

1030.	The coin previously listed does not exist............	—
1031.	1 Ducat ND...	Rare

CHARLES II, 1504-1553
Armored bust. Rev. Arms.

1032.	10 Ducats 1546	Rare

Armored half bust with cap. Rev. Arms between two K's.

1033.	1 Ducat ND...	Rare

Bust with cap. Rev. Arms and "Fert." Only 3 known.

1034. 1 Ducat ND..Very Rare

Ruler on horse. Rev. Arms.

1035. 1 Scudo d'oro ND 10000.00

Arms and "Fert." Rev. Cross.

1036. 1 Scudo d'oro ND 8000.00

Arms. Rev. Ornate cross.

1037. 1 Scudo d'oro ND 7000.00

Arms. Rev. St. Maurice on horse.

1038. 1 Scudo d'oro ND .... Rare

EMANUEL FILIBERT, 1553-1580
Arms. Rev. Cross.

1039. 1 Scudo d'oro ND. Broad type..................... 6000.00

Arms and "Fert." Rev. Cross.

1039a. 1 Scudo d'oro ND. Broad type..................... 6000.00

Oval shield. Rev. Cross.

1039b. 1 Scudo d'oro 1555-71 .... 1500.00

Arms. Rev. Small cross on large cross.

1040. 1 Doppia 1576-80 .... 15000.00
1041. 1 Scudo d'oro 1570-76 ....*...... 2500.00

Bust. Rev. Arms.

1042. 1 Doppia 1570-76 .... 10000.00

Armored bust. Rev. Elephant.

1043. 9 Lire ND... Rare

Busts of the Royal couple. Rev. Serpent.

1044. 3 Filibertos ND.................................. Rare

CHARLES EMANUEL I, 1580-1630

Armored bust. Rev. Arms.

1045. 10 Ducats 1607-28 .... Rare
1046. 10 Scudi d'oro 1623 .... Rare
1047. 4 Scudi d'oro 1586, 87............................ Rare
1048. 2 Doppie 1595, 98, 1601, ND...................... 18000.00
1049. 1 Doppia 1580-1611, ND ....*...... 6000.00

Bust. Rev. Cross.

1050. 1 Scudo d'oro 1627............................... Rare
1051. ½ Scudo d'oro 1627............................... Rare

Bust. Rev. Legend.

1052. 1 Scudo d'oro 1630............................... Rare

Bust. Rev. Compass.

1053. 10 Scudi d'oro 1630 .... Rare

Arms. Rev. Cross.

1054. 1 Doppia 1581.................................... 15000.00
1055. 1 Scudo d'oro 1580-91............................ 5000.00

Madonna. Rev. Arms.

1056. 1 Ducat 1601, 02 .... 1600.00

VICTOR AMADEUS I, 1630-1637
Bust. Rev. Three flags.

1057. 10 Scudi d'oro 1633 .... Rare
1058. 4 Scudi d'oro 1633, 34............................ Rare
1059. 2 Doppie 1632.................................... Rare

Bust. Rev. Arms.

1060. 30 Scudi d'oro 1635 .... Rare
1061. 20 Scudi d'oro 1635 .... Rare
1062. 10 Scudi d'oro 1633, 34, 35, 36 ....*...... Rare
1063. 4 Scudi d'oro 1634, ND........................... Rare
1064. 1 Doppia ND .... Rare

Bust. Rev. Cross.

1065. 10 Scudi d'oro 1635 .... Rare

FRANCIS HYACINT, 1637-1638

Busts of Francis and his mother, Christina. Rev. Madonna.

1066.	8 Scudi d'oro ND		Rare
1067.	4 Scudi d'oro ND	*	Rare

CHARLES EMANUEL II, 1638-1675

Busts of Charles and Christina to right or left. Rev. Arms.

1068.	20 Scudi d'oro 1641		Rare
1069.	10 Scudi d'oro 1641, 68		Rare
1070.	8 Scudi d'oro 1641, ND		Rare
1071.	4 Scudi d'oro 1639-48	*	4000.00
1072.	1 Doppia 1640, 41		Rare

Busts of Charles and Christina. Rev. Arms and value.

1073.	4 Scudi d'oro 1642	Rare

Busts of Charles and Christina. Rev. Madonna.

1074.	8 Scudi d'oro ND	Rare

Arms. Rev. Crossed initials.

1075.	1 Scudo d'oro ND	12000.00

Busts of Charles and Christina. Rev. Crossed initials.

1076.	½ Scudo d'oro ND	16000.00

Youthful bust. Rev. Arms.

1077.	10 Scudi d'oro 1639		Rare
1078.	4 Scudi d'oro 1639, 40	*	Rare

Mature bust. Rev. Arms.

1079.	40 Scudi d'oro 1656	Rare
1080.	30 Scudi d'oro 1656	Rare
1081.	20 Scudi d'oro 1649-71	Rare
1082.	10 Scudi d'oro 1649-71	Rare
1083.	4 Scudi d'oro 1649-54	Rare
1084.	1 Doppia 1650-54	10000.00
1085.	½ Scudo d'oro 1649	Rare

Bust. Rev. Crossed initials.

1085a.	1 Doppia 1670	Rare
1086.	1 Scudo d'oro 1670	Rare

Head. Rev. Arms.

1087.	1 Doppia 1675	6000.00

Head. Rev. Cross.

1088.	1 Scudo d'oro ND	Rare

VICTOR AMADEUS II, 1675-1730

Busts of Victor and Maria Joan. Rev. Arms.

1089.	5 Doppie 1675, 78		Rare
1090.	1 Doppia 1675-80	*	5000.00
1091.	½ Doppia 1675-79		3500.00

Busts of Victor and Maria Joan. Rev. Seated female and cherub.

1092.	2 Doppie 1675-77	Rare

Youthful bust. Rev. Arms and lions.

1093.	20 Scudi d'oro 1684	Rare
1094.	10 Scudi d'oro 1680, 84	Rare

Ruler on horse. Rev. Justice standing.

1095.	5 Doppie 1694	Rare

Youthful bust. Rev. Arms.

1096.	2 Doppie 1680	Rare
1097.	1 Doppia 1680-82	Rare
1098.	½ Doppia 1680, 81	Rare

Older bust. Rev. Arms.

1099.	1 Doppia 1690-1706	Rare
1100.	½ Doppia 1692-1709	Rare

Older bust. Rev. Arms. With title of King of Sicily.

1100a.	1 Doppia 1714-18	Rare

CHARLES EMANUEL III, 1730-1773

Bust. Rev. Arms.

1101.	1 Doppia 1733-41	Rare
1102.	½ Doppia 1733-42	16000.00

Head. Rev. Arms.

1103.	5	Doppie 1755-68	15000.00
1104.	2½	Doppie 1755, 56, 57	11000.00
1105.	1	Doppia 1755-69	2500.00
1106.	½	Doppia 1755-70	* 1600.00
1107.	¼	Doppia 1755-58	3000.00

Bust. Rev. Oval shield of Sardinia.

1108.	5	Doppie 1768, 69	Rare
1109.	2½	Doppie 1768-71 ....*......	8500.00
1110.	1	Doppia 1768-72	2000.00

Eagle. Rev. The Annunciation.

1111.	4	Zecchini 1745, 46 ....*......	7500.00
1112.	1	Zecchino 1743-46	1600.00
1113.	½	Zecchino 1744-46	1200.00

Madonna. Rev. Angel.

1114.	⅙	Zecchino ND	12000.00
1114a.	⅛	Zecchino ND	6000.00

VICTOR AMADEUS III, 1773-1796
Head. Rev. Arms.

1115.	1	Doppia 1773-82	10000.00
1116.	½	Doppia 1773-84	6000.00
1117.	¼	Doppia 1773-85	4000.00

Head. Rev. Eagle.

1118.	5	Doppie 1786	12500.00
1119.	2½	Doppie 1786	5250.00
1120.	1	Doppia 1786-96	1200.00
1121.	½	Doppia 1786-96 ....*......	700.00
1122.	¼	Doppia 1786 ....*......	1400.00

Bust. Rev. Oval shield of Sardinia.

1123.	5	Doppie 1773-84	Rare
1124.	2½	Doppie 1773-84	Rare
1125.	1	Doppia 1773-86 ....*......	4000.00

CHARLES EMANUEL IV, 1796-1802

Head. Rev. Eagle.

1126.	1	Doppia 1797-1800 ....*......	4500.00
1127.	½	Doppia 1797, 98	2500.00

VICTOR EMANUEL I, 1802-1821

Head. Rev. Eagle.

1128.	1	Doppia 1814, 15	15000.00

Head. Rev. Square shield in circle.

1129.	20	Lire 1816-20	700.00

Head. Rev. Oval shield within branches.

1130.	80	Lire 1821 ....*......	9000.00
1131.	20	Lire 1821	6000.00

CHARLES FELIX, 1821-1831

Head. Rev. Arms.

1132.	80	Lire 1823-31. Eagle's head mm.	1250.00
1133.	80	Lire 1824-31. Anchor mm. ....*......	1250.00
1134.	40	Lire 1822-31. Eagle's head mm.	1200.00
1135.	40	Lire 1825, 26. Anchor mm.	1500.00
1136.	20	Lire 1821-31. Eagle's head mm.	275.00
1137.	20	Lire 1824-31. Anchor mm.	800.00

CHARLES ALBERT, 1831-1849

Head. Rev. Arms.

1138.	100	Lire 1832-44. Eagle's head mm.	1100.00
1139.	100	Lire 1832-45. Anchor mm. ....*......	1100.00
1140.	50	Lire 1832-43. Eagle's head mm.	1500.00
1141.	50	Lire 1833, 35, 41. Anchor mm.	1800.00
1142.	20	Lire 1831-49. Eagle's head mm.	150.00

1143.	20 Lire 1831-49. Anchor mm.	150.00
1144.	10 Lire 1832-47. Eagle's head mm. ....*	1200.00
1145.	10 Lire 1833-47. Anchor mm. ....*	1500.00

VICTOR EMANUEL II, 1849-1861

Head. Rev. Arms.

1146.	20 Lire 1850-61. Eagle's head mm.	150.00
1147.	20 Lire 1850-60. Anchor mm. ....*	150.00
1148.	20 Lire 1860. M mm.	400.00
1149.	10 Lire 1850-60. Eagle's head mm.	1200.00
1150.	10 Lire 1850. Anchor mm.	1500.00

(For the later coins of Victor Emanuel II, as King of all Italy, see under Italy, Kings of —).

SAVONA

St. John. Rev. Lily.

1151.	1 Florin ND (1350-96)	2000.00

Madonna and child flanked by two lis. Rev. Eagle. Struck under Louis XII of France.

1152.	2 Ducats ND (1499-1510)	Rare
1153.	1 Ducat ND (1499-1510)	Rare

SAVOY, HOUSE OF

(See Sardinia).

SICILY

(See Messina and Palermo).

SIENA

A. Republic of —

S. Rev. Cross.

1154.	1 Florin ND (1340-1450)	5000.00
1155.	1 Sanese d'oro ND (1375-90) ....*	2000.00
1156.	1 Ducat ND (1450-1550)	2500.00
1157.	½ Ducat 1553-55, ND	4000.00
1158.	½ Scudo d'oro 1549-53	4000.00

Madonna. Rev. Victory standing.

1159.	2 Ducats ND	Rare

She-wolf in shield. Rev. Cross.

1160.	1 Scudo d'oro ND (1533-48)	3000.00

She-wolf. Rev. Cross.

1161.	1 Scudo d'oro 1548-54, ND	4000.00

Madonna. Rev. Cross.

1162.	1 Scudo d'oro 1549	4000.00

Madonna. Rev. St. Victorius standing.

1163.	3 Doppie 1550	Rare

B. Rulers of —

JOHN GALEAZZO, 1390-1404

S. Rev. Cross.

1164.	1 Sanese d'oro ND	3000.00

COSIMO I, 1557-1574
Arms. Rev. Cross.

1165.	1 Scudo d'oro ND	4000.00

HENRY II OF FRANCE, 1547-1559
Madonna and child. Rev. She-wolf.

1166.	4 Ecu d'or 1556	Rare

She-wolf. Rev. Band across oval shield.

1167.	1 Ecu d'or 1557	Rare

S. Rev. Band across oval shield.

1168.	½ Ecu d'or ND	12000.00

SOLFERINO

Marcheses of —

CHARLES GONZAGA, 1643-1678
Bust. Rev. Arms.

1169.	2 Florins ND	12000.00

Ruler standing. Rev. Arms.

1170.   1 Ducat ND.......................................   Rare

SORAGNA

Princes of —

NICHOLAS MELI-LUPI, 1731-1741

Arms. Rev. Eagle.

1171.   1 Scudo d'oro 1731...............................   Rare

SUB-ALPINE REPUBLIC

Helmeted female head. Rev. Value and date. On the Victory of Marengo. Struck at Turin.

1172.   20 Francs. Years 9 and 10 (1800, 01)................   1500.00

TASSAROLO

Counts of —

AUGUSTIN SPINOLA, 1604-1616
Bust. Rev. Arms.

1173.   5 Doppie 1604.......................................   Rare
1174.   2 Doppie 1604.......................................   12000.00

Bust of Rudolph II. Rev. Eagle.
1175.   1 Ducat 1604 ....   12000.00

Soldier standing. Rev. Tablet.
1176.   1 Ducat 1611, 12, ND...............................   4000.00

Soldier standing. Rev. Eagle.
1177.   1 Ducat ND...   3500.00

Soldier standing. Rev. Arms.
1178.   1 Ducat ND...   3500.00

Madonna. Rev. Arms.
1179.   1 Ducat 1614 ....   10000.00

Eagle. Rev. St. Nicholas.

1180.   1 Doppia ND 14000.00

PHILIP SPINOLA, 1616-1688

Bust. Rev. Arms.

1181.   2 Doppie 1629.................................*......   Rare
1182.   1 Doppia 1630......................................   12000.00

Bust. Rev. St. Charles in fire.
1183.   2 Doppie 1640......................................   Rare
1184.   1 Doppia 1640......................................   12000.00

Soldier standing. Rev. Eagle.
1185.   1 Ducat 1637.......................................   2250.00

Soldier standing. Rev. Tablet.
1186.   1 Ducat ND...   2250.00

Rose. Rev. Tablet.
1187.   1 Ducat ND...   5000.00

Eagle. Rev. Bishop.
1188.   2 Doppie ND ....   Rare

TRENTO

Bishops of —

PETER VIGILIO, 1776-1796
Bust. Rev. Arms and eagle.
1189.   1 Ducat 1776.......................................   4000.00

TRESANA

Marcheses of —

WILLIAM II, 1613-1651
St. Ladislas standing. Rev. Madonna.
1190.   1 Ducat 1620 ....   5000.00

St. Louis standing. Rev. Eagle.

1191.   1 Ducat ND.............................. 5000.00

Soldier standing. Rev. Tablet.

1192.   1 Ducat 1619 .... 5000.00

Arab legend on each side. Struck for use in the Levant.

1193.   1 Dinar ND 5000.00

TREVISO

DESIDERIUS, 757-773
Cross. Rev. Star.

1194.   ⅓ Solidus ND........................   Rare

TUSCANY

(For the coins of the Grand Dukes of Tuscany, see under Florence, Leghorn and Pisa).

Government of —

St. John seated. Rev. Lily. Struck at Florence.

1195.   1 Ruspone 1859 .... 8000.00

URBINO

Dukes of —

GUIDOBALD I, 1482-1508

Bust. Rev. Eagle and shield.

1196.   1 Ducat ND............................. 16000.00

FRANCIS MARIA I, 1508-1538

Bust. Rev. Eagle and shield.

1197.   1 Ducat ND............................. 5000.00

Helmeted bust. Rev. Eagle and shield.

1198.   1 Ducat ND............................. 6000.00

LORENZO, 1516-1519
Bust. Rev. Arms.

1199.   1 Ducat ND............................. 16000.00

GUIDOBALD II, 1538-1574
Head. Rev. Arms.

1200.   4 Scudi d'oro ND.......................   Rare

Bust. Rev. Legend.

1201.   1 Ducat ND............................. 16000.00

Arms. Rev. The Annunciation.

1202.   1 Ducat ND............................. 6000.00

St. Helen and cross. Rev. Arms.

1203.   1 Ducat ND............................. 4000.00

Plant. Rev. Winged thunderbolt.

1204.   ¼ Ducat ND............................. 4000.00

FRANCIS MARIA II, 1574-1624

Bust. Rev. Arms.

1205.   20 Scudi d'oro 1604 ....   Rare
1206.   10 Scudi d'oro 1603, 21.............*.....   Rare
1207.   1 Scudo d'oro ND ....*..... 6000.00

Arms. Rev. Tree.

1208.   4 Scudi d'oro ND...................*....11000.00
1209.   1 Scudo d'oro ND ....*...... 5000.00

St. Michael standing. Rev. Arms.

1210.   1 Scudo d'oro ND 2500.00

St. Francis standing. Rev. Fortress.

1211.   1 Scudo d'oro ND 5000.00

VASTO

Marcheses of —

CAESAR D'AVALOS, 1704-1729

Bust. Rev. Arms.

1212.   20 Zecchini 1706........................   Rare
1213.   1 Zecchino 1706....................... 10000.00
1214.   ½ Zecchino 1707 ....*..... 8000.00

VENICE

Doges of —

TYPE I

Doge kneeling before standing figure of St. Mark. Rev. Christ standing within stars. The following coins are undated.

JOHN DANDOLO, 1280-1289

1215.	1 Ducat	2500.00

PETER GRADENIGO, 1289-1311

1216.	1 Ducat	275.00

MARINO ZORZI, 1311-1312

1217.	1 Ducat	4000.00

JOHN SORANZO, 1312-1328

1218.	1 Ducat	350.00

FRANCIS DANDOLO, 1329-1339

1219.	1 Ducat	260.00

BARTHOLOMEW GRADENIGO, 1339-1342

1220.	1 Ducat	260.00

ANDREW DANDOLO, 1343-1354

1221.	1 Ducat	260.00

MARINO FALIER, 1354-1355

1222.	1 Ducat	5500.00

JOHN GRADENIGO, 1355-1356

1223.	1 Ducat	275.00

JOHN DELFINO, 1356-1361

1224.	1 Ducat	260.00

LORENZO CELSI, 1361-1365

1225.	1 Ducat	260.00

MARCO CORNER, 1365-1368

1226.	1 Ducat	260.00

ANDREW CONTARINI, 1368-1382

1227.	1 Ducat	260.00

MICHAEL MOROSINI, 1382

1228.	1 Ducat	1875.00

ANTHONY VENIER, 1382-1400

1229.	1 Ducat	260.00

MICHAEL STENO, 1400-1413

1230.	1 Ducat	260.00

THOMAS MOCENIGO, 1414-1423

1231.	1 Ducat	325.00

FRANCIS FOSCARI, 1423-1457

1232.	1 Ducat	260.00

PASQUALE MALIPIERO, 1457-1462

1233.	1 Ducat	400.00

CHRISTOPHER MORO, 1462-1471

1234.	1 Ducat	400.00

NICHOLAS TRONO, 1471-1474

1235.	1 Ducat	2250.00

NICHOLAS MARCELLO, 1473-1474

1236.	1 Ducat	*	3500.00

PETER MOCENIGO, 1474-1476

1237.	1 Ducat	3000.00

ANDREW VENDRAMIN, 1476-1478

1238.	1 Ducat	700.00

JOHN MOCENIGO, 1478-1485

1239.	1 Ducat	700.00

MARCO BARBARIGO, 1485-1486

1240.	1 Ducat	6000.00

AUGUSTIN BARBARIGO, 1486-1501

1241.	1 Ducat	400.00

LEONARDO LOREDANO, 1501-1521

1242.	1 Ducat	260.00
1243.	½ Ducat	1800.00

ANTHONY GRIMANI, 1521-1523

1244.	1 Ducat	2750.00
1245.	½ Ducat	2250.00

ANDREW GRITTI, 1523-1539

1246.	1 Ducat	275.00
1247.	½ Ducat	2250.00

PETER LANDO, 1539-1545

1248.	1 Ducat	350.00
1249.	½ Ducat	2250.00

FRANCIS DONA, 1545-1553

1250.	1 Zecchino	275.00

MARC ANTHONY TREVISANI, 1553-1554

1251.	1 Zecchino	525.00
1252.	½ Zecchino	2250.00

FRANCIS VENIER, 1554-1556

1253.	1 Zecchino	275.00
1254.	½ Zecchino	2250.00

LORENZO PRIULI, 1556-1559

1255.	1 Zecchino	260.00
1256.	½ Zecchino	3750.00

GIROLAMO PRIULI, 1559-1567

1257.	1 Zecchino	260.00
1258.	½ Zecchino	2250.00

PETER LOREDANO, 1567-1570

1259.	1 Zecchino	260.00
1260.	½ Zecchino	2250.00
1261.	¼ Zecchino	350.00

ALOIS MOCENIGO I, 1570-1577

1262.	2 Zecchini	7500.00
1263.	1 Zecchino	250.00

SEBASTIAN VENIER, 1577-1578

1264.	1 Zecchino	1500.00
1265.	½ Zecchino	2250.00
1266.	¼ Zecchino	1875.00

NICHOLAS DAPONTE, 1578-1585

1267.	1 Zecchino	260.00
1268.	½ Zecchino	2250.00
1269.	¼ Zecchino	1875.00

PASQUALE CICOGNA, 1585-1595

1270.	1 Zecchino	260.00
1271.	½ Zecchino	2250.00
1272.	¼ Zecchino	1875.00

MARINO GRIMANI, 1595-1605

1273.	10 Zecchini	Rare
1274.	1 Zecchino	260.00
1275.	½ Zecchino	400.00
1276.	¼ Zecchino	400.00

LEONARDO DONA, 1605-1612

1277.	15 Zecchini	Rare
1278.	1 Zecchino	325.00
1279.	½ Zecchino	300.00
1280.	¼ Zecchino	300.00

MARC ANTHONY MEMMO, 1612-1615

1281.	1 Zecchino	800.00
1282.	½ Zecchino	1000.00
1283.	¼ Zecchino	1100.00

JOHN BEMBO, 1615-1618

1284.	1 Zecchino	1500.00
1285.	½ Zecchino	2250.00
1286.	¼ Zecchino	1875.00

NICHOLAS DONA, 1618

1287.	1 Zecchino	3250.00
1288.	¼ Zecchino	2500.00

ANTHONY PRIULI, 1618-1623

1289.	5 Zecchini	Rare
1290.	2 Zecchini	3750.00
1291.	1 Zecchino	260.00
1292.	½ Zecchino	400.00
1293.	¼ Zecchino	400.00

FRANCIS CONTARINI, 1623-1624

1294.	1 Zecchino	3000.00
1295.	½ Zecchino	2250.00
1296.	¼ Zecchino	2250.00

JOHN CORNER I, 1625-1629

1297.	1 Zecchino	9000.00
1298.	½ Zecchino	2250.00
1299.	¼ Zecchino	2250.00

NICHOLAS CONTARINI, 1630-1631

1300.	25 Zecchini	Rare
1301.	20 Zecchini	Rare
1302.	15 Zecchini	Rare
1303.	10 Zecchini	Rare
1304.	5 Zecchini	Rare
1305.	3 Zecchini	Rare
1306.	2 Zecchini	Rare
1307.	1 Zecchino	3500.00
1308.	½ Zecchino	1875.00
1309.	¼ Zecchino	1875.00

FRANCIS ERIZZO, 1631-1646

1310.	1 Zecchino	260.00
1311.	½ Zecchino	600.00
1312.	¼ Zecchino	600.00

FRANCIS MOLIN, 1646-1655

1313.	20 Zecchini	Rare
1314.	15 Zecchini	Rare
1315.	12 Zecchini	9000.00
1316.	10 Zecchini	7500.00
1317.	7 Zecchini	11500.00
1318.	1 Zecchino	260.00
1319.	½ Zecchino	1875.00
1320.	¼ Zecchino	1500.00

CHARLES CONTARINI, 1655-1656

1321.	1 Zecchino	400.00
1322.	½ Zecchino	3000.00
1323.	¼ Zecchino	3000.00

FRANCIS CORNER, 1656

1324.	1 Zecchino	3750.00
1325.	½ Zecchino	2250.00

BERTUCCIO VALIER, 1656-1658

1326.	1 Zecchino	400.00
1327.	½ Zecchino	2250.00
1328.	¼ Zecchino	2250.00

JOHN PESARO, 1658-1659

1329.	1 Zecchino	700.00
1330.	½ Zecchino	2250.00
1331.	¼ Zecchino	1500.00

DOMINIC CONTARINI, 1659-1674

1332.	1 Zecchino	260.00
1333.	½ Zecchino	500.00
1334.	¼ Zecchino	500.00

NICHOLAS SAGREDO, 1675-1676

1335.	1 Zecchino	800.00
1336.	½ Zecchino	2250.00
1337.	¼ Zecchino	1500.00

ALOIS CONTARINI, 1676-1684

1338.	1 Zecchino	260.00
1339.	½ Zecchino	2250.00
1340.	¼ Zecchino	1500.00

MARC ANTHONY GIUSTIMANI, 1684-1688

1341.	1 Zecchino	260.00
1342.	½ Zecchino	1000.00
1343.	¼ Zecchino	1750.00

FRANCIS MOROSINI, 1688-1694

1344.	10 Zecchini	10000.00
1345.	8 Zecchini	10000.00
1346.	6 Zecchini	8000.00
1347.	1 Zecchino	260.00
1348.	½ Zecchino	1750.00
1349.	¼ Zecchino	1500.00

SILVESTER VALIER, 1694-1700

1350.	25 Zecchini	Rare
1351.	15 Zecchini	Rare
1352.	12 Zecchini	Rare
1353.	10 Zecchini	11500.00
1354.	1 Zecchino	260.00
1355.	½ Zecchino	1750.00
1356.	¼ Zecchino	1500.00

ALOIS MOCENIGO II, 1700-1709

1357.	10 Zecchini	4500.00
1358.	1 Zecchino	260.00
1359.	½ Zecchino	250.00
1360.	¼ Zecchino	250.00

JOHN CORNER II, 1709-1722

1361.	40 Zecchini	Rare
1362.	36 Zecchini	Rare
1363.	33 Zecchini	Rare
1364.	25 Zecchini	Rare
1365.	20 Zecchini	Rare
1366.	16 Zecchini	Rare

1367.	15 Zecchini	Rare
1368.	12 Zecchini	6000.00
1369.	10 Zecchini	6000.00
1370.	8 Zecchini	4500.00
1370a.	5 Zecchini	4000.00
1371.	2 Zecchini	3000.00
1372.	1 Zecchino	260.00
1373.	½ Zecchino	2000.00
1374.	¼ Zecchino	1750.00

ALOIS MOCENIGO III, 1722-1732

1375.	60 Zecchini	Rare
1376.	50 Zecchini	Rare
1377.	10 Zecchini	5500.00
1378.	4 Zecchini	4000.00
1379.	1 Zecchino	260.00
1380.	½ Zecchino	300.00
1381.	¼ Zecchino	300.00

CHARLES RUZZINI, 1732-1735

1382.	10 Zecchini	7250.00
1383.	3 Zecchini	4000.00
1384.	1 Zecchino	260.00
1385.	½ Zecchino	400.00
1386.	¼ Zecchino	300.00

ALOIS PISANI, 1735-1741

1387.	40 Zecchini	Rare
1388.	30 Zecchini	Rare
1389.	16 Zecchini	Rare
1390.	10 Zecchini	8500.00
1391.	1 Zecchino	260.00
1392.	½ Zecchino	400.00
1393.	¼ Zecchino	300.00

PETER GRIMANI, 1741-1752

1394.	50 Zecchini	Rare
1395.	28 Zecchini	Rare
1396.	25 Zecchini	Rare
1397.	22 Zecchini	Rare
1398.	15 Zecchini	Rare
1399.	10 Zecchini	6000.00
1400.	2 Zecchini	3250.00
1401.	1 Zecchino	260.00
1402.	½ Zecchino	400.00
1403.	¼ Zecchino	400.00

FRANCIS LOREDANO, 1752-1762

1404.	2 Zecchini	3500.00
1405.	1 Zecchino	260.00
1406.	½ Zecchino	400.00
1407.	¼ Zecchino	400.00

MARCO FOSCARINI, 1762-1763

1408.	1 Zecchino	275.00
1409.	½ Zecchino	800.00
1410.	¼ Zecchino	800.00

ALOIS MOCENIGO IV, 1763-1778

1411.	100 Zecchini	Rare
1412.	60 Zecchini	Rare
1413.	50 Zecchini	Rare
1414.	30 Zecchini	Rare
1415.	25 Zecchini	Rare
1416.	20 Zecchini	Rare
1417.	18 Zecchini	Rare
1418.	12 Zecchini	8000.00
1419.	10 Zecchini	7000.00
1420.	8 Zecchini	6000.00
1421.	1 Zecchino	200.00
1422.	½ Zecchino	350.00
1423.	¼ Zecchino	350.00

PAUL RAINIER, 1779-1789

1424.	55 Zecchini	Rare
1425.	50 Zecchini	Rare
1426.	40 Zecchini	Rare
1427.	30 Zecchini	Rare
1428.	24 Zecchini	Rare
1429.	18 Zecchini	Rare
1430.	12 Zecchini	6000.00
1431.	10 Zecchini	6250.00

1432.	8 Zecchini	5000.00
1433.	4 Zecchini	4500.00
1434.	1 Zecchino	200.00
1435.	½ Zecchino	275.00
1436.	¼ Zecchino	275.00

LOUIS MANIN, 1789-1797

1437.	105 Zecchini	Rare
1438.	50 Zecchini	Rare
1439.	10 Zecchini *	6000.00
1440.	9 Zecchini	6250.00
1441.	8 Zecchini	6000.00
1442.	6 Zecchini	7000.00
1443.	5 Zecchini	5000.00
1444.	2 Zecchini	2250.00
1445.	1 Zecchino	250.00
1446.	½ Zecchino	275.00
1447.	¼ Zecchino	275.00

(For Austrian type coins struck at Venice and bearing the "V" mint mark, see under Austria.)

TYPE II

Cross. Rev. Lion in shield. The following coins are undated.

ANDREW GRITTI, 1523-1539

1448.	1 Scudo d'oro	600.00
1449.	½ Scudo d'oro	500.00

PETER LANDO, 1539-1545

1450.	1 Scudo d'oro	1000.00
1451.	½ Scudo d'oro	2250.00

FRANCIS DONA, 1545-1553

1452.	1 Scudo d'oro	2000.00
1453.	½ Scudo d'oro	2250.00

FRANCIS VENIER, 1554-1556

1454.	1 Scudo d'oro	2100.00
1455.	½ Scudo d'oro	2100.00

ANTHONY PRIULI, 1618-1623

1456.	2 Scudi d'oro	3000.00
1457.	1 Scudo d'oro	3750.00

FRANCIS CONTARINI, 1623-1624

1458.	2 Scudi d'oro *	2250.00
1459.	1 Scudo d'oro	3750.00

JOHN CORNER I, 1625-1629

1460.	2 Scudi d'oro	3750.00
1461.	1 Scudo d'oro	1500.00

NICHOLAS CONTARINI, 1630-1631

1462.	2 Scudi d'oro	3000.00
1463.	1 Scudo d'oro	4500.00

FRANCIS ERIZZO, 1631-1646

1464.	2 Scudi d'oro	4500.00
1465.	1 Scudo d'oro	4500.00

FRANCIS CORNER, 1656

1466.	1 Scudo d'oro	6000.00

BERTUCCIO VALIER, 1656-1658

1467.	2 Scudi d'oro	6500.00

NICHOLAS SAGREDO, 1675-1676

1468.	2 Scudi d'oro	6500.00

SILVESTER VALIER, 1694-1700

| 1469. | 2 Scudi d'oro | 7000.00 |
| 1470. | 1 Scudo d'oro | 7000.00 |

JOHN CORNER II, 1709-1722

| 1471. | 1 Scudo d'oro | 6000.00 |

ALOIS MOCENIGO III, 1722-1732

| 1472. | ½ Scudo d'oro | 5500.00 |

CHARLES RUZZINI, 1732-1735

| 1473. | ½ Scudo d'oro | 3000.00 |

ALOIS PISANI, 1735-1741

| 1474. | 2 Scudi d'oro | 6000.00 |
| 1475. | ½ Scudo d'oro | 6000.00 |

PETER GRIMANI, 1741-1752

| 1476. | 1 Scudo d'oro | 6000.00 |

FRANCIS LOREDANO, 1752-1762

1477.	2 Scudi d'oro	6000.00
1478.	1 Scudo d'oro	6000.00
1479.	½ Scudo d'oro	3500.00

MARCO FOSCARINI, 1762-1763

1480.	2 Scudi d'oro	6000.00
1481.	1 Scudo d'oro	4750.00
1482.	½ Scudo d'oro	3750.00

ALOIS MOCENIGO IV, 1763-1778

1483.	2 Scudi d'oro	6000.00
1484.	1 Scudo d'oro	4750.00
1485.	½ Scudo d'oro	4500.00

PAUL RAINIER, 1779-1789

1486.	2 Scudi d'oro	6000.00
1487.	1 Scudo d'oro	4750.00
1488.	½ Scudo d'oro	4750.00

LOUIS MANIN, 1789-1797

1489.	2 Scudi d'oro	1500.00
1490.	1 Scudo d'oro	1200.00
1491.	½ Scudo d'oro	1200.00

TYPE III

Doge kneeling before St. Mark seated. Rev. Lion. The following coins are undated.

LEONARDO DONA, 1605-1612

1492.	2 Ducats	4500.00
1493.	1 Ducat	900.00
1494.	½ Ducat	800.00

NICHOLAS DONA, 1618

| 1495. | 1 Ducat | 6000.00 |

ANTHONY PRIULI, 1618-1623

| 1496. | 1 Ducat | 4500.00 |

JOHN CORNER I, 1625-1629

| 1497. | 1 Ducat | 6000.00 |

DOMINIC CONTARINI, 1659-1674

| 1498. | 10 Ducats | 6000.00 |

TYPE IV

Doge kneeling and lion. Rev. St. Justina standing.

LEONARDO DONA, 1605-1612

| 1499. | 1 Ducat ND | 3000.00 |

TYPE V

Doge kneeling before St. Mark. Rev. Christ on pedestal.

LEONARDO DONA, 1605-1612

| 1500. | 1 Ducat ND | 2250.00 |

TYPE VI

Lion on pedestal. Rev. Value. Struck under the Provisional Government of Venice.

| 1501. | 20 Lire 1848 | 1700.00 |

VENTIMIGLIA

Head of John VI. Rev. Arms.

| 1502. | 2 Zecchini 1725 | Rare |

VERCELLI

DESIDERIUS, 757-773
Cross. Rev. Star.

| 1503. | ⅓ Solidus ND | Rare |

Bust of Charles Emanuel of Sardinia. Rev. Legend. Siege Issue.

| 1503a. | 4 Scudi d'oro 1617 | Rare |

Arms. Rev. Legend. Siege Issue.

| 1504. | 1 Doppia 1638 | Rare |

VERONA

HENRY II, 1013-1024
Cross on each side.

| 1505. | 1 Gold Denarius ND | Rare |

MAXIMILIAN I, 1509-1516

Bust. Rev. St. Zeno seated.

| 1506. | 1 Ducat ND | Rare |

VICENZA

DESIDERIUS, 756-774
Cross. Rev. Star.

| 1507. | ⅓ Solidus ND | Rare |

JAMAICA

Gold coins of Spain or Spanish-American Mints counter-stamped GR (George III of England) in a circular depression.

1.	8 Escudos 1732-1820...............................		Rare
2.	4 Escudos 1733-1820...............................		Rare
3.	2 Escudos 1733-1820........................ *		Rare
4.	1 Escudo 1733-1820...............................		Rare
5.	½ Escudo 1744-1820...............................		Rare

For later issues of Jamaica, see the section "Recent Issues Starting With 1960."

JAPAN

Emperors of —

A. Odd-Shaped Pieces of the Old Coinage

Oval shaped pieces averaging about 150 x 100 millimetres and characterized by seals punched into the metal and by legends applied with ink. The dates given are approximate.

OBANS OR 10 TAEL PIECES

1.	Tensho Oban 1591. Diamond shaped seals.............	Rare
2.	Tensho Naga Oban 1591. Round seals	Rare
3.	Keicho Oban 1601...................................	Rare
4.	Genroku Oban 1695.................................	Rare
5.	Kyoho Oban 1725..................................	25000.00
6.	Tempo Oban 1838.................................	30000.00
7.	Manen Oban 1860 (Size 132 x 80)	15000.00

GORYOBAN OR 5 TAEL PIECES

Type similar to above but averaging about 90 x 50 millimetres and without the ink legends.

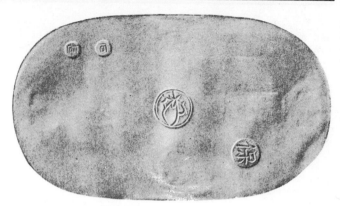

8.	Tempo Goryoban 1837	10000.00

KOBANS OR 1 TAEL PIECES
Type similar to above but averaging about 70 x 40 millimetres.

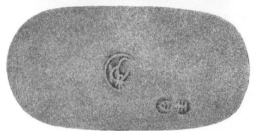

9.	Keicho Koban 1601		8000.00
10.	Genroku Koban 1695.................................		12500.00
11.	Hoei Koban 1710....................................		8000.00
12.	Kyoho Koban 1716 .... *		4000.00
13.	Genbun Koban 1736................................		1500.00
14.	Bunsei Koban 1819.................................		1500.00
15.	Tempo Koban 1837.................................		1500.00
16.	Ansei Koban 1859..................................		7500.00
17.	Manen Koban 1860 (Size 35 x 20)		1250.00

NI-BU OR 2 BU PIECES
Rectangular pieces averaging about 23 x 15 millimetres and bearing legends and floral designs.

18.	Shinbun 2 Bu 1818............................... *		600.00
19.	Sobun 2 Bu 1828................................		500.00
20.	Ansei 2 Bu 1856		100.00
21.	Manen 2 Bu 1860 .... *		250.00
22.	Kaheishi 2 Bu 1868		65.00

ICHI-BU OR 1 BU PIECES
Type similar to above but averaging about 18 x 10 millimetres.

23.	Taiko 1 Bu 1591.................................*......	7500.00
24.	Keicho 1 Bu 1601.................................	800.00
25.	Genroku 1 Bu 1695	1000.00
26.	Hoei 1 Bu 1710...........................	800.00
27.	Kyoho 1 Bu 1716..........................	500.00
28.	Genbun 1 Bu 1736	100.00
29.	Bunsei 1 Bu 1819	250.00
30.	Tempo 1 Bu 1837	350.00
31.	Ansei 1 Bu 1859	2000.00
32.	Manen 1 Bu 1860. (Size reduced)....................	1000.00

NI-SHU OR 2 SHU PIECES
Type similar to above but averaging 13 x 8 millimetres.

33.	Genroku 2 Shu 1695	2000.00
34.	Tempo 2 Shu 1832	25.00
35.	Manen 2 Shu 1860	30.00

IS-SHU OR 1 SHU PIECE
Type similar to above but averaging 10 millimetres square.

36.	Bunsei 1 Shu 1824..................................	200.00

B. Round Pieces of the Old Coinage

Five characters around circle on each side. Size about 20 millimetres.

37.	Taiko Gold coin 1591	8000.00

Four characters around square central hole. Rev. Crest.

38.	Eiraku Gold coin 1593..........................*......	2500.00
39.	Kanei Gold coin 1626	1750.00

Legend and ornaments on each side. Issued by Koshu Province about 1850.

40.	1 Bu. Size 13 millimetres...........................	400.00
41.	2 Shu. Size 11 millimetres.........................	500.00
42.	1 Shu. Size 10 millimetres.........................	500.00
43.	½ Shu. Size 8 millimetres.........................	1000.00
44.	½ Shu. Size 6 millimetres square	850.00

C. The Modern Coinage of Japan

The first modern gold coins of Japan were allied to the U.S. gold standard but in 1897 the gold Yen was devalued by 50% and a new coinage was issued to mark the change.

MUTSUHITO, 1867-1912
(The Meiji Era)

Dragon. Rev. Wreath over crossed banners.

45.	20 Yen. Years 3-13 (1870-80) 18000.00
46.	10 Yen. Years 4-13 (1871-80)	5000.00
47.	5 Yen. Years 3-30 (1870-97)...................*......	2500.00
48.	2 Yen. Years 3-13 (1870-80)	1250.00

Japanese character. Rev. Wreath over crossed banners.

49.	1 Yen. Years 4-13 (1871-80)	600.00

Radiant sun. Rev. Value in wreath. Reduced size coins struck after revaluation of the gold yen in 1897.

50.	20 Yen. Years 30-45 (1897-1912)	1600.00
51.	10 Yen. Years 30-43 (1897-1910) ....*......	600.00
52.	5 Yen. Years 30-45 (1897-1912)	750.00

YOSHIHITO, 1912-1926
(The Taisho Era)

Radiant sun. Rev. Value in wreath.

53.	20 Yen. Years 1-9 (1912-20)...................*......	1600.00
54.	5 Yen. Years 2, 13 (1913, 24)........................	1500.00

HIROHITO, 1926-
(The Showa Era)
Radiant sun. Rev. Value in wreath.

55.	20 Yen. Years 5-7 (1930-32).........................20000.00
56.	5 Yen. Year 5 (1930) 20000.00

JERUSALEM

(Including the Principality of Antioch and the Counties of Edessa and Tripoli).

Crusader Kings of —

BALDWIN I AND II, 1100-1131

Pseudo-Cufic legend on each side.

1.	1 Saracenic Bezant ND	750.00

BOHEMOND I AND II, 1098-1130

Pseudo-Cufic legend on each side, with the letter B on obverse and T on reverse. (Bohemond and Tancred).

2.	1 Saracenic Bezant ND	750.00

CONRAD AND CONRADIN, 1243-1268

Genuine Cufic legend on each side spelling out both the Christian date and phrases relating to Christianity.

3.   1 Bezant 1250-1259 .... 700.00

KOREA

Dragon. Rev. Value. Coins with dates other than those listed below are patterns and are extremely rare.

1.   20 Won 1906 ....* 24000.00
2.   10 Won 1906 ....* 8000.00
3.   5 Won 1908 .... Rare

LATVIA (RIGA)

A. Archbishops of —

WILLIAM, 1554-1563
Bust. Rev. Arms.

1.   1 Ducat 1559 .... 7500.00

B. Polish Kings of —

STEPHAN BATHORI, 1576-1586

Bust. Rev. Riga City arms.

2.   10 Ducats 1586 ....* ...... Rare
3.   5 Ducats 1586 .... Rare
4.   1 Ducat 1584, 85 .... 7000.00

SIGISMUND III, 1587-1632

Bust. Rev. Riga City arms.

5.   1 Ducat 1588, 94, 97, 99, 1619 .... 4500.00

King standing. Rev. City arms.

5a.   1 Ducat 1588 .... 4750.00

C. Swedish Kings of —

GUSTAVE II ADOLPHE, 1611-1632

Bust. Rev. Riga City arms.

6.   1 Ducat 1623 .... Rare

CHRISTINA, 1632-1654
Facing bust. Rev. Riga City arms.

7.   6 Ducats 1644 ....15000.00
8.   5 Ducats 1644, 45 ....15000.00
9.   3 Ducats 1643 ....10000.00

Bust left. Rev. Riga City arms.

10.   1 Ducat 1644 .... 4750.00

Bust right. Rev. Riga City arms.

11.   4 Ducats 1646 .... Rare
12.   3 Ducats 1646 .... Rare
13.   2 Ducats 1646 ....* 8500.00
14.   1 Ducat 1646 .... 4500.00

CHARLES X, 1654-1660

Bust. Rev. City view of Riga.

15.   6 Ducats 1654 .... Rare
16.   5 Ducats 1654 ....* ...... Rare

CHARLES XI, 1660-1697

Bust. Rev. Riga City arms.

17.	2 Ducats 1667		5000.00
18.	1 Ducat 1664, 73	*	4500.00

CHARLES XII, 1697-1718

Bust. Rev. Riga City arms.

19.	1 Ducat 1701, 07	4500.00

LIECHTENSTEIN

Modern government restrikes, all of them bearing the small letter m, exist of numbers 1 and 8-11. The coinage from 1930 to 1952 was based on the Latin Monetary Union standard.

Princes of —

CHARLES, 1614-1627
Bust. Rev. Arms.

1.	10 Ducats 1616	10000.00
2.	6 Ducats 1617	7500.00
3.	5 Ducats 1615	5000.00
4.	4 Ducats 1618	5000.00
5.	3 Ducats 1614, 18	4000.00
6.	2 Ducats 1614, 16	3500.00
7.	1 Ducat 1614, 17, 18	3000.00

JOSEPH JOHN ADAM, 1721-1732
Bust. Rev. Arms.

8.	10 Ducats 1728	10000.00
9.	1 Ducat 1728, 29	3500.00

JOSEPH WENZEL, 1748-1772

Armored bust. Rev. Arms.

10.	1 Ducat 1758	3000.00

FRANCIS JOSEPH I, 1772-1781

Bust. Rev. Arms.

11.	1 Ducat 1778	2750.00

JOHN II, 1858-1929

Head. Rev. Arms.

12.	20 Kronen 1898	*	3000.00
13.	10 Kronen 1898	*	10000.00
14.	10 Kronen 1900		3000.00

FRANCIS I, 1929-1938

Head. Rev. Arms.

15.	20 Franken 1930	1400.00
16.	10 Franken 1930	950.00

FRANCIS JOSEPH II, 1938-

Head. Rev. Arms.

17.	20 Franken 1946	300.00
18.	10 Franken 1946	250.00

Conjoined heads of the Prince and Princess. Rev. Arms.

19.	100 Franken 1952		2500.00
20.	50 Franken 1956	*	250.00
21.	25 Franken 1956		200.00

For later issues, see the section, "Recent Issues Starting With 1960."

LITHUANIA

Polish Kings and Grand Dukes of —

SIGISMUND II, 1544-1572
Bust. Rev. Horseman.

1.	10 Ducats 1562	Rare
2.	1 Ducat 1548-69	3000.00

STEPHAN BATHORI, 1576-1586
Bust. Rev. Arms.

3.	1 Ducat 1586	5000.00

SIGISMUND III, 1587-1632

Bust. Rev. Arms.

4.	10 Ducats 1604-22		Rare
5.	8 Ducats 1592		10000.00
6.	5 Ducats 1618-22	*	5000.00
7.	1 Ducat 1589, 90		4000.00

LADISLAS IV, 1632-1648
Bust. Rev. Arms.

8.	10 Ducats 1639	Rare

JOHN CASIMIR, 1648-1668

Bust. Rev. Horseman.

9.	1 Ducat 1666	4500.00
10.	½ Ducat 1664, 65	2500.00

LIVONIA

A. Army Masters of —

WALTER, 1495-1535
Ruler standing. Rev. Madonna.

1.	10 Ducats 1525	Rare

Ruler standing. Rev. Castle.

2.	2 Ducats 1528	5000.00

Madonna. Rev. Castle.

3.	1 Ducat 1528	3000.00

Arms. Rev. Crossed keys.

4.	½ Ducat 1533	1500.00

HERMAN, 1535-1549
Madonna. Rev. Arms.

5.	1 Florin 1535	3500.00

WILLIAM, 1557-1559
Madonna. Rev. Arms.

6.	1⅓ Ducats 1558, 59	5000.00

GOTTHARD, 1559-1561

Armored bust. Rev. Christ over arms.

7.	2⅜ Ducats ND	*	8000.00
8.	1⅜ Ducats ND		3000.00

B. Swedish Rulers of —

CHRISTINA, 1632-1654

Facing bust. Rev. Arms.

9.	10 Ducats 1645, 48 (1648 Unique)		Rare
9a.	5 Ducats 1645, 48		Rare
10.	2 Ducats 1646	*	6000.00
11.	1 Ducat 1644-48 (1644, 46 rare)	*	3000.00

Bust right. Rev. Arms.

12.	1 Ducat 1648	5000.00

LUXEMBOURG

Grand Dukes of —

JOHN THE BLIND, 1310-1346
St. John. Rev. Lily.

1.	1 Florin ND	1000.00

Ruler standing. Rev. Cross.

2.	1 Royal ND	4500.00

Ruler on throne. Rev. Cross.

3.	1 Ecu ND	3000.00

CHARLES IV, 1346-1353
St. John. Rev. Lily.

4.	1 Florin ND	750.00

WENCESLAS I, 1353-1383

St. John. Rev. Lily.

5.	1 Florin ND	750.00

Ruler under dais. Rev. Arms.

6.   1 Florin ND.. Rare

WENCESLAS II, 1383-1419
St. John. Rev. Eagle.

7.   1 Florin ND.. 4500.00

JOHN OF BAVARIA AND ELIZABETH OF GOERLITZ, 1419-1425
St. Peter standing. Rev. Two shields.

8.   1 Florin ND.. 4500.00

PHILIP OF BURGUNDY, 1443-1467
St. Andrew with cross. Rev. Two shields.

9.   1 Florin ND.. 4000.00

PHILIP OF AUSTRIA, 1482-1506
St. Philip with shield. Rev. Cross.

10.   1 Florin 1502, ND.................................... 5000.00

PHILIP IV OF SPAIN, 1621-1665
Cross. Rev. Arms.

11.   1 Couronne d'or 1632.............................. Rare

CHARLOTTE, 1919-1964

Conjoined heads of Prince Jean of Luxembourg and Princess Josephine Charlotte of Belgium. Rev. Arms; on their marriage. Although without a mark of value, this coin has the same specifications as the standard 20 Franc piece of the Latin Monetary Union.

12.   (20 Francs) 1953................................... 175.00

MALAYA

Native legend on each side. Sultanate coinage struck during the period 1720-60.

1.   1 Mas ND. Octagonal............................. 175.00

JOHORE

ABDUL JALIL, 1699-1719

Inscription. Rev. Inscription.

2.   1 Kupang Mas. Round............................ 175.00
3.   1 Kupang Mas. Octagonal....................... 175.00

TRENGANU

ALFAHDIN SHAH (17th Century)

Inscription. Rev. Inscription.

4.   1 Mas ND (1600-1700)............................ 175.00

MALTA

(The Knights of St. John of Jerusalem at Malta. For earlier coins of the Knights, see under Rhodes).

The coinage of both Malta and Rhodes was produced by the same order of Grand Masters; until 1530 at Rhodes and afterward at Malta.

Grand Masters of —

PHILIPPE VILLIERS, 1521-1534

Ruler kneeling before St. John. Rev. Christ standing.

1.   1 Zecchino ND 3250.00

Bust. Rev. Arms.

2.   1 Zecchino ND 9000.00

PETER DEL PONTE, 1534-1535
Ruler kneeling before St. John. Rev. Christ standing.

3.   1 Zecchino ND .... Unique

JOHN DE HOMEDES, 1536-1553
Ruler kneeling before St. John. Rev. Christ standing.

4.   1 Zecchino 1539, ND 3250.00

JOHN DE LA VALLETTE, 1557-1568
Ruler kneeling before St. John. Rev. Christ standing.

5.   1 Zecchino ND 600.00

PETER DEL MONTE, 1568-1572

Ruler kneeling before St. John. Rev. Christ standing.

6.   1 Zecchino ND 600.00

JOHN DE LA CASSIERE, 1572-1581
Ruler kneeling before St. John. Rev. Christ standing.

7.   1 Zecchino ND 600.00

HUGH DE VERDALA, 1581-1595
Ruler kneeling before St. John. Rev. Christ standing.

8.   1 Zecchino ND 600.00

MARTIN GARZES, 1595-1601
Ruler kneeling before St. John. Rev. Christ standing.

9.   1 Zecchino ND 600.00

ALOFIUS DE WIGNACOURT, 1601-1622
Ruler kneeling before St. John. Rev. Christ standing.

10.   1 Zecchino ND 600.00

LOUIS MENDEZ DE VASCONCELOS, 1622-1623
Ruler kneeling before St. John. Rev. Christ standing.

10a. 1 Zecchino ND 7000.00

ANTHONY DE PAULE, 1623-1636
Ruler kneeling before St. John. Rev. Christ standing.

11. 1 Zecchino ND 2000.00

JOHN PAUL LASCARIS, 1636-1657
Ruler kneeling before St. John. Rev. Christ standing.

12. 1 Zecchino ND 2000.00

GREGORY CARAFFA, 1680-1690

Ruler kneeling before St. John. Rev. Arms.

13. 1 Zecchino ND 2000.00

ADRIEN DE WIGNACOURT, 1690-1697

Ruler kneeling before St. John. Rev. Arms.

14. 4 Zecchini 1695...........................*...... 3000.00
15. 1 Zecchino 1691-96 .... 1500.00

RAYMON PERELLOS, 1697-1720

Bust. Rev. Arms.

16. 4 Zecchini 1717, 18, 19 .... 3000.00

Ruler kneeling before St. John. Rev. Arms.

17. 10 Zecchini 1699.................................... Rare
18. 4 Zecchini 1699, 1705........................... 3250.00
19. 1 Zecchino 1699, 1717, ND ....*...... 1000.00

St. Michael. Rev. Arms.

20. 2 Zecchini ND..................................... 3250.00

MARCANTONIO ZONDADARI, 1720-1722
Bust. Rev. Legend.

21. 4 Zecchini 1721.................................. 5000.00

Bust. Rev. Arms.

22. 4 Zecchini 1722.................................. 5000.00

Ruler kneeling before St. John. Rev. Arms.

23. 1 Zecchino 1722.................................. 1250.00

ANTHONY MANOEL DE VILHENA, 1722-1736

Bust. Rev. Arms.

24. 12 Zecchini 1725.................................. Rare
25. 10 Zecchini 1722.................................. 7500.00
26. 4 Zecchini 1722-28.............................. 2000.00
27. 2 Zecchini 1723-28........................*...... 1500.00

Ruler kneeling before St. John. Rev. Arms.

28. 1 Zecchino 1723, 24, 25, 28....................... 1000.00

EMANUEL PINTO, 1741-1773

Bust. Rev. Arms.

29. 10 Zecchini 1742, ND............................. 4750.00
30. 5 Zecchini 1742, ND............................. Unknown
31. 4 Zecchini 1742, ND............................. 1750.00
32. 2 Zecchini 1742, ND.......................*...... 1250.00
33. 1 Zecchino 1742, ND ....*....... 750.00

Bust to right or left. Rev. Arms on cross.

34. 20 Scudi 1764, 65, 70, 72 .... 1200.00

St. John standing. Rev. Two shields.

35. 20 Scudi 1764 .... 1100.00

St. John standing. Rev. Arms.

36. 10 Scudi 1756, 61, 62, 63 .... 450.00
37.   5 Scudi 1756 ....* 400.00

FRANCIS XIMINES, 1773-1775

Bust in circle. Rev. Two shields.

38. 20 Scudi 1773 .... 1000.00
39. 10 Scudi 1773 ....* 900.00

Bust not in circle. Rev. Two shields.

40. 10 Scudi 1774 .... 750.00

Bust not in circle. Rev. Arms on cross.

41. 20 Scudi 1774 .... 900.00
42. 10 Scudi 1774 ....* 725.00

EMANUEL DE ROHAN, 1775-1797

Bust. Rev. Two shields.

43. 20 Scudi 1778, 81, 82 .... 1250.00
44. 10 Scudi 1778, 82 ....* 900.00
45.   5 Scudi 1779 ....* 500.00

FERDINAND DE HOMPESCH, 1797-1799

St. John standing. Rev. Arms on double eagle. Although dated 1778, this coin is attributed to Hompesch.

46. 20 Scudi 1778 .... Rare

THE SIEGE OF MALTA, 1798-1800

Oblong gold ingot struck by General Vaubois, French defender of the island, during the blockade by the British. Rampant lion. Rev. Value. Size 25 x 20 Millimetres.

47. 17 Scudi, 3 Tari, 5 Grani ND .... Unique

For later issues of Malta, see the section "Recent Issues Starting With 1960."

MARTINIQUE

Gold coins of Brazil or Portugal counterstamped with "22" or "20" (for karats) and a small eagle.

1. 6400 Reis 1727-1804 ....* 2500.00
2. 3200 Reis 1727-1786 .... 2500.00
3. 4000 Reis 1707-1817 .... 2000.00
4. 1000 Reis 1752-1787 .... 2000.00
5.   400 Reis 1725-1796 .... 1500.00
6.   ½ Escudo 1752-1796 .... 1500.00

MEXICO

Mints and mint marks:—

Mo	mm for Mexico City
A or As	mm for Alamos
C or Cn	mm for Culican
Ca or Ch	mm for Chihuahua
Do	mm for Durango
Eo Mo	mm for Tlalpan
Ga	mm for Guadalajara
GC	mm for Guadelupe y Calvo
Go	mm for Guanajuato
Ho	mm for Hermosillo
O or Oa	mm for Oaxaca
Pi	mm for San Luis Potosi
Zs	mm for Zacatecas

The early gold coins of Mexico are known as "cobs", because of their irregular shape, and pieces with a decipherable date are worth twice as much or more than specimens without dates. Full round coins of Philip V, before 1732, are worth three to four times more than the cob specimens. There are five known reverses for the coins of Philip V.

The Escudo system, inherited from the Spanish Kings, was continued under the Republic as late as the 1870's. The Peso, from 1870 to 1905, varied little from that of U.S. gold coinage, the Peso almost being equal to the Dollar. In 1905, the Gold Peso was devalued about one half and the first coins on the new standard appeared in 1905.

The 50 Peso piece or Centenario was struck as a regular circulating medium until 1931. This and other Mexican gold coins minted in the 1940's and later were struck mainly to satisfy the world wide demand for gold coins.

A. Spanish Kings of —

(All coins are from the Mexico City Mint, unless otherwise noted).

CHARLES II, 1665-1700
Arms. Rev. Cross. Cob type.

1.	8 Escudos 1691-1700, ND. Full round type	25000.00
2.	8 Escudos 1679-1701, ND	3500.00
3.	4 Escudos 1693-95, 1701, ND	1500.00
4.	2 Escudos 1701, ND	750.00
5.	1 Escudo 1694, 95, 97, 98, 1701, ND	1000.00

PHILIP V, 1700-1746

Arms. Rev. Cross.

6.	8 Escudos 1702-32, ND. Cob type.........*	2500.00
7.	8 Escudos 1702-32, ND. Full round type	Rare
7a.	4 Escudos 1711-15, ND. Cob type.	1800.00
7b.	2 Escudos 1700-15, ND. Cob type.	750.00
7c.	1 Escudo 1702-04, 07-15, ND. Cob type	675.00

Bust. Rev. Arms.

8.	8 Escudos 1732-47	5000.00
9.	4 Escudos 1732-46	4000.00
10.	2 Escudos 1732-46	950.00
11.	1 Escudo 1732-46...........*	650.00

LOUIS I, 1724
Arms. Rev. Cross.

12.	8 Escudos 1725. Cob type	Rare
12a.	8 Escudos 1725. Full round type	Rare

FERDINAND VI, 1746-1760

Large bust. Rev. Arms.

13.	8 Escudos 1747...........*	Rare
14.	4 Escudos 1747	17000.00
15.	2 Escudos 1747	3700.00
16.	1 Escudo 1747	3000.00

Small bust in high relief. Rev. Arms. The value does not appear on the coins dated from 1752-56.

17.	8 Escudos 1748-56	5000.00
18.	4 Escudos 1748-56...........*	5000.00
19.	2 Escudos 1748-56	2000.00
20.	1 Escudo 1748-56	1200.00

Re-designed bust in lower relief. Rev. Arms.

21.	8 Escudos 1757-59	4400.00
22.	4 Escudos 1757-59...........*	4000.00
23.	2 Escudos 1757-59	1300.00
24.	1 Escudo 1756-59	900.00

CHARLES III, 1759-1788

Small bust. Rev. Arms.

25.	8 Escudos 1760, 61...........*	5000.00
26.	4 Escudos 1760, 61	4000.00
27.	2 Escudos 1760, 61	2000.00
28.	1 Escudo 1760, 61	1700.00

Large bust. Rev. Arms.

29.	8 Escudos 1762-71	5000.00
30.	4 Escudos 1762-71	4000.00
31.	2 Escudos 1762-71...........*	1750.00
32.	1 Escudo 1762-71	1000.00

Older bust of different style. Rev. Arms.

33.	8 Escudos 1772-88 .... *	2000.00
34.	4 Escudos 1772-88 .... *	2000.00
35.	2 Escudos 1772-88	1000.00
36.	1 Escudo 1772-88	475.00

CHARLES IV, 1788-1808

Bust of the previous king, Charles III, with name as "Carol IV." Rev. Arms.

37.	8 Escudos 1789, 90 .... *	2000.00
38.	4 Escudos 1789, 90	2500.00
39.	2 Escudos 1789, 90	800.00
40.	1 Escudo 1789, 90	300.00

Similar to above type but with name as "Carol IIII."

41.	8 Escudos 1790	2200.00
42.	4 Escudos 1790	2750.00

Bust. Rev. Arms.

43.	8 Escudos 1791-1808	1250.00
44.	4 Escudos 1792-1808	2250.00
45.	2 Escudos 1791-1808 .... *	550.00
46.	1 Escudo 1792-1808	300.00

FERDINAND VII, 1808-1822

Large armored bust. Rev. Arms.

47.	8 Escudos 1808-12 .... *	1700.00
48.	4 Escudos 1808-12	2300.00
48a.	2 Escudos 1808-12	Rare
49.	1 Escudo 1809-12	900.00

Large uniformed bust. Rev. Arms.

50.	8 Escudos 1812, 13. Ga mm .... *	Rare
51.	4 Escudos 1812. Ga mm	Rare

Laureate head. Rev. Arms.

52.	8 Escudos 1814-21. Mo mm	1500.00
53.	8 Escudos 1821. Ga mm .... *	4800.00
54.	4 Escudos 1814-20	1250.00
55.	2 Escudos 1814-21	900.00
56.	1 Escudo 1814-20	600.00
57.	½ Escudo 1814-20	350.00

Draped bust. Rev. Arms.

58.	8 Escudos 1821. Ga mm	9500.00

B. Emperors of —

AUGUSTIN ITURBIDE I, 1822-1823

Head. Rev. Eagle on cactus.

59.	8 Escudos 1822	4000.00

Head. Rev. Arms.

60.	8 Escudos 1823		3000.00
61.	4 Escudos 1823	*	3000.00

MAXIMILIAN I, 1864-1867

Head. Rev. Arms.

62.	20 Pesos 1866	2000.00

C. Republic of —

Hand with Liberty Cap over book. Rev. Eagle facing left. The so-called "Hooked neck" or profile eagle.

63.	8 Escudos 1823	7000.00

Hand with Liberty Cap over book. Rev. Eagle facing right.

8 ESCUDOS

64.	Mo mm. 1824-69		750.00
65.	A mm. 1864-72		3000.00
66.	C mm. 1846-70	*	750.00
67.	Ca mm. 1841-71		900.00
68.	Do mm. 1832-70		1300.00
69.	Eo Mo mm. 1828-29		6000.00
70.	Ga mm. 1825-66		1500.00
71.	GC mm. 1845-52		1000.00
72.	Go mm. 1828-70		750.00
73.	Ho mm. 1863-73		1250.00
74.	O mm. 1860-69		1500.00
75.	Zs mm. 1858-71		750.00
76.	Cn mm. 1860		Unknown

(Note: Pi mm., San Luis Potosi, none struck)

4 ESCUDOS

77.	Mo mm. 1825-69	750.00
78.	C mm. 1847, 48	1500.00
79.	Do mm. 1832, 33	1500.00
80.	Eo Mo mm. 1827-30	Unknown
81.	Ga mm. 1844	1500.00
82.	GC mm. 1844-46, 48, 50	1500.00
83.	Go mm. 1829-63	750.00
84.	Ho mm. 1861	2200.00
85.	O mm. 1861	3700.00
86.	Zs mm. 1862	1500.00

2 ESCUDOS

87.	Mo mm. 1825-69	225.00
88.	C mm. 1846-62	400.00
89.	Do mm. 1833-57	1000.00
90.	Eo Mo mm. 1828	2500.00
91.	Ga mm. 1835-70	300.00
92.	GC mm. 1844, 47-50	750.00
93.	Go mm. 1845-62	225.00
94.	Ho mm. 1861	1750.00
95.	O mm. 1858-70	Unknown
96.	Zs mm. 1860, 62, 64	600.00

1 ESCUDO

97.	Mo mm. 1825-69	150.00
98.	C mm. 1846-70	175.00
99.	Do mm. 1832-64	275.00
100.	Eo Mo mm. 1828-30	Unknown
101.	Ga mm. 1825-60	175.00
102.	GC mm. 1844-51	250.00
103.	Go mm. 1845-62	175.00
104.	Ho mm. 1861-73	Unknown
105.	O mm. 1858-70	Unknown
106.	Zs mm. 1853, 60, 62	225.00

½ ESCUDO

107.	Mo mm. 1825-69	100.00
108.	A mm. 1862-72	Unknown
109.	C mm. 1848-67	150.00
110.	Ca mm. 1831-70	Unknown
111.	Do mm. 1833-64	100.00
112.	Eo Mo mm. 1828-30	Unknown
113.	Ga mm. 1825-61	175.00
114.	GC mm. 1843, 46-48, 51	250.00
115.	Go mm. 1845-63	120.00
116.	Ho mm. 1861-73	Unknown
117.	O mm. 1858-70	Unknown
118.	Zs mm. 1860, 62	160.00

Scales and Liberty Cap. Rev. Eagle.

20 PESOS

119.	Mo mm. 1870-1905	*	1000.00
120.	As mm. 1876, 77, 88		3000.00
121.	Ch or Ca mm. 1872-95		1800.00
122.	Cn mm. 1870-1905		1200.00
123.	Do mm. 1870-78		2000.00
124.	Go mm. 1870-1900		1000.00
125.	Ho mm. 1874-76, 88		2750.00
126.	Oa mm. 1870-72, 88		2000.00
127.	Zs mm. 1871-89		2500.00

10 PESOS

128.	Mo mm. 1870-1905	1400.00
129.	As mm. 1874-95	1750.00
130.	Ca mm. 1888	4000.00
131.	Cn mm. 1882-1903	1000.00
132.	Do mm. 1872-84	1000.00
133.	Ga mm. 1870-81, 91	1500.00
134.	Go mm. 1872, 87, 88	1500.00
135.	Ho mm. 1874, 76, 78, 80, 81	2000.00
136.	Oa mm. 1870-86	1100.00
137.	Pi mm. 1888. Pattern	Rare
138.	Zs mm. 1871-95	1000.00

5 PESOS

139.	Mo mm. 1870-1905	700.00
140.	As mm. 1878	1500.00
141.	Ca mm. 1888	2500.00

142. Cn mm. 1873-1903 .... 1000.00
143. Do mm. 1877-79 .... 1500.00
144. Go mm. 1871, 87, 88, 93 .... 1000.00
145. Ho mm. 1874, 77, 88 .... 1500.00
146. Oa mm. 1870-93 .... Unknown
147. Zs mm. 1874-92 .... 750.00

Eagle. Rev. Value.

2½ PESOS

148. Mo mm. 1870-92 .... 800.00
149. As mm. 1888 .... 2500.00
150. Ch mm. 1870-95 .... Unknown
151. Cn mm. 1893 .... 2000.00
152. Do mm. 1870-95 .... Unknown
153. Go mm. 1871, 88 .... 2000.00
154. Ho mm. 1874, 88 .... 2500.00
155. Oa mm. 1870-93 .... Unknown
156. Zs mm. 1872, 73, 75, 78, 88-90 .... 800.00

1 PESO

157. Mo mm. 1870-1905 ....*...... 200.00
158. As mm. 1888 .... 1500.00
159. Ca mm. 1888 .... 1500.00
160. Cn mm. 1873-1905 .... 200.00
161. Go mm. 1870, 71, 88, 90, 92, 94-1900 .... 200.00
162. Ho mm. 1875, 76, 88 .... 1750.00
163. Oa mm. 1870-93 .... Unknown
164. Zs mm. 1872, 75, 78, 88-90 .... 300.00

D. Estados Unidos Mexicanos

Head of Hidalgo to left. Rev. Eagle.

165. 10 Pesos 1905 .... 275.00
166. 10 Pesos 1906-08, 10, 16, 17, 19, 20, 59 .... 210.00
166R. 10 Pesos 1959. Restrike .... 200.00(B)
167. 5   Pesos 1905 .... 550.00
168. 5   Pesos 1906, 07, 10, 18-20, 55 ....*...... 105.00
168R. 5   Pesos 1955. Restrike .... 100.00(B)
169. 2½ Pesos 1918-20, 44-48 ....*...... 52.50
169R. 2½ Pesos 1945. Restrike .... 50.00(B)

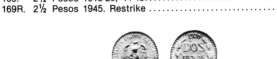

Eagle. Rev. Value in wreath.

170.   2 Pesos 1919, 20, 44-48 .... 42.50
170R. 2 Pesos 1945. Restrike .... 40.00(B)

Aztec Calendar stone. Rev. Eagle.

171.   20 Pesos 1917-21, 59 .... 225.00
171R. 20 Pesos 1959. Restrike .... 210.00(B)

(Numbers 166R, 168R, 169R, 170R, 171R and 172R are bullion coins, i.e.,
coins whose price fluctuates according to the price of gold on the international
market. The price listed is based on gold at $725 per ounce.)

*Winged Victory. Rev. Eagle. The so-called Centenario. The
denomination does not appear on the coins dated 1943.*

172.   50 Pesos 1921-31, 44-47 .... 950.00
172R. 50 Pesos 1947. Restrike .... 925.00(B)
173.   50 Pesos 1943 .... 1100.00

E. Revolutionary Period, 1913-1916

OAXACA STATE

Head of Juarez. Rev. Liberty Cap over scales.

174.   60 Pesos 1916 .... 17000.00

Head of Juarez. Rev. Value in wreath. Struck in low grade gold.

175.   20 Pesos 1915 ....*...... 1000.00
176.   10 Pesos 1915 .... 900.00
177.   5 Pesos 1915 .... 850.00

MOLDAVIA

Princes of —

JOHN HERACLIDES
Crowned head. Rev. Arms.

1.   1 Ducat 1563 .... 8000.00

MONACO

The coinage from 1838 to 1904 was based on the French monetary system and the Latin Monetary Union standard.

Princes of —

LUCIANO, 1505-1523
Crowned arms. Rev. Cross.
1. 1 Scudo d'oro ND .... Rare

HONORE II, 1604-1662

Bust. Rev. Cross of initials.
2. 2 Doppie 1649, 50 .... 9000.00
3. 1 Doppia 1648-60 ....*...... 6000.00
4. ½ Doppia 1650 .... 5000.00

Bust. Rev. Crowned initial.
5. 2 Doppie 1656 .... 10000.00
6. 1 Doppia 1656, 61 .... 6500.00

Bust. Rev. Arms.
7. 5 Doppie 1649 .... Rare

LOUIS I, 1662-1701
Bust. Rev. Two L's.
8. 4 Ducats 1663, 64 .... 10000.00

HONORE V, 1819-1841

Head. Rev. Arms with supporters. These coins were not placed in circulation.
9. 40 Francs 1838 .... 3250.00
10. 20 Francs 1838 ....*...... 3000.00

CHARLES III, 1856-1889

Head. Rev. Arms.
11. 100 Francs 1882, 84, 86............................ 900.00
12. 20 Francs 1878, 79...........................*...... 300.00

ALBERT, 1889-1922

Head. Rev. Arms. The 20 Franc piece was not placed in circulation.
13. 100 Francs 1891-1904 ....*...... 850.00
14. 20 Francs 1892 .... 1500.00

LOUIS II, 1922-1949
(Souvenir gold coins struck from dies also used for minor coins).
Large bust. Rev. Arms.
15. 20 Francs 1947. Normal thickness 1400.00
16. 20 Francs 1947. Double thickness 1450.00
17. 10 Francs 1946. Normal thickness 700.00
18. 10 Francs 1946. Double thickness 1200.00

Head. Rev. Arms.
19. 5 Francs 1945. Normal thickness 1250.00
20. 5 Francs 1945. Double thickness 1300.00
21. 2 Francs ND (1943)............................... 675.00
22. 1 Franc ND (1943) 675.00

RAINIER III, 1949-
(Souvenir gold coins struck from dies also used for minor coins).

Head. Rev. Horseman.
23. 100 Francs 1950. Normal thickness ....*...... 850.00
24. 100 Francs 1950. Double thickness 900.00
25. 50 Francs 1950. Normal thickness 875.00
26. 50 Francs 1950. Double thickness 875.00

Head. Rev. Arms.
27. 20 Francs 1950. Normal thickness ....*...... 650.00
28. 20 Francs 1950. Double thickness 650.00
29. 10 Francs 1950. Normal thickness ....*...... 625.00
30. 10 Francs 1950. Double thickness 625.00

New type head. Rev. Arms. Of smaller size than previous issues of this value.
31. 100 Francs 1956 .... 750.00

For later issues of Monaco, see the section "Recent Issues Starting With 1960."

MONTENEGRO

This country issued gold coins in one year only, 1910, and these pieces conformed to the standards of the Austrian Corona.

Kings of —

NICHOLAS I, 1860-1918

Plain head to right. Rev. Arms.

1.	100 Perpera 1910		9000.00
2.	20 Perpera 1910	*	750.00
3.	10 Perpera 1910	*	500.00

Laureate head to left. Rev. Arms. On the 50th year of both his reign and marriage.

4.	100 Perpera 1910		9500.00
5.	20 Perpera 1910	*	750.00
6.	10 Perpera 1910	*	475.00

MOROCCO

Arab legend on each side. Sultanate coinage struck during the period 1600-1750. With dates from about 1009-1164 A.H.

1.	1 Dinar	225.00
2.	½ Dinar	125.00

Arab legend within star on each side. Struck during the period 1750-1860. With dates from about 1164-1277 A.H.

3.	1 Dinar	225.00
3a.	½ Dinar	125.00

Arab legend. Rev. "1201". Struck at Madrid.

4.	10 Mizquals 1201 A.H. (1786 A.D.)	900.00

Six-pointed star. Rev. Value and date. Struck under French influence and the equivalent of the 20 Franc piece. This coin was not placed in circulation.

5.	4 Ryals 1297 A.H. (1879 A.D.)	2250.00

For later issues of Morocco, see the section "Recent Issues Starting With 1960."

MOZAMBIQUE

Portuguese Kings of —

JOSEPH I, 1750-1777

Arms. Rev. Cross in quadrilobe.

1.	4000 Reis 1755	*	2500.00
2.	2000 Reis 1755		2000.00
3.	1000 Reis 1755		2000.00

MARY II, 1834-1853
"M" in enclosure with various punches and stamps. Rev. Value.

4.	2½ Maticaes ND. Rectangular bar	1500.00
5.	1¼ Maticaes ND. Rectangular bar	1000.00

NEPAL

Kings of —

(The Nepalese Mohar is equal to about ½ of the Indian Mohur. Generally, the 2 and 1 Mohar pieces are of the same size and can be distinguished by different thickness and weight. The Rupee is equal to about 2 Mohars.)

Square and legend. Rev. Circle and legend. Issued from about 1750-1880 and with Saka dates from about 1670-1802.

1.	4 Mohars		1125.00
2.	2 Mohars	*	485.00
3.	1 Mohar		375.00
3a.	½ Mohar		165.00

Inscription in star. Rev. Inscription.

4.	1 Rupee 1735-1771 (1813-1849 A.D.)	450.00

Inscription around triangle. Rev. Inscription around trident.

5.	1 Mohar ND (1809)	950.00

Legend and symbols on each side.

6.	½ Mohar	*	260.00
7.	¼ Mohar	*	185.00
8.	⅛ Mohar		110.00
9.	¹/₁₆ Mohar		110.00
10.	¹/₃₂ Mohar		110.00
11.	¹/₆₄ Mohar		110.00

PRITHVI, 1881-1911

Square between small and large circle. Rev. Circle within panelled legend. With Saka dates from 1803-1833 (1881-1911 A.D.). Up to Saka 1823 (1901 A.D.) the coinage is with plain edge. After Saka 1824 the coinage is with reeded edge and is of much finer workmanship.

12.	4 Mohars	*	1100.00
13.	2 Mohars		675.00
14.	1 Mohar		360.00

Legend and symbols on each side.

15.	½ Mohar	260.00
16.	¼ Mohar	200.00
17.	⅛ Mohar	135.00
18.	¹/₁₆ Mohar	110.00
19.	¹/₃₂ Mohar	110.00
20.	¹/₆₄ Mohar	110.00
21.	¹/₁₂₈ Mohar	90.00

TRIBHUBANA, 1911-1954

Type similar to above. With Samvat dates from 1969-1995 (1912-1938 A.D.).

22.	2 Mohars	*	650.00
23.	1 Mohar		335.00
24.	½ Mohar		185.00

Type similar to above.

25.	2 Rupees 2005 (1948 A.D.)	750.00
26.	1 Rupee 1995-2005 (1938-1948 A.D.)	375.00
27.	½ Rupee 1995-2005 (1938-1948 A.D.)	170.00
28.	¼ Rupee 1995 (1938 A.D.)	90.00

Head of Tribhubana. Rev. Mountain and rising sun in wreath.

29.	1 Rupee 2010 (1953 A.D.)	450.00
30.	½ Rupee 2010 (1953 A.D.)	225.00
31.	¼ Rupee 2010 (1953 A.D.)	110.00
32.	⅛ Rupee 2010 (1953 A.D.)	75.00

MAHENDRA, 1955-

Square between small and large circle. Rev. Circle within panelled legend.

33.	2 Rupees 2012 (1955 A.D.)	335.00
34.	1 Rupee 2012, 19 (1955, 62 A.D.)	150.00
35.	½ Rupee 2012, 19 (1955, 62 A.D.)	80.00
36.	¼ Rupee 2012 (1955 A.D.)	65.00
37.	⅕ Rupee 2012 (1955 A.D.)	60.00

Plumed crown. Rev. Legend with sword and wreath. On Mahendra's coronation.

38.	1 Rupee 2013 (1956 A.D.)	450.00
39.	½ Rupee 2013 (1956 A.D.)	225.00
40.	⅙ Rupee 2013 (1956 A.D.)	1000.00

For later issues, see the section, "Recent Issues Starting With 1960."

NETHERLANDS

Mint and mint marks:—TRA, Torch or lis for Utrecht; HOL for Holland; B for Brussels.

Early Dutch coins were adaptations of types existing in Spain, England, France and the Holy Roman Empire.

The Guilder as a true Dutch denomination was first introduced about 1680 in Zeeland. The Guilder is sometimes also called a Florin.

A. Kings of —

LOUIS NAPOLEON, 1806-1810

Head. Rev. Arms.

1.	20 Guilders 1808, 10		7500.00
2.	10 Guilders 1808, 10	*	6000.00
3.	1 Ducat 1809, 10	*	750.00

Head. Rev. Knight standing.

4.	1 Ducat 1808, 09	1000.00

Knight standing. Rev. Square tablet.

5.	2 Ducats 1806, 07, 08	*	1200.00
6.	1 Ducat 1806, 07, 08. TRA in legend		375.00
6a.	1 Ducat 1806. HOL in legend		1125.00

NAPOLEON, 1810-1814

(For French type coins struck in the Netherlands, see under France.)

WILLIAM I, 1813-1840

Head. Rev. Arms.

7.	10 Guilders 1818-40. Torch or lis mm........*	900.00
8.	10 Guilders 1824-29. B mm............................	900.00
9.	5 Guilders 1827. Torch mm.	800.00
10.	5 Guilders 1826, 27. B mm..........................	800.00

WILLIAM II, 1840-1849

Head. Rev. Arms flanked by value.

11.	10 Guilders 1842......................................	4000.00
12.	5 Guilders 1843......................................	1200.00

Head. Rev. Arms in wreath. Trade coins called "Negotie-penning." The denomination is expressed by the weight of the coin in grams and may be found on the Rev.

13.	20 Guilders or 13.458 Grams 1848	3750.00
14.	10 Guilders or 6.729 Grams 1848 ....*......	3000.00
15.	5 Guilders or 3.3645 Grams 1848	2625.00

WILLIAM III, 1849-1890

Head. Rev. Arms in wreath. Trade coins or "Negotiepenning."

16.	20 Guilders or 13.458 Grams 1850, 51, 53....*......	3375.00
17.	10 Guilders or 6.729 Grams 1850, 51.................	1875.00
18.	5 Guilders or 3.3645 Grams 1850, 51...............	1500.00

Head. Rev. Arms flanked by value.

19.	10 Guilders 1875-89 (1888 rare)	200.00

WILHELMINA, 1890-1948

Girl head with long flowing hair. Rev. Arms. The first two dates are rare.

20.	10 Guilders 1892.............................*......	3750.00
21.	10 Guilders 1895.............................*......	3000.00
22.	10 Guilders 1897....................................	250.00

Large youthful head with coronet. Rev. Arms.

23.	10 Guilders 1898...................................	450.00

Small older head with coronet. Rev. Arms.

24.	10 Guilders 1911-17.................................	180.00(B)
25.	5 Guilders 1912...................................	250.00

Mature head. Rev. Arms.

26.	10 Guilders 1925-33................................	180.00(B)

(Numbers 24 and 26 are bullion coins. The price listed is based on gold at $725 per ounce.)

For trade coins of the Kingdom of the Netherlands bearing the Knight standing, Rev. Legend on tablet motif, see under Netherlands East Indies, numbers 17-22.

For later issues of the Kingdom of the Netherlands, see the section, "Recent Issues Starting With 1960."

B. United Provinces of —, 1576-1795

(The Issues of the United Provinces were succeeded by those of the Batavian Republic, which see.)

Heads of Ferdinand and Isabella of Spain. Rev. Arms on eagle. The coins were struck about 1590 and are undated.

27.	**CAMPEN.**	2 Ducats.....................	1500.00
28.		1 Ducat......................	525.00
29.	**GELDERLAND.**	2 Ducats.....................	2625.00
30.	**OVERYSSEL.**	2 Ducats.....................	1500.00
31.		1 Ducat......................	525.00
32.	**WESTFRISIA.**	2 Ducats.....................	1500.00

33.	ZEELAND.	2 Ducats	*	1500.00
34.		1 Ducat		600.00
35.	ZWOLLE.	2 Ducats		1500.00
36.		1 Ducat		525.00

Bust of Philip II of Spain. Rev. Arms. The coins were struck about 1590 and are undated.

37.	GELDERLAND.	1 Real d'Or	*	2500.00
38.		1 Real d'Or. "England" in title		1500.00
39.		½ Real d'Or		525.00
40.		½ Real d'Or. "England" in title		1125.00
41.	HOLLAND.	1 Real d'Or		1200.00
42.		½ Real d'Or. Bust left		525.00
43.		½ Real d'Or. Bust right		1500.00
44.	OVERYSSEL.	½ Real d'Or		900.00

Royal figure in ship. Rev. Rose or sun in center of crowns.

45.	CAMPEN.	1 Noble ND (1600)		1200.00
46.		½ Noble ND (1600)		900.00
47.		¼ Noble ND (1600)		2000.00
48.	FRISIA.	1 Noble ND (1600)		3500.00
49.		½ Noble ND (1600)		3500.00
50.	GELDERLAND.	1 Noble ND		2000.00
51.		1 Noble 1579		4000.00
52.		½ Noble ND		1500.00
52a.		½ Noble 1579		3500.00
53.	'S-HEERENBERG.	1 Noble ND		Rare
54.	OMMELANDEN.	1 Noble 1579, ND		Rare
55.	OVERYSSEL.	1 Noble 1583, ND	*	1200.00
55a.		½ Noble 1583		Rare
56.		¼ Noble 1583, 85, ND		2000.00
57.	UTRECHT.	1 Noble 1579		3500.00
58.		1 Noble ND (1600)		1200.00
59.		½ Noble 1579		2000.00
60.		½ Noble ND (1600)		900.00
61.		¼ Noble 1579		2000.00
62.	ZEELAND.	1 Noble 1583, 84, 85, ND		1200.00
63.		½ Noble 1583, 85, ND		1100.00

Knight in ship holding seven shields. Rev. Rose and bundle of arrows.

64.	ZEELAND.	1 Noble 1586		Rare
65.		½ Noble 1587, 93, 94, 95		1500.00

Royal figure seated. Rev. Arms within rose.

66.	CAMPEN.	8 Nobles or 4 Souverain d'or ND (1600)		Rare
67.		2 Nobles or 1 Souverain d'or ND (1600)		8500.00

Arms. Rev. Cross.

68.	The coin previously listed will be found as No. 157.			
69.	GELDERLAND.	2 Florins 1577, 78		Rare
70.	HOLLAND.	1 Couronne d'Or 1576, 80, ND		1200.00
71.	UTRECHT.	1 Couronne d'Or 1573-80, ND		1000.00
72.		2 Florins 1577		Rare

Double eagle. Rev. Five shields.

73.	FRISIA.	1 Florin 1617, 18, 19	750.00

Double eagle. Rev. Arms.

74.	FRISIA.	1 Florin 1618, 19	Rare

Orb. Rev. Three shields.

75.	CAMPEN.	1 Florin ND (1612-19)	600.00

Royal figure standing. Rev. Legend (plain or in tablet).

76.	CAMPEN.	2 Ducats 1650, 55-58	*	1125.00
77.		1 Ducat 1596-1676		375.00
78.	DEVENTER.	2 Ducats 1662, 66		1500.00
79.		1 Ducat 1603-66		750.00
80.	ZWOLLE.	2 Ducats 1655, 56, 62		975.00
81.		1 Ducat 1630-76, ND	*	375.00

Royal figure standing. Rev. Three shields.

82.	CAMPEN.	1 Florin 1597	700.00

Royal figure standing. Rev. Arms.

83.	WESTFRISIA.	1 Ducat 1587-1605	400.00

Royal figure standing. Rev. Madonna.

84.	GELDERLAND.	1 Ducat ND (1591)	450.00
85.	OVERYSSEL.	1 Ducat ND (1579)	375.00
86.	UTRECHT.	1 Ducat 1591. Figure between V-D	1125.00
87.	ZWOLLE.	1 Ducat ND (1600)	600.00

William the Silent standing. Rev. Legend.

88.	HOLLAND.	1 Ducat 1583	Rare

Knight standing with shield. Rev. Tablet.

89.	FRISIA.	1 Ducat 1604, 05	975.00

Knight standing. Rev. Tablet.

90.	FRISIA.	2 Ducats 1612, 61	1200.00
91.		1 Ducat 1586-1693	400.00
92.	GELDERLAND.	2 Ducats 1656-1761	1100.00
93.		1 Ducat 1586-1792	300.00
94.	HOLLAND.	2 Ducats 1645-1793	800.00
95.		1 Ducat 1586-1791 ....*	225.00
96.	OVERYSSEL.	1 Ducat 1593-1773	350.00
97.	UTRECHT.	2 Ducats 1652-1794 ....*	600.00
98.		1 Ducat 1587-1794	750.00
99.	WESTFRISIA.	2 Ducats 1660-1780	750.00
100.		1 Ducat 1607-1780	250.00
101.	ZEELAND.	2 Ducats 1646-84	750.00
102.		1 Ducat 1586-1763	350.00

Knight standing. Rev. Circle of shields.

103.	ZEELAND.	30 Guilders 1683, 84, 86, 87	2250.00

Knight standing. Rev. Arms.

104.	ZEELAND.	10 Ducats 1682-87	3750.00

Knight standing between F-D. Rev. Shield.

105.	FRISIA.	1 Ducat ND (1600)	1800.00

Horseman. Rev. Arms. Early style.

106.	FRISIA.	2 Cavaliers 1583. Small type	Rare
107.		1 Cavalier 1582-99. Small type	700.00
108.		1 Cavalier 1607-28. Large type	1500.00
109.		½ Cavalier 1585. Small type	900.00
110.		½ Cavalier 1620-44. Large type	1100.00
111.	GELDERLAND.	1 Cavalier 1582, ND. Small type	Rare
112.		1 Cavalier 1606-28. Large type	1100.00
113.		½ Cavalier 1606-44	900.00
114.	HOLLAND.	1 Cavalier 1606-32 ....*	1100.00
115.		½ Cavalier 1606-45	900.00
116.	OVERYSSEL.	1 Cavalier 1582	Rare

117.		1 Cavalier 1607-20. Large type	1500.00
118.		½ Cavalier 1606-16	1000.00
119.	UTRECHT.	1 Cavalier 1606-25 ....*	1200.00
120.		½ Cavalier 1607-44 ....*	800.00
121.	WESTFRISIA.	1 Cavalier 1621-27	1500.00
122.		½ Cavalier 1621-44	900.00
123.	ZEELAND.	1 Cavalier 1606-44	1500.00
124.		½ Cavalier 1609-48	900.00
124a.	ZWOLLE.	1 Cavalier 1644	5000.00
125.		½ Cavalier 1644	1200.00

Horseman. Rev. Arms. Modern style.

126.	GELDERLAND.	14 Guilders 1750-62	900.00
127.		7 Guilders 1750-62 ....*	600.00
128.	GRONINGEN.	14 Guilders 1761	1000.00
129.		7 Guilders 1761	700.00
130.	HOLLAND.	14 Guilders 1749-63	800.00
131.		7 Guilders 1749-63	500.00
132.	OVERYSSEL.	14 Guilders 1760-63	900.00
133.		7 Guilders 1760-63	600.00
134.	UTRECHT.	14 Guilders 1749-63 ....*	800.00
135.		7 Guilders 1749-63	500.00
136.	WESTFRISIA.	14 Guilders 1749-63	800.00
137.		7 Guilders 1749-63	500.00
138.	ZEELAND.	14 Guilders 1760-64	900.00
139.		7 Guilders 1760-64	600.00

C. Cities and States of —

AMSTERDAM

Knight standing. Rev. Tablet and city shield.

140.	5	Ducats 1673	1875.00
140a.	4½	Ducats 1673	1875.00
141.	4	Ducats 1673	1500.00
141a.	3½	Ducats 1673	1500.00
142.	3	Ducats 1673	1500.00
143.	1	Ducat 1673	525.00

BAAR

Three shields. Rev. Arms on cross.

144.	1 Florin 1445		2000.00

BATAVIAN REPUBLIC

Knight standing. Rev. Tablet. This type was continued under the Kings of the Netherlands.

145.	2 Ducats 1795-1805 ....*		900.00
146.	1 Ducat 1795-1805		300.00

BATENBURG

Barons of —

THIERRY II, 1432-1456
St. Peter. Rev. Floriated cross.

147.	1 Peter d'or ND	Rare

GISEBERT IV, 1516-1525
St. John. Rev. Orb.

148.	1 Florin ND..................................	Rare

WILLIAM, 1556-1573
St. Stephen. Rev. Eagle shield.

149.	2 Ducats ND	1200.00
150.	1 Florin ND..................................	600.00

Christ and Pharisee. Rev. Arms.

151.	2 Ducats ND	Rare

St. Victor standing. Rev. Madonna.

152.	1 Ducat ND...................................	800.00

Bust of Ferdinand. Rev. Madonna.

153.	1 Ducat ND.......................................	800.00

St. Michael. Rev. Ship.

154.	1 Angel 1561, 62, ND..........................	1200.00
155.	½ Angel 1562	Rare

Serpent on cross. Rev. Floriated cross.

156.	1 Couronne d'or ND	1000.00

Arms. Rev. Cross. Portuguese style.

157.	1 Cruzado ND	1000.00

HERMAN THIERRY, 1573-1612

Ruler standing. Rev. Arms.

158.	1 Ducat 1577, 78, 79..........................	800.00

Arms. Rev. Cross.

159.	1 Couronne d'or ND	Rare

Knight standing. Rev. Madonna.

160.	1 Ducat 1579, ND................................	800.00

Knight. Rev. Lion.

161.	1 Ducat ND.....................................	Rare

St. Victor standing. Rev. Arms.

162.	1 Ducat ND.....................................	Rare

St. John. Rev. Arms.

163.	1 Florin ND....................................	Rare

CAMPEN

St. John. Rev. Orb.

164.	1 Florin ND (1525).............................	900.00

Emperor Maximilian seated. Rev. Arms.

165.	1 Real ND......................................	Rare

St. Nicholas. Rev. Orb.

166.	1 Florin ND....................................	Rare

Knight Standing. Rev. Madonna.

166a.	1 Ducat ND	Rare

DEVENTER

St. Lebuin. Rev. Orb.

167.	1 Florin 1488	750.00
168.	1 Florin ND....................................	900.00

Eagle. Rev. Orb.

169.	1 Florin 1523	600.00

Double eagle. Rev. Arms.

170.	1 Florin 1600	Rare
171.	1 Florin ND (1612-37)	600.00

DEVENTER-CAMPEN-ZWOLLE

Orb. Rev. Three or four shields.

172.	1 Florin 1546, ND..............................	800.00

Double eagle. Rev. Three helmeted shields.

173.	1 Florin 1568-79	1200.00

Royal figure standing. Rev. Three shields and orb.

174.	1 Florin 1557	1200.00

DUURSTEDE

Head of Madelinus. Rev. Cross.

175.	1 Triens ND (650-750 A.D.).....................	1500.00

FRANEKER

St. John. Rev. Orb.

176.	1 Florin 1491, 92, ND..........................	Rare

FRIESLAND

Head of Adolphus. Rev. Cross on globe.
176a. 1 Triens ND (650-750 A.D.) .... Rare

Counts of —

GEORGE AND HENRY, 1500-1504
St. John. Rev. Orb.
177. 1 Florin ND .... Rare

GEORGE, 1504-1515
St. John. Rev. Orb.
178. 1 Florin ND .... Rare

St. Bonifacius. Rev. Arms.
179. 1 Florin ND .... Rare

GELDERLAND

Dukes of —

EDWARD, 1361-1371
Lamb. Rev. Cross.
180. 2 Moutons d'or ND .... Rare
181. 1 Mouton d'or ND .... Rare

Lion. Rev. Cross.
182. 1 Lion d'or ND .... Rare

MECHTELD, 1371-1379
Bust under dais. Rev. Two shields.
183. 1 Florin ND .... Rare

MARIE, 1361-1399
Bust under dais. Rev. Arms.
184. 1 Florin ND 1200.00

Arms. Rev. Cross.
185. 1 Couronne d'or ND .... Rare

WILLIAM I, 1377-1402
Bust under dais. Rev. Arms.
186. 1 Florin ND 500.00

St. John. Rev. Arms.
187. 1 Florin ND 800.00

Figure in ship. Rev. Cross.
188. 1 Noble ND .... Rare
189. ½ Noble ND .... Rare

Ruler on throne. Rev. Cross.
190. 1 Chaise d'or ND 4200.00

REINALD IV, 1394-1402
St. John. Rev. Five shields.
191. 1 Florin ND. Struck in Venray .... Rare
192. 1 Florin ND 375.00

St. John. Rev. Two shields.
193. 1 Florin ND. Struck in Nymegen .... Rare

Angel. Rev. Madonna.
194. 1 Florin ND 1500.00

Arms. Rev. Horseman.
195. 1 Florin ND .... Rare

Bust under dais. Two shields.
196. 1 Florin ND .... Rare

St. Peter. Rev. Five shields.
197. 1 Florin ND .... Rare

ARNOLD, 1423-1473
Ruler standing. Rev. Four shields.
198. 1 Florin ND .... Rare
199. The coin previously listed will be found as No. 201.

St. John. Rev. Arms.
200. 1 Florin ND 325.00

St. John. Rev. Five shields.
201. 1 Florin ND .... Rare

Horseman. Rev. Arms.
202. 2 Florins (Cavalier d'or) ND .... Rare
203. 1 Florin ND 600.00
204. ½ Florin ND .... Rare

Arms on cross. Rev. Three shields.
205. 1 Florin ND .... Rare

CHARLES I, 1473-1477
St. Andrew. Rev. Arms.
206. 1 Florin ND 750.00

CHARLES II (MINORITY), 1477-1479
St. John. Rev. Four shields.
207. 1 Florin ND. Struck in Roermond .... Rare

PHILIP THE FAIR (MINORITY), 1482-1494
St. Andrew. Rev. Arms on cross.
208. 1 Florin ND .... Rare

Ruler on throne. Rev. Crowned arms.
209. 1 Real 1487 .... Rare

Ruler in ship. Rev. Cross.
210. ½ Noble 1488 .... Rare

CHARLES II, 1492-1538
St. John. Rev. Arms.
211. 1 Florin ND 250.00

Horseman. Rev. Arms.
212. 1 Florin ND 375.00

Christ. Rev. Three shields.
213. 1 Florin ND 1750.00

Christ. Rev. Four shields.
214. 1 Florin ND .... Rare

CHARLES V OF SPAIN, 1543-1555
Bust with sword and sceptre. Rev. Arms on eagle.
215. 1 Real d'or ND 1200.00
216. 1 Florin ND .... Rare

Arms. Rev. Cross.
217.   1 Couronne 1544, 45, 55 . . . . 650.00

PHILIP II OF SPAIN, 1555-1579
St. Andrew. Rev. Arms.
218.   1 Florin 1568 . . . . 1500.00

Arms between P-P. Rev. Cross.
219.   1 Couronne 1571, 72, 73, 75 . . . . 1200.00

GRONINGEN

St. John. Rev. Orb.
220.   1 Florin 1488, ND . . . .   Rare

St. John. Rev. Double eagle.
221.   1 Florin 1591 . . . . 1500.00

St. Martin. Rev. Orb.
222.   1 Florin ND (1502) 600.00

Double eagle. Rev. Orb.
223.   ½ Florin 1492 . . . .   Rare

'S-HEERENBERG

Counts of —

OSWALD, 1511-1546

St. John. Rev. Four shields.
224.   1 Florin ND 1500.00

WILLIAM IV, 1546-1586

St. Michael. Rev. Ship.
225.   1 Angel ND 1300.00

Bust of St. Oswald. Rev. Madonna.
226.   1 Ducat ND 1000.00

St. Oswald standing. Rev. Arms.
227.   1 Ducat ND . . . .   Rare
228.   1 Ducat 1577 . . . .   Rare

St. Oswald standing. Rev. Madonna.
229.   1 Ducat ND . . . .   Rare

FREDERICK, 1577-1580
Horse carriage. Rev. Cross.
230.   1 Pistolet 1578, 79, ND 1200.00

St. Pancras standing. Rev. Madonna.
231.   1 Florin 1578, 79 . . . .   Rare

St. Pancras standing. Rev. Lion.
232.   1 Ducat ND . . . .   Rare

St. Pancras standing. Rev. Arms.
233.   1 Ducat 1578 . . . .   Rare

St. Martin. Rev. Arms.
234.   1 Florin 1577 . . . .   Rare

Ruler in ship. Rev. Cross. With the arms of the city of Groningen as a counterstamp.
234a.   1 Noble ND . . . .   Unique

HERMAN FREDERICK, 1627-1631
Bust. Rev. Four shields.
235.   1 Florin ND . . . .   Rare

Eagle. Rev. Arms.
236.   1 Florin ND . . . .   Rare

St. Stephen. Rev. Arms.
237.   1 Florin ND 700.00

HOLLAND

Counts of —

WILLIAM V, 1350-1389
Lamb. Rev. Cross.
238.   2 Moutons d'or ND 4000.00
239.   1 Mouton d'or ND 2700.00

Ruler on throne. Rev. Cross.
240.   1 Chaise d'or ND . . . .   Rare

Ruler standing. Rev. Arms.
241.   1 Florin ND 600.00

Horseman. Rev. Cross.
242.   1 Rider ND 3000.00

ALBERT, 1389-1404
Ruler on throne. Rev. Cross.
243.   1 Chaise d'or ND 1200.00

Two lions with shield. Rev. Cross.
244.   1 Chaise d'or ND 4500.00

Ruler standing. Rev. Arms.
245.   1 Florin ND 800.00

Arms. Rev. Cross.

| 246. | 1 Couronne d'or ND | 2500.00 |

WILLIAM VI, 1404-1417
Ruler on throne. Rev. Cross.

247.	2 Chaises d'or ND	Rare
248.	1 Chaise d'or ND	900.00
249.	½ Chaise d'or ND	1000.00
250.	⅓ Chaise d'or ND	1000.00

JOHN, 1421-1425
Ruler on throne. Rev. Cross.

| 251. | 1 Chaise d'or ND | 1000.00 |
| 252. | ½ Chaise d'or ND | 1200.00 |

St. John. Rev. Five shields.

| 253. | 1 Florin ND | 500.00 |

Arms of Bavaria and Holland-Bavaria. Rev. Floriated cross.

| 253a. | ½ Double d'or ND | Unique |

PHILIP THE GOOD, 1425-1428 (AS HEIR)
Ruler on throne. Rev. Cross.

| 254. | 1 Chaise d'or ND | 700.00 |
| 255. | ½ Chaise d'or ND | 600.00 |

PHILIP THE GOOD AND JACQUELINE, 1428-1433
Ruler on throne. Rev. Cross.

| 256. | 1 Chaise d'or ND | 900.00 |
| 257. | ½ Chaise d'or ND | 800.00 |

PHILIP THE GOOD, 1433-1467 (AS COUNT)

Lion. Rev. Arms.

| 258. | 1 Lion d'or ND | 1200.00 |
| 259. | ⅔ Lion d'or ND * | 2500.00 |

St. Andrew. Rev. Arms.

| 260. | 1 Florin ND | Rare |

Knight on horse. Rev. Arms on cross.

| 261. | 1 Rider ND * | 1100.00 |
| 262. | ½ Rider ND | 1800.00 |

MARY, 1477-1482
St. Andrew. Rev. Arms.

| 263. | 1 Florin ND | Rare |

MAXIMILIAN AND PHILIP, 1482-1494
Ruler on throne. Rev. Crowned arms.

| 264. | 1 Real d'or 1487 | ⊛ 7000.00 |

Ruler on ship. Rev. Arms on cross.

| 265. | 1 Noble ND | * | 5000.00 |
| 266. | ½ Noble 1488 | | 1300.00 |

St. Andrew. Rev. Arms.

| 267. | 1 Ducat 1487, 89 | Rare |

PHILIP THE FAIR, 1496-1506
St. Philip. Rev. Cross.

| 268. | 1 Florin ND | 600.00 |
| 269. | ½ Florin ND | 750.00 |

Full length figure. Rev. Arms on cross.

| 270. | 1 Florin ND | 675.00 |

CHARLES V OF SPAIN, 1515-1555
St. Philip. Rev. Cross.

| 271. | 1 Florin ND | 450.00 |
| 272. | ½ Florin ND | Rare |

Bust with sword and orb. Rev. Arms on eagle.

| 273. | 1 Real d'or ND * | 1200.00 |
| 274. | 1 Florin ND | 550.00 |

Arms. Rev. Eagle in shield.

| 275. | ½ Real d'or ND | 450.00 |

Cross. Rev. Arms.

| 276. | 1 Couronne d'or 1543-46, ND | 550.00 |

PHILIP II OF SPAIN, 1555-1581
St. Andrew standing. Rev. Arms.

| 277. | 1 Florin 1567, 68, 69 | 1200.00 |

Cross. Rev. Arms.

| 278. | 1 Couronne d'or 1576, 80, ND | 1500.00 |

MIDDELBURG

Legend in circle. Rev. Blank. Square siege coins.

279.	4 Ducats 1573	Rare
280.	2 Ducats 1573	1500.00
281.	1 Ducat 1573, 74 *	1200.00

NYMEGEN

St. Stephen standing. Rev. Arms.

282.	2 Ducats ND (1500-56) .... *	1100.00
283.	1 Florin ND (1499-1525)	500.00

Bust of Charles V of Spain. Rev. St. Stephen.

284.	1 Ducat ND	Rare

Bust of Emperor Ferdinand. Rev. St. Stephen.

285.	1 Ducat 1558	Rare

St. Stephen seated. Rev. Three shields and orb.

286.	1 Florin 1557	Rare

Arms. Rev. Double eagle.

287.	1 Florin 1569, 1602, 20	Rare

OVERYSSEL

CHARLES V OF SPAIN, 1515-1555
Arms on cross. Rev. Arms.

288.	½ Real ND. Mintmark C on cross	Rare

Bust. Rev. Arms on double eagle.

289.	1 Florin ND. Mintmark C on cross.................	Rare

ROERMOND

St. John. Rev. Lily.

290.	1 Florin ND (1343-61)	Rare

UTRECHT

Bishops of —

ARNOLD, 1371-1378
St. Martin in dais. Rev. Arms.

291.	1 Florin ND.......................................	Rare

FLORIS, 1379-1393

Bust in dais. Rev. Two shields.

292.	1 Florin ND..	1500.00

Bust in dais. Rev. Eagle on shield.

293.	1 Florin ND..	1500.00

Ruler seated. Rev. Cross.

294.	1 Chaise d'or ND.................................	2000.00

FREDERICK, 1394-1423
St. Peter. Rev. Four shields.

295.	1 Florin ND....................................	Rare

St. Peter. Rev. Five shields.

296.	1 Florin ND....................................	1500.00

St. John. Rev. Arms.

297.	1 Florin ND....................................	375.00

St. John. Rev. Three shields.

298.	1 Florin ND....................................	Rare

St. John. Rev. Four shields.

299.	1 Florin ND....................................	1500.00

ZWEDER, 1425-1426
St. John. Rev. Five shields.

300.	1 Florin ND....................................	Rare

RUDOLPH (BISHOP-ELECT), 1426-1433
St. Martin. Rev. Arms.

301.	1 Florin ND....................................	650.00

St. John. Rev. Arms.

302.	1 Florin ND....................................	1500.00

St. John. Rev. Four shields.

303.	1 Florin ND....................................	Rare

Two shields. Rev. Eagle.

304.	1 Florin ND....................................	Rare

RUDOLPH, 1433-1455
St. Martin. Rev. Arms.

305.	1 Florin ND....................................	275.00

WALRAVEN, 1433-1450
St. Martin. Rev. Arms.

306.	1 Florin ND....................................	Rare

DAVID, 1455-1496
St. Martin. Rev. Arms.

307.	1 Florin ND....................................	300.00

King David behind shield. Rev. Ornate floriated cross.

308.	1 Harpe d'or ND.................................	1200.00

Half length bust with harp. Rev. Arms.

309.	½ Florin 1492	1700.00

King David seated. Rev. Arms.

310.	1 Florin 1492	1800.00

Christ seated. Rev. Four shields.

311.   1 Florin ND 1000.00

ENGELBERT, 1481-1483
St. Martin. Rev. Arms.

312.   1 Florin ND .... Rare

FREDERICK, 1496-1516
St. John. Rev. Five shields.

313.   1 Florin ND 500.00

Christ seated. Rev. Four shields.

314.   1 Florin ND .... Rare

Bishop seated. Rev. Arms on cross.

315.   1 Florin ND .... Rare

PHILIP, 1517-1524
Seated figure. Rev. Arms.

316.   1 Florin ND 1500.00

PHILIP II OF SPAIN, 1555-1579
St. Andrew. Rev. Arms.

317.   1 Florin 1568 .... Rare

---

VIANEN

Barons of —

HENRY, 1556-1568
St. Michael. Rev. Arms on ship.

318.   1 Angel ND 1300.00

Arms. Rev. Cross.

319.   1 Couronne d'or ND .... Rare

Bust of St. Henry. Rev. Madonna.

320.   1 Ducat ND 900.00

St. John. Rev. Four shields.

321.   1 Florin ND .... Rare

ZWOLLE

St. Michael. Rev. Orb.

322.   1 Florin ND (1488-1519) 800.00

Double eagle. Rev. Helmeted arms.

323.   1 Florin ND (1590-1612) 600.00

St. John Standing. Rev. Double eagle with state arms on long cross.

324.   1 Goldgulden ND .... Unique

---

NETHERLANDS EAST INDIES

A. Java Coinage

Symbol. Rev. Incuse square. Struck during the Hindu period, 896-1158. The largest piece weighs about 10 grams.

1.	96 Krisnalas ND	1500.00
2.	24 Krisnalas ND ....*	275.00
3.	12 Krisnalas ND	275.00
4.	6 Krisnalas ND	200.00

"B" (Batavia) counterstamped on Dutch Ducats during the period 1686-1700.

5.   1 Ducat. Dates before 1700 .... 1800.00

Dutch lion in square counterstamped on Japanese gold Kobans of the Keicho era, 1596-1614.

6.   1 Koban ND 6000.00

"Java" (in Arabic) counterstamped on the obverse of Dutch Ducats during the period 1753-1761.

7.   1 Ducat. Dates before 1761 .... 600.00

Native legend with Christian date. Rev. Native legend. The "Rupee" (also known as mohur) coinage was struck from dies that were also used for silver coins. The issues from 1808-1816 were struck under foreign occupation; under the French from 1808-1811, and under the British from 1811-1816.

8.	2 Java Ducats 1746, 47, 48	2000.00
9.	1 Java Ducat 1744, 45, 46 ....*	1500.00
10.	2 Gold Rupees 1783	2400.00
11.	1 Gold Rupee 1766-97 ....*	1800.00
12.	½ Gold Rupee 1766-1807 ....*	900.00
13.	¼ Gold Rupee 1766	1500.00
14.	1 Gold Rupee 1808-16	1200.00
15.	½ Gold Rupee 1813-16	1200.00

B. Sumatra Coinage

Native legend on each side. Struck under the Sultans of Atjeh during the period 1297-1760.

16.   1 Mas ND 100.00

C. Coinage under the Kingdom of the Netherlands

Knight standing. Rev. Legend in square tablet. This type was struck exclusively for use in the East Indies beginning in 1814. They were also used as trade coins among the Dutch banks. The type does not change from ruler to ruler.

17.	1 Ducat 1814-40. (William I). Utrecht Mint. Torch mm.	400.00
18.	1 Ducat 1824-30. Brussels Mint. Palm branch mm ..	600.00
19.	1 Ducat 1841. (William II)	425.00
20.	2 Ducats 1854, 67. (William III)	Rare
21.	1 Ducat 1849-85. (William III)	300.00
22.	1 Ducat 1894-1937. (Wilhelmina).........*	85.00(B)

(Number 22 is a bullion coin. The price listed is based on gold at $725 per ounce.)

NEWFOUNDLAND

Head of Queen Victoria of Great Britain. Rev. Value and date.

1. 2 Dollars 1865-88 (1880 Rare) 250.00

NORWAY

A. Danish Kings of —

(Only those coins of the Danish kings with distinctive Norwegian designs are listed below. Other issues of the Danish kings, although struck at the Kongsberg, Norway mint, are listed under Denmark.)

FREDERICK III, 1648-1670

Crowned bust facing. Rev. Lion.

1. 1 Ducat 1660 .... Rare

Laureate bust. Rev. Lion.

2.	1 Portugaloser 1665, 68, 69	Rare
3.	2 Ducats 1665 ....*	Rare
4.	1 Ducat 1665, 68, 69	12000.00
5.	½ Ducat 1666, ND	5000.00

CHRISTIAN V, 1670-1699

Laureate bust. Rev. Lion.

6.	4 Ducat 1671	Rare
7.	3 Ducats 1671, 73, 78	Rare
8.	2 Ducats 1673, ND.........*	7000.00
9.	1 Ducat 1673, ND	6000.00
10.	½ Ducat ND	5000.00

Laureate head. Rev. Lion. Thick flan.

11. 2 Ducats ND .... Rare

Ruler on horse. Rev. Lion.

12. 3 Ducats 1673 .... Rare

Crowned C5 and lion. Rev. Long cross.

13.	1 Louis d'or 1673, 84, 85.........*	Rare
14.	½ Louis d'or 1684, 85	Rare

B. Swedish Kings of —

OSCAR II, 1872-1905

Head. Rev. Lion shield and two values.

15.	5 Species-20 Kroner 1874, 75	475.00
16.	2½ Species-10 Kroner 1874	800.00

Head. Rev. Lion shield.

17.	20 Kroner 1876-1902	450.00
18.	10 Kroner 1877, 1902	700.00

C. Independent Kings of —

HAAKON VII, 1905-1957

Crowned head. Rev. St. Olaf standing.

19.	20 Kroner 1910	450.00
20.	10 Kroner 1910	450.00

PARAGUAY

Lion seated before pole bearing the Liberty Cap. Rev. Justice seated. This coin was not placed in circulation.

1.	4 Pesos 1867	11500.00

Lion seated before pole bearing the Liberty Cap. Rev. Arms within wreath.

1a.	4 Fuertes 1867	Unique

Lion standing before pole bearing the Liberty Cap. Rev. Value in wreath, star above.

2.	5 Pesos 1873	15000.00

For later issues of Paraguay, see the section, "Recent Issues Starting With 1960."

PERSIA (IRAN)

Shahs of —

It will be noted that the Shahs did not picture themselves on their coinage until recent times, the first portrait piece appearing in 1854. Note: Due to revisions, the numbering has been changed from previous editions.

ISMAIL I, 1502-1524

Arab legend on each side. With dates from about 907-930 A.H.

1.	1 Ashrafi ....*	100.00
2.	¼ Ashrafi	85.00

TAHMASP I, 1524-1576
Arab legend on each side. With dates from about 930-984 A.H.

3.	1 Ashrafi	150.00
4.	⅔ Ashrafi	125.00

MOHAMMED KHUDABANDA, 1578-1587
Arab legend on each side. With dates from about 985-996 A.H.

5.	1½ Ashrafi	200.00
6.	1 Ashrafi	100.00

ABBAS I, 1587-1629
Arab legend on each side. With dates from about 996-1038 A.H.

7.	2 Ashrafis	200.00
8.	1 Ashrafi	150.00
9.	½ Ashrafi	75.00

HUSSEIN, 1694-1722
Arab legend on each side. With dates from about 1105-1135 A.H.

10.	1 Ashrafi	75.00

TAHMASP II, 1722-1731

Arab legend on each side. With dates from about 1135-1144 A.H.

11.	1 Ashrafi	75.00

ASHRAF, 1725-1729
Arab legend on each side. With dates from about 1137-1142 A.H.

12.	1 Ashrafi	75.00

ABBAS III, 1731-1736
Arab legend on each side. With dates from about 1144-1148 A.H.

13.	1 Ashrafi	60.00

NADIR, 1736-1747

Arab legend on each side. With dates from about 1148-1158 A.H.

14.	1 Ashrafi ....*	60.00
15.	2 Mohurs	200.00
16.	1 Mohur ....*	75.00
16a.	⅓ Mohur	55.00
16b.	¼ Mohur	45.00

RUKH, 1748-1750
Arab legend on each side. With dates from about 1161-1163 A.H.

17.   1 Mohur... 110.00

KERIM KHAN, 1750-1779

Arab legend on each side. With dates from about 1163-1193 A.H.

18.   1 Mohur...*...... 80.00
19.   ½ Mohur... 60.00
20.   ¼ Mohur... 50.00

Arab legend. Rev. Legend in star shaped pattern.

21.   1 Mohur... 150.00

MOHAMMED HASAN KHAN, 1750-1759
Arab legend on each side. With dates from about 1163-1172 A.H.

22.   1 Mohur... 85.00
23.   ¼ Mohur... 60.00

ABUL FATH KHAN, 1779
Arab legend on each side.

24.   ¼ Mohur 1193 A.H................................. 200.00

SADIK KHAN, 1779-1782
Arab legend on each side. With dates from about 1193-1196 A.H.

25.   1 Mohur... 85.00
26.   ¼ Mohur... 60.00

ALI MURAD KHAN, 1779-1785
Arab legend on each side. With dates from about 1193-1199 A.H.

27.   1 Mohur... 85.00
28.   ¼ Mohur... 60.00

JAAFAR KHAN, 1785-1789
Arab legend on each side. With dates from about 1199-1203 A.H.

29.   1 Mohur... 85.00

LUTFALI KHAN, 1789-1794
Arab legend on each side. With dates from about 1203-1209 A.H.

30.   ¼ Mohur... 75.00

AKA MOHAMMED KHAN, 1794-1797

Arab legend. Rev. Embellished legend with date in panel.

31.   1 Toman 1209 A.H. (1794 A.D.)...................... 225.00

FATH ALI, 1797-1834

Arab legend on each side. With dates from about 1212-1250 A.H.

32.   5 Tomans... 275.00
33.   2 Tomans... 135.00
34.   1 Toman...................................*..... 75.00
35.   ½ Toman... 60.00
36.   ⅔ Toman... 60.00
37.   ⅓ Toman... 40.00

Ruler on horse. Rev. Legend.

38.   2 Tomans 1239 A.H. (1823 A.D.).................... 500.00
39.   ⅔ Toman 1236 A.H. (1820 A.D.).................... 275.00

Ruler seated on throne. Rev. Legend in panel or star as indicated.

40.   ½ Toman 1249 A.H. (1833 A.D.). Panel............... 135.00
41.   ½ Toman 1249 A.H. (1833 A.D.). Star............... 160.00

MOHAMMED, 1834-1848

Arab legend on each side.

41a.   3 Mohurs 1251 A.H. (1835 A.D.).................... 600.00

Lion. Rev. Legend in square.

42.   ½ Toman 1262 A.H. (1846 A.D.).................... 85.00

Arab legend on each side.

43.   ½ Toman 1250-1264 A.H. (1834-48 A.D.)............. 60.00

HASAN SALAR, REBEL, 1848-1850

Arab legend on each side.

44.   ½ Toman 1265 A.H. (1848 A.D.)..................... 135.00

NASREDIN, 1848-1896
(The coinage of this ruler is dated from 1265-1314 A.H.).

Arab legend on each side in either a circle, square or octogram.

45.   1 Toman..*...... 60.00
46.   ½ Toman... 45.00
47.   ¼ Toman... 35.00

Toughra in wreath. Rev. Legend in wreath.

48.   2 Tomans 1281 A.H. (1864 A.D.)..................... 325.00

Half-length uniformed bust facing. Rev. Legend.

49.   2 Tomans 1271 A.H. (1854 A.D.).............*...... 160.00
50.   1 Toman 1273-91 A.H. (1856-74 A.D.)........*...... 85.00
51.   ⅕ Toman 1274 A.H. (1857 A.D.)..................... 35.00

Lion. Rev. Legend in wreath or circle.

52.   10 Tomans... Unknown
53.   5 Tomans (Medal of Bravery)...........*.... 750.00
54.   2 Tomans.. Unknown
55.   1 Toman 1296 A.H. (1879)...................... 250.00
56.   ½ Toman 1296, 98, 1308 A.H. (1879, 81, 91).... 175.00
57.   ⅕ Toman 1295 A.H. (1878).................... 150.00

Bust. Rev. Legend in wreath or circle.

58.   25 Tomans 1000.00
59.   10 Tomans   1297, 1311 A.H. (1880, 93) .. * 3500.00
60.   2 Tomans 1297, 99 A.H. (1880, 82) ..... * 275.00
61.   1 Toman 1297 A.H. (1880), No Obverse legend 200.00
62.   1 Toman 1297-1312 A.H. (1880-94) 150.00
63.   ½ Toman 1297-1305 A.H. (1880-87) 150.00
64.   ⅕ Toman 1297-1303 A.H. (1880-85) 75.00

Bust. Rev. Legend. On the Shah's return from Europe.

65.   2 Tomans 1307 A.H. (1889).................... 700.00
66.   1 Toman 1307 A.H. (1889)..................... 250.00

Bust. Rev. Legend. On bank officials visit to mint.

67.   2 Tomans 1308 A.H. (1890).................... 700.00

MUZAFFAREDIN, 1896-1907
(The coinage of this ruler is dated from 1314-1325 A.H.).

Uniformed bust with plumed hat. Rev. Legend in wreath.

68.   10 Tomans 1314 A.H. (1896) 4000.00
69.   2 Tomans 1316-23 A.H. (1898-1905) .... * 275.00
70.   1 Toman 1316-21 A.H. (1898-1903) ..... * 175.00
71.   ½ Toman 1316-24 A.H. (1898-1906) 90.00
72.   ⅕ Toman ND, 1324 A.H. (1906) 150.00

Same type as above but with Persian characters at each side of bust on Obv. On his birthday.

73.   2 Tomans 1322 A.H. (1904 A.D.).............. 500.00

Lion. Rev. Legend in wreath.

74.   2 Tomans 1311 A.H...........................*.... 350.00
75.   1 Toman 1314 A.H. (1896)....................*.... 275.00
76.   ½ Toman 1314-15 A.H. (1896-97) 200.00
77.   ⅕ Toman 1309 A.H............................ 175.00

MOHAMMED ALI, 1907-1909

Uniformed bust with plumed hat. Rev. Legend in wreath.

| 78. | 1 Toman 1326, 27 A.H. (1908, 09 A.D.) .. * .... | 250.00 |
| 79. | ½ Toman 1326 A.H. (1908 A.D.) .... * .... | 200.00 |

Lion. Rev. Legend in wreath.

| 80. | 1 Toman 1324 A.H. (1907 A.D.)............... | 300.00 |
| 81. | ½ Toman 1324-25 A.H. (1907-08 A.D.) .... | 225.00 |

AHMED, 1909-1925

(The coinage of this ruler is dated from 1327-1344 A.H.).
Lion. Rev. Legend.

| 82. | ½ Toman 1328-30 A.H. (1910-12) .... | 175.00 |
| 83. | ⅕ Toman 1332-41 A.H. (1914-21) .... | 150.00 |

Bust with plumed hat. Rev. Legend.

84.	1 Toman 1331-43 A.H. (1913-24) .... *	175.00
85.	½ Toman 1331-43 A.H. (1913-24)	75.00
86.	⅕ Toman 1331-43 A.H. (1913-24)	50.00

Bust with plumed hat. Rev. Lion. On the 10th year of reign.

| 87. | 5 Tomans 1337 A.H. (1919 A.D.)........ * .... | 2000.00 |

RIZA KHAN PAHLEVI, 1925-1941

*(The Persian calendar was changed to the solar year during
this reign, causing 1304 S.H. to fall in 1925 A.D.)*

Lion. Rev. Legend.

88.	5 Pahlevi 1305 S.H. (1926 A.D.)	1000.00
89.	2 Pahlevi 1305 S.H. (1926 A.D.)	450.00
90.	1 Pahlevi 1305 S.H. (1926 A.D.)	250.00
91.	1 Toman 1305 S.H. (1926 A.D.)........ *	300.00

Bust with plumed hat. Rev. Legend.

92.	5 Pahlevi 1306-08 S.H. (1927-29 A.D.) ... *	750.00
93.	2 Pahlevi 1306-08 S.H. (1927-29 A.D.) ... *	250.00
94.	1 Pahlevi 1306-08 S.H. (1927-29 A.D.)	150.00

Head left with military cap. Rev. Lion.

| 95. | 1 Pahlevi 1310 S.H. (1931 A.D.) .... | 1000.00 |
| 96. | ½ Pahlevi 1310-15 S.H. (1931-36 A.D.) .. * .... | 300.00 |

MOHAMMED RIZA PAHLEVI, 1942-1979

Lion. Rev. Legend.

| 97. | 1 Pahlevi 1322-24 S.H. (1943-45 A.D.) .... | 150.00 |
| 98. | ½ Pahlevi 1320-23 (1941-44 A.D.) .... | 85.00 |

Head. Rev. Lion. These coins appear in red gold.

99.	5 Pahlevi 1339-55 S.H., 2535-36 M.S. (1959-79 A.D.).............................	650.00(B)
100.	2½ Pahlevi 1339-55 S.H., 2535-36 M.S. (1959-79 A.D.).............................	350.00(B)
101.	1 Pahlevi 1330-55 S.H., 2535-36 M.S. (1950-79 A.D.)..................... *	150.00(B)
102.	½ Pahlevi 1330-55 S.H., 2535-36 M.S. (1950-79 A.D.) .... *	85.00(B)
103.	¼ Pahlevi 1332-35 S.H. (1953-55 A.D.)	75.00(B)
104.	¼ Pahlevi 1336-55 S.H., 2536-37 M.S. (1956-79 A.D.) large flan	35.00(B)

(Numbers 99-104 are bullion coins. The price listed is based on gold at $725 per ounce.)

For later issues of Persia, see under Iran in the section, "Recent Issues Starting With 1960."

PERU

Mints and mint marks:—L, LM, ME or monogram for Lima; C or CO for Cuzco. Peru struck gold coins as a regular circulating medium of exchange until 1950. Gold pieces minted after 1950 were not legal tender. Since 1862 Peru has used four standards in the minting of its gold coins. These standards are: the French monetary system for Soles of 1863, the English Pound for the Libra denominations 1898-1964, the U.S. gold Dollar for the 50 Soles (equivalent to 20 Dollars) 1930-1931, and the price of gold at $35.00 per ounce for Soles minted since 1950.

A. Spanish Kings of —
CHARLES II, 1665-1700

Pillars and date. Rev. Cross. Cob type.

1.	8 Escudos 1696-1701 ....*	3500.00
2.	4 Escudos 1696-1701	2500.00
3.	2 Escudos 1696-1701. L mm	1000.00
4.	2 Escudos 1698. C mm	1300.00
5.	1 Escudo 1696-1701. L mm	750.00
6.	1 Escudo 1698. C mm.......................	1000.00

PHILIP V, 1700-1746

Pillars and date. Rev. Cross. Cob type.

7.	8 Escudos 1702-46........................	1750.00
8.	4 Escudos 1702-46........................	1750.00
9.	2 Escudos 1700, 02-46...............*......	1000.00

Crude castle. Rev. Cross.

10.	1 Escudo 1702-46.........................	1500.00

LOUIS I, 1724
Pillars and date. Rev. Cross. Cob type.

11.	8 Escudos 1724, 25......................	4000.00

FERDINAND VI, 1746-1760

Pillars and date. Rev. Cross. Cob type.

12.	8 Escudos 1747-50.................*.....	1300.00
13.	4 Escudos 1747-50.......................	5000.00
14.	2 Escudos 1747-50.......................	1000.00
15.	1 Escudo 1747-50........................	750.00

Large bust with flowing wig. Rev. Arms with value.

16.	8 Escudos 1751, 52, 53..................	3000.00
17.	4 Escudos 1751, 52.....................	Rare
18.	2 Escudos 1751, 52, 53...............*.....	1000.00
19.	1 Escudo 1751, 52.......................	750.00

Smaller bust. Rev. Arms without value.

20.	8 Escudos 1754-60................*......	3000.00
21.	4 Escudos 1757, 58.....................	5000.00
22.	2 Escudos 1758, 59.....................	1500.00
23.	1 Escudo 1754, 57, 59	750.00

CHARLES III, 1759-1788

Small armored bust. Rev. Arms.

24.	8 Escudos 1761, 62.....................	6000.00
25.	4 Escudos 1761, 62.....................10000.00
26.	2 Escudos 1761, 62..................*.....	2000.00
27.	1 Escudo 1761, 62......................	1000.00

Large bust. Rev. Arms without value.

28.	8 Escudos 1763-72.....................	6000.00
29.	4 Escudos 1769, 70....................	4000.00
30.	2 Escudos 1765-72.................*	1750.00
31.	1 Escudo 1766-72......................	750.00

Bust. Rev. Arms with value.

32.	8 Escudos 1771-89..................*......	1500.00
33.	4 Escudos 1777-88.....................	2000.00
34.	2 Escudos 1772-89.....................	1000.00
35.	1 Escudo 1772-89......................	300.00

CHARLES IV, 1788-1808

Bust of the previous King, Charles III. Rev. Arms.

36.	8 Escudos 1789, 90, 91................	2000.00
37.	4 Escudos 1789, 91.................*......	2000.00
38.	2 Escudos 1790, 91...................	800.00
39.	1 Escudo 1789, 90, 91	500.00

Bust. Rev. Arms.

40.	8 Escudos 1792-1808	1500.00
41.	4 Escudos 1792-1808	1500.00
42.	2 Escudos 1792-1808 ....*	500.00
43.	1 Escudo 1792-1808...................	200.00

FERDINAND VII, 1808-1824

Bust in uniform. Rev. Arms.

44.	8 Escudos 1808-12	*	2500.00
45.	4 Escudos 1809, 10		3500.00
46.	2 Escudos 1809-11		1500.00
47.	1 Escudo 1810, 12		800.00

Large draped bust. Rev. Arms.

48.	8 Escudos 1812	2500.00
49.	4 Escudos 1812	3000.00

Small draped bust. Rev. Arms.

50.	8 Escudos 1812, 13, 14	*	1700.00
51.	4 Escudos 1812, 13		2500.00
52.	2 Escudos 1812, 13		900.00
53.	1 Escudo 1812, 13		500.00

Laureate head. Rev. Arms.

54.	8 Escudos 1814-21. ME mm.	*	1400.00
55.	8 Escudos 1824. CO mm		3000.00
56.	4 Escudos 1814-21		1500.00
57.	2 Escudos 1814-21		800.00
58.	1 Escudo 1814-21		300.00
59.	½ Escudo 1814-21		1000.00

B. Republic of —

Llama, tree and cornucopia. Rev. Wreath and place of minting.

60.	½ Escudo 1826. Cuzco		160.00
61.	½ Escudo 1826. Lima	*	120.00

Liberty standing holding shield and pole; the place of minting in the legend. Rev. Arms.

62.	8 Escudos 1826-55. Lima		1150.00
63.	8 Escudos 1826-45. Cuzco		1550.00
64.	4 Escudos 1828, 50, 53-55. Lima	*	600.00
65.	2 Escudos 1826-29, 50, 51, 53-55. Lima		400.00
66.	1 Escudo 1826-55. Lima		150.00
67.	1 Escudo 1830-46. Cuzco		200.00
67a.	½ Escudo 1829-39. Lima		175.00

Liberty seated facing left. Rev. Arms.

68.	8 Escudos 1862, 63		1000.00
69.	4 Escudos 1863		Rare
70.	20 Soles 1863	*	850.00
71.	10 Soles 1863		500.00
72.	5 Soles 1863		300.00

Indian head. Rev. Arms. The 1, ½ and ⅕ Libra pieces struck after 1950 were not legal tender.

73.	1 Libra 1898-1967	*	170.00(B)
74.	½ Libra 1902-66		85.00(B)
75.	⅕ Libra 1906-67		55.00(B)

(Numbers 73-75 are bullion coins. The price listed is based on gold at $725 per ounce.)

Arms. Rev. Motto.

76.	5 Soles 1910	130.00

Head of the Inca Indian Chief, Manco Capoc. Rev. Inca emblems.

77.	50 Soles 1930-31	2700.00

Liberty seated facing right. Rev. Arms. None of these pieces were legal tender.

78.	100 Soles 1950-70 (1952, 58 rare)		980.00(B)
79.	50 Soles 1950-69 (1952, 58 rare)		490.00(B)
80.	20 Soles 1950-69 (1952, 58 rare) *		195.00(B)
81.	10 Soles 1956-69 *		100.00(B)
82.	5 Soles 1956-69		50.00(B)

(Numbers 78-82 are bullion coins. The price listed is based on gold at $725 per ounce.)

For later issues, see under Peru in the section, "Recent Issues Starting With 1960."

C. Republican States of —

NORTH PERU

Liberty standing holding shield and pole. Rev. Arms and "Estado Nor Peruano."

87.	8 Escudos 1836, 38 *		5000.00
88.	4 Escudos 1838		Rare
89.	2 Escudos 1838		3000.00
90.	1 Escudo 1838		1000.00

SOUTH PERU

Sun over flags and "Estado Sud Peruano". Rev. Volcano and castle and below "Federacion".

91.	8 Escudos 1837	2000.00

Obv. similar to above but with legend "Repub. Sud Peruano". Rev. similar to above but with "Confederacion."

92.	8 Escudos 1837, 38	2100.00

Radiant sun. Rev. Value in wreath.

93.	1 Escudo 1838	750.00
94.	½ Escudo 1838	900.00

PHILIPPINE ISLANDS

Spanish Rulers of —

ISABELLA II, 1833-1868

Head. Rev. Arms.

1.	4 Pesos 1861-68 *		300.00
2.	2 Pesos 1861-68 *		150.00
3.	1 Peso 1861-68		125.00

ALFONSO XII, 1875-1886

Head. Rev. Arms.

4.	4 Pesos 1880-82, 85	1000.00

For later issues of the Philippines, see the section, "Recent Issues Starting With 1960."

POLAND

Other coins of the Kings of Poland will be found under Danzig, Latvia, Lithuania and Germany-Elbing.

A. Kings of —

LADISLAS LOKIETEK, 1306-1333
King on throne. Rev. St. Stanislas.

1.	1 Ducat ND	Rare

SIGISMUND I, 1506-1548
Bust. Rev. Arms.

2.	1 Ducat 1528-48	1600.00

STEPHAN BATHORI, 1576-1586
Bust. Rev. Arms.

3.	1 Ducat 1586	5000.00

SIGISMUND III, 1587-1632

Bust. Rev. Arms.

4.	100 Ducats 1621	Rare
5.	90 Ducats 1621	Rare
6.	60 Ducats 1621	Rare

7.	20 Ducats 1614, 17	1800.00
8.	10 Ducats 1588-1628, ND	10000.00
9.	5 Ducats 1596-1623 ....*	4000.00
10.	4 Ducats 1611, 12	4000.00
11.	3 Ducats 1599, 1612	2600.00
12.	2 Ducats 1610	1800.00
13.	1 Ducat 1588-1630, ND....................*	800.00

LADISLAS IV, 1632-1648

Bust. Rev. Arms.

14.	10 Ducats 1635, 36	12000.00
15.	5 Ducats 1642, 45, 47............................	5000.00
16.	1 Ducat 1639-44 ....*	900.00

JOHN CASIMIR, 1648-1668

Bust. Rev. Arms.

17.	10 Ducats 1661	12000.00
18.	5 Ducats 1649-52, ND............................	5000.00
19.	2 Ducats 1650-67 ....*	2200.00
20.	1 Ducat 1649-62 ....*	900.00
21.	½ Ducat 1653-62, ND............................	900.00

Bust. Rev. Eagle.

| 22. | 2 Ducats 1650.................................... | 2000.00 |

Ruler standing. Rev. Arms.

| 23. | 1 Ducat 1649..................................... | 1200.00 |

MICHAEL KORYBUT, 1669-1673

Bust. Rev. Arms.

| 24. | 2 Ducats 1671................................... | 4500.00 |

JOHN III SOBIESKI, 1674-1696

Bust. Rev. Arms.

| 25. | 2 Ducats ND .... | 4500.00 |
| 26. | 1 Ducat 1682, 83............................* | 1800.00 |

AUGUST II AND AUGUST III, 1697-1763
(See under Germany-Saxony).

STANISLAS AUGUST, 1764-1795

Head. Rev. Arms.

27.	3 Ducats 1794 ....*	3000.00
28.	1½ Ducats 1794	1500.00
29.	1 Ducat 1765. Armored bust	1500.00

Initials on star. Rev. Arms.

| 30. | 1 Ducat 1766..................................... | 1250.00 |

Head. Rev. Value in square.

| 31. | 1 Ducat 1766-79 .... | 750.00 |

Ruler standing. Rev. Value in square.

| 32. | 1 Ducat 1766, 67, 70, 71, 72 .... | 800.00 |

Head. Rev. Legend.

| 33. | 1 Ducat 1780-95 .... | 650.00 |

B. Russian Czars of —

ALEXANDER I, 1815-1825

Plain head. Rev. Eagle.

34.	50 Zloty 1817-19. Oblique milling.............*	700.00
35.	25 Zloty 1817-19. Oblique milling	500.00
36.	50 Zloty 1819-23. Straight milling	700.00
37.	25 Zloty 1820-25. Straight milling ....*	500.00

Laureate head. Rev. Value and date in wreath.

| 38. | 50 Zloty 1827-29 .... | 1200.00 |
| 39. | 25 Zloty 1828-33 .... | 750.00 |

NICHOLAS I, 1825-1855

Eagle. Rev. Two values as indicated.

40.	20 Zloty-3 Roubles 1834-40. St. Petersburg mm *.....	325.00
41.	20 Zloty-3 Roubles 1841. St. Petersburg mm	Rare
42.	20 Zloty-3 Roubles 1834-40. Warsaw Mint	1500.00

C. Revolution 1830-1831

Knight standing. Rev. Tablet. Dutch type coin bearing the mint mark of a small eagle.

| 43. | 1 Ducat 1831 .... | 350.00 |

D. Republic of —

Crowned head of Boleslaus. Rev. Eagle. On the 900th Anniversary of Poland.

| 44. | 20 Zloty 1925 .... | 160.00 |
| 45. | 10 Zloty 1925 .... | 90.00 |

For later issues, see the section ''Recent Issues Starting With 1960.''

E. Cities of —

GNESEN

Bishops of —

STANISLAUS SZEMBEK, 1706-1721

Bust. Rev. Arms.

| 46. | 1 Ducat 1721 .... | 2250.00 |

KRAKAU

Bishops of —

CAJETAN SOLTYK, 1759-1782

Bust. Rev. Legend.

| 47. | 1 Ducat 1762 .... | 1250.00 |

THORN

Polish Kings of —

SIGISMUND III, 1587-1632

Bust. Rev. Arms.

| 48. | 1 Ducat 1630 .... | 800.00 |

City view. Rev. Legend.

| 49. | 5 Ducats 1629 .... | 3000.00 |

LADISLAS IV, 1632-1648

Bust. Rev. Arms.

| 50. | 1 Ducat 1633-48 .... | 800.00 |

JOHN CASIMIR, 1648-1668

Bust. Rev. Arms.

| 51. | 2 Ducats 1660-68 .... * ...... | 1800.00 |
| 52. | 1 Ducat 1649-67 .... | 800.00 |

Bust. Rev. City view.

53.	5 Ducats 1655, 59 .... *	3750.00
54.	4 Ducats 1655	3750.00
55.	3 Ducats 1655	2250.00

MICHAEL KORYBUT, 1669-1673

Bust. Rev. Arms.

| 56. | 2 Ducats 1671 .... | 3000.00 |

Bust. Rev. City view.

57.   2 Ducats 1670, ND 1750.00

AUGUST II OF SAXONY, 1697-1733

Bust. Rev. Arms.

58.   1 Ducat 1702 .... 1000.00

WARSAW

Saxon Grand Dukes of —

FREDERICK AUGUST

Head. Rev. Arms.

59.   1 Ducat 1812, 13 .... 1250.00

PORTUGAL

Mints and mint marks:—
A   mm for Angra (Azores)
B   mm for Braga
C   mm for Ceuta (Morocco)
L   mm for Lisbon
P   mm for Porto
T   mm for Toro

Other coins of the Portuguese Kings will be found under Brazil, India-Cochin, India-Diu, India-Goa, India-Malacca and Mozambique.

A. Kings of —

SANCHO I, 1185-1211
(Mints: Braga, Coimbra)

Ruler on horse. Rev. Cross of five shields with a star in each angle.

1.   1 Morabitino ND 4000.00

ALFONSO II, 1211-1223
(Mints: Braga, Coimbra, Lisbon)
Ruler on horse. Rev. Cross of five shields with three stars and a cross in angles.

2.   1 Morabitino ND 6000.00

SANCHO II, 1223-1248
(Mints: Braga, Lisbon)
Ruler on horse. Rev. Cross of five shields.

3.   1 Morabitino ND 8000.00

ALFONSO III, 1248-1279
Ruler on horse. Rev. Cross of five shields.

4.   1 Morabitino ND .... Unknown

PEDRO I, 1357-1367
(Dobras and Half Dobras are mentioned in contemporary documents as existing, but no specimen of either coin has yet been discovered.)

FERDINAND, 1367-1383
(Mints: Lisbon, Porto)

Ruler standing. Rev. Ornate floriated cross in quadrilobe.

5.   1 Dobra ND ....*...... 6500.00
6.   ½ Dobra ND .... Rare

Ruler standing. Rev. Cross of five shields in circle.

7.   1 Dobra ND ....*...... 4500.00

DUARTE, 1433-1438
(Mint: Lisbon)

Crowned E in octolobe. Rev. Crowned shield.

8.   1 Escudo ND .... Unique

ALFONSO V, 1438-1481
(Mints: Lisbon, Porto, Toro, Ceuta)

Arms. Rev. Cross in ornamental frame.

9.   1 Cruzado ND 600.00

Crown over ALFQ. Rev. Shield.

10.   1 Escudo ND 8500.00

Crowned shield. Rev. Castle. Struck for Ceuta.

11.   ½ Escudo ND .... Rare

Crowned shield. Rev. Quarterod arms. Struck for Toro.

12.   1 Escudo ND .... Rare

JOHN II, 1481-1495
(Mints: Lisbon, Porto)

Ruler on throne. Rev. Shield.

13.   1 Justo ND.. 6000.00

Ruler standing. Rev. Shield.

14.   1 Justo ND 7500.00

Hand holding sword. Rev. Arms.

15.   ½ Justo ND.. 1000.00

Arms. Rev. Cross in ornamental frame.

16.   1 Cruzado ND 550.00

MANUEL I, 1495-1521
(Mint: Lisbon)

Arms. Rev. Cross of Jerusalem.

17.   1 Portuguez (10 Ducats) ND 7500.00

Arms. Rev. Cross.

18.   1 Cruzado ND 600.00
19.   ¼ Cruzado ND 2500.00

JOHN III, 1521-1557
(Mints: Lisbon, Porto)

Arms. Rev. Cross of Jerusalem in plain field.

20.   1 Portuguez ND 9000.00

Arms. Rev. Cross of Jerusalem in ornate field.

20a.   1 Portuguez ND 7000.00

Arms. Rev. Cross.

21.   1 Cruzado ND (23 mm) 450.00
21a.   1 Cruzado ND (27 mm) 3500.00

Arms. Rev. Cross of Calvary.

22.   1 Cruzado Calvario ND 425.00

St. Vincent standing. Rev. Arms.

| 23. | 1 San Vincente ND | * | 1000.00 |
| 24. | ½ San Vincente ND | | 850.00 |

SEBASTIAN, 1557-1578
(Mints: Lisbon, Porto)

St. Vincent standing. Rev. Arms.

| 25. | 1 San Vincente ND | | 1000.00 |
| 26. | ½ San Vincente ND | * | 1000.00 |

Arms. Rev. Cross of Jerusalem.

27.	1 Engenhoso 1562-66. (Long cross)	*	1250.00
28.	1 Engenhoso ND. (Long cross)		1500.00
29.	500 Reais (1 Cruzado) ND. (Short cross)	*	400.00

HENRY I, 1578-1580
(Mint: Lisbon)

Arms. Rev. Cross of Jerusalem.

| 30. | 500 Reais (1 Cruzado) ND | | 6000.00 |

THE GOVERNORS, 1580
(Mint: Lisbon)

Arms. Rev. Cross of Jerusalem.

| 31. | 1 Cruzado ND | | Rare |

ANTONIO I, 1580-1583
(Mints: Lisbon, Angra)
Arms. Rev. Cross of Jerusalem.

| 32. | 500 Reais (1 Cruzado) ND | | 9000.00 |

Arms. Rev. Floriated cross. Struck for the Azores. Both coins are the same size; the 2000 Reis is identified by a counterstamp.

| 33. | 2000 Reis ND | * | 4000.00 |
| 34. | 1000 Reis ND | | 5000.00 |

Arms. Rev. Cross of St. George. Struck for the Azores.

| 35. | 1000 Reais ND | | 8000.00 |

PHILIP I (PHILIP II OF SPAIN), 1580-1598
(The following coins are from the Lisbon Mint, unless otherwise noted.)
Arms. Rev. Cross of St. George.

36.	4 Cruzados ND		4500.00
37.	2 Cruzados ND		3000.00
38.	1 Cruzado ND		2500.00

Arms. Rev. Cross of Jerusalem.

| 39. | 500 Reis (1 Cruzado) ND | | 8000.00 |

PHILIP II (PHILIP III OF SPAIN), 1598-1621

Arms. Rev. Cross of St. George.

40.	4 Cruzados ND		2000.00
41.	2 Cruzados ND		2500.00
42.	1 Cruzado ND	*	2250.00

PHILIP III (PHILIP IV OF SPAIN), 1621-1640

Arms. Rev. Cross of St. George.

43.	4 Cruzados ND	*	3000.00
44.	2 Cruzados ND		1750.00
45.	1 Cruzado ND		2000.00

JOHN IV, 1640-1656

Arms. Rev. Cross of St. George.

46.	4 Cruzados 1642-52	*	2000.00
47.	2 Cruzados 1642, 46, 47		1750.00
48.	1 Cruzado 1642, 47		1500.00
49.	The coin previously listed does not exist.		

Counterstamped coinage for use in Portugal only.

49a.	Crowned 10U in square over Portuguez (10000 Reis)		Rare
49b.	Crowned 4U in square over 4 Cruzados (4000 Reis)		2000.00
49c.	Crowned 1U in square over 1 Cruzado (1000 Reis)		1250.00

ALFONSO VI, 1656-1683

(For counterstamped coinage issued for both Portugal and colonies, see under Brazil.)

Arms. Rev. Cross of St. George.

49d.	4 Cruzados 1660, 63		3500.00
49e.	2 Cruzados 1660		3000.00

Arms. Rev. Cross of Jerusalem.

50.	4000 Reis (Moeda) 1663-66		2750.00
51.	2000 Reis (½ Moeda) 1663, 66		2000.00
51a.	1000 Reis (¼ Moeda) 1663, 66		2500.00

PETER, PRINCE REGENT, 1667-1683

(For counterstamps, see under Brazil.)

Arms. Rev. Cross in quadrilobe.

52.	4400 Reis (Moeda) 1668-74	*	2250.00
53.	2200 Reis (½ Moeda) 1668-74		1750.00
54.	1100 Reis (¼ Moeda) 1668, 71		1750.00

Arms. Rev. Cross of Jerusalem.

55.	4000 Reis (Moeda) 1677-82		1250.00
56.	2000 Reis (½ Moeda) 1677-82		1000.00
57.	1000 Reis (¼ Moeda) 1677-81	*	600.00

PETER II, 1683-1706

(For counterstamps, see under Brazil.)

Arms. Rev. Cross.

58.	4000 Reis (Moeda) 1688-1706		850.00
59.	2000 Reis (½ Moeda) 1683-1706		600.00
60.	1000 Reis (¼ Moeda) 1683-1706		350.00

JOHN V, 1706-1750

Bust. Rev. Arms. The 24 and 16 Escudo pieces are essais and were not placed in circulation. From 1722 through 1732, the design of the arms changed every year.

61.	Dobra of 24 Escudos 1731		Rare
62.	Dobra of 16 Escudos 1731		Rare
63.	Dobra of 8 Escudos 1722. L mm		6000.00
63a.	Dobra of 8 Escudos 1723-32. No mm		2250.00
64.	Dobra of 4 Escudos (Peca) 1722. L mm		2500.00
65.	Dobra of 4 Escudos (Peca) 1723-50. No mm	*	900.00
66.	Dobra of 2 Escudos (½ Peca) 1722. L mm		1250.00
67.	Dobra of 2 Escudos (½ Peca) 1723-50. No mm		750.00
68.	1 Escudo (1600 Reis) 1722. L mm		200.00
69.	1 Escudo (1600 Reis) 1723-50. No mm		150.00
70.	½ Escudo (800 Reis) 1722. L mm		325.00
71.	½ Escudo (800 Reis) 1723-50. No mm		250.00

Arms. Rev. Cross. The 8000 Reis piece is an essai and was not placed in circulation.

72.	8000 Reis (2 Moedas) 1711		Rare
73.	4000 Reis (Moeda) 1707-22. No mm		400.00
74.	4000 Reis (Moeda) 1712-14. P mm		550.00
75.	2000 Reis (½ Moeda) 1707-25. No mm		275.00
76.	2000 Reis (½ Moeda) 1713, 14. P mm		350.00
77.	1000 Reis (Quartinho) 1707-47. No mm		125.00
78.	1000 Reis (Quartinho) 1713. P mm		300.00

Cross. Rev. Crown over name.

79.	400 Reis (Cruzado) 1717-48		100.00

JOSEPH I, 1750-1777

Bust. Rev. Arms.

80.	4 Escudos (6400 Reis) 1750-76		650.00
81.	2 Escudos (3200 Reis) 1750-76	*	500.00
82.	1 Escudo (1600 Reis) 1750-76		225.00
83.	½ Escudo (800 Reis) 1750-76		150.00

Arms. Rev. Cross.

84.	1000 Reis (Quartinho) 1749-69 .... 150.00

Cross. Rev. Crown over name.

85.	400 Reis (Cruzado) 1752-76 .... 75.00

MARY I AND PETER III, 1777-1786

Conjoined busts. Rev. Arms.

86.	4 Escudos (6400 Reis) 1777-85 .... * 650.00
87.	2 Escudos (3200 Reis) 1778, 84 .... 550.00
88.	1 Escudo (1600 Reis) 1777-85 .... 225.00
89.	½ Escudo (800 Reis) 1777-84 .... 135.00

Arms. Rev. Cross.

90.	1000 Reis (Quartinho) 1777-84 .... 135.00

Cross. Rev. Crown over name.

91.	400 Reis (Cruzado) 1777-85 .... 100.00

MARY I, 1786-1816

Bust with widow's veil. Rev. Arms.

92.	4 Escudos (6400 Reis) 1786, 87 .... 1000.00
93.	1 Escudo (1600 Reis) 1787 .... 900.00
94.	½ Escudo (800 Reis) 1787, 88 .... * 700.00

Bust with ornamental headdress. Rev. Arms.

95.	4 Escudos (6400 Reis) 1789-99 .... * 650.00
96.	2 Escudos (3200 Reis) 1789 .... 650.00
97.	1 Escudo (1600 Reis) 1789-96 .... 275.00
98.	½ Escudo (800 Reis) 1789-96 .... 165.00

Arms. Rev. Cross.

99.	1000 Reis (Quartinho) 1787-1800 .... 325.00

Cross. Rev. Crown over name.

100.	400 Reis (Cruzado) 1787-96 .... 90.00

JOHN, PRINCE REGENT, 1799-1816

Bust. Rev. Plain arms.

101.	4 Escudos (Peca) 1802 .... 1650.00

Bust. Rev. Ornamental arms.

102.	4 Escudos (Peca) 1804-16 .... 775.00
103.	2 Escudos (½ Peca) 1805, 07 .... 775.00
104.	1 Escudo 1807 .... * 550.00
105.	½ Escudo 1805, 06 .... 300.00

Cross. Rev. Crown over name.

106.	400 Reis (Cruzado) 1807 .... 165.00

JOHN VI, 1816-1826

Bust. Rev. Arms.

107.	4 Escudos (Peca) 1818-24 .... 800.00
108.	2 Escudos (½ Peca) 1818-23 .... * 800.00
109.	1 Escudo 1818-21 .... 550.00
110.	½ Escudo 1818-21 .... 275.00

Arms. Rev. Cross.

111.	1000 Reis (Quartinho) 1818-21 .... 165.00

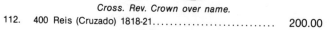

Cross. Rev. Crown over name.

112.	400 Reis (Cruzado) 1818-21 .... 200.00

PETER IV, 1826-1828

Laureate head. Rev. Arms.

113.	4 Escudos (Peca) 1826, 28 .... 2000.00
114.	2 Escudos (½ Peca) 1827 .... * 1750.00

MICHAEL I, 1828-1834

Small laureate bust. Rev. Arms in clinging palms.

115.	4 Escudos (Peca) 1828	*	2250.00
116.	2 Escudos (½ Peca) 1828		2000.00

Large laureate bust with collar. Rev. Arms in spreading palms.

117.	4 Escudos (Peca) 1830, 31	*	1750.00
118.	2 Escudos (½ Peca) 1830, 31		1500.00

MARY II, 1834-1853

Head with upswept hair. Rev. Arms.

119.	4 Escudos (Peca) 1833	4500.00

Draped bust with diadem. Rev. Arms.

120.	4 Escudos (Peca) 1833-35	1100.00

Head. Rev. Arms.

121.	5000 Reis 1836-51	*	450.00
122.	2500 Reis 1836-53		275.00
123.	1000 Reis 1851		165.00

During this reign, the Brazilian 20,000 Reis pieces of the Minas Mint, 1724-27, were counterstamped with the arms of Portugal, giving these coins a decreed legal value of 30,000 Reis.

124.	20,000 Reis 1724-27. Counterstamped	3300.00

PETER V, 1853-1861

Head. Rev. Arms. The 10,000 Reis piece is an essai and was not placed in circulation.

			Rare
125.	10000 Reis 1861		
126.	5000 Reis 1860, 61	*	275.00
127.	2000 Reis 1856-60		200.00
128.	1000 Reis 1855		135.00

LOUIS I, 1861-1889

Young head. Rev. Small arms in palms.

129.	5000 Reis 1862, 63	*	275.00
130.	2000 Reis 1864-66		225.00

Older head. Rev. Large draped arms.

131.	10000 Reis 1878-89	*	675.00
132.	5000 Reis 1867-89		385.00
133.	2000 Reis 1868-88		250.00

Head. Rev. Value.

134.	1000 Reis 1879	1400.00

CHARLES I, 1889-1908

Head. Rev. Arms. This coin is an essai and was not placed in circulation.

135.	5000 Reis 1895	2500.00

B. Republic, 1910-1926

Seated female. Rev. Arms. This coin is an essai and was not placed in circulation.

136.	5 Escudos 1920	2200.00

RHODES

(The Knights of St. John of Jerusalem at Rhodes)

Most of the coinage is of Venetian style and type.

Grand Masters of —

DIEUDONNE DE GOZON, 1346-1353

Ruler kneeling before St. John. Rev. Angel seated on Sepulcher of Christ.

1.   1 Zecchino ND 4500.00

PIERRE DE CORNILLAN, 1354-1355
Ruler kneeling before St. John. Rev. Angel seated on Sepulcher of Christ.

2.   1 Zecchino ND 5750.00

ANTOINE FLUVIAN, 1421-1437

Ruler kneeling before St. John. Rev. Christ standing.

3.   1 Zecchino ND 4500.00

JACQUES DE MILLY, 1454-1461
Ruler kneeling before St. John. Rev. Christ standing.

4.   1 Zecchino ND 4500.00

JEAN BAPTIST ORSINI, 1467-1476
Ruler kneeling before St. John. Rev. Christ standing.

5.   1 Zecchino ND 1500.00

PIERRE D'AUBUSSON, 1476-1503
Ruler kneeling before St. John. Rev. Christ standing.

6.   1 Zecchino ND 900.00

EMERIC D'AMBOISE, 1503-1512
Arms. Rev. Lamb.

7.   2 Ducats ND 5750.00
8.   1 Ducat ND..................................*..... 5750.00

Ruler kneeling before St. John. Rev. Christ standing.

9.   1 Zecchino ND 900.00

FABRIZIO DEL CARRETTO, 1513-1521
Bust with cap. Rev. Arms. (This may be a medal).

10.   10 Zecchini ND................................... Rare

Ruler kneeling before St. John. Rev. Christ standing.

11.   1 Zecchino ND 900.00

PHILIPPE VILLIERS
At Rhodes 1521-1522 and at Malta 1530-1534.
(For the coinage of this Grand Master and of his successors see under Malta).

ROUMANIA

The entire gold coinage of Roumania is based on the Latin Monetary Union standard. The 12½ Lei piece of 1906 is the only example of this denomination in the Union's coinage. The 50, 25 and 12½ Lei pieces struck in 1906, and the 50 and 25 Leis of 1922 are broad and thin and are struck in imitation of Ducat coinage to represent the equivalent of 4, 2 and 1 Ducat pieces. The commemorative coins of 1939 and 1940 (numbers 13-20) are rare and seldom appear.

Kings of —

CAROL I, 1866-1914

Young head with side whiskers. Rev. Value.

1.   20 Lei 1867, 68 .... 2000.00

Older head with whiskers. Rev. Value.

2.   20 Lei 1870.. 600.00

Head. Rev. Arms.

3.   20 Lei 1883-90 .... 160.00

Old head of 1906. Rev. Young head of 1867. On the 40th year of reign.

4.   100 Lei 1906.................................*..... 1750.00
5.   20 Lei 1906....................................... 275.00

Uniformed bust. Rev. Ruler on horse. On the 40th year of reign.

6.   50 Lei 1906....................................... 650.00

Uniformed bust. Rev. Eagle. On the 40th year of reign.

7.	25	Lei 1906..	500.00
8.	12½	Lei 1906................................*......	250.00

FERDINAND I, 1914-1927

Head. Rev. Arms. On his Coronation.

9.	100	Lei 1922................................*......	2250.00
10.	20	Lei 1922..	450.00

Crowned bust. Rev. Crowned bust of Marie. On his Coronation.

11.	50	Lei 1922..	1250.00
12.	25	Lei 1922................................*......	700.00

CAROL II, 1930-1940
Commemorative Coins on the Centennial of Birth of Carol I.

Head. Rev. Large arms.

13.	100	Lei 1939..	5000.00
14.	20	Lei 1939................................*......	850.00

Head. Rev. Angel over shield.

15.	100	Lei 1939..	5000.00

Head. Rev. Eagle over shield.

16.	20	Lei 1939..	850.00

Commemorative Coins on the 10th year of his Reign.

Head and legend within ornamental circle. Rev. Small crown over large monogram.

17.	100	Lei 1940..	4250.00
18.	20	Lei 1940................................*......	450.00

Head and legend only. Rev. Large crown over small monogram.

19.	100	Lei 1940..	4000.00
20.	20	Lei 1940..	450.00

MICHAEL I, 1940-1947

Conjoined heads of three Roumanian Kings, with dates 1601, 1918, 1944. Rev. Eagle within circle of shields. Although without the mark of value, this coin has the same specifications as the standard 20 Lei coin.

21.	(20 Lei) 1944..		170.00

RUSSIA

Most of the early gold coins (numbers 1-61) exist as later re-strikes (Novodels).

Russia affords us the only example of platinum coins actually being struck for circulation, and the 12, 6 and 3 Rouble coins of this metal are highly prized.

At the time platinum was discovered in the Ural Mountains it was worth so much less than gold that a 3 Rouble platinum coin weighing 10.3600 grams was the equal of a 3 Rouble gold coin weighing only 3.4900 grams. As a matter of fact, gold coins began to be counterfeited in platinum or struck in platinum at government mints (unofficially) from original dies. The platinum coins were then gold plated, and since platinum is slightly denser than gold and passes the same chemical tests as gold does, the gilded coins became indistinguishable from all-gold coins. These platinum coins are also highly prized.

The 3 Rouble gold piece struck from 1869 to 1885 is the Russian equivalent of the 1 Ducat. The 10 and 5 Rouble pieces struck from 1886 to 1894 and then re-valued in 1897 to 15 and 7½ Roubles, were struck according to the Latin Monetary Union standard and are equal to 40 and 20 Franc pieces.

NOTE: Due to extensive revisions, the numbering has been changed from previous editions.

A. Czars of —

VLADIMIR, 978-1015
Bust. Rev. Bust of Christ.

1.	1 Solidus ND......................................		Rare

IVAN III, 1462-1505

Hungarian state emblem. Rev. St. Vladislav.

2. 1 Ducat 1484. Hermitage Museum .... Unique

IVAN IV, THE TERRIBLE, 1533-1584
Eagle on each side.

3. 5 Ducats ND .... Rare

Eagle. Rev. Legend.

4. ½ Ducat ND........................... 2000.00
5. ¼ Ducat ND........................... 1750.00

Ruler on horse. Rev. Legend.

6. ½ Gold Kopeck (Denga) ND 2000.00

THEODORE, 1584-1598
Eagle. Rev. Legend.

7. 1 Ducat ND............................ 2000.00

Ruler on horse. Rev. Legend.

8. 1 Ducat ND............................ 2000.00

BORIS GODUNOV, 1598-1605
Bust with sceptre. Rev. Eagle.

9. 1 Ducat ND........................... Rare

Ruler on horseback. Rev. Legend.

10. ½ Gold Kopeck (Denga) ND 2000.00

DEMETRIUS (PRETENDER), 1604-1606
Bust with sceptre. Rev. Eagle.

11. 12 Ducats ND .... Rare

Eagle on each side.

12. 12 Ducats ND .... Rare
13. 11 Ducats ND .... Rare
14. 10 Ducats ND .... Rare
15. 1 Ducat ND .... Rare
16. 1 Gold Kopeck ND .... Rare
17. ½ Gold Kopeck (Denga) ND .... Rare

BASIL SHUISKY, 1606-1610
St. George. Rev. Eagle.

18. 5 Ducats ND (2 known)...................... Rare
19. 1 Ducat ND .... Rare

Eagle. Rev. Legend.

20. ½ Ducat................................. 2500.00
21. ¼ Ducat ND............................. 2000.00

Ruler on horse. Rev. Legend.

22. 1 Gold Kopeck ND .... * 2000.00
23. ½ Gold Kopeck ND 1500.00

LADISLAS, 1610-1612

Ruler on horse. Rev. Legend.

24. 1 Gold Kopeck ND 1000.00

MICHAEL, 1613-1645

Eagle on each side.

25. 4 Ducats ND .... * 3000.00
26. 1 Ducat ND .... Rare
27. ⅔ Ducat ND 1750.00

Eagle. Rev. Legend.

28. ½ Ducat ND 2000.00
29. ¼ Ducat ND 1000.00

Ruler on horse. Rev. Legend.

30. 1 Gold Kopeck ND ....* 1000.00
31. ½ Gold Kopeck ND 1000.00

ALEXIS, 1645-1676
Eagle on each side.

32. 10 Ducats ND .... Rare
33. 8 Ducats ND .... Rare
34. 3 Ducats ND .... Rare
35. 1½ Ducats ND .... Rare
36. 1 Ducat ND............................. Rare

Bust with sceptre. Rev. Bust of Christ.

37. 2 Ducats ND .... Rare

Eagle. Rev. Legend.

38. ½ Ducat ND........................... 2000.00
39. ¼ Ducat 1654, ND........................... 1250.00
40. 1 Gold Kopeck ND ....* 1500.00
41. ½ Gold Kopeck ND 900.00

THEODORE ALEXEIVITCH, 1676-1682

Eagle on each side.

42. 2 Ducats ND (Same as No. 43, double thick) 2500.00
43. 1 Ducat ND............................. 2000.00

SOPHIA, REGENT FOR PETER I AND IVAN V, 1682-1689

Bust of Sophia. Rev. Busts of Peter I and Ivan V.

44. 5 Ducats ND .... Rare
45. 3 Ducats ND .... Rare
46. 2 Ducats ND 2500.00
47. 1½ Ducats ND 2000.00

48.	1 Ducat ND........................ *	1750.00
49.	⅔ Ducat ND........................	1700.00
50.	½ Ducat ND........................	1500.00
51.	¼ Ducat ND........................ *	1200.00

Eagle. Rev. Legend.

52.	4 Ducats ND	3500.00
53.	3 Ducats ND	3000.00
54.	2 Ducats ND	2500.00

Eagle on each side.

55.	1½ Ducats ND...................... *	1500.00
56.	1 Ducat ND.......................	1250.00

IVAN V, CO-CZAR WITH PETER I, 1682-1696
Eagle on each side.

57.	9 Ducats ND	Rare
58.	6 Ducats ND, Novodels only..............	Rare
59.	2½ Ducats ND........................	Rare

Ruler on horse. Rev. Legend.

60.	1 Gold Kopeck ND	1000.00

PETER I, THE GREAT, 1682-1725
Ruler on horse. Rev. Legend.

61.	1 Gold Kopeck ND	1200.00

Bust. Rev. Eagle.

62.	13 Ducats 1705.......................	9000.00
63.	12 Ducats 1702. Dated March 1	Rare
64.	10 Ducats 1702. Dated March 1	10000.00
65.	8 Ducats 1702. Dated February 1	8000.00
66.	8 Ducats 1702. Dated March 1	8000.00
67.	7 Ducats 1702. Dated January 10	8000.00
68.	6 Ducats 1702. Dated February 1	6000.00
69.	5 Ducats 1702. Dated February 1	6000.00
70.	4 Ducats 1714................... *	6000.00
71.	3 Ducats 1702. Dated February 1	3500.00
72.	2 Ducats 1701, 02, 14	3500.00
73.	1 Ducat 1701-07. Date in Slavic numerals.	2000.00
74.	1 Ducat 1710, 11. Date in Arabic numerals. Eagle holding 4 maps in its beaks and talons.. *	2500.00
75.	1 Ducat 1710-14. Date in Arabic numerals	1500.00
76.	1 Ducat 1716. With Latin inscription	1500.00

Bust. Rev. St. Andrew.

77.	2 Roubles 1718, 20-25..................	850.00

Bust. Rev. Ruler on horse. Struck as a military reward for officers.

78.	4 Ducats 1706. For Battle of Kalish............	4500.00
79.	4 Ducats 1708. For Battle of Leesno	4500.00
80.	2 Ducats 1706. For Battle of Kalish...........	3500.00
81.	2 Ducats 1708. For Battle of Leesno	3500.00
82.	1 Ducat 1706. For Battle of Kalish..... *	3000.00
83.	1 Ducat 1708. For Battle of Leesno...... *	3000.00

Crown on cushion. Rev. Crown and legend. On the Coronation of Catherine I.

84.	1 Ducat 1724........................	1000.00

CATHERINE I, 1725-1727

Bust. Rev. St. Andrew.

85.	2 Roubles 1726, 27	2000.00

PETER II, 1727-1730

Bust. Rev. Eagle.

86.	1 Ducat 1729........................	2500.00

Crown on pedestal. Rev. Crown over legend. On his Coronation.

87.	1 Ducat 1728........................	1000.00

Bust. Rev. St. Andrew.

88.	2 Roubles 1727, 28	1500.00

ANNE, 1730-1740

Bust. Rev. Eagle.

89.	1½ Ducats 1738	Unique
90.	1 Ducat 1730, 38, 39 .... *	2500.00

Crown. Rev. Legend. On her Coronation.

91.	1 Ducat 1730........................	800.00

Crowned bust. Rev. Eagle and trophies. On the Peace with Turkey.

92.	1 Ducat 1739........................	750.00

Crowned bust. Rev. Legend. On her death.

93.	1 Ducat 1740........................	750.00

ELIZABETH, 1741-1762

Bust. Rev. St. Andrew.

94.	2 Ducats 1749, 51	1800.00
95.	1 Ducat 1749, 51-53	750.00

Bust. Rev. Eagle. The 5 Rouble piece is a pattern.

96.	2 Ducats 1749, 51	1750.00
97.	1 Ducat 1742-44, 46-49, 51-53, 55, 57 .. *	750.00
98.	5 Roubles 1755	5000.00
99.	2 Roubles 1756, 58	400.00
100.	1 Rouble 1756-58	250.00

Bust. Rev. Crowned initials.

101.	½ Rouble or Poltina 1756	200.00

Bust. Rev. Eagle to left on clouds. This issue was not placed in circulation.

102.	2 Roubles 1756	Rare
103.	1 Rouble 1756	2000.00

Bust. Rev. Cross of four shields.

104.	20 Roubles 1755	Unique
105.	10 Roubles 1755-59 .... *	2000.00
106.	10 Roubles 1757. Larger bust. Pattern	4000.00
107.	5 Roubles 1755-59	2000.00

Tomb. Rev. Crown over legend. On her death.

108.	1 Ducat 1761	750.00

PETER III, 1762

Bust. Rev. Cross of four shields.

109.	10 Roubles 1762	4000.00
110.	5 Roubles 1762 .... *	2500.00

Bust. Rev. Eagle.

111.	1 Ducat 1762	2000.00

CATHERINE II, THE GREAT, 1762-1796

Bust. Rev. Cross of four shields.

112.	10 Roubles 1762-83, 85-86, 95-96 .... *	900.00
113.	5 Roubles 1762-78, 80-86, 88-92, 94-96	700.00

Bust. Rev. Eagle.

114.	10 Ducats 1762	Rare
115.	2 Ducats 1796	2500.00
116.	1 Ducat 1763, 66, 96	800.00
117.	2 Roubles 1766, 85 .... *	450.00
118.	1 Rouble 1779	275.00

Bust. Rev. Crowned initials.

119.	½ Rouble or Poltina 1777, 78	200.00

Crown. Rev. Legend. On her Coronation.

120.	1 Ducat 1762	750.00

Bust. Rev. Flying eagle.

121.	1 Ducat 1766	600.00

Ceres seated. Rev. Caduceus. On the Peace with Turkey.

122.	1 Ducat 1774	750.00

Olive Branch. Rev. Legend. On the Peace with Sweden.

123.	1 Ducat 1790	750.00

Knight standing. Rev. Tablet. Dutch type (design similar to No. 124, which see). This coin repeats in detail the design of the Dutch Ducat and differs only in the mintmaster's sign. It was originally intended for use in foreign trade but gradually became current at home. First struck under Catherine II, it was issued for more than a century, during which the minting of it was the subject of great secrecy. It was last issued in 1868, when Dutch government protests brought an end to its mintage.

124.	1 Ducat 1768, 69, 81, 84-86, 91, 92	250.00

PAUL I, 1796-1801

Cross of four crowned initials. Rev. Tablet.

125.	5 Roubles 1798-1801 .... *	1000.00
126.	1 Ducat 1797	1500.00

Eagle. Rev. Tablet.

127.	1 Ducat 1796...........................	2000.00

Knight standing. Rev. Tablet. Dutch type (same type as No. 105a, which see).

128.	1 Ducat 1800, 01	250.00

ALEXANDER I, 1801-1825

Cross of four shields. Rev. Legend. The 10 and 5 Roubles of 1803 are unique.

129.	10 Roubles 1802-05, 09	*	2500.00
130.	10 Roubles 1806......................		Rare
131.	5 Roubles 1802-05		1200.00
132.	5 Roubles 1806......................		Unknown

Eagle. Rev. Legend in wreath.

133.	5 Roubles 1817-19, 22-25	325.00

Knight standing. Rev. Tablet. Dutch type (same type as No. 105a, which see).

134.	1 Ducat 1802, 03, 05, 06, 18	250.00

NICHOLAS I, 1825-1855

Conjoined busts of the Czar and Czarina. Rev. As indicated. These coins were not placed in circulation.

135.	10 Roubles 1836. Rev. Initials		4000.00
136.	10 Roubles 1836. Rev. Value and date. (36 struck)	*	8000.00

Eagle. Rev. Legend in four lines.

137.	5 Roubles 1826-31	250.00

Eagle. Rev. Value and date.

138.	5 Roubles 1832-55	*	200.00
139.	5 Roubles 1842-49. Warsaw mint..............		1200.00

Eagle. Rev. Value and date. With additional legend indicating gold from the Kolywan Mines.

140.	5 Roubles 1832.....................	2750.00

Eagle. Rev. Value and date.

141.	Platinum 12 Roubles 1830-45		5000.00
142.	Platinum 6 Roubles 1829-45		2500.00
143.	Platinum 3 Roubles 1828-45	*	500.00

Knight standing. Rev. Tablet. Dutch type (same type as No. 105a, which see). Coins bearing the date 1849 were struck until 1868.

144.	1 Ducat 1831, 49	200.00

ALEXANDER II, 1855-1881

Eagle. Rev. Value and date. The 25 Rouble piece was not placed in circulation.

145.	25 Roubles 1876......................		12000.00
146.	5 Roubles 1855-81	*	200.00
147.	3 Roubles 1869-81		375.00

ALEXANDER III, 1881-1894

Eagle. Rev. Value and date.

148.	5 Roubles 1881-85	*	150.00

149.   3 Roubles 1881-85 . . . .   375.00

Head. Rev. Eagle.

150.   10 Roubles 1886-94 . . . .   600.00
151.   5 Roubles 1886-94 . . . . * 135.00

NICHOLAS II, 1894-1917

*Head. Rev. Eagle in circle, legend around. These coins were
not placed in circulation. The numbers struck appear in parentheses.*

152.   37½ Roubles or 100 Francs 1902 (225) . . . . * 7500.00
153.   25 Roubles or 2½ Imperials 1896 (300), 98 (150)   6000.00
154.   15 Roubles or 1 Imperial 1895 (5). Pattern 8000.00
155.   10 Roubles or 1 Imperial 1895-97. Pattern   4000.00
156.   10 Roubles or ⅔ Imperial 1895 (5). Pattern 7000.00
157.   5 Roubles or ½ Imperial 1895 (36), 96 (33).
        Pattern . . . . * . . .   4000.00
158.   5 Roubles or ⅓ Imperial 1895 (5). Pattern 6000.00

Head. Rev. Eagle.

159.   15 Roubles 1897 . . . .   275.00
160.   7½ Roubles 1897 . . . .   175.00
161.   10 Roubles 1898-1904, 06, 09-11 . . . .   210.00(B)
162.   5 Roubles 1897-1904, 06-07, 09-11 . . . . * . . . .   100.00(B)

B. Soviet Union (U.S.S.R.) —

Sower scattering seed. Rev. Hammer and Sickle.

163.   10 Roubles or 1 Chervonetz 1923, 25 . . . .   400.00

(Numbers 161 and 162 are bullion coins. The price listed is based on gold
at $725 per ounce.)
(For later issues of the Soviet Union see the section, "Recent Issues Starting
With 1960," under "Russia."

SAINT MARTIN

*Gold coins of Brazil counterstamped on Obv. with "22" or
"20" (for karats), a small H and a small negro head.*

1.   6400 Reis 1727-1804 . . . . 10000.00

SAINT VINCENT

*Gold coins of Brazil counterstamped three times along the
outer edge of the Obv. with an S and usually with a
plugged hole in the center.*

1.   6400 Reis 1787-1804 . . . . 10000.00

SALVADOR

Liberty head. Rev. Arms.

1.   20   Pesos 1892 . . . .   4500.00
2.   10   Pesos 1892 . . . .   3000.00
3.   5   Pesos 1892 . . . . * 1500.00
4.   2½   Pesos 1892 . . . .   1500.00

*Conjoined heads of Alvarada (1525) and Quinonez (1925).
Rev. Arms. On the 400th year of Salvador.*

5.   20 Colones 1925 . . . .   4500.00

For later issues, see the section, "Recent Issues Starting With 1960."

SAN MARINO

St. Marinus standing. Rev. Three towers.

1.   20 Lire 1925 . . . .   2250.00
2.   10 Lire 1925 . . . .   1500.00

For later issues of San Marino, see the section, "Recent Issues
Starting With 1960."

SAUDI ARABIA

Arab legend in circle on each side.

1.   1 Saudi Pound 1370 A.H. (1951) 180.00

Palm tree over crossed swords. Rev. Value and date.
2.   1 Saudi Pound 1377 A.H. (1957-58)................. 180.00
(Note: For the gold coins struck at the Philadelphia Mint, see under United States of America, following the 50 Dollar gold pieces).

SCOTLAND

Kings of —

DAVID II, 1329-1371
Ruler in ship. Rev. Ornate cross.
1.   1 Noble ND .... Rare

ROBERT III, 1390-1406

Crowned shield. Rev. St. Andrew with long cross.
2.   1 Lion ND.. 2500.00
3.   ½ Lion ND.. Unknown

Crowned shield. Rev. St. Andrew with short cross.
4.   1 Lion ND.. 2750.00

Crowned shield. within border. Rev. St. Andrew with long cross.
5.   ½ Lion ND.. Unknown

Crowned shield. Rev. St. Andrew without cross.
6.   1 Lion ND.. 2500.00

Shield. Rev. Cross of St. Andrew.
7.   ½ Lion or Demy ND............................... 1750.00

JAMES I, 1406-1437

Lion in diamond shaped square. Rev. Cross of St. Andrew in border.
8.   1 Demy ND....................................... 1750.00
9.   ½ Demy ND................................*...... 2500.00

JAMES II, 1437-1460

Lion in diamond shaped square. Rev. Cross of St. Andrew in border.
10.   1 Demy ND....................................... 2250.00

Crowned shield. Rev. St. Andrew with cross.
11.   1 Lion ND.................................*..... 3000.00
12.   ½ Lion ND....................................... 4500.00

JAMES III, 1460-1488

Ruler on horse. Rev. Shield on long cross.
13.   1 Rider ND...............................*...... 2250.00
14.   ½ Rider ND...............................*...... 3500.00
15.   ¼ Rider ND..................................... 3500.00

Unicorn. Rev. Star with wavy rays.
16.   1 Unicorn ND.............................*...... 3500.00
17.   ½ Unicorn ND................................... Unknown

JAMES IV, 1488-1513

Unicorn. Rev. Star with wavy rays.
18.   1 Unicorn ND.............................*...... 3000.00
19.   ½ Unicorn ND............................*....... 3000.00

Crowned shield. Rev. St. Andrew with cross.
20.   1 Lion ND................................*...... 3500.00
21.   ½ Lion ND....................................... 4500.00

JAMES V, 1513-1542

Unicorn. Rev. Star.
22.   1 Unicorn ND.............................*...... 2500.00
23.   ½ Unicorn ND................................... 3000.00

Shield and value. Rev. Cross with thistles in angles.
24.   20 Shillings or 1 Crown. ND 2500.00

Bust with hat. Rev. Arms.
25.   1 Ducat or Bonnet piece 1539, 40 . . . . * 5500.00
26.   ⅔ Ducat or Bonnet piece 1540 . . . .   5500.00
27.   ⅓ Ducat or Bonnet piece 1540 . . . .   Rare

MARY, 1542-1567

Crowned shield. Rev. Floriated cross.
28.   1 Crown ND 3500.00

Crowned shield. Rev. Crown over MR or Maria monogram.
29.   20 Shillings 1543 . . . . * 4500.00
30.   1 Lion or 44 Shillings 1553 . . . .   3500.00
31.   ½ Lion or 22 Shillings 1553 . . . . * 3500.00

Crowned shield between M and R. Rev. Crown over Maria monogram.
32.   1 Lion 1557 . . . .   Rare

Bust. Rev. Crowned shield.
33.   3 Pounds or 1 Ryal 1555, 57, 58 . . . . * 7000.00
34.   1½ Pounds or ½ Ryal 1555, 57, 58 . . . .   7000.00

*Busts of Mary and Francis of France facing each other.
Rev. Floriated cross.*
35.   1 Ducat or 60 Shillings 1558 . . . .   Rare

Shield. Rev. Cross of four crowned M's.
36.   1 Crown 1561 . . . .   Unique

JAMES VI, 1567-1625

Half length figure. Rev. Shield.
37.   20 Pounds 1575, 76 . . . .   Rare

Youthful bust. Rev. Shield between divided date.
38.   1 Ducat 1580 . . . .   6750.00

Lion holding sword and sceptre. Rev. Cross of four IR's.
39.   1 Lion Noble 1584, 85, 86, 88 . . . .   6750.00
40.   ⅔ Lion Noble 1584, 85, 87 . . . . * 6750.00
41.   ⅓ Lion Noble 1584 . . . .   Rare

Shield on ship. Rev. Cross in embellished border.
42.   1 Thistle Noble ND 4000.00

Bust with high hat. Rev. Seated lion.

43.   1 Hat Piece 1591-93 .... 6750.00

Ruler on horse. Rev. Crowned shield.

44.   1 Rider 1593, 94, 95, 98, 99, 1601 ....*...... 2250.00
45.   ½ Rider 1593, 94, 95, 98, 99, 1601 .... 2250.00

Sword and sceptre. Rev. Crowned shield.

46.   1 Sword and Sceptre Piece 1601-04 ....*...... 1000.00
47.   ½ Sword and Sceptre Piece 1601-04 .... 1000.00

Crowned bust with orb and sceptre. Rev. Arms.

48.   1 Unite (20 Shillings or 1 Sceptre) ND 2500.00

Crowned bust. Rev. Arms.

49.   2 Crowns or ½ Unite ND 1250.00
50.   1 Britain Crown ND ....*...... 1000.00
51.   ½ Crown ND ....*...... 1000.00

Crowned rose. Rev. Crowned thistle.

52.   1 Thistle Crown ND 850.00

CHARLES I, 1625-1649

Crowned bust of Charles with orb and sceptre. Rev. Arms.

53.   1 Unite ND.............................. 2250.00

Crowned bust of Charles. Rev. Arms.

54.   2 Crowns or ½ Unite ND....................*...... 3500.00
55.   1 Britain Crown ND............................... Very Rare

*Crowned bust of Charles with orb and sceptre. Rev. Arms.
Briot's coinage.*

56.   1 Unite ND... 2750.00

Crowned bust of Charles. Rev. Arms. Briot's coinage.

57.   2 Crowns or ½ Unite ND....................*...... 3000.00
58.   1 Britain Crown ND............................... 3500.00
59.   ½ Britain Crown ND............................... 3000.00

WILLIAM II (III OF ENGLAND), 1694-1702

Bust with small rising sun below. Rev. Arms.

60.   1 Pistole 1701 ....*...... 5500.00
61.   ½ Pistole 1701 .... 5500.00

SERBIA

19th century Serbian coinage is based on the Latin Monetary Union standard.

Kings of —

STEPHAN DUSHAN, 1331-1355
Standing royal couple. Rev. Christ seated.

1. 3 Ducats ND .... Rare

STEPHAN UROSH, 1346-1370
Ruler on horse. Rev. Helmet and insignia.

2. 1 Solidus or Ducat ND 6000.00

MILAN OBRENOVICH IV, 1868-1889

Head by Tasset with full title in legend. Rev. Value.

3. 20 Dinars 1879...................................... 285.00

New head by Scharff with short title. Rev. Value.

4. 20 Dinars 1882...................................... 175.00
5. 10 Dinars 1882...................................... 140.00

SIAM (Thailand)

Kings of —

A. Gold Bullet Money of the Bangkok Dynasty

A roughly round shaped piece of gold, a portion of which dimples back on itself. The clear portion of the "Bullet" bears a mark which has been counterstamped on it and identifies it. The various marks used by the respective Kings are described below. These issues are without dates.

PRA NANG KLAO, 1824-1851
Palace mark (A crude gateway).

1. 1 Tical... 525.00
2. ⅛ Tical... 275.00
3. ¹⁄₁₆ Tical... 225.00

Crude flower mark.

4. ⅛ Tical... 225.00

Three leaves of the bale-fruit tree.

5. ⅛ Tical... 225.00

MONGKUT, 1851-1868
Marks of the Chakra and the Siamese Crown.

6. 4 Ticals 600.00
7. 2 Ticals 450.00
8. 1 Tical... 400.00
9. ½ Tical... 200.00
10. ¼ Tical... 150.00
11. 1½ Ticals. Elliptical shape......................... 135.00

Waterpot mark.

12. ¼ Tical... 900.00
13. ⅛ Tical... 135.00
14. ¹⁄₁₆ Tical... 125.00

B. Conventional or Standard Gold Coins

The conventional or standard gold coins are of far greater scarcity than the earlier bullet money.

FIRST ISSUE OF MONGKUT (1863)

Crown between umbrellas with a few leaf scrolls in the field. Rev. Elephant in beaded circle within a chakra with narrow spokes.

15. 8 Ticals ND................................. * 725.00
16. 4 Ticals ND................................. * 400.00
17. 2 Ticals ND 300.00

SECOND ISSUE OF MONGKUT (1864)

Crown between umbrellas with flamboyant leaves in the field. Rev. Elephant in ornamental circle within a chakra with wide spokes. The coins of this issue are the same size as the corresponding silver coins of these values.

17a. 4 Ticals ND .... Rare
18. 2 Ticals ND................................. * 7500.00
19. 1 Tical ND 2000.00
20. ½ Tical ND 1500.00
21. ¼ Tical ND 650.00
22. ⅛ Tical ND 450.00
23. ¹⁄₁₆ Tical ND 425.00

MISCELLANEOUS ISSUES OF MONGKUT
Large crown between flower sprays. Rev. Legend.

24. 2 Ticals ND .... Rare

Chakra over crown flanked by waterpots. Rev. Blank.

25. 2 Ticals ND .... Rare

CHULALONGKORN, 1868-1910

Bust. Rev. Crown and umbrellas.

26. 2 Ticals ND 250.00

For later issues, see under Thailand in the section, "Recent Issues Starting With 1960."

SOUTH AFRICA

Only 837 specimens were struck of the Burgers Pound of 1874. The ½ Pound of 1893 is very rare, as are also the English type Pounds and ½ Pounds of 1923 and 1924. South Africa became a republic in 1961 and adopted the decimal system for its coinage. The 2 Rand denomination is equivalent to the Pound.

A. Presidents of —

Head of Thomas Francois Burgers. Rev. Arms.

1.　1 Pound 1874......................... 5250.00

Head of Krueger. Rev. Arms.

2.　1 Pound 1892-1900.........................*...... 150.00
3.　½ Pound 1892-97................................ 125.00

ZAR in script letters. Rev. EEN POND. The so-called Veld Pound struck at Pilgrims Rest.

4.　1 Pound 1902...................................... 2250.00

B. British Sovereigns of —

GEORGE V, 1910-1936

Head. Rev. St. George. This is the same type as the English Pound but with the distinguishing South African mint mark SA on ground below horse.

5.　1 Pound 1923-32.................................. 200.00(B)
6.　½ Pound 1923-26.................................. 200.00

GEORGE VI, 1937-1952

Head. Rev. Springbok.

7.　1 Pound 1952. Proof............................... 225.00
8.　½ Pound 1952. Proof.............................. 200.00

(Number 5 is a bullion coin. The price listed is based on gold at $725 per ounce.)

ELIZABETH II, 1952-1960

Head. Rev. Springbok.

9.　1 Pound 1953-60. Proof........................... 225.00
10.　½ Pound 1953-60. Proof.......................... 200.00

For later issues of South Africa, see the section, "Recent Issues Starting With 1960."

SPAIN

Mints and mint marks:—

B, Ba, BA or 8-pointed star	mm for Barcelona
B or Bo	mm for Burgos
C crowned	mm for Cadiz
C plain	mm for Catalonia
Ca, CA or cup	mm for Cuenca
G	mm for Granada
M, MD, M crowned or 6-pointed star	mm for Madrid
M, PM or diamond	mm for Majorca
PA or PP	mm for Pamplona
S or 7-pointed star	mm for Seville
T, To or TOLE	mm for Toledo
V or VA	mm for Valencia
V or VD	mm for Valladolid
Z or CA	mm for Zaragoza
Aqueduct	mm for Segovia

Geographically, Spanish coinage is the most universal in the annals of world numismatics. At one time or another, Spain had control over much of the world and her coinage followed the course of empire. The Spanish series is, therefore, the most far flung of all national coinages, extending beyond the borders of Continental Spain into the following areas:

Europe: Portugal; Belgium (see Brabant and Flanders); France (see Besancon, Dole, Navarre, Provence and Rousillon); Italy (see Cagliari, Messina, Milan and Naples); Netherlands (see Gelderland, Holland, and United Provinces).

America: Bolivia, Chile, Colombia, Guatemala, Mexico and Peru.

Orient: Philippine Islands.

The Spanish and Spanish-American gold Doubloon was the most popular coin of its day. Most of the coinage was struck from gold mined in the American colonies.

After the Escudo-Real standard was abandoned about 1850, Spain adopted the Latin Monetary Union standard and the first coin on the new standard was struck in 1869.

(The Houses of Castile and Leon)

A. Kings of —

ALFONSO VIII, 1158-1214

Arab legend on each side with the addition of "ALF" on Obv. Struck in the style of the Arab Dinars of the period.

1.　1 Maravedi ND 1750.00

ALFONSO X, 1252-1284

Castle. Rev. Lion.

2.	1 Dobla ND..	2500.00

ALFONSO XI, 1312-1350
Castle. Rev. Lion.

3.	1 Dobla of 20 Maravedis ND	3000.00

PETER I, 1350-1369

Crowned bust. Rev. Arms.

4.	12 Doblas ND		Rare
5.	10 Doblas ND		Rare
6.	1 Dobla of 35 Maravedis ND	*	2500.00
7.	20 Maravedis ND.................................		2000.00

Castle. Rev. Lion.

8.	1 Dobla ND...............................	3000.00
9.	15 Maravedis ND...........................	2000.00

HENRY II, 1368-1379

Ruler on horse. Rev. Arms.

10.	1 Dobla of 35 Maravedis ND	3250.00

HENRY III, 1390-1406
Castle. Rev. Lion.

11.	1 Dobla of 20 Maravedis ND	2700.00

JOHN II, 1406-1454

Shield. Rev. Arms.

12.	1 Dobla de la Banda ND..........................	1250.00

HENRY IV, 1454-1474
Castle. Rev. Lion.

13.	1 Castellano ND.............................	2000.00
14.	½ Castellano ND	1750.00

Ruler on throne. Rev. Arms.

15.	5 Enriques or 5 Doblas ND		Rare
16.	1 Enrique or Dobla ND	*	2500.00
17.	½ Enrique or ½ Dobla ND.................		1250.00

Shield. Rev. Arms.

18.	1 Dobla de la Banda ND.......................	3000.00

ALFONSO DE AVILA, 1465-1468
Ruler on horse. Rev. Arms.

19.	1 Dobla ND.....................................	2250.00
20.	½ Dobla ND....................................	2000.00

FERDINAND V AND ISABELLA I, 1476-1516

Crowned busts facing each other. Rev. Arms on eagle.

21.	50 Excelentes ND. Seville		Very Rare
22.	20 Excelentes ND. Seville		20000.00
23.	10 Excelentes ND. Seville or Segovia..........	*	12000.00
24.	4 Excelentes ND. Burgos	*	8000.00
25.	4 Excelentes ND. Segovia		3500.00
25a.	4 Excelentes ND. Seville		5000.00
26.	2 Excelentes ND. Burgos		1000.00
27.	2 Excelentes ND. Granada		1400.00
28.	2 Excelentes ND. Seville		950.00
29.	2 Excelentes ND. Toledo	*	1000.00
30.	2 Excelentes ND. Segovia		1100.00
31.	2 Excelentes ND. Cuenca....................		2100.00

Crowned busts facing each other. Rev. Arms without eagle.

32.	1 Excelente ND. Burgos		2000.00
33.	1 Excelente ND. Cuenca.........................		2000.00
34.	1 Excelente ND. Granada		950.00
35.	1 Excelente ND. Seville.....................	*	900.00
36.	1 Excelente ND. Toledo		1500.00
36a.	1 Excelente ND. Segovia		1750.00
37.	1 Castellano ND. Seville........................		1750.00
38.	1 Castellano ND. Toledo		1100.00
38a.	1 Castellano ND. Segovia.......................		950.00
39.	½ Castellano ND. Seville........................		1200.00
40.	½ Castellano ND. Toledo		950.00
40a.	½ Castellano ND. Segovia.......................		1500.00
41.	1 Ducat ND. Seville.............................		600.00

Crowned figures seated on thrones. Rev. Two shields on eagle.

42.	4 Ducats (Double Castellano) ND. Seville	7500.00

Crowned F. Rev. Crowned Y.

43.	½ Excelente ND. Burgos	1800.00
43a.	½ Excelente ND. Granada	800.00
44.	½ Excelente ND. Seville	800.00
44a.	½ Excelente ND. Toledo	1100.00

CHARLES I AND JOHANNA, 1516-1556

Crowned arms. Rev. Cross.

44b.	1 Escudo ND. Cuenca	*	1500.00
45.	1 Escudo ND. Seville		375.00
45a.	1 Escudo ND. Toledo		500.00
46.	1 Escudo ND. Segovia		800.00
46a.	1 Escudo ND. Burgos	*	2500.00

PHILIP II, 1556-1598

Crowned arms. Rev. Cross. With or without poorly showing dates.

47.	4 Escudos 1589, 91, 93, ND. Seville. Cob Type *	600.00
48.	4 Escudos 1591, 92, ND. Madrid. Cob type	3500.00
48a.	4 Escudos ND. Burgos. Cob type	3000.00
49.	4 Escudos 1597. Barcelona. Modern style	3500.00
49a.	4 Escudos 1587. Segovia. Modern style	4000.00
49b.	4 Escudos ND. Toledo. Cob type	1200.00
49c.	4 Escudos ND. Valladolid. Cob type	3500.00
50.	2 Escudos ND. Burgos. Cob type	800.00
50a.	2 Escudos ND. Cuenca. Cob type	1400.00
51.	2 Escudos 1591. Madrid. Modern style	1400.00
52.	2 Escudos ND. Granada. Cob type	800.00
53.	2 Escudos 1588-97, ND. Seville. Cob type	500.00
54.	2 Escudos 1590-97, ND. Toledo. Cob type	350.00
54a.	2 Escudos ND. Valladolid. Cob type	1200.00
54b.	2 Escudos 1597. ND. Segovia. Cob type	1400.00
54c.	2 Escudos 1587. Segovia. Modern style	3500.00
55.	1 Escudo ND. Granada. Cob type	800.00
55a.	1 Escudo ND. Toledo. Cob type	700.00
56.	1 Escudo 1570, 90, 95, ND. Seville	400.00
56a.	1 Escudo ND, Segovia	1200.00

PHILIP III, 1598-1621

Arms. Rev. Cross. The cobs with or without poorly showing dates.

57.	100 Escudos 1609, 18. Segovia	Very Rare
58.	8 Escudos 1613, Seville. Cob type	3000.00
59.	8 Escudos 1610, 11, 14, 15, Segovia. Modern style	4500.00
59a.	8 Escudos 1615. Segovia. Cob type	4000.00
60.	8 Escudos 1615. Toledo. Cob type	4000.00
61.	4 Escudos 1613, 15. Seville. Cob type	2250.00
62.	4 Escudos 1607, 08, 11, Segovia. Modern style	4000.00
62a.	4 Escudos 1615. Segovia. Cob type	1100.00
62b.	4 Escudos 1615. Toledo. Cob type	1500.00
63.	2 Escudos 1601, 10-13, 17, 19, 20. Seville. Cob type	700.00
64.	2 Escudos 1607, 10. Segovia. Modern style	1500.00
64a.	2 Escudos 1615. Segovia. Cob type	700.00
65.	2 Escudos 1615, 16, 20. Madrid. Cob type	900.00
65a.	2 Escudos 1603, 14. Toledo. Cob type	700.00

66.	1 Escudo 1607, 08. Segovia. Modern style	*	900.00
67.	1 Escudo 1615. Segovia. Cob type		950.00
67a.	1 Escudo 1610. Seville. Cob type		350.00

Crowned arms. Rev. Cross with castles and lions in the angles. Struck from dies used for the silver 50 Real coin.

68.	Gold 50 Reales 1620. Segovia	Rare

PHILIP IV, 1621-1665

Arms. Rev. Cross. The cobs with or without poorly showing dates.

69.	100 Escudos 1623, 31, 33, 38, 59, 61. Segovia	Very Rare
70.	8 Escudos 1630, 62, ND. Madrid. Cob type	2500.00
71.	8 Escudos 1627-65. Seville. Cob type	1650.00
72.	8 Escudos 1627-55. Segovia. Modern style *	Rare
73.	4 Escudos 1631-51, ND. Madrid. Cob type	1000.00
74.	4 Escudos 1630-47. Seville. Cob type	850.00
74a.	4 Escudos 1651, 59. Segovia. Cob type	2000.00
75.	4 Escudos 1655. Segovia. Modern style	3000.00
75a.	2 Escudos 1625, 28, 51, 61. Madrid. Cob type	1000.00
76.	2 Escudos 1621, 61. Seville. Cob type	500.00
76a.	2 Escudos 1628-33. Cuenca. Cob type	900.00
77.	2 Escudos 1653, 56, Barcelona. Cob type	2500.00
78.	2 Escudos 1651-52. Segovia. Modern style	2500.00
79.	1 Escudo 1636. Madrid. Cob type	700.00
80.	1 Escudo 1627-28, 39. Segovia. Cob type	500.00

Crowned chain arms. Rev. Cross.

80a.	8 Escudos 1652. Pamplona	Rare

Bust. Rev. Chain arms.

80b.	4 Escudos ND. Pamplona	3500.00

Crowned arms. Rev. Cross with castles and lions in the angles. Struck from dies used for the silver 50 Real coin.

81.	Gold 50 Reales 1626. Segovia	Rare

CHARLES II, 1665-1700

Arms. Rev. Cross. The cobs with or without poorly showing dates.

82.	8 Escudos 1697, 99. Barcelona. Cob type	Rare
83.	8 Escudos 1666, 68, 85, 93. Poorly dated. Madrid. Cob type	Rare
84.	8 Escudos 1668-99. Seville. Cob type	3000.00
85.	8 Escudos 1699, 1700. Seville. Modern style	3000.00
86.	8 Escudos 1682-88. Segovia. Modern style *	2500.00
86a.	8 Escudos 1688. Toledo. Cob type	Rare
86b.	4 Escudos 1676, 79, 97, 99. Barcelona. Cob type	2600.00
87.	4 Escudos 1661, 65. Poorly dated. Madrid. Cob type	1500.00
87a.	4 Escudos 1667, 88. Seville. Cob type	1400.00
88.	4 Escudos 1699, 1700. Seville. Modern style	1400.00
89.	4 Escudos 1683, 86-87, 99, 1700. Segovia. Modern style	1750.00
89a.	2 Escudos 1683, 93. Madrid. Cob type	3000.00
90.	2 Escudos 1688-90, 99. Seville. Cob type	1750.00

91.	2 Escudos 1683. Segovia. Modern style.............	3500.00
92.	1 Escudo 1689-90. Madrid. Cob type................	2500.00
93.	1 Escudo 1672, 87, 99, 1700. Seville. Cob type.....	1350.00
94.	1 Escudo 1674, 79, 83. Segovia. Modern style	3500.00

PHILIP V, 1700-1746

Bust with long hair. Rev. Arms.

95.	8 Escudos 1728-30. Madrid	Rare
96.	8 Escudos 1729-38. Seville...................*	7500.00
97.	4 Escudos 1732-34. Madrid	3500.00
98.	4 Escudos 1729-33. Seville......................	9000.00
99.	2 Escudos 1729-34. Madrid	1000.00
100.	2 Escudos 1730-42. Seville..................*	1400.00
101.	1 Escudo 1729-42. Madrid......................	500.00
102.	1 Escudo 1729-33. Seville......................	700.00
103.	½ Escudo 1738-46. Madrid.....................	200.00
104.	½ Escudo 1738-46. Seville.....................	150.00

Arms. Rev. Cross. The cobs with or without poorly showing dates.

104a.	8 Escudos 1701. Burgos. Cob type	7000.00
104b.	8 Escudos 1701. Barcelona. Cob type............	7000.00
105.	8 Escudos 1719-27. Madrid	Rare
106.	8 Escudos 1703-19. Poorly dated. Madrid. Cob type.	2000.00
107.	8 Escudos 1708-23. Segovia	Rare
108.	8 Escudos 1701-29. Seville..................*	6000.00
109.	4 Escudos 1710, 19, 23, 27. Madrid	9000.00
110.	4 Escudos 1701-29. Seville.....................	10000.00
111.	4 Escudos 1725. Cuenca.......................	Rare
111a.	4 Escudos 1721. Segovia......................	Rare
112.	4 Escudos 1707. Valencia......................	7500.00
113.	2 Escudos 1707. Valencia......................	2900.00
114.	2 Escudos 1711, 23. Madrid...................	2600.00
115.	2 Escudos 1701-26. Seville....................	1600.00
116.	2 Escudos 1719. Seville. Cob type...............	Unknown
117.	1 Escudo 1719, 21, 23, 27, 28. Madrid............	600.00
118.	1 Escudo 1701-23. Seville.....................	700.00
119.	1 Escudo 1729. Madrid. Cob type.................	400.00

LOUIS I, 1724

Arms. Rev. Cross.

120.	8 Escudos 1724. Segovia	Rare
121.	4 Escudos 1724. Segovia ....* ...	Rare
122.	2 Escudos 1724. Seville. Cob type................	Unknown
123.	2 Escudos 1724. Seville. Modern style.............	3500.00

FERDINAND VI, 1746-1759

Bust. Rev. Arms.

124.	8 Escudos 1747, 48. Seville........................	8000.00
125.	8 Escudos 1747, 49, 50. Madrid....................	8000.00
126.	4 Escudos 1748. Madrid ....*	4500.00
126a.	4 Escudos 1747, 49. Seville......................	7500.00
127.	2 Escudos 1749. Madrid	3000.00

Plain head. Rev. Arms.

128.	2 Escudos 1749. Seville	2000.00
129.	½ Escudo 1746-59. Madrid.......................	175.00
130.	½ Escudo 1746-59. Seville...................*	125.00

Arms. Rev. Cross. Cob type.

| 131. | 8 Escudos 1752, 55. Seville........................ | Unknown |
| 132. | 2 Escudos 1751, 54. Seville....................... | Unknown |

CHARLES III, 1759-1788

Bust or plain head. Rev. Arms.

| 133. | ½ Escudo 1759-71. Madrid...................* ...... | 150.00 |
| 134. | ½ Escudo 1759-71. Seville....................... | 125.00 |

Young bust. Rev. Arms.

| 135. | 8 Escudos 1760. Madrid .... | Rare |
| 136. | 4 Escudos 1761. Madrid .... | Rare |

Older bust. Rev. Arms.

137.	8 Escudos 1771-88. Madrid ....*	3750.00
138.	8 Escudos 1762-88. Seville...................*	2500.00
139.	4 Escudos 1772-88. Madrid	500.00
140.	4 Escudos 1772-88. Seville......................	500.00
141.	2 Escudos 1772-88. Madrid	250.00
142.	2 Escudos 1773-77, 79, 87, 88. Seville..............	275.00
143.	1 Escudo 1772-88. Madrid......................	100.00
144.	1 Escudo 1773-87. Seville.....................	125.00
145.	½ Escudo 1772-88. Madrid.....................	150.00
146.	½ Escudo 1773-88. Seville......................	100.00

CHARLES IV, 1788-1808

Bust. Rev. Arms.

147.	8 Escudos 1788-1805. Madrid	2000.00
147a.	8 Escudos 1790, 91. Seville...............	Rare
148.	4 Escudos 1788-1803. Madrid ......*	750.00
148a.	4 Escudos 1801, 08. Seville.............	5000.00
149.	2 Escudos 1788-1808. Madrid	250.00
150.	2 Escudos 1790-1808. Seville	300.00
151.	1 Escudo 1788-1807	100.00
152.	½ Escudo 1788-96. Madrid...........	1200.00

JOSEPH NAPOLEON BONAPARTE, 1808-1814

Head. Rev. Arms. All with M mm.

153.	320 Reales 1810, 12. Laureate head ....*	Rare
154.	80 Reales 1809, 10. Plain head............	1000.00
155.	80 Reales 1811, 12, 13. Laureate head	900.00

FERDINAND VII, 1808-1833

Broad draped bust. Rev. Arms.

156.	2 Escudos 1808, 09. Seville..........	350.00
156a.	2 Escudos 1811. Cadiz	1250.00

Draped laureate bust. Rev. Arms.

157.	8 Escudos 1811. Cadiz..............	6000.00
158.	2 Escudos 1811. Cadiz.............*	700.00
159.	2 Escudos 1813. Madrid	450.00
160.	2 Escudos 1809. Seville	400.00

Laureate bust with high collar. Rev. Arms.

161.	2 Escudos 1812-14. Madrid	800.00

Plain or laureate head. Rev. Arms. The large plain C mm. is for Catalonia. The small crowned C mm. is for Cadiz.

162.	8 Escudos 1813, 14. Catalonia...........	12000.00
163.	8 Escudos 1814-20. Madrid	2500.00
164.	4 Escudos 1814-24. Madrid ......*	900.00
165.	2 Escudos 1811-14. Cadiz...........	400.00
166.	2 Escudos 1811-14. Catalonia........	3500.00
167.	2 Escudos 1814-33. Madrid	500.00
168.	2 Escudos 1815-33. Seville..........	400.00
169.	1 Escudo 1817. Madrid	1000.00
170.	½ Escudo 1817. Madrid	125.00

Plain older head. Rev. Arms.

171.	320 Reales 1822, 23. Madrid	3750.00
172.	160 Reales 1822. Madrid ....*	1500.00
173.	80 Reales 1822, 23. Madrid	700.00
174.	80 Reales 1822, 23. Barcelona	700.00
175.	80 Reales 1823. Seville	1600.00

ISABELLA II, 1833-1868

Head right with hair combed up. Rev. Arms.

176.	80 Reales 1836-48. Barcelona ......*	500.00
177.	80 Reales 1834-48. Madrid	500.00
178.	80 Reales 1836-48. Seville	500.00

Head left with hair combed down. Rev. Arms.

179.	1 Doblon or 100 Reales 1850, 51. Madrid ...*	550.00
180.	1 Doblon or 100 Reales 1850. Barcelona	2500.00
180a.	1 Doblon or 100 Reales 1850, Seville	3000.00

Head left with hair combed down. Rev. Arms in palms.

181.	100 Reales 1854, 55.................	800.00

Draped laureate bust. Rev. Arms in palms.

182.	100 Reales 1856-62	.........................*	350.00
183.	40 Reales 1861-63	....	200.00
184.	20 Reales 1861-63	....	200.00

Draped laureate bust. Rev. Draped arms. The 10 Escudos value is equal in size and weight to the 100 Reales value.

185.	100 Reales 1863-64	....	300.00
186.	40 Reales 1864	....	200.00
187.	10 Escudos 1865-68	..........................*	250.00
188.	4 Escudos 1865-68	....	175.00
189.	2 Escudos 1865	....	250.00

PROVISIONAL GOVERNMENT, 1870

Hispania standing. Rev. Arms.

190.	100 Pesetas 1870	....	Rare

AMADEO I, 1871-1873

Head. Rev. Arms.

191.	100 Pesetas 1871	...............................*	Rare
192.	25 Pesetas 1871	....	Rare

ALFONSO XII, 1874-1885

Young head. Rev. Arms.

†193.	25 Pesetas 1876-81	....	300.00
†194.	10 Pesetas 1878, 79 (1879 rare)	....	350.00

†Note: There are official government restrikes of these coins with the dates 19-61 and 19-62 in the small stars on the obverse. These will be found under Spain in the section, "Recent Issues Starting With 1960."

Older bearded head. Rev. Arms.

195.	25 Pesetas 1881-85	....	300.00

ALFONSO XIII, 1886-1931

Large baby head. Rev. Arms.

†196.	20 Pesetas 1889, 90	....	350.00

Child head with curly hair. Rev. Arms.

197.	20 Pesetas 1892	....	3250.00

Juvenile head. Rev. Arms.

†198.	100 Pesetas 1897	....	2750.00
†199.	20 Pesetas 1899	...............................*	600.00

Uniformed bust. Rev. Arms.

200.	20 Pesetas 1904	....	5000.00

B. Cities and Kingdoms of —

ARAGON

Kings of —

PETER IV, 1336-1387

St. John standing. Rev. Lily.

201.	1 Florin ND.........................*......	350.00
202.	½ Florin ND...........................	500.00
203.	¼ Florin ND...........................	500.00

JOHN I, 1387-1396
St. John standing. Rev. Lily.

204.	1 Florin ND...........................	300.00
205.	½ Florin ND...........................	450.00

MARTIN, 1396-1410
St. John standing. Rev. Lily.

206.	1 Florin ND...........................	300.00
207.	½ Florin ND...........................	600.00

FERDINAND I, 1412-1416
St. John standing. Rev. Lily.

208.	1 Florin ND...........................	600.00
209.	½ Florin ND...........................	700.00

ALFONSO V, 1416-1458
St. John standing. Rev. Lily.

210.	1 Florin ND...........................	450.00
211.	½ Florin ND...........................	500.00

JOHN II, 1458-1479
Crowned bust. Rev. Shield and dragon.

212.	1 Timbre ND	Rare

Crowned bust. Rev. Crowned arms.

213.	1 Escudo ND	2000.00
214.	¼ Escudo ND	1000.00

FERDINAND II AND ISABELLA, 1479-1504
Crowned heads facing each other. Rev. Arms.

214a.	1 Ducat ND. Zaragoza	1100.00

FERDINAND II (FERDINAND V OF SPAIN), 1479-1516

Crowned bust. Rev. Crowned arms.

215.	4 Ducats ND. Bust left	4000.00
216.	2 Ducats ND. Bust left	2000.00
217.	1 Ducat ND. Bust right ....*......	1200.00

CHARLES AND JOHANNA, 1516-1555

Crowned busts facing each other. Rev. Arms.

217a.	100 Ducats 1528 ....Very Rare
218.	50 Ducats 1520 ....Rare
219.	20 Ducats 1520 ....10000.00
220.	2 Ducats ND ....*...... 2700.00

Arms. Rev. Value. Siege coin of the Napoleonic Wars.

221.	20 Pesetas 1812-14	1500.00

CATALONIA

Barcelona Mint

Princes of —

BERENGUER RAMON I, 1018-1035
Arab legend in circle within Latin legend. Rev. Arab legend.

222.	1 Mancuso ND	2000.00

PEDRO OF PORTUGAL, 1464-1466
Crowned bust facing. Rev. Arms.

223.	1 Pacifico or Ducat ND..........................	2200.00
224.	½ Pacifico or ½ Ducat ND	2200.00

RENE OF ANJOU, 1466-1472

Crowned bust facing. Rev. Arms.

225.	1 Pacifico or Ducat ND......................*......	3500.00
226.	½ Pacifico or ½ Ducat ND	2500.00
227.	¼ Pacifico or ¼ Ducat ND	1000.00

FERDINAND II (FERDINAND V OF SPAIN), 1479-1516

Crowned bust. Rev. Arms.

228.	4 Principats or 4 Ducats ND......................	4000.00
229.	2 Principats or 2 Ducats ND......................	1750.00
230.	1 Principat or Ducat ND....................*.....	750.00
231.	½ Principat or ½ Ducat ND......................	600.00

St. John. Rev. Lily.

231a.	1 Florin ND......................................	750.00

CHARLES AND JOHANNA, 1516-1555

Crowned busts facing each other. Rev. Arms.

232.	2 Principats 1521, 31, 32, ND	Rare

Initials I and C in circle. Rev. Arms.

233.	½ Principat ND	2000.00

PHILIP II, 1556-1598
Cross of Jerusalem. Rev. Arms.

233a.	4 Escudos 1597. Barcelona	Rare

PHILIP III, 1598-1621

Bust. Rev. Arms.

234.	⅓ Trentin 1618	750.00

Busts of Ferdinand and Isabella facing each other. Rev. Arms.

234a.	5 Trentines ND	Rare

PHILIP IV, 1621-1665
Bust. Rev. Arms.

235.	⅓ Trentin 1625	800.00

Busts of Ferdinand and Isabella facing each other. Rev. Arms. Struck under Philip III and Philip IV.

236.	1 Trentin 1622-32, ND	2500.00
237.	½ Trentin 1626, 30, 41, ND . . . .*	1200.00

LOUIS XIII OF FRANCE (COUNT OF BARCELONA), 1641-1643
Laureate head. Rev. Cross of eight L's. Issued during French rule in Catalonia.

237a.	2 Escudos 1642	Rare

PRIVATE ISSUE, 1900
Empty throne. Rev. St. George slaying dragon. Private contribution coins without denomination but corresponding to the contemporary Spanish gold coins.

238.	(100 Pesetas) 1900	—
239.	(20 Pesetas) 1900	—

LEON

Kings of —

FERDINAND II, 1157-1188
Crowned bust. Rev. Lion and globe.

240.	1 Maravedi ND	4000.00

ALFONSO IX, 1188-1230

Crowned bust. Rev. Lion walking.

241.	1 Maravedi Alfonsi ND	3000.00

MAJORCA

Kings of —

PETER IV, 1343-1387

Ruler on throne. Rev. Cross potent.

242.	1 Gold Real ND . . . .*	2000.00
243.	½ Gold Real ND	1500.00
244.	¼ Gold Real ND	1000.00
245.	⅛ Gold Real ND	750.00

FERDINAND II (FERDINAND V OF SPAIN), 1479-1516

Bust. Rev. Arms.

246.	1 Ducat ND . . . .*	850.00
246a.	½ Ducat ND	850.00

CHARLES I, 1516-1556

Bust. Rev. Arms.

247.	1 Ducat ND	600.00

Bust. Rev. Square shield.

247a.	½ Ducat ND	750.00

PHILIP II, 1556-1598
Arms. Rev. Square shield.

247b.	2 Escudos ND	1000.00
247c.	1 Escudo ND	1000.00

PHILIP III, 1598-1621

Arms. Rev. Square shield.

248.	4 Escudos ND	3000.00
249.	2 Escudos ND . . . .*	1500.00
250.	1 Escudo ND	Unknown

PHILIP IV, 1621-1665
Arms. Rev. Square shield.

251.	4 Escudos 1648	2000.00

Crowned bust. Rev. Arms.

252.	2 Ducats ND	Unknown

CHARLES II, 1665-1700

Arms. Rev. Square shield.

252a.	8 Escudos 1689		7000.00
253.	4 Escudos 1698............................ *		4000.00
254.	2 Escudos 1678, 89, 98..........................		1500.00
255.	1 Escudo 1698...................................		850.00
256.	½ Escudo 1695...................................		700.00

PHILIP V, 1700-1746

Bust. Rev. Arms.

257.	2 Escudos 1723	1750.00

Bust. Rev. Arms and tree.

258.	2 Escudos ND....................................	1000.00
259.	1 Escudo ND.....................................	1000.00

Bust. Rev. Square Shield

259a.	½ Escudo 1703, ND..........................	4000.00

Arms. Rev. Square shield.

260.	4 Escudos 1704	8000.00
261	2 Escudos ND, 1723, 26....................	1500.00
261a.	1 Escudo ND....................................	7500.00

CHARLES III, 1700-1724
Arms. Rev. Square shield.

262.	4 Escudos 1707	4000.00
262a.	2 Escudos 1707, ND	2250.00

VALENCIA

Kings of —

ALFONSO V OF ARAGON, 1416-1458

Dragon over shield. Rev. Square shield.

263.	1 Timbre or ⅔ Ducat ND.................... *	1400.00
264.	½ Timbre ND	1000.00

JOHN II, 1458-1479

Bust facing. Rev. Arms.

265.	1 Ducat ND..	2750.00

FERDINAND AND ISABELLA, 1479-1504

Crowned heads facing each other. Rev. Arms.

266.	4 Ducats ND	4000.00
267.	2 Ducats ND	Unknown
268.	1 Ducat ND........................... *	1000.00

Initials F and I crowned. Rev. Arms.

269.	½ Ducat ND..	800.00

FERDINAND II (FERDINAND V OF SPAIN), 1504-1516

Bust right or left. Rev. Square shield.

270.	4 Ducats ND	2500.00
271.	2 Ducats ND .... *	1000.00
272.	1 Ducat ND......................................	800.00
273.	½ Ducat ND.......................................	500.00

Initial F. Rev. Arms.

274.	½ Ducat ND.......................................	750.00

St. John. Rev. Lily.

274a.	1 Florin ND.......................................	525.00

CHARLES I, 1517-1556

Bust. Rev. Square shield.

275.	4 Coronas or 4 Ducats ND	2250.00
276.	2 Coronas or 2 Ducats ND .... *	1500.00
277.	1 Corona or 1 Ducat ND..........................	1000.00

Cross of Jerusalem. Rev. Square shield.

278.	4 Coronas or 4 Ducats ND	2500.00
279.	2 Coronas or 2 Ducats ND	1000.00
280.	1 Corona or 1 Ducat ND................... *	750.00

PHILIP II, 1556-1598
Cross of Jerusalem. Rev. Square shield.
281.   4 Coronas or 4 Escudos ND...................... 2500.00

PHILIP IV, 1621-1665
Cross of Jerusalem. Rev. Square shield.
282.   1 Escudo ND or poorly dated..................... 600.00

CHARLES II, 1665-1700
Cross of Jerusalem. Rev. Square shield.
283.   1 Escudo 1688, 93-95, 1700, ND................. 550.00

Dragon over shield. Rev. Square shield.
284.   1 Escudo 1688.................................. 400.00

Arms. Rev. Square shield.
285.   ½ Escudo ND.................................... 450.00

SWEDEN

This section in the catalogue is devoted to the coinage struck in Sweden proper. Additional coins of the Swedish Kings will be found under Esthonia, Latvia, Livonia and in Germany under Augsburg, Bremen and Verden, Elbing, Erfurt, Furth, Hesse-Cassel, Mayence, Nuremberg, Osnabruck, Pomerania, Stettin and Wurzburg.

Sweden was on the Ducat standard as late as 1868. After that, a brief coinage was made on the Latin Monetary Union and a Carolin or 10 Franc piece was struck from 1868 to 1872. The modern coinage of Sweden is based on the standards of the Scandinavian Monetary Union, to which Denmark and Norway also subscribed.

Kings of —

ERIC XIV, 1560-1568

Head. Rev. Jehova in Hebrew characters over Sceptre.
1.   1 Goldgulden 1568................................. Rare

JOHN III, 1568-1592

Bust in circle. Rev. Heart shaped shield within inscribed circle.
2.   20 Ducats or 2 Portugalosers ND................... Unique
3.   10 Ducats or 1 Portugaloser ND................... Rare
4.   5 Ducats or ½ Portugaloser or 2 Rosenobles ND.*. Rare

Bust in circle. Rev. Christ over shield.
5.   5 Ducats or ½ Portugaloser or 2 Rosenobles 1576.   Rare

Crowned sheaf with value and date. Rev. Arms in circle.
6.   48 Marks 1590............................   Rare
7.   24 Marks 1590............................   Rare
8.   12 Marks 1590............................   Rare

Crowned sheaf and value. Rev. Three crowns and date.
9.   6 Marks 1590, 91..........................   Rare

Rampant lion in circle. Rev. Three crowns and value.
10.   3 Marks 1590.............................   Rare

Crowned bust. Rev. Quartered arms.
11.   1 Hungarian Gulden 1569, 73 ....   Rare

Crowned bust. Rev. Shield with three crowns.
12.   1 Crown Gulden 1569, 70..................   Rare

CHARLES IX, 1560-1611
Bust. Rev. Value.
13.   8 Marks 1587, 89, 99, 1603. Square ....   Rare

Laureate or crowned bust. Rev. Arms.
14.   16 Marks 1606-11 .... 8000.00

Bust. Rev. Crown over three shields.
15.   6 Marks 1609.............................. 4000.00

Sheaf. Rev. Hebrew "Jehova."
16.   10 Marks 1610. Square..................... 10000.00
17.   5 Marks 1610, 11. Square.................. 8000.00

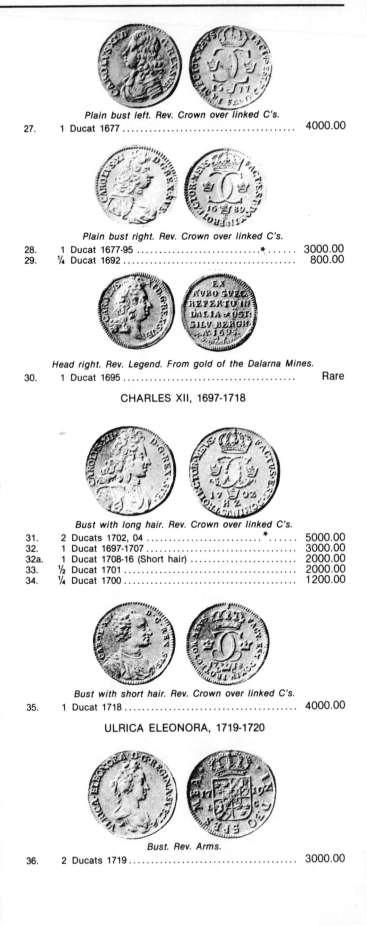

GUSTAVE II ADOLPHE, 1611-1632
Bust. Rev. Arms.

18.	16 Marks 1615, 24	15000.00

Sheaf. Rev. Hebrew "Jehova."

19.	10 Marks 1616, 26. Square ....*	8000.00
20.	5 Marks 1612. Square	Unknown

Bust. Rev. Arms supported by lions.

21.	5 Ducats 1620	Rare

CHARLES X, 1654-1660

Bust. Rev. Arms.

22.	10 Ducats 1654	Rare
23.	1 Ducat 1654-60, ND ....*	7000.00

CHARLES XI, 1660-1697

Bust right. Rev. Arms.

24.	1 Ducat 1662-65	5000.00

Bust or head left. Rev. Cross of arms.

25.	1 Ducat 1666-69	4000.00

Laureate bust left. Rev. Crown over linked C's.

26.	1 Ducat 1670-76, ND	4000.00

Plain bust left. Rev. Crown over linked C's.

27.	1 Ducat 1677	4000.00

Plain bust right. Rev. Crown over linked C's.

28.	1 Ducat 1677-95 ....*	3000.00
29.	¼ Ducat 1692	800.00

Head right. Rev. Legend. From gold of the Dalarna Mines.

30.	1 Ducat 1695	Rare

CHARLES XII, 1697-1718

Bust with long hair. Rev. Crown over linked C's.

31.	2 Ducats 1702, 04 ....*	5000.00
32.	1 Ducat 1697-1707	3000.00
32a.	1 Ducat 1708-16 (Short hair)	2000.00
33.	½ Ducat 1701	2000.00
34.	¼ Ducat 1700	1200.00

Bust with short hair. Rev. Crown over linked C's.

35.	1 Ducat 1718	4000.00

ULRICA ELEONORA, 1719-1720

Bust. Rev. Arms.

36.	2 Ducats 1719	3000.00

Bust. Rev. Crown over linked UE.

37.   1 Ducat 1719, 20 .... 2500.00

FREDERICK I, 1720-1751

Bust. Rev. Crown over linked FR or FF.

38.   1 Ducat 1720-28 .... 3000.00

Bust. Rev. Cross of eight F's.

39.   1 Ducat 1728, 29, 32.............................. 2000.00
40.   ¼ Ducat 1730, 33, 40............................. 400.00

Bust. Rev. Crowned shield.

41.   1 Ducat 1734-50 .... 1750.00
42.   ½ Ducat 1735, 38 .... 1000.00

Bust. Rev. Crowned shield with sun rising from bottom left.
From gold mined in China.

43.   1 Ducat 1738-50 .... 1700.00

Bust. Rev. Crowned shield, and below, the small arms of
Smaland, indicating gold from the Adelfors Mines.

44.   1 Ducat 1741-50 .... 4000.00
45.   ½ Ducat 1741, 46, 47............................. 2500.00

ADOLPHE FREDERICK, 1751-1771

Head. Rev. Crowned shield.

46.   1 Ducat 1751-71 ....*...... 2500.00
47.   ½ Ducat 1754, 55 .... 1500.00
48.   ¼ Ducat 1754, 55 .... 600.00

Head. Rev. Crowned shield and legend indicating gold from
the Dalarna Mines.

49.   1 Ducat 1751, 54 .... 6000.00

Head. Rev. Crowned shield, and below, the small arms of
Smaland, indicating gold from the Adelfors Mines.

50.   1 Ducat 1752-70 .... 5000.00

GUSTAVE III, 1771-1792

Head. Rev. Crowned shield.

51.   1 Ducat 1771-92 .... 1750.00

Head. Rev. Crowned shield, and below, the small arms of
Smaland, indicating gold from the Adelfors Mines.

52.   1 Ducat 1771-86 .... 4000.00

GUSTAVE IV ADOLPHE, 1792-1809

Head. Rev. Crowned shield.

53.   1 Ducat 1793-98 .... 1750.00

Armored bust. Rev. Crowned shield.

54.   1 Ducat 1799-1809 ....   1500.00

Head. Rev. Crowned shield, and below, the small arms of Smaland, indicating gold from the Adelfors Mines.

55.   1 Ducat 1796 ....   7000.00

Armored bust. Rev. Similar to above.

56.   1 Ducat 1801 ....   6000.00

Armored bust. Rev. Crowned shield, and below, the small arms of Dalarna, indicating gold from the Dalarna Mines.

57.   1 Ducat 1804 ....   5000.00

CHARLES XIII, 1809-1818

Head with title as King of Sweden. Rev. Crowned shield.

58.   1 Ducat 1810-14 ....   1500.00

Head with title as King of Sweden and Norway. Rev. Crowned shield.

59.   1 Ducat 1815, 16, 17 ....   1500.00

Head. Rev. Crowned shield, and below, the small arms of Dalarna, indicating gold from the Dalarna Mines.

60.   1 Ducat 1810 ....   3500.00

CHARLES XIV, 1818-1844

Head. Rev. Crowned shield.

61.   1 Ducat 1818-29 ....   1500.00

Head. Rev. Arms.

62.   4 Ducats 1837-43 ....*......   4000.00
63.   2 Ducats 1830-43 ....   3000.00
64.   1 Ducat 1830-43 ....   1200.00

OSCAR I, 1844-1859

Head. Rev. Arms.

65.   4 Ducats 1846, 50 ....   5000.00
66.   2 Ducats 1850, 52, 57.......................*......   3500.00
67.   1 Ducat 1844-59 ....   1000.00

CHARLES XV, 1859-1872

Head. Rev. Arms.

68.   1 Ducat 1860-68 ....   1000.00

Head. Rev. Crowned shield. With two values as indicated.

69.   1 Carolin-10 Francs 1868-72.......................   500.00

OSCAR II, 1872-1907

Head. Rev. Arms.

70.   20 Kronor 1873-1902 ....*......   350.00
71.   10 Kronor 1873-1901 ....   175.00

Head. Rev. Value.

72.   5 Kronor 1881-1901 ....   150.00

GUSTAVE V, 1907-1950

Head. Rev. Arms.

73.   20 Kronor 1925 ....   950.00

Head. Rev. Value.

74.   5 Kronor 1920 ....   200.00

SWITZERLAND

Switzerland, though small in area, has produced a body of coinage that for historical interest, variety of type and numismatic value, rivals that of any major power of the world, past or present.

A. Confederation of —

Cross on shield. Rev. Value. Not placed in circulation.

1.   20 Francs 1871 ....   4000.00

Girl head. Rev. Cross on shield. Not placed in circulation.

2.   20 Francs 1871 ....   7000.00

Helvetia seated. Rev. Value and date. Not placed in circulation.

3.   20 Francs 1873. Two dots and mintmark .....*......   2000.00
4.   20 Francs 1873. Two dots, no mintmark 3000.00

Girl head. Rev. Cross on shield.

5.   20 Francs 1883, 86, 89-96 ....* 185.00
6.   20 Francs 1888 ....   8500.00

Girl head against Alps background. Rev. Cross on shield.

7.   20 Francs 1897-1949 ....   175.00(B)

(Number 7 is a bullion coin. The price listed is based on gold at $725 per ounce.)

Girl head against Alps background. Rev. Value and date.

8.   100 Francs 1925 ....*......   7500.00
9.   10 Francs 1911 ....   300.00
10.   10 Francs 1912-22 ....   125.00

COMMEMORATIVE ISSUES

The following 100 Franc pieces were struck by the Berne Mint for the Federal Shooting Festivals.

Rifleman standing. Rev. Oval shield. Valid during the Fribourg Shooting Festival.

11.   100 Francs 1934 ....   2250.00

Rifleman kneeling. Rev. Legend over shield. Valid during the Lucerne Shooting Festival.

12.   100 Francs 1939 ....   750.00

B. Cantons, Ecclesiastical Princes and Cities of —

APPENZELL (INNER-RHODEN)

St. Mauritius standing. Rev. Legend in cartouche.

13.	1 Ducat 1737 ....*......	7500.00
14.	1 Ducat 1739	Rare

BASEL

A. City of —

Coinage as a mint of the Holy Roman Empire.

Madonna standing. Rev. Orb. With the name of Sigismund.

15.	1 Goldgulden ND. (1419-33). As King...............	600.00
16.	1 Goldgulden ND. (1433-37). As Emperor...........	600.00
17.	1 Goldgulden ND. Without his name........*......	1000.00

Madonna standing. Rev. Orb. With the name of Albert II.

18.	1 Goldgulden ND. (1437-39)	1500.00

Madonna standing. Rev. Orb. With the name of Frederick III.

19.	1 Goldgulden ND. (1440-51). As King...............	650.00
20.	1 Goldgulden ND. (1451-93). As Emperor...........	600.00
21.	1 Goldgulden ND. With Weinsberg shield...........	750.00
22.	1 Goldgulden 1491, 92, 93	5000.00

Madonna standing. Rev. Orb. With the name of Maximilian I.

23.	1 Goldgulden 1502, 03. With Weinsberg shield......	6000.00
24.	1 Goldgulden 1505-09. With Konigstein-Munzenberg shield................................*......	5000.00

City Coinage

Madonna standing, Basel arms at feet. Rev. Orb. With the name of Pope Julius II.

25.	1 Goldgulden 1512. Museum of Basel	Unique

Madonna standing. Rev. Arms on cross. With the name of Pope Julius II.

26.	1 Goldgulden 1513..................................	6000.00

Madonna standing. Rev. Arms on cross. With the name of Maximilian I.

27.	1 Goldgulden 1516.................................	5000.00

Madonna standing. Rev. Arms on cross. With the name of the City of Basel.

28.	1 Goldgulden 1520, 21.....................*......	5000.00
29.	1 Goldgulden 1524, 25, 28, 33, 38, 39..............	6000.00

Arms. Rev. Double eagle.

30.	4 Ducats ND (about 1570)	Rare

Arms on cartouche. Rev. Orb.

31.	2 Goldgulden ND. (17th Century)....................	4000.00
32.	1 Goldgulden ND. (17th Century)....................	1600.00

Basilisk with arms. Rev. Orb.

33.	2 Goldgulden ND. (17th Century)....................	8000.00

Basilisk with arms. Rev. Double eagle.

34.	2 Goldgulden ND. (17th Century)....................	8000.00

Arms on cartouche. Rev. Liberty cap on pole.

35.	2 Goldgulden ND. (18th Century)....................	6000.00
36.	1 Goldgulden ND. (18th Century)....................	1500.00

Northern view of the city. Rev. Basilisk and arms within eight shields.

37.	25 Ducats ND. (1700-10)............................	Rare
38.	20 Ducats ND. (1700-10)....................*......	Rare
39.	15 Ducats ND. (1700-10)....................*......	Rare

Northeastern view of the city. Rev. Basilisk holding shield with eight small arms.

40.	12 Ducats ND. (1700-30)............................	17500.00
41.	10 Ducats ND. (1700-30)............................	15000.00

Northwestern view of the city. Rev. Two basilisks holding arms.

42.   8 Ducats ND. (about 1700)......................... 15000.00

Northeastern view of the city. Rev. Arms within eight shields.

43.   6 Ducats ND. (17th Century)...................... 10000.00

Northwestern view of the city. Rev. Arms within eight shields.

44.   4 Ducats ND. (17th Century).................*..... 6000.00
45.   3 Ducats ND. (17th Century)....................... 4500.00
46.   2 Ducats ND. (17th Century)....................... 4500.00

Legend on cartouche. Rev. Basilisk with arms.

47.   2 Ducats ND. (18th Century)....................... 7500.00
48.   1 Ducat ND. (18th Century).................*..... 3000.00
49.   ½ Ducat ND. (18th Century)....................... 2000.00

Arms in cartouche. Rev. Double eagle.

50.   1 Ducat ND. (1620-50)............................. 3000.00

Legend in square cartouche. Rev. Arms in oval cartouche.

51.   1 Ducat ND. (17th Century)........................ 2750.00

Basilisk and oval shield. Rev. Value and name.

52.   ½ Ducat ND. (1750-80)............................. 3000.00
53.   ¼ Ducat ND. (1750-80)............................. 2500.00

Arms on cross. Rev. Double eagle.

54.   1 Goldgulden 1621, 22......................*...... 4500.00
55.   1 Goldgulden 1623.............................. Rare

Arms on cartouche. Rev. Double eagle.

56.   1 Ducat 1640...................................... 3000.00

Legend on cartouche. Rev. Basilisk with arms.

57.   1 Ducat 1653...................................... 4000.00

Legend on cartouche. Rev. Arms. Angel's head above.

58.   10 Ducats 1676.................................... Rare

Eastern view of the city. Rev. Basilisk with arms.

59.   20 Ducats 1741................................. Rare
60.   12 Ducats 1741................................. Rare
61.   10 Ducats 1741................................. Rare
62.   8 Ducats 1741.................................15000.00
63.   6 Ducats 1741.................................12500.00
64.   5 Ducats 1740.......................*......10000.00
65.   4 Ducats 1740................................. 9000.00
66.   3 Ducats 1740................................. 9000.00

Northwestern view of the City. Rev. Basilisk with arms, shields below.

67.   2 Ducats 1743................................. 8500.00
68.   1 Ducat 1743.......................*...... 7500.00
69.   ⅔ Ducat 1743................................. 5500.00

Value on drapery, liberty cap above. Rev. Basilisk with arms.

70.   2 Ducats ND. (1750-1800) 4500.00

Denomination in wreath. Rev. Arms, liberty cap above.

71.   2 Ducats 1795.................................... Rare

Arms, liberty cap above. Rev. Tripod.

72.   1 Duplone 1795 .... 3000.00

Arms, liberty cap above. Rev. Legend in wreath.

73.   1 Duplone 1795, 96 .... 2000.00

"Show Pieces" of Basel

Basilisk with arms and eight shields. Rev. Plancus standing.

74.   12 Ducats ND. (17th Century) 8500.00
75.   8 Ducats ND. (17th Century) 7000.00
76.   6 Ducats ND. (17th Century) 6000.00

Northern view of the city. Rev. Plancus standing.

77.   3 Ducats ND. (17th Century) .... Rare

Double eagle. Rev. Plancus standing.

78.   1 Ducat ND. (1620-50) 3500.00

Northwestern view of the city. Rev. Hen.

79.   3 Ducats ND. (17th Century) 3000.00

Western view of the city behind arms held by griffins. Rev. Hen.

80.   10 Ducats ND. (17th Century) .... * 8000.00
81.   6 Ducats ND. (17th Century) .... * 6000.00
82.   5 Ducats ND. (17th Century) 5500.00

Northern view of the city. Rev. The Adoration by the shepherds.

83.   3 Ducats ND. (1680-1700) 3000.00
84.   2 Ducats ND. (1680-1700) 2500.00

Northern view of the city. Rev. The Adoration by the three Magi.

85.   3 Ducats ND. (1680-1700) 3000.00
86.   2 Ducats ND. (1680-1700) .... * 2500.00

The Adoration by the shepherds. Rev. The Adoration by the three Magi.

87.   3 Ducats ND. (1680-1700) 2500.00
88.   2 Ducats ND. (1680-1700) 2000.00

B. Bishops of —

JOHN FRANCIS OF SCHONAU, 1651-1656
Legend on shield. Rev. St. Henry standing.

88a.   1 Ducat 1654 .... Rare

JOHN CONRAD I OF ROGGENBACH, 1656-1693

Legend on shield. Rev. St. Henry standing.

88b.   1 Ducat 1662 .... Rare

JOHN CONRAD II OF REINACH-HIRZBACH, 1705-1737
Bust. Rev. Double eagle with arms.

88c.   2 Ducats 1716 .... Very Rare
88d.   1 Ducat 1716 .... Rare

BERNE

One-headed eagle over arms. Rev. St. Vincent standing.

89.	4 Goldgulden 1492	*	20000.00
90.	3 Goldgulden 1492		18000.00
91.	2 Goldgulden 1492		16000.00

Two-headed eagle over arms. Rev. St. Vincent standing.

92.	2 Ducats 1600	*	7000.00
93.	1 Ducat 1600	*	5000.00
94.	½ Ducat 1601		4500.00

Bear and two-headed eagle below seven shields, within circle of 20 shields. Rev. St. Vincent standing.

95.	10 Ducats 1501	Rare
96.	9 Ducats 1501	Rare
97.	8 Ducats 1501	Rare
98.	6 Ducats 1501 *	20000.00
99.	5 Ducats 1501	17000.00

Arms. Rev. St. Peter standing.

100.	1 Goldgulden ND. (1479 1500)	10000.00

Arms. Rev. Bust of St. Vincent.

101.	1 Goldgulden ND. (1500-30)	Rare

Two-headed eagle over arms. Rev. Orb with name of Frederick II.

102.	1 Goldgulden ND. (16th Century)	8500.00
103.	1 Goldgulden 1590, 94	Rare

Eagle over arms. Rev. Cross.

104.	2 Goldgulden ND. (1490-1550)	Rare
105.	1 Goldgulden ND. (1490-1550)	Rare
106.	½ Goldgulden ND. (1490-1550)	Rare
107.	½ Goldgulden 1554, 56, 62, 90	Rare

Arms. Rev. Eagle with name of Frederick II.

108.	1 Goldgulden 1530. Swiss National Museum	Unique
109.	1 Goldgulden 1537, 39. Single head eagle ..*	10000.00
110.	1 Goldgulden 1566. Double eagle	Rare

Arms. Rev. Cross.

111.	4 Ducats ND. (16th Century)	Rare

Arms. Rev. Legends as illustrated.

112.	3 Ducats ND. (16th Century). Legend in seven lines *	15000.00
113.	3 Ducats ND. (16th Century). Circular legend..*	Rare
114.	2 Ducats ND. (16th Century). Legend in seven lines.	12000.00

Arms. Rev. Double eagle.

115.	3 Ducats 1659	11000.00
116.	2 Ducats 1658	9000.00
117.	2 Ducats ND. (1645-1665)	10000.00
118.	1 Ducat 1658 *	6000.00

Arms supported by bear and lion. Rev. Crowned cartouche supported by bears.

119.	4 Ducats ND. (about 1700)	7000.00

Arms. Rev. Value and date between branches.

120.	2 Ducats 1679	5000.00
121.	1 Ducat 1679	5000.00
122.	1 Ducat 1679. (Rev. Cartouche)	5000.00

Bear and lion holding arms. Rev. Legend and value in cartouche with floral wreath.

123.	12 Ducats 1681	22000.00
124.	10 Ducats 1681	20000.00
125.	4 Ducats 1680, 84. Without floral wreath on Rev. *..	9000.00

Crowned arms on branches. Rev. Legend in cartouche.

133.	10 Ducats ND. (18th Century)	20000.00
134.	8 Ducats ND. (18th Century)	17000.00
135.	6 Ducats ND. (18th Century) .... *	15000.00
136.	4 Ducats ND. (18th Century)	9000.00
137.	4 Ducats ND. (18th Century). Value on Rev.........	9000.00

Crown over two shields and value. Rev. Male and female holding drapery.

126.	3 Ducats 1680, 84, 97, 1707................ *	7000.00
127.	3 Ducats 1699 (one shield on Obv.).................	8000.00
128.	3 Ducats 1734 (cartouche on Rev.)..................	10000.00

Arms supported by bear and lion. Rev. Male and female at altar.

138.	10 Ducats ND. (1700-1710)	18000.00
139.	8 Ducats ND. (1700-1710)	Rare
140.	7 Ducats ND. (1700-1710)	Rare
141.	6 Ducats ND. (1700-1710)	15000.00
142.	5 Ducats ND. (1700-1710)	12000.00
143.	4 Ducats ND. (1700-1710) .... *	8000.00

Crowned arms. Rev. Male and female at altar.

144.	5 Ducats ND. (18th Century)........................	12000.00
145.	4 Ducats ND. (18th Century)	8000.00

Crowned arms on branches. Rev. Legend in cartouche.

129.	3 Ducats 1734......................................	12500.00

Bear holding arms in circle of shields. Rev. Male and female at altar.

146.	8 Ducats ND. (1700-1710). She-bear nursing.........	Rare
147.	5 Ducats 1700, ND. (1700-1710)	12000.00
148.	4 Ducats ND. (1700-1710)	8000.00

Arms. Rev. Male and female holding drapery.

130.	2 Ducats 1698......................................	7000.00
131.	1 Ducat 1697, 1718	2500.00

Bear in cartouche. Rev. Angel with shield.

149.	1 Ducat 1696.......................................	5000.00

Crowned arms supported by bear and lion. Rev. View of the city, with small arms above.

132.	10 Ducats ND. (1680-1720)	22000.00

Arms supported by bear and lion. Rev. Bear holding shield.

150.	6 Ducats 1701......................................	Rare
151.	5 Ducats 1701......................................	15000.00
152.	4 Ducats 1701.............................. *	10000.00

Two lions holding arms and cap. Rev. Legend and value on shield.

153.   2 Ducats 1703, 19, 27, 71 .... 5000.00

Arms. Rev. Cross.

154.   ½ Ducat 1718 .... 2000.00
155.   ½ Ducat 1781 .... 4000.00
156.   ¼ Ducat 1707, 31, 66, 77, 78, 81, ND. (1800) . * 2000.00

Crowned arms. Rev. Legend and value in cartouche.

157.   3 Ducats 1772 .... 8500.00
158.   2 Ducats 1789 .... * 6000.00
159.   1 Ducat 1725, 41, 88, 89, ND. (1772) .... * 2500.00
160.   ½ Ducat 1714, 17, 19 .... 1750.00

Crowned arms. Rev. Value and date in wreath, legend around.

161.   8 Ducats 1796 .... 17000.00
162.   8 Ducats 1798 .... Rare
163.   6 Ducats 1796 .... 15000.00
164.   4 Ducats 1796, 98 .... 11000.00
165.   4 Ducats 1825 .... 15000.00
166.   2 Ducats 1796 .... * 3000.00
167.   1 Ducat 1793 (Oval shield) Rare; 94 .... * 2000.00

Crowned arms. Rev. Legend in wreath.

168.   2 Duplones 1793-96 .... 2000.00
169.   1 Duplone 1793-96 .... * 1250.00

Crowned arms. Warrior standing.

170.   6 Duplones or 12 Ducats 1795. (Struck from
          thaler dies) .... Rare
171.   4 Duplones or 8 Ducats 1797 .... 15000.00
172.   2 Duplones 1794, 96, 97, 98 .... * 4000.00
173.   1 Duplone 1793, 97, 1819, 29 .... 2500.00
174.   ½ Duplone 1797 .... 1500.00

*Arms. Rev. Crowned monogram. Without the mark of value
and not placed in circulation.*

175.   (10 Francs) ND. (About 1810) 8500.00

CHUR

A. Bishops of —

PETER II, 1581-1601

Bust of St. Luke. Rev. Double eagle.

176.   7 Ducats ND 15000.00

JOHN V, 1601-1627

Bust of St. Luke. Rev. Double eagle.

177.   7 Ducats 1613 .... 14000.00
178.   7 Ducats 1615 .... 14000.00
179.   7 Ducats ND .... * 8500.00
180.   1 Goldgulden ND. (Name of Matthias) 1500.00
181.   1 Goldgulden ND. (Name of Ferdinand II) 2500.00

Arms. Rev. Double eagle.

182.   2 Ducats ND .... Rare

JOSEPH, 1627-1635
Arms. Rev. Double eagle.

182a.   1 Ducat ND .... Rare

JOHN VI, 1636-1661
Arms. Rev. Double eagle.

183.	1 Ducat 1636, 49, 52	Rare

ULRIC VI, 1661-1692
Arms. Rev. Double eagle.

184.	6 Ducats 1664	Rare
185.	1 Ducat 1664	Rare

ULRIC VII, 1692-1728
Arms. Rev. Double eagle.

186.	10 Ducats 1720	Rare

Arms. Rev. Bust of St. Luke.

187.	1 Ducat 1693	Rare
188.	1 Ducat 1697 (broad flan).....................	Rare
189.	1 Ducat 1713	8500.00

JOSEPH BENEDICT, 1728-1754

Bust. Rev. Arms.

190.	10 Ducats 1736, 37	Rare
191.	8 Ducats 1747	18000.00
192.	7 Ducats 1749 ....*.....	15000.00
193.	6 Ducats 1749	Rare
194.	5 Ducats 1749	13000.00
195.	1 Ducat 1749	5000.00

JOHN ANTHONY, 1755-1777

Arms. Rev. Madonna.

196.	1 Ducat 1767	6500.00

B. City of —

Bust of St. Luke. Rev. Double eagle.

197.	1 Goldgulden ND. (Name of Ferdinand II)..........	2500.00

St. Luke standing. Rev. Double eagle.

198.	1 Goldgulden 1618 (Name of Matthias)	5000.00

Arms. Rev. Double eagle.

199.	2 Ducats 1633. (Name of Ferdinand II).............	12000.00
200.	1 Ducat 1634, 36, 37 (Name of Ferdinand II)........	8000.00
201.	1 Ducat 1638, 39, 41, 42, 44 (Name of Ferdinand III)	9000.00

EINSIEDELN

Abbots of —

BEATUS, 1780-1808
Arms. Rev. Madonna of Einsiedeln.

202.	1 Ducat 1783	3000.00

FISCHINGEN

Abbots of —

FRANCIS, 1688-1728

Arms. Rev. St. Ida with stag.

203.	2 Ducats 1726. Thick flan....................	*	6000.00
204.	1 Ducat 1726		5000.00

FRIBOURG

Eagle over fortress. Rev. Floriated cross.

205.	2 Florins 1597. Swiss National Museum		Unique
206.	1 Florin 1594, 97............................	*	10000.00
207.	1 Florin 1599		8500.00
208.	1 Florin 1619, 20		Rare
209.	½ Florin ND. (About 1510)...................		5000.00
210.	½ Ecu d'or 1610. 2.18 g. Berne Museum		Unique

Eagle over fortress. Rev. Bust of St. Nicholas.

211.	1 Florin 1587 ....*.....		12000.00
212.	1 Florin 1594		Rare

Eagle over fortress. Rev. St. Nicholas standing.

213.	1 Ducat ND. (About 1550)........................	10000.00

Eagle over fortress. Rev. Cross in quadrilobe.

214.	1 Quadruple or 2 Duplones 1622		Rare
215.	1 Duplone or 1 Pistole 1622		Rare
216.	1 Duplone or 1 Pistole 1635	*	9000.00

Arms. Rev. Sun.

228.	1 Ecu d'or au Soleil ND. (1540-50)	*	10000.00
229.	3 Pistoles 1771	*	6500.00
230.	1 Small Pistole of 35 Florins 1752-55, 57, 58, 62, 70	*	2500.00

GENEVA

Arms. Rev. Value.

231.	20 Francs 1848	1850.00
232.	10 Francs 1848	2000.00

Double eagle and arms. Rev. Sun.

217.	1 Quadruple 1635, 37, 38, 40-42, 44-46	*	10000.00
218.	1 Ecu-Pistolet 1562-68, 74-76, 80-83, 85, 86, 1634		3000.00
219.	1 Ecu-Pistolet 1569, 78, 79		Rare
220.	1 Pistole 1634, 36, 38-42		6000.00

Double eagle over arms. Rev. Quadrilobe.

221.	1 Pistole 1594. (Struck from 3 Sols dies)	Unique

GRISONS

Canton of —

Three shields. Rev. Value.

233.	16 Francs 1813	7500.00

Double eagle. Rev. Legend in tablet.

222.	2 Ducats 1654, 58-60, 62, 63, 66		6000.00
223.	2 Ducats 1656, 57, 64, 90	*	5000.00
224.	1 Ducat 1644, 46, 48-51, 54		3000.00
225.	1 Ducat 1647, 52, 67		Rare

HALDENSTEIN

Barons of —

THOMAS I, 1609-1628
Bust. Rev. Double eagle.

234.	7 Ducats 1617	18000.00
235.	4 Ducats 1617	15000.00
236.	2 Ducats 1617	Rare

Arms. Rev. Double eagle.

226.	1 Large Pistole of 40 Florins 1722, 24	3500.00
227.	1 Small Pistole of 35 Florins 1772	3750.00

Double eagle. Rev. Ruler kneeling before seated Christ.

237.	1 Goldgulden ND	3000.00

Double eagle. Rev. Ruler kneeling before standing Christ.

238.	1 Goldgulden 1618		Rare
239.	1 Goldgulden ND		6000.00

JULIUS OTTO I, 1628-1666
Ruler standing. Rev. Double eagle.

240.	1 Ducat 1638, 42, 49		8000.00

THOMAS II, 1667
Bust facing. Rev. Double eagle.

241.	1 Ducat 1667		Rare

GUBERT, 1733
Bust. Rev. Arms.

242.	6 Ducats 1733		Rare
243.	5 Ducats 1733		Rare
244.	1 Ducat 1733		Rare

THOMAS III, 1747-70
Bust. Rev. Arms.

245.	1 Ducat 1767		Rare

HELVETIAN REPUBLIC

Warrior standing. Rev. Value.

246.	32 Francs 1800	*	7500.00
247.	16 Francs 1800		2500.00

LAUSANNE

Bishops of —

BENOIT, 1476-1491
Bust. Rev. Arms.

248.	1 Ducat ND. Lausanne Museum		Unique

AYMON, 1491-1517
Bust. Rev. Arms.

249.	1 Ducat ND		6500.00

LUCERNE

Eagle over arms. Rev. Bust of St. Leodegar.

250.	4 Ducats ND. (16th Century)	*	20000.00
251.	3 Ducats ND. (16th Century)		Rare

Eagle over arms. Rev. Bust of St. Leodegar facing.

252.	4 Ducats ND		Rare
253.	2 Ducats 1603		Rare

Arms. Rev. St. Leodegar standing.

254.	6 Ducats 1698		10000.00
255.	5 Ducats 1698		9500.00
256.	4 Ducats 1698		9000.00

Value in cartouche. Rev. St. Leodegar and St. Maurice standing.

257.	1 Ducat ND. (1695-1700)		6000.00

Double eagle over arms. Rev. Bust of St. Leodegar facing.

258.	1 Ducat 1639		7500.00

Crowned arms. Rev. St. Leodegar and Church.

259.	2 Ducats 1675. (Broad flan)		10000.00

Warrior with shield seated. Rev. St. Leodegar seated.

260.	5 Ducats 1695		Rare
260a.	4 Ducats 1695 (Berne Museum)		Unique
261.	2 Ducats 1695		10000.00

St. Leodegar seated. Rev. Legend in cartouche.

262.	10 Ducats 1714		Rare
263.	5 Ducats 1714		12500.00

Arms. Rev. Legend in cartouche.

264.	5 Ducats 1714		10000.00

St. Leodegar standing. Rev. Value in cartouche.

265.	3 Ducats 1714		8500.00
266.	2 Ducats 1714	*	7500.00
267.	1 Ducat 1715		5000.00
268.	1 Ducat 1725		8000.00

Arms supported by wild men. Rev. Value.

269.	5 Ducats 1741		13000.00
270.	4 Ducats 1741		15000.00
271.	3 Ducats 1741		10000.00
272.	2 Ducats 1741	*	6000.00
273.	1 Ducat 1741	*	3500.00

Crowned arms. Rev. Value in wreath.
274. 24 Munzgulden 1794, 96 .... * 7000.00
275. 12 Munzgulden 1794, 96 .... 1850.00

Crowned arms. Rev. Warrior seated.
276. 20 Francs 1807 .... 5000.00
277. 10 Francs 1804 .... * 1500.00

MESOCCO

Marcheses of —

GIAN GIACOMO, 1487-1518
Arms: Three crosses. Rev. Cross.
278. 1 Scudo d'oro del sole ND 10000.00

Arms: Lily of France. Rev. Cross.
279. 1 Scudo d'oro del sole ND .... Rare

Arms: Three scallops. Rev. Cross.
280. 1 Scudo d'oro del sole ND .... Rare

Orb. Rev. Madonna.
281. 1 Zecchino ND. City Museum, Brescia, Italy .... Unique

MURI

Abbots of —

PLACIDUS, 1684-1723
Bust. Rev. View of the Abbey.
282. 5 Ducats 1720 .... 7000.00

Bust. Rev. Arms of the Zurlauben family.
283. 1 Ducat 1720 .... 4000.00

NEUCHATEL

Counts of —

HENRY I, 1575-1595
Bust. Rev. Arms.
284. 1 Ecu Pistolet .... Unique

HENRY II, 1595-1663
Bust. Rev. Arms.
285. 2 Pistoles 1603 .... Rare
286. 2 Pistoles 1618 .... Rare

Bust right. Rev. Arms.
287. 2 Pistoles 1631. Berne Museum .... Unique

MARIE, 1694-1707

Bust. Rev. Arms.
288. 4 Pistoles 1694. Neuchatel Museum .... Unique
289. 2 Pistoles 1694 .... * 20000.00

Cross of four M's, "16" (Kreuzer) in center. Rev. Arms.
290. 1 Pistole (2 Ducats) 1694. Neuchatel Museum ...... Unique
291. ½ Pistole (1 Ducat) 1694 .... Rare

(For the gold coins struck by the kings of Prussia for Neuchatel, see under Germany-Prussia.)

OBWALDEN (UNTERWALDEN)

Arms. Rev. St. Nicholas von der Flue standing.
292. 8 Ducats 1728 .... Rare

Double eagle with arms of Obwalden. Rev. Legend in rectangular cartouche.
293. 1 Ducat 1726 .... 8500.00

Legend in rectangular cartouche. Rev. St. Nicholas von der Flue standing.
294. 1 Ducat 1726 .... 3500.00

Legend in cartouche. Rev. St. Nicholas von der Flue kneeling to right.

295.	5 Ducats 1732	Rare
296.	1 Ducat 1725	Rare
297.	1 Ducat 1730	3000.00
298.	1 Ducat 1743 ....*	1500.00
299.	1 Ducat 1787 (St. Nicholas to left and facing)	1700.00
300.	1 Ducat 1787. "Niederberger"—restrike by Durussel.	600.00

Arms. Rev. St. Nicholas kneeling slightly to left.

301.	1 Ducat 1774	6500.00

RHEINAU

Abbots of —

GEROLD II, 1697-1735

Arms. Rev. View of the Abbey.

302.	1 Ducat 1710	4000.00

Bust. Rev. Arms.

303.	2 Ducats 1723	6500.00

Arms. Rev. St. Fintan standing.

304.	2 Ducats 1723 ....*	6500.00
305.	1 Ducat 1723	3750.00

ST. GALLEN

A. City of —

Bear. Rev. Double eagle.

306.	4 Ducats 1620. Square. Museum of St. Gallen	Unique
307.	3 Ducats 1618, 19. Museum of St. Gallen...........	Unique
308.	2 Ducats 1621 ....*	8500.00

B. Abbots of —

BEDA, 1767-1796

Arms. Rev. St. Gallus on throne.

309.	1 Ducat 1773 ....*	5000.00
310.	1 Ducat 1774. (Date on Obv.)	4500.00

Arms. Rev. Bear with stick of firewood.

311.	1 Ducat 1781	4500.00

SCHAFFHAUSEN

Ram jumping out from city gate. Rev. Double eagle.

312.	20 Ducats 1656	Rare
313.	1 Goldgulden 1622................................	Rare

Arms. Rev. Double eagle.

314.	1 Ducat 1633 ....*	4500.00
315.	1 Ducat 1657 (overstruck on 1633 Ducat), ND (1658).	3500.00

SCHWYZ

Crowned double eagle over arms. Rev. Floriated cross. Struck at Bellinzona, 1510-20.

316.   1 Scudo d'oro ND .... Rare

St. Martin on horseback, and beggar. Rev. Madonna.

317.   1 Ducat ND (1621), 1653 ....*...... 5500.00
318.   1 Ducat 1674 .... Rare

Lion holding shield. Rev. Legend.

319.   1 Ducat ND (1779), 1781, 88, 90.................... 6000.00

Lion holding shield. Rev. Legend.

320.   1 Ducat 1844 .... 7000.00

SION (WALLIS)

Bishops of —

HILDEBRAND, 1565-1604

Floriated cross. Rev. St. Theodul over arms.

321.   1 Ducat ND....................................... 10000.00

ADRIEN III, 1640-1646

Mitre and crosier over arms of Riedmatten. Rev. Eagle over arms of Wallis. Struck from Kreuzer dies.

322.   1 Ducat ND....................................... 10000.00

SOLOTHURN

Eagle over arms. Rev. Bust of St. Ursus. Struck from Dicken dies.

323.   3 Ducats ND. (16th Century) .... Rare

Arms. Rev. St. Ursus standing in oval trilobe.

324.   1 Ducat 1630. Museum of Berne.................... Unique
325.   ½ Ducat 1630 ....*..... Rare

Double eagle and arms. Rev. St. Ursus standing in oval trilobe.

326.   1 Ducat ND (about 1630)......................... Unique

Crowned arms. Rev. St. Ursus standing.

327.   1 Ducat 1768 ....10000.00
328.   2 Duplones 1787, 96.............................. 4500.00
329.   2 Duplones 1797, 98.............................. 3700.00
330.   1 Duplone 1787, 96, 97 ....*..... 2250.00
331.   1 Duplone 1798 .... 2500.00
332.   ½ Duplone 1787, 96 ....*..... 1500.00
333.   ¼ Duplone 1789, 96 .... 850.00

Crowned oval shield. Rev. St. Ursus standing.

333a.   32 Franken 1813.................................. Rare
334.   16 Franken 1813.................................. 8500.00
335.   8 Franken 1813.................................. 8500.00

URI

Floriated cross over arms. Rev. St. Martin on horseback and beggar.

336.   1 Pistole ND. Small size. (17th Century) ....*...... 6000.00
337.   1 Pistole 1613. Large size .... Rare

Legend and value. Rev. St. Martin standing and beggar.

338.   1 Ducat 1701 .... Rare
339.   1 Ducat 1704 (overstruck on 1701 Ducat) 8000.00

Arms. Rev. St. Martin on horseback and beggar.

340.   1 Ducat 1720 .... 3000.00
341.   1 Ducat 1736 (overstruck on 1720 Ducat)....*...... 2500.00

URI, SCHWYZ AND UNTERWALDEN

Three shields, double eagle and crossed keys. Rev. Floriated cross. Presumably struck at Bellinzona before 1520. Only a rubbing of this piece is known.

342. 1 Scudo d'oro ND .... Unknown

Same Obv. as above. Rev. St. Martin on horseback and beggar. Struck at Bellinzona.

343. 1 Ducat ND (about 1520)......................... Rare

Double eagle over three arms. Rev. Floriated cross. Naples type, struck at Altdorf.

344. 1 Gold Krone ND (about 1561) ....*......18000.00
345. 1 Gold Krone 1556................................. Unique

Three arms in triangular composition. Rev. Floriated cross. Struck from Broad-Batzen dies.

346. 1 Pistole 1569. Museum of Berne.................. Unique

URI AND UNTERWALDEN

Crowned double eagle over two arms. Rev. Floriated cross. North Italian type, struck at Bellinzona after 1508.

347. 1 Scudo d'oro ND 18000.00

ZUG

Arms. Rev. Crowned double eagle. Struck from ⅛ Assis dies.

348. ⅛ Ducat ND. (17th Century) .... Rare

Bust of St. Oswald. Rev. Double eagle and arms.

349. 1 Ducat 1691. Museum of Winterthur .... Unique
350. 1 Goldgulden 1615................................ Unique

Arms. Rev. Legend.

351. 1½ Ducats 1692 .... Rare

Arms. Rev. Value.

352. ½ Ducat 1692 .... 4000.00

ZURICH

Eagle and large arms. Rev. Charlemagne on throne.

353. 1 Goldgulden ND (about 1510)..................... 5000.00

Arms in trilobe. Rev. Double eagle in shield. Gothic script.

354. 1 Goldgulden 1526.............................12000.00
355. 1 Goldgulden 1527..........................*......12000.00

Two lions with three shields and crown. Rev. Circle of nine shields around arms of Zurich. "Schnabeltaler" dies.

356. 10 Ducats 1559 ....*......20000.00
357. 9 Ducats 1559 ....18000.00
358. 8 Ducats 1559 ....15000.00

Arms on double eagle. Rev. Floriated cross.

359. 1 Gold Krone ND (about 1560)..............*..... 6500.00
360. 1 Gold Krone 1631............................ 7500.00
361. ½ Gold Krone ND (about 1560)..............*...... 3000.00

Eagle and small Zurich shield. Rev. Charlemagne on throne.

362. 1 Goldgulden ND (about 1600)..............*...... 7500.00
363. 1 Goldgulden ND (about 1600). Charlemagne on double trilobe........................... Rare
364. ½ Goldgulden ND (about 1600) .... Unique

Small Zurich shield in quadrilobe. Rev. Crowned double eagle.

365.   1 Goldgulden 1622...................... 6000.00

Eagle and shield. Rev. Charlemagne with orb standing right.

366.   1 Ducat ND (about 1600)........................ 6000.00

Double-headed eagle and shield. Rev. Charlemagne standing with sword, facing.

367.   ½ Ducat ND. (End of 16th Century). Broad flan...... 7500.00

Charlemagne on throne. Rev. Saints Regula and Felix standing and carrying their heads.

368.   1 Ducat ND (about 1607)...................... 8000.00

Legend in wreath. Rev. Charlemagne on throne.

369.   2 Ducats ND (about 1620) 8500.00
370.   1 Ducat ND (about 1620).................*...... 6500.00

Lion with shield. Rev. Double eagle.

371.   4 Ducats 1624 ....*...... 8500.00
372.   4 Ducats 1622. (From ½ Taler dies) .... Rare
373.   4 Ducats 1629............................ Rare
374.   2 Ducats 1624............................ 7000.00
375.   2 Ducats 1629. (Date in exergue on Rev.).......... 7000.00

Warrior standing. Rev. Legend in wreath.

376.   ½ Ducat 1639 ....*...... 3500.00
377.   ¼ Ducat 1639 .... 3500.00

Large arms between branches. Rev. Legend. Struck from 20 Schilling dies.

378.   2 Ducats ND. (17th Century)................ Rare

Two lions holding arms and wreath. Rev. Crowned double eagle.

379.   4 Ducats 1640, 41 .... 10000.00
380.   2 Ducats 1641 ....*...... 7000.00

Legend in wreath. Rev. Two lions and one shield.

381.   1 Ducat 1641, 43 .... 3500.00

Legend in wreath. Rev. Two lions and two shields.

382.   1 Ducat 1646, 48 (Rare), 49, 50.............. 4000.00

Legend in wreath. Rev. Lion and arms.

383.   4 Ducats 1666 .... Rare
384.   2 Ducats 1673. (IUSTICIA ET CONCORDIA) 8500.00
385.   2 Ducats ND, 1645, 61, 62, 73 (Rare), 80, 84, 97 * ... 3000.00
386.   ½ Ducat 1641, 45, 49, 51, 66, 70.................. 2000.00
387.   ¼ Ducat 1645, 49 .... 1500.00

Date in wreath. Rev. Lion and arms.

388.	½ Ducat 1671, 77, 92, 1702	*	2000.00
389.	¼ Ducat 1671, 77, 92, 1702		1500.00

Two lions and arms. Rev. Western view of the city.

400.	10 Ducats 1724, 25	*	25000.00
401.	8 Ducats 1723		Rare

Two lions holding two shields and wreath. Rev. Legend in cartouche.

390.	15 Ducats 1649	20000.00
391.	8 Ducats 1646	18000.00
392.	6 Ducats 1647	15000.00

Two lions and arms. Rev. Legend in cartouche.

402.	2 Ducats 1707-76. 1707 is Rare	4750.00

Legend in wreath. Rev. Arms in cartouche.

393.	1 Ducat 1651	4500.00

Lion and arms. Rev. Legend in wreath or cartouche.

403.	1 Ducat 1702-1810	*	2500.00
404.	½ Ducat 1707-76. 1723 is Rare	*	1250.00
405.	¼ Ducat 1707-67		850.00

Arms. Rev. Date in wreath.

394.	½ Ducat 1654, 62	1000.00
395.	¼ Ducat 1654, 66	850.00

Bust of Zwingli to left. Rev. Legend. On the Reformation.

406.	1 Ducat 1719	800.00

Lion and shield. Rev. Western view of the city.

396.	10 Ducats ND. (17th Century). Northern view of the city within bulwarks	25000.00
396a.	8 Ducats 1739	Rare
397.	6 Ducats 1739	Rare
398.	5 Ducats 1720, 24, 30 (Rare), 33, 40, 53 ..... *	20000.00
399.	4 Ducats 1720, 28	Rare

Bust of Zwingli to right. Rev. Legend. On the Reformation.

407.	1 Ducat 1819	650.00

SYRIA

Eagle. Rev. Legend in rectangular panel.
1. 1 Pound 1950 .... 180.00
2. ½ Pound 1950 .... 80.00

TANGIER

Hercules standing. Rev. Legend, weight and fineness. A private bank issue of Tangier.
1. 1 Hercules ND (1954) 350.00

TIBET

Tibetan style lion. Rev. Stylized design in circle.
1. 20 Srangs 1917-20 .... 650.00

TIERRA DEL FUEGO

Julius Popper, who struck these coins, was a South American adventurer. This coinage may be considered as a territorial issue of Argentina.

The name Popper centered over crossed hammers and pickaxe. Rev. Value in circle.
1. 5 Gramos 1889 .... 5000.00
2. 1 Gramo 1889 .... 1000.00

TRANQUEBAR

Danish Kings of —

CHRISTIAN VII, 1766-1808

Monogram. Rev. The God Vishnu.
1. 1 Pagoda ND 325.00

TUNIS

A. Beys of —

MOHAMMED, 1855-1859 AND MOHAMMED AL-SADIK, 1859-1882

Three line Arab legend in open wreath. Rev. Arab date and value.
1. 100 Piastres 1272-85. A.H. (1855-68) ....*...... 700.00
2. 80 Piastres 1272 A.H. (1855) 350.00
3. 50 Piastres 1272-97 A.H. (1855-92) 300.00
4. 40 Piastres 1272 A.H. (1855) 300.00
5. 25 Piastres 1273-1300 A.H. (1853-82) 150.00
6. 20 Piastres 1272 A.H. (1855) 140.00
7. 10 Piastres 1272-88 A.H. (1855-71) 100.00
8. 5 Piastres 1272-94 A.H. (1855-76) 60.00

B. French Protectorate of —

The only 10 Franc piece that it is normally possible to obtain is dated 1891. All other dates are very rare.

New type legend in closed wreath. Rev. Arab date and value.
9. 25 Piastres 1300, 02 A.H. (1883, 85) 250.00

French value. Rev. Arab value and date. Two denominations appear on this coin, the old Tunisian value of 25 Piastres and the new French equivalent of 15 Francs.
10. 15 Francs-25 Piastres 1304, 08 A.H. (1887, 91)
    No mm 250.00
11. 15 Francs-25 Piastres 1307, 08 A.H. (1889, 90)
    A mm. ....*.... 300.00

Arab legend in wreath. Rev. French name, value and date. Very small amounts were coined of the 20 Franc pieces of 1894-96, 1902, 05-28 and of the 10 Franc pieces from 1892-1928.
12. 20 Francs 1891-1928 ....*...... 175.00
13. 10 Francs 1891-1928 .... 100.00

Arab legend in vertical panel. Rev. Value and date in circle.

14.   100 Francs 1930-37 . . . . 225.00

Arab legend in vertical panel. Rev. Large date. Without the mark of value, although the coins have the same specifications as the preceeding issues. Only about 30 pieces were struck in each year.

15.   (100 Francs) 1938-55 . . . . 850.00

TURKESTAN, CHINESE

Native legend on each side. Struck during the period 1865-1877 by the rebel, Yakub Beg. With dates from about 1290-1295 A.H.

1.   1 Tilla 225.00

Four Chinese characters in circle. Rev. Dragon, and in English, "Sungarei . . . 2 Mace".

2.   2 Mace ND (1906) . . . . Rare

Dragon. Rev. Four Chinese characters in circle.

3.   2 Mace ND (1907) . . . . * 600.00
4.   1 Mace ND (1907) 475.00

TURKEY

As is typical of the Arab-Asian Empires (which see) the coinage of the Ottoman Sultans was of the same general type over a period of about 400 years. It was, therefore, not felt necessary to describe the coinage of each Sultan, since such a catalogue would be more a chronological list of names than of coin types.

A. Ottoman Sultans of —

MOHAMMED II, 1451, TO MUSTAFA IV, 1808

Arab legend on each side. This general type was used by the Sultans from 1451 to 1808; with dates from about 943-1223 A.H.

1.   1 Sequin . . . . * 60.00
2.   ½ Sequin 50.00
3.   ¼ Sequin 40.00

AHMED III, 1703, TO MAHMUD II, 1839

Toughra as main motif. Rev. Arab legend. This general type was used by the Sultans from 1703 to 1839; with dates from about 1116-1254 A.H.

3a. 10   Sequins 2000.00
4.   6   Sequins 600.00
5.   5   Sequins 325.00
6.   4   Sequins 260.00
7.   3   Sequins 200.00
8.   2   Sequins 130.00
9.   1½ Sequins 100.00
10.   1   Sequin . . . . * . . 65.00
11.   ½ Sequin 35.00
12.   ¼ Sequin 30.00

ABDUL MEJID, 1839-1861

Toughra in plain field. Rev. Legend, accession date 1255 and regnal year. All coins bear the accession date 1255 in Arabic numerals, in addition to other numerals for the regnal year, which indicate the precise date of coinage.

13.   20 Piastres. Years 1, 3, 5 (1839, 41, 43) 45.00
14.   10 Piastres. Years 1-2 (1839-40) 35.00
15.   5 Piastres. Years 1-5 (1839-43) 30.00

Toughra and regnal date. Rev. Legend and accession date.

16.   500 Piastres. Year 18 (1856) 800.00
17.   250 Piastres. Year 18 (1856) . . . . * 400.00
18.   100 Piastres. Years 5-23 (1843-61) 175.00
19.   50 Piastres. Years 6-23 (1844-61) 85.00
20.   25 Piastres. Years 6-23 (1844-61) 70.00

Type as above but with the name of the city of Adrianople (Edirne) added to the legend on coins with regnal date 8, thus commemorating the Sultan's visit to that city.

21.   100 Piastres. Year 8 (1846) 175.00
22.   50 Piastres. Year 8 (1846) 150.00

ABDUL AZIZ, 1861-1876

Same type as above but with the accession date 1277.

23.	500 Piastres. Years 7-13 (1867-73)	....	800.00
24.	250 Piastres. Years 7, 9 (1867, 69)	....	400.00
25.	100 Piastres. Years 1-14 (1861-74)	.... *	175.00
26.	50 Piastres. Years 1, 7, 9 (1861, 67, 69)	....	85.00
27.	25 Piastres. Years 1-7 (1861-67)	....	70.00

Type as above but with the name of the city of Brusa added to the legend on coins with regnal dates 1 or 2, thus commemorating the Sultan's visit to that city.

28.	100 Piastres. Year 1 (1861)	....	225.00
29.	50 Piastres. Year 1 (1861)	....	170.00
30.	25 Piastres. Year 1 (1861)	....	125.00

MURAD V, 1876

Toughra without flower to right and regnal year 1. Rev. Legend and accession date 1293.

31.	100 Piastres. Year 1 (1876)	....	300.00
32.	50 Piastres. Year 1 (1876)	....	200.00
33.	25 Piastres. Year 1 (1876)	....	125.00

ABDUL HAMID II, 1876-1909
Standard Gold Coins

Same type as above but with the accession date, 1293, and a flower to the right of the toughra.

34.	500 Piastres. Years 1-2 (1876-77)	....	800.00
35.	250 Piastres. Years 1-2 (1876-77)	....	400.00
36.	100 Piastres. Years 1-6 (1876-81)	....	175.00
37.	50 Piastres. Years 1-6 (1876-81)	....	85.00
38.	25 Piastres. Years 3-6 (1878-81)	....	70.00

Same type and accession date as above, but with the inscription "al-Ghazi" (i.e., fighter of infidels) in place of the flower.

39.	500 Piastres. Years 7-32 (1899-1907)	....	800.00
40.	250 Piastres. Years 7-32 (1899-1907)	....	400.00
41.	100 Piastres. Years 7-34 (1899-1909)	....	175.00
42.	50 Piastres. Years 7-34 (1899-1909)	....	85.00
43.	25 Piastres. Years 7-32 (1899-1907)	....	70.00

De Luxe Gold Coins

Group of military weapons. Rev. Legend with accession date 1293. Although very large and quite thin, this, like all De Luxe coins prior to 1926, is of standard weight.

44.	500 Piastres. Years 26-33 (1901-08)	....	750.00

Toughra. Rev. Legend. Ornamental wreath on each side. With accession date 1293.

45.	250 Piastres. Years 24-33 (1899-1908)	.... *	400.00
46.	100 Piastres. Years 29-33 (1904-08)	....	200.00
47.	50 Piastres. Years 28-31 (1903-06)	....	125.00
48.	25 Piastres. Years 27, 30 (1902, 05)	....	90.00
49.	12½ Piastres. Year 30 (1905)	....	75.00

MOHAMMED V, 1909-1918
Standard Gold Coins

Same type as previous issues but with the accession date 1327 and the inscription "Rashad" (the Sultan's name) to the right of the toughra.

50.	500 Piastres. Years 1-4 (1909-12)	.... *	800.00
51.	250 Piastres. Years 1-6 (1909-14)	....	400.00
52.	100 Piastres. Years 1-7 (1909-15)	....	175.00
53.	50 Piastres. Years 2-5 (1910-13)	....	85.00
54.	25 Piastres. Years 1-6 (1909-14)	....	70.00

Type as above, but with the inscription "al-Ghazi" instead of "Rashad."

55.	500 Piastres. Year 10 (1918)	....	800.00
56.	250 Piastres. Year 7 (1915)	....	400.00
57.	100 Piastres. Years 7-10 (1915-18)	.... *	175.00
58.	50 Piastres. Year 9 (1917)	....	85.00
59.	25 Piastres. Year 7 (1915)	....	70.00

Type as above but with the name of a city replacing Constantinople on coins with regnal dates 1, 2 or 3. The following cities may be read in Arabic on the coins, which thus commemorate the Sultan's visit to that city:— Adrianople (Edirne), Brusa, Kossova, Monastir, Salonica (Selanik).

60.	500 Piastres. Year 2 (1910). Edirne	....	750.00
60a.	500 Piastres. Year 3 (1911). Kossova	....	750.00
60b.	500 Piastres. Year 3 (1911). Monastir	....	750.00
60c.	500 Piastres. Year 3 (1911). Selanik	....	800.00
61.	100 Piastres. Year 1 (1909). Brusa	....	275.00
61a.	100 Piastres. Year 2 (1910). Edirne	....	275.00
61b.	100 Piastres. Year 3 (1911). Kossova	....	275.00
61c.	100 Piastres. Year 3 (1911). Monastir	....	275.00
61d.	100 Piastres. Year 3 (1911). Selanik	....	300.00
62.	50 Piastres. Year 1 (1909). Brusa	....	175.00
62a.	50 Piastres. Year 2 (1910). Edirne	....	175.00

62b.	50 Piastres. Year 3 (1911). Kossova	175.00
62c.	50 Piastres. Year 3 (1911). Monastir..................	175.00
62d.	50 Piastres. Year 3 (1911). Selanik	200.00
63.	25 Piastres. Year 1 (1909). Brusa....................	90.00

De Luxe Gold Coins

Similar to No. 44 but with the accession date 1327.

64. 500	Piastres. Years 2-8 (1910-16) ....*......	1000.00

Similar to Nos. 45-49, but with the accession date 1327.

65. 250	Piastres. Years 2-8 (1910-16)	300.00
66. 100	Piastres. Years 2-8 (1910-16)	400.00
67. 50	Piastres. Years 2-8 (1910-16)	175.00
68. 25	Piastres. Years 2-8 (1910-16)	85.00
69. 12½	Piastres. Years 2-6 (1910-14)	70.00

MOHAMMED VI, 1918-1921
Standard Gold Coins

Same type as previous issues but with the accession date 1336.

70.	500 Piastres. Years 2-3 (1919-20)	950.00
71.	250 Piastres. Year 1 (1918)	500.00
72.	100 Piastres. Year 1 (1918).........................	175.00
73.	50 Piastres. Years 1, 5 (1918, 22)....................	85.00
74.	25 Piastres. Years 1-2 (1918-19)	70.00

De Luxe Gold Coins

Same general type as the previous issue of De Luxe Gold Coins but with the accession date 1336.

75.	500 Piastres. Years 1-4 (1918-21)	1000.00
76.	250 Piastres. Years 2-3 (1919-20)	300.00
77.	100 Piastres. Years 2-3 (1919-20)	200.00
78.	25 Piastres. Years 2-3 (1919-20)	65.00

B. Republic of —

I. REGULAR ISSUES
Standard Gold Coins

Star, legend and Mohammedan year within crescent. Rev. Legend and corresponding Christian year (in Arabic numerals).

79.	500 Piastres 1926-29 ....*.....	900.00
80.	250 Piastres 1926-28	500.00
81.	100 Piastres 1926-29	250.00
82.	50 Piastres 1926-28	100.00
83.	25 Piastres 1926-29	75.00

De Luxe Gold Coins

Sunburst and crescent. Rev. Date and wreath. As the De Luxe coins of the Sultans, these pieces are highly decorative. They are very large and thin but of standard weight.

84.	500 Piastres 1927, 28	1100.00
85.	250 Piastres 1927, 28	300.00
86.	100 Piastres 1927, 28 ....*......	200.00
87.	50 Piastres 1927, 28	85.00
88.	25 Piastres 1927, 28	75.00

II. SPECIAL COMMEMORATIVE ISSUES
The following coins do not bear the marks of value but are of the same sizes and weights as the previous issues.

PRESIDENT KEMAL ATATURK
Standard Gold Coins

Head and below "Ankara". Rev. Legend and date 1923, with two additional numerals below, which must be added to 1923 to determine the exact year of issue.

89.	500 Piastres 1943-	850.00(B)
90.	250 Piastres 1943-	400.00(B)
91.	100 Piastres 1943- ....*......	175.00(B)
92.	50 Piastres 1943-	85.00(B)
93.	25 Piastres 1943-	70.00(B)

(Numbers 89-93 are bullion coins. The price listed is based on gold at $725 per ounce.)

De Luxe Gold Coins

Head in circle of stars. Rev. Legend in circle of stars, date below.

94.	500 Piastres 1942-44, 47-48, 50- ....*......	800.00
95.	250 Piastres 1942-44, 46-	400.00
96.	100 Piastres 1942-44, 48-	150.00
97.	50 Piastres 1942-44, 46, 48-	85.00
98.	25 Piastres 1942-44, 46, 48-	70.00

PRESIDENT ISMET INONU
Standard Gold Coins

Head and below "Ankara". Rev. Legend and date 1923, with two additional numerals below, which must be added to 1923 to determine the exact year of issue.

99.	500 Piastres 1943-49	*	850.00
100.	250 Piastres 1943-49		400.00
101.	100 Piastres 1943-49		175.00
102.	50 Piastres 1943-49		80.00
103.	25 Piastres 1943-49		70.00

De Luxe Gold Coins

Head in wreath. Rev. Legend and date.

104.	500 Piastres 1943-47		800.00
105.	250 Piastres 1944-47		400.00
106.	100 Piastres 1944-47	*	150.00
107.	50 Piastres 1944-47		80.00
108.	25 Piastres 1944-47		70.00

For later issues of Turkey, see the section, "Recent Issues Starting With 1960."

UNITED STATES OF AMERICA

Mints and mint marks:—

Without mint mark for Philadelphia (Pennsylvania)
C   mm for Charlotte (North Carolina)
CC   mm for Carson City (Nevada)
D   mm for Dahlonega (Georgia, 19th century)
D   mm for Denver (Colorado, 20th century)
O   mm for New Orleans (Louisiana)
S   mm for San Francisco (California)

The initial gold coinage, 1795-1834, was of sterling purity, .916⅔ Fine. In 1834, the fineness was reduced to .899¼ and at the same time, the weight of the coins themselves was also reduced, the 5 Dollar piece, for example, going from 135 to 129 grains, and the 2½ Dollar piece in proportion. In 1837, the fineness was increased to .900, at which point it remained until the end of gold coinage in 1933. United States gold coins dated before 1808 do not show the mark of value. The Philadelphia Mint coined 20 Dollar gold pieces dated 1933, but this date is not listed in the catalogue since the coins were not released officially and possession of this one date is illegal.

There is also in existence, a large amount of so-called coins of ¼, ½ and 1 Dollar denominations. Most of these coins are octagonal and they are sometimes called California gold coins or charms. They were privately struck in California or other western areas until the early years of this century. They are not included in this book since they do not form a part of regular U.S. coinage. On the other hand, the coinage of Territorial and Pioneer Gold, privately minted, has been included because these pieces are collected for their historic interest.

A. Coinage of the Official U.S. Government Mints

(The valuations are for the commonest date of the respective mint.)

1 DOLLAR

Liberty Head. Rev. Value. Small size.

1.	No mm. 1849-54		375.00
2.	C mm. 1849-53		450.00
3.	D mm. 1849-54	*	500.00
4.	O mm. 1849-53		375.00
5.	S mm. 1854		400.00

Small Liberty Head with feather head-dress. Rev. Value. Large size.

6.	No mm. 1854, 55		550.00
7.	C mm. 1855		750.00
8.	D mm. 1855	*	2750.00
9.	O mm. 1855		700.00
10.	S mm. 1856		600.00

Large Liberty Head with feather head-dress. Rev. Value. Large size.

11.	No mm. 1856-89		350.00
12.	C mm. 1857, 59		500.00
13.	D mm. 1856-61		600.00
14.	S mm. 1857-60, 1870	*	400.00

COMMEMORATIVE ISSUES

Different Obverses as indicated. Rev. Value and date.
For the Louisiana Purchase Exposition.

15.	1903. Head of Jefferson		900.00
16.	1903. Head of McKinley		900.00

Head on each side. For the Lewis & Clark Exposition.

17.	1904, 05	2000.00

Panama Canal laborer. Rev. Value.
For the Panama-Pacific Exposition.

18.	1915	1000.00

Head of William McKinley. Rev. Memorial Building.
For the McKinley Memorial.

19.	1916, 17	850.00

Bust of U.S. Grant. Rev. Cabin.
For the Grant Memorial.

20.	1922	*	1500.00
21.	1922. Same but with star on Obv.		1500.00

2½ DOLLARS (QUARTER EAGLES)

(The reverses bear various types of eagles.)

Liberty Head without stars. Rev. Eagle.

22. No mm. 1796 .... 17500.00

Liberty Head with stars. Rev. Eagle.

23. No mm. 1796-98, 1802, 04-07 .... 6000.00

Draped bust of Liberty with round cap. Rev. Eagle.

24. No mm. 1808 .... 16500.00

Liberty Head with round cap. Rev. Eagle.

25.	No mm. 1821, 1824-27	*	7500.00
26.	No mm. 1829-34. Size reduced		6500.00

Liberty Head with ribbon. Rev. Eagle. Without motto on Rev.

27.	No mm. 1834-39	*	375.00
28.	C mm. 1838, 39		500.00
29.	D mm. 1839		500.00
30.	O mm. 1839		425.00

Liberty Head with Coronet. Rev. Eagle.

31.	No mm. 1840-1907	*	275.00
32.	No mm. 1848-"Cal" over eagle		12500.00
33.	C mm. 1840-44, 46-52, 54-56, 58, 60		450.00
34.	D mm. 1840-57, 59		450.00
35.	O mm. 1840, 42, 43, 45-47, 50-52, 54, 56, 57		300.00
36.	S mm. 1854, 56-63, 65-73, 75-79		300.00

Indian Head. Rev. Eagle. With designs and legends incused.

37.	No mm. 1908-15, 26-29		300.00
38.	D mm. 1911, 14, 25 (1911 Rare)	*	300.00

COMMEMORATIVE ISSUES

Columbia on mythical sea horse. Rev. Eagle.
For the Panama-Pacific Exposition.

39. 1915 .... 3500.00

Liberty Standing. Rev. Independence Hall.
For the Philadelphia Sesquicentennial.

40. 1926 .... 750.00

3 DOLLARS

Liberty Head with feather head-dress. Rev. Value and date.

41.	No mm. 1854-89	*	750.00
42.	D mm. 1854		5000.00
43.	O mm. 1854		850.00
44.	S mm. 1855-57, 60, 70		750.00

4 DOLLARS (STELLA)

Liberty Head with flowing hair. Rev. Star.

45. No mm. 1879, 80. Patterns only 30000.00

Liberty Head with coiled hair. Rev. Star.

46.   No mm. 1879, 80. Patterns only 75000.00

5 DOLLARS (HALF EAGLES)

(The reverses bear various types of eagles.)

Liberty Head. Rev. Small eagle.

47.   No mm. 1795-98 .... 10000.00

Liberty Head. Rev. Large, heraldic eagle.

48.   No mm. 1795, 1797-1807 .... 4000.00

Draped bust of Liberty with round cap. Rev. Eagle.

49.   No mm. 1807-12 .... 4000.00

Liberty Head with round cap. Rev. Eagle.

50.   No mm. 1813-29 .... 5000.00
51.   No mm. 1829-34. Size reduced 10500.00

Liberty Head with ribbon. Rev. Eagle. Without motto on Rev.

52.   No mm. 1834-38 ....* 450.00
53.   C mm. 1838 .... 2000.00
54.   D mm. 1838 .... 2000.00

Liberty Head with coronet. Rev. Eagle. Without motto.

55.   No mm. 1838-65 ....* 275.00
56.   C mm. 1839-44, 46-61 .... 500.00
57.   D mm. 1839-61 .... 500.00
58.   O mm. 1840-47, 51, 54-57 .... 400.00
59.   S mm. 1854-66 .... 325.00

Liberty Head with coronet. Rev. Eagle. With Motto.

60.   No mm. 1866-1908 ....* 250.00
61.   O mm. 1892-94 .... 400.00
62.   S mm. 1866-88, 92-1906 .... 250.00
63.   CC mm. 1870-84, 90-93 .... 375.00
64.   D mm. 1906, 07 .... 250.00

Indian Head. Rev. Eagle. With designs and legends incused.

65.   No mm. 1908-15, 1929 ....* 400.00
66.   O mm. 1909 .... 1500.00
67.   S mm. 1908-16 .... 400.00
68.   D mm. 1908-11, 1914 .... 450.00

10 DOLLARS (EAGLES)

(The reverses bear various types of eagles.)

Liberty Head. Rev. Small eagle.

69.   No mm. 1795-97 .... 12500.00

Liberty Head. Rev. Large heraldic eagle.

70.   No mm. 1797-1801, 03, 04 .... 6500.00

Small Liberty Head. Rev. Eagle. Without motto.

71. No mm. 1838, 39... 1750.00

Large Liberty Head. Rev. Eagle. Without motto.

72. No mm. 1840-65.................................*...... 400.00
73. O mm. 1841-60... 400.00
74. S mm. 1854-66... 400.00

Liberty Head. Rev. Eagle. With motto.

75. No mm. 1866-1907..............................*..... 400.00
76. O mm. 1879-83, 88, 92-95, 97, 99, 1901, 03, 04, 06...... 400.00
77. S mm. 1866-74, 76-89, 92-1903, 05-07.................. 400.00
78. CC mm. 1870-84, 90-93................................. 450.00
79. D mm. 1906, 07.. 400.00

Indian Head. Rev. Eagle. Without motto.

80. No mm. 1907. With period before and after the
        Rev. legend....................................10000.00
81. No mm. 1907, 08. Without periods..............*...... 850.00
82. D mm. 1908.. 850.00

Indian Head. Rev. Eagle. With motto.

83. No mm. 1908-15, 26, 32, 33....................*..... 600.00
84. S mm. 1908-16, 20, 30................................. 600.00
85. D mm. 1908-11, 14.................................... 600.00

20 DOLLARS (DOUBLE EAGLES)

(The reverses bear various types of eagles.)

Liberty Head. Rev. Eagle. Without motto.

86. No mm. 1850-65................................*...... 900.00
87. No mm. 1861. Rev. by Paquet.......................... Rare
88. O mm. 1850-61.. 1500.00
89. S mm. 1854-66... 900.00
90. S mm. 1861. Rev. by Paquet........................... Rare

Liberty Head. Rev. Eagle. With motto and "Twenty D."

91. No mm. 1866-76.................................*...... 850.00
92. S mm. 1866-76... 850.00
93. CC mm. 1870-76.. 900.00

Liberty Head. Rev. Eagle. With motto and "Twenty Dollars."

94. No mm. 1877-1907..............................*...... 850.00
95. S mm. 1877-85, 1887-1907.............................. 850.00
96. CC mm. 1877-79, 82-85, 89-93.......................... 900.00
97. D mm. 1906, 07.. 850.00

*Liberty standing (St. Gaudens type) with date in Roman Numerals.
Rev. Flying Eagle.*

98. No mm. 1907. Very high relief (concave) and
        very wide edge...................................... Rare
99. No mm. 1907. Normal high relief with wire or
        flat edge.......................................*...... 9500.00

Liberty standing with date in usual numerals. Rev. Eagle. Without motto.

100.	No mm. 1907, 08	.................................*......	850.00
101.	D mm. 1908	....	850.00

Liberty standing. Rev. Eagle. With motto.

102.	No mm. 1908-15, 20-29, 31, 32	....	850.00
103.	S mm. 1908-11, 13-16, 20, 22, 24-27, 30	.........*......	850.00
104.	D mm. 1908-11, 13, 14, 23-27, 31	....	850.00

50 DOLLARS

Head of Minerva. Rev. Owl. Commemorative issue for the Panama-Pacific Exposition.

105.	1915. Round coin	....	35000.00
106.	1915. Octagonal coin	...........................*......	25000.00

GOLD COINAGE FOR FOREIGN COUNTRIES
(Gold coins struck at the Philadelphia Mint in 1945 and 1946 for use in Saudi Arabia.)

Weight and fineness in three line rectangular tablet. Rev. Eagle and "U.S. Mint, Philadelphia, U.S.A."

107.	4 Saudi Pounds ND	...........................*......	900.00
108.	1 Saudi Pound ND	....	325.00

B. Coinage of the Territorial and Private Mints

(Pioneer Gold)

BALDWIN & CO.

San Francisco, California

Horseman with lariat. Rev. Eagle.

109.	10 Dollars 1850	....	30000.00

"Baldwin & Co" on head band of liberty. Rev. Eagle.

110.	5 Dollars 1850	....	7000.00
111.	10 Dollars 1851	....	20000.00
112.	20 Dollars 1851	....	25000.00

AUGUST BECHTLER

Rutherford, North Carolina

Value and legend. Rev. Weight and legend. The coins are undated but were struck from 1831 to 1842.

113.	1 Dollar ND. One variety	.....................*......	850.00
114.	5 Dollars ND. Three varieties	....	2500.00

CHRISTOPHER BECHTLER

Rutherford, North Carolina

Value and legend. Rev. Weight and legend. The coins are undated but were struck from 1831 to 1842.

115.	1 Dollar ND. Four varieties	....	900.00
116.	2½ Dollars ND. Seven varieties	................*.....	3000.00
117.	5 Dollars ND. Six varieties	....	3000.00
118.	5 Dollars August 1, 1834. Two varieties	.....*......	4000.00

BLAKE & CO.

Sacramento, California
Stamping machine. Rev. Value and legend.

119.	20 Dollars 1855	....	Rare

BLAKE & AGNELL

Sacramento, California

*Square shaped ingot with name, weight, fineness and value
stamped on both sides.*

120. $23.30 1855 .... Rare

EPHRAIM BRASHER

New York

*Radiant sun over mountains. Rev. Eagle with "EB" punched
on either the wing or breast. The famous Brasher
Doubloon.*

121. Doubloon 1787 ....* ..... Very Rare
122. ½ Doubloon 1787 .... Unique

*Cross of Jerusalem and "EB" punch mark. Rev. Pillars with
"Brasher" below. An imitation of a Lima Mint 8 Escudos
dated 1742.*

123. 8 Escudos or Doubloon (1787) .... Rare

CALIFORNIA & SIERRA CO.

California

Rectangular ingot with various punch marks and lettered edges.

124. $36.57 1860 .... Rare

CINCINNATI MINING & TRADING CO.

San Francisco, California

Indian Head. Rev. Eagle.

125. 5 Dollars 1849 .... Rare
126. 10 Dollars 1849 .... Rare

CLARK, GRUBER & CO.

Denver, Colorado

View of Pikes Peak. Rev. Eagle.

127. 10 Dollars 1860 ....* 7500.00
128. 20 Dollars 1860 .... 25000.00

"Clark & Co." on head band of Liberty. Rev. Eagle.

129. 2½ Dollars 1860 .... 1750.00
130. 5 Dollars 1860 .... 2000.00

"Pikes Peak" on head band of Liberty. Rev. Eagle.

131. 2½ Dollars 1861 ....* 1500.00
132. 5 Dollars 1861 ....* 2500.00
133. 10 Dollars 1863 .... 3750.00
134. 20 Dollars 1861 .... 9000.00

J.J. CONWAY & CO.

Georgia Gulch, Colorado

*Name of company. Rev. Value and "Pikes Peak". Undated
but struck in 1861.*

135. 2½ Dollars ND .... Rare
136. 5 Dollars ND .... Rare
137. 10 Dollars ND .... Rare

DUBOSQ & CO.

San Francisco, California

"Dubosq & Co." on head band of Liberty. Rev. Eagle.

138. 5 Dollars 1850 .... Rare
139. 10 Dollars 1850 .... Rare

DUNBAR & CO.

San Francisco, California

"Dunbar & Co." on head band of Liberty. Rev. Eagle.

140. 5 Dollars 1851 .... Rare

AUGUSTUS HUMBERT

U.S. Assayer of gold, San Francisco, California.

Eagle. Rev. Four line legend in tablet.

141. 10 Dollars 1852 ....* 1750.00
142. 20 Dollars 1852 .... 7000.00

Eagle. Rev. Small 50, star or circle in center of reverse.
Octagonal shaped with lettered edge.

143.   50 Dollars 1851. Five varieties 9000.00

Eagle. Rev. Machine made criss-cross of circular lines.
Octagonal shaped with reeded edge.

144.   50 Dollars 1851, 52. Three varieties 5000.00

KELLOGG & CO.

San Francisco, California

"Kellogg & Co." on head band of Liberty. Rev. Standard Eagle.

145.   20 Dollars 1854, 55 .... 2500.00

Obv. Similar to above. Rev. Eagle holding shield.

146.   50 Dollars 1855 ....   Rare

KELLOGG & HEWSTON

San Francisco, California

Rectangular ingot with various punch marks and name along edge.

147. $49.50 ND. (1860)......................................   Rare

F.D. KOHLER

State Assayer, San Francisco and Sacramento, California
Rectangular gold ingots bearing name, weight, fineness and value.

148. $36.55 1850 ....   Rare
149. $37.31 1850 ....   Rare
150. $40.07 1850 ....   Rare
151. $41.68 1850 ....   Rare
152. $45.34 1850 ....   Rare
153. $50.00 1850 ....   Rare
154. $54.09 1850 ....   Rare

MASSACHUSETTS & CALIFORNIA CO.

San Francisco, California

Arms supported by bear and stag. Rev. Value in wreath.

155.   5 Dollars 1849. Four varieties......................   Rare

MINERS BANK

San Francisco, California

Name and value. Rev. Eagle.

156.   10 Dollars 1849 ....10000.00

MOFFAT & CO.

San Francisco, California

"Moffat & Co." on head band of Liberty. Rev. Eagle.

157.   5 Dollars 1849, 50 .... 1250.00
158.   10 Dollars 1849, 52 .... 2500.00
159.   20 Dollars 1853 ....*...... 2500.00

Rectangular ingots bearing legends, values and weights.

160. $ 9.43 ND (1849-1853)............................... Unique
161. $14.25 ND (1849-1853)............................... Unique
162. $16.00 ND (1849-1853)...............................   Rare

THE MORMONS

Salt Lake City, Utah

Eye and Bishop's Mitre. Rev. Clasped hands.

163.	2½	Dollars 1849	*	4000.00
164.	5	Dollars 1849, 50	*	2000.00
165.	10	Dollars 1849	*	35000.00
166.	20	Dollars 1849	*	20000.00

Lion. Rev. Beehive on breast of eagle.

167.	5	Dollars 1860	8000.00

NORRIS, GRIEG & NORRIS

San Francisco, California

Eagle. Rev. Legend.

168.	5	Dollars 1849. Plain or reeded edge	2500.00

OREGON EXCHANGE CO.

Oregon City, Oregon

Beaver and initials. Rev. Legend.

169.	5	Dollars 1849	10000.00
170.	10	Dollars 1849	30000.00

J.S. ORMSBY

San Francisco, California

"J.S.O." Rev. Value. Undated but struck in 1849.

171.	5	Dollars ND	Rare
172.	10	Dollars ND *	Rare

PACIFIC CO.

San Francisco, California

Liberty Cap. Rev. Eagle.

173.	5	Dollars 1849 *	Rare
174.	10	Dollars 1849	Rare

JOHN PARSONS & CO.

Tarryall Mines, Colorado

Stamping machine. Rev. Eagle and "Pikes Peak Gold." Undated but struck in 1861.

175.	2½	Dollars ND	Rare
176.	5	Dollars ND	Rare

Rectangular ingot bearing name and various legends.

177.	20	Dollars 1860	Unique

SHULTS & CO.

San Francisco, California

"Shults & Co." on head band of Liberty. Rev. Eagle.

178.	5	Dollars 1851	15000.00

TEMPLETON REID

Lumpkin County, Georgia

Legend on each side.

179.	2½	Dollars 1830	Rare
180.	5	Dollars 1830	Rare
181.	10	Dollars 1830	Rare
182.	10	Dollars ND	Rare

TEMPLETON REID

San Francisco, California
Legend on each side.

183.	10 Dollars 1849	....	Rare
184.	25 Dollars 1849	....	Unknown

UNITED STATES ASSAY OFFICE OF GOLD

San Francisco, California

Eagle. Rev. Legend in tablet.

185.	10 Dollars 1852, 53. Two varieties	...........*	1500.00
186.	20 Dollars 1853. Two varieties	....	2000.00

Eagle. Rev. Machine made criss-cross of circular lines. Octagonal shaped.

187.	50 Dollars 1852. Two varieties	....	7500.00

WASS, MOLITOR & CO.

San Francisco, California

"W.M. & Co." on head band of Liberty. Rev. Eagle.

188.	5 Dollars 1852	....	3500.00
189.	10 Dollars 1852, 55. Two varieties	...........*	3500.00
190.	20 Dollars 1855. Two varieties	....	12500.00

Liberty head. Rev. Name and value.

191.	50 Dollars 1855	....	15000.00

Arms. Rev. Value in wreath. These coins are patterns and were not placed in circulation.

1.	40 Reales 1854	....	Rare
2.	1 Doblon 1870	...........................*	Rare
3.	5 Pesos 1870	....	Rare
4.	2 Pesos 1870	....	Rare
5.	1 Peso 1870	....	Rare
5a.	50 Centesimos 1870	....	Rare

Head of Artigas. Rev. Value and dates 1830 and 1930. On the Centennial of the Republic. 100,000 were reported struck, but only 14,415 were issued.

6.	5 Pesos 1930	....	275.00

VATICAN CITY (ROME)

Papal coinage closely follows Italian Issues insofar as coinage standards are concerned.

Popes of —

A. Coinage struck at Rome

POPULAR GOVERNMENT, 1305
Arms. Rev. St. John.

1.	1 Florin ND	....	Rare

JOHN XXII, 1316-1334
INNOCENT VI, 1352-1362
URBAN V, 1362-1370
CLEMENT VII, 1378-1394
(See under France-Avignon).

THE ROMAN SENATE, 1350-1439

Senator kneeling before St. Peter. Rev. Christ.

2.	1 Ducat ND	....	700.00

ALEXANDER V, 1409-1410
JOHN XXIII, 1410-1415
MARTIN V, 1421-1428
(See under Vatican-Bologna).

EUGENE IV, 1431-1447

Arms. Rev. St. Peter.

3.   1 Ducat ND................................ 3000.00

NICHOLAS V, 1447-1455
Crossed Keys. Rev. St. Peter and St. Paul.

4.   3 Ducats ND .... Rare

Keys. Rev. Pope seated.

5.   1 Ducat ND................................ Rare

Arms. Rev. St. Peter.

6.   1 Ducat ND................................ 900.00

CALIXTUS III, 1455-1458

Arms. Rev. St. Peter in ship.

7.   1 Ducat ND................................ 2750.00

Arms. Rev. St. Peter standing.

8.   1 Ducat ND................................ 2500.00

Arms. Rev. St. Peter and St. Paul.

9.   1 Ducat ND................................ Rare

PIUS II, 1458-1464
St. Peter and St. Paul. Rev. Ship at Sea.

10.   2 Ducats ND .... Rare

Arms. Rev. Ship at sea.

11.   1 Ducat ND................................ Rare

Arms. Rev. St. Peter.

12.   1 Ducat ND................................ 1350.00

PAUL II, 1464-1471
Christ and St. Peter. Rev. Eight apostles in ship.

13.   4 Ducats 1464, 65 .... Rare

Arms. Rev. Christ and St. Peter.

13a.   2 Ducats 1464 .... Rare

Arms. Rev. Christ and St. Peter.

14.   1 Ducat 1464 .... 7000.00

Arms. Rev. Pope kneeling before St. Peter.

15.   2 Ducats ND ....*...... Rare
15a.   1 Ducat 1464, ND.................... 6000.00

Arms. Rev. Pope kneeling before Christ.

16.   1 Ducat ND................................ 2500.00

Arms. Rev. St. Peter.

17.   2 Ducats ND .... Unknown
18.   1 Ducat ND................................ 3000.00

Arms. Rev. Two apostles.

19.   1 Ducat ND................................ 1500.00

Arms. Rev. St. Veronica.

20.   1 Ducat ND................................ 3000.00

SIXTUS IV, 1471-1484
Christ and St. Peter in landscape. Rev. Apostles in ship.

21.   10 Fiorini di camera 1475............... Rare

Arms. Rev. Christ and St. Peter.

22.   2 Ducats ND .... Rare

Arms. Rev. St. Peter in ship.

23.	1 Fiorino di camera 1475, ND	1000.00

Arms. Rev. Pope kneeling before Christ.

24.	1 Ducat ND	Rare

Arms. Rev. Two apostles.

25.	1 Ducat ND	1700.00

INNOCENT VIII, 1484-1492

Arms. Rev. St. Peter in ship.

26.	1 Fiorino di camera ND	950.00

Arms. Rev. Two apostles.

27.	1 Ducat ND	2500.00

ALEXANDER VI BORGIA, 1492-1503
Bust. Rev. Arms.

28.	3 Ducats 1495, 1500	Rare

Arms. Rev. Christ and St. Peter; apostles in ship to left.

29.	5 Fiorini di camera ND	Rare

Arms. Rev. St. Peter in ship.

30.	2 Fiorini di camera ND .... *	4500.00
31.	1 Fiorino di camera ND	950.00

Two apostles. Rev. Legend.

32.	1 Ducat ND	Rare

PIUS III, 1503
Arms. Rev. St. Peter in ship.

33.	1 Fiorino di camera ND	Rare

JULIUS II, 1503-1513
Bust. Rev. Pastoral scene.

34.	4 Ducats ND	Rare

Bust. Rev. St. Peter sealed.

35.	3 Ducats ND	Rare

Bust. Rev. Two apostles in ship.

36.	2 Fiorini di camera ND	12000.00

Bust. Rev. Two apostles kissing.

37.	2 Fiorini di camera ND	Rare

Bust. Rev. St. Peter in ship.

38.	2 Fiorini di camera ND	Rare

Arms. Rev. Two apostles in ship.

39.	2 Fiorini di camera ND	7500.00
40.	1 Fiorino di camera ND .... *	950.00

Arms. Rev. St. Peter in ship.

41.	2 Fiorini di camera ND	6500.00
42.	1 Fiorino di camera ND	950.00

LEO X, 1513-1521

Bust. Rev. The three Magi.

43.	2½ Ducats ND .... *	Rare
44.	2 Ducats ND	Rare

Arms. Rev. Two apostles in ship.

45.	2 Fiorini di camera ND	6500.00
46.	1 Fiorino di camera ND .... *	2250.00

Arms. Rev. Two apostles standing.

47.	1 Ducat ND	2500.00

Arms. Rev. St. Peter in ship.

48.	1 Fiorino di camera ND	2000.00

SEDE VACANTE, 1521

Arms. Rev. St. Peter in ship.

49.	1 Fiorino di camera ND	11000.00

ADRIAN VI, 1522-1523

Arms. Rev. St. Peter in ship.

50.	2 Fiorini di camera ND	*	Rare
51.	1 Fiorino di camera ND		6000.00

SEDE VACANTE, 1523
Arms. Rev. St. Peter in ship. Trident mintmark in reverse legend.

51a.	1 Fiorino di camera ND	Rare

CLEMENT VII, 1523-1534

Birth of Christ. Rev. Pope opening the Holy Door.

52.	5 Ducati 1525	Rare

Bust. Rev. Angel and St. Peter.

53.	2 Ducats ND	Rare

Bust. Rev. Christ standing.

54.	2 Ducats ND	Rare

Pope and Emperor Charles V standing. Rev. Two apostles.

55.	2 Ducats ND	Rare

Arms. Rev. Two apostles.

56.	3 Ducats ND	Rare

Arms. Rev. Two apostles in ship.

57.	2 Fiorini di camera ND	Rare

Arms. Rev. St. Peter.

58.	2 Ducats ND	Rare

Arms. Rev. St. Peter in ship.

59.	2 Fiorini di camera ND	*	5500.00
60.	1 Fiorino di camera ND		1250.00

Arms. Rev. St. Peter seated.

61.	2 Ducats ND	Rare

PAUL III, 1534-1549
Bust. Rev. Christ among the Doctors.

61a.	3 Fiorini di camera ND	Rare

Bust. Rev. St. Peter in ship.

62.	2 Fiorini di camera ND	Rare

Arms. Rev. St. Paul in ship.

63.	1 Fiorino di camera ND	6500.00

Arms. Rev. St. Peter in ship.

64.	1 Fiorino di camera ND	1650.00

Arms. Rev. St. Paul standing. There are several varieties of the standing figure.

65.	1 Scudo d'oro ND	700.00
65a.	½ Scudo d'oro ND	Rare

Arms. Rev. Pope seated.

65b.	1 Scudo d'oro ND	Rare

JULIUS III, 1550-1555

Bust. Rev. St. Peter in ship.

66.	1 Fiorino di camera 1551	Rare

Arms. Rev. St. Peter.

67.	1 Scudo d'oro ND	12000.00

Arms. Rev. The Holy Door.

68.	1 Scudo d'oro 1550	14000.00

Arms. Rev. Bust of Christ.

69.	1 Scudo d'oro 1551, 52, ND	4000.00

SEDE VACANTE, 1555

Arms. Rev. St. Peter.

70.	1 Scudo d'oro 1555	Rare

PAUL IV, 1555-1559
Arms. Rev. St. Paul.

71.	1 Scudo d'oro ND	Rare

Arms. Rev. St. Peter.

72.	1 Scudo d'oro ND	Rare

SEDE VACANTE, 1559
Arms. Rev. St. Peter.

73.	1 Scudo d'oro 1559	Rare

PIUS IV, 1559-1565
(See under Vatican-Bologna).

PIUS V, 1566-1572
Bust. Rev. St. Peter in ship.

74.	2 Fiorini di camera 1566...........................	Rare
75.	1 Fiorino di camera ND	Rare

Arms. Rev. St. Peter kneeling before Christ.

76.	4 Scudi d'oro ND..................................	Unknown

GREGORY XIII, 1572-1585
Bust. Rev. The Holy Door.

77.	1 Scudo d'oro 1575................................	Rare
78.	The coin previously listed may be found under Vatican-Ancona, No. 311.	
79.	The coin previously listed has been found to be a medal.	

Arms. Rev. St. Peter raising girl.

79a.	1 Scudo d'oro ND	Rare

Arms. Rev. St. Peter.

80.	1 Scudo d'oro 1581, ND	8500.00

Bust. Rev. Madonna seated.

81.	1 Scudo d'oro ND	10000.00

Bust. Rev. St. Paul.

82.	1 Scudo d'oro ND	Rare

Arms. Rev. The Holy Door.

83.	1 Scudo d'oro 1575...............................	Rare

Arms. Rev. St. Peter in ship.

84.	1 Scudo d'oro 1575, 76	Rare

Arms. Rev. Bust of Christ.

85.	1 Scudo d'oro 1577-82, ND	5250.00

SIXTUS V, 1585-1590

Arms. Rev. Bust of Christ.

86.	1 Scudo d'oro 1585, 87, 88	6500.00

Arms. Rev. St. Peter.

87.	1 Scudo d'oro 1585...............................	Rare

SEDE VACANTE, 1590
Arms. Rev. St. Peter and angel.

88.	4 Scudi d'oro 1590	Rare

Arms. Rev. Roma seated.

89.	1 Scudo d'oro 1590...............................	Rare

Arms. Rev. Bust of Christ.

90.	1 Scudo d'oro 1590...............................	Rare

URBAN VII, 1590
GREGORY XIV, 1590-1591
(See under Vatican-Bologna).

SEDE VACANTE, 1591
Arms. Rev. David with harp.

91.	4 Scudi d'oro 1591	Rare

INNOCENT IX, 1591-1592
(See under Vatican-Bologna).

CLEMENT VIII, 1592-1605
Bust. Rev. Justice and Peace standing.

92.	4 Scudi d'oro 1598	Rare

Bust. Rev. The Church seated.

93.	4 Scudi d'oro ND.................................	Rare

Bust. Rev. The Lateran Church.

94.	1 Scudo d'oro ND	Rare

Arms. Rev. The Church seated.

95.	1 Scudo d'oro ND	10000.00

Arms. Rev. Pope kneeling.

96.	1 Scudo d'oro ND	10000.00

Arms. Rev. Dove.

97.	1 Scudo d'oro ND	Rare

SEDE VACANTE, 1605
Arms. Rev. The Church seated.

98.	4 Scudi d'oro 1605	Rare
99.	1 Scudo d'oro 1605...............................	Rare

PAUL V, 1605-1621

Bust. Rev. St. Paul seated.

100.	4 Scudi d'oro 1606, 07...........................	10000.00

Bust. Rev. St. Paul standing.

| 101. | 4 Scudi d'oro 1609 | 10000.00 |
| 102. | 1 Scudo d'oro 1617 ....*...... | 3500.00 |

Arms. Rev. Bust of St. Paul.

| 103. | 4 Scudi d'oro 1608, 09 | 8000.00 |
| 104. | 1 Scudo d'oro 1607, 15 ....*...... | 2000.00 |

Arms. Rev. Busts of St. Peter and St. Paul.

| 105. | 1 Scudo d'oro 1609 | 3000.00 |

Arms. Rev. St. Paul standing.

| 106. | 2 Scudi d'oro ND | 6500.00 |

Arms. Rev. St. Paul seated.

| 107. | 4 Scudi d'oro 1617 | 9000.00 |
| 108. | 1 Scudo d'oro 1606, 11 ....*...... | 2750.00 |

GREGORY XV, 1621-1623
Bust. Rev. Madonna standing.

| 109. | 1 Scudo d'oro 1622 | 8500.00 |

Bust. Rev. Church of St. Mary the Major.

| 110. | 1 Scudo d'oro 1622 | 7000.00 |

Arms. Rev. Madonna standing.

| 111. | 4 Scudi d'oro ND ....*...... | 15000.00 |
| 112. | 2 Scudi d'oro ND | 12000.00 |

Arms. Rev. St. Paul standing.

| 113. | 2 Scudi d'oro ND | 14000.00 |

SEDE VACANTE, 1623
Arms. Rev. Christ standing.

| 114. | 4 Scudi d'oro 1623 | Rare |
| 114a. | 2 Scudi d'oro 1623 | Rare |

URBAN VIII, 1623-1644

Bust. Rev. The Holy Door.

| 115. | 1 Scudo d'oro 1625 | 3500.00 |

Bust. Rev. Madonna standing.

| 116. | 4 Scudi d'oro 1634 | 16000.00 |
| 117. | 1 Scudo d'oro 1627-36, ND ....*...... | 3500.00 |

Bust. Rev. St. Michael standing.

| 118. | 4 Scudi d'oro 1634 | 17500.00 |
| 119. | 1 Scudo d'oro 1629, 36 | 3000.00 |

Bust. Rev. Bust of Christ.

| 120. | 1 Scudo d'oro 1630 | 3000.00 |

Arms. Rev. Madonna standing.

| 121. | 2 Scudi d'oro 1624 | 12000.00 |
| 122. | 1 Scudo d'oro 1642, 43, ND | 3000.00 |

Arms. Rev. Busts of St. Peter and St. Paul.

| 123. | 2 Scudi d'oro 1624 | 10000.00 |
| 123a. | 1 Scudo d'oro ND | 6000.00 |

Bust. Rev. Busts of St. Peter and St. Paul.

| 123b. | 2 Scudi d'oro ND | Rare |

Arms. Rev. The Holy Door.

| 124. | 1 Scudo d'oro 1625 | 2500.00 |

Arms. Rev. Bust of St. Paul.

| 125. | 1 Scudo d'oro 1627 | 3000.00 |

Arms. Rev. St. Michael standing.

| 126. | 1 Scudo d'oro 1642, 43, ND | 3000.00 |

INNOCENT X, 1644-1655
Bust. Rev. Arms.

| 127. | 4 Scudi d'oro 1647 | Rare |

Bust. Rev. The Holy Door.

| 128. | 4 Scudi d'oro 1650 | Rare |

Arms. Rev. Bust of St. Peter.

| 129. | 2 Scudi d'oro 1652 | Rare |
| 130. | 1 Scudo d'oro 1644, 52 ....*...... | 10000.00 |

Arms. Rev. Head of St. Peter.

| 130a. | 2 Scudi d'oro ND | Rare |

Arms. Rev. Madonna standing.

| 131. | 1 Scudo d'oro 1645, 52 | 10000.00 |

Arms. Rev. The Holy Door.

| 132. | 2 Scudi d'oro 1651 | Rare |

SEDE VACANTE, 1655

Arms. Rev. Dove.

133.　4 Scudi d'oro 1655 .... Rare
134.　2 Scudi d'oro 1655.........................*......17500.00

ALEXANDER VII, 1655-1667

Arms. Rev. Money chest.

135.　4 Scudi d'oro ND................................. Rare

Arms. Rev. Legend.

136.　2 Scudi d'oro ND.........................*...... Rare
137.　1 Scudo d'oro ND 7500.00

SEDE VACANTE, 1667
Arms. Rev. Dove.

138.　1 Scudo d'oro 1667............................... 10000.00

CLEMENT IX, 1667-1669

Arms. Rev. Madonna.

139.　4 Scudi d'oro ND.........................*...... Rare
140.　2 Scudi d'oro ND................................ 9500.00
141.　1 Scudo d'oro ND 5750.00

SEDE VACANTE, 1669
Arms. Rev. Dove.

142.　4 Scudi d'oro 1669 .... Rare
143.　2 Scudi d'oro 1669.............................15000.00
144.　1 Scudo d'oro 1669............................. 8000.00

CLEMENT X, 1669-1676

Bust. Rev. St. Peter.

145.　2 Scudi d'oro 1670 .... Rare

Arms. Rev. St. Venantius.

146.　2 Scudi d'oro ND...............................11000.00

Bust. Rev. King David.

147.　4 Scudi d'oro 1673 .... Rare

Arms. Rev. The Holy Door.

148.　1 Scudo d'oro 1675................................. 7500.00

Arms. Rev. King David.

149.　4 Scudi d'oro ND................................. Rare

Arms. Rev. St. Peter and St. Paul.

150.　2 Scudi d'oro ND.................................10000.00

Arms. Rev. St. Peter.

151.　1 Scudo d'oro ND 5500.00

Arms. Rev. Madonna.

152.　1 Scudo d'oro ND .... Rare

INNOCENT XI, 1676-1689

Bust. Rev. Madonna and four saints.

153.　4 Scudi d'oro 1676, 77............................. Rare

Arms. Rev. Madonna seated.

153a.　4 Scudi d'oro 1676 .... Rare

Bust. Rev. Holy figure among clouds.

154.　4 Scudi d'oro 1678 .... Rare

Bust. Rev. Legend.

155.　4 Scudi d'oro 1681, 82, 85 .... Rare

Arms. Rev. Religion seated.

156.　2 Scudi d'oro 1678 .... Rare

Arms. Rev. Legend.

157.	4 Scudi d'oro 1687	20000.00
158.	2 Scudi d'oro 1677-87...............................	11000.00
159.	1 Scudo d'oro 1684, ND ....*	5000.00

Arms. Rev. Madonna.

160.	1 Scudo d'oro ND	5000.00

Arms. Rev. Bust of Madonna.

161.	1 Scudo d'oro ND	5000.00

Arms. Rev. Bust of St. Peter.

162.	1 Scudo d'oro ND	5000.00

SEDE VACANTE, 1689
Arms. Rev. Dove.

163.	4 Scudi d'oro 1689	Rare
163a.	2 Scudi d'oro 1689	Rare

ALEXANDER VIII, 1689-1691

Bust. Rev. St. Peter and St. Paul.

164.	4 Scudi d'oro 1689	17500.00

Bust. Rev. The Church standing.

165.	16 Scudi d'oro 1690	Rare

Bust. Rev. Two oxen.

166.	4 Scudi d'oro 1690	14000.00

Bust. Rev. St. Bruno.

167.	4 Scudi d'oro 1690	Rare

Bust. Rev. St. Magnus and St. Bruno.

168.	4 Scudi d'oro 1690	17000.00

Arms. Rev. St. Bruno.

169.	2 Scudi d'oro 1689	10000.00

Arms. Rev. St. Peter.

170.	1 Scudo d'oro 1689.................................	5500.00

Arms. Rev. Busts of St. Peter and St. Paul.

171.	1 Scudo d'oro 1690.................................	4250.00

Arms. Rev. Altar.

172.	2 Scudi d'oro 1690	12500.00

SEDE VACANTE, 1691

Arms. Rev. Dove.

173.	2 Scudi d'oro 1691	Rare

INNOCENT XII, 1691-1700

Bust. Rev. Fountain.

174.	4 Scudi d'oro 1694	15000.00

Bust. Rev. Noah's Ark.

175.	2 Scudi d'oro 1697	11000.00

Bust of St. Peter. Rev. Arms.

176.	1 Scudo d'oro 1691, 92	5000.00
177.	½ Scudo d'oro 1694................................	3000.00

Arms. Rev. St. Paul.

178.　2 Scudi d'oro 1692 .... 10000.00

Arms. Rev. Plant.

179.　1 Scudo d'oro 1694 .... 9500.00

Arms. Rev. The Holy Door.

180.　2 Scudi d'oro 1699 .... 12000.00
181.　1 Scudo d'oro 1700 .... 4500.00
182.　½ Scudo d'oro 1694 .... 4000.00

Arms. Rev. Corn ears in vessel.

183.　1 Scudo d'oro 1697 .... 4000.00

SEDE VACANTE, 1700
Arms. Rev. Dove.

184.　1 Scudo d'oro 1700 .... 7500.00

CLEMENT XI, 1700-1721

Bust. Rev. The Holy Door.

185.　2 Scudi d'oro 1700 .... 9000.00

Bust. Rev. Piety and Discord.

186.　4 Scudi d'oro 1706 .... Rare

Bust. Rev. Arms.

187.　1 Scudo d'oro 1710 .... 5000.00

Bust. Rev. Star over sea.

188.　½ Scudo d'oro 1716 .... 4000.00

Bust. Rev. Bust of St. Peter.

189.　½ Scudo d'oro 1717 .... 950.00

Bust. Rev. Legend.

190.　2 Scudi d'oro 1710, 14 .... 9500.00

Bust of St. Paul facing right or left. Rev. Arms.

191.　2 Scudi d'oro 1702, 05 .... Unknown
192.　1 Scudo d'oro 1702-09 .... * 4000.00

Arms. Rev. Madonna.

193.　4 Scudi d'oro 1706 .... Rare

Arms and globe. Rev. Legend.

194.　2 Scudi d'oro 1706 .... Rare

Arms. Rev. Anchor.

195.　1 Scudo d'oro 1706 .... 5000.00

Arms. Rev. Charity standing.

196.　4 Scudi d'oro 1707 .... Rare

Arms. Rev. Three females.

197.　4 Scudi d'oro 1707 .... Rare

Arms. Rev. St. Francis kneeling.

198.　2 Scudi d'oro 1707 .... 12000.00

Arms. Rev. St. Francisca.

199.　2 Scudi d'oro 1709 .... 12000.00

Arms. Rev. Bust of St. Peter.

200.　½ Scudo d'oro 1709, 16, 17 .... 1250.00

Arms. Rev. Various legends.

201.　2 Scudi d'oro 1712 .... 10000.00
202.　1 Scudo d'oro 1711-18 .... * 2500.00
203.　½ Scudo d'oro ND 1500.00

Arms. Rev. Bow and arrow.

204.　1 Scudo d'oro 1716 .... 5500.00

Arms. Rev. Religion seated.

205.　1 Scudo d'oro 1718 .... Unknown

Arms. Rev. Faith standing.

206.　1 Scudo d'oro 1718 .... 2250.00

Arms. Rev. Olive tree.

207.   1 Scudo d'oro 1720 .... 5000.00

Three mountains. Rev. Star over sea.

208.   ½ Scudo d'oro 1706 .... 4000.00

SEDE VACANTE, 1721
Arms. Rev. Dove.

209.   2 Scudi d'oro 1721 .... 13000.00
210.   1 Scudo d'oro 1721 .... 7000.00

INNOCENT XIII, 1721-1724

Bust. Rev. Eagle.

211.   1 Scudo d'oro 1724 .... 6500.00

Arms. Rev. Legend.

212.   1 Scudo d'oro 1722 .... 5000.00

Arms. Rev. Eagle.

213.   ½ Scudo d'oro 1724 .... 3000.00

SEDE VACANTE, 1724
Arms. Rev. Dove.

214.   1 Scudo d'oro 1724 .... 10000.00

BENEDICT XIII, 1724-1730

Arms. Rev. The Holy Door.

215.   2 Scudi d'oro 1725 ....12000.00
216.   1 Scudo d'oro 1725 ....* 5000.00

The Church seated. Rev. Rose and value.

217.   1 Zecchino 1729 .... 3000.00

SEDE VACANTE, 1730
Arms. Rev. Dove.

218.   2 Scudi d'oro 1730 .... 11000.00

Arms on cross and value. Rev. The Church seated.

219.   1 Zecchino 1730 .... 4000.00

CLEMENT XII, 1730-1740

Bust. Rev. Various legends.

220.   1 Scudo d'oro 1735, 38, 39 .... 1300.00

Arms. Rev. The Church seated.

221.   2 Zecchini 1731, 39 ....* 6000.00
222.   1 Zecchino 1738, 39, ND 550.00
223.   ½ Zecchino 1739 .... 350.00

Arms. Rev. Legend.

224.   1 Scudo d'oro 1734-36, 38 .... 800.00

Legend. Rev. Bust of St. Peter.

225.   ½ Scudo romano ND 1800.00

SEDE VACANTE, 1740
Arms. Rev. The Church seated.

226.   2 Zecchini 1740 .... 7000.00
227.   1 Zecchino 1740 .... 1250.00
228.   ½ Zecchino 1740 .... 1250.00

Legend. Rev. Bust of St. Peter.

229.   ½ Scudo romano 1740 .... 350.00

BENEDICT XIV, 1740-1758

Arms. Rev. The Church seated.

230.	2 Zecchini 1748	*	4000.00
231.	1 Zecchino 1740-56, ND		375.00
232.	½ Zecchino 1740-55		300.00

Legend. Rev. Bust of St. Peter.

233.	½ Scudo romano 1741, ND		200.00

Arms. Rev. Bust of St. Peter.

234.	½ Scudo romano 1751		250.00

SEDE VACANTE, 1758
Arms. Rev. The Church seated.

235.	1 Zecchino 1758		2250.00

CLEMENT XIII, 1758-1769

Arms. Rev. The Church seated.

236.	2 Zecchini 1759, 66	*	2000.00
237.	1 Zecchino 1758-69		375.00
238.	½ Zecchino 1758, 67		375.00

SEDE VACANTE, 1769
Arms. Rev. The Church seated.

239.	1 Zecchino 1769		2000.00

CLEMENT XIV, 1769-1774

Arms. Rev. The Church seated.

240.	1 Zecchino 1769-73	*	400.00
241.	½ Zecchino 1769		375.00

SEDE VACANTE, 1774
Arms. Rev. The Church seated.

242.	1 Zecchino 1774		1250.00

PIUS VI, 1774-1799
Arms. Rev. The Church seated.

243.	1 Zecchino 1775-84		475.00
244.	½ Zecchino 1796		1000.00

Lily. Rev. St. Peter seated.

245.	2 Doppie romane or 60 Paoli 1776, 77	*	2750.00
246.	1 Doppia or 30 Paoli 1776-91		575.00
247.	½ Doppia or 15 Paoli 1776-87		350.00

PIUS VII, 1799-1823

Arms. Rev. St. Peter seated.

248.	1 Doppia romana 1800-23. R mm	*	450.00
249.	1 Doppia 1815-21. B mm		650.00

SEDE VACANTE, 1823

Arms. Rev. St. Peter seated.

250.	1 Doppia romana 1823. R mm		4000.00
251.	1 Doppia 1823. B mm	*	2500.00

LEO XII, 1823-1829

Bust. Rev. Faith standing.

252.	2 Zecchini 1828. R mm		4000.00

Arms. Rev. The Church seated.

252a.	2 Zecchini 1824. No mm. (Rome)		Rare

Arms. Rev. Faith seated left.

253.	2 Zecchini 1824, 25. R mm		2500.00

Arms. Rev. St. Peter seated.

254.	1 Doppia 1823, 29. R mm	*	1400.00
255.	1 Doppia 1824. B mm		1500.00

SEDE VACANTE, 1829

Arms. Rev. St. Peter seated.

256.	1 Doppia 1829. R mm	*	4000.00
257.	1 Doppia 1829. B mm		2250.00

PIUS VIII, 1829-1830

Bust. Rev. St. Peter and St. Paul standing. Without the mark of value. This is a pattern.

258.   20 Scudi 1830. B mm ....   Rare

SEDE VACANTE, 1830

Arms. Rev. Dove.

259.   1 Doppia 1830. R mm 4000.00

GREGORY XVI, 1831-1846

Bust. Rev. St. Peter and value.

260.   1 Doppia 1833, 34. R mm...................*.....   3000.00
261.   1 Doppia 1834. B mm 2500.00

Bust. Rev. St. Peter and St. Paul.

262.   5 Scudi 1834. R mm..............................   Rare

Bust. Rev. Value.

263.   10   Scudi 1835-45. R mm............................   2000.00
264.   10   Scudi 1835-36, 40-42, 45. B mm..................   2500.00
265.   5   Scudi 1835-46. R mm..........................   1900.00
266.   5   Scudi 1835, 41-43. B mm 1500.00
267.   2½   Scudi 1835-45. R mm..........................   650.00
268.   2½   Scudi 1835-36, 40, 42-44, 46. B mm ....*......   650.00

SEDE VACANTE, 1846

Arms. Rev. Dove.

269.   5 Scudi 1846. R mm.............................   5000.00

PIUS IX, 1846-1878

Bust. Rev. Value.

270.   10   Scudi 1850, 56. R mm.............................   4000.00
271.   5   Scudi 1846-48, 50, 54. R mm.................   1500.00
272.   5   Scudi 1846. B mm.............................   2000.00
273.   2½   Scudi 1848, 55-63. R mm ....*.....   375.00
274.   2½   Scudi 1854, 56-59. B mm 400.00
275.   1   Scudo 1853-57. R mm. Small size..............   250.00
276.   1   Scudo 1853, 54. B mm. Small size........*.....   250.00
277.   1   Scudo 1858-65. R mm. Large size 250.00
278.   100 Lire 1866, 68, 69.............................   6000.00
279.   50   Lire 1868, 70 ....   6000.00
280.   20   Lire 1866-70 ....*.....   250.00
281.   10   Lire 1866, 67, 69.............................   450.00
282.   5   Lire 1866, 67..............................*......   1250.00

PIUS XI, 1922-1937

Bust. Rev. Christ standing.

283.   100 Lire 1929-35 ....*......   500.00
284.   100 Lire 1933 (1934). On the Holy Year and
            showing both dates.........................   450.00
285.   100 Lire 1936, 37. Size reduced. (1937 rare)...........   500.00

PIUS XII, 1939-1958

Bust. Rev. Christ standing.

286.   100 Lire 1939, 40, 41................................   600.00

Bust. Rev. Charity seated with children.

287.   100 Lire 1942-47 ....*......   700.00
288.   100 Lire 1948-49 ....   400.00

Crowned bust. Rev. Opening of the Holy Door. On the Holy Year of 1950.
289.　100 Lire 1950 . . . . 375.00

Bust. Rev. Charity standing.
290.　100 Lire 1951-56 . . . . 1000.00

Bust. Rev. Arms.
291.　100 Lire 1957-58 . . . . 400.00

JOHN XXIII, 1958-1963

Bust. Rev. Arms.
292.　100 Lire 1959 . . . . 2000.00

B. Papal Coinage struck outside of Rome

These issues are distinguishable from those of the Rome Mint by differences of type, legend or arms.

ANCONA

PAUL III, 1464-1471
Arms. Rev. St. Peter and St. Paul.
292a.　1 Ducat ND . . . . Rare

SIXTUS IV, 1471-1484
Arms. Rev. St. Peter and St. Paul.
293.　1 Ducat ND . . . . Rare

INNOCENT VIII, 1484-1492
Arms. Rev. St. Peter in ship.
294.　1 Fiorino di camera ND 6000.00

Arms. Rev. Two saints.
295.　1 Ducat ND . . . . Unknown

ALEXANDER VI BORGIA, 1492-1503
Arms. Rev. St. Peter.
296.　1 Ducat ND . . . . Unknown

Arms. Rev. St. Peter in ship.
297.　1 Fiorino di camera ND 4000.00

Knight on horse. Rev. St. Quiriacus.
298.　1 Ducat ND . . . . Unknown

JULIUS II, 1503-1513

Arms. Rev. St. Peter in ship.
299.　1 Ducat ND 6000.00

Knight on horse. Rev. St. Quiriacus.
299a.　1 Ducat ND . . . . Rare

LEO X, 1513-1521

Knight on horse. Rev. St. Quiriacus.
300.　2 Ducats ND . . . . * . . . . . Rare
301.　1 Ducat ND 6000.00

Arms. Rev. Apostles in ship.
301a.　1 Ducat ND . . . . Rare

Arms. Rev. St. Peter and St. Paul.
302.　1 Ducat ND 5500.00

ADRIAN VI, 1522-1523
Knight on horse. Rev. St. Quiriacus.
303.　1 Ducat ND 20000.00

Arms. Rev. Two saints.
304.　1 Ducat ND 20000.00

CLEMENT VII, 1523-1534
Knight on horse. Rev. St. Quiriacus.
305.　1 Ducat ND 12000.00

Arms. Rev. Two saints.
306.　1 Ducat ND 10000.00

Arms. Rev. Cross.
307.　1 Scudo d'oro ND 8000.00

ANONYMOUS COINAGE, 1500-1600
Knight on horse. Rev. St. Quiriacus.

308.	2 Ducats ND	Rare
309.	1 Ducat ND	6000.00

GREGORY XIII, 1572-1585
Bust. Rev. The Holy Door.

310.	1 Scudo d'oro 1575	Rare

Bust. Rev. Charity standing.

311.	1 Scudo d'oro 1576, ND	Rare

Arms. Rev. Charity standing.

312.	1 Scudo d'oro ND	9000.00

SIXTUS V, 1585-1590
Arms. Rev. Legend.

313.	2 Scudi d'oro 1585	Unknown

Arms. Rev. Madonna.

314.	4 Scudi d'oro 1586	Rare

Arms. Rev. Cross.

315.	1 Doppia 1586	Rare
316.	1 Scudo d'oro 1586	10000.00

AVIGNON

(See under France-Cities).

BOLOGNA

URBAN VI, 1378-1389
Lion, letter "B" to left. Rev. St. Peter.

316a.	1 Ducat ND	2000.00

ALEXANDER V, 1409-1410
Sun and shield. Rev. St. Peter.

317.	1 Ducat ND	Rare

St. Peter. Rev. Arms.

318.	1 Ducat ND	Unknown

JOHN XXIII, 1410-1415
Arms. Rev. St. Peter.

319.	1 Ducat ND	10000.00

MARTIN V, 1421-1428
Lion; "M" or head of stag to left. Rev. St. Peter with or without arms to right.

320.	1 Ducat ND	5000.00

Arms. Rev. St. Peter.

321.	1 Ducat ND	8000.00

ANONYMOUS COINAGE, 1350-1450
Lion. Rev. St. Peter.

322.	1 Bolognino d'oro ND	2000.00

EUGENE IV, 1431-1447
Arms. Rev. St. Peter.

323.	1 Ducat ND	8000.00

NICHOLAS V, 1442-1455
Lion. Rev. St. Peter, small keys and tiara in field.

323a.	1 Ducat ND	Rare

PIUS II, 1458-1464
Lion. Rev. St. Peter between arms.

324.	1 Ducat ND	12000.00

PAUL II, 1464-1471
Lion. Rev. St. Petronius seated.

324a.	2 Ducats ND	Rare

Arms. Rev. St. Peter.

325.	1 Ducat ND	12000.00

Lion. Rev. St. Peter between arms.

326.	1 Ducat ND	8000.00

SIXTUS IV, 1471-1484
Arms. Rev. St. Peter.

327.	1 Ducat ND	Rare

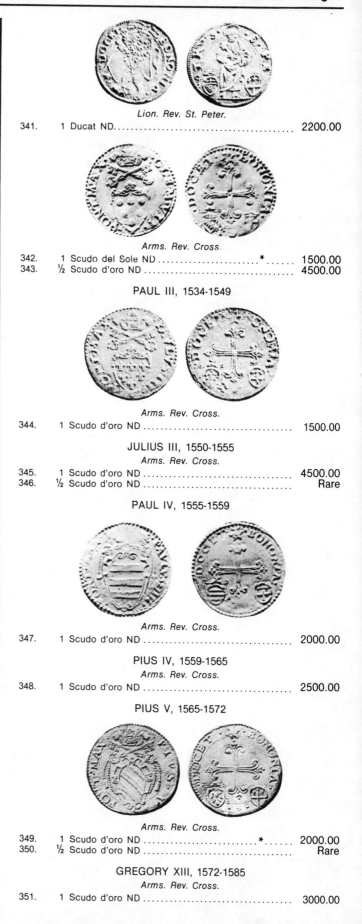

INNOCENT VIII, 1484-1492
Arms. Rev. St. Peter.

328. 1 Ducat ND.. Rare

Lion. Rev. St. Peter.

329. 1 Ducat ND.. 9000.00

ALEXANDER VI BORGIA, 1492-1503

Arms. Rev. St. Peter.

330. 1 Ducat ND.. 1500.00

PIUS III, 1503
Arms. Rev. St. Peter.

331. 1 Ducat ND.. Rare

JULIUS II, 1503-1513
Arms. Rev. St. Peter.

332. 1 Ducat ND.. 1000.00

Arms. Rev. St. Peter between arms.

332a. 1 Ducat ND 1200.00

Bust. Rev. St. Petronius seated.

333. 2 Ducats ND ....*...... Rare
334. 1 Ducat ND.. Unknown

LEO X, 1513-1521
Bust. Rev. St. Petronius seated.

335. 2 Ducats ND .... Rare

Bust. Rev. St. Peter.

336. 1 Ducat ND.. Rare

Arms. Rev. St. Peter.

337. 1 Ducat ND.. 1500.00

Arms. Rev. St. Peter in ship.

337a. 1 Florino di camera ND .... Rare

Lion. Rev. St. Peter.

338. 1 Ducat ND.. 2000.00

CLEMENT VII, 1523-1534
Bust of St. Petronius. Rev. Legend.

339. 10 Ducats 1529 .... Rare
340. 3 Ducats 1529 .... Rare

Lion. Rev. St. Peter.

341. 1 Ducat ND.. 2200.00

Arms. Rev. Cross.

342. 1 Scudo del Sole ND ....*...... 1500.00
343. ½ Scudo d'oro ND 4500.00

PAUL III, 1534-1549

Arms. Rev. Cross.

344. 1 Scudo d'oro ND 1500.00

JULIUS III, 1550-1555
Arms. Rev. Cross.

345. 1 Scudo d'oro ND 4500.00
346. ½ Scudo d'oro ND .... Rare

PAUL IV, 1555-1559

Arms. Rev. Cross.

347. 1 Scudo d'oro ND 2000.00

PIUS IV, 1559-1565
Arms. Rev. Cross.

348. 1 Scudo d'oro ND 2500.00

PIUS V, 1565-1572

Arms. Rev. Cross.

349. 1 Scudo d'oro ND ....*...... 2000.00
350. ½ Scudo d'oro ND .... Rare

GREGORY XIII, 1572-1585
Arms. Rev. Cross.

351. 1 Scudo d'oro ND 3000.00

Bust. Rev. Felsina seated.

351a.   4 Scudi d'oro ND ....   Rare

SIXTUS V, 1585-1590

Arms. Rev. Cross.

352.   1 Doppia ND ....* 8000.00
353.   1 Scudo d'oro ND 3500.00

URBAN VII, 1590 (13 DAYS)

Arms. Rev. Cross.

354.   1 Doppia ND ....   Rare

GREGORY XIV, 1590-1591

Arms. Rev. Cross.

355.   1 Doppia ND ....   Rare

INNOCENT IX, 1591-1592
Arms. Rev. Cross.

356.   1 Doppia ND ....   Rare

CLEMENT VIII, 1592-1605
Arms. Rev. Cross.

357.   1 Doppia ND 7500.00
Arms. Rev. Cross and date.
357a.   1 Doppia 1597-99 ....   Rare

ANONYMOUS COINAGE, 1500-1600
St. Peter. Rev. Lion.

358.   1 Bolognino d'oro ND 2000.00

INNOCENT X, 1644-1655
Arms. Rev. Cross.

359.   4 Scudi d'oro 1654 ....   Rare
360.   1 Doppia 1654 ....   Rare
361.   1 Scudo d'oro 1654 ....   Rare

ALEXANDER VII, 1655-1667

Arms. Rev. Cross.

362.   4 Scudi d'oro 1655-59 ....* 7500.00
363.   2 Doppia 1655-58, 60, 61, 66 ....   6000.00
364.   1 Scudo d'oro 1655-64, 66 ....   3500.00

CLEMENT IX, 1667-1669
Arms. Rev. Cross.

365.   4 Scudi d'oro 1667 ....   Rare
366.   2 Scudi d'oro 1667 ....   Unknown
367.   1 Scudo d'oro 1667 ....   Unknown

CLEMENT X, 1669-1676
Arms. Rev. Cross.

368.   8 Scudi d'oro 1671 ....   Unknown
369.   4 Scudi d'oro 1673 ....   Unknown
370.   2 Scudi d'oro 1673 ....   Unknown
371.   1 Scudo d'oro 1671 ....   Unknown

CLEMENT XI, 1700-1721
Arms. Rev. Cross.

372.   1 Doppia 1714, ND ....   Rare
373.   1 Scudo d'oro 1713 ....   Rare

CLEMENT XII, 1730-1740
Arms. Rev. Cross.

374.   1 Scudo d'oro 1732, 36 ....   Rare

Two shields. Rev. Lion.

375.   1 Zecchino 1737, 38 ....   8000.00

SEDE VACANTE, 1740
Lion. Rev. Two shields.

376.   1 Zecchino 1740 ....   6000.00

BENEDICT XIV, 1740-1758

Bust. Rev. Felsina standing.

377.   2 Zecchini 1741, 42 ....   Rare
378.   1 Zecchino 1741, 42 ....* 6000.00
379.   The coin previously listed has been found to be a medal.

Lion. Rev. Two shields.

380.   1 Zecchino 1746 ....   5000.00

Arms. Rev. Cross.

381.   1 Zecchino 1751 ....   Rare
382.   The coin previously listed does not exist ....   —

CLEMENT XIV, 1769-1774

Lion. Rev. Two shields.

383.   1 Zecchino 1771 ....   5500.00

PIUS VI, 1774-1799

Lily. Rev. Two shields.

384.	4 Doppia 1786, 87	2250.00
385.	2 Doppia 1778, 80, 81, 86, 87, 96. (60 Paoli)........	1200.00
386.	1 Doppia 1778, 80, 85-89, 91-92, 94-95. (30 Paoli) * . .	500.00
387.	½ Doppia 1778-80, 87-88, 91-92. (15 Paoli)	400.00

Lily. Rev. Arms.

388.	½ Doppia 1778	4000.00

Bust. Rev. Temple.

389.	1 Zecchino 1782	6000.00

Arms. Rev. St. Petronius over two shields.

390.	10 Zecchini 1786, 87	7000.00
391.	5 Zecchini 1787	5500.00
392.	2 Zecchini 1786, 87	3000.00
393.	1 Zecchino 1778-80, 86, 87, ND .... *	3000.00
394.	½ Zecchino 1786	4000.00
395.	100 Bolognini (Scudo d'oro) ND	Unknown

(Later coinage of the Bologna Mint is of the same type as that of the Rome Mint and will be found under Vatican-Rome described with "B mm").

CAMERINO

PAUL III, 1534-1549

Arms. Rev. St. Paul.

396.	1 Scudo d'oro ND	Rare

FERRARA

PAUL V, 1605-1621

Bust. Rev. St. George and St. Maurelius.

397.	4 Scudi d'oro 1620	Rare

FOLIGNO

PAUL II, 1464-1471

Arms. Rev. St. Peter kneeling before Christ.

398.	1 Zecchino ND	Unknown

LEO X, 1513-1521
Lion. Rev. St. Peter and St. Paul.

399.	2 Doppio Ducato ND	Rare

Arms. Rev. St. Felician.

400.	1 Ducat ND	Unknown

MACERATA

SIXTUS IV, 1471-1484
Arms. Rev. St. Peter in ship.

401.	1 Fiorino di camera ND	Rare

INNOCENT VIII, 1484-1492

Arms. Rev. St. Peter in ship.

402.	1 Fiorino di camera ND	8000.00

ADRIAN VI, 1522-1523
Arms. Rev. St. Peter in ship.

403.	1 Fiorino di camera ND	Rare

GREGORY XIII, 1572-1585
Arms. Rev. The Holy Door.

403a.	1 Scudo d'oro 1575	Rare

MANTOVA

PIUS II, 1458-1464
Arms. Rev. St. Peter. With "Diete Mantova."

403b.   1 Ducat ND.. 9000.00

MODENA

LEO X, 1513-1521

Bust. Rev. St. Geminianus seated.

404.   1 Ducat ND................................... Rare

ADRIAN VI, 1522-1523
Bust. Rev. St. Geminianus seated.

405.   1 Ducat ND................................... Unknown

CLEMENT VII, 1523-1534

Bust. Rev. St. Geminianus seated.

406.   1 Ducat ND..19000.00

Arms. Rev. St. Geminianus seated.

407.   1 Ducat ND....................................... 9000.00

PARMA

LEO XII, 1513-1521
St. John and St. Hillary. Rev. Christ and Madonna.

408.   1 Ducat ND.. Rare

ADRIAN VI, 1522-1523
St. John and St. Hillary. Rev. Christ and Madonna.

409.   1 Zecchino ND .... Unknown

CLEMENT VII, 1523-1534
Arms. Rev. Christ and Madonna.

410.   2 Ducats 1526 .... Unknown

Arms. Rev. Madonna.

411.   1 Ducat ND..................................... Unknown

PAUL III, 1534-1549

Arms. Rev. Pallas seated.

412.   1 Scudo d'oro ND 2000.00

Arms. Rev. Cross.

413.   ½ Scudo d'oro ND .... Rare

PERUGIA

LEO X, 1513-1521
Arms. Rev. Griffin.

414.   1 Ducat ND.. Rare

St. Herculanus. Rev. Griffin.

415.   1 Ducat ND.. Rare

PAUL III, 1534-1549

Arms. Rev. Griffin and shield.

416.   1 Scudo d'oro ND 12000.00

Arms. Rev. Griffin in square.

417.   1 Scudo d'oro ND 12000.00

JULIUS III, 1550-1555
Arms. Rev. Cross.

418.   1 Scudo d'oro ND .... Unknown

PIACENZA

ADRIAN VI, 1522-1523
Bust. Rev. Legend.

419.   1 Doppia ND .... Unknown

Bust. Rev. Keys.

420.   1 Zecchino ND .... Unknown

CLEMENT VII, 1523-1534

Bust. Rev. St. Anthony on horse.

421.   1 Ducat ND..   Rare

PAUL III, 1534-1549

Arms. Rev. Cross.

422.   1 Scudo d'oro ND ....*...... 1250.00
423.   ½ Scudo d'oro ND .... Rare

RAVENNA

LEO X, 1513-1521

Arms. Rev. St. Appolinaris.

424.   1 Ducat ND.. Rare

SPOLETO

PIUS II, 1458-1464
Arms. Rev. St. Peter. With "DUC SPOL."

424a. 1 Ducat ND.. Rare

PAUL II, 1464-1471

Arms. Rev. St. Peter.

425.   1 Ducat ND.. Rare

VENEZUELA

Venezuelan coinage is based on the Latin Monetary Union standard. The 100, 50 and 5 Bolivar pieces of 1875 are of exceptional rarity and are specimen proofs marked "ESSAI." Rare essais also exist of the 25 Bolivar piece.

Head of Bolivar. Rev. Arms. The values are expressed on the Rev. by the weight of the coins in grams.

1.   100 Bolivares (20 Venezolanos) 1875 (32.2580 Grams)..   Rare
2.   100 Bolivares 1886-89 (32.2580 Grams) ....*...... 1250.00
3.   50 Bolivares (10 Venezolanos) 1875, 88 (16.1290 Grams).................................... Rare
4.   25 Bolivares (5 Venezolanos) 1875 (8.0645 Grams)....   350.00
5.   20 Bolivares 1879-1912 (6.4516 Grams) 150.00
6.   10 Bolivares 1930 (3.2258 Grams) ....*......   175.00
7.   5 Bolivares (1 Venezolano) 1875 (1.6129 Grams).....   Rare

For later issues, see the section "Recent Issues Starting With 1960."

WALLACHIA

Voivods of —

MICHAEL THE BRAVE, 1600-1601

Bust with furred hat. Rev. Legend.

1.   10 Ducats 1600.................................. Rare
2.   5 Ducats 1600...........................*...... Rare

CONSTANTINE BRENCOVAN, 1688-1714

Bust with furred hat. Rev. Arms. On the 25th year of reign.

3.   5 Ducats 1713................................... Rare

YEMEN

YAHA BIN MOHAMMED, 1904-1948

Inscription in circle. Rev. Inscription.

1.   ¼ Imadi 1365 A.H. (1947)............................ 700.00

AHMED HAMID AL-DIN, 1948-1963

Inscription on crescent. Rev. Inscription.

2.   1 Imadi 1377 A.H. (1958)..................... * 1500.00
3.   ½ Imadi 1370 A.H. (1951)............................ 750.00
4.   ¼ Imadi 1370-77 A.H. (1951-58) 450.00

YUGOSLAVIA

A. Kings of —

ALEXANDER I, 1921-1934

Head. Rev. Value and date.

1.   20 Dinars 1925.................................... 250.00

Conjoined heads of the King and Queen, with counterstamp of sword for Bosnia or ear of wheat for Serbia. Rev. Eagle.

2.   4 Ducats 1931, 32, 33............................. 875.00

Head, with counterstamp of sword for Bosnia or ear of wheat for Serbia. Rev. Eagle.

3.   1 Ducat 1931, 32, 33.............................. 150.00

B. Cities of —

RAGUSA (DUBROVNIK)

St. Blasius standing. Rev. Christ amid stars.

4.   1 Gold Perper or 2 Doppia 1618, 83 .... Rare

LAIBACH (LJUBLIANA)

Bishops of —

THOMAS GRONN, 1599-1630

Bishop holding cross, facing angel. Rev. Legend.

5.   3 Ducats 1599 .... Rare

For later issues, see the section "Recent Issues Starting With 1960."

ZANZIBAR

The two gold coins are of extraordinary rarity. The author knows of only four specimens of the 5 Rial piece and only one of the 2½ Rial piece which was last noted in 1938. The coins were struck at the Brussels Mint.

SULTAN SA'ID, 1870-1888

Arab legend. Rev. Arab legend and date, with value in Christian numerals.

1.   5   Rials 1299 A.H. (1881) .... Rare
2.   2½ Rials 1299 A.H. (1881) .... Rare

PART II.

RECENT ISSUES STARTING WITH 1960

RECENT ISSUES STARTING WITH 1960

As in the first part of this book, the author has sought to include in this section all types of gold coins which will be found in the numismatic marketplace. Among such coins are the proliferation of issues which in recent years have been intended primarily for the consumption of collectors and investors rather than as a circulating medium of exchange.

There is no unanimity of opinion among numismatists regarding the status of these issues as coins. While they have been included herein, their publication does not constitute an endorsement or recommendation, but rather a desire on the part of the publisher to make this book as complete as possible.

COLLECTOR'S COINS

Commencing with 1960, there has been a marked increase in the issuance of what have become known as collector's coins. These pieces are generally commemorative in nature, struck in limited quantities, and intended for and marketed primarily to collectors rather than for use in everyday commerce in their country of origin.

BULLION COINS

Bullion coins are issued to satisfy the desire on the part of many people to hold gold bullion in coin form. They are issued at a modest premium over their gold value and may be either current issues or restrikes of older coins. In contrast to numismatic coins, they are often traded in large quantities, without regard for date, mint mark or condition.

Among the current issues of bullion coins are the following:

> Canadian 50 Dollars
> Chilean Condores
> British Sovereigns of Elizabeth II
> Iranian Pahlevis
> Netherlands Ducats

> Russian 10 Roubles
> South African Rands and Krugerrands
> Turkish Standard gold coins

Rather than issue bullion coins with new designs, some countries have chosen to re-issue older, more established coins. Known as restrikes, these coins continue to bear the original date of issue although struck at a much later time. Restrikes have the same weight and fineness as the original coins and are often difficult for those with untrained eyes to distinguish from the originals. Such coins have been issued primarily by:

> Austria
> Hungary
> Mexico

Restrikes have also been produced by Spain with one important difference—in addition to bearing the date of the original issue, the coins also have the date of restriking. This date can be found in the small stars on the obverse of each coin. The Spanish restrikes are listed in this section; all others can be found in Part I, with the original coins.

When the letter "R" appears after a number, it indicates that the coin is a restrike.

THE VALUATIONS AND STATE OF PRESERVATION

The valuations in this section are for uncirculated (mint state) specimens or for proof specimens, where indicated, and for the commonest date or variety of the type.

AMOUNTS MINTED

Thought was given to including the amounts minted for each of the following issues. However, the editor's research has shown that as a result of the increase in the price of gold, a significant number of the coins have already been melted, and therefore, to indicate the actual number struck would not serve as a realistic guide to rarity.

NOTE: VALUATIONS ARE BASED ON A GOLD PRICE OF $725.00 PER OUNCE.

AFGHANISTAN

(For previous issues, see Part I.)

MOHAMMED ZAHIR, 1933-1973

Throne room. Rev. Legend in wreath. Royal presentation tokens.

42.	2	Tilla of 8 grams 1339 S.H./1380 A.H. (1961 A.D.) ..	500.00
43.	1½	Tilla of 6 grams 1349-50 S.H. (1971-72 A.D.)......	450.00
44.	1	Tilla of 4 grams 1339 S.H./1390-91 A.H. (1961 A.D.)	350.00

Marco Polo sheep. Rev. Arms. For the world wildlife conservation program.

45.	10,000 Afghani 1978.........................	700.00
	Proof	750.00

AJMAN

Different obverses as indicated. Rev. Crossed flags. Struck in proof only.

1.	100 Riyals 1970. Head of Lenin......................	455.00
2.	50 Riyals 1970. Bust of Nasser	220.00
3.	25 Riyals 1970. Bust of Nasser ....*......	110.00

Bow of Venetian gondola. Rev. Crossed flags over sultan. Struck in proof only.

4.	100 Riyals 1970....................................	455.00
5.	50 Riyals 1970....................................	220.00
6.	25 Riyals 1970....................................	110.00

Fish. Rev. Crossed flags over sultan. Struck in proof only.

7.	75 Riyals 1970....................................	325.00

Different obverses as indicated. Rev. Value in Arabic numerals. Struck in proof only.

8.	25 Riyals 1970. Martin Luther King, Jr.		110.00
9.	25 Riyals 1970. George Marshall ....*		110.00
10.	25 Riyals 1970. Mahatma Ghandi		110.00
11.	25 Riyals 1970. Jan Palach		110.00
12.	25 Riyals 1970. Albert Schweitzer		110.00
13.	25 Riyals 1970. Bertrand Russell		110.00
14.	25 Riyals 1970. Albert Luthuli		110.00
15.	25 Riyals 1970. Dag Hammarskjold		110.00

ALBANIA

(For previous issues, see Part I.)

Different obverses as indicated. Rev. Arms. Struck in proof only.

18.	500 Leks 1968, 70. Bust of Skanderbeg	2075.00
19.	200 Leks 1968, 70. Woman's head	825.00
20.	100 Leks 1968, 70. Girl picking fruit	415.00
21.	50 Leks 1968, 70. Fortress and viaduct	210.00
22.	20 Leks 1968, 70. Sword and helmet in wreath	80.00

ANGUILLA

Different obverses as indicated. Rev. Arms. Struck in proof only.

1.	100 Dollars 1967. People in circle	1000.00
2.	20 Dollars 1967. Two mermaids	200.00
3.	10 Dollars 1967. Underwater scene	100.00
4.	5 Dollars 1967. Church	50.00

AUSTRIA

Official government restrikes have been issued. They are listed in Part I since they bear the date of the original coin rather than the date of the new minting.

Knight on horse. Rev. Arms. On the 1000th Anniversary of Austria.

797.	1,000 Schillings 1976	255.00

BAHAMAS

Bust of Queen Elizabeth II. Different reverses as indicated.

1.	100 Dollars 1967. Columbus landing on San Salvador		850.00
		Proof	900.00
2.	50 Dollars 1967. Columbus' ship, the Santa Maria		425.00
		Proof	450.00
3.	20 Dollars 1967. Lighthouse		170.00
		Proof	180.00
4.	10 Dollars 1967. Fortress		85.00
		Proof	90.00

Bust of Queen Elizabeth II with new legend. Different reverses as indicated.

5.	100 Dollars 1971 (39.94 grams). Arms..........*		850.00
		Proof	900.00
6.	100 Dollars 1972 (31.95 grams). Arms		685.00
		Proof	725.00
7.	50 Dollars 1971 (19.97 grams). The Santa Maria*		425.00
		Proof	450.00
8.	50 Dollars 1972 (15.97 grams). The Santa Maria......		340.00
		Proof	360.00
9.	20 Dollars 1971 (7.99 grams). Lighthouse.....*		170.00
		Proof	180.00
10.	20 Dollars 1972 (6.38 grams). Lighthouse.............		135.00
		Proof	145.00
11.	10 Dollars 1971 (3.99 grams). Fortress ....*		85.00
		Proof	90.00
12.	10 Dollars 1972 (3.19 grams). Fortress		65.00
		Proof	70.00

Bust of Queen Elizabeth II. Different reverses as indicated. On independence from Great Britain.

13.	100 Dollars 1973. New coat of arms		200.00
		Proof	225.00
14.	50 Dollars 1973. Crawfish..........................		100.00
		Proof	110.00
15.	20 Dollars 1973. Four flamingoes		40.00
		Proof	45.00
16.	10 Dollars 1973. Tobacco dove......................		20.00
		Proof	22.50

Bust of Queen Elizabeth II. Rev. Two Flamingoes. Independence Day coin.

17.	50 Dollars 1973......................................		210.00
		Proof	225.00

Bust of Queen Elizabeth II. Different reverses as indicated. The date of issue appears on the reverse. The obverse carries the date 1973, which is the year of independence.

18.	200 Dollars 1974-77. Arms		235.00
		Proof	260.00

19.	150 Dollars 1974-77. Crawfish		175.00
		Proof	200.00
20.	100 Dollars 1974-77. Four flamingoes		115.00
		Proof	125.00
21.	50 Dollars 1974-77. Tobacco dove..............		60.00
		Proof	70.00

Two flamingoes. Rev. Arms. On the first anniversary of independence.

22.	100 Dollars 1974.............................		210.00
		Proof	225.00

Parrot. Rev. Arms. On the second and third anniversaries of independence.

23.	100 Dollars 1975-76		210.00
		Proof	225.00

Arms. Rev. Two flamingoes. The 1974 issue was struck in 1976. Struck in proof only.

24.	2,500 Dollars 1974, 77		8700.00

Different obverses as indicated. Rev. Arms. On the 5th anniversary of independence. Struck in proof only.

25.	100 Dollars 1978. Bust of Prince Charles	290.00
26.	100 Dollars 1978. Bust of Milo B. Butler	290.00

Bust of Princess Anne. Rev. Arms. On her visit and the 250th anniversary of Parliament. Struck in proof only.

27.	250 Dollars 1979	225.00

BAHRAIN

Bust of Isa Bin Sulman. Rev. Arms. On the opening of Isa Town.

1.	10 Dinars 1968		400.00
		Proof	600.00

BARBADOS

Ship. Rev. Arms. On the 350th anniversary of discovery.

1.	100 Dollars 1975		75.00
		Proof	80.00

Hands reaching to a document. Rev. Arms. On the human rights campaign.

2.	200 Dollars 1979 (24mm)	170.00
3.	200 Dollars 1979 (27mm). Proof	210.00

Three symbolic figures of adult and children. Rev. Arms. On the Year of the Child.

4.	100 Dollars 1979 (21mm)	85.00
5.	100 Dollars 1979 (20mm). Proof	105.00

BELIZE

Arms. Rev. National Assembly Building below Mayan symbols.

1.	100 Dollars 1975		80.00
		Proof	80.00

Arms. Rev. Mayan design.

2.	100 Dollars 1976		72.00
		Proof	75.00

Arms. Rev. Statue of Mayan sun god.

3.	100 Dollars 1977		72.00
		Proof	75.00

Arms. Rev. Mayan deity Itzamna - lord of the heavens.

4.	100 Dollars 1978		72.00
		Proof	75.00

Arms. Rev. Jaguar.

5.	250 Dollars 1978		200.00
		Proof	200.00

Arms. Rev. Angelfish.

6.	100 Dollars 1979		72.00
		Proof	75.00

Eight-pointed star surrounded by flora. Rev. Arms.

7.	100 Dollars 1979		72.00
		Proof	75.00

Moorish Idol fish. Rev. Arms. Struck in proof only.

8.	100 Dollars 1980	75.00

BERMUDA

Bust of Queen Elizabeth II. Rev. Bird in flight. Struck in proof only.

1.	20 Dollars 1970	900.00

Bust of Queen Elizabeth II. Rev. Parliamentary Mace of Bermuda and the Royal Monograms. On the Royal Visit.

2.   100 Dollars 1975 . . . .   165.00
                                                Proof 175.00

Bust of Queen Elizabeth II. Rev. The "Deliverance," first ship built in Bermuda. On the Queen's Silver Jubilee.

3.   100 Dollars 1977 . . . .   170.00
                                                Proof 175.00

Bust of Queen Elizabeth II. Rev. Sailboat. On the Queen's Silver Jubilee.

4.   50 Dollars 1977 . . . .   85.00
                                                Proof 87.50

BHUTAN

Bust of Maharaja Jigme Wangchuk. Rev. Sacred thunderbolt on Buddhist wheel of life. On the 40th anniversary of the coronation of the king's father. Only 72 pieces were struck of each of the platinum denominations.

1.   5 Sertums 1966 . . . .   855.00
                                                Proof 900.00
2.   2 Sertums 1966 . . . .   340.00
                                                Proof 375.00
3.   1 Sertum 1966 . . . . * 170.00
                                                Proof 195.00
4.   Platinum 5 Sertums 1966 . . . .   Rare
5.   Platinum 2 Sertums 1966 . . . .   Rare
6.   Platinum 1 Sertum 1966 . . . .   Rare

Bust of young girl. Rev. Emblem.

7.   1 Sertum 1970 . . . .   170.00

BIAFRA

Arms. Rev. Eagle. On the second anniversary of independence. Although dated 1969, these coins were issued in 1970, after the collapse of the Republic. Struck in proof only.

1.   25 Pounds 1969 . . . .   1700.00
2.   10 Pounds 1969 . . . .   850.00
3.   5 Pounds 1969 . . . . * 340.00
4.   2 Pounds 1969 . . . .   170.00
5.   1 Pound 1969 . . . .   85.00

BOTSWANA

Portrait of President Seretse Khama. Rev. Arms.

1.   10 Thebe 1966 . . . .   240.00

Bust of President Seretse Khama. Rev. Arms. On the tenth anniversary of independence.

2.   150 Pula 1976 . . . .   335.00
                                                  Proof 340.00

Arms. Rev. Brown hyena. For the world wildlife conservation program.

3.   150 Pula 1978 . . . .   700.00
                                                  Proof 750.00

BRAZIL

(For previous issues, see Part I.)

Heads of Peter I and President Medici. Rev. Map. On the sesquicentennial of independence.

126.   300 Cruzeiros 1972 . . . .   200.00

BRITISH VIRGIN ISLANDS

QUEEN ELIZABETH II, 1952-

Head. Rev. The Royal Tern.
1.   100 Dollars 1975 . . . . 150.00
                                    Proof   150.00

Bust of Queen Elizabeth II. Rev. Arms. On her 50th birthday.
2.   100 Dollars 1976 . . . . 150.00
                                    Proof   150.00

Bust of Queen Elizabeth II. Rev. Crown. On her Silver Jubilee.
3.   100 Dollars 1977 . . . . Rare
                                    Proof   150.00

*Bust of Queen Elizabeth II. Rev. Symbols of the British monarchy.
On the 25th anniversary of her coronation.*
4.   100 Dollars 1978 . . . . 150.00
                                    Proof   150.00

Bust of Queen Elizabeth II. Rev. Bust of Sir Francis Drake.
5.   100 Dollars 1979 . . . . 150.00
                                    Proof   150.00
*Bust of Queen Elizabeth II. Rev. The "Golden Hind." On the 400th
anniversary of Drake's global circumnavigation.*
6.   100 Dollars 1980 . . . . 150.00
                                    Proof   150.00

BRUNEI

*Bust of Sultan Hassanal Bolkiah. Rev. Coronation crown. On the
tenth anniversary of his coronation. Struck in proof only.*
1.   1,000 Dollars 1978 . . . . 1070.00

BULGARIA

(For previous issues, see Part I.)
Republic of —

*Standing figures of Saints Cyril and Methodius. Rev. Value
above shield. On the 1100th anniversary of the Slavic
alphabet. Struck in proof only.*
9.   20 Leva 1963 . . . . * 350.00
10.   10 Leva 1963 . . . . 175.00

*Head of Premier Dimitrov. Rev. Flag above value. On the
20th anniversary of the People's Republic. Struck in proof
only.*
11.   20 Leva 1964 . . . . * 350.00
12.   10 Leva 1964 . . . . 175.00

BURMA

(For previous issues, see Part I.)

Peacock. Rev. Eight-pointed star. Issued by the government in exile.
8.   4 Mu 1971 . . . . 185.00
9.   2 Mu 1971 . . . . 92.50
10.   1 Mu 1971 . . . . * 45.00

BURUNDI

*Uniformed bust of King Mwambutsa IV. Rev. Arms. Inde-
pendence commemorative. Struck in proof only.*
1.   100 Francs 1962 . . . . * 670.00
2.   50 Francs 1962 . . . . 335.00
3.   25 Francs 1962 . . . . 170.00
4.   10 Francs 1962 . . . . 67.50

Uniformed facing bust of King Mwambutsa IV. Rev. Arms.
On the 50th anniversary of his reign. Struck in proof only.

5.	100 Francs 1965	.............................*	630.00
6.	50 Francs 1965	....	315.00
7.	25 Francs 1965	....	155.00
8.	10 Francs 1965	....	65.00

Bust of President Micombero, Rev. Arms. On the first anniversary of
the Republic.

9.	100 Francs 1967	....	630.00
10.	50 Francs 1967	....	315.00
11.	25 Francs 1967	....	155.00
12.	20 Francs 1967	....	130.00
13.	10 Francs 1967	....	65.00

CAMEROUN

Bust of President El Hadj Ahmadou Ahidjo. Different reverses
as indicated. On the 10th anniversary of independence.
Struck in proof only.

1.	20,000 Francs 1970. Coat of arms	....	1470.00
2.	10,000 Francs 1970. Two elk	....	735.00
3.	5,000 Francs 1970. Official seal of Cameroun	....	370.00
4.	3,000 Francs 1970. Horns of elk	....	220.00
5.	1,000 Francs 1970. Geometric design	....	72.50

CANADA

(For previous issues, see Part I.)

QUEEN ELIZABETH II, 1952-

Bust. Rev. Arms. On the 100th Anniversary of Confederation.
Struck in proof only.

5.	20 Dollars 1967	....	400.00

Bust of Queen Elizabeth II. Rev. Athena standing, her left hand on
the shoulder of an athlete. On the 1976 Montreal Olympics.

6.	100 Dollars 1976 (27mm)	....	180.00
7.	100 Dollars 1976 (25mm) Proof	....	360.00

Bust of Queen Elizabeth II. Rev. Bouquet of flowers. On her Silver
Jubilee. Struck in proof only.

8.	100 Dollars 1977	....	360.00

Bust of Queen Elizabeth II. Rev. Twelve Canadian geese. Struck in
proof only.

9.	100 Dollars 1978	....	360.00

Bust of Queen Elizabeth II. Rev. Boys and girls holding hands
around globe. On the International Year of the Child. Struck in
proof only.

10.	100 Dollars 1979	....	360.00

Bust of Queen Elizabeth II. Rev. Maple Leaf.
11. 50 Dollars 1979- . . . . 745.00 (B)
(Number 11 is a bullion coin. The price listed is based on gold at $725 per ounce.)
Bust of Queen Elizabeth II. Rev. Inuit paddling kyak, iceberg behind. Struck in proof only.
12. 100 Dollars 1980. . . . . 360.00

CAPE VERDE ISLANDS

Map over star. Rev. Bonito. On the first anniversary of independence. Struck in proof only.
1. 2,500 Escudos 1976 . . . . 150.00

CAYMAN ISLANDS

Head of Queen Elizabeth II. Rev. Conjoined heads of Queen Elizabeth and Prince Philip. For the 25th wedding anniversary of the Royal couple.
1. 25 Dollars 1972 . . . . 185.00
                                                              Proof 195.00

Bust of Winston Churchill. Rev. Arms. On the 100th anniversary of his birth.
2. 100 Dollars 1974 . . . . 265.00
                                                              Proof 275.00

Bust of Queen Elizabeth II. Rev. Busts of the five earlier sovereign queens of England.
3. 100 Dollars 1975-77 . . . . 265.00
                                                              Proof 275.00

Bust of Queen Elizabeth II. Rev. Individual busts of the five earlier sovereign queens of England. Struck in proof only.
4. 50 Dollars 1977. Queen Mary I 130.00
5. 50 Dollars 1977. Queen Elizabeth I 130.00
6. 50 Dollars 1977. Queen Mary II 130.00
7. 50 Dollars 1977. Queen Anne 130.00
8. 50 Dollars 1977. Queen Victoria. 130.00
Bust of Queen Elizabeth II. Rev. Arms of the United Kingdom. On the Queen's Silver Jubilee.
9. 100 Dollars 1977. . . . . 265.00
                                                              Proof 275.00
Bust of Queen Elizabeth II. Different reverses as indicated. On the 25th anniversary of her coronation. Struck in proof only.
10. 100 Dollars 1978. Legend 265.00
11. 50 Dollars 1978. Ampulla 130.00
12. 50 Dollars 1978. Orb 130.00
13. 50 Dollars 1978. St. Edward's crown 130.00
14. 50 Dollars 1978. Chair 130.00
15. 50 Dollars 1978. Sceptre 130.00
16. 50 Dollars 1978. Spoon 130.00

CENTRAL AFRICAN REPUBLIC (EMPIRE)

Bust of President Jean Bedel Bokassa. Different reverses as indicated. Struck in proof only.

1. 20,000 Francs 1970. Native food products. 1470.00
2. 10,000 Francs 1970. UN symbol; 3 co-joined
         female heads. 735.00
3. 5,000 Francs 1970. Olympic wrestlers. 370.00
4. 3,000 Francs 1970. Martin Luther King 220.00
5. 1,000 Francs 1970. Coat of arms. 72.50

Different obverses as indicated. Rev. Arms.
6.   25,000 CFA Francs 1978. Bust of Bokassa I 320.00
7.   10,000 CFA Francs 1978. 3 Busts 125.00

CENTRAL AMERICAN REPUBLICS

Tree. Rev. Rising sun over mountains. Issued by the Union of Central American Banks on the tenth anniversary of the Central American Bank of Economic Integration for Honduras, Guatemala, El Salvador, Nicaragua and Costa Rica. Struck in proof only.
1.   50 Pesos 1970 . . . .   420.00

CHAD

The following issues were all struck in 1970 in proof only.

Head of President Tombalbaye. Rev. Arms. On the 10th anniversary of independence.

1. 20,000 Francs 1970 . . . .   1470.00

Uniformed bust of General De Gaulle. Rev. Arms above Cross of Lorraine.

2. 10,000 Francs 1960 . . . .   735.00

Head of General Leclerc. Rev. Palm trees, buildings and arms.

3.   5,000 Francs 1941 . . . .   370.00

Head of Governor Eboue. Rev. Map and arms.

4.   3,000 Francs 1940 . . . .   220.00

Head of Commandant Lamy. Rev. Nude girl and arms.

5.   1,000 Francs 1900 . . . .   72.50

CHILE

(For previous issues, see Part I.)

Liberty head with coiled hair. Rev. Arms. Two values appear on these coins.
54.   100 Pesos—10 Condores 1926, 32, 46-63 . . . . . .*   425.00(B)
55.   50 Pesos — 5 Condores 1926, 58, 61-62, 65, 67,
          68, 74 . . . .   210.00(B)
56.   20 Pesos— 2 Condores 1926, 58-59, 61 . . . . . .*   100.00(B)

(Numbers 54-56 are bullion coins. The price listed is based on gold at $725 per ounce.)

427

Bust of Chiang Kai-shek. Rev. Two cranes and flowers. On his 80th birthday.

17. 2000 Yuan 1966 (Year 55) 700.00

CHINA (PEOPLE'S REPUBLIC)

Different obverses as indicated. Rev. Arms. Struck in proof only.

57.	500 Pesos 1967. Liberty head and flag	2130.00
58.	200 Pesos 1967. O'Higgins and San Martin	
	on horseback	850.00
59.	100 Pesos 1967. Liberty head and coining machine ...	425.00
60.	50 Pesos 1967. Bust of O'Higgins	210.00

Winged woman with outstretched arms. Rev. Arms. On the third anniversary of the new government.

61.	500 Pesos 1976	2150.00
	Proof	2250.00
62.	100 Pesos 1976	420.00
	Proof (100 minted)	Rare
63.	50 Pesos 1976	210.00
	Proof	225.00

Different obverses as indicated. Rev. Arms. On the 30th anniversary of the republic. Struck in proof only.

1.	400 Yuan 1979. T'ien An Men Square...........	375.00
2.	400 Yuan 1979. Monument of People's Heroes.....	375.00
3.	400 Yuan 1979. Great Hall of the People	375.00
4.	400 Yuan 1979. Mao Zedong Mausoleum ....,	375.00

Boy and girl watering flower. Rev. Arms. On the International Year of the Child. Struck in proof only.

5. 450 Yuan 1979 .... 385.00

NATIONALIST CHINA

(For previous issues, see Part I.)

Head of Dr. Sun Yat-sen. Rev. Value in floral wreath. On the 100th anniversary of his birth.

15.	2000 Yuan 1965 (Year 54).....................	700.00
16.	1000 Yuan 1965 (Year 54).....................	350.00

COLOMBIA

(For previous issues, see Part I.)

Head of Pope Paul VI. Rev. Arms and value. On the 39th International Eucharistic Congress of Bogota. Struck in proof only.

112.	1500 Pesos 1968.....................................	1350.00
113.	500 Pesos 1968.....................................	450.00
114.	300 Pesos 1968.....................................	270.00
115.	200 Pesos 1968.....................................	180.00
116.	100 Pesos 1968..................................... *	90.00

Uniformed bust of Bolivar. Different reverses as indicated. Struck in proof only.

117. 1500 Pesos 1969. Bust of Santander 1350.00
118. 500 Pesos 1969. Bust of Rondon 450.00
119. 300 Pesos 1969. Bust of Anzoategui 270.00
120. 200 Pesos 1969. Bust of Soublette.................... 180.00
121. 100 Pesos 1969. Bust of Paris 90.00

Different obverses as indicated. Rev. Emblem of the 6th Pan American Games. For the 1971 games in Cali. Struck in proof only.

122. 1500 Pesos 1971. Indian figures on raft .... * 1350.00
123. 500 Pesos 1971. Indian goddess with son 450.00
124. 300 Pesos 1971. Indian prophet and teacher 270.00
125. 200 Pesos 1971. Indian running....................... 180.00
126. 100 Pesos 1971. Indian throwing spear 90.00

Indian urn. Rev. Value. To commemorate the 50th Anniversary of The Bank of The Republic of Colombia.

127. 1500 Pesos 1973..................................... 400.00
Proof 425.00

Bust of Guilermo Valencia. Rev. Arms. On the centenary of his birth. Struck in proof only.

128. 2000 Pesos 1973................................. * 270.00
129. 1500 Pesos 1973.................................... 180.00
130. 1000 Pesos 1973.................................... 90.00

Bust of the explorer Rodrigo De Bastidas. Rev. Tairona Indian sculpture. On the 450th anniversary of the founding of the city of Santa Marta. Struck in proof only.

131. 2000 Pesos 1975.................................... 180.00
132. 1000 Pesos 1975.................................... 90.00

Arms of the city of Medellin. Rev. Three orchids. On the 300th anniversary of the city.

133. 2,000 Pesos 1975.................................. 180.00
134. 1,000 Pesos 1975.................................. 90.00
Arms. Rev. Ocelot. For the world wildlife conservation program.
135. 10,000 Pesos 1979........................... 700.00
Proof 750.00

COMOROS

Bust of Said Mohamed Cheikh. Different reverses as indicated.

1. 20,000 Francs 1976. Coelecanth fish 125.00
Proof 130.00
2. 10,000 Francs 1976. Colibri hummingbird 62.50
Proof 65.00

CONGO

Military bust of President Joseph Kasavubu. Rev. Elephant. On the 5th anniversary of independence. Struck in proof only.

1. 100 Francs 1965 .... * 675.00
2. 50 Francs 1965 .... 335.00
3. 25 Francs 1965 .... 165.00

Military bust of Kasavubu. Rev. Palm trees. Struck in proof only.

4. 20 Francs 1965 ....*...... 130.00
5. 10 Francs 1965 .... 65.00

COOK ISLANDS

Bust of Queen Elizabeth II. Rev. Head of Winston Churchill, Parliament Building, and flag. On the 100th anniversary of his birth.

1. 100 Dollars 1974 .... 360.00
   Proof 385.00

Bust of Queen Elizabeth II. Rev. Ship between busts of Captain James Cook and King George III. On the 200th anniversary of Cook's second Pacific voyage.

2. 100 Dollars 1975 .... 200.00
   Proof 210.00

Bust of Queen Elizabeth II. Rev. Jugate busts of Benjamin Franklin and James Cook. On the Bicentennial of the United States.

3. 100 Dollars 1976 .... 200.00
   Proof 210.00

Bust of Queen Elizabeth II. Rev. Royal cipher amid waves and native flora. On her Silver Jubilee.

4. 100 Dollars 1977 .... 200.00
   Proof 210.00

Bust of Queen Elizabeth II. Rev. Bust of James Cook. On the 250th anniversary of Cook's birth.

5. 250 Dollars 1978 .... 345.00
   Proof 355.00

Bust of Queen Elizabeth II. Rev. Captain Cook and two shipmates going ashore. On the bicentennial of Cook's discovery of Hawaii.

6. 200 Dollars 1978 .... 300.00
   Proof 310.00

Bust of Queen Elizabeth II. Rev. Pacific flora and fauna. On the 200th anniversary of Cook's return to England.

7. 200 Dollars 1979 .... 300.00
   Proof 310.00

Bust of Queen Elizabeth II. Rev. Profile bust of the sea god Tangaroa. Struck in proof only.

8. 100 Dollars 1979 .... 210.00

COSTA RICA

(For previous issues, see Part I.)

Different obverses as indicated. Rev. Arms. Struck in proof only.

23.	1000 Colones 1970. Map, waves, sun and mountains...	4100.00
24.	500 Colones 1970. Bust of Jesus Jimenez	1560.00
25.	200 Colones 1970. Juan Santamaria and cannon	625.00
26.	100 Colones 1970. Native art	310.00
27.	50 Colones 1970. Figure on globe	155.00

Arms. Rev. Great anteater. For the world wildlife conservation program.

28.	1500 Colones 1974....................................		700.00
		Proof	750.00

CUBA

(For previous issues, see Part I.)
Bust of Carlos Manuel de Cespedes. Rev. Arms.

8.	100 Pesos 1977	255.00

Abstract symbol. Rev. Arms. On the meeting of "non-aligned nations" in Havana.

9.	100 Pesos 1979	255.00

CYPRUS

(For previous issues, See Part I.)

Bust of Archbishop Makarios III. Rev. Map. On his death.

6.	50 Pounds 1978............................		340.00
		Proof	350.00

CZECHOSLOVAKIA

(For previous issues, see part I.)
Different obverses as indicated. Rev. Arms.

19.	10 Ducats 1978. View of Prague	800.00
20.	5 Ducats 1978. Seal of St. Charles University.....	400.00
21.	2 Ducats 1978. King Charles IV seated	160.00
22.	1 Ducat 1978. Head Of King Charles IV	80.00

DAHOMEY

Different obverses as indicated. Rev. Arms. Struck in proof only.

1.	25000 CFA Francs 1971. 3 Presidents		1865.00
2.	10000 CFA Francs 1971. Hippopotami		745.00
3.	5000 CFA Francs 1971. 5 Animals		375.00
4.	2500 CFA Francs 1971. 3 Dancers.......	*	185.00

DOMINICA

Bust of Queen Elizabeth II. Different reverses as indicated. On independence.

1.	300 Dollars 1978. Arms		390.00
		Proof	425.00
2.	150 Dollars 1978. Parrot over islands		200.00
		Proof	225.00

DOMINICAN REPUBLIC

(For previous issues, see Part I.)

Three interlocking rings. Rev. Arms. For the XII Central American and Caribbean Games.

2.	30 Pesos 1974	245.00
	Proof	260.00

Pre-Columbian Indian artifact. Rev. Arms. On the opening of the Pueblo Viejo mine.

3.	100 Pesos 1975	210.00
	Proof	215.00

Head of Juan Pablo Duarte. Rev. Arms. On the centennial of his death.

4.	200 Pesos 1977	575.00
	Proof	585.00

Bust of Pope John Paul II. Rev. Arms. On his visit.

5.	250 Pesos 1979	585.00
6.	100 Pesos 1979	225.00

EGYPT

(For previous issues, see Part I.)

United Arab Republic, 1958-1971

Aswan Dam. Rev. Inscription.

44.	5 Pounds 1960 .... *	865.00
45.	1 Pound 1960	175.00

Diversion of the Nile. Rev. Inscription. The weight of the Pound was reduced in 1964 from 8.5 grams to 5.2 grams. The 10 Pound coin struck in that year weighs 52 grams and is the heaviest gold coin minted since 1915.

46.	10 Pounds 1964. Reduced weight .... *	1050.00
	Proof	1100.00
47.	5 Pounds 1964. Reduced weight	530.00
	Proof	550.00

Koran on globe. Rev. Inscription in circle. On the 1400th Anniversary of the Koran.

48.	5 Pounds 1968	530.00

Bust of Gamal Abdel Nasser. Rev. Legend and value. In honor of the late President.

49.	5 Pounds 1970	530.00
50.	1 Pound 1970 .... *	160.00

Arab Republic of Egypt, 1971-

National Bank of Egypt building. Rev. Legend, value and date. On the 75th anniversary of the National Bank.

51.	5 Pounds 1973	*	530.00
52.	1 Pound 1973		160.00

Soldier crossing Suez Canal. Rev. Legend, value and date. On the 1973 Yom Kippur War.

53.	5 Pounds 1974	500.00

Bust of King Faisal of Saudi Arabia. Rev. Legend, value, and date. On his death.

54.	5 Pounds 1976	400.00
55.	1 Pound 1976	200.00

Head of Om Kholsum. Rev. Legend, value, and date. On the death of the Egyptian singer.

56.	5 Pounds 1976	*	400.00
57.	1 Pound 1976		200.00

View of the Suez Canal. Rev. Legend, value, and date. On its reopening.

58.	5 Pounds 1976	400.00

On the Economic Union.

59.	5 Pounds 1977	400.00

Bust of President Anwar Sadat. Rev. Inscription. On the peace initiative. Struck in proof only.

60.	100 Pounds 1979	640.00
61.	50 Pounds 1979	320.00

EQUATORIAL GUINEA

Different obverses as indicated. Rev. Arms above crossed tusks. Struck in proof only.

1.	5000 Pesetas 1970. Head of President Macias	1475.00
2.	1000 Pesetas 1970. Jules Rimet soccer cup and scenic views	295.00
3.	500 Pesetas 1970. Bust of Pope John XXIII	145.00
4.	500 Pesetas 1970. Bust of Lenin	145.00
5.	500 Pesetas 1970. Bust of Lincoln	145.00
6.	500 Pesetas 1970. Bust of Ghandi	145.00
7.	250 Pesetas 1970. Naked Maja	72.50
8.	250 Pesetas 1970. Praying hands	72.50

Different obverses as indicated. Rev. Arms above crossed tusks. On the centennial of Rome as a capital city. Struck in proof only.

9.	750 Pesetas 1970. Roma standing	220.00
10.	750 Pesetas 1970. Forum and Coliseum	220.00
11.	750 Pesetas 1970. Roma seated	220.00
12.	750 Pesetas 1970. Winged head of Roma	220.00

Bust of President Macias Nguema Biyogo. Different reverses as indicated. On the tenth anniversary of his election. Struck in proof only.

13.	10,000 Ekuele 1978. Agricultural implements ······	270.00
14.	5,000 Ekuele 1978. Bank building ·············	145.00

ETHIOPIA

(For previous issues, see Part I.)

Bust of Haile Selassie. Rev. Arms. On his 75th birthday. Struck in proof only.

30.	200 Dollars 1966 ·····································	1675.00
31.	100 Dollars 1966 ·····································	840.00
32.	50 Dollars 1966 ·····································	420.00
33.	20 Dollars 1966 ································* ····	165.00
34.	10 Dollars 1966 ·····································	82.50

Different obverses as indicated. Rev. Lion. In commemoration of the 5 modern Ethiopian monarchs. Struck in proof only.

35.	100 Dollars 1972. Bust of Haile Selassie·········	840.00
36.	50 Dollars 1972. Bust of Theodros II············	420.00
37.	50 Dollars 1972. Bust of Yohannes IV ··········	420.00
38.	50 Dollars 1972. Bust of Menelik II ············	420.00
39.	50 Dollars 1972. Bust of Zewditu ··············	420.00

Arms. Rev. Walia ibex. For the world wildlife conservation program.

40.	500 Bir 1979 ·························	700.00
	Proof	750.00

FALKLAND ISLANDS

Bust of Queen Elizabeth II. Rev. Sheep. Struck in proof only.

1.	5 Pounds 1974 ·····························	850.00
2.	2 Pounds 1974 ·····························	340.00
3.	1 Sovereign 1974 ·························	170.00
4.	½ Sovereign 1974 ·························	85.00

Bust of Queen Elizabeth II. Rev. Sea lion. For the world wildlife conservation program.

5.	150 Pounds 1979 ·························	700.00
	Proof	750.00

FIJI

Bust of Queen Elizabeth II. Rev. King Ratu Seru Cakobau. On the 100th anniversary of cession to Great Britain.

1.	100 Dollars 1974-75 ························	365.00
	Proof	375.00

Bust of Queen Elizabeth II. Rev. King Ratu Seru Cakobau.

2.	100 Dollars 1975 ·························	365.00

Bust of Queen Elizabeth II. Rev. Banded iguana. For the world wildlife-conservation program.

3.	250 Dollars 1978 ·························	700.00
	Proof	750.00

FUJAIRAH

GABON

Head of President Leon Mba. Rev. Arms. Dated 1960 but
struck and released in 1965 to commemorate independence.
Struck in proof only.

1. 100 Francs 1960 .... * 670.00
2. 50 Francs 1960 .... 335.00
3. 25 Francs 1960 .... 165.00
4. 10 Francs 1960 .... 67.50

Different obverses as indicated. Rev. Arms. Struck in proof only.

1. 200 Riyals 1969. Bust of Alsharqi..................... 865.00
2. 100 Riyals 1969. Heads of Apollo 11 astronauts....... 430.00
3. 100 Riyals 1969. Heads of Apollo 12 astronauts....... 430.00
4. 50 Riyals 1969. Olympic rings, torch and legend..... 215.00
5. 25 Riyals 1969. Bust of President Nixon 110.00

*Bust of President Bongo. Different reverses as indicated.
Struck in proof only.*

5. 20,000 Francs 1969. Apollo 11 on launching pad....... 1470.00
6. 10,000 Francs 1969. Apollo 11 landing on moon 735.00
7. 5,000 Francs 1969. Tribal masks 365.00
8. 3,000 Francs 1969. Arms............................. 220.00
9. 1,000 Francs 1969. Woodcutter 72.50

*Different obverses as indicated. Rev. Arms (same type as
previous issue). Struck in proof only.*

6. 100 Riyals 1970. Head of Pope Paul and map
of Australia 430.00
7. 100 Riyals 1970. Head of Pope Paul and 2 cathedrals. 430.00
8. 100 Riyals 1970. Apollo 13 emblem 430.00
9. 100 Riyals 1971. Apollo 14 emblem 430.00

GAMBIA

*Bust of Sir Dawda Kairaba Jawara. Rev. Sitatunga. For the world
wildlife conservation program.*

1. 500 Dalasis 1977 .... 700.00
Proof 750.00

GIBRALTAR

Bust of Queen Elizabeth II. Different reverses as indicated. On the 250th anniversary of the use of British sterling in the colony.

1.	100 Pounds 1975. Arms	665.00
	Proof	700.00
2.	50 Pounds 1975. Madonna and Child	330.00
	Proof	350.00
3.	25 Pounds 1975. Lion	165.00
	Proof	175.00

GREAT BRITAIN

(For previous issues, see Part I.)

ELIZABETH II, 1952-

Bust. Rev. St. George slaying dragon. A few specimen sets of 5 Pound, 2 Pound, Sovereign and ½ Sovereign pieces were struck in 1953 for presentation and to maintain the series. None were made available and all are now in official custody.

275.   1 Sovereign 1957-59, 62-68 .... 200.00(B)

Mature bust. Rev. St. George slaying dragon. The 1979 issue was struck in proof only.

276.   1 Sovereign 1974, 76, 79 .... 200.00(B)

(Numbers 275 and 276 are bullion coins. The price listed is based on gold at $725 per ounce.)

GREECE

(For previous issues, see Part I.)

CONSTANTINE II, 1964-

Phoenix bird and soldier. Rev. Arms and value. Issued in 1970 by the Bank of Greece to mark the 1967 revolution.

12.	100 Drachmai 1967 ....*	775.00
13.	20 Drachmai 1967	350.00

On joining the Common Market.

14.	10,000 Drachmai 1979	425.00

GUINEA

Different obverses as indicated. Rev. Arms. Struck in proof only.

1.	10,000 Francs 1969. Bust of Ahmed Sekou Toure	840.00
2.	5,000 Francs 1969. Views of Munich and other Olympic sites	420.00
3.	2,000 Francs 1969. Apollo 11 landing on moon	170.00
4.	1,000 Francs 1969. Conjoined heads of John Kennedy and Robert Kennedy	85.00

Different obverses as indicated. Rev. Arms. Struck in proof only.

5.	2,000 Francs ND (1970). Soyuz in flight	170.00
6.	2,000 Francs ND (1970). Apollo 13 insignia...........	170.00

Series A. (.900 fine gold).

Different obverses as indicated. Rev. Arms. Struck in proof only.

7.	5,000 Francs 1970. Head of Nasser	420.00
8.	5,000 Francs 1970. Head of Echnaton	420.00
9.	5,000 Francs 1970. Head of Chephren	420.00
10.	5,000 Francs 1970. Head of Cleopatra	420.00
11.	5,000 Francs 1970. Head of Nefertiti	420.00
12.	5,000 Francs 1970. Head of Ramses III	420.00
13.	5,000 Francs 1970. Head of Toutankhamon	420.00
14.	5,000 Francs 1970. Head of Tiyi	420.00

Different obverses as indicated. Rev. Arms.

15.	2,000 Sylis 1977. Head of Mao Tse Tung	120.00
		Proof	125.00
16.	2,000 Sylis 1977. Head of Sekou Toure	120.00
		Proof	125.00
17.	1,000 Sylis 1977. Head of Nkrumah	60.00
		Proof	62.50
18.	1,000 Sylis 1977. Head of Makeba	60.00
		Proof	62.50

Different obverses as indicated. Rev. Arms. Struck in proof only.

1.	1000 Gourdes 1967-70. Bust of Duvalier	4100.00
2.	200 Gourdes 1967-70. Native running with machete	825.00
3.	100 Gourdes 1967-70. Girl holding machete	410.00
4.	50 Gourdes 1967-70. Voodoo dancer	205.00
5.	20 Gourdes 1967-70. Native holding machete	82.50

GUYANA

Arawak indian casting gold upon the water. Rev. Arms. On the tenth anniversary of independence. Only 100 pieces were struck in uncirculated condition.

1.	100 Dollars 1976	100.00
		Proof	65.00

El Dorado kneeling. Rev. Arms. Only 100 pieces were struck in uncirculated condition.

2.	100 Dollars 1977	100.00
		Proof	65.00

Series B. (.585 fine gold).   Series C. (.900 fine gold).

Different obverses as indicated. Rev. Arms. Struck in proof only.

6.	500 Gourdes 1969. Three artists	2070.00
7.	250 Gourdes 1969. Bust of Christophe	1035.00
8.	60 Gourdes 1969-70. Bust of Petion.	270.00
9.	40 Gourdes 1969-70. Bust of Dessalines	180.00
10.	30 Gourdes 1969-70. The Citadelle	135.00

Different obverses as indicated. Rev. Arms. Struck in proof only.

11.	200 Gourdes 1971. Native and palm trees	825.00
12.	100 Gourdes 1971. Chief Stalking Turkey	410.00
13.	100 Gourdes 1971. Chief Billy Bowlegs	410.00
14.	100 Gourdes 1971. Chief Red Cloud	410.00
15.	100 Gourdes 1971. Chief War Eagle	410.00
16.	100 Gourdes 1971. Chief Geronimo	410.00
17.	100 Gourdes 1971. Chief Joseph Nez Perce	410.00
18.	100 Gourdes 1971. Chief Sitting Bull	410.00
19.	100 Gourdes 1971. Chief Osceola	410.00
20.	100 Gourdes 1971. Chief Playing Fox	410.00
21.	50 Gourdes 1971. 4 Soldiers	205.00

Different obverses as indicated. Rev. Arms. For the second anniversary of the accession of President Jean Claude Duvalier.

22. 1000 Gourdes 1973. Jean Claude Duvalier.............. 300.00
    Proof 310.00
23. 500 Gourdes 1973. Mother holding child.............. 150.00
    Proof 155.00
24. 500 Gourdes 1973. Girl holding conch shell.......... 150.00
    Proof 155.00
25. 200 Gourdes 1973. 2 whimsical football players...... 60.00
    Proof 62.50
26. 100 Gourdes 1973. Christopher Columbus............. 30.00
    Proof 32.50

American Revolution battle scene. Rev. Arms. On the bicentennial of the United States.

27. 1000 Gourdes 1974 .... 275.00
    Proof 300.00

Young woman lighting Olympic flame. Rev. Arms. For the 1976 Olympic Games in Innsbruck and Montreal.

28. 500 Gourdes 1974, 75 .... 135.00
    Proof 150.00

Bust of Pope Paul VI, praying hands, and view of St. Peter's Square. Rev. Arms. On the Holy Year of 1975.

29. 200 Gourdes 1974, 75 .... 60.00
    Proof 65.00

Two Haitian women with arms raised. Rev. Arms. On International Women's Year.

30. 200 Gourdes 1975 .... 60.00

Soccer ball. Rev. Arms. On the World Cup tournament in Argentina.

31. 500 Gourdes 1977 .... 175.00
    Proof 180.00

Map of Europe. Rev. Arms. On the 20th anniversary of the European Common Market.

32. 500 Gourdes 1977 .... 175.00
    Proof 180.00

Flags on interlocking gears. Rev. Arms.

33. 500 Gourdes 1977 .... 175.00
    Proof 180.00

Olympic flames. Rev. Arms. On the 1980 Moscow Olympics.

34. 500 Gourdes 1977 .... 175.00
    Proof 180.00

Busts of Francois and Jean-Claude Duvalier. Rev. Arms.

35. 500 Gourdes 1977 .... 175.00
    Proof 180.00

Sailboat. Rev. Arms.

36. 250 Gourdes 1977 .... 85.00
    Proof 90.00

Busts of Menachem Begin and Anwar Sadat. Rev. Arms. On the Egyptian president's visit to Jerusalem.

37.	250 Gourdes 1977		85.00
		Proof	90.00

Bust of Charles A. Lindbergh over the "Spirit of St. Louis." Rev. Arms. On the 50th anniversary of his Transatlantic flight.

38.	250 Gourdes 1977		85.00
		Proof	90.00

Kneeling figure breaking chains of bondage. Rev. Arms. On the furtherance of the campaign for human rights.

39.	250 Gourdes 1977		85.00
		Proof	90.00

HONG KONG

Bust of Queen Elizabeth II. Rev. Arms. On the Royal Visit.

1.	1000 Dollars 1975		400.00
		Proof	900.00

Bust of Queen Elizabeth II. Rev. Dragon. First of the annual Chinese New Year coins.

2.	1,000 Dollars 1976		775.00
		Proof	1000.00

Bust of Queen Elizabeth II. Rev. Snake.

3.	1,000 Dollars 1977		425.00
		Proof	525.00

Bust of Queen Elizabeth II. Rev. Horse.

4.	1,000 Dollars 1978		425.00
		Proof	525.00

Bust of Queen Elizabeth II. Rev. Goat.

5.	1,000 Dollars 1979		400.00
		Proof	500.00

Bust of Queen Elizabeth II. Rev. Monkey.

6.	1,000 Dollars 1980		400.00
		Proof	500.00

HUNGARY

(For previous issues, see Part I.)

Official government restrikes have been issued. They are listed in Part I since they bear the date of the original coin rather than the date of the new minting.

People's Republic, 1945-

Bust of Liszt. Rev. Lyre.

101.	500 Florins 1961	880.00
102.	100 Florins 1961	175.00
103.	50 Florins 1961	87.50

Bust of Bartok. Rev. Lyre.

104.	500 Florins 1961	*	880.00
105.	100 Florins 1961		175.00
106.	50 Florins 1961		87.50

Bust of Nicholas Zrinyi. Rev. The defense of Szigetvar. On the 400th anniversary of the war against the Turks.

106a.	1000 Forint 1966		1750.00
106b.	500 Forint 1966	*	880.00
106c.	100 Forint 1966		175.00

Bust of Kodaly. Rev. Peacock. On the composer's 85th birthday.

106d. 1000 Forint 1967 . . . . 1750.00
106e. 500 Forint 1967 . . . . * 880.00

Bust of Dr. Ignaz Semmelweis. Rev. Arms. On the 150th anniversary of the birth of the obstetrician who conquered childbed fever.

106f. 1000 Forint 1968 . . . . 1750.00
106g. 500 Forint 1968 . . . . 880.00
106h. 200 Forint 1968 . . . . 350.00
106i. 100 Forint 1968 . . . . * 175.00
106j.   50 Forint 1968 . . . . 87.50

ICELAND

Head of Sigurdsson. Rev. Arms.

1.   500 Kronur 1961 . . . . 400.00
                                              Proof   525.00

Viking ship with Ingolfur Arnarson. Rev. Sea eagle, dragon, bull, and giant with spear. On the 1100th anniversary of settlement.

2. 10,000 Kronur 1974 . . . . 325.00
                                              Proof   425.00

INDONESIA

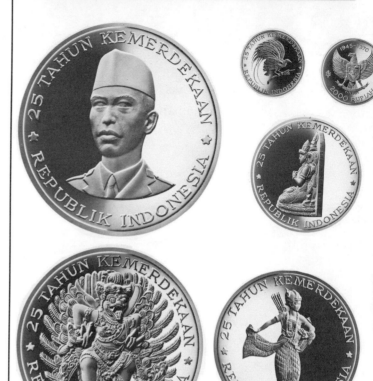

Different obverses as indicated. Rev. Bird flanked by BI monogram (Bank of Indonesia). Struck in proof only.

1. 25,000 Rupiah 1970. Bust of Suharto 1300.00
2. 20,000 Rupiah 1970. Deity 1035.00
3. 10,000 Rupiah 1970. Balinese dancer 510.00
4.   5,000 Rupiah 1970. Idol 255.00
5.   2,000 Rupiah 1970. Plumed bird 100.00

Arms. Rev. Komodo dragon. For the world wildlife conservation program.

6. 100,000 Rupiah 1974 . . . . 700.00
                                              Proof   750.00

IRAN (PERSIA)

(For previous issues, see Part I.)

MOHAMMED RIZA PAHLEVI, 1942-1979
(In 1976, the dating was changed to the Monarchic system. 1355 S.H. became 2535 M.S.)

Head. Rev. Lion. These coins appear in red gold.

99.	5 Pahlevi 1339-55 S.H., 2536-37 M.S. (1959-79 A.D.)	650.00(B)
100.	2½ Pahlevi 1339-55 S.H., 2536-37 M.S. (1959-79 A.D.)	350.00(B)
101.	1 Pahlevi 1330-55 S.H., 2536-37 M.S. (1950-79 A.D.) *	150.00(B)
102.	½ Pahlevi 1330-55 S.H., 2536-37 M.S. (1950-79 A.D.) *	85.00(B)
103.	¼ Pahlevi 1332-35 S.H. (1953-56 A.D.)	75.00(B)
104.	¼ Pahlevi 1336-55 S.H., 2536-37 M.S. (1956-79 A.D.) large flan	35.00(B)

(Numbers 99-104 are bullion coins. The price listed is based on gold at
$725 per ounce.)

Bust. Rev. Inscription. Commemorative.

105.	2½ Pahlevi 1338 S.H. (1960 A.D.)	350.00

*Different obverses as indicated. Rev. Arms. For the coronation
of the Imperial couple and the 2500th anniversary of the
Persian Monarchy. Struck in proof only.*

106.	2,000 Rials 1971. Shah and Empress	400.00
107.	1,000 Rials 1971. Persepolis ruins	200.00
108.	750 Rials 1971. Cylinder of Cyprus	125.00
109.	500 Rials 1971. Winged griffin	75.00

*Busts of the Shah and his father. Rev. Lion. On the 50th anniversary
of the Pahlevi dynasty.*

110.	10 Pahlevi 2535-36 M.S. (1976-77)	1500.00
111.	10 Pahlevi 2537-38 M.S. (1978-79)	1500.00

Islamic Republic, 1979 -
Mosque. Rev. Inscription.

112.	1 Pahlevi (?) 1358 S.H. (1979)	175.00
113.	½ Pahlevi (?) 1358 S.H. (1979)	100.00

IRAQ

*Busts of two soldiers. Rev. Value and inscription for the
golden jubilee of the Iraqi Army.*

1.	5 Dinars 1971	290.00
	Proof	300.00

ISLE OF MAN

*Head of Queen Elizabeth II. Rev. Arms in shield. On the
200th anniversary of England's purchase of the Isle of
Man.*

1.	5 Pounds 1965 *	850.00
	Proof	900.00
2.	1 Pound 1965	170.00
	Proof	185.00
3.	½ Pound 1965	85.00
	Proof	100.00

Bust of Queen Elizabeth II. Rev. Viking warrior on horseback.

4.	5 Pounds 1973-77	850.00
	Proof	900.00
5.	2 Pounds 1973-77	340.00
	Proof	375.00
6.	1 Sovereign 1973-77 *	170.00
	Proof	185.00
7.	½ Sovereign 1973-77	85.00
	Proof	100.00

*Bust of Queen Elizabeth II. Rev. Viking warrior on horseback,
triskelis below. On the millenium of Tynwald. Struck in proof
only.*

8.	5 Sovereigns 1979	900.00
9.	2 Sovereigns 1979	375.00
10.	1 Sovereign 1979	185.00
11.	½ Sovereign 1979	100.00

ISRAEL

Israel was established as a republic in 1948. The 20 Pound piece is
equivalent to the English Pound. Proof coins bear the Hebrew letter
"Mem."

Small head of Herzl. Rev. Menorah.

1.	20 Pounds 1960	650.00

Small head of Weizmann. Rev. Menorah. Struck in proof only.

2.	100 Pounds 1962	650.00
3.	50 Pounds 1962 *	650.00

Menorah. Rev. Cornucopia. On the National Bank Jubilee.

4. 50 Pounds 1964 . . . . 1000.00
Proof 5000.00

Emblem of the Israel Defense Forces. Rev. The Wailing Wall. On Israel's victory in the six-day Middle East war. Struck in proof only.

5. 100 Pounds 1967 . . . . 600.00

Temple of Solomon. Rev. Panoramic view of Jerusalem. On the 20th anniversary of independence. Struck in proof, but without a "Mem."

6. 100 Pounds 1968 . . . . 550.00

Hebrew word "Shalom." Rev. Legend, helmet and sapling. In memory of fallen comrades. Struck in proof only.

7. 100 Pounds 1969 . . . . 500.00

Disk behind vertical panels. Rev. Menorah. Dedicated to Soviet Jewry's struggle for freedom. Struck in proof only.

8. 100 Pounds 1971 . . . . 500.00

Part of the Israeli Declaration of Independence. Rev. Menorah. On the 25th anniversary of independence. Struck in proof only.

9. 200 Pounds 1973 . . . . * 600.00
10. 100 Pounds 1973 . . . . 300.00
11. 50 Pounds 1973 . . . . 150.00

Small head of Ben-Gurion. Rev. Menorah. On his death. Struck in proof only.

12. 500 Pounds 1974 . . . . 600.00

Stylized Star of David. Rev. Value. On the 25th anniversary of State of Israel Bonds. Struck in proof only.

13. 500 Pounds 1975 . . . . 425.00

Olive tree. Rev. value. On the 30th anniversary of statehood. Struck in proof only.

14. 1,000 Pounds 1978 . . . . 250.00

Olive branch. Rev. Arms, value and inscription. On the peace treaty with Egypt. Struck in proof only.

15.   5,000 Pounds 1980 . . . .   350.00

IVORY COAST

Bust of President Felix Houphouet Boigny. Rev. Arms. Struck in proof only.

1.   100 Francs 1966 . . . .   675.00
2.   50 Francs 1966 . . . .   335.00
3.   25 Francs 1966 . . . . * 165.00
4.   10 Francs 1966 . . . .   67.50

JAMAICA

(For previous issues, see Part I.)

Three ships and map. Rev. Arms. To commemorate the tenth anniversary of Independence.

6.   20 Dollars 1972 . . . .   185.00
                                          Proof   195.00

Bust of Christopher Columbus. Rev. Arms.

7.   100 Dollars 1975 . . . .   165.00
                                          Proof   185.00

Bust of Admiral Horatio Nelson in front of map and ship. Rev. Arms. Only 100 pieces were struck in uncirculated.

8.   100 Dollars 1976 . . . .   200.00
                                          Proof   165.00

Queen Elizabeth II seated holding orb and sceptre. Rev. Arms. On her Silver Jubilee. Struck in proof only.

9.   250 Dollars 1978 . . . .   900.00
10.   100 Dollars 1978 . . . .   235.00

Crowned bust of Prince Charles holding sceptre. Rev. Arms. On the tenth anniversary of his investiture as Prince of Wales. Struck in proof only.

11.   250 Dollars 1979 . . . .   900.00
12.   100 Dollars 1979 . . . .   235.00

JERSEY

Bust of Queen Elizabeth II. Different reverses as indicated. For the Royal 25th wedding anniversary.

1.   50 Pounds 1972. Jersey Arms 485.00
                                          Proof   495.00
2.   25 Pounds 1972. English Royal Arms 240.00
                                          Proof   250.00
3.   20 Pounds 1972. Shell 200.00
                                          Proof   210.00
4.   10 Pounds 1972. Ancient Gold Jewelry 100.00
                                          Proof   105.00
5.   5 Pounds 1972. Shrew 50.00
                                          Proof   52.50

JORDAN

Bust of King Hussein. Different reverses as indicated. Struck in proof only.

1.   25 Dinars 1969. Dome of the Rock.................... 1450.00
2.   10 Dinars 1969. Bust of Pope Paul VI............... 580.00
3.   5 Dinars 1969. Treasury Building.................... 290.00
4.   2 Dinars 1969. Forum of Jepagh.................... 115.00

Bust of King Hussein. Rev. Arms. On his Silver Jubilee. Struck in proof only.
5.   25 Dinars 1977............................. 315.00

Bust of King Hussein. Rev. Holebara Bustard bird. For the world wildlife conservation program.
6.   50 Dinars 1977............................. 700.00
                                    Proof 750.00

KATANGA

Bananas. Rev. Baluba cross.
1.   5 Francs 1961.................................... 280.00

KENYA

Bust of President Jomo Kenyatta. Different reverses as indicated.
1.   500 Shillings 1966. Mt. Kenya........................ 800.00
                                    Proof 850.00
2.   250 Shillings 1966. Cockerel 400.00
                                    Proof 425.00
3.   100 Shillings 1966. Kenyatta's fly whisk.............. 160.00
                                    Proof 170.00

KIRIBATI

Arms. Rev. Large meeting hut. On independence.
1.   150 Dollars 1979............................. 340.00

KUWAIT

Value in Arabic in center circle. Rev. Dhow sailing left.
1.   5 Dinars 1961.................................... 2000.00

LAOS

Bust of King Sri Savang Vatthana. Rev. Three-headed elephant. On the king's coronation.
1.   80,000 Kip 1971.................................... 1675.00
2.   40,000 Kip 1971.................................... 840.00
3.   20,000 Kip 1971.................................*..... 420.00
4.   8,000 Kip 1971.................................... 165.00
5.   4,000 Kip 1971.................................... 82.50

Bust of King Sri Savang Vatthana above three-headed elephant. Different reverses as indicated. Struck in proof only.

6. 100,000 Kip 1975. Buddha figure 150.00
7. 50,000 Kip 1975. That Luang temple 75.00
8. 50,000 Kip 1975. Laotian girl 75.00

LESOTHO

Bust of King Moshoeshoe in tribal regalia. Rev. Arms. Struck in proof only.

1. 4 Maloti 1966 .... * 340.00
2. 2 Maloti 1966 .... 170.00
3. 1 Maloti 1966 .... 85.00

Head of undraped King Moshoeshoe. Rev. Arms. Patterns. Only seven pattern sets were prepared.

4. 20 Maloti 1966 .... Rare
5. 10 Maloti 1966 .... Rare
6. 4 Maloti 1966 .... Rare
7. 2 Maloti 1966 .... Rare

Bust of King Moshoeshoe in tribal regalia. Different reverses as indicated. To commemorate the work of the F.A.O. (Food and Agriculture Organization) of the United Nations. Struck in proof only.

8. 20 Maloti 1969. Sheep 1700.00
9. 10 Maloti 1969. Water buffalo....................... 850.00
10. 4 Maloti 1969. Ram................................ 340.00
11. 2 Maloti 1969. Farmer 170.00
12. 1 Maloti 1969. Horseman 85.00

Bust of King Moshoeshoe II. Rev. Man on horse. On the tenth anniversary of independence. Struck in proof only.

13. 100 Maloti 1976 .... 185.00

Bust of Queen Elizabeth II. Rev. Arms. On the tenth anniversary of independence and the 45th anniversary of the commonwealth.

14. 50 Maloti 1976 .... 95.00

LIBERIA

Head of President Tubman. Rev. Arms and value.

1. 20 Dollars 1964. Red gold 390.00
                                        Proof 400.00
2. 20 Dollars 1964. Yellow gold....................... 700.00

Head of President Tubman. Rev. Providence Island.

3. 25 Dollars 1965..................................... 490.00
                                        Proof 500.00

Bust of President Tubman. Rev. Arms and value. Not officially released.

4. 30 Dollars 1965............................*...... 315.00
5. 12 Dollars 1965..................................... 125.00

Different obverses as indicated. Rev. Arms. On the inauguration of President Tolbert.

6. 20 Dollars 1972. Bust of Tolbert 700.00
7. 10 Dollars 1972. Bust of Liberty 350.00
8. 5   Dollars 1972. Ship 175.00
9. 2½ Dollars 1972. The Capitol 85.00

Bust of President Tolbert. Rev. Scene at Providence Island. On the 150th anniversary of founding.

10.   25 Dollars 1972 .... 650.00

Bust of President Tolbert. Different reverses as indicated. On his inauguration. Struck in proof only.

11.   400 Dollars 1976. Map (25 struck)............... 1140.00
12.   200 Dollars 1976. Tolbert blowing horn (100 struck) 570.00
13.   100 Dollars 1976. People stretching upwards
       (175 struck)............................. 285.00

Bust of founding president Joseph Jenkins Roberts. Rev. Arms. On the 130th anniversary of nationhood.

14.   100 Dollars 1977............................. 230.00
                                        Proof 230.00

Elephant. Rev. Arms. O.A.U. commemorative. Struck in proof only.

15.   100 Dollars 1979............................. 230.00

LIECHTENSTEIN

(For previous issues, see Part I.)

Head of Prince Franz Joseph II. Rev. Arms. On the 100th anniversary of the Landesbank, Liechtenstein's national bank. Not released for circulation.

22.   50 Franken 1961............................*...... 250.00
23.   25 Franken 1961.................................. 250.00

MACAO

Ruins of St. Paulo. Rev. Racing Car. On the 25th anniversary of the Macao Grand Prix. Struck in proof only. Varieties exist with and without commercial logotypes on the car.
1.   500 Patacas 1978 . . . .   170.00

Arms, Rev. Goat. On the Chinese New Year. Struck in proof only.
2.   500 Patacas 1979 . . . .   170.00

Arms. Rev. Monkey. On the Chinese New Year
3.   1,000 Patacas 1980 . . . .   350.00

MALAWI

Bust of Dr. Hastings Kamuzu Banda. Rev. Male and female Nyala. For the world wildlife conservation program.
1.   250 Kwacha 1978 . . . .   700.00
                                                                     Proof   750.00

MALAYSIA

Bust of President Abdul Rahman. Rev. Parliament building.
1.   100 Ringgit 1971 . . . .   400.00
                                                                     Proof   650.00

Head of Tun Abdul Razak surrounded by 14 flags. Rev. Arms. On the third 5 year plan.
2.   200 Ringgit 1976 . . . .   150.00
                                                                     Proof   155.00

Emblem of the Employees Provident Fund. Rev. Value and inscription. On its 25th anniversary.
3.   250 Ringgit 1976 . . . .   160.00
                                                                     Proof   165.00

Arms. Rev. Tapir. For the world wildlife conservation program.
4.   500 Ringgit 1976 . . . .   700.00
                                                                     Proof   750.00

Bajau horseman. Rev. Arms. On the Ninth Southeast Asia Games.
5.   200 Ringgit 1977 . . . .   150.00
                                                                     Proof   155.00

MALI

Head of President Modibo Keita. Rev. Arms.

1.	100 Francs 1967		670.00
2.	50 Francs 1967		335.00
3.	25 Francs 1967	*	165.00
4.	10 Francs 1967		65.00

MALTA (ISLAND OF)

(For previous issues, see Part I.)

Different obverses as indicated. Rev. Arms.

48.	50 Pounds 1972. Statue of Neptune	700.00
49.	20 Pounds 1972. "Merill" bird	255.00
50.	10 Pounds 1972. Stone stove	125.00
51.	5 Pounds 1972. Map, hand holding torch	65.00

Different obverses as indicated. Rev. Arms.

52.	50 Pounds 1973. Castle	320.00
53.	20 Pounds 1973. Fountain	130.00
54.	10 Pounds 1973. Watchtower	65.00

Different obverses as indicated. Rev. Arms.

55.	50 Pounds 1974. Likeness of first Maltese coin	320.00
56.	20 Pounds 1974. Boat	130.00
57.	10 Pounds 1974. National flower	65.00

Different obverses as indicated. Rev. Arms.

58.	50 Pounds 1975. Ornamental stone balcony	320.00
59.	20 Pounds 1975. Fresh water crab	130.00
60.	10 Pounds 1975. Maltese falcon	65.00

Different obverses as indicated. Rev. Arms.

61.	50 Pounds 1976. Statue of Neptune	320.00
62.	20 Pounds 1976. Storm Petrel	125.00
63.	10 Pounds 1976. Swallow-tail butterfly	62.50

Different obverses as indicated. Rev. Arms.

64.	100 Pounds 1977. Sculpture "Les Gavroches"	680.00
	Proof	690.00
65.	50 Pounds 1977. Pottery	340.00
	Proof	350.00
66.	25 Pounds 1977. Ancient Coin	170.00
	Proof	175.00

MALTA (ORDER OF)
Sovereign Military Order of Malta.

The Sovereign Military Order of Malta had its origin in 1099 as the Sovereign Military Hospitaller Order of St. John of Jerusalem, which moved its headquarters to Malta in 1530.

In 1798 the Order left the island and established its current home in Rome in 1834. Because the coins issued by the Order-in-exile are a continuation of a previously legitimate numismatic series, they have been included herein.

St. John the Baptist standing holding pennon of the Order. Rev. Maltese Cross.

1.	10 Scudi 1961	170.00
2.	5 Scudi 1961	85.00

Paschal lamb with the pennon of the Order. Rev. Crowned arms.

3.	10 Scudi 1962, 63 (1962 Rare)	270.00

St. John the Baptist standing holding the pennon of the Order. Rev. Crowned arms.

4.	5 Scudi 1962, 63 (1962 Rare)	100.00

Uniformed facing bust of Grand Master De Mojana. Rev. Paschal lamb with the pennon of the Order.

5.	10 Scudi 1964	170.00

Uniformed facing bust of Grand Master De Mojana. Rev. St. John the Baptist standing holding pennon of the Order.

6.	5 Scudi 1964	85.00

Uniformed facing bust of Grand Master De Mojana. Rev.
Crowned arms.

7.   10 Scudi 1965, 66..................................   170.00

Uniformed facing bust of Grand Master De Mojana. Rev. St. John
    the Baptist standing handing the pennon of the Order to
    kneeling Grand Master.

8.   5 Scudi 1965, 66..................................   85.00

Uniformed bust of Grand Master De Mojana. Rev. Crowned arms.

9.   10 Scudi 1967 ....   170.00

Uniformed bust of Grand Master De Mojana. Rev. Two Oval
    shields.

10.   10 Scudi 1968 ....   170.00

Uniformed bust of Grand Master De Mojana. Rev. St. John
    the Baptist standing handing the pennon of the Order to
    kneeling Grand Master.

11.   10 Scudi 1969 .... *......   170.00
12.   5 Scudi 1967, 68, 71-...............................   85.00

Uniformed bust of Grand Master De Mojana. Rev. Crowned
    Maltese cross.

13.   5 Scudi 1969, 70..................................   85.00

Uniformed bust of Grand Master De Mojana. Rev. St. John
the Baptist standing holding the pennon of the Order.

14.   10 Scudi 1970, 72, 74...........................   170.00

Uniformed bust of Grand Master De Mojana. Rev. Paschal
lamb with the pennon of the Order on globe.

15.   10 Scudi, 1971, 73.................................   170.00

Uniformed bust of Grand Master De Mojana. Rev. Crowned Arms.

16.   10 Scudi 1975-76 ....   170.00

Uniformed bust of Grand Master De Mojana. Rev. St. John baptizing
    Jesus.

17.   10 Scudi 1977-78 ....   170.00

Uniformed bust of Grand Master De Mojana. Rev. Castle.

18.   10 Scudi 1979 ....   170.00

MAURITANIA

Crescent and star. Rev. Mine entrance, hopper, and conveyor belt.
    On the 15th anniversary of independence.

1.   500 Ouguiya 1975 ....   555.00

MAURITIUS

Bust of Queen Elizabeth II. Rev. Native scene. Independence commemorative.

1.   200 Rupee 1971.. 335.00
                                                Proof   800.00

Bust of Queen Elizabeth II. Rev. Mauritius flycatcher. For the world wildlife conservation program.

2.   1,000 Rupees 1975........................... 700.00
                                              Proof   750.00

Bust of Prime Minister Ramgoolam. Rev. Assembly building. On the tenth anniversary of independence.

3.   1,000 Rupees 1978........................... 195.00
                                              Proof   285.00

MEXICO

Official government restrikes have been issued. They are listed in Part I since they bear the date of the original coin rather than the date of the new minting.

MONACO

(For previous issues, see Part I.)

Conjoined heads of Prince Rainier and Princess Grace. Rev. Crowned arms. On their 10th wedding anniversary.

32.   200 Francs 1966....................................... 700.00
                                                Proof   875.00

Head of Prince Ranier. Rev. Arms. On the 25th anniversary of his reign. Struck in proof only.

33.   3,000 Francs 1974 .... 750.00
34.   Platinum 2,000 Francs 1974................... 500.00
35.   Platinum 1,000 Francs 1974................... 275.00

MONGOLIA

Arms. Rev. Two native horses. For the world wildlife conservation program.

1.   750 Tugrug 1976 .... 700.00
                                             Proof   750.00

MOROCCO

(For previous issues, see Part I.)

Head of King Hassan. Rev. Arms. On the king's birthday.

6.   250 Dirhams 1975, 77........................ 135.00
                                             Proof   145.00

Head of King Hassan. Rev. Arms between map and ear of wheat.

7.   500 Dirhams 1979........................... 270.00

MUSCAT AND OMAN

SAID BIN TAIMUR
Crossed daggers. Rev. Value.

1.   15 Rials 1381 A.H. (1962) 225.00

NEPAL

(For previous issues, see Part I.)

Crested crown. Rev. Sword and wreath. On the coronation of King Birendra Bir Bikran.

41.   1 Rupee 2031 (1974) ....   * 210.00
42.   ½ Rupee 2031 (1974) 105.00
43.   ¼ Rupee 2031 (1974) 52.50

Bust of King Birendra. Rev. Indian rhino. For the world wildlife conservation program.
44.　1,000 Rupees 1975 . . . . 700.00
　　　　　　　　　　　　　　　　　　　　　Proof　750.00

NETHERLANDS

(For previous issues, see Part I.)

Knight standing. Rev. Legend in square tablet.
26a.　1 Ducat 1960, 72, 74-76, 78 . . . . 90.00(B)
(Number 26a is a bullion coin. The price listed is based on gold at $725 per ounce.)

NETHERLANDS ANTILLES

Head of Queen Juliana. Rev. The "Andrew Doria." On the bicentennial of the United States.
1.　200 Guilders 1976 . . . . 165.00
　　　　　　　　　　　　　　　　　　　　　Proof　175.00

Head of Queen Juliana. Rev. Peter Stuyvesant standing.
2.　200 Guilders 1977 . . . . 165.00
　　　　　　　　　　　　　　　　　　　　　Proof　175.00
Head of Queen Juliana. Rev. Head of King Willem I. On the 150th anniversary of the central bank.
3.　100 Guilders 1978 . . . . 140.00
　　　　　　　　　　　　　　　　　　　　　Proof　150.00

NICARAGUA

Bust of poet Ruben Dario. Rev. Arms within triangle. On the centenary of the poet.
1.　50 Cordobas 1967 . . . . 400.00

Arms. Different reverses as indicated.
2.　2000 Cordobas 1975. Astronaut and colonial girl 360.00
　　　　　　　　　　　　　　　　　　　　　Proof　365.00
3.　1000 Cordobas 1975. Liberty Bell 180.00
　　　　　　　　　　　　　　　　　　　　　Proof　185.00
4.　500 Cordobas 1975. Naked maiden with seedling 90.00
　　　　　　　　　　　　　　　　　　　　　Proof　95.00
5.　500 Cordobas 1975. Spanish colonial church 90.00
　　　　　　　　　　　　　　　　　　　　　Proof　95.00
6.　200 Cordobas 1975. Pieta 35.00
　　　　　　　　　　　　　　　　　　　　　Proof　37.50

NIGER

Bust of President Hamani. Rev. Arms flanked by flags. Issued in 1965 on the 5th anniversary of independence. Struck in proof only.
1.　100 Francs 1960 . . . . 675.00
2.　50 Francs 1960 . . . . 335.00
3.　25 Francs 1960 . . . . *. . . . 165.00
4.　10 Francs 1960 . . . . 67.50

Different obverses as indicated. Rev. Arms. Struck in proof only.
5.	100 Francs 1968. Bust of President Hamani...........	675.00
6.	50 Francs 1968. Lion	335.00
7.	25 Francs 1968. Big horn sheep	165.00
8.	10 Francs 1968. Two ostriches......................	67.50

OMAN

(Rebel Issue.) Arms in center circle. Different reverses as indicated.

1.	500 Ryals 1971. Mosque	850.00
2.	200 Ryals 1971. Secretary bird holding snake	340.00
3.	100 Ryals 1971. Carnation	170.00
4.	50 Ryals 1971. Sailboat .... *	85.00

Arms. Rev. Tahr. For the world wildlife conservation program.
5.	75 Rials 1977	700.00
	Proof	750.00

PAKISTAN

The Astor Markhor goat. Rev. Arms. For the world wildlife conservation program.
1.	3,000 Rupees 1976....................	700.00
	Proof	750.00

Bust of Mohammed Ali Jinnah. Rev. Arms. On the centennial of the birth of Pakistan's founder.
2.	500 Rupees 1976...........................	95.00
	Proof	105.00

Monument. Rev. Legend. On the inauguration of the Islamic Summit Minar, Lahore.
3.	1,000 Rupees 1977.........................	190.00
	Proof	200.00

Bust of poet Allama Mohammad Iqbal. Rev. Value. On the centennial of his birth.
4.	500 Rupees 1977..........................	95.00
	Proof	105.00

PANAMA

Bust of Balboa. Rev. Arms. On the 500th anniversary of his birth.
1.	100 Balboas 1975-77	170.00
	Proof	175.00

Balboa kneeling holding sword and banner. Rev. Arms. On the 500th anniversary of his birth.
2.	500 Balboas 1975-76	875.00
	Proof	885.00

Bust of Simon Bolivar. Rev. Arms. On the 150th anniversary of the
    Pan-American Congress.
3.   Platinum 150 Balboas 1976 . . . .   270.00
                                            Proof   280.00

Map of the Americas. Rev. Arms. On the 30th anniversary of the
    Organization of American States.
4.   500 Balboas 1978 . . . .   900.00
                                            Proof   875.00

Dove orchid. Rev. Arms.
5.   100 Balboas 1978 . . . .   170.00
                                            Proof   175.00

Flag. Rev. Arms. On the 75th anniversary of independence.
6.   75 Balboas 1978 . . . .   125.00
                                            Proof   125.00

Jaguar head. Rev. Arms. Struck in proof only.
7.   500 Balboas 1979 . . . .   875.00

Flag and map of Panama. Rev. Arms. On the Panama Canal Treaty.
8.   Platinum 200 Balboas 1979 . . . .   270.00
                        Turtle. Rev. Arms.
9.   100 Balboas 1979 . . . .   170.00
                                            Proof   175.00

Pre-Columbian condor sculpture. Rev. Arms. Struck in Proof only.
10.   100 Balboas 1980 . . . .   175.00

PAPUA NEW GUINEA

Head of Prime Minister Michael Somare. Rev. Bird of Paradise
    and value. On attaining independence.
1.   100 Kina 1975 . . . .   200.00
                                            Proof   210.00

Crest of the Bank of Papua New Guinea. Rev. Bird of paradise
    above string of shells. On the first anniversary of independence.
2.   100 Kina 1976 . . . .   250.00
                                            Proof   200.00

Papuan hornbill. Rev. Arms.
3.   100 Kina 1977 . . . .   210.00
                                            Proof   200.00

Bird Wing butterfly. Rev. Arms.

4.   100 Kina 1978 .... 210.00
                                          Proof 200.00

Four faces. Rev. Arms.

5.   100 Kina 1979 .... 210.00
                                          Proof 200.00

PARAGUAY

(For previous issues, see Part I.)

*Bust of Stroessner. Rev. Lion seated before pole bearing the
Liberty Cap. Only 50 pieces were struck for presentation
purposes.*

3.   10,000 Guaranies 1968 .... Rare

Bust of General Stroessner. Rev. Arms.

4.   4,500 Guaranies 1972 .... 670.00
5.   3,000 Guaranies 1972 .... 445.00
6.   1,500 Guaranies 1972 .... 225.00

*Bust of Alessandro Manzoni. Rev. Arms. On the 100th
anniversary of his death.*

7.   4,500 Guaranies 1973 ....* 670.00
8.   3,000 Guaranies 1973 .... 445.00
9.   1,500 Guaranies 1973 .... 225.00

*Bust of Winston Churchill. Rev. Arms. On the 100th
anniversary of his birth.*

10.   4,500 Guaranies 1974 .... 670.00
11.   3,000 Guaranies 1974 .... 445.00
12.   1,500 Guaranies 1974 .... 225.00

PERU

(For previous issues, see Part I.)

Republic of —

*Indian head. Rev. Arms. The 1, ½ and ⅕ Libra pieces
struck after 1950 were not legal tender.*

73.   1 Libra 1898-1967 ....* ..... 170.00(B)
74.   ½ Libra 1902-66 .... 85.00(B)
75.   ⅕ Libra 1906-67 .... 37.50(B)

Head of the Inca Indian Chief, Manco Capoc. Rev. Inca emblems.

77R.   50 Soles 1967-70 .... 500.00

*Liberty seated facing right. Rev. Arms. None of these pieces
were legal tender.*

78.   100 Soles 1950-69 (1952, 58 rare)...................... 980.00(B)
79.   50 Soles 1950-69 (1952, 58 rare).....................* 490.00(B)
80.   20 Soles 1950-69 (1952, 58 rare)...............* 195.00(B)
81.   10 Soles 1956-69.............................* 100.00(B)
82.   5 Soles 1956-69................................. 50.00(B)

(Numbers 73-75 and 78-82 are bullion coins. The price listed is based on
gold at $725 per ounce.)

*Replica of the first Peruvian coin, an 8 Reales. Rev. Arms.
On the 400th anniversary of the Lima Mint.*

83.   100 Soles 1965.............................* 1000.00
84.   50 Soles 1965 .... 500.00

Arms. Rev. Winged Victory. On the centennial of the defeat
of the Spanish fleet in the naval battle of 1866.

| 85. | 100 Soles 1966 ....* ...... | 1000.00 |
| 86. | 50 Soles 1966 .... | 500.00 |

Monument. Rev. Arms. On the 150th anniversary of the Battle of
Ayacucho.

| 87. | 1 Sol 1976 .... | 490.00 |
| 88. | ½ Sol 1976 .... | 195.00 |

Different obverses as indicated. Rev. Arms. On the centenary of the
War of the Pacific.

89.	100,000 Soles 1979. Admiral Grau	715.00
90.	100,000 Soles 1979. Colonel Bolognesi	715.00
91.	100,000 Soles 1979. Colonel Caceres	715.00
92.	50,000 Soles 1979. Alfonso Ugarte.	355.00
93.	50,000 Soles 1979. Francisco Calderon	355.00
94.	50,000 Soles 1979. Captain Aguirre	355.00

PHILIPPINES

(For previous issues, see Part I.)

Head of Pope Paul VI. Rev. Head of President Ferdinand E.
Marcos. On the Pope's visit to the Philippines. Demone-
tized at the time of issue.

| 5. | 1 Piso 1970 .... | 600.00 |

Bust of President Marcos. Rev. Arms. On the third anniversary of the New Society Program.

| 6. | 1000 Piso 1975 .... | 210.00 |
| | Proof | 220.00 |

Emblems of the organizations of the International Monetary Fund.
Rev. Map. On their 1976 meeting in Manila.

| 7. | 1,500 Pisos 1976 .... | 430.00 |
| | Proof | 440.00 |

Busts of President and Mrs. Marcos. Rev. Presidential seal. On the
5th anniversary of the "New Society." Struck in proof only.

| 8. | 5,000 Pisos 1977 .... | 1625.00 |

Bust of President Marcos. Rev. Seal of the Central Bank. On the 5th anniversary of the "New Society."

9. 1,500 Pisos 1977 . . . . 425.00
              Proof 435.00

View of mint building. Rev. Arms. On the inauguration of the security printing plant-gold refinery-mint.

10. 1,500 Pisos 1978 . . . . 425.00
              Proof 435.00

POLAND

(For previous issues, see Part I.)
Different obverses as indicated. Rev. Arms.

60. 500 Zlotych 1976. Bust of Kosciuszko 625.00

61. 500 Zlotych 1976. Bust of Pulaski 625.00

Head of Frederic Chopin. Rev. Arms. Struck in proof only.

62. 2,000 Zlotych 1977 . . . . 210.00

Ski-jumper in flight. Rev. Arms. On the Lake Placid Winter Olympic Games.

63. 2,000 Zlotych 1980 . . . . 200.00

RAS AL KHAIMA

Different obverses as indicated. Rev. Legend and value. On the centenary of Rome as a capital city. Struck in proof only.

1. 200 Riyals 1970. Romulus, Remus and wolf 865.00
2. 150 Riyals 1970. Liberty standing; a building;
    Romulus, Remus and wolf 650.00
3. 100 Riyals 1970. World War I victory 435.00
4. 75 Riyals 1970. The city of Rome 325.00
5. 50 Riyals 1970. "The kingdom of Italy" . . . . . * 215.00

Different obverses as indicated. Rev. Value. Champions of Sport series. Struck in proof only.

6. 200 Riyals 1970. Busts of members of Italian
       soccer team 865.00
7. 150 Riyals 1970. Bust of Gimondi, Italian cyclist 650.00
8. 100 Riyals 1970. Jules Rimet soccer cup 435.00
9. 75 Riyals 1970. Bust of Rivera, Italian soccer player . 325.00
10. 50 Riyals 1970. Bust of Riva, Italian soccer player . . . 215.00

RHODESIA

Head of Queen Elizabeth II. Different reverses as indicated. On the first anniversary of independence. Struck in proof only.

1. 5 Pounds 1966. Arms 875.00
2. 1 Pound 1966. Lion with elephant tusk in forepaw . . 375.00
3. 10 Shillings 1966. Sable antelope 135.00

RUSSIA

(For previous issues, see Part I.)

Sower scattering seed. Rev. Hammer and sickle.

163. 10 Roubles or 1 Chervonetz 1923, 25, 76- . . . . 195.00 (B)
(Number 163 is a bullion coin. The price listed is based on gold at $725 per ounce.)

Different obverses as indicated. Rev. Arms. Struck in platinum. On the 1980 Moscow Olympic Games.

164. 150 Roubles 1977. Olympic symbols 450.00
              Proof 475.00
165. 150 Roubles 1978. Discus thrower 450.00
              Proof 475.00
166. 150 Roubles 1979. Two wrestlers 450.00
              Proof 475.00
167. 150 Roubles 1979. Chariot race 450.00
              Proof 475.00
168. 150 Roubles 1980. Ancient runners 450.00
              Proof 475.00

ST. THOMAS AND PRINCE

Different obverses as indicated. Rev. Arms.

1.	2,500 Dobras 1977. People around globe	....	135.00
		Proof	140.00
2.	2,500 Dobras 1977. World friendship	....	135.00
		Proof	140.00
3.	2,500 Dobras 1977. 3 interlocking circles	....	135.00
		Proof	140.00
4.	2,500 Dobras 1977. Dancers and musicians	....	135.00
		Proof	140.00
5.	2,500 Dobras 1977. Mother and child	....	135.00
		Proof	140.00

EL SALVADOR

(For previous issues, see Part I.)

Different obverses as indicated. Rev. Arms and bust. For the 150th anniversary of Central American Independence.

6.	200 Colones 1971. Colonial church	....	495.00
7.	100 Colones 1971. Map	....	245.00
8.	25 Colones 1971. Salvador Dali sculpture, "La Fecundidad"	....	60.00

Statue of Independence and bust. Rev. Arms. For the 150th anniversary of Central American Independence.

9.	50 Colones 1971	....	125.00

Different obverses as indicated. Rev. Arms. On the 1980 Moscow Olympic Games.

169.	100 Roubles 1977. Stadium	....	365.00
		Proof	385.00
170.	100 Roubles 1978. Rowing stadium	....	365.00
		Proof	385.00
171.	100 Roubles 1979. Velodrome	....	365.00
		Proof	385.00
172.	100 Roubles 1979. Indoor sports arena	....	365.00
		Proof	385.00
173.	100 Roubles 1980. Olympic symbol over globe and palm branch	....	365.00
		Proof	385.00
174.	100 Roubles 1980. Olympic flame	....	365.00
		Proof	385.00

RWANDA

Bust of President Gregoire Kayibanda. Rev. Arms. Independence commemorative. Struck in proof only.

1.	100 Francs 1961	....	630.00
2.	50 Francs 1961	....	315.00
3.	25 Francs 1961	....	160.00
4.	10 Francs 1961	.... *	75.00

Arms. Rev. Sun over mountains. On the 18th annual Governor's
    Assembly.
10. 250 Colones 1977 .... 340.00
                           Proof 360.00

SAN MARINO

(For previous issues, see Part I.)

Arms. Rev. Saint Marinus.

3.	2 Scudi 1974	............................*	125.00
4.	1 Scudo 1974	....	62.50

Arms. Rev. Value.

5.	2 Scudi 1975	........................* ...	125.00
6.	1 Scudo 1975	.... *	62.50

Female head. Rev. 3 castle towers.

7.	5 Scudi 1976. Head left	1700.00
8.	2 Scudi 1976. Head right	200.00
9.	1 Scudo 1976. Head right	100.00

Allegorical head of Democracy. Rev. 3 castle towers.

10.	5 Scudi 1977	320.00
11.	2 Scudi 1977	125.00
12.	1 Scudo 1977	62.50

Facing head of Liberty. Rev. Arms.

13.	10 Scudi 1978	640.00
14.	2 Scudi 1978	125.00
15.	1 Scudo 1978	62.50

Three plumes. Rev. Clasped hands.

16.	2 Scudi 1979	125.00
17.	1 Scudo 1979	62.50

SENEGAL

Arms. Rev. Value and date. On the eighth anniversary of
    independence. Struck in proof only.

1.	100 Francs 1968	....	670.00
2.	50 Francs 1968	....	335.00
3.	25 Francs 1968	.............................*	165.00
4.	10 Francs 1968		65.00

Bust of President Leopold Sedar Senghor. Rev. Arms. On the 25th
    anniversary of the Eurafrique program.

5.	2,500 Francs 1975	.... *	850.00
		Proof	850.00
6.	1,000 Francs 1975	....	350.00
		Proof	350.00
7.	500 Francs 1975	....	175.00
		Proof	175.00
8.	250 Francs 1975	....	125.00
		Proof	125.00

SEYCHELLES

Bust of President James R. Mancham. Rev. Giant tortoise. On
    independence.

1.	1,000 Rupees 1976	....	340.00
		Proof	350.00

Arms. Rev. Black Paradise flycatcher. For the world wildlife
    conservation program.

2.	1,500 Rupees 1978	....	700.00
		Proof	750.00

SHARJAH

Different obverses as indicated. Rev. Palm tree above crossed flags. Struck in proof only.

1. 200 Riyals 1970. Head of Khalid bin Mohamed
   Al-Qasimi 870.00
2. 100 Riyals 1970. Bust of Napoleon.................... 435.00
3. 100 Riyals 1970. Bust of Bolivar 435.00
4. 50 Riyals 1970. "Jules Rimet" soccer cup and globe. 215.00
5. 25 Riyals 1970. Mona Lisa........................... 105.00

SIERRA LEONE

Lion's head. Rev. Map and value. On the 5th anniversary of independence.

1. 1 Golde 1966 .... 1145.00
   Proof 1175.00
2. ½ Golde 1966 .... 570.00
   Proof 585.00
3. ¼ Golde 1966 .... *...... 285.00
   Proof 295.00
4. Palladium 1 Golde 1966........................... 1250.00
5. Palladium ½ Golde 1966 .... 750.00
6. Palladium ¼ Golde 1966 .... 325.00

Bust of Dr. Siaka Stevens. Rev. Arms. On his 70th birthday.
7. 10 Golde 1975 .... 700.00
   Proof 800.00

SINGAPORE

Crest of the Republic. Rev. Raffles lighthouse.
1. 150 Dollars 1969 .... 535.00
   Proof 750.00

Arms. Different reverses as indicated. On the tenth anniversary of independence.

2. 500 Dollars 1975. Head of lion....................... 725.00
   Proof 750.00
3. 250 Dollars 1975. Four hands clasped together 365.00
   Proof 375.00
4. 100 Dollars 1975. High-rise buildings................. 145.00
   Proof 150.00

SOLOMON ISLANDS

Bust of Queen Elizabeth II. Rev. Arms. On sovereignty. Struck in proof only.
1. 100 Dollars 1978............................. 195.00

SOMALIA

Bust of President Osman. Rev. Arms. On the 5th anniversary of independence.

1.	500 Shillings 1965	1470.00
2.	200 Shillings 1965	735.00
3.	100 Shillings 1965 ....*.....	365.00
4.	50 Shillings 1965	180.00
5.	20 Shillings 1965	90.00

Arms. Different reverses as indicated. On the 10th anniversary of independence.

6.	500 Shillings 1970. Building..........................	1470.00
7.	200 Shillings 1970. Camel...........................	735.00
8.	100 Shillings 1970. Girl carrying fruit	365.00
9.	50 Shillings 1970. Man holding vase	180.00
10.	20 Shillings 1970. Stylized atomic symbol	90.00

Arms. Rev. Different reverses as indicated. On the First anniversary of the revolution of 1969.

11.	200 Shillings 1970. Monument	735.00
12.	100 Shillings 1970. Hand, helmet and rifle	365.00
13.	50 Shillings 1970. Ear of corn	180.00

SOUTH AFRICA

(For previous issues, see Part I.)

Republic of, 1960 —

Bust of Riebeck. Rev. Springbok.

11.	2 Rand 1961- ....*		170.00(B)
		Proof	175.00
12.	1 Rand 1960-		85.00(B)
		Proof	87.50

Bearded bust of President Paul Kruger (1883-1902). Rev. Springbok. Without the mark of value. Intended as a trade coin for distribution through banks outside South Africa.

13.	1 Krugerrand 1967-		745.00(B)
		Proof	775.00

(Numbers 11-13 are bullion coins. The price listed is based on gold at $725 per ounce.)

SOUTH KOREA

Different obverses as indicated. Rev. Arms. Struck in proof only.
1. 25,000 Won 1970. King Sejong the Great............... 2030.00
2. 20,000 Won 1970. Crown of Silla Dynasty.............. 1625.00
3. 5,000 Won 1970. Turtle ship 400.00
4. 2,500 Won 1970. Queen Sunduk...................... 200.00
5. 1,000 Won 1970. Great South Gate.................... 80.00

Bust of President Chung Hee Park. Rev. The presidential coat of arms. Struck in proof only.
6. 10,000 Won 1970....................................... 810.00

SPAIN

(For previous issues, see Part I.)

The following coins are official government restrikes with the dates 19-61 or 19-62 in the small stars on the obverse.

Young head of Alfonso XII. Rev. Arms.
193R. 25 Pesetas 1876. Restrike (19-61 Rare)......... 350.00
194R. 10 Pesetas 1978. Restrike (19-61 Rare)......... 125.00

Large baby head of Alfonso XIII. Rev. Arms.
196R. 20 Pesetas 1887. Restrike (19-61 Rare)......... 250.00

Juvenile head of Alfonso XIII. Rev. Arms.
198R. 100 Pesetas 1897. Restrike (19-61 Rare)......... 800.00
199R. 20 Pesetas 1896. Restrike (19-61 Rare)......... 250.00

SUDAN

Arms. Rev. Scimitar-horned onyx. For the world wildlife conservation program.
1.   100 Pounds 1976 .... 700.00
                                        Proof 750.00

Map of Africa. Rev. Arms. On the O.A.U. meeting in Khartoum.
2.   50 Pounds 1978........................... 370.00
3.   25 Pounds 1978........................... 175.00

SURINAM

Hand holding flag over map. Rev. Arms. On the first anniversary of independence.
1.   100 Gulden 1976 .... 140.00
                                        Proof 145.00

SWAZILAND

Head of King Sobhuza II. Rev. Arms. Independence commemorative. Struck in proof only.
1.   1 Lilangeni 1968................................. 650.00

Bust of King Sobhuza II. Different reverses as indicated. On the King's 75th birthday.

2.	25 Emalangeni 1974. Conjoined busts of young King and mother	580.00
3.	20 Emalangeni 1974. Child standing	465.00
4.	10 Emalangeni 1974. Maiden standing	230.00
5.	5 Emalangeni 1974. Arms	115.00

Bust of King Sobhuza II. Different reverses as indicated. On the king's 75th birthday.

6.	100 Emalangeni 1975. Swazi maiden		180.00
		Proof	185.00
7.	50 Emalangeni 1975. Greater kudu		90.00
		Proof	92.50

TANZANIA

Head of President Nyerere. Rev. Cheetah. For the world wildlife conservation program.

1.	1500 Shilingi 1974		700.00
		Proof	750.00

THAILAND (SIAM)

(For previous issues, see under "Siam" in Part I.)

Head of Queen Sirikit. Rev. Queen's initials and floral wreath. On her 36th birthday.

1.	600 Baht 1968	*	315.00
2.	300 Baht 1968		155.00
3.	150 Baht 1968		75.00

Bust of King Phumiphol. Rev. Monogram on throne, parasol above. On the 25th anniversary of the King's reign.

4.	800 Baht 1971		420.00
5.	400 Baht 1971	*	210.00

Bust of King Phumiphol. Rev. White-eyed river martin. For the world wildlife conservation program.

6.	2,500 Baht 1975		700.00
		Proof	750.00

Conjoined busts of Prince Vajiralongkorn and Princess Soamsawalii. Rev. Arms. On their wedding.

7.	2,500 Baht 1977	315.00

Bust of King Phumiphol. Rev. Royal monogram. On his 50th birthday.

8.	5,000 Baht 1978	630.00

Bust of Prince Vajiralongkorn. Rev. Emblem of the staff college. On his graduation.

9.   3,000 Baht 1978 . . . .   315.00

Bust of Princess Sirindhorn. Rev. Arms. On her investiture.

10.   2,500 Baht 1978 . . . .   315.00

TOGO

Bust of President-General Eyadema. Rev. Arms. On his tenth anniversary in power. Struck in proof only.

1.   50,000 CFA Francs 1977 . . . .   ———
2.   25,000 CFA Francs 1977 . . . .   ———

TONGA

Standing figure of Queen Salote Tupou III. Rev. Arms.

1.   1 Koula 1962 . . . .   700.00
                                                        Proof   725.00
2.   ½ Koula 1962 . . . . * 345.00
                                                        Proof   350.00
3.   Platinum 1 Koula 1962 . . . .   Rare
4.   Platinum ½ Koula 1962 . . . .   Rare

Bust of Queen Salote Tupou III Rev. Arms.

5.   ¼ Koula 1962 . . . . * 175.00
                                                        Proof   180.00
6.   Platinum ¼ Koula 1962 . . . .   Rare

Bust of King Taufa'ahau Tupou IV. Rev. Arms. On the king's coronation.

7.   Palladium 1 Hau 1967 . . . .   425.00
8.   Palladium ½ Hau 1967 . . . .   225.00
9.   Palladium ¼ Hau 1967 . . . . * 125.00

Bust of Tupou IV. Rev. Arms. On the king's 50th birthday. Same design as the previous issue but with a counter-stamp to the left of the bust.

10.   Palladium 1 Hau 1968 . . . . * . . .   425.00
11.   Palladium ½ Hau 1968 . . . . * 225.00
12.   Palladium ¼ Hau 1968 . . . .   125.00

Different obverses as indicated. Rev. Arms. On the centenary of the Constitution.

13.   100 Pa'anga 1975. King Taufa'ahau 425.00
                                                        Proof   430.00
14.   75 Pa'anga 1975. Queen Salote 320.00
                                                        Proof   325.00
15.   50 Pa'anga 1975. King George II 210.00
                                                        Proof   215.00
16.   25 Pa'anga 1975. King George I 105.00
                                                        Proof   110.00

TRINIDAD AND TOBAGO

Two scarlet ibises. Rev. Arms.

1.   100 Dollars 1976 . . . .   85.00
                                                        Proof   72.50

TUNISIA

Head of President Habib Bourguiba. Rev. Minaret of Grand Mosque at Kairouan. On the 10th anniversary of the Republic.

1.   40 Dinars 1967 . . . .   1600.00
2.   20 Dinars 1967 . . . .   800.00
3.   10 Dinars 1967 . . . . * 400.00
4.   5 Dinars 1967 . . . .   200.00
5.   2 Dinars 1967 . . . .   80.00

TURKEY

(For previous issues, see Part I.)

II. SPECIAL COMMEMORATIVE ISSUES
The following coins do not bear the marks of value but are of the same sizes and weights as the previous issues.

PRESIDENT KEMAL ATATURK
Standard Gold Coins

Head and below "Ankara". Rev. Legend and date 1923, with two additional numerals below, which must be added to 1923 to determine the exact year of issue.

89.	500 Piastres 1943-74	850.00 (B)
90.	250 Piastres 1943-74	400.00 (B)
91.	100 Piastres 1943-74 .... *	175.00 (B)
92.	50 Piastres 1943-74	85.00 (B)
93.	25 Piastres 1943-74	70.00 (B)

(Numbers 89-93 are bullion coins. The price listed is based on gold at $725 per ounce.)

De Luxe Gold Coins

Head in circle of stars. Rev. Legend in circle of stars, date below.

94.	500 Piastres 1942-44, 47-48, 50-74	800.00
95.	250 Piastres 1942-44, 46-74	400.00
96.	100 Piastres 1942-44, 48-74 .... *	150.00
97.	50 Piastres 1942-44, 46, 48-74	85.00
98.	25 Piastres 1942-44, 46, 48-76	70.00

(For numbers 99-108, see Part I.)

Bust of Ataturk. Rev. Shooting star. On the 50th anniversary of the Republic.

109.	500 Lira 1973	150.00

Different obverses as indicated. Rev. Value in wreath. For the F.A.O. program. 550 pieces of each were struck in proof only.

110.	1,000 Lire 1978. Mother nursing child	340.00
111.	500 Lire 1978. Bride in Anatolian costume.	170.00

TURKS AND CAICOS ISLANDS

Bust of Winston Churchill. Rev. Arms. On the 100th anniversary of his birth.

1.	100 Crowns 1974 ....*	210.00
	Proof	220.00
2.	50 Crowns 1974	105.00
	Proof	110.00

Bust of Queen Elizabeth II. Different reverses as indicated. Commemorating the "Age of Exploration."

3.	100 Crowns 1975. Two spacecraft in orbit.............	145.00
	Proof	150.00
4.	50 Crowns 1975. Columbus and three ships	72.50
	Proof	75.00
5.	25 Crowns 1975. Arms..............................	36.00
	Proof	37.50

Bust of Queen Elizabeth II. Rev. Four portraits of Queen Victoria.

6.	100 Crowns 1976-77........................	210.00
	Proof	220.00

Bust of Queen Elizabeth II. Rev. Busts of George Washington and George III facing. On the bicentennial of the United States.

7.	50 Crowns 1976	65.00
	Proof	70.00

Bust of Queen Elizabeth II. Rev. Four portraits of George III.

8.	100 Crowns 1977	210.00
	Proof	220.00

Bust of Queen Elizabeth II. Rev. Crown and date in wreath. On the Silver Jubilee.

9. 50 Crowns 1977 . . . . 105.00
                                          Proof 110.00

Bust of Queen Elizabeth II. Different reverses as indicated. On the 25th anniversary of her coronation. Struck in proof only.

10. 50 Crowns 1978. Lion of England 105.00
11. 50 Crowns 1978. Griffin of Edward III 105.00
12. 50 Crowns 1978. Red Dragon of Wales. 105.00
13. 50 Crowns 1978. Unicorn of Scotland 105.00
14. 50 Crowns 1978. Greyhound of Richmond 105.00
15. 50 Crowns 1978. White horse of Hanover . . * 105.00
16. 50 Crowns 1978. Blackbull of Clarence . . . . * 105.00
17. 50 Crowns 1978. Yale of Beaufort . . . . * 105.00
18. 50 Crowns 1978. Falcon of the Plantagenets * 105.00
19. 50 Crowns 1978. White lion of Mortimer . . . * 105.00

Bust of Queen Elizabeth II. Rev. Two athletes. On the XI Commonwealth Games. Struck in proof only.

20. 100 Crowns 1978 . . . . 210.00

Bust of Queen Elizabeth II. Rev. Head of Prince Charles and princely implements. On the tenth anniversary of his investiture. Struck in proof only.

21. 100 Crowns 1979 . . . . 210.00

TUVALU

Bust of Queen Elizabeth II. Rev. Hut. Struck in proof only.

1. 50 Dollars 1976 . . . . 340.00

UGANDA

Different obverses as indicated. Rev. Arms. Struck in proof only.

1. 1000 Shillings 1969. Bust of Pope Paul VI 2900.00
2. 500 Shillings 1969. Pope Paul VI on globe 1450.00
3. 100 Shillings 1969. Pope Paul VI on map of Africa 290.00
4. 50 Shillings 1969. Martyrs' shrine 145.00

UM-AL-QAWAIN

Different obverses as indicated. Rev. Arms. Struck in proof only.
1. 200 Riyals 1970. Bust of Ahmed Bin Rashid Almoalla.   870.00
2. 100 Riyals 1970. 2 antelopes leaping..................   435.00
3. 50 Riyals 1970. Cannon and Fort 215.00
4. 25 Riyals 1970. Cannon............................   110.00

VENEZUELA

(For previous issues, see Part I.)

Cock of the Rock. Rev. Arms. For the world wildlife conservation
program.
8. 1,000 Bolivares 1975 ....   700.00
                                          Proof   750.00

WESTERN SAMOA

Head of Chief Malietoa Tanumafili II. Rev. Paul Revere on horse,
map behind. On the bicentennial of the United States. Struck in
proof only.
1. 100 Tala 1976...............................   330.00
Weightlifter. Rev. Arms. On the 1976 Montreal Olympics. Struck in
proof only.
2. 100 Tala 1976...............................   330.00
Bust of Queen Elizabeth II over island scene. Rev. Arms. On her
Silver Jubilee. Struck in proof only.
3. 100 Tala 1977...............................   330.00

Bust of Charles Lindbergh below "Spirit of St. Louis." Rev. Arms.
On the 50th anniversary of his trans-Atlantic flight. Struck in
proof only.
4. 100 Tala 1977.............................   330.00
Bust of C.K. Smith and Pacific map. Rev. Arms. On the 50th
anniversary of the first trans-Pacific flight. Struck in proof only.
5. 100 Tala 1978.............................   330.00
Three runners. Rev. Arms. On the XI Commonwealth Games. Struck
in proof only.
6. 100 Tala 1978.............................   330.00

YEMEN ARAB REPUBLIC

(For previous issues, see Part I.)

Arms. Different reverses as indicated. Struck in proof only.
5. 50 Ryals 1969. Lion................................   1025.00
6. 30 Ryals 1969. Head of Azzubairi 615.00
7. 20 Ryals 1969. Apollo 11 moon landing.............   410.00
8. 20 Ryals 1969. Camel..............................   410.00
9. 10 Ryals 1969. Gazelles...........................   205.00
10. 5 Ryals 1969. Falcon head........................   100.00

Different obverses as indicated. Rev. Arms.
11. 100 Rials 1975. Arab Jerusalem.................   380.00
                                            Proof   390.00
12. 75 Rials 1975. Olympic torch and athletes 285.00
                                            Proof   290.00
13. 50 Rials 1975. Mona Lisa....................   190.00
                                            Proof   195.00
14. 25 Rials 1975. Oil rigs 95.00
                                            Proof   100.00
15. 20 Rials 1975. Mosque.....................   75.00
                                            Proof   80.00

YUGOSLAVIA

(For previous issues, see Part I.)

Bust of President Tito. Rev. Arms. On the 25th anniversary
of the Council of National Liberation.
6. 1000 Dinars 1968 ....   1640.00
7. 200 Dinars 1968...........................*......   325.00

People holding flags; above, a panoramic view of the town of Jajce. Rev. Arms.

8.	500 Dinars 1968	820.00
9.	100 Dinars 1968...............................*......	165.00

Bust of President Tito. Different reverses as indicated. On the VIII Mediterranean Games.

10.	5,000 Dinar 1979. Building	615.00
11.	2,500 Dinar 1979. Stadium	365.00
12.	2,000 Dinar 1979. Indoor stadium................	245.00
13.	1,500 Dinar 1979. Rings	185.00

ZAIRE

(For previous issues, see under "Congo.")

Bust of President Mobutu. Rev. Leopard. For the world wildlife conservation program.

1.	100 Zaires 1975		700.00
		Proof	750.00

ZAMBIA

Bust of President Kaunda. Rev. African wild dogs. For the world wildlife conservation program.

1.	200 Kwacha 1979...........................		700.00
		Proof	750.00

Appendix

THE PRINCIPAL GOLD COINS OF THE WORLD

The tables below show the major characteristics of the principal gold coins of the world—Their original value in U.S. gold dollars, their weight, their fineness, and their gold content in troy ounces.

ORIGINAL VALUE IN U.S. GOLD DOLLARS

This column shows the relationship to each other of the principal gold coins of the world in terms of U.S. gold dollars.

The period of time used in arriving at the original exchange value is the so-called "Golden Age" of gold coinage—most of the 19th century and until the outbreak of World War I in 1914. It was during this period that a true international gold standard was in existence.

This standard came to an unofficial end in 1914 and to an official end in 1933, when following an outbreak of universal monetary failures, the world price of gold was raised to $35.00 per ounce.

During this stable period of about 100 years, the face value of U.S. gold coins was based on the legal value of $20.67183 per ounce of pure or fine gold. The original exchange values listed in the tables below are in terms of U.S. gold dollars based on U.S. gold coins struck during the period of 1837-1933.

For those gold coins of the world struck before 1837 or after 1933, the values have been determined by judging the weight and fineness of the coins as though they had been struck during the period 1837-1933.

In addition to its historic interest, the column of "Original Values" will be especially useful when one wants to estimate quickly the relative size of a gold coin with which he is not familiar. Since all of the comparative values are based on the same fixed standard ($20.67183 per ounce of fine gold), one can compare any coin with a U.S. gold piece of the same equivalent value.

For example, the table shows that a 100 Lire piece of Italy is valued at $19.29. This coin should be slightly smaller in size than a U.S. $20 gold piece, valued at $20.00. Similarly, a 50 Franc of France, valued at $9.65, should be about the size of a U.S. $10 gold piece. And the 20 Kroner of Denmark is equivalent to a U.S. $5 gold piece.

Further comparisons can be made of the weight and fineness of the coins using the appropriate columns in the tables.

GOLD CONTENT IN TROY OUNCES

The valuations assigned to the coins in this book are a general guide to their numismatic value and represent the approximate figure at which a coin would change hands between a well informed buyer and a well informed professional numismatist. Reflected in a coin's price are such diverse factors as rarity, condition, demand, and availability, which along with the known bullion value of the coin, combine to establish a market price for the piece.

Most gold coins currently sell at a premium over the bullion value and changes in the free market price of gold are reflected, to some degree, in coin prices, especially in the more common issues.

The bullion value of any coin can be determined by using the column in the tables below, entitled, "Gold Content in Troy Ounces." This gives the number of troy ounces of fine gold that each piece contains. To calculate the bullion value of a coin, multiply this figure by the current price of gold bullion on the free market. Any amount above this figure that a coin is valued at represents its numismatic worth, i.e., the value that collectors place on it based on its scarcity, condition, mintage, etc.

Example: Bullion Value Calculation

Given coin: 1957 Sovereign of Great Britain.
Given price of gold bullion: $725 per troy ounce.

Turning to the "Gold Content in Troy Ounces" column in the tables below, we see that the 1957 British Sovereign contains 0.2354 fine troy ounces. of gold.

0.2354 (troy ounces) x $725 (price per ounce) = $170.66 (bullion value)

Knowing the fine gold content also enables the reader to determine the precise amount, in dollars and cents, that he is paying per ounce of gold for a given coin. This is calculated by dividing the price of the coin by its fine gold content.

Example: Cost per Ounce of Gold in a Coin

Given coin: 1957 Sovereign of Great Britain.
Given retail price of coin: $200.00

$$\frac{\$200.00 \text{ (coin price)}}{0.2354 \text{ (troy ounces)}} = \$849.62 \text{ (cost per troy ounce)}$$

In consulting these tables it should be borne in mind that the fractions or multiples of a given gold coin are always in exact proportion as regards weight and value.

Some coinages that were struck over a century or more inevitably tend to show variations in weight, fineness or both and the figures given below for such coinages are for typical or average specimens of the coins in question.

Table I is confined to those coins of the same denomination and value, but of different national origin, which circulated in many countries over a long period of time, enjoying international acceptance.

Table II shows the principal gold coins of specific countries.

TABLE I

In this table especially (because the coinages extended over hundreds of years), the figures in the Gram and Fineness columns are approximate and are for average, familiar specimens.

The column, "Gold Content in Troy Ounces," was provided through the courtesy of David L. Ganz.

Name of Coin	Where Circulated and Ultimate Dates of Coinage	Original Value in U.S. Gold Dollars	Weight of Coin in Grams	Purity or Fineness	Gold Content in Troy Ounces
THE DINAR	Africa and Asia, 660-1902				
3 Dinars		$ 7.80	12.6000	.975	.3950
2 Dinars		5.20	8.4000	.975	.2633
1 Dinar		2.60	4.2000	.975	.1317
½ Dinar		1.30	2.1000	.975	.0658
¼ Dinar		.65	1.0500	.975	.0329
THE DUCAT	All Europe, 1280-1972				
100 Ducats		229.00	350.0000	.986	11.0952
50 Ducats		114.50	175.0000	.986	5.5476
20 Ducats		45.80	70.0000	.986	2.2190
10 Ducats		22.90	35.0000	.986	1.1095
5 Ducats		11.45	17.5000	.986	.5548
4 Ducats		9.16	14.0000	.986	.4438
3 Ducats		6.87	10.5000	.986	.3329
2 Ducats		4.58	7.0000	.986	.2219
1 Ducat		2.29	3.5000	.986	.1109
½ Ducat		1.15	1.7500	.986	.0555
¼ Ducat		.58	.8750	.986	.0277
⅛ Ducat		.29	.4375	.986	.0139
1/16 Ducat		.15	.2188	.986	.0069
1/32 Ducat		.08	.1094	.986	.0035

Name of Coin	Where Circulated and Ultimate Dates of Coinage	Original Value in U.S. Gold Dollars	Weight of Coin in Grams	Purity or Fineness	Gold Content in Troy Ounces
THE ESCUDO	Spain and Spanish-America, 1598-1873				
8 Escudos		$ 16.00	27.0674	.875	.7614
4 Escudos		8.00	13.5334	.875	.3807
2 Escudos		4.00	6.7667	.875	.1904
1 Escudo		2.00	3.3834	.875	.0952
½ Escudo		1.00	1.6917	.875	.0476
THE FLORIN	All Europe, 1200-1896	Similar to the Ducat.			
THE GOLDGULDEN	Same as the Florin.				
THE MOHUR	Asia, 1200-1947 See Table II, under India.				
THE POUND	British Empire, 1817-1979 See Table II, under Great Britain.				
THE SEQUIN	Ottoman Empire, 1451-1839 See Table II, under Turkey.				

TABLE II

Country and Denomination	Period of Coinage	Original Value in U.S. Gold Dollars	Weight of Coin in Grams	Purity or Fineness	Gold Content in Troy Ounces
AFGHANISTAN					
1 Tilla	1896-1919	2.75	4.6000	.900	.1331
5 Amani	1921	13.50	22.7500	.900	.6583
2 Amani	1921-1925	5.40	9.1000	.900	.2633
1 Amani	1921-1925	2.70	4.5500	.900	.1316
½ Amani	1921-1925	1.35	2.2750	.900	.0658
2½ Amani	1925-1928	8.97	15.0000	.900	.4340
1 Amani	1925-1928	3.59	6.0000	.900	.1736
½ Amani	1925-1928	1.79	3.0000	.900	.0087
1 Habibi (30 Rupees)	1929	2.75	4.6000	.900	.1331
20 Afghani	1929-1930	3.59	6.0000	.900	.1736
10,000 Afghani	1978	20.00	33.4370	.900	.9675
AJMAN					
100 Riyals	1970	12.38	20.7000	.900	.6279
75 Riyals	1970	9.29	15.5300	.900	.4494
50 Riyals	1970	6.19	10.3500	.900	.2995
25 Riyals	1970	3.09	5.1750	.900	.1497
ALBANIA					
100 Francs	1926-1938	19.29	32.2580	.900	.9334
50 Francs	1938	9.65	16.1290	.900	.4667
20 Francs	1926-1938	3.86	6.4516	.900	.1867
10 Francs	1927	1.93	3.2258	.900	.0933
500 Leks	1968-1970	59.00	98.7400	.900	2.8569
200 Leks	1968-1970	23.62	39.4900	.900	1.1427
100 Leks	1968-1970	11.81	19.7500	.900	.5715
50 Leks	1968-1970	5.90	9.8700	.900	.2857
20 Leks	1968-1970	2.36	3.9500	.900	.1143
ANGUILLA					
100 Dollars	1967	29.53	49.3700	.900	1.4286
20 Dollars	1967	5.90	9.8700	.900	.2856
10 Dollars	1967	2.95	4.9300	.900	.1427
5 Dollars	1967	1.47	2.4600	.900	.0712
ARGENTINA					
5 Pesos	1881-1896	4.82	8.0645	.900	.2334
2½ Pesos	1881-1884	2.41	4.0322	.900	.1167
AUSTRIA					
1 Souverain d'or or Sovrano	1781-1800	6.86	11.0600	.919	.3268
½ Souverain d'or or Sovrano	1781-1800	3.43	5.5300	.919	.1634
1 Sovrano	1820-1856	6.86	11.3320	.900	.3279
½ Sovrano	1820-1856	3.43	5.6660	.900	.1639
1 Krone	1858-1866	6.66	11.1110	.900	.3215
½ Krone	1858-1866	3.33	5.5550	.900	.1607
8 Florins-20 Francs	1870-1892	3.86	6.4516	.900	.1867
4 Florins-10 Francs	1870-1892	1.93	3.2258	.900	.0933

Country and Denomination	Period of Coinage	Original Value in U.S. Gold Dollars	Weight of Coin in Grams	Purity or Fineness	Gold Content in Troy Ounces
100 Corona	1908-1915	20.26	33.8753	.900	.9802
20 Corona	1892-1916	4.05	6.7750	.900	.1960
10 Corona	1892-1912	2.03	3.3375	.900	.0980
100 Schillings	1926-1938	14.12	23.5240	.900	.6807
25 Schillings	1926-1938	3.53	5.8810	.900	.1702
1,000 Schillings	1976	7.27	12.1500	.900	.3516
BAHAMAS					
100 Dollars	1967-1971	24.33	39.9400	.916⅔	1.1771
100 Dollars	1972	19.46	31.9500	.916⅔	.9416
50 Dollars	1967-1971	12.16	19.9710	.916⅔	.5886
50 Dollars	1972	9.73	15.9710	.916⅔	.4709
20 Dollars	1967-1971	4.87	7.9880	.916⅔	.2354
20 Dollars	1972	3.89	6.3800	.916⅔	.1880
10 Dollars	1967-1971	2.43	3.9943	.916⅔	.1162
10 Dollars	1972	1.94	3.1900	.916⅔	.0940
100 Dollars	1973	5.65	14.5400	.585	.2735
50 Dollars-Crawfish	1973	2.83	7.2700	.585	.1367
20 Dollars	1973	1.13	2.9000	.585	.0545
10 Dollars	1973	.56	1.4500	.585	.0273
50 Dollars-Flamingoes	1973	6.08	15.6448	.585	.2943
(Note: The 1973 series was struck in .585 gold for issue and in .750 gold for presentation.)					
200 Dollars	1974-1977	6.65	10.9200	.916⅔	.3218
150 Dollars	1974-1977	4.99	8.1900	.916⅔	.2414
100 Dollars-4 Flamingoes	1974-1977	3.33	5.4600	.916⅔	.1609
50 Dollars	1974-1977	1.66	2.7300	.916⅔	.0805
100 Dollars-Independence Day Issues	1974-1976	5.99	18.0145	.500	.2896
2,500 Dollars	1974, 1977	248.00	407.2611	.916⅔	12.0000
100 Dollars	1978	8.29	13.6100	.916⅔	.4010
250 Dollars	1979	6.45	10.7800	.900	.3119
BAHRAIN					
10 Dinars	1968	9.75	16.0000	.916⅔	.4715
BARBADOS					
100 Dollars	1975	2.06	6.2100	.500	.0998
200 Dollars-Uncirculated	1979	4.86	8.1200	.900	.2350
200 Dollars-Proof	1979	6.04	10.1000	.900	.2923
100 Dollars-Uncirculated	1979	2.43	4.0600	.900	.1175
100 Dollars-Proof	1979	3.02	5.0500	.900	.1461
BELGIUM					
100 Francs	1853-1912	19.29	32.2580	.900	.9334
40 Francs	1834-1841	7.72	12.9032	.900	.3733
25 Francs	1847-1850	4.82	8.0645	.900	.2334
20 Francs	1835-1914	3.86	6.4516	.900	.1867
10 Francs	1849-1912	1.93	3.2258	.900	.0933

Country and Denomination	Period of Coinage	Original Value in U.S. Gold Dollars	Weight of Coin in Grams	Purity or Fineness	Gold Content In Troy Ounces
BELIZE					
100 Dollars	1975-1980	2.06	6.2100	.500	.0998
250 Dollars	1978	5.26	8.8000	.900	.2546
BERMUDA					
20 Dollars	1970	4.87	7.9881	.916⅔	.2354
100 Dollars	1975	4.20	7.0300	.900	.2260
100 Dollars	1977	4.85	8.1000	.900	.2344
50 Dollars	1977	2.42	4.0500	.900	.1172
BHUTAN					
5 Sertums	1966	24.37	40.0000	.916⅔	1.1789
2 Sertums	1966	9.75	16.0000	.916⅔	.4715
1 Sertum	1966-1970	4.87	8.0000	.916⅔	.2358
BIAFRA					
25 Pounds	1969	48.67	79.8805	.916⅔	2.3543
10 Pounds	1969	24.33	39.9403	.916⅔	1.1771
5 Pounds	1969	9.73	15.9761	.916⅔	.4709
2 Pounds	1969	4.87	7.9881	.916⅔	.2354
1 Pound	1969	2.43	3.9940	.916⅔	.1177
BOLIVIA					
1 Onza	1868	21.53	35.9991	.900	1.0417
35 Grams Pure Gold	1952	23.30	38.9000	.900	1.1256
14 Grams Pure Gold	1952	9.31	15.5600	.900	.4502
7 Grams Pure Gold	1952	4.65	7.7800	.900	.2251
3½ Grams Pure Gold	1952	2.33	3.8900	.900	.1126
BOTSWANA					
10 Thebe	1966	6.76	11.3000	.900	.3270
150 Pula	1976	9.61	15.7800	.916⅔	.4651
150 Pula	1978	20.00	33.4370	.900	.9675
BRAZIL					
20,000 Reis	1724-1727	32.77	53.6000	.916⅔	1.5797
10,000 Reis	1724-1727	16.38	26.8000	.916⅔	.7899
4,000 Reis	1703-1727	6.54	10.7200	.916⅔	.3159
2,000 Reis	1703-1727	3.27	5.3600	.916⅔	.1580
1,000 Reis	1708-1727	1.64	2.6800	.916⅔	.0790
400 Reis	1725-1730	.65	1.0720	.916⅔	.0316

(The above six coins were struck under the national system and bear the cross of Jerusalem. The first three coins below were struck under the colonial system and bear a plain cross, except for the dates from 1823 to 1833 of the 4,000 Reis piece, which show the Brazilian emperor.)

Country and Denomination	Period of Coinage	Original Value in U.S. Gold Dollars	Weight of Coin in Grams	Purity or Fineness	Gold Content In Troy Ounces
4,000 Reis	1695-1833	4.93	8.2000	.916⅔	.2417
2,000 Reis	1695-1793	2.47	4.1000	.916⅔	.1208
1,000 Reis	1696-1787	1.24	2.0500	.916⅔	.0604
12,800 Reis	1727-1733	17.47	28.6000	.916⅔	.8429
6,400 Reis	1727-1833	8.74	14.3000	.916⅔	.4215
3,200 Reis	1727-1786	4.37	7.1500	.916⅔	.2107
1,600 Reis	1727-1784	2.19	3.5750	.916⅔	.1054
800 Reis	1727-1786	1.10	1.7875	.916⅔	.0527
400 Reis	1730-1734	.55	0.8938	.916⅔	.0263
20,000 Reis	1849-1922	10.93	17.9296	.916⅔	.5284
10,000 Reis	1849-1922	5.46	8.9648	.916⅔	.2642
5,000 Reis	1854-1859	2.73	4.4824	.916⅔	.1321
300 Cruzeiros	1972	10.18	16.6500	.920	.4925
BRITISH VIRGIN ISLANDS					
100 Dollars	1975-1980	4.25	7.1000	.900	.2054
BRUNEI					
1000 Dollars	1978	30.46	50.0000	.916⅔	1.4736
BULGARIA					
100 Leva	1894-1912	19.29	32.2580	.900	.9334
20 Leva	1894-1912	3.86	6.4516	.900	.1864
10 Leva	1894	1.93	3.2258	.900	.0933
20 Leva	1963-1964	10.10	16.8900	.900	.4887
10 Leva	1963-1964	5.05	8.4500	.900	.2443
BURMA					
5 Rupees	1880	2.09	3.5000	.900	.1013
4 Rupees	1852-1878	1.70	2.8000	.900	.0812
2 Rupees	1852-1880	.85	1.4000	.900	.0405
1 Rupee	1852-1880	.43	.7000	.900	.0203
4 Mu	1971	5.31	8.0000	.999	.2569
2 Mu	1971	2.66	4.0000	.999	.1285
1 Mu	1971	1.33	2.0000	.999	.0642
BURUNDI					
100 Francs	1962	19.14	32.0000	.900	.9259
50 Francs	1962	9.57	16.0000	.900	.4630
25 Francs	1962	4.78	8.0000	.900	.2315
10 Francs	1962	1.91	3.2000	.900	.0926
100 Francs	1965	17.94	30.0000	.900	.8680
50 Francs	1965	8.97	15.0000	.900	.4340
25 Francs	1965	4.47	7.5000	.900	.2170
10 Francs	1965	1.79	3.0000	.900	.0868
CAMEROUN					
20,000 Francs	1970	41.87	70.0000	.900	2.0255
10,000 Francs	1970	20.93	35.0000	.900	1.0127
5,000 Francs	1970	10.46	17.5000	.900	.5064
3,000 Francs	1970	6.28	10.5000	.900	.3038
1,000 Francs	1970	2.09	3.5000	.900	.1013

Country and Denomination	Period of Coinage	Original Value in U.S. Gold Dollars	Weight of Coin in Grams	Purity or Fineness	Gold Content In Troy Ounces
CANADA					
20 Dollars	1967	10.93	18.2733	.900	.5287
10 Dollars	1912-1914	10.00	16.7181	.900	.4838
5 Dollars	1912-1914	5.00	8.3591	.900	.2419
100 Dollars-Uncirculated	1976	5.17	13.3375	.583	.2501
100 Dollars-Proof	1976-1980	10.34	16.9655	.916⅔	.5000
50 Dollars	1979	20.67	31.1035	.999	1.0000
CAPE VERDE ISLANDS					
2,500 Escudos	1976	5.14	8.6000	.900	.2488
CAYMAN ISLANDS					
25 Dollars	1972	5.23	15.7500	.500	.2532
100 Dollars	1974-1978	7.54	22.6801	.500	.3646
50 Dollars	1977-1978	3.76	11.3400	.500	.1820
CENTRAL AFRICAN REPUBLIC (EMPIRE)					
20,000 Francs	1970	41.87	70.0000	.900	2.0255
10,000 Francs	1970	20.93	35.0000	.900	1.0127
5,000 Francs	1970	10.47	17.5000	.900	.5064
3,000 Francs	1970	6.28	10.5000	.900	.3038
1,000 Francs	1970	2.09	3.5000	.900	.1013
25,000 Francs	1978	9.18	15.3500	.900	.4442
10,000 Francs	1978	3.67	6.1400	.900	.1777
CENTRAL AMERICAN REPUBLICS					
50 Pesos	1970	11.63	20.0000	.900	.5787
CHAD					
20,000 Francs	1970	41.87	70.0000	.900	2.0255
10,000 Francs	1970	20.93	35.0000	.900	1.0127
5,000 Francs	1970	10.47	17.5000	.900	.5064
3,000 Francs	1970	6.28	10.5000	.900	.3038
1,000 Francs	1970	2.09	3.5000	.900	.1013
CHILE					
10 Pesos	1853-1890	9.15	15.2000	.900	.4398
5 Pesos	1858-1873	4.58	7.6000	.900	.2199
2 Pesos	1857-1875	1.84	3.0400	.900	.0880
1 Peso	1860-1873	.92	1.5200	.900	.0440
20 Pesos	1896-1917	7.30	11.9500	.916⅔	.3522
10 Pesos	1895-1901	3.65	5.9990	.916⅔	.1762
5 Pesos	1895-1900	1.83	2.9990	.916⅔	.0881
100 Pesos	1926-1963	12.20	20.3397	.900	.5885
50 Pesos	1926-1962	6.10	10.1698	.900	.2943
20 Pesos	1926-1961	2.44	4.0680	.900	.1177
500 Pesos	1967	60.80	101.6500	.900	2.9413
200 Pesos	1967	24.33	40.6700	.900	1.1768
100 Pesos	1967	12.16	20.3300	.900	.5883
50 Pesos	1967	6.08	10.1600	.900	.2940
500 Pesos	1976	61.91	102.27	.900	2.9600
50 Pesos	1976	5.99	10.15	.900	.2900
CHINA					
20 Dollars-Republic	1919	9.00	14.8000	.900	.4283
10 Dollars-Republic	1916-1919	4.50	7.4000	.900	.2141
10 Dollars-Yunnan	1919	5.40	9.0000	.900	.2602
5 Dollars-Yunnan	1919	2.70	4.5000	.900	.1301
2,000 Yuan-Nationalist	1965	17.94	30.0000	.900	.8681
1,000 Yuan-Nationalist	1965	8.97	15.0000	.900	.4340
2,000 Yuan-Nationalist	1966	18.06	31.0600	.950	.9487
400 Yuan-People's Republic	1979	10.30	16.9000	.916⅔	.4981
450 Yuan-People's Republic	1979	10.46	17.1700	.916⅔	.5060
COLOMBIA					
20 Pesos	1859-1877	19.29	32.2580	.900	.9334
10 Pesos	1856-1877	9.65	16.1290	.900	.4667
5 Pesos	1856-1885	4.82	8.0645	.900	.2333
2 Pesos	1856-1876	1.93	3.2258	.900	.0977
1 Peso	1856-1878	.96	1.6129	.900	.0467
10 Pesos	1919-1924	9.73	15.9761	.916⅔	.4708
5 Pesos	1913-1930	4.87	7.9881	.916⅔	.2354
2½ Pesos	1913-1928	2.43	3.9940	.916⅔	.1177
1,500 Pesos	1968-1971	38.58	64.5000	.900	1.8663
500 Pesos	1968-1971	12.86	21.5000	.900	.6221
300 Pesos	1968-1971	7.72	12.9000	.900	.3733
200 Pesos	1968-1971	5.14	8.6000	.900	.2488
100 Pesos	1968-1971	2.57	4.3000	.900	.1244
1,500 Pesos-Bank	1973	11.42	19.1000	.900	.5527
2,000 Pesos	1973	7.72	12.9000	.900	.3733
1,500 Pesos-Valencia	1973	5.14	8.6000	.900	.2488
1,000 Pesos	1973-1975	2.57	4.3000	.900	.1244
2,000 Pesos	1975	5.14	8.6000	.900	.2488
10,000 Pesos	1979	20.00	33.4370	.900	.9675
COMOROS					
20,000 Francs	1976	3.67	6.1400	.900	.1777
10,000 Francs	1976	1.84	3.0700	.900	.0888
CONGO					
100 Francs	1965	18.73	32.2300	.900	.9326
50 Francs	1965	9.56	15.9800	.900	.4624
25 Francs	1965	4.79	8.0000	.900	.2315
20 Francs	1965	3.79	6.3400	.900	.1835
10 Francs	1965	1.91	3.1900	.900	.0923

Country and Denomination	Period of Coinage	Original Value in U.S. Gold Dollars	Weight of Coin in Grams	Purity or Fineness	Gold Content in Troy Ounces
COOK ISLANDS					
100 Dollars	1974	10.19	16.7185	.916⅔	.4927
100 Dollars	1975	5.74	9.6000	.900	.2778
200 Dollars	1978-1979	9.93	16.6000	.900	.4803
250 Dollars	1978	10.71	17.9000	.900	.5179
COSTA RICA					
10 Pesos	1870-1876	8.60	14.3000	.875	.4023
5 Pesos	1867-1875	4.30	7.1500	.875	.2011
2 Pesos	1866-1876	1.72	2.8600	.875	.0805
1 Peso	1864-1872	.86	1.4300	.875	.0402
20 Colones	1897-1900	9.31	15.5600	.900	.4502
10 Colones	1897-1900	4.65	7.7800	.900	.2251
5 Colones	1899-1900	2.33	3.8900	.900	.1126
2 Colones	1897-1928	.93	1.5560	.900	.0450
1,000 Colones	1970	116.06	194.0400	.900	5.6147
500 Colones	1970	44.57	74.5200	.900	2.1562
200 Colones	1970	17.82	29.8000	.900	.8623
100 Colones	1970	8.91	14.9000	.900	.4311
50 Colones	1970	4.46	7.4500	.900	.2156
1,500 Colones	1974	20.00	33.4370	.900	.9675
CUBA					
20 Pesos	1915-1916	20.00	33.4370	.900	.9675
10 Pesos	1915-1916	10.00	16.7185	.900	.4838
5 Pesos	1915-1916	5.00	8.3592	.900	.2419
4 Pesos	1915-1916	4.00	6.6872	.900	.1935
2 Pesos	1915-1916	2.00	3.3436	.900	.0968
1 Peso	1915-1916	1.00	1.6718	.900	.0484
100 Pesos	1977-1979	7.31	12.0000	.916⅔	.3537
CYPRUS					
50 Pounds	1978	9.73	15.9800	.916⅔	.3537
CZECHOSLOVAKIA					
10 Ducats	1929-1978	22.87	34.9000	.986	1.1065
5 Ducats	1929-1978	11.43	17.4500	.986	.5532
5 Ducats-Commemorative	1929	13.11	20.0000	.986	.6341
4 Ducats	1928	9.15	13.9600	.986	.5073
3 Ducats	1929	7.64	12.0000	.986	.3804
2 Ducats	1923-1978	4.57	6.9800	.986	.2213
1 Ducat	1923-1978	2.29	3.4900	.986	.1106
1 Ducat-Commemorative	1929	2.62	4.0000	.986	.1268
DAHOMEY					
25,000 CFA Francs	1970	53.16	88.8800	.900	2.5718
10,000 CFA Francs	1970	21.26	35.5500	.900	1.0287
5,000 CFA Francs	1970	10.63	17.7700	.900	.5142
2,500 CFA Francs	1970	5.31	8.8800	.900	.2569
DANISH WEST INDIES					
10 Daler-50 Francs	1904	9.65	16.1290	.900	.4667
4 Daler-20 Francs	1904-1905	3.86	6.4516	.900	.1867
DANZIG					
25 Gulden	1923-1930	4.87	7.9881	.916⅔	.2354
DENMARK					
2 Christian d'or	1826-1870	8.00	13.3000	.903	.3827
1 Christian d'or	1775-1869	4.00	6.6500	.903	.1913
20 Kroner	1873-1931	5.36	8.9606	.900	.2592
10 Kroner	1873-1917	2.68	4.4803	.900	.1296
DOMINICA					
300 Dollars	1978	11.48	19.2000	.900	.5556
150 Dollars	1978	5.74	9.6000	.900	.2778
DOMINICAN REPUBLIC					
30 Pesos	1955	17.85	29.6220	.900	.8571
30 Pesos	1974	7.00	11.7000	.900	.3385
100 Pesos	1975	5.98	10.0000	.900	.2894
200 Pesos	1977	16.48	31.0000	.800	.7973
250 Pesos	1979	16.74	27.9900	.900	.8099
100 Pesos	1979	6.52	10.9000	.900	.3154
ECUADOR					
10 Sucres	1899-1900	4.87	8.1360	.900	.2354
1 Condor	1928	5.00	8.3592	.900	.2419
EGYPT					
500 Piastres	1861-1960	24.70	42.5000	.875	1.1956
100 Piastres	1839-1960	4.94	8.5000	.875	.2391
50 Piastres	1839-1958	2.47	4.2500	.875	.1196
20 Piastres	1923-1938	.99	1.7000	.875	.0478
10 Piastres	1839-1909	.49	.8500	.875	.0239
5 Piastres	1839-1909	.25	.4250	.875	.0120
10 Pounds	1964	30.26	52.0000	.875	1.4628
5 Pounds	1955-1960	24.71	42.5000	.875	1.1956
5 Pounds	1964-1977	15.12	26.0000	.875	.7314
1 Pound	1955-1960	4.94	8.5000	.875	.2391
1 Pound	1970-1977	4.65	8.0000	.875	.2251
½ Pound	1958	2.47	4.2500	.875	.1196
100 Pounds	1979	18.28	30.0000	.916⅔	.8842
50 Pounds	1979	9.14	15.0000	.916⅔	.4421

Country and Denomination	Period of Coinage	Original Value in U.S. Gold Dollars	Weight of Coin in Grams	Purity or Fineness	Gold Content in Troy Ounces
EQUATORIAL GUINEA					
5,000 Pesetas	1970	42.18	70.5200	.900	2.0405
1,000 Pesetas	1970	8.43	14.1000	.900	.4080
750 Pesetas	1970	6.32	10.5700	.900	.3058
500 Pesetas	1970	4.22	7.0500	.900	.2040
250 Pesetas	1970	2.11	3.5200	.900	.1019
10,000 Ekuele	1978	7.78	12.7620	.916⅔	.3761
5,000 Ekuele	1978	4.24	6.9600	.916⅔	.2052
ETHIOPIA			About		
2 Warks	1889-1917	8.37	14.0000	.900	.4051
1 Wark	1889-1931	4.19	7.0000	.900	.2026
½ Wark	1889-1931	2.09	3.50000	.900	.1013
¼ Wark	1889	1.05	1.7500	.900	.0506
⅛ Wark	1889	.52	.8750	.900	.0253
200 Dollars	1966	47.85	80.0000	.900	2.3149
100 Dollars	1966-1972	23.92	40.0000	.900	1.1574
50 Dollars	1966-1972	11.96	20.0000	.900	.5787
20 Dollars	1966	4.79	8.0000	.900	.2315
10 Dollars	1966	2.39	4.0000	.900	.1157
500 Bir	1979	20.00	33.4370	.900	.9675
FALKLAND ISLANDS					
5 Pounds	1974	24.33	39.9400	.916⅔	1.1771
2 Pounds	1974	9.74	15.9800	.916⅔	.4710
1 Sovereign	1974	4.87	7.9900	.916⅔	.2355
½ Sovereign	1974	2.43	3.9900	.916⅔	.1176
150 Pounds	1979	20.00	33.4370	.900	.9675
FIJI					
100 Dollars	1974-1975	10.42	31.3634	.500	.5042
250 Dollars	1978	20.00	33.4370	.900	.9675
FINLAND					
20 Markkaa	1878-1913	3.86	6.4516	.900	.1867
10 Markkaa	1878-1913	1.93	3.2258	.900	.0933
200 Markkaa	1926	5.10	8.4210	.900	.2437
100 Markkaa	1926	2.55	4.2105	.900	.1218
FRANCE (Until 1803, the figures are an average of familiar pieces)					
1 Ecu d'or	1266-1641	2.25	3.4000	.963	.1053
1 Chaise d'or	1285-1422	3.15	4.7000	1.000	.1511
1 Royal d'or	1285-1461	2.81	4.2000	1.000	.1350
1 Lion d'or	1328-1350	3.28	4.9000	1.000	.1575
1 Pavillion d'or	1328-1350	3.42	5.1000	1.000	.1640
1 Ange d'or	1328-1350	4.86	7.2500	1.000	.2331
1 Franc a Cheval	1350-1461	2.61	3.8900	1.000	.1251
1 Mouton d'or	1350-1422	3.15	4.7000	1.000	.1511
1 Franc a Pied	1350-1380	2.56	3.8200	1.000	.1228
1 Salut d'or	1380-1461	2.61	3.8900	1.000	.1251
1 Heaume d'or	1380-1422	3.12	5.1000	.916⅔	.1503
1 Henry d'or	1550-1559	2.28	3.6000	.958	.1109
2 Louis d'or	1640-1792	8.10-10.40	13.40-17.20	.916⅔	.3949-.5069
1 Louis d'or	1640-1793	4.05-5.20	6.70-8.60	.916⅔	.1975-.2535
½ Louis d'or	1640-1784	2.03-2.65	3.35-4.30	.916⅔	.0987-.1267
100 Francs	1855-1913	19.29	32.2580	.900	.9334
50 Francs	1855-1904	9.65	16.1290	.900	.4667
40 Francs	1803-1839	7.72	12.9039	.900	.3734
20 Francs	1803-1914	3.86	6.4516	.900	.1867
10 Francs	1854-1914	1.93	3.2258	.900	.0933
5 Francs	1854-1889	.96	1.6129	.900	.0467
100 Francs	1929-1936	3.94	6.5500	.900	.1895
FUJAIRAH					
200 Riyals	1969	24.80	41.4600	.900	1.1997
100 Riyals	1969-1971	12.40	20.7300	.900	.5998
50 Riyals	1970	6.20	10.3600	.900	.2998
25 Riyals	1970	3.10	5.1800	.900	.1499
GABON					
100 Francs	1960	19.14	32.0000	.900	.9259
50 Francs	1960	9.57	16.0000	.900	.4630
25 Francs	1960	4.79	8.0000	.900	.2315
10 Francs	1960	1.91	3.2000	.900	.0926
20,000 Francs	1969	41.87	70.0000	.900	2.0255
10,000 Francs	1969	20.93	35.0000	.900	1.0127
5,000 Francs	1969	10.47	17.5000	.900	.5064
3,000 Francs	1969	6.28	10.5000	.900	.3038
1,000 Francs	1969	2.09	3.5000	.900	.1013
GAMBIA					
500 Dalasis	1977	20.00	33.4370	.900	.9675
GERMAN EAST AFRICA					
15 Rupees	1916	4.48	7.5000	.900	.1728
GERMAN NEW GUINEA					
20 Marks	1895	4.76	7.9650	.900	.2305
10 Marks	1895	2.38	3.9825	.900	.1152

Country and Denomination	Period of Coinage	Original Value in U.S. Gold Dollars	Weight of Coin in Grams	Purity or Fineness	Gold Content in Troy Ounces
GERMANY					
20 Marks	1871-1915	4.76	7.9650	.900	.2305
10 Marks	1872-1914	2.38	3.9825	.900	.1152
5 Marks	1877-1878	1.19	1.9913	.900	.0576
10 Taler	1742-1857	7.96	13.3000	.900	.3848
5 Taler	1699-1856	3.98	6.6500	.900	.1924
2½ Taler	1699-1855	1.99	3.3200	.900	.0961
1 Carolin	1726-1782	4.90	9.7000	.770	.2401
½ Carolin	1726-1737	2.45	4.8500	.770	.1201
¼ Carolin	1726-1736	1.23	2.4250	.770	.0600
10 Gulden	1819-1842	4.16	6.8500	.904	.1991
5 Gulden	1819-1835	2.08	3.4250	.904	.0995
1 Krone	1857-1870	6.66	11.1110	.900	.3215
½ Krone	1857-1869	3.33	5.5550	.900	.1608
1 Pistole	Same as the 5 Taler piece above				
1 Frederick d'or (or other name)	Same as the 5 Taler piece above				
GIBRALTAR					
100 Pounds	1975	18.95	31.1040	.916⅔	.9167
50 Pounds	1975	9.48	15.5520	.916⅔	.4584
25 Pounds	1975	4.74	7.7760	.916⅔	.2292

GREAT BRITAIN (Until 1663, the figures are an average of familiar pieces)

Country and Denomination	Period of Coinage	Original Value in U.S. Gold Dollars	Weight of Coin in Grams	Purity or Fineness	Gold Content in Troy Ounces
1 Noble	1327-1483	5.29	8.0000	.9948	.2559
1 Angel	1422-1625	3.31	5.0000	.9948	.1599
1 Ryal	1485-1625	8.59	13.0000	.9948	.4158
1 Sovereign	1485-1525	7.93	12.0000	.9948	.3838
1 Sovereign	1526-1547	7.31	12.0000	.916⅔	.3537
1 Sovereign	1551-1625	7.93	12.0000	.9948	.3838
1 George Noble	1509-1547	2.75	4.5000	.916⅔	.1326
3 Pounds (Triple Unite)	1642-1644	16.50	27.0000	.916⅔	.7958
20 Shillings (1 Unite or Laurel)	1603-1663	5.50	9.0000	.916⅔	.2653
2 Crowns or 10 Shillings	1603-1663	2.75	4.5000	.916⅔	.1326
1 Crown or 5 Shillings	1509-1663	1.38	2.2500	.916⅔	.0663
½ Crown or 2½ Shillings	1509-1625	.69	1.1250	.916⅔	.0332
5 Guineas	1668-1777	25.50	41.7500	.916⅔	1.2305
2 Guineas	1664-1777	10.20	16.7000	.916⅔	.4922
1 Guinea	1663-1813	5.10	8.3500	.916⅔	.2461
½ Guinea	1669-1813	2.55	4.1750	.916⅔	.1230
⅓ Guinea	1797-1813	1.70	2.7834	.916⅔	.0820
¼ Guinea	1718-1762	1.28	2.0875	.916⅔	.0615
5 Pounds	1820-1953	24.33	39.9403	.916⅔	1.1771
2 Pounds	1820-1953	9.73	15.9761	.916⅔	.4707
1 Pound (Sovereign)	1817-1979	4.87	7.9881	.916⅔	.2354
½ Pound (½ Sovereign)	1817-1953	2.43	3.9940	.916⅔	.1177
GREECE					
100 Drachmae	1876-1967	19.29	32.2580	.900	.9334
50 Drachmae	1876	9.65	16.1290	.900	.4667
40 Drachmae	1852	7.72	12.9039	.900	.3734
20 Drachmae	1833-1967	3.86	6.4516	.900	.1867
10 Drachmae	1876	1.93	3.2258	.900	.0933
5 Drachmae	1876	.96	1.6129	.900	.0467
10,000 Drachmae	1979	11.96	20.000	.916⅔	.3537
GUATEMALA					
20 Pesos	1869-1878	19.29	32.2580	.900	.9334
16 Pesos	1863-1869	15.44	25.8078	.875	.7259
10 Pesos	1869	9.65	16.1290	.900	.4667
8 Pesos	1864	7.72	12.9039	.875	.3630
5 Pesos	1869-1878	4.82	8.0645	.900	.2333
4 Pesos	1861-1869	3.86	6.4516	.875	.1815
2 Pesos	1859	1.93	3.2258	.875	.0907
1 Peso	1859-1860	.96	1.6129	.875	.0454
4 Reales (½ Peso)	1859-1864	.48	.8065	.875	.0227
20 Quetzals	1926	20.00	33.4370	.900	.9675
10 Quetzals	1926	10.00	16.7185	.900	.4838
5 Quetzals	1926	5.00	8.3592	.900	.2419
GUINEA					
10,000 Francs	1969	23.93	40.0000	.900	1.1574
5,000 Francs	1969-1970	11.96	20.0000	.900	.5787
2,000 Francs	1969-1970	4.79	8.0000	.900	.2315
1,000 Francs	1969	2.39	4.0000	.900	.1157
2,000 Sylis	1977	3.51	5.8700	.900	.1699
1,000 Sylis	1977	1.76	2.9350	.900	.0850
GUYANA					
100 Dollars	1976	1.90	5.7400	.500	.0920
100 Dollars	1977	1.85	5.5800	.500	.0897
HAITI					
1,000 Gourdes	1967-1969	118.12	197.4800	.900	5.7142
500 Gourdes	1969	59.06	151.9000	.585	2.8567
250 Gourdes	1969	29.53	75.9500	.585	1.4285
200 Gourdes	1967-1971	23.62	39.4900	.900	1.1427
100 Gourdes	1967-1971	11.81	19.7500	.900	.5715
60 Gourdes	1969-1970	7.08	18.2200	.585	.3713
50 Gourdes	1967-1971	5.90	9.8700	.900	.2856
40 Gourdes	1969-1970	4.72	12.1500	.585	.2475
30 Gourdes	1969-1970	3.54	9.1100	.585	.1856
20 Gourdes	1967-1969	2.36	3.9500	.900	.1143
1,000 Gourdes	1973	8.71	14.5600	.900	.4213
500 Gourdes	1973	4.35	7.2800	.900	.2107
200 Gourdes	1973	1.74	2.9100	.900	.0842
100 Gourdes	1973	.87	1.4500	.900	.0420
1,000 Gourdes	1974	7.76	13.0000	.900	.3762
500 Gourdes	1974	3.89	6.5000	.900	.1881
200 Gourdes	1975	1.73	2.9000	.900	.0839
500 Gourdes	1977	5.08	8.5000	.900	.2460
250 Gourdes	1977	2.54	4.2500	.900	.1230
HEJAZ					
1 Dinar	1923	4.39	7.2166	.916⅔	.2127
HONDURAS					
20 Pesos	1888-1908	19.29	32.2580	.900	.9334
10 Pesos	1871-1889	9.65	16.1290	.900	.4667
5 Pesos	1871-1913	4.82	8.0640	.900	.2334
1 Peso	1871-1922	.96	1.6120	.900	.0467
HONG KONG					
1,000 Dollars	1975-1980	9.74	15.9760	.916⅔	.4710
HUNGARY					
8 Florins-20 Francs	1870-1892	3.86	6.4516	.900	.1867
4 Florins-10 Francs	1870-1892	1.93	3.2258	.900	.0934
100 Korona	1907-1908	20.26	33.8753	.900	.9802
20 Korona	1892-1916	4.05	6.7750	.900	.1960
10 Korona	1892-1915	2.03	3.3875	.900	.0980
500 Forint	1961	25.15	38.3800	.986	1.2167
100 Forint	1961	5.03	7.6760	.986	.2431
50 Forint	1961	2.52	3.8380	.986	.1217
1,000 Forint	1966-1968	50.31	84.1040	.900	2.4336
500 Forint	1966-1968	25.15	42.0520	.900	1.2168
200 Forint	1968	10.06	16.8210	.900	.4867
100 Forint	1966-1968	5.03	8.4100	.900	.2433
50 Forint	1968	2.52	4.2050	.900	.1217
ICELAND					
10,000 Kronur	1974	9.27	15.5000	.900	.4485
500 Kronur	1961	5.36	8.9604	.900	.2593
INDIA					
200 Mohurs	1628-1658	1,416.00	2332.0000	.916⅔+	68.7300 +
100 Mohurs	1556-1707	708.00	1166.0000	.916⅔+	34.3650 +
5 Mohurs	1556-1627	35.40	58.3000	.916⅔+	1.7183 +
2 Mohurs	1556-1835	14.16	23.3200	.916⅔	.6873
1 Mohur	1200-1947	7.08	11.6600	.916⅔	.3437
½ Mohur	1200-1947	3.54	5.8300	.916⅔	.1718
⅓ Mohur	1200-1947	2.37	3.8867	.916⅔	.1146
¼ Mohur	1200-1947	1.77	2.9150	.916⅔	.0859
⅙ Mohur	1200-1947	1.18	1.9435	.916⅔	.0573
⅛ Mohur	1200-1947	.89	1.4575	.916⅔	.0430
1/16 Mohur	1500-1820	.45	.7288	.916⅔	.0215
1/32 Mohur	1500-1820	.23	.3644	.916⅔	.0107
10 Rupees (⅔ Mohur)	1862-1879	4.72	7.7740	.916⅔	.2292
5 Rupees (⅓ Mohur)	1820-1879	2.36	3.8870	.916⅔	.1146
15 Rupees	1918	4.87	7.9881	.916⅔	.2354
1 Pagoda (crude style)	1200-1868	1.60	3.0000	.800	.0772
(The following for Cutch-Bhuj)					
100 Kori	1866	11.35	18.7000	.916⅔	.5511
50 Kori	1873-1874	5.68	9.3500	.916⅔	.2756
25 Kori	1862-1870	2.84	4.6750	.916⅔	.1378
(The following for Madras; modern style coinage)					
2 Pagodas	(1810)	3.56	5.8500	.916⅔	.1724
1 Pagoda	(1810)	1.78	2.9250	.916⅔	.0862
(The following for Travancore)					
2 Pagodas	1877-1924	3.12	5.1000	.916⅔	.1503
1 Pagoda	1877-1924	1.56	2.5500	.916⅔	.0752
½ Pagoda	1881-1924	.78	1.2750	.916⅔	.0376
¼ Pagoda	1881-1924	.39	.6375	.916⅔	.0188
INDONESIA					
25,000 Rupiah	1970	36.91	61.7100	.900	1.7856
20,000 Rupiah	1970	29.53	29.3700	.900	1.4286
10,000 Rupiah	1970	14.76	24.6800	.900	.7141
5,000 Rupiah	1970	7.38	12.3400	.900	.3571
2,000 Rupiah	1970	2.95	4.9300	.900	.1427
100,000 Rupiah	1974	20.00	33.4370	.900	.9675
IRAQ					
5 Dinars	1971	8.27	13.5700	.916⅔	.3998
ISLE OF MAN					
5 Pounds	1965	24.33	39.9403	.916⅔	1.1771
1 Sovereign	1965	4.87	7.9881	.916⅔	.2354
½ Sovereign	1965	2.43	3.9940	.916⅔	.1177
(Note: Proof specimens of the 1965 issue were struck in .980 fine.)					
5 Pounds	1973-1979	24.26	39.8134	.916⅔	1.1734
2 Pounds	1973-1979	9.70	15.9253	.916⅔	.4694
1 Sovereign	1973-1979	4.85	7.9627	.916⅔	.2347
½ Sovereign	1973-1979	2.43	3.9813	.916⅔	.1173
ISRAEL					
100 Pounds	1962-1967	16.25	26.6800	.916⅔	.7363
50 Pounds	1962-1964	8.13	13.3400	.916⅔	.3932
20 Pounds	1960	4.87	7.9880	.916⅔	.2354
100 Pounds	1968-1969	13.29	25.0000	.800	.6430
100 Pounds	1971	13.16	22.0000	.900	.6366
200 Pounds	1973	16.15	27.0000	.900	.7813
100 Pounds	1973	8.07	13.5000	.900	.3906

Country and Denomination	Period of Coinage	Original Value in U.S. Gold Dollars	Weight of Coin in Grams	Purity or Fineness	Gold Content In Troy Ounces
50 Pounds	1973	4.19	7.0000	.900	.2025
500 Pounds	1974	16.75	28.0000	.900	.8102
500 Pounds	1975	11.96	20.0000	.900	.5787
1,000 Pounds	1978	7.17	12.0000	.900	.3472
5,000 Pounds	1980	10.34	17.2800	.900	.5000
ITALY					
100 Lire	1832-1927	19.29	32.2580	.900	.9334
80 Lire	1821-1831	15.44	25.8078	.900	.7468
50 Lire	1832-1927	9.65	16.1290	.900	.4667
40 Lire	1806-1848	7.72	12.9039	.900	.3734
20 Lire	1800-1927	3.86	6.4516	.900	.1867
10 Lire	1832-1927	1.93	3.2258	.900	.0933
5 Lire	1863-1865	.96	1.6129	.900	.0467
100 Lire	1931-1936	5.25	8.7990	.900	.2546
50 Lire	1931-1936	2.63	4.3995	.900	.1273
100 Lire	1937	3.10	5.1900	.900	.1502

(The following for Florence:
80 Florins = 10 Zecchini = 200 Paoli = 133⅓ Lire)

Country and Denomination	Period of Coinage	Original Value in U.S. Gold Dollars	Weight of Coin in Grams	Purity or Fineness	Gold Content In Troy Ounces
80 Florins	1827-1828	21.66	32.6180	1.000	1.0487
1 Ruspone (3 Zecchini)	1719-1859	6.93	10.4610	1.000	.3363
1 Zecchino	1712-1853	2.31	3.4870	1.000	.1121

(The following for Naples: 30 Ducati = 10 Ducats = 10 Oncie)

Country and Denomination	Period of Coinage	Original Value in U.S. Gold Dollars	Weight of Coin in Grams	Purity or Fineness	Gold Content In Troy Ounces
6 Ducati	1749-1785	5.12	8.8200	.875	.2481
4 Ducati	1749-1782	3.42	5.8800	.875	.1654
2 Ducati	1749-1772	1.71	2.9400	.875	.0827
30 Ducati	1818-1856	25.00	37.8670	.996	1.2126
15 Ducati	1818-1856	12.50	18.9330	.996	.6063
6 Ducati	1826-1856	5.00	7.5730	.996	.2425
3 Ducati	1818-1856	2.50	3.7860	.996	.1212

(For the following, please see Table I)

Country and Denomination	Period of Coinage	Original Value in U.S. Gold Dollars
1 Doppia	1280-1815	Equal to 2 Ducats
1 Florin	1250-1500	Equal to 1 Ducat
1 Scudo d'oro	1300-1750	Equal to 1 Ducat
1 Zecchino	1500-1800	Equal to 1 Ducat
1 Genovino	1200-1415	Equal to 1 Ducat

Country and Denomination	Period of Coinage	Original Value in U.S. Gold Dollars	Weight of Coin in Grams	Purity or Fineness	Gold Content In Troy Ounces
IVORY COAST					
100 Francs	1966	19.14	32.0000	.900	.9259
50 Francs	1966	9.57	16.0000	.900	.4630
25 Francs	1966	4.79	8.0000	.900	.2315
10 Francs	1966	1.91	3.2000	.900	.0926
JAMAICA					
20 Dollars	1972	5.23	15.7484	.500	.2532
100 Dollars	1975-1976	4.68	7.8300	.900	.2263
100 Dollars	1978-1979	6.78	11.3400	.900	.3281
250 Dollars	1978-1979	25.85	43.2219	.900	1.2507
JAPAN					
20 Yen	1870-1880	19.94	33.3332	.900	.9645
10 Yen	1871-1880	9.97	16.6666	.900	.4823
5 Yen	1870-1897	4.98	8.3333	.900	.2411
2 Yen	1870-1880	1.96	3.3333	.900	.0965
1 Yen	1871-1880	.98	1.6666	.900	.0482
20 Yen	1897-1932	9.97	16.6666	.900	.4823
10 Yen	1897-1910	4.98	8.3333	.900	.2411
5 Yen	1897-1930	2.49	4.1666	.900	.1206
JERSEY					
50 Pounds	1972	13.79	22.6300	.916⅔	.6670
25 Pounds	1972	7.25	11.9000	.916⅔	.3507
20 Pounds	1972	5.64	9.2600	.916⅔	.2729
10 Pounds	1972	2.83	4.6400	.916⅔	.1368
5 Pounds	1972	1.60	2.6200	.916⅔	.0772
JORDAN					
25 Dinars	1969	41.34	69.1100	.900	1.9997
10 Dinars	1969	16.53	27.6400	.900	.7998
5 Dinars	1969	8.27	13.8200	.900	.3999
2 Dinars	1969	3.30	5.5200	.900	.1597
25 Dinars	1977	8.97	15.0000	.900	.4340
50 Dinars	1977	20.00	33.4370	.900	.9675
KATANGA					
5 Francs	1961	7.97	13.3300	.900	.3857
KENYA					
500 Shillings	1966	23.15	38.0000	.916⅔	1.1199
250 Shillings	1966	11.57	19.0000	.916⅔	.5600
100 Shillings	1966	4.63	7.6000	.916⅔	.2240
KIRIBATI					
150 Dollars	1979	9.74	15.9800	.916⅔	.4710
KOREA					
20 Won	1906-1910	9.97	16.6666	.900	.4823
10 Won	1906-1909	4.98	8.3333	.900	.2411
5 Won	1908-1909	2.49	4.1666	.900	.1206
KUWAIT					
5 Dinars	1961	8.27	13.5715	.916⅔	.4000
LAOS					
80,000 Kips	1971	47.85	80.0000	.900	2.3149
40,000 Kips	1971	23.93	40.0000	.900	1.1574
20,000 Kips	1971	11.96	20.0000	.900	.5787
8,000 Kips	1971	4.79	8.0000	.900	.2315
4,000 Kips	1971	2.39	4.0000	.900	.1157
100,000 Kips	1975	4.38	7.3200	.900	.2118
50,000 Kips	1975	2.19	3.6600	.900	.1059
LESOTHO					
20 Maloti	1966-1969	48.67	79.8810	.916⅔	2.3522
10 Maloti	1966-1969	24.33	39.9400	.916⅔	1.1771
4 Maloti	1966-1969	9.73	15.9760	.916⅔	.4709
2 Maloti	1966-1969	4.87	7.9880	.916⅔	.2354
1 Maloti	1966-1969	2.43	3.9940	.916⅔	.1177
100 Maloti	1976	5.38	9.0000	.900	.2604
50 Maloti	1976	2.69	4.5000	.900	.1302
LIBERIA					
20 Dollars — Red Gold	1964	11.16	18.6500	.900	.5397
20 Dollars — Yellow Gold	1964	12.38	18.6500	.999	.5990
30 Dollars	1965	8.97	15.0000	.900	.4340
25 Dollars	1965	13.94	23.3120	.900	.6746
12 Dollars	1965	3.59	6.0000	.900	.1736
20 Dollars	1972	20.00	33.4370	.900	.9675
10 Dollars	1972	10.00	16.7185	.900	.4838
5 Dollars	1972	5.00	8.3592	.900	.2419
2½ Dollars	1972	2.50	4.1796	.900	.1209
25 Dollars	1972	14.09	23.3120	.910	.6820
400 Dollars	1976	14.36	24.0000	.900	.6945
200 Dollars	1976	7.17	12.0000	.900	.3472
100 Dollars	1976	3.59	6.0000	.900	.1736
100 Dollars	1977-1979	6.54	10.9300	.900	.3613
LIECHTENSTEIN					
20 Kronen	1898-1900	4.05	6.7750	.900	.1960
10 Kronen	1898-1900	2.03	3.3375	.900	.0966
100 Franken	1952	19.29	32.2580	.900	.9334
20 Franken	1930-1946	3.86	6.4516	.900	.1867
10 Franken	1930-1946	1.93	3.2258	.900	.0933
50 Franken	1956-1961	6.84	11.2900	.900	.3267
25 Franken	1956-1961	3.42	5.6450	.900	.1633
LUXEMBOURG					
20 Francs	1953	3.86	6.4516	.900	.1867
MACAO					
500 Patacas	1978-1979	4.85	7.9600	.916⅔	.2340
1,000 Patacas	1980	9.73	15.9700	.916⅔	.4707
MALAWI					
250 Kwacha	1978	20.00	33.4370	.900	.9675
MALAYSIA					
100 Ringgit	1971	11.34	18.6200	.916⅔	.5488
200 Ringgit	1976-1977	4.37	7.3000	.900	.2112
250 Ringgit	1976	6.14	10.2600	.900	.2969
MALI					
100 Francs	1967	19.14	32.0000	.900	.9259
50 Francs	1967	9.57	16.0000	.900	.4630
25 Francs	1967	4.79	8.0000	.900	.2315
10 Francs	1967	1.91	3.2000	.900	.0926
MALTA (Island of)					
20 Scudi	1764-1778	9.00	16.0000	.840	.4321
10 Scudi	1756-1782	4.50	8.0000	.840	.2161
5 Scudi	1756-1779	2.25	4.0000	.840	.1080
50 Pounds	1972	18.28	30.0000	.916⅔	.9645
20 Pounds	1972	7.31	12.0000	.916⅔	.3537
10 Pounds	1972	3.66	6.0000	.916⅔	.1768
5 Pounds	1972	1.83	3.0000	.916⅔	.0884
50 Pounds	1973-1976	9.14	15.0000	.916⅔	.4421
20 Pounds	1973-1976	3.66	6.0000	.916⅔	.1768
10 Pounds	1973-1976	1.83	3.0000	.916⅔	.0884
100 Pounds	1977	19.45	31.9600	.916⅔	.9419
50 Pounds	1977	9.74	15.9800	.916⅔	.4710
25 Pounds	1977	4.87	7.9900	.916⅔	.2355
MALTA (Military Order of)					
10 Scudi	1961	4.87	8.0000	.916	.2354
5 Scudi	1961	2.44	4.0000	.916	.1178
10 Scudi	1962	4.89	8.0000	.920	.2366
5 Scudi	1962	2.45	4.0000	.920	.1183
10 Scudi	1963-1979	4.79	8.0000	.900	.2315
5 Scudi	1963-1979	2.39	4.0000	.900	.1157
MAURITANIA					
500 Ouguiya	1975	15.98	26.0000	.920	.7690
MAURITIUS					
200 Rupees	1971	9.48	15.5600	.916⅔	.4586
1,000 Rupees	1975	20.00	33.4370	.900	.9675
1,000 Rupees	1978	9.74	15.9800	.916⅔	.4710
MEXICO					
20 Pesos	1870-1905	19.72	33.8400	.875	.9520
10 Pesos	1870-1905	9.86	16.9200	.875	.4760
5 Pesos	1870-1905	4.93	8.4600	.875	.2380
2½ Pesos	1870-1893	2.47	4.2300	.875	.1190

Country and Denomination	Period of Coinage	Original Value in U.S. Gold Dollars	Weight of Coin in Grams	Purity or Fineness	Gold Content in Troy Ounces
1 Peso	1870-1905	.99	1.6900	.875	.0476
50 Pesos	1921-1947	24.90	41.6666	.900	1.2057
20 Pesos	1917-1959	9.97	16.6666	.900	.4823
10 Pesos	1905-1959	4.98	8.3333	.900	.2411
5 Pesos	1905-1955	2.49	4.1666	.900	.1206
2½ Pesos	1918-1948	1.25	2.0833	.900	.0603
2 Pesos	1919-1948	1.00	1.6666	.900	.0482
MONACO					
100 Francs	1882-1904	19.29	32.2580	.900	.9334
40 Francs	1838	7.72	12.9039	.900	.3734
20 Francs	1838-1892	3.86	6.4516	.900	.1867
2 Francs	1943	9.57	16.0000	.900	.4630
1 Franc	1943	4.79	8.0000	.900	.2315
100 Francs Normal	1950	15.25	25.5000	.900	.7379
100 Francs Double thick	1950	30.50	51.0000	.900	1.4757
50 Francs Normal	1950	12.26	20.5000	.900	.5932
50 Francs Double thick	1950	24.52	41.0000	.900	1.1864
20 Francs Normal	1950	8.67	14.5000	.900	.4196
20 Francs Double thick	1950	17.35	29.0000	.900	.8391
10 Francs Normal	1950	6.28	10.5000	.900	.3038
10 Francs Double thick	1950	12.56	21.0000	.900	.6077
100 Francs	1956	7.34	12.0000	.900	.3472
200 Francs	1966	19.57	32.0000	.920	.9465
MONGOLIA					
750 Tugrug	1976	20.00	33.4370	.900	.9675
MONTENEGRO					
100 Perpera	1910	19.29	33.8753	.900	.9802
20 Perpera	1910	3.86	6.7750	.900	.1960
10 Perpera	1910	1.93	3.3875	.900	.0980
MOROCCO					
4 Ryals	1879	3.86	6.4516	.900	.1867
250 Dirhams	1975-1977	3.93	6.4500	.916⅔	.1901
500 Dirhams	1979	7.72	12.9000	.900	.3733
MUSCAT AND OMAN					
15 Rials	1962	4.87	7.9878	.916⅔	.2354
NEPAL					
4 Mohars	1750-1938	14.00	23.0500	.916⅔	.6793
2 Mohars	1750-1938	7.00	11.5250	.916⅔	.3397
1 Mohar	1750-1938	3.50	5.7625	.916⅔	.1698
½ Mohar	1750-1938	1.75	2.8813	.916⅔	.0849
¼ Mohar	1750-1911	.88	1.4406	.916⅔	.0425
⅛ Mohar	1750-1911	.44	.7203	.916⅔	.0212
1⁄16 Mohar	1750-1911	.22	.3602	.916⅔	.0106
1/32 Mohar	1750-1911	.11	.1801	.916⅔	.0053
1/64 Mohar	1750-1911	.06	.0901	.916⅔	.0027
1/128 Mohar	1881-1911	.03	.0450	.916⅔	.0013
2 Rupees	1948-1955	7.02	11.5246	.916⅔	.3397
1 Rupee	1938-1962	3.51	5.7623	.916⅔	.1698
½ Rupee	1938-1962	1.76	2.8813	.916⅔	.0849
¼ Rupee	1955	1.77	2.9100	.916⅔	.0858
1/5 Rupee	1955	1.42	2.3300	.916⅔	.0687
1/6 Rupee	1956	1.29	2.1100	.916⅔	.0622
1 Rupee	1974	6.09	10.0000	.916⅔	.2947
½ Rupee	1974	3.05	5.0000	.916⅔	.1473
¼ Rupee	1974	1.52	2.5000	.916⅔	.0737
1,000 Rupees	1975	20.00	33.4370	.900	.9675
NETHERLANDS					
20 Guilders	1808-1810	8.34	13.6500	.916⅔	.4023
10 Guilders	1808-1810	4.17	6.8250	.916⅔	.2012
20 Guilders	1848-1853	8.04	13.4580	.900	.3966
10 Guilders	1818-1933	4.02	6.7290	.900	.1947
5 Guilders	1826-1912	2.01	3.3645	.900	.0974
14 Guilders	1749-1764	6.10	9.9300	.916⅔	.2927
7 Guilders	1749-1764	3.05	4.9650	.916⅔	.1463
1 Ducat	1960-1978	2.28	3.4940	.983	.1104
NETHERLANDS ANTILLES					
200 Guilders	1976-1977	4.75	7.9500	.900	.2300
100 Guilders	1978	4.02	6.7200	.900	.1944
NETHERLANDS EAST INDIES					
1 Ducat	1814-1937	2.28	3.4940	.983	.1104
NEWFOUNDLAND					
2 Dollars	1865-1888	2.00	3.3283	.916⅔	.0981
NICARAGUA					
50 Cordobas	1967	19.14	32.0000	.900	.9259
2,000 Cordobas	1975	10.34	17.2800	.900	.5000
1,000 Cordobas	1975	5.74	9.6000	.900	.2778
500 Cordobas	1975	3.23	5.4000	.900	.1563
200 Cordobas	1975	1.26	2.1000	.900	.0608
NIGER					
100 Francs	1960-1968	19.14	32.0000	.900	.9259
50 Francs	1960-1968	9.57	16.0000	.900	.4630
25 Francs	1960-1968	4.79	8.0000	.900	.2315
10 Francs	1960-1968	1.91	3.2000	.900	.0926
NORWAY					
20 Kronor	1874-1910	5.36	8.9606	.900	.2593
10 Kronor	1874-1910	2.68	4.4803	.900	.1296
OMAN					
500 Ryals	1971	24.38	40.0000	.917	1.1793
200 Ryals	1971	9.75	16.0000	.917	.4717
100 Ryals	1971	4.87	8.0000	.917	.2359
50 Ryals	1971	2.44	4.0000	.917	.1179
75 Ryals	1977	20.00	33.4370	.900	.9675
PAKISTAN					
3,000 Rupees	1976	20.00	33.4370	.900	.9675
500 Rupees	1976-1977	2.74	4.5000	.916⅔	.1326
1,000 Rupees	1977	5.48	9.0000	.916⅔	.2652
500 Rupees	1977	2.22	3.6400	.916⅔	.1073
PANAMA					
100 Balboas	1975-1980	4.88	8.1600	.900	.2361
500 Balboas	1975-1979	24.94	41.7000	.900	1.2066
150 Balboas-Platinum	1976	——	9.3000	.999	.2990
200 Balboas-Platinum	1978	——	9.3100	.999	.2990
75 Balboas	1978	3.52	10.6000	.500	.1704
PAPUA NEW GUINEA					
100 Kina	1975-1979	5.72	9.5700	.900	.2769
PARAGUAY					
10,000 Guaranies	1968	27.52	46.0083	.900	1.3313
4,500 Guaranies	1972-1974	19.08	31.9000	.900	.9230
3,000 Guaranies	1972-1974	12.74	21.3000	.900	.6163
1,500 Guaranies	1972-1974	6.40	10.7000	.900	.3096
PERSIA (IRAN)					
1 Ashrafi	1500-1750	2.25	3.5000	.975	.1097
25 Tomans	1848-1896	43.00	71.9252	.900	2.0812
20 Tomans	1848-1896	34.40	57.4880	.900	1.6635
10 Tomans	1848-1925	17.20	28.7440	.900	.8317
5 Tomans	1848-1925	8.60	14.4372	.900	.4178
2 Tomans	1848-1925	3.44	5.7489	.900	.1664
1 Toman	1848-1927	1.72	2.8744	.900	.0832
½ Toman	1848-1925	.86	1.4372	.900	.0416
1/5 Toman	1858-1925	.34	.5749	.900	.0166
5 Pahlevi	1927-1930	5.66	9.5900	.900	.2775
2 Pahlevi	1927-1930	2.26	3.8360	.900	.1110
1 Pahlevi	1927-1930	1.13	1.9180	.900	.0555
5 Pahlevi	1961-1979	24.35	40.6799	.900	1.7771
2½ Pahlevi	1961-1979	12.17	20.3399	.900	.5885
1 Pahlevi	1932-1979	4.80	8.1359	.900	.2354
½ Pahlevi	1932-1979	2.40	4.0680	.900	.1177
¼ Pahlevi	1950-1979	1.20	2.0340	.900	.0585
2,000 Rials	1971	15.59	26.0600	.900	.7541
1,000 Rials	1971	7.97	13.0300	.900	.3770
750 Rials	1971	5.84	9.7700	.900	.2827
500 Rials	1971	3.89	6.5100	.900	.1884
PERU					
20 Soles	1863	19.29	32.2580	.900	.9334
10 Soles	1863	9.65	16.1290	.900	.4667
5 Soles	1863	4.82	8.0645	.900	.2334
1 Libra	1898-1967	4.87	7.9881	.916⅔	.2354
½ Libra	1902-1966	2.43	3.9940	.916⅔	.1177
1/5 Libra	1906-1967	.97	1.5976	.916⅔	.0471
50 Soles	1930-1931	20.00	33.4370	.900	.9675
100 Soles	1950-1969	28.00	46.8071	.900	1.3544
50 Soles	1950-1969	14.00	23.4035	.900	.6772
20 Soles	1950-1969	5.60	9.3614	.900	.2709
10 Soles	1956-1969	2.80	4.6807	.900	.1354
5 Soles	1956-1969	1.40	2.3404	.900	.0677
1 Sol	1976	14.00	23.4000	.900	.6771
½ Sol	1976	5.59	9.3500	.900	.2705
100,000 Sols	1979	20.43	33.5300	.916⅔	.9882
50,000 Sols	1979	10.20	16.7500	.916⅔	.4937
PHILIPPINE ISLANDS					
4 Pesos	1861-1862	3.86	6.7661	.875	.1903
2 Pesos	1861-1868	1.93	3.3830	.875	.0952
1 Peso	1861-1868	.96	1.6915	.875	.0476
1 Piso	1970	11.78	19.7000	.900	.5700
1,000 Pisos	1975	5.95	9.9500	.900	.2879
1,500 Pisos	1976	12.29	20.5500	.900	.5946
5,000 Pisos	1977	46.51	77.7588	.900	2.2500
1,500 Pisos	1977-1978	12.23	20.4500	.900	.5917
POLAND					
50 Zloty	1817-1829	6.04	9.8000	.916⅔	.2888
25 Zloty	1817-1833	3.02	4.9000	.916⅔	.1444
20 Zloty-3 Roubles	1834-1840	2.26	3.4500	.980	.1087
20 Zloty	1925	3.86	6.4516	.900	.1867
10 Zloty	1925	1.93	3.2258	.900	.0933
500 Zloty	1976	17.91	29.9500	.900	.8666
2,000 Zloty	1977-1980	4.79	8.0000	.900	.2315

PORTUGAL

Country and Denomination	Period of Coinage	Original Value in U.S. Gold Dollars	Weight of Coin in Grams	Purity or Fineness	Gold Content in Troy Ounces
4 Cruzados	1580-1652	9.15	14.0000	.986	.4438
2 Cruzados	1580-1647	4.58	7.0000	.986	.2219
1 Cruzado	1438-1647	2.29	3.5000	.986	.1109
4,000 Reis	1663-1722	6.54	10.7200	.916⅔	.3159
2,000 Reis	1663-1725	3.27	5.3600	.916⅔	.1579
1,000 Reis	1663-1821	1.64	2.6800	.916⅔	.0790
400 Reis	1717-1821	.65	1.0720	.916⅔	.0316
8 Escudos	1717-1732	17.47	28.6000	.916⅔	.8429
4 Escudos	1722-1835	8.74	14.3000	.916⅔	.4215
2 Escudos	1722-1831	4.37	7.1500	.916⅔	.2107
1 Escudo	1722-1821	2.19	3.5750	.916⅔	.1054
½ Escudo	1722-1821	1.10	1.7875	.916⅔	.0527
5,000 Reis	1836-1851	5.92	9.5600	.916⅔	.2818
2,500 Reis	1838-1853	2.96	4.7800	.916⅔	.1409
1,000 Reis	1851	1.48	2.3900	.916⅔	.0704
10,000 Reis	1878-1889	10.81	17.7350	.916⅔	.5227
5,000 Reis	1860-1889	5.40	8.8675	.916⅔	.2613
2,000 Reis	1856-1888	2.16	3.5470	.916⅔	.1045
1,000 Reis	1855-1879	1.08	1.7735	.916⅔	.0523

RAS AL KHAIMA

200 Riyals	1970	24.76	41.4000	.900	1.1979
150 Riyals	1970	18.57	31.0500	.900	.8985
100 Riyals	1970	12.38	20.7000	.900	.5990
75 Riyals	1970	9.29	15.5300	.900	.4494
50 Riyals	1970	6.19	10.3500	.900	.2995

RHODESIA

5 Pounds	1966	24.33	39.9403	.916⅔	1.1771
1 Pound	1966	4.87	7.9881	.916⅔	.2354
10 Shillings	1966	2.43	3.9940	.916⅔	.1177

ROUMANIA

100 Lei	1906-1940	19.29	32.2580	.900	.9334
50 Lei	1906-1922	9.65	16.1290	.900	.4667
25 Lei	1906-1922	4.82	8.0645	.900	.2334
20 Lei	1867-1944	3.86	6.4516	.900	.1867
12½ Lei	1906	2.41	4.0323	.900	.1167

RUSSIA (Platinum coinage, as well as the Rouble gold coinage of 1718-1825 were of variable weight and fineness.)

25 Roubles	1876	19.90	32.7000	.916⅔	.9637
10 Roubles	1836	7.96	13.0800	.916⅔	.3842
5 Roubles	1826-1885	3.98	6.5400	.916⅔	.1928
3 Roubles	1869-1885	2.38	3.9000	.916⅔	.1149
12 Roubles-Platinum	1830-1845	9.52	41.5000	about .975	1.3343
6 Roubles-Platinum	1829-1845	4.76	20.7500	about .975	.6671
3 Roubles-Platinum	1828-1845	2.38	10.3750	about .975	.3336
10 Roubles	1886-1894	7.72	12.9039	.900	.3734
5 Roubles	1886-1894	3.86	6.4516	.900	.1867
15 Roubles	1897	7.72	12.9039	.900	.3734
7½ Roubles	1897	3.86	6.4516	.900	.1867
37½ Roubles	1902	19.29	32.2580	.900	.9334
25 Roubles	1896-1908	19.29	32.2580	.900	.9334
10 Roubles	1898-1979	5.15	8.6026	.900	.2489
5 Roubles	1897-1910	2.57	4.3013	.900	.1245
150 Roubles-Platinum	1977-1980	——	15.5500	.999	.4993
100 Roubles	1977-1980	10.33	17.2800	.900	.5001

RWANDA

100 Francs	1965	17.94	30.0000	.900	.8681
50 Francs	1965	8.97	15.0000	.900	.4340
25 Francs	1965	4.47	7.5000	.900	.2170
10 Francs	1965	2.21	3.7000	.900	.1085

ST. THOMAS AND PRINCE

2,500 Dobras	1977	3.88	6.4800	.900	.1875

EL SALVADOR

20 Pesos	1892	19.29	32.2580	.900	.9334
10 Pesos	1892	9.65	16.1290	.900	.4667
5 Pesos	1892	4.82	8.0645	.900	.2334
2½ Pesos	1892	2.41	4.0323	.900	.1167
20 Colones	1925	9.31	15.5600	.900	.4502
200 Colones	1971	14.12	23.6000	.900	.6829
100 Colones	1971	7.06	11.8000	.900	.3414
50 Colones	1971	3.53	5.9000	.900	.1707
25 Colones	1971	1.76	2.9500	.900	.0854
250 Colones	1977	9.74	15.9800	.916⅔	.4710

SAN MARINO

20 Lire	1925	3.86	6.4516	.900	.1867
10 Lire	1925	1.93	3.2258	.900	.0933
2 Scudi	1974-1979	3.66	6.0000	.916⅔	.1769
1 Scudo	1974-1979	1.83	3.0000	.916⅔	.0884
5 Scudi	1976-1977	9.14	15.0000	.916⅔	.4421
10 Scudi	1978	18.28	30.0000	.916⅔	.8842

SAUDI ARABIA

1 Saudi Pound	1951-1957	4.87	7.9881	.916⅔	.2354

SENEGAL

Country and Denomination	Period of Coinage	Original Value in U.S. Gold Dollars	Weight of Coin in Grams	Purity or Fineness	Gold Content in Troy Ounces
100 Francs	1968	19.14	32.0000	.900	.9259
50 Francs	1968	9.57	16.0000	.900	.4630
25 Francs	1968	4.79	8.0000	.900	.2315
10 Francs	1968	1.91	3.2000	.900	.0926
2,500 Francs	1975	24.33	39.9300	.916⅔	1.1768
1,000 Francs	1975	9.72	15.9500	.916⅔	.4701
500 Francs	1975	4.85	7.9600	.916⅔	.2346
250 Francs	1975	2.42	3.9800	.916⅔	.1173

SERBIA

20 Dinars	1879-1882	3.86	6.4516	.900	.1867
10 Dinars	1882	1.93	3.2258	.900	.0933

SEYCHELLES

1,000 Rupees	1976	9.74	15.9800	.916⅔	.4710
1,000 Rupees	1978	20.00	33.4370	.900	.9675

SHARJAH

200 Riyals	1970	24.80	41.4600	.900	1.1997
100 Riyals	1970	12.40	20.7300	.900	.5998
50 Riyals	1970	6.20	10.3600	.900	.2998
25 Riyals	1970	3.10	5.1800	.900	.1499

SIAM

8 Ticals	1851-1868	4.50	7.8400	.900	.2269
4 Ticals	1851-1868	2.25	3.9200	.900	.1134
2 Ticals	1851-1907	1.13	1.9600	.900	.0567

SIERRA LEONE

1 Golde	1966	32.63	54.5450	.900	1.5783
½ Golde	1966	16.31	27.2730	.900	.7891
¼ Golde	1966	8.16	13.6360	.900	.3946

SINGAPORE

150 Dollars	1969	15.21	24.8830	.920	.7360
500 Dollars	1975	20.67	34.5594	.900	1.0000
250 Dollars	1975	10.34	17.2797	.900	.5000
100 Dollars	1975	4.13	6.9119	.900	.2000

SOLOMON ISLANDS

100 Dollars	1978	5.60	9.3700	.900	.2711

SOMALIA

500 Shillings	1965-1970	41.87	70.0000	.900	2.0255
200 Shillings	1965-1970	16.75	28.0000	.900	1.0128
100 Shillings	1965-1970	8.37	14.0000	.900	.5064
50 Shillings	1965-1970	4.19	7.0000	.900	.2532
20 Shillings	1965-1970	1.67	2.8000	.900	.1266

SOUTH AFRICA, REPUBLIC

2 Rand	1961-1980	4.87	7.9881	.916⅔	.2354
1 Rand	1961-1980	2.43	3.9940	.916⅔	.1177
1 Krugerrand	1967-1980	20.67	33.9305	.916⅔	1.0000

SOUTH KOREA

25,000 Won	1970	57.90	96.8000	.900	2.8010
20,000 Won	1970	46.32	77.4400	.900	2.2408
10,000 Won	1970	23.16	38.7200	.900	1.1204
5,000 Won	1970	11.58	19.3600	.900	.5602
2,500 Won	1970	5.79	9.6800	.900	.2801
1,000 Won	1970	2.31	3.8700	.900	.1120

SPAIN

10 Doblas	1350-1369	22.84	34.9000	.986	1.1064
5 Doblas	1454-1474	14.70	22.5000	.986	.7133
1 Dobla	1252-1474	2.94	4.5000	.986	.1427
½ Dobla	1454-1474	1.47	2.2500	.986	.0713
1 Excelente	1476-1516	Equal to 1 Ducat			
Escudo Coinage	1516-1833	See Table I with the following exceptions regarding fineness.			
Escudo Coinage	1516-1772	——	——	.916⅔	——
Escudo Coinage	1773-1785	——	——	.900	——
Escudo Coinage	1786-1833	——	——	.875	——
320 Reales	1810-1823	15.54	27.0000	.875	.7596
160 Reales	1822	7.72	13.5000	.875	.3798
80 Reales	1809-1848	3.86	6.7500	.875	.1899
100 Reales or 10 Escudos	1850-1868	4.97	8.3500	.900	.2416
40 Reales or 4 Escudos	1861-1868	1.98	3.3400	.900	.0968
20 Reales or 2 Escudos	1861-1865	.99	1.6700	.900	.0483
100 Pesetas	1870-1897	19.29	32.2580	.900	.9334
25 Pesetas	1871-1885	4.82	8.0645	.900	.2334
20 Pesetas	1889-1904	3.86	6.4516	.900	.1867
10 Pesetas	1878	1.93	3.2258	.900	.0933

SUDAN

100 Pounds	1976	20.00	33.4370	.900	.9675
50 Pounds	1978	10.66	17.5000	.916⅔	.5158
25 Pounds	1978	5.03	8.2500	.916⅔	.2435

SURINAM

100 Gulden	1976	4.02	6.7200	.900	.1944

Country and Denomination	Period of Coinage	Original Value in U.S. Gold Dollars	Weight of Coin in Grams	Purity or Fineness	Gold Content in Troy Ounces
SWAZILAND					
1 Lilangeni	1968	17.27	28.3500	.916⅔	.8355
25 Emalangeni	1974	16.62	27.7800	.900	.8038
20 Emalangeni	1974	13.30	22.2300	.900	.6432
10 Emalangeni	1974	6.65	11.1200	.900	.3218
5 Emalangeni	1974	3.33	5.5600	.900	.1609
100 Emalangeni	1975	5.17	8.6400	.900	.2500
50 Emalangeni	1975	2.58	4.3195	.900	.1250
SWEDEN					
1 Carolin or 10 Francs	1868-1872	1.93	3.2258	.900	.0933
20 Kronor	1873-1925	5.36	8.9606	.900	.2593
10 Kronor	1873-1901	2.68	4.4803	.900	.1296
5 Kronor	1881-1920	1.34	2.2401	.900	.0648
SWITZERLAND					
20 Francs	1871-1947	3.86	6.4516	.900	.1867
10 Francs	1911-1922	1.93	3.2258	.900	.0933
100 Francs	1925	19.29	32.2580	.900	.9334
100 Francs	1934	15.50	25.9000	.900	.7494
100 Francs	1939	10.50	17.5000	.900	.5064
6 Duplones	1794	27.60	45.8400	.900	1.3264
4 Duplones	1797-1798	18.40	30.5600	.900	.8843
2 Duplones	1793-1798	9.20	15.2800	.900	.4421
1 Duplone	1787-1829	4.60	7.6400	.900	.2211
½ Duplone	1787-1796	2.30	3.8200	.900	.1105
¼ Duplone	1789-1796	1.15	1.9100	.900	.0055
32 Franken	1800	9.20	15.2800	.900	.4421
16 Franken	1800-1813	4.60	7.6400	.900	.2211
8 Franken	1813	2.30	3.8200	.900	.1105
24 Munzgulden	1794-1796	9.20	15.2800	.900	.4421
12 Munzgulden	1794-1796	4.60	7.6400	.900	.2211
20 Francs (Geneva)	1848	3.86	7.6000	.750	.1833
10 Francs (Geneva)	1848	1.93	3.8000	.750	.0916

(Other denominations are similar to those of France, Germany or Italy)

Country and Denomination	Period of Coinage	Original Value in U.S. Gold Dollars	Weight of Coin in Grams	Purity or Fineness	Gold Content in Troy Ounces
SYRIA					
1 Pound	1950	4.06	6.7500	.900	.1953
½ Pound	1950	2.03	3.3750	.900	.0977
TANZANIA					
1,500 Shillingi	1974	20.00	33.4370	.900	.9675
THAILAND					
600 Baht	1968	8.97	15.0000	.900	.4340
300 Baht	1968	4.49	7.5000	.900	.2170
150 Baht	1968	2.24	3.7500	.900	.1085
800 Baht	1971	11.96	20.0000	.900	.5787
400 Baht	1971	5.98	10.0000	.900	.2894
2,500 Baht	1975	20.00	33.4370	.900	.9675
2,500 Baht	1977	8.97	15.0000	.900	.4340
3,000 Baht	1978	8.97	15.0000	.900	.4340
5,000 Baht	1978	17.97	30.0000	.900	.8680
TONGA					
1 Koula	1962	19.80	32.5000	.916⅔	.9578
½ Koula	1962	9.90	16.2500	.916⅔	.4789
¼ Koula	1962	4.95	8.1250	.916⅔	.2395

(Note: A small quantity of proof specimens of the 1962 issue were struck in .999 fine gold.)

Country and Denomination	Period of Coinage	Original Value in U.S. Gold Dollars	Weight of Coin in Grams	Purity or Fineness	Gold Content in Troy Ounces
1 Hau-Palladium	1967-1968	——	63.5000	.980	——
½ Hau-Palladium	1967-1968	——	32.0000	.980	——
¼ Hau-Palladium	1967-1968	——	16.0000	.980	——
100 Pa'anga	1975	12.19	20.0000	.916⅔	.5895
75 Pa'anga	1975	9.13	15.0000	.916⅔	.4420
50 Pa'anga	1975	6.09	10.0000	.916⅔	.2947
25 Pa'anga	1975	3.05	5.0000	.916⅔	.1474
TRINIDAD AND TOBAGO					
100 Dollars	1976	2.06	6.2100	.500	.0998
TUNIS					
100 Piastres	1855-1864	11.90	19.4920	.900	.5640
80 Piastres	1855	9.52	15.5936	.900	.4512
50 Piastres	1855-1867	5.95	9.7460	.900	.2820
40 Piastres	1855	4.76	7.7968	.900	.2256
25 Piastres	1857-1882	2.98	4.8730	.900	.1410
20 Piastres	1855	2.38	3.8984	.900	.1128
10 Piastres	1855-1871	1.19	1.9492	.900	.0560
5 Piastres	1864-1872	.60	.9746	.900	.0282
20 Francs	1891-1928	3.86	6.4516	900	.1867
15 Francs	1886-1891	2.90	4.8387	.900	.1400
10 Francs	1891-1928	1.93	3.2258	.900	.0933
100 Francs	1930-1955	3.94	6.5500	.900	.1895
TUNISIA					
40 Dinars	1967	45.46	76.0000	.900	2.1991
20 Dinars	1967	22.73	38.0000	.900	1.0996
10 Dinars	1967	11.36	19.0000	.900	.5498
5 Dinars	1967	5.68	9.5000	.900	.2749
2 Dinars	1967	2.27	3.8000	.900	.1099
TURKEY					
5 Sequins	1703-1839	8.00	15.0000	.800	.3858
4 Sequins	1703-1839	6.40	12.0000	.800	.3086
3 Sequins	1703-1839	4.80	9.0000	.800	.2315
2 Sequins	1703-1839	3.20	6.0000	.800	.1543
1 Sequin	1451-1839	1.60	3.0000	.800	.0772
½ Sequin	1451-1839	.80	1.5000	.800	.0386
¼ Sequin	1451-1839	.40	.7500	.800	.0193
500 Piastres	1839-1975	21.98	36.0829	.916⅔	1.0634
250 Piastres	1839-1975	10.99	18.0414	.916⅔	.5317
100 Piastres	1839-1975	4.40	7.2166	.916⅔	.2127
50 Piastres	1839-1975	2.20	3.6083	.916⅔	.1063
25 Piastres	1839-1975	1.10	1.8041	.916⅔	.0532
12½ Piastres	1909-1918	.55	.9021	.916⅔	.0266
500 Piastres	Deluxe since 1926	21.37	35.0800	.916⅔	1.0339
250 Piastres	Deluxe since 1926	10.69	17.5400	.916⅔	.5169
100 Piastres	Deluxe since 1926	4.27	7.0160	.916⅔	.2068
50 Piastres	Deluxe since 1926	2.14	3.5080	.916⅔	.1034
25 Piastres	Deluxe since 1926	1.07	1.7540	.916⅔	.0517
500 Lire	1973	3.65	6.0000	.916⅔	.1768
1,000 Lire	1978	9.75	16.0000	.916⅔	.4716
500 Lire	1978	4.87	8.0000	.916⅔	.2358
TURKS AND CAICOS ISLANDS					
100 Crowns	1974	5.99	18.0145	.500	.2896
50 Crowns	1974	2.99	9.0073	.500	.1448
100 Crowns	1975	4.13	12.4417	.500	.2000
50 Crowns	1975	2.06	6.2208	.500	.1000
25 Crowns	1975	1.03	3.1104	.500	.0500
100 Crowns	1976-1979	5.98	18.0100	.500	.2895
50 Crowns	1976	1.94	5.8400	.500	.0939
50 Crowns	1977-1978	2.99	9.0073	.500	.1448
TUVALU					
50 Dollars	1976	9.74	15.9800	.916⅔	.4710
UGANDA					
1,000 Shillings	1969	82.67	138.2400	.900	4.0001
500 Shillings	1969	41.34	69.1200	.900	2.0001
100 Shillings	1969	8.27	13.8200	.900	.4000
50 Shillings	1969	4.13	6.9100	.900	.2000
UM-AL-QAWAIN					
200 Riyals	1970	24.80	41.4600	.900	1.1997
100 Riyals	1970	12.40	20.7300	.900	.5998
50 Riyals	1970	6.20	10.3600	.900	.2998
25 Riyals	1970	3.10	5.1800	.900	.1499
UNITED STATES					
50 Dollars	1915	50.00	83.5920	.900	2.4188
20 Dollars	1850-1933	20.00	33.4370	.900	.9675
10 Dollars	1795-1804	10.68	17.4957	.916⅔	.5156
10 Dollars	1838-1933	10.00	16.7185	.900	.4838
5 Dollars	1795-1833	5.34	8.7480	.916⅔	.2578
5 Dollars	1834-1836	5.00	8.3592	.899¼	.2417
5 Dollars	1837-1929	5.00	8.3592	.900	.2419
4 Dollars	1879-1880	4.00	6.6872	.900	.1935
3 Dollars	1854-1889	3.00	5.0154	.900	.1451
2½ Dollars	1796-1833	2.67	4.3740	.916⅔	.1289
2½ Dollars	1834-1836	2.50	4.1796	.899¼	.1208
2½ Dollars	1837-1929	2.50	4.1796	.900	.1209
1 Dollar	1849-1889	1.00	1.6718	.900	.0484
4 Saudi Pounds	1945-1946	19.48	31.9522	.916⅔	.9417
1 Saudi Pound	1945-1946	4.87	7.9881	.916⅔	.2354
URUGUAY					
5 Pesos	1930	5.20	8.4800	.916⅔	.2499
VATICAN					
4 Doppia	1786-1787	13.04	21.8000	.900	.6308
2 Doppia	1776-1777	6.52	10.9000	.900	.3154
1 Doppia	1776-1834	3.26	5.4500	.900	.1577
½ Doppia	1776-1787	1.63	2.7250	.900	.0788
10 Scudi	1835-1856	10.36	17.3000	.900	.5006
5 Scudi	1835-1854	5.18	8.6500	.900	.2503
2½ Scudi	1835-1863	2.59	4.3250	.900	.1251
1 Scudo	1853-1865	1.04	1.7300	.900	.0501
100 Lire	1866-1870	19.29	32.2580	.900	.9334
50 Lire	1868-1870	9.65	16.1290	.900	.4667
20 Lire	1866-1870	3.86	6.4516	.900	.1867
10 Lire	1866-1869	1.93	3.2258	.900	.0933
5 Lire	1866-1867	.96	1.6129	.900	.0467
100 Lire	1929-1935	5.25	8.7990	.900	.2546
100 Lire	1936-1959	3.18	5.2000	.900	.1504

(Other denominations are the same as those of Italy.)

Country and Denomination	Period of Coinage	Original Value in U.S. Gold Dollars	Weight of Coin in Grams	Purity or Fineness	Gold Content in Troy Ounces
VENEZUELA					
100 Bolivares	1875-1889	19.29	32.2580	.900	.9334
50 Bolivares	1875-1888	9.65	16.1290	.900	.4667
25 Bolivares	1875	4.82	8.0645	.900	.2334
20 Bolivares	1879-1912	3.86	6.4516	.900	.1867
10 Bolivares	1930	1.93	3.2258	.900	.0933
5 Bolivares	1875	.96	1.6129	.900	.0467
1,000 Bolivares	1975	20.00	33.4370	.900	.9675
WESTERN SAMOA					
100 Tala	1976-1978	9.47	15.5500	.916⅔	.4583
YEMEN ARAB REPUBLIC					
50 Ryals	1969	29.31	49.0000	.900	1.4178
30 Ryals	1969	17.59	29.4000	.900	.8507
20 Ryals	1969	11.72	19.6000	.900	.5671
10 Ryals	1969	5.86	9.8000	.900	.2836
5 Ryals	1969	2.93	4.9000	.900	.1418
75 Rials	1975	8.16	13.6500	.900	.3950

Country and Denomination	Period of Coinage	Original Value in U.S. Gold Dollars	Weight of Coin in Grams	Purity or Fineness	Gold Content in Troy Ounces
YUGOSLAVIA					
20 Dinars	1925	3.86	6.4516	.900	.1867
1,000 Dinars	1968	46.77	78.2000	.900	2.2628
500 Dinars	1968	23.39	39.1000	.900	1.1314
200 Dinars	1968	9.35	15.6400	.900	.4526
100 Dinars	1968	4.68	7.8200	.900	.2263
5,000 Dinar	1979	17.65	29.5000	.900	.8536
2,500 Dinar	1979	10.41	17.4000	.900	.5035
2,000 Dinar	1979	7.06	11.8000	.900	.3414
1,500 Dinar	1979	5.26	8.8000	.900	.2546
ZAIRE					
100 Zaires	1975	20.00	33.4370	.900	.9675
ZAMBIA					
200 Kwacha	1979	20.00	33.4370	.900	.9675
ZANZIBAR					
5 Rials	1881	5.00	8.3592	.900	.2419
2½ Rials	1881	2.50	4.1796	.900	.1209

WEIGHTS AND MEASURES

A. The purity or fineness of gold coins

The fineness of gold coins ranges from about .500 fine to 1.000 fine or pure gold. Chemically pure, unalloyed gold is considered to be 1.000 fine or 24 karats. The term "Fine gold" as used in banking and government circles refers to gold of 1.000 fineness.

24 Karats	=	1.000	Fine
23 Karats	=	.958⅓	Fine
22 Karats	=	.916⅔	Fine
21 Karats	=	.875	Fine
20 Karats	=	.833⅓	Fine
18 Karats	=	.750	Fine
14 Karats	=	.583⅓	Fine

It will be noted that .900 fine gold (the standard of U.S. gold coins and of most other countries) would be about 21.6 Karats.

B. The weight of gold coins

The troy and metric systems are used in weighing gold coins or precious metals in general. The weight of gold coins is usually expressed in grams.

1	Troy Ounce	=	31.103½ Grams
1	Troy Ounce	=	480 Grains
1	Troy Ounce	=	20 Pennyweight
12	Troy Ounces	=	1 Troy Pound
32.15	Troy Ounces	=	1 Kilogram
1	Gram	=	15.432 Grains
1	Gram	=	0.643 Pennyweight
1,000	Grams	=	1 Kilogram
24	Grains	=	1 Pennyweight
5,760	Grains	=	1 Troy Pound
15,432	Grains	=	1 Kilogram
240	Pennyweight	=	1 Troy Pound
643.01	Pennyweight	=	1 Kilogram
1	Kilogram	=	2.68 Troy Pounds

Comparisons of Grains and Grams

Grains		Grams
1	=	.0648
10	=	.648
15.432	=	1
20	=	1.30
25	=	1.62
35	=	2.27
50	=	3.24
75	=	4.86
100	=	6.48
125	=	8.10
150	=	9.72
175	=	11.34
200	=	12.96
250	=	16.20
300	=	19.44
350	=	22.68
400	=	25.92
450	=	29.16
500	=	32.40
1000	=	64.80

Equivalents of the Troy and Avoirdupois systems

(The Troy Pound consists of 12 Ounces; the Avoirdupois Pound of 16 Ounces.)

Avoirdupois			Troy or Metric
1	Ounce	=	437.50 Grains
1	Ounce	=	18.2291 Pennyweight
1	Ounce	=	28.3495 Grams
1	Ounce	=	0.9114 Ounce
1	Ounce	=	0.0625 Pound
1	Pound	=	7,000 Grains
1	Pound	=	291.666 Pennyweight
1	Pound	=	14.5833 Ounces
1	Pound	=	453.5926 Grams
35.2740	Ounces	=	1 Kilogram
2.2046	Pounds	=	1 Kilogram

C. Inches and Millimeters

The diameter or size of coins is usually expressed in millimeters. The table below shows the relationship between the millimeter scale and the more familiar inch scale.

Inches	Millimeters
¼	6.35
½	12.70
¾	19.05
1	25.40
1¼	31.75
1½	38.10
1¾	44.45
2	50.80

THE MOHAMMEDAN CALENDAR

This table shows the Christian or A.D. years of corresponding Mohammedan or A.H. years, and will enable one to ascertain at a glance the correct Christian year of those Afro-Asian coins which are dated according to the Mohammedan Calendar.

Year 1 A.H. of this Calendar began on July 16, 622 A.D. (A.H. is Anno Hegira, meaning in the year of Mohammed's flight from Mecca to Medina.)

A.H.	A.D.	A.H.	A.D.	A.H.	A.D.	A.H.	A.D.
1	622	1000	1591	1200	1785	1300	1882
10	631	1010	1601	1210	1795	1305	1887
20	640	1020	1611	1215	1800	1310	1892
30	650	1030	1620	1220	1805	1315	1897
40	660	1040	1630	1225	1810	1320	1902
50	670	1050	1640	1230	1814	1325	1907
60	679	1060	1650	1235	1819	1330	1911
70	689	1070	1659	1240	1824	1335	1916
80	699	1080	1669	1245	1829	1340	1921
90	708	1090	1679	1250	1834	1345	1926
100	718	1100	1688	1255	1839	1350	1931
200	815	1110	1698	1260	1844	1355	1936
300	912	1120	1708	1265	1848	1360	1941
400	1009	1130	1717	1270	1853	1365	1946
500	1106	1140	1727	1275	1858	1370	1950
600	1203	1150	1737	1280	1863	1375	1956
700	1300	1160	1747	1285	1868	1380	1961
800	1397	1170	1756	1290	1873	1385	1965
900	1494	1180	1766	1295	1878	1390	1970
		1190	1776			1395	1975
						1400	1980

FOREIGN LANGUAGE NUMERALS

Chart courtesy of Gilbert C. Heyde, F.R.N.S

479

GENERAL REFERENCES

From the hundreds of books and catalogues consulted in the preparation of this work, the following are suggested as general sources of reference.

AFGHANISTAN. Wilson, London, 1841.

AMERICAS, THE. References are for all countries in The Americas. Raymond, "The Gold Coins of North and South America", New York, 1937; Raymond, "Standard Catalogue of United States Coins", New York, 1954; Yeoman, "A Guide Book of United States Coins", Racine, 1975; Santos Leitao, "Brazil Coinage", Rio de Janeiro, 1960; Vidal Quadras, "Collection of Spanish Gold Coins", Barcelona, 1892; Tolra, "Collection of Spanish Gold Coins", Barcelona, 1936; Christensen, "The Ubilla-Echevez Collection", Hoboken, 1964; Harris, "Gold Coins of the Americas", Florence, Alabama, 1971.

ANNAM. Schroeder, Berlin Museum, 1898.

ARAB-ASIAN EMPIRES. Berlin Museum, 1898 and British Museum, 1941, 1956 for Arab-Byzantine and Arab-Sassanian issues.

AUSTRALIA. Deacon, Melbourne, 1952.

AUSTRIA. Miller-Aichholz, Vienna, 1948; Cejnek, Vienna, 1935; Horsky Collection, Frankfurt, 1910; Jaeckel, Basel, 1956; Bernhart and Roll (For Slazburg), Munich, 1930.

BELGIUM. Dupriez, Brussels, 1949; Gaillard, Ghent, 1854; Nussbaum; Delmonte, Amsterdam, 1964.

BULGARIA. Ljubica, Zagreb, 1875.

CEYLON. Codrington, Colombo, 1924.

CHINA. Kann, Hong Kong, 1954.

CYPRUS. Schlumberger, Paris, 1877.

DANZIG. Hutten-Czapski, St. Petersburg, 1871.

DENMARK. Schou, Copenhagen, 1926.

ETHIOPIA. Anzani, Rome, 1926.

EUROPE. Schlumberger, Munich, 1967.

FRANCE. Ciani, Paris, 1926; F. Poey d'Avant, Paris, 1838; La-Faurie, Paris, 1951, 1956; Monsieur V. Guilloteau, Paris, 1943.

GERMANY. General reference works consulted:—Jaeger, Basel, 1956; Kohler, Hannover, 1759; Soothe, Hamburg, 1784; Reimmann, Frankfurt, 1892; Rudolph, Dresden, 1911.

Specialized reference works consulted:

City	Author	Place and Date
Aachen	Menadier	Berlin 1913
Anhalt	Mann	Hannover 1907
Augsburg	Forster	Leipzig 1910, 1914
Baden	Wielandt	Karlsruhe 1955
Bamberg	Heller	Bamberg 1839
Bavaria	Beierlein	Munich 1894, 1900, 03, 06
Bentheim	Kennepohl	Frankfurt 1927
Brandenburg-Franconia	Schroetter	Halle 1927, 29
Bremen	Jungk	Bremen 1875
Brunswick	Fiala	Prague 1910
Cologne	Noss	Cologne 1926
Dortmund	Meyer	Vienna 1883
Eichstadt	Gebhardt	Halle 1924
Einbeck	Buck	Leipzig 1939
Emden	Knyphausen	Hannover 1872
Erfurt	Leitzman	Weissensee 1864
Frankfurt	Joseph and Fellner	Frankfurt, 1896, 1903
Fulda	Schneider	Fulda 1826
Hamburg	Gaedechens	Hamburg 1850
Hanau	Suchler	Hanau 1897
Hesse	Hoffmeister	Hannover 1880 and Prince Alexander, Darmstadt, 1877-85
Hildesheim	Buck	Leipzig 1937
Julich Cleve Berg	Noss	Munich 1929
Lauenburg	Schmidt	Ratzeburg 1884 and Dorfmann, Ratzeburg, 1940
Lippe	Grote	1867
Lubeck	Behrens	Berlin 1905
Magdeburg	Schroetter	Magdeburg 1909
Mansfeld	Tornau	Prague 1937
Mayence	Prince Alexander	Darmstadt 1882
Mecklenburg	Evers	Schwerim 1799
Minden	Stange	Munster 1913
Moers	Noss	Munich 1927
Munster	Niessert	Coesfeld 1839, 1841
Nassau	Isenbeck	Wiesbaden 1890
Nordhausen	Lejeune	Dresden 1910
Nuremberg	Kellner	Grunwald 1957
Oettingen	Loeffelholz	Oettingana 1883
Osnabruck	Kennepohl	Munich 1938
Paderborn	Weingartner	Munster 1882
Palatinate	Noss	Munich 1938 and Exter, Zweibrucken, 1759, 1775
Prussia	Schroetter	Berlin 1902-25 and Bahrfeldt, Halle, 1913
Quedlinburg	Duning	Quedlinburg 1886
Rantzau	Meyer	Vienna 1882
Ratzeburg	Bahrfeldt	Schwerin 1913
Regensburg	Plato	Regensburg 1779
Reuss	Schmidt and Knab	Dresden 1907
Rosenberg	Friedensburg and Seger	Breslau 1901
Rostock	Grimm	Berlin 1905
Salm	Joseph	Frankfurt 1914
Saxony	Tentzel	Dresden 1705, 1714 and Baumgarten, Dresden 1812
Schauenburg	Weinmeister	Berlin
Schleswig-Holstein	Lange	Berlin 1908, 1912
Schwarzburg	Fischer	Heidelberg 1904
Silesia	Friedensburg and Seger	Breslau 1901
Solms	Joseph	Frankfurt 1912
Speyer	Harster	Speyer 1882
Stolberg	Frederick	Dresden 1911
Stralsund	Bratring	Berlin 1907
Teutonic Order	Waschinski	Gottingen 1952
Treves	Noss	Bonn 1916
Ulm	Binder	Stuttgart 1846
Wallenstein	Meyer	Vienna 1886
Wismar	Grimm	Berlin 1897
Worms	Joseph	Darmstadt 1906
Wurttemberg	Ebner	Stuttgart 1910-1915

GREAT BRITAIN. Brooke, London, 1932; Seaby, London, 1965; Spink, London, 1950.

HOLY ROMAN EMPIRE. Same as Austria.

HUNGARY. Same as Austria and Rethy, Budapest, 1899. For Transylvania: Resch, Hermannstadt, 1901.

INDIA. Calcutta Museum, 1906; Delhi Museum, 1936; British Museum, 1892; Marsden, London, 1823; Meili Collection of Schulman, Amsterdam, 1910.

IRELAND. Seaby, London, 1970.

ISRAEL. Kadman, Tel-Aviv, 1963.

ITALY. "Corpus Nummorum Italicorum" by King Victor Emanuele III, Rome, 1910-1943.

JAPAN. Jacobs and Vermuele, New York, 1953.

JERUSALEM. Schlumberger, Paris, 1877.

MALTA. Schembri, London, 1910.

NETHERLANDS. Stephanik, Amsterdam, 1904; Schulman, Amsterdam, 1946.

NETHERLANDS EAST INDIES. Netcher, Batavia, 1863; Bucknill, London, 1931; Scholten-Schulman, Amsterdam, 1953.

POLAND. Hutten-Czapski, St. Petersburg, 1871.

PORTUGAL. Vaz, Lisbon, 1948; Batalha-Reis, Lisbon, 1956.

RHODES. Schlumberger, Paris, 1877.

RUSSIA. Schubert, St. Petersburg, 1855; Severin, New York, 1958; Spassky, Amsterdam, 1967; Spassky, Leningrad, 1961; Petrov, Moscow, 1899; Mikhailovich, St. Petersburg, 1888-1914.

SCOTLAND. Stewart, London, 1955.

SERBIA. Ljubica, Zagreb, 1875.

SIAM. Le May, Bangkok, 1932.

SOUTH AFRICA. Kaplan, Germiston, 1950.

SPAIN. Vidal Quadras, Barcelona, 1892; Tolra, Barcelona, 1936; Lopez-Chaves and Yriarte, Madrid, 1968; Heiss, Madrid, 1865; Vicenti, Madrid, 1974; Cayon-Castan, Madrid, 1974.

SWEDEN. Levin, Stockholm, 1887; Brunn Collection, Frankfurt, 1914; Gluck-Hesselblad, Stockholm, 1953; Ahlstrom, Stockholm, 1967.

SWITZERLAND. Divo-Tobler, Zurich, 1967, 1974.

TUNIS. Monsieur V. Guilloteau, Paris, 1943.

TURKEY. British Museum, 1883.

VATICAN. "Corpus Nummorum Italicorum" by King Victor Emanuele III, Rome, 1910-1943.

GENERAL. Yeoman, "Modern World Coins," Racine, Wisconsin, 1978; Krause, "Standard Catalog of World Coins", Iola, Wisconsin, 1979.

INDEX